CW00928058

# MINI
## The Racing Story

## John Baggott

The Crowood Press

First published in 1999 by
The Crowood Press Ltd
Ramsbury, Marlborough
Wiltshire SN8 2HR

© John Baggott 1999


All rights reserved. No part of this publication may be reproduced or transmitted in any form or by any means, electronic or mechanical, including photocopy, recording, or any information storage and retrieval system, without permission in writing from the publishers.

**British Library Cataloguing-in-Publication Data**
A catalogue record for this book is available from the British Library.


ISBN 1 86126 254 X

Typeset by Carreg Limited, Ross-on-Wye, Herefordshire

Printed and bound by The Bath Press

# Contents

# Foreword

**by Ken Tyrrell**

In 1964 I managed the works Mini team in the European Touring Car Championship and found myself involved in the hurly-burly world of management and tactics in a totally different form of racing. I thought I knew about managing a single-seater team, but touring cars were a different ballgame!

The way the championship was scored that season, class-winners could win the overall title if they kept winning each race, so that our Minis stood as good a chance as the bigger cars. It wasn't only winning, but winning by the greatest margin which would also help on title count-backs. Hillclimbs were included and we won at Mont Ventoux only to find out that there weren't enough entries to make a class. From then on we took a full class everywhere we went with anyone who would come along with their Minis! I even drove in one hillclimb myself...

At the race in Hungary, in order to win by the maximum amount, we wanted all of the Minis we controlled to be as far behind as possible in second place, third and fourth. The marshals couldn't understand why, at all our stops to refuel, we were washing windscreens, windows, even the whole car to lose time. Saab were up to the same game but they didn't do it in the pits – they stopped out on the circuit and had *lunch*!

That Mini championship season seemed to be a different drama at every race! We were quickest by far at Spa – first, second and third on the grid – and if everything held together we would be 1–2–3 in the race. Because of the continuous high speed at Spa we were having a problem with the oil getting to the gearbox bearings, but in the race we were running 1–2–3 so comfortably that we arranged for them to cross the finishing line together. As luck would have it, one of our cars had trouble with its gearbox and the other two waited for him, but as they came down from the last corner to the finishing line, a DKW caught up and passed them on the grass! We were beaten into second place by half a car's length!

I got my own back on DKW at one of the hillclimbs – and also got myself into trouble with BMC competitions boss, Stuart Turner. We were beaten by a DKW but it was pointed out to me that the DKW didn't have carpets and Group 2 regs demanded carpets. I put in a protest which was upheld and we won our class. If we hadn't (although we didn't know it at the time) we wouldn't have won the championship. Stuart Turner gave me a right bollocking. He said 'BMC *never* protest.'

The final round was a four-hour refuelling race at Monza and *all* the class-winners were equal on points, so it was wide open. This was when Alan Mann, who was running the works Ford team, pulled a fast one. He wanted to stop us winning our class so he brought an Anglia which wasn't normally competitive but might be at Monza with its long straights and no chicanes in those days. His trump card was in bringing an extra Lotus Cortina, whose job was to tow the Anglia in its slipstream! That was *good*. Very clever tactics. The Cortina would come in and refuel, wait for the Anglia, and then resume towing again. We had a problem with icing carburettors and Warwick Banks was running second with a slight misfire, but over at Ford they were having trouble getting the fuel in. They ran out in the closing laps and we won the race and the championship.

As a postscript I'll tell a story against myself that Warwick may remember. At one of his refuelling stops late in the race he started unbuckling his harness and climbing out of the car. I asked him what he was doing and he said he was going for a pee. I pushed him back in and said, 'Do it in the car, we're trying to win a championship here!' And we did. Sorry about that, Warwick.

Ken Tyrrell

# Acknowledgements

When I started my research for this history, a friend and fellow motor sport enthusiast warned me that my problem would not be what to put in, but what to leave out! However, without the assistance of many people, my task would have been impossible and there would have been nothing to include in the first place.

When I sought assistance from Mini Cooper enthusiast Pete Flanagan, his view was that this was a book that should always have been written. Throughout my year of research, Pete was a constant source of information about things Cooper in particular, and things Mini in general. Dave Woodgate and Steve Gardiner have been generous in lending me cuttings from their accumulated back numbers of magazines, delving ever further into their respective lofts to satisfy my requests for more facts. Robert Young, the Cooper Register archivist, has also provided material.

Jeffrey Parish of the Mini Se7en Racing Club assembled and copied for me the club's championship results since 1966 – no mean task. The Cooper Register, the GTM Owners Club, the Mini Marcos Owners Club and the Unipower Register have patiently dealt with my questions on their respective marques. I heartily recommend any of these organizations to owners.

I have gleaned information from past issues of *Autocar & Motor*, *Autosport*, *Cars and Car Conversions*, *Classics*, *Classic and Sportscar*, *Mini Magazine*, *Mini World*, *Motor*, *Motoring News* and *Motor Racing*. To their editors and reporters past and present, thank you.

The following competitors, team managers, tuners and enthusiasts have taken me down their own memory lane to enable me to tell the Mini racing story:

John Aley, Janice Allen, Brian Archer, Sally Aspinall, Gilles Baillarguet, Clive Baker, Peter Baldwin, Warwick Banks, Tony Barnard, Tony Barron, Andy Barton, Rod Bathgate, Ian Bax, Sedric Bell, Steve Bell, Tom Bewick, Geoff Bird, Jonathan Bird, David Blackridge, John Blanckley, Tony Blore, Jimmy Blumer, Bill Blydenstein, Len Bosshard, David Boyer, Andrew Bradshaw, John Brigden, Ralph Broad, Jonathan Buncombe, Roger Bunting, Peter Burnham, Jim Burrows, Paul Butler, Mike Campbell Cole, Andrew Cannings, Kevin Card, Christabel Carlisle, Tony Chamings, Andrew Charman, Mike Chittenden, Bill Cole, Nick Cole, Jim Conroy, Tim Conroy, Peter Cooper, Tina Cooper, Peter Cope, Ian Cornick, Ken Costello, Tom Coulthard, Barbara Cowell, Chris Cramer, Dave Cross, Bob Curl, Ian Curley, Alan Curnow, Julian Cutler, Jack Daniels, Phil Darbyshire, Val Dare-Bryan, Martin Davidson, John Davies, Tony Davies, Gordon Dawkins, Peter Day, Russell Dell, Ginger Devlin, Chris Dobson, Lionel Dodkins, Dave Dorrington, Alan Edis, Rod Embley, David Enderby, Roger Enever, John Fenning, John Fitzpatrick, Angus Fogg, Dave Forster, Mark Forster, Bob

6

Fox, Gordon Franks, Mike Fry, Fred Game, Roger Garland, Nigel Gaymer, Paul Gaymer, Geoff Gilkes, Brian Gillibrand, Jeff Goodliff, Chris Gow, Ron Graham, Norman Grimshaw, Monty Guildford, Martin Hadwen, Barry Hall, Gary Hall, Ian Hall, James Hall, Steve Hall, Peter Handforth, John Handley, Derek Hanwell, Ian Hargreaves, Paul Harmer, Terry Harmer, Steve Harris, Brian Harvey Graham Hatfield, Peter Hawthorne, Matt Hayman, Lawrence Heasman, Andrew Hedges, Brian Heerey, Howard Heerey, Peter Hepponstall, David Hipperson, Norman Hodson, Mike Horrocks, Jack Hosker, Richard Hudson-Evans, Margaret Hughes, Gerry Hulford, Paul Ivey, John Jackson, Mike Jackson, Susan Jones, Chris Judge, Peter Kaye, John Kelly, Bob Kemp, Terry Keneham, Peter Kitchen, Roy Lacock, John Lafferty, Charles Lampton, Tony Lanfranchi, Chris Lawrence, Richard Laws, Max Le Grand, Peter Leslie, Adam Lesniewski, Jonathan Lewis, Graham Lloyd, Tony Loader, Richard Longman, Glen Mabbs, Liz Maddison, Tony Maggs, John Maguire, Denise Manderscheid, Dean Marks, Jem Marsh, David Marshall, Gerry Marshall, Ginger Marshall, Wayne Martin, Sue Mason, John Matthews, Tony Matthews, Peter May, Jimmy McClements, Jim McDougall, John Miles, Bob Milloy, Dave Morgan, Jon Mowatt, Steve Neal, Bob Neville, Roly Nix, Martin Nott, David Oldham, Alf Otley, Nick Ouroussoff, Jeffrey Parish, Donald Parker, James Parker, Bill Piper, John Playfoot, Peter Porter, Tim Powell, Bill Price, Harry Ratcliffe, Brian Redman, John Rhodes, Bill Richards, Simon Ridge, Steven Roberts, Stan Robinson, Ralph Saunders, Chris Seaman, Peter Shepherd, Bryan Slark, Barry Smith, Enid Smith, Eric Smith, Steve Soper, Gordon Spice, Phil Spurling, Adrian Standing, Allan Staniforth, Paul Stanworth, Gary Streat, Jerry Sturman, Glyn Swift, Nick Swift, Paul Taft, John Terry, James Thacker, Marie Tièche, Chris Tyrrell, Ken Tyrrell, Ernie Unger, Micki Vandervell, Julian Vereker, Julian Vernaeve, Richard Wager, Basil Wales, Reg Ward, Patrick Watts, Richard and Wendy Way, Jack Wheeler, Phil Whitehead, Jim Whitehouse, Sir John Whitmore, Derek Wilkins, Barrie Williams, Richard Williamson, Pen Wills, Colin Woolard, Robert Young.

Rob Willig and Paul Emmelkamp assisted with translations.

As well as providing her usual proof-reading expertise, my wife Jane has assisted me with my research and now claims to know almost as much about Minis as she does about MG Midgets.

Many photographers have made a contribution to this book. Not all the prints I have been lent bear the name of the person behind the lens, but the cameramen include: Peter Baldwin, Howard Barker, S. Boothroyd, Roger Bowyer, Eric Bryce, Mike Campbell Cole, Andrew Cannings, Ken Cope, Peter Cope, Hugh Coster, Peter Day, Dave Forster, John Gaisford, Monty Guildford, Mary Harvey, Gerry Hulford, Steve Jones, B.S. Kreisky, Dave Leonard, Maureen Magee, John March, David Marshall, Lynton Money, Eddie Regan, Andrew Roberts, Fred Scatley, Seaman Photographer, Evan Selwyn-Smith, H.P. Severt, Eric Smith, Roger Standish, Chris Todd, Peter Trevellick, John Whitmore, Tim Whittington. I apologize for any photographers who have been omitted because I have been unable to trace them. Jeffrey Parish, of the Mini Se7en Racing Club, and Enid Smith from the BARC Press Office, have kindly provided prints from their archives.

# Introduction

When Alec Issigonis designed the Mini, did he ever imagine that not only would it still be in production forty years after its introduction, but that examples, some surely modified beyond his wildest dreams, would still be racing all over the world?

The Mini made its first major circuit appearance at the traditional Brands Hatch Boxing Day meeting in 1959. Four examples took part in the race for saloon cars, one driven by Sir John Whitmore; he would go on to win the British Saloon Car Championship in a Don Moore-tuned Mini, before progressing to bigger things. With the introduction of the Austin and Morris Mini Cooper S, in 1963, the Mini's competitiveness was raised to a higher level. From 1071, 970 and 1275 versions, still more power was sought. Following the advent of the eight-port head and injection, furtive minds began to plan ways to mate Ford and Hillman Imp engines with the Mini gearbox, in a continued quest for extra horsepower. Their efforts, mostly combining with the engineering expertise of the likeable Gordon Allen, led to a significant number of hybrid Special Saloon Minis.

Mini Se7en racing was introduced in 1966, followed in 1969 by a super formula, which became the basis of the Mini Miglia series. Both these one-marque championships are still running today and invariably provide the closest and most exciting races on the programme. Leyland backed the 1275GT Challenge, which ran from 1976 to 1980.

BMC/Leyland usually concentrated their direct factory competition effort on rallying but, on occasions, ran their own cars at the circuits. However, over the years, the works backed a number of privately owned teams to enter Minis in national and international races on their behalf. The Cooper Car Company was the best known and arguably the most successful of these teams. Other outfits such as British Vita Racing (1968 European Touring Car Champions), Broadspeed and Equipe Arden (1969 British Saloon Car Champions) also chalked up their fair share of victories, sometimes using the same drivers as Cooper.

During the 1960s, the Mini engine and drive train found its way into the front, or, in some cases, the back of a plethora of GT and kit cars, most of which utilized glass-fibre bodies. These vehicles also had their racing history, some even taking on the might of Porsche and Ferrari in the classic events at Le Mans and the Nurburgring. While examples of the Cox GTM and Mini Marcos may still be seen today, sightings of other makes, such as Camber and Unipower, are now extremely rare.

When Minis race against larger, more powerful machinery, the crowd loves the David and Goliath aspect. A Mini snapping at the heels of a Jaguar or a Lotus Cortina delights the spectators at historic races today, just as it did their fathers at saloon events three decades ago. Long may it continue to do so.

# 1   Minis on the Track

Sir Alec Issigonis originally designed the Mini to combat the bubble-car threat to BMC's market share as a result of the Suez crisis. He started work on the project in March 1957, just seven months later there were two prototypes on the road and the car was ready for launch in August 1959. According to Jack Daniels, the Chief Design and Development Engineer on the project, the company and the designers were aware from the very beginning of the tremendous cornering ability of this compact, easy-to-drive four-seater. They also knew it would be quick – indeed, the engine capacity had had to be reduced by 100cc, from the intended 948cc, to make the car more suitable for the type of customer that was envisaged for it.

While some of the BMC drivers admitted to dicing with Jaguars when driving the Mini prototypes on their twisting 100-mile (160-km) testing route in the Cotswolds, the Mini was not initially seen as a car for racing. However, when John Cooper suggested that it might have racing potential, Issigonis went along with it, despite any initial misgivings that his Mini had originally been designed as a car for the people.

## BOXING DAY 1959

The traditional Boxing Day meeting at Brands Hatch in 1959 marked the first major race outing of the Austin Seven and Morris Mini Minor, as they were then known. Four were entered in the Yuletide Trophy Race for saloon cars: Austins for Sir John Whitmore and K. Jack, while R.W. De Selincourt and J.G. Armstrong were driving Morris examples.

Despite being less than two months old, Whitmore's red car, 616 HKM, had already worked hard for its living. Whitmore had collected the car, which had white stripes over its roof, from his friend Tony Coleman's Folkestone Motor Company on

*Ralph Broad (46) tries to drive all the way round the outside of Timo Makinen (43) at Silverstone's Becketts Corner. BMC liked their rally drivers to have occasional race outings, to hone their tarmac skills.*

5 November. Ten days later, he drove it in the RAC Rally. Following the repair of a bent wing, which had been damaged on the rally, the car was resprayed dark blue. It appeared in this livery at Brands, complete with four Amal carburettors.

The Yuletide Trophy Race at Brands in 1959 was a wet race, but the spectators were impressed at the way Whitmore managed to get his Mini through the corners. As he recalls, 'They could all be taken flat out, if I sort of threw the little brick at it.'

Whitmore's race ended in retirement after a puncture, picked up while running sixth overall, the leading Mini. Both Mini Minors also retired, leaving Jack's Austin Seven as the only finisher. Based on these inauspicious results, who would have guessed that the Mini would rise to such heights in motor sport, and that it would still be racing forty years later?

## JOHN HANDLEY

Rally enthusiast John Handley, who became very well known for his exploits behind the wheel of racing Minis, was the first to acquire a Mini with the specific intention of using it in competition. When the car was launched, each dealer was told to keep at least one car in the showroom, but Handley managed to persuade his local garage to part with their only example. Having taken delivery of Austin Mini 4700 RE on a Wednesday, Handley drove it along to his local Hagley and District Light Car Club meeting. There, to the great amusement of his fellow members, he announced his intentions to rally his new acquisition.

True to his word, Handley, with navigator Tony Moy, competed in the 1959 Worcestershire Rally, held on the first weekend in September, just days after

Handley had bought the car. During that event, he became the first owner to discover that the floor pans of the early cars leaked, when he saw the rubber mats floating in the foot well. Although the pair finished the event, Handley does not recall where they were placed; he points out, however, that they were both quite green.

For the next four years, John Handley continued to use 4700 RE for rallies, sprints, hillclimbs, races and even the odd production car trial; it was a period during which, he says, he was 'learning his craft'. Prominent BRDC member Max Trimble would enter the Mini in his name, to enable Handley to compete in the support races at the British Grand Prix and International Trophy meetings. Early on, Jim Whitehouse had been called upon to modify the Mini's cylinder head. Until 1961, the car was also Handley's daily means of transport.

## PETER KAYE

Peter Kaye sold his Morris 1000 to finance the purchase of grey Austin Seven PHL 282, and immediately set about preparing it for the 1960 season. In February, his attempted drive from Yorkshire to Downton, to obtain tuning parts from Daniel Richmond, was abandoned at Oxford, as the result of a broken windscreen. The factory fitted a new one for free.

For Peter Kaye, Mini success came on his first time out, with a class win at the Castle Howard Hillclimb on 10 April 1960. The Easter Meeting at Rufforth in Yorkshire, his local circuit, on 16 April 1960, marked his Mini race debut.

Kaye soon discovered the problems of regularly revving the 850 engine to 8,000rpm. The crank oil seal failed, spraying oil on to the clutch. The 'solution' was a packet of Fullers Earth in the toolbox; having removed the starter motor, he would ask someone to depress the pedal while he tipped some of the powder in to soak up the oil.

By 1961, the engine had been bored out to 960cc, using modified A40 Devon pistons, fitted with Speedwell cam, Arden manifolds and a head from Downton. The block had been modified to take cam bearings, after the original hole in the casting had worn to an oval shape resulting in a broken oil pump drive. The car was quick and took many awards in races, sprints and hillclimbs. In 1962, Kaye replaced his 850 with a Cooper.

*Allan Staniforth competing at Rufforth in 1963. The front number plate doubles as splash guard for the distributor, the air scoop feeds twin choke down-draught Solex on a self-fabricated manifold.*

## ALLAN STANIFORTH

*Daily Mirror* reporter Allan Staniforth was another early Morris Mini Minor competitor. His cream version 4929 WU, purchased in January 1960, was third to Kaye at Castle Howard, and also ran at the Rufforth Easter meeting. The car had one of the first full harnesses, stitched for him in girth webbing by a Leeds saddler. He modified the 850 engine by fitting a Sprite cam and Lucas Sport distributor, used an A35 pulley to reduce the dynamo speed and removed two fan blades. Just before that first hillclimb, he fitted a Barwell big valve head with a pair of one-and-one-eighth SUs and hand-made ram pipes.

Tyres proved a perennial headache to early Mini competitors. Staniforth started by running them at 27F 24R, but later tried 40psi in the fronts, in an attempt to stabilize them. Blistering was a constant problem. By June, he had graduated to a twin-choke Solex carburettor on a split Siamese port head. Eventually, one of the splitter tongues, made from 16-gauge mild steel and welded to the manifold, vibrated free and exited through the head and

exhaust, with no major damage. All Staniforth heard was a slight rattle.

Without access to a dyno, Staniforth used 0–60mph road-test runs to check the effectiveness of his modifications. During 1960, his runs improved from 23.8 seconds to 14.8 seconds. In 1962, he had his best Mini year; he had become a hillclimb specialist, and took fifteen class records and wins from seventeen outings. In 1963, he purchased a second-hand Downton Mini, 464 ANU, one of the cars that had become known as 'Mini Ton Bombs', the first to do 100mph. When it came to a routine engine rebuild, Allan discovered few mysteries inside. He continued to compete in a Mini until 1965, when he built the first Terrapin, a Mini-engined single-seater.

## CHRISTABEL CARLISLE

Having spectated at Brands with a group of family and friends, Christabel Carlisle decided that watching motor sport was noisy and boring. She vowed that, if she ever visited a racetrack again, it would be as a competitor. This Kensington piano teacher already had an 850 Mini, CMC 77, which had been bought for her as a twenty-first birthday present by her family. Her uncle had provided a Sprite cylinder head to increase the car's performance. She is happy to admit that she had never had a mechanical bent, but she felt that her musician's ear would be able to tell if something was not running properly.

In 1960, Christabel Carlisle broke into club racing. She entered her first event without ever having driven on a circuit before, so a test session was hurriedly booked at Silverstone. Luckily, Marcus Chambers happened to be there with the BMC team. Even at that early stage, he was impressed with her consistent lap times and, at the end of the day, he asked Jack Sears to drive her round to show her the racing lines.

Christabel Carlisle's first race was at Silverstone on 18 June 1960, one of the seven outings required to gain signatures to qualify for a National Licence. On this occasion, she failed to gain a signature,

*Christabel Carlisle gets CMC 77 on to three wheels in one of her early races at Brands Hatch, in 1961. At the time, she thought the car was sounding a bit noisy, but only knew the reason why back in the pits after the race.*

having hit too many straw bales trying to get to grips with the Mini's understeer characteristics on the track. By the end of the season, however, she had qualified, having managed to keep the whole thing a secret from the family by 'staying with friends' when she was actually at races.

Christabel had kept in touch with Marcus Chambers during 1960, and had been grateful for the spare parts she had been able to scrounge from BMC's competition department. She was delighted to be told at the end of the year that Chambers had arranged for her to receive full backing. She would race as a privateer in a BMC-supplied Mini, which would still carry CMC 77; Castrol had retained the services of Don Moore to run the car. The Carlisle family was now informed of Christabel's racing aspirations.

In April 1961, Christabel entered the BRSCC's first-ever race exclusively for Minis. After an entertaining drive, she finished second behind Graham Burrows. Her first International was at Silverstone, on 8 July 1961. To compete at this level, she needed to upgrade her National Licence. This was normally a mere formality, but it was pointed out that some women who had competed in previous Internationals had crashed, leading to adverse publicity for the sport. Christabel managed to persuade the organizers that she would not indulge in such folly. She soon had to eat her words, however. During the Friday practice session, she ran wide on to the grass and, in regaining the circuit, a wheel dug in, rolling the car. While she sought out the clerk of the course to apologize, Marcus Chambers arranged for the mechanics to return the car to Abingdon and rebuild it into another shell.

At 6pm, Christabel found time to phone home and report what had happened. She was too late; Mr Carlisle had already read of his daughter's escapade in the *London*

*Christabel Carlisle (CMC 77) heads Mick Clare (YMJ 681) and John Aley (JRA 85) in the Archie Scott Brown memorial meeting at Snetterton, June 1961. Miss Carlisle is wearing overalls run up in flameproof material by her dressmaker.*

*Evening Standard*, and was not impressed. However, not wanting to let the team down, Christabel was determined to race the next day. It was her first-ever wet event and she finished fifth in class, twelfth overall from seventeen starters.

Her parents relented and came to watch her race at Snetterton on 28 July, where she led Mick Clare until the last lap, when he dodged out of her slipstream to win by half a wheel. Her father was impressed at her sporting gesture as she shook hands with Clare after the race, while she herself mentally noted her adversary's move for future outings. At Brands on 1 October she had another stirring dice, this time with Vic Elford, in the small class of the Saloon Car Race. Despite leading for most laps, she had to give best to Elford and again finished second.

Christabel Carlisle was now consistently dicing with the works team Minis but, under the terms of her support, it was not really the 'done thing' to beat them. On 28 April 1962, at Aintree, she executed the manoeuvre that she had learnt from Mick Clare on Tony Maggs, to split the works cars, and came home third. The result – Love, Whitmore, Carlisle, Maggs – spoiled the hoped-for Cooper Car Company 1, 2, 3.

*Christabel Carlisle and Don Moore at Silverstone on 12 May 1962. Moore invariably took his caravan to meetings, and his wife Babs provided sandwiches and endless cups of tea.*

*Christabel Carlisle in CMC 77 in front of the works cars of John Love and John Whitmore at the Crystal Palace Whit Monday meeting in 1962. Christabel's chance of victory was taken from her, half a lap from the finish, when the clutch failed. Her personal registration number was bought as a present by her brother and sister.*

She recalls one outing at Mallory at around the same time when, glancing out of the passenger window as she rounded Gerard's Bend, she saw a wheel fly by. She was soon to realize that it was one of her own, as her car failed to make the corner and skidded to a halt on three wheels and a brake drum.

Christabel also took part in some long-distance and European events. Ken Tyrrell ran the car in Denmark for two races at the Roskilde Ring, in August 1962. The narrowness of the circuit made pole position essential, so the local drivers baulked her to prevent the Mini setting a decent time. Tyrrell protested, she was allowed another run, got pole and won both races, having led from start to finish. In June 1963, her uncle Christopher McLaren joined her to drive the middle stint in the Nurburgring 1,000km race, the outing resulting in a class win for the Mini. Christabel and American co-driver Denise McCluggage won the ladies' award, and were third in class in the Motor Six-Hour Race at Brands in July 1963.

During that summer, Christabel, unhappy with the 'team orders' situation, began to enjoy the racing less, and decided to hang up her helmet. Her last outing was on 20 July 1963 when, from a class of fifteen cars, she was third behind John Whitmore and Paddy Hopkirk.

## BRIAN REDMAN

Well-known racing driver Brian Redman was one of many who cut their teeth in Minis. He had his first outing in 1960, when he competed in the road car that he used to make his living – travelling the country selling mop heads. The car was highly modified, with Downton head, Alexander road/race cam, twin inch-and-a-half SUs and a Peco exhaust system.

Redman's driving impressed Daniel Richmond, who asked him to join the Downton team for the Silverstone Six-Hour Relay. Redman turned up at the circuit for practice; when Richmond saw the hotchpotch of tuning parts under the bonnet, he commented, 'Can't possibly work old boy – everything has to be matched.' After the practice, in which Redman's times had been up at the front end of the team, Richmond handed him a brown paper parcel. Inside was a brand new Formula Junior cylinder head, which Brian fitted that night ready for the race proper the next day. However, 1960 was the year in which all the Minis were withdrawn from the Silverstone race, when the front wheels started pulling over the nuts.

Redman's Mini was used for races, sprints and hillclimbs throughout the season, sometimes competing under the Team Red Rose banner. Brian Redman even drove it all the way from Burnley in Lancashire to Goodwood in Sussex just for a six-lap handicap race, because he was so keen to race at the circuit. By the end of the year the engine was sounding a little tired, to say the least, so Redman sold the Mini to Rodney Bloor at Sports Motors of Manchester. It was replaced by an XK 140, which was then itself replaced by a Morgan Plus 4. Despite this move to a new marque, Brian Redman was to reappear later in the 1960s, from time to time, in one of the Vita Minis.

On 1 September 1966, Redman was one of a number of drivers invited to take part in a BMC test day at Silverstone. His laps in one of Donald Healey's works Sprites went according to plan, but, when he got behind the wheel of Don Moore's Mini 1394 ND, all did not go so well. He crashed so heavily that the seat came loose and he ended up in the back of the car. Despite this, Don Moore offered him a drive the following season, but by this time Redman already had a contract elsewhere and was about to embark on a very successful professional career.

Redman now lives in America and occasionally races Minis there in vintage events. In his view, 'They are the most fun of everything!'

## DOC SHEPHERD

Doc Shepherd took up racing late in life, when he 'got too old to play polo'. In 1959, driving his Austin A40, he was the man to

*John Aley (JRA 85) leads Doc Shepherd (VCE 613) and the 105E Anglia of Doc Merifield into Stowe Corner at Snetterton, 19 March 1961.*

beat in saloon cars. However, rather than resting on his laurels, he decided he had better see what the Mini was all about. He acquired one as a road car, and got the engine bored out from 848 to 872cc. Over time, he also changed the cam and had a modified head fitted and the car thus became a full-blown competition car.

Shepherd took a class win in the Snetterton MRC Sprint on 1 November 1959 in VCE 613, and in saloon car races began mixing it with fellow Mini men John Aley and Sir John Whitmore. It was not until his sixtieth birthday, on 13 June 1960, that Shepherd again appeared in a Mini. According to him, it was 'a lousy birthday, because Aley was quicker than me in practice'.

In racing, Shepherd neither expected nor gave any quarter and apparently drove round the circuit as if he were on his own, intent purely on winning. During his 1961 Mini outings he had one notable win at Crystal Palace, as well as a spectacular retirement at Aintree as a result of the car skidding along the tarmac on its roof. The car was then re-shelled into a new road Mini WER 113.

Shepherd always felt that the Mini's understeering characteristics did not fit in with his driving style; he preferred rear-wheel drive, which he found more predictable. Later in the 1961 season he decided to revert to rear-wheel drive and sold his Mini.

## MARTIN DAVIDSON

When Doc Shepherd decided to sell WER 113 in 1961, an advertisement duly appeared in *Autosport*. Martin Davidson, a motoring enthusiast who was doing his articles at law, managed to buy a copy of the magazine the day before it was officially available. He was the first to reply

and inspect the Mini, and bought it straight away, both as a car for sprints, as well as for everyday transport. On 21 September 1961, Davidson competed in his first sprint at Goodwood, winning the saloon car class, beating, among others, a 1200cc Mini prepared by Daniel Richmond of Downton Engineering. Having done fairly well in other end-of-season sprints, he went to a couple of general racing test days at Brands Hatch. When he got his lap times down to 67.2, his mates, including long-time drinking partner Gerry Marshall, told him he had to go racing.

The 1962 Mallory Park Easter Monday meeting saw Davidson on the grid for his first race, which he won, along with the next three. That first win resulted in problems at home. Davidson's family had been unaware of his burgeoning career in this hazardous sport, but one of his father's friends had seen the names of the Mallory Park winners in the *Daily Telegraph* and had unwittingly let the cat out of the bag. Following heated debates, and threats to cancel his articles, the young Davidson left home. In an effort to keep the peace, he entered future races under the name of 'Harry Martin', derived from his first name and from a long-standing nickname.

Martin Davidson's Mini was driven on the road to and from the race circuits and he still used it to get about every day. The night before his next meeting at Brands the crankshaft broke – this was to become something of a regular occurrence. On Saturday morning, before practice, he bought a new crank from University Motors, and got a local garage to rebuild the bottom end. There was no time to get it balanced, so he scrounged a lift to the circuit and qualified in a friend's Mini. In the race on Sunday, he had to start from the back of the grid as he was not racing the car in which he had practised. By lap seven, he had caught the leaders and on the next tour he took the lead along the main straight. However, erstwhile leader Barry Hall was having none of it, and the subsequent contact between the two pitched Davidson's car into the concrete wall that protected the paddock tunnel.

Gerry Marshall, who was in the pits, ran across the track and dragged his pal out of the car. (Marshall was quite an athlete and had won many a pint betting on his own sprinting prowess.) The outcome of Davidson's accident was a broken jaw, the loss of a number of teeth and, initially, no recollection of ever having been in a motor race. Jack Wheeler, whose Sprite Martin subsequently co-drove in endurance races, believes that his weight, or rather lack of it, saved him from more serious injury. Once Davidson was on the road to recovery, he was visited by Dean Dellamont, a top official at the RAC, who presented him with his full licence, telling him he had satisfied them by almost completing the requisite six races.

The remains of the car were taken back to Davidson's garage, a lock-up in Lancaster Mews close to the premises of the legendary John Sprinzel. The front of the body had absorbed most of the impact, so a shell with rear-end damage was found at a breaker's yard near Brands and the two good halves were grafted together. Davidson continued to campaign the car, with good results. At the end of the season, the 850 motor was sold for good money and Martin decided to move up a class.

A 997cc engine was built and the car now entered as a Mini Cooper. Among Davidson's achievements in 1963 was a new Brands lap record.

In 1964, Davidson only did four races; one of these was a spur-of-the-moment entry at Evanton Circuit in Scotland. He and his girlfriend had taken the Cooper on a touring holiday, and saw that the local car club was organizing its first-ever meeting at an old airfield near Inverness. There were races in the morning, including an open saloon car event, and a sprint in the afternoon; he had to have a go. Having entered (fortunately, he always kept his racing licence in the car), he borrowed a crash helmet and went out to practise. As he had not gone to Scotland with a view to racing, the car did not have its decent set of tyres – they were practically bald! It started to drizzle at the beginning of the race, and adhesion was not helped by the tufts of grass growing between the concrete sections of the old runway and mud running on to the track in a couple of places. It was a twelve-car field and, despite a spin at the first corner, Davidson had a hell of a dice with local driver Mike White in a Jag, to come second overall and win the smaller class. In the afternoon sprint, he beat the Jag to win the saloons outright, and take third-fastest time of day. He came home from his holiday with three trophies.

During his time in the Mini, Davidson had notched up thirty-five wins, but in 1965 he decided to sell the car. It was advertised once again in the columns of *Autosport*, this time as the 'Imp Eater', for £645. The night before they were due to demonstrate it to a potential purchaser at Brands, Jack Wheeler and Davidson went to the lock-up to measure all the suspension angles, to enable them to build another, even-quicker Mini at a future date. No two measurements were the same! The following day, all seemed to be going well; the buyer had agreed to a deal, when Davidson, still wearing his double-breasted overcoat, decided to do just one more lap to try and break the record. It proved to be a bad move – someone spun in front of him, and once more he had a damaged Mini. The deal could only go ahead as agreed after more repairs.

# GERRY MARSHALL

During 1961, Gerry Marshall was placed in Eelmore Plain sprints, driving Minis hired from a Wembley garage for road use. Subsequently, he was to compete in his own Mini, YCD 436, originally built for Tim Farr by Frank Hamlin. Farr, a law student, did a couple of events in the car and then swapped it with Marshall for his road car of the time, a smart Riley 1.5. When Marshall returned home with his new acquisition, his father was less than impressed; instead of the Riley, his son now drove a two-tone Mini, painted in white and primer. Like many racers of the era, YCD 436 was based on an accident-damaged road car; while Frank had made an excellent job of welding the new front on, it had never been painted.

Brian Claydon built Marshall a new 998cc engine, based on a prototype Riley Elf block. After several sprints, which produced some class wins, Marshall's first race was at Snetterton on Easter Monday 1964. He beat Mac Ross in his Mini, BMR 10, to take the class. Wanting more, he raced at Snetterton again the next two weekends, taking two class wins, plus a third overall in the Unlimited Saloon Race, after snapping at the heels of Albert Betts' 3.4 Jaguar. Following a hurried rebuild, as the result of a roll at Mallory, Marshall notched up his first overall win, by 22 seconds, at Brands Hatch in April. He also sliced 1.6 seconds off the lap record.

At about this time Marshall met up with Bill McGovern, who was then in the furniture business and ran a VX 490. Marshall invited him to join his crowd at the John Lyon at Wembley, the local car enthusiast's watering hole. This was situated on a roundabout at the end of a dual carriageway used by the regulars as a drag strip. In 1963, McGovern bought a new 1071 Mini Cooper S, CMK 855A, which he started racing. Later, he ran a 1275S before moving to Hillman Imps, where he really made his name.

Having made his mark, Gerry Marshall, along with Chris Montague and Bill McGovern, all had their first International race on the Brands GP circuit towards the end of the season. On the very first lap of the race, Marshall got it wrong at Hawthorns, went off into the undergrowth and missed several trees before one finally stopped him. On the second lap, McGovern had a spectacular end-over-end roll at Paddock, and, next time round, Montague had a less spectacular off at the same corner.

Marshall's car was sold at the end of the year, to pay bills and to buy an engagement ring, but he missed racing and, in his own words, 'moped about'. His fiancée, used to his gibes that she was wearing his Mini Cooper on her finger, told him he had better get another car. He came to an agreement with Mike Walton that they would use Walton's racing wheels, tyres and 970S lump in Marshall's road Cooper, and would share the car at meetings. In 1965, results were again good, with Marshall occasionally beating the works-backed cars. Robbie Gordon then took the car on, for driver Julian Hasler. Marshall also drove another of Gordon's Minis, a 1275S, to a class win at the 1965 Snetterton 500km, in August.

During the 1966/7 seasons, Marshall mostly raced Elans and TVRs, but he did do International meetings at Monza and the Nurburgring in a 1275S. During a testing session of his Elan at Snetterton, Marshall also tried Bill Blydenstein's lightweight, short-stroke 850 Mini. Subsequently, Blydenstein wanted to sell the car, and offered it first to Marshall. A deal was struck, and Ken Eyers and Marshall acquired the car between them to race just for fun when other commitments permitted.

Marshall did two races breaking the 850-lap record at Brands as well as a couple of hillclimbs, taking a class record at Woburn. At the end of the season, Bill Blydenstein offered Marshall a drive in his Vauxhalls. Eyers bought out Marshall's half-share of the Mini, and the rest is history, as Blydenstein, Marshall and the subsequent DTV Vauxhalls, including Big Bertha and Baby Bertha, became legendary.

## TONY LANFRANCHI

In 1965, Alexander Engineering, based at Haddenham Airfield, asked Yorkshireman Tony Lanfranchi to drive their Cooper S, EKX 210B, in the British Saloon Car Championship. The car, which was blue with a cream bonnet, was looked after by chief mechanic Fred Hillyer. Lanfranchi's dice of the season was with John Fitzpatrick at Silverstone on 15 May. They were slipstreaming and place-swapping throughout the whole race until Lanfranchi won the class, by about three inches. At the end of the season, he finished second in the 1001cc to 1300cc class, with team-mate John Lewis fourth in class.

## RON AND ROB MASON

Ron Mason and his son Rob were both noted Mini drivers during the late 1960s. Rob won the Wills and BBC Grandstand trophies at a televised Lydden meeting. In 1968 and 1969, he was a leading contender in a green car prepared by Don Moore, recording seventeen wins in 1968, including a victory at Brands on his twenty-first birthday.

In 1969, Rob Mason walked away unscathed from a big accident at Silverstone's Copse Corner, despite the fact that the front of the roof was nearly level with the wings. Coming into the corner he had slid off on someone else's oil, hit the bank and rolled, with the car ending up spinning round on its roof. Just as he thought it was all over, he was hit by another Mini, which set him spinning again.

Rob Mason enjoyed success in 1971 in the Glacier/Hepolite Special Saloon Car Championship. He dominated his class, with seven wins, and took the class championship. He then went on to race Hillman Imps for George Bevan. Ron was a leading contender in the early years of the Mini Miglia series and, like his son, also did Special Saloons in a Mini.

## TEAM SPEEDWELL OF HARROW

Three racing friends in the Harrow area contacted Tim Conroy who worked at Speedwell, the tuning firm set up by Graham Hill and John Sprinzel, and suggested that the company might like to back their efforts. Roger Bunting (A35), Barry Hall (Mini) and John Miles (Sprite) received parts free or at a substantial discount, and in return entered their cars in events under the 'Team Speedwell of Harrow' banner.

In 1961, Barry Hall had borrowed £513 from his dad and bought a brand-new red 850 Mini, 659 CXH. He joined the local Harrow Car Club (when Steve Soper's father was club secretary), and by the end of the year had done a couple of the club's sprints. After meeting Roger Bunting and Peter Kitchen, he decided to go racing the following season.

As part of the team, Hall got a Speedwell CS5 cam and longer, lower wishbones to give the Mini just a little more negative camber. Soon, the car looked so evil on the road that Hall had to dig out his old bicycle to get to work on; the car continued to develop into an out-and-out racer. It was still taxed and driven to the circuits. In the event of a race retirement, Roger Bunting was persuaded to trailer it home, his own car being driven on the road – illegal, of course. Hall's main claim to fame was the setting of the class record at Brands – 1:10.8. However, it was immediately broken the following week before it had even been printed in the programme.

## JOHN ALEY

John Aley was one of many drivers to make the transition from A35 to Mini. He had originally become involved in Cambridge Racing, a team of undergraduates who raced three A35s, and through this had established a connection with BMC. He recalls that, when the Mini first came out, very few drivers could get to grips with front-wheel drive and make it go properly. The average clubman found it

easier to make a 105E Anglia or an A35 competitive. In his opinion, it was the small tuning concerns slaving away in the background that finally cracked the Mini's handling.

While he was still having success with the A35, Aley bought a Mini as a road car and, for a bit of a laugh, entered it in the odd event. The outcome surprised several people, including Aley himself, so he had the car converted for Group 2 and began regularly to win races. He soon decided that it would be better if he prepared his own car, and employed New Zealander Frank Hamlin; before long, they began working on friends' cars as well.

One of John Aley's memorable Mini outings was in 1961, at the grandly named GP of La Chatre, held on closed roads around the French town. He left his work (as a motor claims assessor) on the Friday evening, picked up his wife Jean and headed for the night boat, where he met up with two pals who had brought his Mini Pick-Up, full of spares. On the other side of the Channel, they drove to La Chatre, arriving in time for Saturday practice, after which they adjourned to a local bar for a drinking session.

*Neck and neck into Club at Silverstone during the BRDC International Trophy Meeting on 6 May 1961, John Aley in his road car (7771 NK) and John Whitmore (TMO 840). Whitmore narrowly beat Aley to win the class. Marcus Chambers had sold Whitmore this ex-works rally car, previously driven by Tom Clark, for £350.*

The organization of the event involved a large number of local people; even the Mayor and the fire brigade had turned out to help. Before the race on Sunday morning, Aley had to get involved with officials of another kind when he had to rescue one of his friends from the *gendarmes*. It seems that, rather the worse for wear, his errant friend had tried to move a car that did not belong to him. After persuading the officer not to press charges, Aley got down to the purpose of the trip – winning the race – which he accomplished most efficiently. Having attended the presentation ceremony in the town square, and the obligatory party that followed, the team drove to the port and just made the early-morning boat. Aley was back at his desk by Monday lunch-time having gained some useful funds from BMC and other manufacturer's bonus schemes which paid handsomely for an outright win.

On subsequent outings across the Channel (including a successful outing at Montlhéry, when he won the Paris Cup), Aley would take out British car spares to sell, and bring back Fiat and DKW parts for willing buyers in the UK. Although he was occasionally able to persuade race organizers to pay him start money or to provide free hotel accommodation, money was always tight in those days, and this unofficial import-export activity helped to cover expenses. Grand Prix drivers had similar money problems in the 1960s – they were not paid huge retainers then – and they would often take part in any half-decent European saloon car race to earn much-needed funds.

In the course of his job as an insurance engineer, Aley covered 600-750 miles (950-1200km) a week travelling to inspect damaged vehicles. The team decided to set up his road car, a Mini saloon (JRA 85), in exactly the same way as the racer, so that he gained wide experience of the car's han-

dling characteristics in all weathers and on a vast range of surfaces. He was, in effect, practising as he went about his daily business.

Finding himself preparing more and more cars for club racers, Aley took the plunge, gave up his insurance job and set himself up in business, John Aley Racing, in a small workshop at the bottom of his garden. One of his projects was to build a small run of £400 competition Minis – second-hand cars that were road legal, and built up to virtually Group 2 spec, enabling impecunious club racers to make a start in motor sport. He does not recall the venture making him a great deal of money – he probably did too good a job on them!

After any rust had been repaired, the cars were resprayed, the suspension was lowered, the brakes upgraded, and additional instruments and safety harness fitted in the stripped-out cockpit. The rebuilt 850cc engine had new cam, Blydenstein head and ran on inch-and-a-half SUs. The racer came complete with a new set of Dunlop SP tyres and the little details the

*John Aley receives the winner's flowers after taking victory in the 1961 Grand Prix de La Chatre. His wife Jean is more concerned with the headlight, broken in a first-lap shunt, as the car still has to be driven home to England.*

*Having blown his Cooper S up in practice for the 1965 Nurburgring Six Hours, John Aley persuaded the organizers to allow him to drive his road car, a standard 850 Traveller. He finished sixth in class, and the club came up with a special award for him.*

scrutineers like to check, such as laminated screen, catch tank and double throttle springs. Aley was not promising that they would be race winners, but reckoned that a half-decent driver should get round Brands in about 69 seconds. About eighteen were built.

Aley also expanded into the bolt-on tuning market, selling various stage conversions for Mini, Viva, and other vehicles. The world-famous Aleybar came about almost by accident. Aley was preparing a Sebring Sprite for Mike Ducker, and ended up buying the car and using it at a few events. At some time, the car had been fitted with an old American rollover bar and Aley was interested to hear young men in the paddock comment that, if they could get one of the bars, they might be able to persuade their parents that it would be safe to go motor racing. One morning, Aley came down to breakfast and announced to his wife and mechanic (who lodged with them) that he had had a really good idea. They would make roll bars for the six most popular cars and sell them to racing

enthusiasts in a kit, complete with nuts, bolts and mounting brackets. Mrs Aley and the mechanic told him to go back to bed! Aley went ahead anyway, and produced the first kits, costing £9/15/6d. The rest is history.

Having sold Aleybars, and then buying the firm back again for a while, John Aley is no longer involved in manufacturing roll bars. However, his idea has made an enormous contribution to motor sport, eventually resulting in rollover bars becoming mandatory.

## JIMMY BLUMER

Jimmy Blumer, now proprietor of Roseberry Service Station in Middlesborough, had a good grounding in motor sport, having competed in his first Monte Carlo Rally in 1950, at the age of just 18. After doing the event six years running, he moved into sprints and hillclimbs and then to circuit racing. In the

*Jimmy Blumer and Bunty Richmond with UHR 850, the Downton development Mini, an early car that was very successfully raced by Blumer. It also had many hillclimb outings with Daniel Richmond at the wheel, and was a regular class winner at Wiscombe Park.*

*Jimmy Blumer (168), followed by Mick Clare (166), hounds Jeff Uren's Ford Zephyr through Bottom Bend at the 1960 Brands Hatch August Bank Holiday meeting, the first to be held on the 2.65-mile Grand Prix Circuit.*

late 1950s, he was frequently asked to race other people's cars, and had some memorable outings in Derek Murray's Downton-tuned Austin A 35 pick-up in 1957/8. These included class wins at the Blagdon Sprint in Northumberland, and the Catterick Hillclimb. He also raced it at Oulton Park and Charterhall, again taking class wins.

By 1960, Blumer was campaigning his own Cooper Monaco. One day, when he was racing it at Aintree, he was approached in the paddock assembly area by someone who asked if she was speaking to Jimmy Blumer and told him that she wanted to talk about his driving record. Blumer replied that he would be pleased to talk to her but that she would have to wait until after the race.

That person was Bunty Richmond, the wife of Daniel Richmond and the organizational power behind his Downton Engineering tuning concern. After the race, the Richmonds asked Blumer if he had heard the rumours about the new little car that BMC was bringing out. He had, and he was surprised to learn that

Downton had been promised one to race and develop. He was offered the drive, which he accepted. When the business-like Bunty Richmond pointed out that they could not afford to pay him but that they could probably run to expenses, his response was, 'Who asked for money?'

One of Blumer's most memorable outings in the Downton Mini, UHR 850, appropriately running a modified 850cc engine, was at the first meeting to be held on the new Grand Prix Circuit at Brands Hatch, on 1 August 1960. During practice for the saloon car race, Blumer broke a wheel out in the country. (This was a common occurrence – the early wheels were not strong enough for racing and the centres pulled out.) He got out on the grass by the nearest marshal's post, watched the detached wheel bounce along the track, failed to get out of its way, and was hit on the leg by it.

On the next lap, the same fate befell John Adams in the Speedwell Mini. He parked *his* three-wheeler at the same marshal's post, and Blumer teased him with

23

*To the crowd's delight, Blumer beat the Zephyr, but Mick Clare just failed to get by. After the race, Bunty Richmond drove the Downton Mini home to Wiltshire and took it shopping the next morning.*

the comment 'What Speedwell do today, Downton did yesterday!'

Blumer's car was recovered to the paddock, a new wheel was fitted and the scrutineer was persuaded that the same thing would not happen again. In the race, Blumer had a ding-dong with Jeff Uren driving the works Ford Zodiac. This 'David and Goliath' epic resulted in a class third for the Mini in the up to 1500 class! In Blumer's own words, 'The race was terrific fun and it didn't do any harm for Downton.' He was asked to complete a lap of honour, usually reserved for class and overall winners, and the crowd showed their enthusiasm for the little car and its driver.

Daniel Richmond claimed that the car was achieving 0 to 100mph in 27 seconds. BMC soon addressed the wheel problem, making a stronger version, stamped with the MG logo, for easy recognition by the scrutineers. In the meantime, Bunty Richmond drove the Mini home after the race at Brands Hatch, and then used it to go shopping the next morning.

In 1963, Downton joined with the Cooper Team for a three-car assault at the Spa round of the European Touring Car Championship. Practice times were good. Before the race, the Cooper team manager Ken Tyrrell agreed with the three drivers that if, as expected, they were running class 1, 2 and 3 at the finish, they should cross the line in formation. Everything was going according to plan, with Sir John Whitmore leading from Jimmy Blumer and Bill Blydenstein. On the last lap, however, Blydenstein popped his gearbox and dropped back. Whitmore and Blumer tried to communicate with each other in sign language whether they should wait for him or not. Meanwhile, the works DKW capitalized on their hesitation and roared past to win the class. The Mini formation thus came home in 2, 3, 4, instead of 1, 2, 3!

Within a couple of weeks of first meeting the Richmonds, Blumer visited their premises in Wiltshire and established business, as well as driving, links with the company, with his Roseberry Service

Station becoming the area agent for Downton products. Bunty Richmond was quick to point out that dealings would be based strictly on a cash-on-delivery basis. When racing in the south, Blumer invariably stayed with the Richmonds, sharing fine wine with them and lingered over many a dinner table. On such occasions, it was not uncommon for Daniel Richmond to start to draw out the solution of some engineering problem on a paper napkin or cigarette packet, while apparently remaining fully involved in the conversation.

Downton maintained a good record, often beating Speedwell and Alexander cars, and gaining excellent publicity in the motoring press. Often, at Newcastle Motor Club meetings held on the RAF Ouston Airfield circuit, Jimmy Blumer would be driving in four or five races, competing in the Mini, in his Cooper Monaco, and in other people's cars too. He professes to have had the most fun in the Mini 850; it also kept him relatively dry, unlike the single-seaters and sports cars.

At the end of the 1962 season, Blumer was offered a deal to drive for Ford, and left his position as the Downton team driver. Bunty Richmond teasingly calling him a traitor but they still ended up enjoying dinner together after races.

## JANSPEED ENGINEERING LTD

### Jan Odor

Another tuner to cut his teeth on Minis was Hungarian refugee Jan Odor, who arrived in the UK in 1958 and become an odd-job man for Daniel Richmond at Downton. There, his expertise soon became apparent. First, he found a rusty lathe in bits in the corner of the workshop, assembled the machine and got it working. Next, he persuaded Richmond to let him rebuild a worn-out Bentley cylinder head that had been brought in by a customer and was considered beyond saving. He completed the job to an excellent standard. It turned out that Odor had completed two years' training as machinist in a Budapest locomotive works, and, with Daniel Richmond's encouragement, he began to use his skills on many other projects. He soon became an integral part of the Downton team.

Determined to set up on his own, Odor left Downton in 1962. Tom Sawyer, a Downton customer whose racing Mini Cooper had been looked after by Odor, offered to capitalize the new business, in return for a partnership. Janspeed Engineering Ltd was born.

*Spa 1962 – the formation finish that did not go quite to plan. The Cooper team (left to right), John Whitmore, Jimmy Blumer and Bill Blydenstein, about to lose the class on the finishing line to Holvoet's DKW.*

Sawyer's Cooper was raced with continuing success. On one occasion, Odor met John Cooper in the paddock at Goodwood and enquired if his company would supply him with close-ratio gears and wide wheels. Cooper replied 'no', adding that Odor's car was already going fast enough! The Mini was campaigned until it was written off at Brands. Odor graduated to preparing a BMC-engined Formula 3 car for John Fenning to drive, and did some hillclimbs himself in a modified A35 van.

## John Fenning

John Fenning first met Jan Odor while he was on crutches following a road accident. The pair hit it off straight away, and Fenning was subsequently Odor's choice to drive the red and black Janspeed Morris Mini Cooper, 2705 MW, in the 1963 British Touring Car Championship. Fenning had a good season, enjoying many dices with John Whitmore whom he described as 'a driver and a half'.

One of the most memorable races between Fenning and Whitmore was at Goodwood on Easter Monday, 15 April 1963:

> We were at it hammer and tongs the whole race but I just could not make a passing move stick. It was real door-handle stuff. Anyway, I had it sussed, I was going to get him at the chicane on the last lap. I tried to drive round the inside of him on entry, Whitty leant on me and I demolished the chicane for the second time in my career. Determined to finish, I stuck it in reverse and backed out straight into Christabel's path and she stuffed me up the arse.

The class result was 1 Sir John Whitmore (93), 2 Christabel Carlisle (92), and 3 John

*After his race-long dice with John Whitmore at Goodwood on 15 April 1963, John Fenning (2705 MW) was determined to snatch victory at the chicane on the last lap, but it was not to be. Having got it wrong and hit the wall, Fenning then reversed out into the path of Christabel Carlisle (CMC 77). The dented boot lid and wing can be seen as they dash for the line.*

Fenning (98). Although he did not win, Fenning did set the fastest lap, 1:48.6 (79.86mph/128kph) on lap 9, breaking the existing record. After the race, the two Johns were hauled up in front of the stewards for door-handling.

Like John Aley, Fenning became involved in motor sport safety products, founding Willans, the harness manufacturers, in 1969. Fenning himself did not wear a harness in single-seaters until 1967, when he adapted an ex-government pilot's harness, bought, still in its cellophane packet, from a surplus store. He shortened it on an old shoemaker's sewing machine, and made special fittings to bolt it into the car. Subsequently, he started producing similar harnesses for other people, selling about twelve in his first year. Purpose-built Willans belts are now seen in competition cockpits throughout the world.

## The Other Janspeed Minis

In 1965, two Janspeed 1000cc Cooper S club cars were raced by Terry Kirby, who worked in the Janspeed cylinder-head shop, and Ralph Wilding. Between them, they notched up some good results. Over the winter Jan Odor decided to build an 850 Mini, but the following season seems to have had few small-class races and the car did not have many outings. However, Tom Sawyer, who never claimed to be a particularly fast driver, did chop two seconds off the record in the car at a hillclimb. As it was getting so little use, the car was converted to a 1293S and won first time out, at Castle Combe, in the hands of Geoff Mabbs.

In the summer of 1967, Janspeed Engineering moved into a new factory. Janspeed products, particularly exhaust manifolds, continue to be used world-wide, although Jan Odor himself has now retired.

## JACK DAVIES

Among the many club racers who used Downton was Sussex driver Jack Davies. He competed in Autocross, sprints, hillclimbs and circuit races in a Mini Cooper S, bought in 1964 as a family car for himself, his wife and his two sons. (Those two boys, Tony and John, were destined to follow their father into motor sport.) From 1966 to 1975, Jack Davies won more than 400 awards with the car, which he still owns today.

After doing a few local Autocross events, Davies heard that Sevenoaks and District Motor Club was holding an evening test session at Brands. He immediately joined the club and went along, and that was the beginning of this racing career. In 1969, he

*Jack Davies gets one wheel in the air at the Eight Clubs Silverstone meeting on 7 June 1969. His car had just returned from Downton Engineering after a rebuild. The engine featured special titanium con rods and, running on split Weber 45s, produced 130bhp. Davies still owns the car and has won over 400 awards in it.*

competed at Boxing Day Brands, in front of the TV cameras. His fame was short-lived. Derek Foy and he tangled on the start line and Davies ended up in the barriers.

Weekend family outings centred around Davies' racing, and he would often perform at two different circuits on consecutive days. On one such occasion, he was having a good race at Lydden on the Sunday when he had to take to the grass to avoid a spinning Anglia. A wheel dug in, the Mini gently rolled over into the bank, and the screen popped out, caused by pressure from a large dent in the roof. Not wanting to spoil his Bank Holiday Monday outing at Croft, Davies went home for a few hours' sleep before setting off northwards at the crack of dawn. Half-way up the M1, he called into a windscreen company, got a new screen fitted, and persuaded the fitter to knock out the roof roughly into the bargain. The car made practice in plenty of time.

# MICK CLARE

Cambridge garage proprietor Mick Clare was another driver who started in single-seaters, and was inspired to buy himself one of the new Minis after watching them race. His races in 1960 were in a near-standard 850 car, YMJ 681. His first modification was to fabricate cooling ducts for the front brakes from a cut-down oil can and some rubber tubing. Assisted by his son Terry, he gas-flowed his cylinder heads with the aid of cigar smoke, then tested the car down the road behind the garage.

Mick Clare started the 1961 season with a win at the BRSCC Snetterton Spring Meeting, beating John Aley at an average speed of 72.33mph (115.7kph). Alexander Engineering then asked him to race under their team banner; they would supply some cash, together with tuning parts, while the Clares would still do their own cylinder heads. More success followed.

Clare moved up to a 997 Cooper for the 1962 season, and was one of the few privateers to be able to keep up with the Cooper Car Company cars. At Goodwood, however, he was frustrated at constantly being out-braked by the Cooper cars. After practice, he strolled over and observed that their Minis were fitted with larger discs and callipers. After a quick visit to the men from Girling, he himself was also similarly equipped.

The 1071S was introduced in April 1962, and Mick Clare got one in time for the British Grand Prix meeting at Aintree on 21 July, where he came fourth in class.

In June 1963, at Mallory Park, the handlebar-moustachioed man from Cambridge achieved every privateer's dream and beat the works team. It was not an easy race by any means. He managed to get in front on the first lap and, in an effort to stay ahead, braked much too late for Shaws Hairpin.

The car went completely sideways, pretty well setting itself up for the corner and he kept the lead. The problems were subsequently found to have resulted from oil from a detached breather pipe spraying on to the nearside brake disc.

Under normal circumstances, any driver might have pulled off but, sensing the chance of a unique victory, Clare pressed on. To add to his problems, the bonnet popped up onto its safety catch, and he quite expected to be black-flagged. Perhaps the marshals turned a blind eye because he was in front? As he was running a 4.2 diff, he could do the whole circuit, except the hairpin, in top. He was straight-lining The Esses at 8,000rpm, using lots of grass verge on entry and just missing it on the exit. It was a spectacular drive that had the crowd on its feet, and secured Mick Clare a fine victory.

The next weekend, at Goodwood, he was once again up among the Cooper boys. In a do-or-die effort, he got past them going round the outside of St Marys. He slipstreamed Mike Young's Anglia, but the Ford's wider rubber meant that the Mini was unable to pass. After the race, the

*Cambridge driver Mick Clare was noted for his speed behind the wheel; in the paddock, his trademark handlebar moustache made him stand out from the crowd.*

scrutineers went over the Mini with a fine-tooth comb, convinced that its remarkable progress must be as the result of some rule infringement. As expected, they found nothing untoward.

By 1964, Mick Clare had progressed to a 1275S bearing the number MC 58. The April meeting at Aintree witnessed the end of his fine record. During the race, a car in the gaggle of saloons in front of him braked too early for a bend. Having put the car slightly sideways to miss it, Clare floored the throttle to try and get round everyone else. He went too wide and demolished the brick boilerhouse, hitting it at about 85mph (135kph). He was dragged from the car, and immediately asked for a pain-killing injection so that he could watch the end of the race. Later, at the hospital, doctors discovered a broken wrist and broken leg, as well as a couple of cracked ribs.

Nine months later, Clare was fit enough to make a return in the repaired S, but his damaged ankle, now twisted, did not aid his driving style. From always being a front-runner before the accident, he was now finishing fourth and fifth, so he decided to call it a day. John Wales continued to campaign the car during 1965 and 1966.

## STEVE McQUEEN

Film star Steve McQueen was a great motor sport enthusiast, racing many types of car both in America and Europe, as well as sharing an interest in motorcycles with Sir John Whitmore. Having secured the 1961 British Saloon Car Championship in the penultimate round, Whitmore opted to lend the Hollywood star his Mini for the last race at Brands on 1 October. McQueen enjoyed a good dice with Vic Elford and Christabel Carlisle, and came home third in class.

*Brands Hatch start line 1961: John Whitmore talks to Steve McQueen, who is strapped into Whitmore's first racing Mini, ready for the off. McQueen came third in the race.*

# BARRIE 'WHIZZO' WILLIAMS

During a career spanning forty years of Autocross, sprints, racing and rallying, Barrie Williams drove many Minis on the track. He had rallied them on and off since 1962, enjoyed a couple of circuit outings in his faithful rally 1071S, 120 MNP, and had previous race experience in a Morris 1000. He recalls that early Mini racers used Michelin Xs; when the steel bands came through the outer wall, they would turn them round so that they were inside, out of the scrutineers' sight. You could tell if a car was really motoring, because the bands would spark as they struck the tarmac.

At Mallory Park in 1965, Barrie Williams drove Liz McKechnie's metallic-blue Broadspeed-built 999S. Williams had raced an Anglia for Liz's brother Alan. The blue Mini had been rebuilt following a big accident at Mallory, which had led to Liz's virtual retirement. Williams raced the car at many circuits during the season, then a 1275 lump was put in it and he took it to Sweden, and to Spain for a European Championship Race.

The Spanish race took place at Jarama, during the European Formula 2 weekend of 22/23 July 1967. Williams towed the Mini to Spain on the back of his Austin A40 Farina, discovering on arrival that he was in the same hotel as the Grand Prix drivers. The next morning, two of the drivers, having missed their ride to the circuit, scrounged a lift with Williams. The A40 was full, so they had to ride in the racer, on the trailer. Having indulged in a little horseplay with one of the local drivers, Williams found himself entering a roundabout too quickly. Looking in the mirror, he saw that Piers Courage's reactions were on the ball. Sitting in the Mini's driving seat, he had it on full opposite lock!

Williams recalls that practice had its

*Barrie Williams in the McKechnie Racing Organisation's Broadspeed-built Mini in 1965.*

high and its low points. The high point was when he achieved a circuit first for a Mini, putting in a scorching lap to claim a front-row grid position. The low point was when one of the adjustable shock absorbers broke, pitching the car into the barriers; the marshals added insult to injury by frog-marching him to an ambulance for a compulsory trip to the medical centre. When he arrived back in the paddock, the Mini was a sorry state. The officials were disappointed that it seemed unlikely it would race, but the Brabham mechanics came up with a solution. Their team had use of the facilities at a Madrid garage that also happened to be the local BMC dealers. Williams dragged the remains of the Mini onto his trailer and drove to Madrid. The local mechanics cut off the front end, hand-beat all the body panels back to shape and then spot-welded them back on.

During practice, one of Williams' friends had seen that, while the award for the first Austin home in the Saloon Car Race was rather insignificant, the trophy for the first Morris was an enormous silver cup. While the mechanics were completing the welding, Williams removed the grille from a brand-new Mini, and borrowed the dynamo and distributor to replace the damaged items on his own car. He replaced the grille on the showroom car, to conceal the fact that the items were missing. He then had the Morris badges removed from his car, so that they would be eligible for the better award. A local driver, who was also competing in a Mini, suggested they go to his flat, as he had the other spares needed to complete the repair. The flat was better stocked than Special Tuning at Abingdon. The man produced suspension components from the wardrobe and three tyres from under a bed, then drove them back to the workshop in the early hours, going through all the red lights and stopping at the green ones.

The reassembled car was sprayed with aerosols and, after a couple of hours snatched sleep, Williams drove back to the circuit. He thought all his troubles were over, but an alert official on the starting grid pointed out that the regulations required competing cars to have carpets and a spare wheel. The Mini lacked both. One of the crew ran back to the paddock, ripped the carpets out of a friend's Cortina and took one of the wheels off the trailer. He rushed back to the grid, threw the trailer wheel in the boot and stuffed the carpet behind the driver's seat.

Compared with the events of the previous twenty-four hours, the race was fairly uneventful. Williams' damaged radiator grille fell out on the first lap, and he finished third overall and won the class. But, most importantly, as the driver of the first Morris to cross the finishing line, Barrie Williams is still the proud owner of that fine silver trophy.

After totalling HCJ 870D, a brand-new 1275S, in the 1966 RAC Rally, Williams had the car rebuilt as a racer, and notched up a class second in the 1967 Snetterton 500km race. Tony Lanfranchi was nominated as second driver for this three-hour race, but Williams just managed to go the whole distance on the fuel in the twin tanks and decided against a pit stop. In any event, he says, he was faster than Lanfranchi in that particular car. Another good result in that car was a third in the 1967 TT at Oulton Park.

Having made friends during previous racing trips to Sweden, Barrie Williams was invited to take part in a Trotterling event – car racing on a gravel oval usually used for horse-trotting races – at Ärjang, close to the Norwegian border. One of the locals lent him some road tyres to replace the nobblies that were on the car, and warned him to cover the headlights and leading edge of the front wings with foam rubber to protect them from the flying gravel. The cars raced six at a time, starting on a 3 x 3 grid – 'basically one enormous drift', according to Williams. Even up against local drivers in works-backed cars designed for the surface, he won all his heats and the final, and used the day's prize money to buy an engagement ring for his Swedish fiancée.

Barrie Williams had known Harry Ratcliffe for a long time and, as well as having occasional drives for the Vita team, had worked for him as workshop manager for a couple of years. In 1969, when the team moved on from Minis, he purchased KDK 319F, a 970S and raced it privately in the British Touring Car Championship. It proved so reliable that he hardly spent a penny on it all season, only checking the tappets and changing the diff pawls, and, when he was feeling particularly flush, splashing out on a new set of plugs. It was a year's cheap motor sport, with good results.

At the end of the season, Williams was called upon by the oil company to whom he was contracted to be part of a three-man

*Barrie Williams using his ex-Vita Mini to good effect in the Guards 200 at Brands Hatch in 1969; he finished third.*

team to test a proposed new lubricant. He was joined by a motorcycle racer and by Formula Vee driver Fred Saunders for two days of slogging round Snetterton, with pit stops for fuel and to enable the technicians to check oil consumption and viscosity. The three drivers took part on the basis that, if they experienced engine problems, the company would pay for a rebuild. With this in mind, Saunders put in his spare engine and drove his car round with great verve, determined to get a new one. Despite circulating at below the Formula Vee lap record, he did not succeed.

The idea of the new product was that, in addition to excellent lubrication properties, it should have the same distinctive smell as one of the company's more expensive products. To this end, the boffins had added a special ingredient. The second part of the test took place at the MOD test track at Chobham in Surrey. The three drivers were asked to lap at a steady speed and to throttle back opposite the slip road, where the assembled experts would be sniffing. A 70mph (110kph) speed limit was in force, and Williams was soon called in by the officer in charge, who, unim-

pressed by his 100mph (160kph) lap, reprimanded him. Much to Williams' amusement, the sniffers were by now lying on their stomachs in an effort to detect that smell. Not surprisingly, the oil was never put into production.

Williams yearned for 1300 power again and swapped the 'Vitamin' for a larger-engined example built by Wally Dick, who used to look after John Rhodes' cars. KDF 319F was sold to a policeman who used it on the road, while Williams raced the 1300.

In 1995, Williams drove Norman Grimshaw's Historic Touring Car, a 1964 1293S, at Donington Park and thoroughly enjoyed himself. He found he was setting lap times that would match a Fiesta XR2. He recalls, 'When I got out of the car, I could not get the grin off my face.' Grimshaw now owns 120 MNP and arranged that, after a rebuild, Williams would drive it in the Rallysprint at the 1998 Coys Historic Weekend. The car was not finished in time. The bonnet and boot lid, complete with registration numbers, were swapped over on to Grimshaw's own road rally S, and Williams took that round; he did not spare his right foot, and was quickest in two out of three runs. His adversary asked how an old boy like him could still drive so fast; Williams just smiled. At the awards dinner in November, which coincided with his sixtieth birthday, he received a trophy for outstanding performance, as well as 'a super choccie cake, which I very quickly cut up and passed round those on my table, before it ended up in someone's face'.

## JULIAN VEREKER AND THE COBURN 850S

Working for Coburn Improvements, a tuning firm who operated from the ground floor of a converted coach house at 7 Netherhall Gardens, Hampstead, North London, Julian Vereker was ideally placed to make his own Mini special. While many racing cars passed through the ground-floor workshop, the flat upstairs was, over the years, home to many names in the motor sport world including Martin Davidson, Jack Wheeler and John Brown. Julian Vereker's pale blue Austin Mini ended up as what he called an 850S. The engine was based on a late 1098 Midget block, with 2in main bearings; in it were a Blydenstein 340/320 racing cam, a 970S crank with specially modified Cooper S rods and Fiat 500 pistons. The cylinder head was based on an 11-stud Formula Junior casting that had been well worked, and incorporated large nimonic steel valves, with lightened valve gear and followers. It had a Weber 45 on a Derrington inlet with Janspeed exhaust manifold. The transmission had straight-cut S gears and a very low, 4.6 final drive. It revved to 9,000 and pulled 80bhp at 7,200.

A great deal of thought went into building the engine. The machining was done by Bill Flowers, the son of the owner of Mill Hill Engineering, whose main business was the rebuilding of bus engines. The 1275 rods needed to be bushed to accept the Fiat gudgeon pin and would only go in the block from the bottom. The pistons had to be fitted afterwards and, to allow for this, the block had to be machined to allow the big ends to come up high enough to allow the rods to protrude sufficiently for the pistons to go on. As they were from an air-cooled engine, these had to be at 100 degrees before the pin would fit; once in, it was secured by a wire circlip. Julian made various gadgets to simplify the assembly.

It was not only the engine of YXN 554 that was special. All the suspension angles had been modified, and the car had been lowered and fitted with special Koni shock absorbers. The front S disc brakes were augmented by Minifin drums, with VG 95 linings, on the rear. The car ran on Dunlop Green Spot four-band racing tyres.

In common with the cars of many racers of his time, Julian Vereker's Mini was not only street legal, it was his only form of everyday transport. It was road-tested by *Cars and Car Conversions* who found it 'quite amazingly flexible: you can potter through the Hampstead traffic at under 2,000rpm in top gear if you feel like it, the engine ticks over at 1,000rpm, smoothly, relatively quietly and with no sign of temperament.' It seemed that Vereker had come up with a winner. During 1966, the little car covered 7,000 road miles (over 11,000km), and started and finished eighteen races. Vereker's tally: five second places, four thirds and three fourths. The Mini was fast as well as reliable – it went through the Oulton Park speed trap at 103mph (165kph), and is claimed to have seen off an Elan while on a holiday trip, fully laden with luggage. According to Vereker, its reliability came from the fact that the cam did not maximize the valve lift, unlike those used by many of his contemporaries. His concept was to use a gentle lift and utilize the flow of exhaust gases to the maximum, thus his tuned length long centre branch exhaust system.

For the 1967 season, Vereker's car was improved still further and began to produce 83bhp at 8,200rpm, giving a top speed of 114mph (182.5kph). A limited slip differential was fitted and the bodywork was painted in the Coburn colours of royal blue with gold roof and bonnet.

Vereker was one of only four drivers to get hold of a set of the new Firestone slick tyres, which the company had only just started to make for Minis. One day he was called by his old college friend Chris Parry who worked in the Firestone Competition

*Julian Vereker leads a Hillman Imp and a field of Minis at Brands Hatch early in the 1967 season.*

Department. Firestone had four sets of the slick tyres for sale at £36 a set on a first-come, first-served basis. It would take Vereker an hour to drive to Brentford and he did not have £36, but he knew that he would regret it if he did not have the tyres. He went straight round to see his bank manager, Norman Bill, for a loan. Bill pointed out that tyres wore out and that, in any case, he would also need special wheels for them, a fact which Vereker had forgotten. However, he was persuaded that the tyres would win races and increased Vereker's overdraft by £94 to cover the new equipment. Vereker drove straight to Essex and got the first set. Once he had had the tyres fitted to the car on $5^1/_2$in (13.75cm) Minilites, he found that they were good for two seconds a lap round the Brands Club Circuit.

In 1967, Vereker again completed every race he started, winning seventeen and never finishing outside the points. Despite not completing the full season, he won the Free Formula 850 championship, scoring 54 points, beating Bob Riley and Frank Reynolds, who were both on 38 points. One memorable race was at Mallory in

May. Having qualified fourth, he was up the front from the flag. Bob Fox got past, but went off at the next corner. Malcolm Quickfall, driving his Langrop Engineering-prepared car, overtook Vereker on the straight, then the pair were locked in battle for the rest of the race. On the last lap, Vereker out-fumbled Quickfall through The Esses and then got it sideways in front of Quickfall at Shaws Hairpin, forcing him to brake. In the dash to the line, Vereker got it by a headlamp rim.

Julian Vereker had only gone racing to prove that he could build engines and, having done that, he decided to retire. Racing and working in the tuning business had proved very time-consuming. The car was advertised in September for £650, with the original wheels and Dunlop tyres, and was sold to Peter Baldwin. Vereker then sold the Minilites with the Firestones, which the bank manager had looked upon as a depreciating asset, for more than he had paid, after using them for the best part of a season.

Part of the way through the year, Daniel Richmond had persuaded Vereker to leave

Coburn and go and work for him at Downton. A big bust-up with Bunty Richmond meant that he only stayed for six months before leaving to join Janspeed towards the end of the year. He now runs his audio business from the former Janspeed premises, which he bought from Jan Odor in the early 1970s.

## SIMON RIDGE

Simon Ridge competed in Special Saloon Minis from 1965 to 1975. For his first two seasons, he drove his car to and from the circuit, but a coming-together with Dave Morgan at the Mallory hairpin caused the pair some problems. Both had to botch up their cars in order to drive them home again. Both had to hammer suspension components straight; Morgan had to tie his passenger door shut with rope and

Ridge had to get south of London, where he knew the roads, before dark, as he had no headlights. The following season, each invested in a basic £45 Mike Cannon trailer.

By 1970, Simon Ridge was being sponsored by Automex. That season, he did thirty-four races, won nine and came second thirteen times. He had now bought a spare engine and gearbox and worked on the basis that he did eight races with one unit then swapped them over, giving him time to rebuild the one that had just come out, so that it was ready to go back in after the next eight outings. He also had to work in a quick re-shell after a race at Crystal Palace on 3 October. Taking avoiding action to miss a spinning Anglia, he went through the ambulance entrance in the infield sleeper wall and hit a tree. It was a televised meeting and his wife and mother-in-law were sitting at home watching in

*Simon Ridge on his way to a win at Crystal Palace in 1970.*

horror, while Murray Walker gave the viewers all the details.

Despite this setback, 1970 was Ridge's most successful year. Competing in three championships, he had good results in all of them. He won the Janspeed Challenge Trophy, came second to Roger Williamson in the Hepolite-Glacier Championship and was second to John Turner in the Atlantic Petroleum series. Points scorers in the latter were rewarded with petrol vouchers from the company – these proved very useful, as he was now towing with an ex-police Wolseley fitted with a Healey 3000 engine.

Simon Ridge had only one outing in 1971, in a friend's car. He had entered the Trumps Moto-Pop Midsummer Night's Motor Race Meeting at Crystal Palace, on the evening of 18 June. As well as a full race programme, the event included per-

formances by Manfred Mann, Desmond Decker and Humphrey Lyttleton, as well as a fashion show and an appearance by the Penthouse Pets! Needless to say, the 'midsummer' weather did not oblige. Ridge's race was black-flagged when he was lying fifth, owing to a flooded circuit.

In 1973, Ridge bought an ex-Nick Cole 1300 Mini for £250 from Roger Holgate. The price was realistic as the car had been stripped to a shell and all the running gear was inside, in boxes. He competed in this until 22 June 1975, when he hung up his helmet. During his ten years in Special Saloons, Ridge did 109 races, notching up eighteen wins, forty-five seconds and eleven third places. In his view, it was a privilege to be part of the club scene in the mid-1960s; by 1975, he was witnessing a certain change of mood and seeing the spirit of the era vanishing.

## JAMES HUNT

Simon Ridge was indirectly responsible for world-famous racing driver James Hunt becoming involved in motor sport. This resulted in some friction between the families, as Hunt did not go to medical school as intended. Simon Ridge's brother Chris was James Hunt's tennis partner. Hunt happened to arrive at the Ridges' house in Surrey one day when Simon was preparing his car for its next outing. He showed considerable interest in the car, so Ridge offered him some spare tickets to Silverstone the following day. The date was 28 August 1965, the day before Hunt's eighteenth birthday, and the invitation was accepted.

*1968: James Hunt stands on the grid beside the car of Simon Ridge, the person who first sparked his interest in motor racing.*

James Hunt turned up at the appointed hour in his mother's Mini van, to follow Ridge to Silverstone. The back was full of boxes of old squash bottles filled with water, to feed the van's leaky radiator. Throughout the journey, Ridge had to keep an eye on the mirror and stop every time the Mini van needed to replenish the radiator.

After watching the race, Hunt announced that he was going to be a racing driver. Ridge reminded him that being a racing driver was not a job and that he did it just for fun, but he agreed to help him get started. He knew Mike Pigneguy and arranged for Hunt to pay him £45 for the ex-Mac Ross racing Mini that had been written off at Mallory. He found another shell; the plan was to swap all the running gear over from the damaged racer to the new shell. Part of the way through the project, Hunt decided to finish the job himself.

Having (in his view) completed the car, James Hunt entered three races at Snetterton, but immediately encountered one or two problems with the scrutineers. First, they observed that, instead of being fitted with the obligatory laminated windscreen, the car only had the toughened one that had been in the shell of the original road car. They were not impressed when he offered to remove both front and rear screens. The regulations in force at the time also provided that all saloon cars should be fitted with a passenger seat. In an attempt to comply with this, Hunt had used bits of an old Meccano set to fit a small, metal-framed motorist's picnic chair. He did not get a race.

On his second attempt, Hunt passed scrutineering but encountered mechanical problems during practice. It was almost third-time lucky at Brands Hatch on 8 October 1967, when J.S.H. Hunt made the grid and was doing quite well, despite two cars spinning off in front of him. On lap five, an observant marshal noticed car number 214 was leaking oil and Hunt was duly black-flagged. He decided that enough was enough, sold the Mini and used the money as a down payment on an Alexis Formula Ford.

This was the first rung on Hunt's ladder to his World Championship. Coincidentally, when Simon Ridge climbed out of his own Mini after his last-ever race, in June 1975, the Brands Hatch commentator announced that he had heard on the radio that James Hunt had just won his first Grand Prix.

## DAVID MORGAN

Unfortunately, David Morgan's connection with James Hunt relates to a clash between the two during a Crystal Palace F3 race in 1970; as a result, Morgan was called up before a tribunal. It seems that the driving was getting a bit cut and thrust and Morgan ended up as the scapegoat.

Young David Morgan started his racing at an early age, in pedal cars, but had his first taste of Mini power when his father let him drive his Speedwell-tuned Mini van at a Brands Hatch public test day, circa 1964. Morgan's father had raced an XK 120 and, when that had been written off, had acquired a couple of Mini shells, with a view to one day turning them into a racer. After his drive round Brands, David Morgan was fired with enthusiasm and soon commandeered the project. His first-ever race was at Mallory and resulted in him collecting his spinning friend, Simon Ridge.

Morgan could not afford racing tyres and had to rely on Pirelli Cinturatos, quite soft road tyres. He 'upgraded' his 850 for a short-stroke 997, which he found to be slower and success eventually came when he got himself a 998 Cooper engine. His first win was at Lydden Hill in 1966, when he beat the local circuit expert in his Anglia. Now the Mini sported one of the first sets of Minilites complete with proper racing rubber. He had also asked Tony Bunton of Carlow Engineering to build him a 970S power unit, which ran a down-draught Weber 48 and revved to 10,000rpm. This appreciably increased the top end.

The 1967 season saw a sponsored drive from Bob Henderson of Minnow Carburettors, with Morgan's car running a set of his carbs and, much to Morgan's disgust, a silencer. Henderson believed that the practice, then popular, of running an open exhaust decreased the power output. He was also offered a 'works' engine, which had been built by Downton, but found little or no improvement from the Carlow Engineering version that he had previously used. Morgan continued his winning ways, but now admits that, while the Fish gave greater torque, his old 48 produced a greater maximum speed. Towards the end of the season, Tony Bunton offered Morgan a drive in his 1300S and he won a race in it at Brands.

Saloon car fans of the day must still remember the famous 1000cc dice that David Morgan had at Brands with Alan Peer (Anglia) and Bernard Unett (Fraser Imp). Unett spun in the early stages and had to make up ground. Morgan was just in front as the three of them rounded Clearways for the last time, but they crossed the line virtually three abreast. The verdict just went to the Anglia, with the Mini second.

Morgan used to tow the racing-car trailer on the back of a Mark 7 Jaguar, loaded with spares and his team of helpers. While the Jag was capable of maintaining a good cruising speed, the load left the acceleration a little bit to be desired. On runs to Cadwell Park, Morgan utilized Lincolnshire's flat terrain to the full. By standing on the transmission tunnel with his head out of the sun roof, one of his mates could tell Morgan if any cars were approaching, or whether it was safe to straight-line the bend. In this way, the team were able to travel at a fairly constant 110mph (175kph). On a good day, an early-morning run from Surrey to Cadwell could be done in just over three hours – a creditable time, given the roads of the day.

After F3, David Morgan moved to Formula Atlantic before retiring from the cockpit in 1982 and becoming a race engineer. In 1998, he was working in this position with an American Indycar team.

# 2   Bigger and Better

Throughout the 1960s, the Mini seemed unstoppable on the British club scene, with drivers and tuners continuing to work together to wring just a little more out of their cars. As the years went by, an increasing number of competitors switched to the model to enjoy their motor sport to the full.

## THE CHARLES CLARK MINIS

From 1964 to 1968, Charles Clark, the BMC dealers from Chapel Ash, near Wolverhampton, backed a two-car Mini racing team, driven by three of their salesmen, Ian Mitchell, Phil Darbyshire, and Tony Matthews (who also acted as team manager). Phil Darbyshire and Ian

Mitchell had been racing their own 1000cc road cars for some while, Mitchell eventually taking his off the road to make it an all-out racer. Darbyshire won the 'Absolutely Standard Old Boy Race' at Mallory, his Cooper naturally in road trim.

Picking their moment, at the end of a good business week, the three salesmen managed to persuade Clark's Managing Director Billy Stokes to back the team. Clarks bought Ian Mitchell's car and ordered a new 1275S. The team colours of Fiesta yellow with a white roof came about by accident. A Clark's customer also had an S on order and had requested a yellow one, so the sales manager put the racer through as yellow as well, on the basis that his customer would get the one that came through first. After delivery of the

*Team Charles Clark: (left to right) Tony Matthews, Ian Mitchell, Nick Brise (Joint MD) and Phil Darbyshire, June 1964.*

yellow 1275S, both racers were taken to John Rhodes for preparation, with Downton being entrusted with the engines. Clarks did the bodywork in house.

The cars took awards at local sprints and hillclimbs, as well as many places in races throughout the UK. On consecutive weekends at Mallory, Phil Darbyshire broke a wheel at Gerrards and Ian Mitchell put the 1275 through the advertising hoarding at The Esses; both cars needed new shells. Tony Matthews had both cars out again at Brands a fortnight later and managed to keep the cost quiet. While Mitchell mainly campaigned the 1275 car, the drivers did occasionally swap and John Rhodes and Peter Hawthorne sometimes had outings in them as well.

In the early days of the team, the BARC would not allow cars to be entered in the name of a company, so Tony Matthews would put them in the programme under his own name. Eventually, the BARC relented, but Matthews still had to fight to be allowed to display the sponsor's name on the car. This was permitted, provided the letters were no more than an inch (2.5cm) high.

Tony Matthews was not allowed to forget the time when Ian Mitchell ran out of petrol two laps from the end, while leading a race. Nearly every member of the workshop staff brought him in a can of lighter fuel on the Monday morning after the weekend.

The 1965 Ilford Films Championship went to the last round at Brands, where either Ian Mitchell or local driver Ken Costello could win the class. Mitchell's clutch went in practice; having no spare, he loaded the Mini back on the trailer. On discovering Mitchell's problem, Ken Costello went home and got a spare and helped fit it as well. Mitchell won the race, depriving Costello of class honours. Costello said that he raced to enjoy a good dice and that there was no point in winning if his main rival was not competing.

*Phil Darbyshire at the 1965 Mallory Park Boxing Day meeting, rounding the Devil's Elbow, leading Ted Williams in his Anglia. The Mini finished second overall in the race, for saloons up to 1000cc.*

At the start of the 1966 season, the 1275 engine failed. Unable to get parts in time, Tony Matthews instructed mechanic Derek Harris to bolt it together with what bits he had, including one odd piston. Ian Mitchell went on to have his most successful year, taking twenty-six wins and securing the title of King of Mallory.

## KEN COSTELLO

Although better known for putting a V8 engine in an MGB before BMC did, Ken Costello was also renowned for his racing exploits in Minis. At one time, he held six simultaneous lap records at Brands, Castle Combe, Crystal Palace, Mallory and Lydden. He started with an 850 and ended his final races, some years later, in a white S with a gold roof. If possible, he would do two meetings in a weekend, one on Saturday and one on Sunday. Crystal Palace was his favourite track, despite the fact that there was nowhere to go if you got it wrong. He reckons he did about 400 races – building and preparing all his own cars and engines – and never retired as a result of mechanical failure. He enjoyed the spirit of racing in those days: if you nudged another driver during the race, you went over and apologized afterwards. He recalls once tapping another competitor going into the hairpin at Mallory, seeking him out and offering to pay for the cracked lamp lens.

During his 1000cc days, Costello was up against Ginger Paine in George Bevan's Austin A40 in a race at Brands. The practice was wet and the pair were at it hammer and tongs for the whole session. Having had more than his required dose of adrenalin, Costello would willingly have gone home after that. The race turned out to be a bit of an anti-climax, the contrasting dry conditions meaning that Costello's Mini did not have enough power to stay in front. His cars were always set up with lots of positive rather than negative camber, which is why they were so competitive in the wet. During one wet race at Mallory, he was leading when, two laps from home, the oil pressure dropped; he eased up, dropped the revs to 6,000 and stroked it home for a win. On stripping down the engine, he found the oil-pump spindle had broken, so he had some made out of EN36 nickel chrome steel. The bearings were not marked, which he puts down to the use of Molyslip.

On another occasion at Oulton, Costello practised out of session and had to start from the back of the grid. As he lined up, he noticed the temperature rising. To make things worse, two front-row drivers started to creep forward before the starter dropped the flag; Costello made the marshals push them back and switched off the engine while he was waiting. When the race was finally ready for the off, he had a flat battery and, by the time he had received a push start, he thought he might just as well drive straight back to the paddock. As he was thinking this, he noticed that he was already overtaking people and decided to keep going. Despite his ten-second penalty, he came second and might well have won, given another lap.

One day, while driving his Mini on the road, Costello had a bit of a dice with a Jaguar. As luck would have it, both drivers pulled into the same petrol station and the Jag driver turned out to be a salesman at Cripps Garage of Sidcup, the local Leyland dealers. When he discovered that Costello raced, he proposed a chat with the boss to see if he could get some backing. The subsequent meeting resulted in a sponsorship deal. The car was entered as a Cripspeed Mini and Costello was able to avail himself of the company's rolling-road facilities.

*Micki Vandervell in her white Cooper S (149) at Maggotts, Silverstone, August 1970. This car replaced an earlier green version, which was written off at the same circuit. Micki enjoyed her racing so much that she even competed with her wrist in plaster, following a water-skiing accident.*

In October 1965, Costello had a good dice with John Cannadine's similar S at Lydden Hill, then in its first year as a tarmac circuit, in its short form, with the hairpin only half-way up the hill. The pair were the only ones really in the race and, on this occasion, Costello was not only beaten into second place but also lost the lap record to his adversary; Cannadine lopped 0.2 seconds off the previous best time to set the new record at 40.4.

For 1966, an engine with an aluminium eight-port head and four Amal carburettors was built. Setting it up on the rollers, Costello was delighted to find he had gained another 10bhp on the top end and could not wait to get the car on the track. On its next outing, however, he found that it was two seconds a lap slower; the torque was down and he was losing time coming out of the corners.

Costello may be the only driver to have had his engine stripped to check that it was not *smaller* than its stated capacity. Having run in the up-to-1300 class in the Redex series at Brands one week, he noticed there was a Spring Grove round the next weekend, but that it was for cars in the 1301-to-2000cc class. He had an S block in his garage that had been bored plus 30, giving a capacity of 1304cc. He had pistons and rods on the shelf, so he built up a new bottom end to use with his existing head. He turned up on spec and managed to persuade Nick Syrett to let him go out and practise. As first reserve he got on the grid, where mechanical maladies forced another competitor to withdraw. On the line, Syrett told him he wanted him to go straight to the scrutineering bay after the race to check that his engine was big enough. He won the race and the engine was legal by 4cc.

*Twice National Hillclimb Champion Chris Cramer began his competition career in a Mini. Here, his S rounds a bend at Prescott, in 1970. That year he had eighteen wins and four second places. The car held class records at sixteen hills.*

Ken Costello's best year was probably 1967, when he won the Redex Saloon Car Championship, broke eight lap records and also took the 1300 class in the Mini Se7en series.

## MICKI VANDERVELL

Micki Vandervell worked at Stoke Mandeville Hospital and had her Minis tuned at the nearby premises of Alexander Engineering. She made her competition debut in Autocross during 1968, moving to circuit racing in 1970. She was somewhat nonplussed by the motoring journalists' fascination with the fact that she was the niece of Tony Vandervell, of Vanwall F1 fame; she did not really know him that well.

Micki Vandervell regularly competed in Special Saloon Minis, as well as the 1275GT, VPP 80J, in Production Saloons,

and went on to drive all manner of cars in the course of her racing. The motoring press of the time referred to her as 'a fast lady, in the nicest possible sense'.

## CHRIS CRAMER

Chris Cramer is probably best known as 1980 and 1985 British National Hillclimb Champion, but he started motor sport in 1966, sprinting his mildly tuned road 1071S. The next year, he breathed on it a bit more and, at the suggestion of fellow competitor Doc Blackridge, tried his hand on the hills and discovered that hillclimbing was for him. In 1968, Cramer and two friends paid £75 for a Mark 1 Mini, an MOT failure found in a farmyard, and started work on what was to be Cramer's first purpose-built competition car. It was powered by the 1071S engine from his original car, now highly modified, and painted in a distinctive mustard yellow. One official at Prescott, the noted hill for the historic fraternity, described it as 'that nasty little yellow tin can on four wheels that goes indecently fast'.

With the change of the class structure, dividing the classes at 1000cc and 1300cc, Cramer found that, although he could finish in the top three, the 1071 was too small for a class win against the 1300s. He decided that it would be more competitive in the smaller class, so he went to Jeff Goodliff at BVRT and got him to build a 998 with a difference – it had TJ injection and a cross-flow head. Now the results started to come, and Cramer took the 1969 Prescott Total Trophy and was runner-up in the Gold Cup. In 1970, he won both the Shell Leaders National Hillclimb Championship and the Prescott Gold Cup Competition overall. He was also second overall in the Castrol/BARC Champion-

ship. Cramer was always a competitive driver; Major Charles Lampton, one of Wiscombe's founders, recalls him as a young man, cornering the Mini on two wheels.

Cramer decided on something different for 1971 and bought a Terrapin – a sports racing car version rather than the usual single-seater. He started work on the car ready to install his existing Mini engine for the start of the season. The Terrapin design was such that the Mini engine was installed in the back of the car, but, unlike many other Mini derivatives, staying the same way round. The chassis preparation took longer than anticipated and Cramer continued running the Mini until the middle of the year, when he eventually swapped the engine over. He did not get on with it, recalling, 'I was a bit like a cat, but that car used up rather too many of my nine lives.'

*Alec Poole (86) in the Complan Mini, flanked by Jim McClements (81) and Jackie Patterson (84), Bishopscourt 1969.*

The Mini rolling shell had been sold to finance the project, so he had to use the Terrapin for the rest of the season. He sold the car but kept the engine, using the top end on a Sprite block to power his next mount – an in-line 'A' Series powered Mallock. He set sixteen class records on the hills with his Mini.

## THE COMPLAN MINI

Sometimes referred to as the 'Cotton Reel Mini' in reference to its 8 x 13in (20 x 32.5cm) Brabham wheels, this machine was the brainchild of Alec Poole and Henry Freemantle, with invaluable technical assistance from Syd Enever, head of the MG Experimental Department at Abingdon where Poole worked. The car was powered by an eight-port 1300 engine with Lucas fuel injection, *and* a Holset 3LD turbocharger, which was restricted to a maximum manifold pressure of 15psi.

The fuel pump was run at higher than normal pressure, with the injectors set at the lower pressure of 30/35psi. The compression ratio was lowered to 8:1 by machining the con rods with eighth-of-an-inch shorter centres and the clutch had stronger springs to cope with the increased torque. Not surprisingly, with the impeller spinning at very high revs, there was a risk of overheating. To counteract this, the car ran two Mini radiators, one on either side of the engine. The car had a Vita coil-sprung beam axle. On test, the engine produced nearly 200bhp at the flywheel, but was de-tuned for reliability. At 4,000rpm it gave 100bhp, rising to 160bhp at 6,000rpm, with peak power of 185bhp at 7,500rpm.

This Mini had started life as Alec's joint project with fellow Abingdon employee Bob Neville. The pair had bought a new shell and Neville had then used ex-rally

*The turbocharged fuel-injected engine from Alec Poole's Complan Mini. Built in 1969, it produced nearly 200bhp.*

subframes and suspension components, due for the scrap pile, to build it up to a rolling shell. When he was ready to do his maiden event, Neville rang Alec Poole in Ireland and asked if he could borrow the engine from his road Unipower. It was a Group 2 spec 1275 unit, so it was quite suitable. When Neville moved on to race MGs, Poole acquired his share of the car and it later became the Complan Mini, the car being named after the sponsor's product.

Alec Poole, who mainly raced the car in Ireland from 1969 to 1971, says that it pulled 142mph (227kph) on the long straight at Phoenix Park, running a 3.75 final drive. Bob Neville recalls watching one race and asking Poole afterwards why he had overtaken another car on a somewhat unusual line. Poole told him that

*Terry Harmer (223) leads Martin Raymond (224) at Crystal Palace on 3 August 1968. Harmer held his position to the flag.*

when the turbo came in, the car went where it wanted to go.

Roger Enever had a one-off outing in the car at the BRDC Silverstone meeting, towards the end of 1970. He had an overall win and recorded the fastest lap of the race, at 88.78mph (142kph).

## TERRY HARMER

Spectating at Bill Chesson's Lydden Hill Circuit near Dover, I have witnessed many a dice featuring the forceful style of Terry Harmer. Probably the best-known of the Rob Roy Racing With D.J. Bond Team drivers, Harmer invariably took the laurels, although he modestly says that he had a lot of luck. He had his first-ever race on 20 March 1966, in a mildly modified road 998cc Cooper, and took his first win at Brands. Later that year, he bought a proper racer, which, after a little work, produced some results. In 1967, he made a brief foray into 1300s – a short engine was under £100 in those days.

When funds permitted, Harmer had Downton rebuild his 970S and he got hold of some of the latest Firestones, second-hand. A Brands test proved that he had

found the right formula. He set a 60.4-second lap, passing George Bevan's Imp driven by his son Peter. In the pits George Bevan came up to him to say, 'I see you've got your 1300 engine back in again, Terry.' Harmer had to reply, 'Sorry George, it's a 1000, same as your Imp.' Apparently, Bevan senior told his son if he did not go quicker he would put Bill McGovern in the car; McGovern subsequently got the drive.

On 15 October, Harmer put his car on pole at Brands Hatch and, despite fluffing the start, got to the front at Druids on the first lap to take a win. He was so confident on the eighth tour that he was seen waving to his sister, who he had spotted in the crowd on South Bank. Doing his lap of honour – which was to be the first of many during a successful career – he soon found out how hard it was to hold the chequered flag, wave to the crowd and steer, all at the same time!

By 1968, the Downton 970S was producing about 105bhp and the plan was to do as many races as possible so that the season paid for itself. Race entries were around £3 and the organizing clubs were paying £25 prize money for a win. The Mini Se7en Club was also running a championship, with Mini drivers amassing

*Terry Harmer looks for a way past the Les Nash Anglia in a Group 2 race on the Brands Hatch Grand Prix Circuit in 1968. He had to give best to the Anglia and finished second in the up-to-1000cc class.*

points for top three placings in every saloon car race in the country. By working on his car all night, two or three days a week, Terry Harmer managed to do fifty-six races in the season, sometimes competing in four races at two different circuits in a weekend. He had eighteen wins, fourteen seconds and seven thirds and won the Mini Championship. Unfortunately, the prize fund from the factory, which had been hinted at, never materialized.

However, the biggest disappointment of the year was missing out on the Redex Saloon Car Championship at the last round, at Mallory Park. Having put the car on pole, Harmer needed one point to win. In the race, his Mini went on to three cylinders, taking three laps to clear; by this time he was a lap down and finished the race out of the points. His final total tied with Imp man Ray Calcutt, who took the crown by virtue of having the greater number of race wins. To add insult to injury, Harmer's season did not pay for itself either. Over the winter, he built his own 1300 engine; designed for low down torque rather than maximum power, it produced 120bhp.

In 1969, Terry Harmer raced in various classes, not by choice but out of necessity, owing to mechanical maladies. He ran the 1300, his old 970 and a 1000 borrowed from Martin Raymond. He broke the Brands GP Circuit lap record with the 970; on the lap, his brakes had failed, the lap after that, the engine let go. He also shared with Bob Jones the Group 5 Mini that Jones co-owned with Paul Hutton, in a British Touring Car round two-hour race at Brands. After a pit stop that lost them a minute, they came home fourth after tailing race winner Rob Mason for the last part of the race. The £45 prize money was equivalent to nearly two weeks' wages.

Harmer managed three Special Saloon wins in early 1970, before he pinched the running gear in March to complete the D.J. Bond-sponsored Group 5 Mini built for the British Saloon Car Championship. He finished the year fourth in class and used the car in Group 5 trim to get pole in a wet Special Saloon race at Mallory. He was forced to retire at the end of lap one when a dirty fuse stopped the wipers. Lack of funds prevented much racing in the early part of 1971, but in September he

*In front of the old Brands Hatch clubhouse, Terry Harmer and John Thurlow do the last-minute checks before Paul Harmer's first race, in June 1969. Meanwhile, the driver chats to his girlfriend, who has been allowed to sit on the wing of his Ford Anglia.*

bought Rob Mason's well-known Don Moore 1300 Mini, when Mason changed his allegiance to Imps. Harmer raced this car with great success until 1973.

Harmer's outstanding race during this period was an outright win at a wet Brands Hatch on 1 April 1973. He beat Nick Whiting's Escort by thirteen seconds, only to be told by the stewards that he had been given a jump-start penalty. They let him explode before telling him that it was only a ten-second penalty, so he had still won the race. April Fool?

With marriage just around the corner, the car was sold soon after this outing but, in November, Harmer purchased a semi space frame 1300 from Chris Bruce. He campaigned this until 1976 and was always a leading contender, when he could afford to race. He remembers 1974 as the year everybody in Special Saloons was going quicker and quicker; he himself cracked the 53-second mark at Brands Hatch for the first time.

In 1975, Harmer planned to have a serious crack at the Simoniz Championship. By mid-season he had a three-win advan-

tage, and then his employers went bust. Harmer soon got another job with D.J. Bond who continued to pay entry fees and travelling costs, but he was short on funds to maintain the car and had to miss several rounds which eroded his lead. By the last round he had dropped to third. With double points on offer he turned out for the final race and got enough points to get back to second in the championship, which was won by Peter Baldwin.

After a few 1275GT outings in 1975, Harmer completed his Mini-racing era in 1977 and 1978, sharing the car with Paul Soames. During his twelve-year run in Special Saloon Minis, Terry Harmer had competed in 217 races and recorded eighty wins, forty-seven seconds and twenty-three third places.

## PAUL HARMER

Currently better known for writing articles and taking photographs for *Mini World*, former Brands Hatch Press Officer Paul Harmer was no mean driver behind

*Paul Harmer driving his Harmer Motor Group Mini in a Kent Messenger 1000cc Special Saloon Championship race at Brands Hatch in 1970.*

*Paul Butler behind the wheel of the Automex Mini at Brands in 1971. He lived so close to his local circuit, Crystal Palace, that he usually managed to get home for lunch on race days.*

the wheel of a racing Mini in the early 1970s. In 1969, motivated by brother Terry's involvement, Paul had his first outing in his 850 Mini, EUV 59C. Result: one broken con rod. Next year, a one-litre steel-shelled special saloon was built, largely with the help of the D.J. Bond mechanics. The car was soon sorted and Paul Harmer was doing 57- and 57.2-second laps round Brands. These times, he recalls, were good for the front row until the Bevan Imps came on the scene. Despite the increased opposition however, he still managed seven wins and a dozen or so second places.

At Brands in 1970, the small-capacity Special Saloon grid saw the two Bevan Imps of Calcutt and Willcocks on the front row beside Guildford's Oselli Mini, with the brothers Harmer on row two. When the flag dropped, the Harmers were off the line like scalded cats, to be in positions one and two by Paddock; it must have been rare for two brothers to be in such a situation. Paul kept the Imps at bay for most of the race, but they forced a way by in the

closing stages; Terry and Paul finished first and fourth, respectively.

Paul Harmer's best day's racing was on 27 June 1971, when he had two races for free at Brands. He had entered two events at the Romford Enthusiasts Car Club meeting. After practice, he was called to race control where an embarrassed official told him that the timekeepers had not recorded a time for him. He was offered a full refund of his entry fees – three guineas (£3.15) – and told he could still race, but that he would have to start both events from the back of the grid, with a ten-second penalty.

He finished sixth in the up-to-1000cc encounter, and was determined to make a better showing in the All Comers Saloon Car Challenge. He made a blinding start and, as the laps went by, overtook cars left, right and centre, but recalls being too busy to watch for pit signals and having no idea of his position, or how many laps there were to go. Rounding Clearways, he reeled in another car and then, coming on to the start-finish straight, suddenly saw the

chequered flag being readied and realized that he was chasing the race leader. He nipped out of the tow and tried a dash for the line, but just failed. Still, coming through from last to second in ten laps, winning a tankard plus £5 prize money, and no entry fees, wasn't a bad day out.

## PAUL BUTLER

Paul Butler started racing karts and later drove his Sprite, also part of the Bond team, to several successes in Modsports events. He also raced a Mini sponsored by David Dickerson's Automex concern in Sutton. This car was usually raced, with a great deal of success, by Simon Ridge. At a sleety Brands on 6 December 1970, Dickerson offered Butler a drive in the car against Ridge in a D.J. Bond Mini. Butler got up to third place, but then spun the unfamiliar car out of contention in the poor conditions. The race was won by Mick Osborne's Dayglo-red Mini, with Ridge second and Peter Baldwin third. Butler consoled himself by setting fastest lap.

At the opening race of the Brands 1971 season, Butler made no mistakes, winning the race for Saloons under 1000cc in convincing fashion. He particularly enjoyed racing at Crystal Palace (he lived close enough to the track to be able to go home for lunch). On one occasion, he lost the clutch and struggled on, making crash changes. Eventually, he missed changing down for South Tower Corner, and discovered how hard the railway sleepers lining the bend were!

Sometimes the early-morning journey to a circuit could be more harrowing than the race itself. Butler recalls an instance when he and fellow Mini man Mo Mendham, who ran his tuning business from the garage at the back of his parent's pub in Watford, were both on their way to Mallory Park. As Butler approached the Watford junction on the M1, he saw the Mendham Mk 2 Jaguar coming up the slip road, complete with Mini on the trailer. Both drivers speeded up, racers on or off the track! Soon, both cars were doing more than 70mph (113kph), and their respective trailers were becoming rather unstable. The more powerful Jag got in front and Butler was able to witness its trailer starting to slide from side to side, smoke pouring off the tyres, with three pairs of syn-

*Paul Hutton (106), Bernard Bird (105) and Ian Bax (110) dispute the class lead at Crystal Palace. The drivers had survived a start-line shunt that took out a couple of headlights. Bax went on to win the 1300 class.*

chronized eyeballs in the back of the Jag following its progress. Sense took over, both cars slowed down and the trailers were stabilized.

## IAN BAX

Ian Bax started Mini club racing in 1965. In his first two seasons he won three races at Brands and one at Lydden, the car being entered in the name of Sydney Greene. Syd Greene owned Gilby Engineering and, as well as being a great friend of Dick Jacobs, of MG racing fame, built his own F1 car in 1961. He allowed Ian Bax to use the Gilby Engineering name to get trade support for the Mini, and Bax thanked him by entering under his name.

Bax would be the first to admit that his own car preparation left a lot to be desired. Fortunately, he met up with Peter Vickers (who still builds Mini Miglias today), and handed over all the preparation to him. In 1967, Bax moved on to the British Touring Car Championship, running the Mini in

the under-one-litre class. In 1968, he was fourth in class at the end of the year, with seconds at the British GP meeting at Brands, plus Crystal Palace.

In 1970, touring cars had to run to Group 2 spec and, despite being up against the works Escorts and works/Britax Minis, Bax amassed enough points to secure fifth in class at the end of the year, with third places at Brands and Crystal Palace being his best results. He also did some club races and, despite the car's Group 2 weight of approximately 14cwt (710kg), picked up five class wins. A bigger budget was now needed in order to be competitive in Touring Cars, so from 1971–74 Bax reverted to club racing. After the closure of Crystal Palace, his other local circuit, at the end of the 1972 season, he raced mainly at Brands and Lydden.

During this period the car had eighteen class wins, held the lap record at Brands and set a record at Lydden that would stand for four years. There were many dices with the likes of Terry Harmer, Bob Jones and Paul Hutton and Bax often beat visiting 'stars' such as Jonathan

Buncombe and Geoff Wood at Brands, using his local knowledge. The car had now been trimmed down to 10cwt (510kg), had an eight-port Norman Abbott head and was producing 140bhp. Even this level of power was not enough to stay with the new breed of Ford-powered Special Saloon Minis, so the car was sold to Japan where it won its first race. Ian Bax and long-time racing partner John Wilmshurst turned their attentions to racing MG Midgets.

Despite this move away from Minis, Bax was tempted by the announcement of the inaugural Willhire 24-Hour Race at Snetterton in 1980. He acquired and prepared an ex-Steve Harris 1275GT to enter with co-drivers John Wilmshurst and Bob Humphries, who would be having his first-ever race. The trio finished second in the up to 1600cc class. According to Bax, this was the first time a 1275 Mini had finished a twenty-four-hour event.

Motor sport gets into the system and, in 1990, after a long lay-off, Bax had two outings at Brands in Bob Humphrey's Vickers-built Mini Miglia; he set fastest lap in one race. He is still involved today, instructing at the Ian Taylor Racing School and acting as a clerk of the course for the BARC, of which he is now Vice Chairman.

## TONY BARNARD

An engineer, Sussex-based Tony Barnard worked for both Elva cars and Nerus Engineering before deciding to go racing. He recalls doing his first hillclimb in 1965 and then sharing a Mini Se7en before doing Free Formula 850 and a bit of Mini 1000. He had many race and hill class wins, including one at his local Bodiam Hillclimb, where he held the class record.

*Minis were always out in abundance in the Seven Fifty Motor Club Six-Hour Relay. Peter Shepherd's 1300 car at Woodcote, Silverstone during the 1973 event.*

53

On one occasion there, he had to take to the escape road, going through the fence and ending up in a field with a bull. In June 1969, he rolled end over end at Brands' Paddock Hill Bend; this destroyed the car and forced retirement, as other responsibilities meant there were no funds to repair the car.

By the end of 1971, Barnard had rebuilt the Mini and succumbed to the urge to go racing again. In 1973, he accepted an offer for the car from a New Zealander who wanted to race for a year, but bought it back from him at the end of the season. He remained a regular competitor at Lydden Hill. After practice for a 1000cc event, he noticed that one of his callipers had distorted due to overheating. Determined not to miss the race, he arranged to borrow one of Peter Shepherd's brakes from his 1300cc car. However, the pair were in consecutive races, which meant a very quick change, working with red-hot metal.

As Tony Barnard Racing, Barnard the engineer prepared many local cars, including Peter Shepherd's Mini, as well as single-seaters for Will Arif and Paul Sleeman, who won the 1983 *Autosport* Golden Helmet award.

## PETER SHEPHERD

Peter Shepherd started his racing in a Terrier, moving to Mini Se7en with a self-built car in 1968. The 1971 season saw him in Free Formula 850 with an early form of fuel injection which fellow Mini competitor Richard Jockle had come up with. The system still utilized the original SU fuel pump, which resulted in surges of power, but Richard Owen, who was later to become a successful racing car designer, perfected a balance tank to get around the problem. Shepherd used a pocketed block, which led to frequent head-gasket failure

– it was not uncommon to have to change the gasket between practice and the race. The introduction of a competition head gasket cured the problem.

Oselli Engineering of Oxford were approached to build a more powerful engine and this proved to be a good investment. In 1970, David Oldham decided that Oselli should get involved in building bigger engines and Shepherd was joined by Geoff Gilkes in the Oselli 1300 team. As well as a good selection of circuit class wins, Shepherd took places at some hill-climbs, regularly taking the Mini to Jersey. Later, he would defect to the hills completely, in a Harrison single-seater.

## TONY YOULTEN

Although he raced with support from *Cars and Car Conversions*, Tony Youlten managed to persuade the magazine to let him keep his car, which ran in the up-to-1300 class, in its distinctive bright yellow and mustard livery. At Brands on 13 March 1968, he was third in class with his reliable Richard Miles engine. He had an eventful outing at the Thruxton Easter International Meeting, when, after a reasonable practice session, just about everything went wrong in the race. In the early stages, he spun while avoiding an errant Cortina and Camaro; having restarted, he managed to spin at the chicane, which dislodged a battery lead. After fixing this, he was on his way again and still managed third in class.

## COLIN HINE

A good friend of *Cars and Car Conversions* editor Richard Hudson-Evans, Colin Hine raced his Mini in the Triple C Team. He had a good run of Silverstone outings in

*Jonathan Buncombe (60) bought a Mk 2 grille to make his Mk 1 Mini look like the latest model. He fights off 'Lydden Maestro' Colin Youle to beat him during this 1968 race.*

1970. On 25 July, after a race-long dice with Paddy McNally and Jack Davies, he managed to split them and come home second. The next weekend he came fourth in the Triplex round and he was running second in class on 14 August but was forced to retire when the condenser cried 'enough'. Determined to maximize the car's performance, he changed the familiar Clubman front for the more aerodynamic saloon shape, and changed his Weber 45 for the Dellorto version, as he had heard that these were giving a horsepower advantage.

In 1971, Hine had an active season, with his development work producing a good tally of places. Having broken the crank while leading his class in September, he had to carry out an unexpected rebuild. He also planned to use the close season to lighten the car dramatically and modify the rear suspension. However, his racing career was nearly cut short after returning from honeymoon to find he had been burgled. He lost his trailer, lots of spares and a set of wets, although the police did recover his Vauxhall Cresta tow car, badly damaged.

## JONATHAN BUNCOMBE

Hampshire driver Jonathan Buncombe, whose father used to compete in an AC Bristol, first appeared in a Mini in 1966, moving from sprints and Autocross to the circuits the following year. He competed in a 1293 club car, with an engine tuned by Planet Engineering from Brightlingsea. By 1968, he had amassed sufficient funds to go to local tuners Downton, whom he had held in high regard since his days as a schoolboy enthusiast. That season, he chalked up almost twenty second places, being regularly beaten by Richard Longman and also having good competitive drives against Don Currie.

For 1969, Buncombe went to Group IV. His mother bought him a brand-new Cooper, which was taken straight from the showroom, unregistered, and stripped out for the track, and powered by a 1293 Downton engine. Buncombe invariably finished his races first of the private entrants and occasionally managed to beat some of the works-backed cars, too. At Thruxton, his local circuit, he got past the Cooper and Britax team cars and at one

*The 1972 Wiggins Teape Dice of the Year was awarded to Jonathan Buncombe (62) and Rob Mason (61) in the Don Moore Mini, for this race at Mallory. The lead changed three times a lap for twenty laps. Buncombe won the race and the Wiggins Teape Championship.*

stage was leading both the Broadspeed Escorts as well, but one managed to find a way through at the chicane on the last lap, giving Buncombe another second. He finished the year seventh, behind the six works cars.

Throughout the season, Buncombe had aspired to a Mini works drive for the next year; based on performance, he must have been at the top of the list, but Lord Stokes' withdrawal from racing put paid to that plan. Buncombe endured a disastrous season in a BMW 2002, having sold the Group IV Mini to a Californian who won an American championship with it.

In 1971, Richard Longman, who was moving to Formula 3, asked Buncombe if he would like to represent Longman and Company in the Osram GEC Championship. The deal was that Buncombe built and prepared the rolling shell and Longmans would take care of the engine, with Steve Harris coming to the meetings to look after it. Longman and Harris, along with their respective other halves, travelled many miles to circuits all over the UK in the Buncombe Cortina 1600E. The four of them often slept in the car, to keep costs down.

Jonathan Buncombe won the 1300 class

*Motospeed double act, Paul and brother Greg Taft, dispute the lead at Lodge, Oulton Park in 1974.*

*Former* Cars and Car Conversions *writer John Brigden's car on the main straight at Lydden Hill in 1977.*

sixteen times out of eighteen rounds. His one failure was when he lost a lap at Brands because the throttle stuck, although he still crossed the line to keep the 100 per cent finish record. The missing round was at Silverstone, where he won

his (very wet) race, but the event for the up-to-850 cars, in which his championship rival Graeme Janzen competed, was abandoned, along with the rest of the programme, as conditions worsened. This round was excluded from the end-of-year results, Buncombe's win counted for nothing, and Buncombe and Janzen shared the championship.

During that 1971 championship year, Buncombe broke the lap records at Cadwell Park, Castle Combe, Crystal Palace and Thruxton. The car for this impressive performance was a five-port Mini with carburettoration (albeit an early split Weber set-up), rather than an eight-porter with injection, which had been homologated and was becoming the norm. There was great satisfaction in doing so well in a five-port Mini, which many of his competitors considered was hardly suitable for motor sport at that level.

Buncombe had a good start to the 1972 season, with seconds at Brands and Thruxton and a surprise win at Oulton Park, where the previously invincible

*When Lord March invited John Cooper to enter a Mini Cooper S in the first Goodwood Festival in 1993, John Brigden was asked to represent him in his rally S, EUO 868C. Left to right, Ken Tyrrell, John Cooper and John Brigden.*

Escort of Vince Woodman had problems. The car was running in Group 2 trim, which increased the weight by 1.5cwt (75kg), adversely affecting the tyres in the closing stages of the race. Buncombe could usually out-qualify his Dagenham-mounted rival and keep ahead of him for the first five laps, but then the tyres went off and Woodman would get by. Steve Harris continued to experiment with the engine, wringing every extra ounce of power out of it.

Buncombe had a hell of a dice with Vince Woodman at Silverstone, with regular place-changing and one of them getting below the lap record every other lap. They were going faster and faster into each corner until the inevitable happened. Woodman was in front as the pair approached Stowe, but he left his braking too late and Buncombe suddenly had a sideways Escort in front of him. Locking up all four wheels, he vividly remembers his rival's eyes popping out of his head inside his full-face helmet as he waited for the impact.

The Mini hit the Ford's 'A' post hard but, after the impact, the pair optimistically set off to continue the battle. Woodman did not appreciate that his front offside suspension was only attached by the top strut, with the wheel hanging out of the side of the car. He three-wheeled through the next bend but, as soon as the damaged corner made contact with the ground, he was off into the undergrowth. Buncombe retired with a burst radiator and tyres like thrupenny bits. That race is still a topic of conversation when the two of them meet.

The Buncombe team now travelled to meetings in luxury, as Jonathan Buncombe had bought Rob Walker's old Thames Trader F1 transporter; it was much more comfortable for sleeping than the Cortina. He finished the year in the top five and took the class. Occasionally, he would have a non-championship outing with the Longman development eight-port engine. Looking back on his Mini days, Buncombe has great memories of racing as a young man, but considers that he and his rivals were all less worldly-wise than the young drivers of today.

## JOHN BRIGDEN

Kent-based writer and PR man John Brigden started his racing career at the same 1975 Thruxton meeting as Jonathan Palmer, driving a 1959-shelled Se7en. During those early days, he admits that the team was noted for needing push-starts off the line. After two seasons of sharing the car in Se7ens, Brigden decided to upgrade it to a 1293 Special Saloon for 1976. He worked for *Cars and Car Conversions* from 1977 to 1980, where he got his hands on many goodies that were sent to the magazine for appraisal. One such item was the new Aldon lightweight alloy trailing arm rear end, which replaced the subframe. Apart from saving 60lb (25kg), this modification enabled Brigden to dial out some understeer by adjusting the rear camber and castor angles.

On moving to Pembury, John Brigden found a kindred spirit in his new neighbour, Roger Tolliday, whom he describes as 'the sort of chap for whom a Haynes workshop manual was normal bedtime reading'. Tolliday helped to keep the car going in a period when Special Saloons were getting more professional and expensive. Brigden had some placings in the car, but the proliferation of BDA engines forced him out of racing in 1983.

Brigden was closely involved in the early issues of *Mini World*, was later appointed as PR consultant to British Motor Heritage and became a Mini driver to be reckoned with in historic rallying.

## JIMMY McCLEMENTS

One of a vast band of Irish Mini drivers who started their motor sport in driving tests, Jimmy McClements obtained sponsorship to race his car from his employers, Kane of Comber, the local BMC dealers. He found that the car control learnt in the driving tests was an invaluable grounding for other motor sport disciplines. In his early seasons of racing he was doing twenty-five to thirty meetings a year.

In 1969, he won the Irish Saloon Car championship in a 1293 Riley Elf. Many Irish drivers ran Elfs or Wolseley Hornets, due to a surplus of Mark 1 shells in Ireland that were sold off at £45 each.

McClements bought two, so that he had a spare. The grille was normally a very expensive item, especially when the shell had cost only 45 quid, so the car's badge depended on where a grille could be scrounged. Archie Phillips' father had a Riley dealership, so his car was inevitably an Elf, while Alec Poole's dad ran a Wolseley franchise, so he drove a Hornet.

Through his Downton connections, Jimmy McClements got hold of a rare Weslake cross-flow head, which he used on the engine of the new car built for the 1971 season. This ran a pair of Weber 45s, producing tremendous low-down torque. Working for Kanes, who were also his sponsors, McClements considered racing

*Jimmy McClements, Riley Elf 1070 RZ, and Eddie Regan, Wolseley Hornet SZJ 1, head the saloon field at Bishopscourt in 1969. The reason so many of the Riley and Wolseley derivatives were raced in Ireland was a surplus of shells, which were sold off at £45 each. The badge drivers raced under depending on where they could obtain the cheapest grille.*

almost as part of his job. He always ensured that his car was immaculately turned out and always made time at events to talk to the spectators and answer their questions. Over the years, he surely indirectly influenced the purchase of many cars from the company as a result of his good PR at the tracks. In 1974, he competed in a series at Ingliston where, apart from getting the award for the best-prepared car, he often beat the DTV Vauxhalls.

Bishops Court, one of the Irish circuits, had a long right-hand bend, which any driver worth his salt took flat out. Overlooking the corner was a steep bank, always lined with spectators. If they sensed a driver backing off, the crowd would all shout 'chicken', or make suitable noises and arm movements. Very few of the local drivers backed off!

Jimmy McClements was out of racing from 1985 to 1991, when he bought a KAD Mini.

*Chris Judge driving his immaculately prepared Gas Warm Mini in the 1993 BRSCC Modified Saloon Car Championship. He was a regular points scorer in the series.*

## CHRIS JUDGE

A good grounding of three years in autotests, production car trials and a few rallies led Chris Judge to try his hand at sprinting his street-legal Mark 1 Cooper in 1977. The next year, a friend talked him into entering the same car, now a little more developed, in a TEAC Special Saloon race at Lydden. On the first lap he made contact with the spinning Mini of Phil Whitehead; Whitehead retired on the spot, but Judge continued, with a minor dent, to complete his first-ever motor race. Back in the paddock, Whitehead revealed that he was thinking of selling the car and a deal was struck – Judge bought the Jack Whitehead Garage ST 970S for £600, minus the wets.

Chris Judge ran the car in Special Saloon races, sprints and hillclimbs from 1978 to 1981, taking many awards and class records. When the class structure changed, in 1982, a 1000cc engine was no longer competitive so Ian Hargreaves at Avonbar was commissioned to build a 1300 unit. Judge recalls that Hargreaves taught him a lot about setting up both car and engine.

The 1986 season produced eleven wins from twelve outings. Judge then ran a fibreglass-bodied space-frame car, from 1989 to 1992, winning in it at Brands first time out and continuing a front-runner thereafter.

For 1993, Judge decided to move to the Modified Saloon class, introduced to attract drivers put off by the spiralling costs of building and running a competitive Special Saloon. He built a new car, which became the well-known 'Gas Warm Mini', in which he had one win and many places. He was BARC National Sprint Class Champion five times and has been a regular winner of regional speed championships since 1977.

# 3 The Works and Works-Supported Teams

While the BMC factory did prepare some cars of their own for racing, they preferred to concentrate on rallying and, in the main, were represented on the circuits by private teams. These teams received varying degrees of works backing.

## COOPER MINI RACING TEAM

### John Cooper

The most famous of the private BMC-backed teams was the Cooper Mini Racing Team, headed by John Cooper, who conceived and designed the Mini Cooper with racing in mind. He persuaded the factory to build, within a very short space of time, 1,000 Mini Coopers and, subsequently, 1,000 Cooper Ss. This meant that the models could be homologated to race as production-based, rather than prototype, cars.

Cooper had a unique relationship with BMC, perhaps because of his friendship with Alec Issigonis. He inspired huge loyalty from the staff in the competitions department and would usually get what he wanted from them in the way of parts. If it could not be got out of the front door in time – there was always an 'unreasonable' deadline – the lads would set to and make it unofficially and deliver it via the back door. The Cooper S was to make a lasting impression.

*John Love (72) leads the grid off the line closely followed by John Whitmore (73), Oulton Park, September 1962.*

## John Love

South African driver John Love and team-mate Sir John Whitmore dominated their class for the Cooper Team in the 1962 British Saloon Car Championship. Love won seven out of the eight rounds in the series and set the fastest lap on four occasions. He won the championship, beating Peter Harper's Sunbeam Rapier by three points.

During the 1962 season, the team tended to share cars with the Tyrrell-backed duo who were originally briefed to do the European series for BMC. However, they ended up doing quite a few of the British rounds in order to help the Cooper team consolidate the championship.

At the BRSCC-organized August Bank Holiday Monday meeting at Brands Hatch, Love was joined by Bill Blydenstein to score a works 1, 2 in the class.

## Tony Maggs

As a member of the Cooper Formula Junior and Formula 1 Teams, South African Tony Maggs was occasionally drafted into a Mini. A 1962 outing particularly sticks in his mind, at a time when Christabel Carlisle was posing a threat to the team's championship aspirations. Maggs backed John Love up at Aintree; his brief from Cooper was to 'get in there, keep her occupied and for gawd's sake keep her out of his hair'. He obeyed instructions, but admits that he was surprised at Carlisle's speed and impressed by her consistent attempts to outbrake him into the bends. He achieved his objective but, looking back on the race, reflects that 'it was not one of those drives that one loves to remember, or feels proud of'.

## Sir John Whitmore

In 1961, John Whitmore was sponsored by

*Sideways motoring: John Whitmore (99) and John Aley (101) delight the crowds at South Tower Bend, Crystal Palace in 1961. Whitmore's car was an Austin Seven, but the weekend it went racing at the Roskilde Ring, it changed its identity to a Morris Mini Minor.*

*John Whitmore (right), 1961 British Saloon Car Champion, with Don Moore holding the trophy and Ray Simpson from Castrol (left). Whitmore secured the crown in the 850 Mini he is leaning on, an ex-works rally car bought from Marcus Chambers for £350.*

Castrol to race a Lotus 20 Formula Junior. However, try as he might, Don Moore, his engine builder, could not make the car's BMC engine match the Ford engines of the works cars. Moore suggested that if Whitmore supplied a Mini, he would build him an engine that would hopefully be competitive in saloons. Whitmore paid £350 to the factory for TMO 840, a rather tired ex-rally car; it was rebuilt, painted green and fitted with the promised Moore engine.

Whitmore had started to race Minis for fun, but having got Don Moore's backing, he decided that he must aim to win the Saloon Car Championship. He won at Goodwood, Aintree, Oulton and Snetterton, and added two seconds and a third place to take the championship. Christabel Carlisle, his main opponent

throughout the season, was second, with John Aley third.

John Cooper asked Whitmore to drive for his team in 1962 and he stayed for 1963 as well, describing the experience as 'two great years'. John Love was his first team-mate and, having allowed Love to out-fumble him at the season's inaugural race at Snetterton on 14 April, Whitmore had to demur to team orders for the rest of the year. The pair finished in first and second places in every race.

The Aintree round in April was probably John Whitmore's most spectacular of the year. Having passed Love, he was pursuing Alan Hutcheson in his Riley 1.5 (third) and Peter Harper's Sunbeam (fifth). He went through Melling flat-out and sideways at about 105mph (170kph). He managed to get the little car straightened out

63

again before outbraking his competitors into Tatts, as the spectators roared their approval. On the last lap, Whitmore waited for his team mate to catch up and take the class – the result was Love, Whitmore, Carlisle – having made his point.

Whitmore was number one driver for 1963 with Paddy Hopkirk in the second car, rally commitments permitting. As in 1962, a third car was run at certain races. For some reason, which no one can remember, the team missed the first round at Snetterton on 30 March and Mick Clare won. John Whitmore then won the class in all nine of the races in which he competed, with Hopkirk taking victory at Mallory on 3 July when Whitmore had another driving commitment. The team also missed the Oulton Park round on 21 September, where Edward Lewis scored in his Mini Cooper.

Despite winning nine out of twelve races, John Whitmore lost the championship to Jack Sears by two points. It was particularly galling, because Sears had driven Fords in two different classes and his total score, before dropped rounds, was 75 to Whitmore's 77. However, the correct-ed points read Sears 71, Whitmore 69. From their limited outings, Paddy Hopkirk was sixth and Tim Mayer eighteenth. Tony Maggs and John Rhodes also had occasional outings for the team that year.

## 'Smoky' John Rhodes

Of all the drivers who drove for Cooper, John Rhodes had probably the most spectacular driving style, enthralling the spectators and, usually, keeping the opposition at bay.

Rhodes always wanted to go racing but could not afford to. Luckily for him, a friend came up with the money and they were able to buy a Formula Junior, virtually in kit form, with the intention of sharing it. Rhodes used his mechanical expertise to build the car. After his first race, the friend said 'never again' and Rhodes ended up driving the car for the rest of the season. The following year, several other pals fancied a go, so Rhodes ended up building three more cars, using workshop space at John Cooper's premises at Surbiton. This is how he met Ginger

*The British crowds loved the epic David and Goliath battles between the Minis and the Jaguars. John Whitmore harries a Jag at Brands Hatch on 6 October 1962. The layout at Brands, with its tight corners, was ideal to enable the Minis to climb all over the more powerful cars.*

*John Rhodes gets the tyres smoking as he demonstrates his famous cornering technique. The left arm is in the air while the right is in the door pocket.*

Devlin, the team manager of the Cooper Mini Racing Team.

In 1964, John Rhodes, now driving various machinery, was testing a Bob Gerrard F1 car at Silverstone. Devlin was there on the same day with his drivers John Love and Tony Maggs in the Cooper S. After sorting out Gerrard's car, Rhodes asked Devlin if he could have a drive in one of the Minis; within a few laps he was on the pace. Having just stepped out of an F1 car, he found the Mini lacking in power when he got to the first bend and the brakes did not seem to be up to much either. He started to put the car sideways to scrub off speed – the Rhodes driving style began to develop and the nickname 'Smoky' began to stick.

As a result of that test, John Rhodes got to meet John Cooper and they shook hands on a drive. From that day on, Rhodes became dedicated to the Mini and, although he occasionally drove other cars, he was never happier than when he was behind the wheel of a Mini Cooper. While Rhodes' driving style became a firm favourite with the spectators, Dunlop was not happy with what it did to their tyres. Certainly, the tyres would usually go off before the end of the race, and Dunlop once recorded a temperature of 250°F (120 °C) on the shoulder of one of them.

Rhodes always capitalized on his ability to make a good start, often leading the class early in the race and relying on his sideways driving to keep the opposition at bay until the end. Because of its Formula 1 pedigree, the Cooper Mini team was very professional, with a long round of testing prior to each race to ensure the correct set-up for every circuit. Rhodes would utilize the procedure now favoured for Formula 1 qualifying: an out lap, a quick lap and an in lap. To enable valid comparisons, Rhodes says it was vital for him to drive each quick lap to within one-fifth of a second of the previous lap. The team would often take four or five cars to a test, and Rhodes would choose the one that he found to be best suited to the particular track.

65

*Paddy Hopkirk (left) and John Rhodes (right) on the Brands Hatch start line just before the 1969 Six-Hour race. They finished third in class, seventh overall.*

John Rhodes won the 1.3-litre class of the British Touring Car Championship from 1965 to 1968. He probably had his best year in 1967, at 39 years of age. Although he only won his class in three races, including the support event to the Race of the Champions at Brands on 12 March, he invariably finished in the points. He concluded the year third overall in the series, as well as winning the class. During his four-year run he chalked up nineteen victories. In 1968, Rhodes also took Division Two of the European Touring Car Championship; this result was particularly impressive, given that he was competing with cars up to 1.6 litres, although, by then, the Mini Coopers were running eight-port heads and fuel injection giving a very useful 120bhp. John says the team had eight cars, but in the main he tended to stick to his particular favourite. By the

end of the year, the shell of that car was, literally, coming apart at the seams.

Rhodes' view is that drivers in that era were more competitive than today. A team would test up to six drivers and the fastest man would get the drive, without taking account of how much sponsorship one particular person could bring with them. Drivers spent a lot of time in close proximity to each other, either in tents, caravans or, if times were good, in a hotel and there was always a friendly atmosphere before and after the races. The touring car fraternity even had an impromptu pop group.

At this time Jack Brabham was racing a Chevrolet Camaro. John Rhodes had a momentous dice with him at Oulton Park. 'Black Jack' pulled away from the Mini down the straight, but Rhodes made ground in the corners and invariably got up the inside of the larger car going through Old Hall, with slight body contact being made. One lap later, Brabham was getting a bit fed up with this and was clearly seen steering the car with one hand and shaking his fist at Rhodes with the other. When the two met up after the race, Brabham apologized for letting off steam in the heat of the moment.

## John Handley

John Handley joined the Cooper team from Broadspeed in 1966, as number two driver to Rhodes. He was paid £100 per race, plus a percentage of any prize and bonus money, and at the same time carried on working in his full-time job selling bearings for the family business. In his time with the Cooper team, he did more testing than racing; drivers turning up to qualify on race day knew exactly what time they were going to do, because they had tested there a few days before. The only exceptions were at Snetterton and Silverstone, where the wind direction could make a difference.

Although he had more Mini experience, Handley was happy in his role helping his number one. He would frequently 'give him a tow' during practice. If Handley was driving a larger-capacity car, he would allow Rhodes to slipstream him and the car would reach a top speed of 120mph (190kph). In Handley's experience, at Nurburgring, 'towing' a 1000 with a 1300 could cut twenty seconds off the smaller car's lap time – quite a few places on the grid.

In common with many Mini drivers before him, Handley had a wheel go with near disastrous consequences. It happened at Hawthorns on the Brands GP Circuit, during practice. The front nearside rim split and the car rolled into a ditch. Handley was dazed more than knocked out, but it seemed dark and he could smell petrol, so, for a brief moment, he thought his time had come. They took him back to the pits in the ambulance and, after he had been pronounced fit to drive, Ginger Devlin took him over to the spare car and firmly told him to go out in it and qualify.

Handley particularly remembers one dice he had with Paddy Hopkirk, on 30 October 1966 at Brands. Hopkirk was having an outing in one of the British Vita Minis. The two drivers changed places about four times on each lap, but Handley was in front when it mattered most – when the chequered flag dropped.

## Ginger Devlin

Ginger Devlin helped build the prototype 500cc Cooper racing car in 1946. He left the company two years later, rejoined them in 1955, and was soon one of the team's Formula 1 mechanics. In 1962, John Cooper asked him to take charge of the Cooper Mini Racing Team and he held the position of team manager until Lord Stokes pulled the plug on racing in 1969. Devlin ran one team for the British Saloon Car Championship and, when Ken Tyrrell concentrated on single-seaters, another for the European Championship.

Devlin organized many test days for the team, running his own and, often, other drivers. Stuart Turner, BMC Competitions Manager, liked to get his rally drivers into the racers to give them some circuit experience and John Cooper would also arrange for drivers to come along. Devlin's test days often ended up like a driving who's who, with Rauno Aaltonen, John Fitzpatrick, Denny Hulme, Jackie Stewart and Julian Vernaeve among the famous names who attended.

On race days, Devlin's first job was to get the cars to the circuit in raceable condition; ideally, they would have been set up on Abingdon's rolling road a few days before. He always made sure each driver scrubbed in all their new tyres, and a spare set of pads which were then taken off and marked. When John Rhodes was in the team, it was vital that he was first in line for practice, the car running the tyres and pads from the last race. This meant that Rhodes would set his fastest time on his first rolling lap before his tyres went off or he got involved with traffic. Rhodes recalls Ginger Devlin always getting him out at the head of the queue.

The race strategy was for Rhodes to make the best start possible and try and get up among the cars in the larger classes, then use them as a buffer between him and the others in his own class. He usually made a four-second gap on that first lap and then kept it for the rest of the race.

Initially, the team's engines were supplied by Eddie Maher from the Morris engine factory at Coventry. Later, they were prepared by Daniel Richmond's crew at Downton; they were well placed to tweak the Cooper S engines, as Richmond

had done a lot of consultancy work on the S. According to Devlin, it was a sad day when Richmond's services were dispensed with by Harry Webster, the man brought in by Lord Stokes to take on the role of chief engineer. Apparently, Webster called Richmond to a meeting, said something to the effect that he knew him as the man responsible for all the Cooper S warranty claims, and then told him that his services were no longer required. Those in the know realized that the Cooper S was warranty-intensive because its powerful engine took its toll on other parts of the car.

## The Britax-Cooper-Downton Team

When Lord Stokes cut BMC's budgets in 1969 and withdrew works support for his team, John Cooper decided to carry on with Minis for what would be one final year. Safety equipment manufacturer Britax provided financial support and Downton provided the engines, leading to

*Steve Neal powers his Britax-Cooper Downton car through Becketts at Silverstone in 1969. The two black lines on either side of the bonnet badge helped the pits tell the two cars apart.*

*Gordon Spice enjoyed his 1969 season in the Britax-Cooper Downton team. Team manager Ginger Devlin admits that Gordon's dry-sumped engine was marginally more powerful than his team-mate's.*

the team's new name. Steve Neal, who had declined the third seat in a three-car factory team, was signed as one driver. Gordon Spice, his former Arden team-mate, became the other.

Downton built lightweight standard-stroke engines with eight-port down-draught heads for the season. These featured a titanium flywheel with sintered steel insert and twin-plate clutch. Spice's engine was dry-sumped, using an MGB oil pump and 1-gallon (4.5-litre) tank under the offside front wing. This set-up gave an extra 4bhp. Ginger Devlin instructed the team to go for class wins and Spice and Neal enjoyed a hectic season. On 16 August, Neal beat the factory car of Rhodes at the Oulton Park Gold Cup Meeting. At the end of the year, Spice, who had won the class twice, was fifth overall in the championship, second in class and Neal finished fourth in class.

The team received invitations to race in Europe but, despite the offer of good start money, they were not interested. However, Gordon Spice still had his 1967 privateer

car, which he painted in team colours and raced across the Channel when he could. He enjoyed some good outings in Germany and at the Jyallandsbring in Denmark and the start and prize money came in very useful too.

## KEN TYRRELL AND HIS DRIVERS

Ken Tyrrell ran the Mini Cooper racing activities in Europe from 1962 to 1964. The team was run from Tyrrell's premises near Ripley in Surrey, with Roger Bailey in charge of the day-to-day arrangements. In 1964, Ken Tyrrell ran the works 970 Cooper Ss in the European Touring Car Championship with drivers Warwick Banks, a British commercial pilot, and Julian Vernaeve, a Belgian garage proprietor. At the Swiss hillclimb round there was a shortage of drivers in the class, so Tyrrell himself competed.

### Julian Vernaeve

Julian Vernaeve had his first circuit race at Spa in 1950, driving an Austin A40. After doing well in a number of rallies with diverse machinery, he went back to the circuits in 1960 in a Mini with an 850cc engine supplied by Don Moore. (Moore had been recommended by John Aley and Vernaeve describes him as the most honest man he ever met in motor sport.) This car ended the DKW domination of the small class in Europe.

In 1964, Vernaeve won European Championship races at Zolder, Belgium and Budapest as well as taking the hill-climb in his native Belgium. Having done so many competitive events in a Mini, it is hardly surprising that he describes the car as 'enjoyable fun' and 'an easy car to change direction in'.

Competing in a Mini from 1960 to 1973, Vernaeve amassed a formidable collection of eighty-nine first places: thirty races, twenty-four hillclimbs, thirty-two rallies and three slaloms. Among these was the Tour de France, taking in events at major circuits and hillclimbs, which he won in 1969 with Paddy Hopkirk. In his final Mini year, Vernaeve was second in the Belgian Touring Car Championship.

## Warwick Banks

Warwick Banks had a great grounding in Minis, having rallied CMC 77 (Christabel Carlisle's old racer) with John Handley in a number of events, including the Tour of Corsica and the RAC. The pair were lucky to get to Corsica at all. As they were crossing France in Handley's Riley 1.5, the tow bar tore loose from the boot floor. The first they knew of the problem was when the Mini and its trailer, the tow bar still attached, overtook them. It ran on to a wide grass verge and ploughed to a halt. They had to lash the empty trailer to the back bumper of the tow car and drive in convoy the rest of the way to Marseilles to catch the ferry to Corsica.

Warwick Banks had his first drive in a Mini Cooper on a race track when Ken Tyrrell invited him to a Goodwood test in March 1964, prior to the start of the season. As a result, he got the drive in the team's Group 2 970 Cooper S and ended up winning the 1964 European Touring Car Championship, which comprised five hillclimbs (best three to count) and ten races (best seven to count). The scoring system was based on class wins. Banks won the crown in convincing style by taking nine class victories.

The first hillclimb was a $13^1/_2$-mile (21.5km) course at Mont Ventoux in France, which rose to 6,261ft (2280m) above sea level. Banks won his class and

*Warwick Banks in the thick of it at the Silverstone International Trophy Meeting in May 1965; he went on to record a class win.*

broke the class record by over $1^1/_2$ minutes, only to be told that, as there were fewer than five starters in his class, the result would not count towards his championship scores. After that event, Ken Tyrrell drafted in extra Minis, if required, to ensure there were always enough starters.

When it came to the race on the old banked circuit at Monza, Banks had a 100 per cent record of wins. Ford, which had a similar number of Cortina victories in the large-capacity class, decided they had to do something about it. They put out John Young in an Anglia to try and snatch the small class from the Mini's grasp. To aid Young's progress, one of the Cortinas gave the Anglia 'a tow' and he built up quite a lead; however, the plan misfired when Young ran out of fuel. At Zandvoort, Banks arranged a tow for himself behind Rob Slotemaker's 1275S during official practice and they shared the front row, outqualifying the other twenty-six competitors. The two Minis finished first and third overall.

The Budapest round was 269 miles (430km) long and part of the circuit was over cobbled streets, which were lethal in the wet. As the class winner's margin of victory at this event was to be used in case of a tie, Tyrrell had to be careful when planning the strategy for his team of Minis. While Banks needed to win by the maximum margin, Tyrrell also had to ensure that the other drivers completed the required 91 per cent of the winner's race distance to qualify as finishers. As a result, some of the other drivers had exceptionally long fuel stops. Tyrrell recalls bemused marshals beckoning his cars out of their pit, while the mechanics seemed determined to wash not just the windows but the entire car before allowing it to rejoin the race. Banks was not allowed the luxury of an extended stop, however; when he came in, he brought the car to a halt and opened the door to get out. Tyrrell asked him where he was going and Banks replied that he needed a pee. Tyrrell told him there was no time and that, if it was really urgent, he would have to do it in the car; he slammed the door.

In 1965, again driving a Mini Cooper for the Tyrrell Team, Warwick Banks tackled the British Saloon Car Championship, which turned out to be a real cliffhanger. Banks' worst outing of the year was at Crystal Palace, when he was punted off by private entrant John Cannadine in a 1275S. After the race, Banks went over to the other driver to remonstrate with him; Cannadine retorted that, as he was in a 970cc car, he had no right to be ahead of one with a 1275cc engine. When John Cooper heard this he was angrier than Banks had ever seen him.

The outcome of the series – between Banks and Roy Pierpoint in his Ford Mustang – hinged on the last race at Oulton Park. Pierpoint spun out at Old Hall early on, necessitating a restart. The team pulled out another car for him to drive and he came second in class to Jack Brabham; this meant that Banks, who had won his class, took the title and was awarded the trophy. During the year, he had recorded six class wins from eight starts, with victories at Brands (twice), Oulton (twice), Snetterton, and Silverstone.

Three weeks later, Brabham's car was protested on some minor point and the appeal was upheld; this meant that Roy

*A classic Mini sideways racing shot taken at Silverstone's Club Corner during the British Grand Prix Meeting on 10 July 1965. Rauno Aaltonen leads Warwick Banks and Harry Ratcliffe. Many of the crowd are watching the race from portable grandstands, which they brought with them.*

Pierpoint was the champion. The following month, Pierpoint went on a shooting trip with Warwick Banks, who duly handed over the silverware. The regulations had been very tightly policed that year. John Whitmore had many times claimed that Banks' car was not legal and threatened to protest him, but had decided not to. After the end of the season, however, he pointed out that the hinge-down mechanism on the rear number plate had been removed and that the car did not, therefore, conform to Group 2 regulations. The team had, in all innocence, removed the flap to stop it rattling. Sportingly, neither Whitmore nor his team had reported it to the officials; to be honest, it had provided no advantage.

## BROADSPEED

The Broadspeed team was founded in late 1962, its members being Don Jackson, Peter Tempest, John Fitzpatrick, Jeff May, Eric Barnard and Ralph Broad. Broad was a meticulous engineer and racing driver who ran a small business in Sparkbrook, Birmingham. In 1959, he bought one of the first 850 Minis to come off the Longbridge production line and was soon driving it in all forms of motor sport. One of his first circuit races in 111 CON was on the original Silverstone club circuit, where he won the class and broke the up-to-850 lap record.

In 1963, the team fielded a brace of Group 3 850 Minis with Broad and Fitzpatrick at the wheel and Jeff May as team manager. The cars were painted in Broad's favourite colour, Rolls Royce Regal Red, with a silver roof, and this was to become the Broadspeed livery for many years. Broad's preparation was so meticulous that Broadspeed's better-handling Minis were often up among the cars run by John Cooper. One day, after he had lapped Brands in what was then considered to be an indecently quick 66 seconds, the scrutineers decided to take a look at exactly what Fitzpatrick had under the bonnet. After removing the head and carefully checking, they confirmed that the engine was indeed 848cc, exactly as it should have been. Broad then replaced the head, using the same gasket.

Ralph Broad attributed his engines' ability to rev to 8,000 and above and thus to produce more power than other 850s, to one thing: meticulous balancing. The crank was a work of art – it was shot-blasted, all corners were carefully

*John Terry at the wheel of the Broadspeed car during the Spa 24-Hour Race.*

radiused and every other moving component had received detailed attention. The superb handling resulted from the car being lowered to the absolute maximum.

For the 1964 season, two 1071S versions were prepared for Ralph Broad and John Handley to race in selected International events, but they were soon upgraded to 1293cc. A 998 Cooper was also driven by various drivers at home and abroad, with the object of beating the works cars. The team had many successes.

Handley, who first drove for the team in the 1963 Oulton Park Gold Cup when he deputized for the unavailable Fitzpatrick, had a good year in his car, 3210 VT. He remembers a race at Zolder that made everyone sit up and take notice of Broadspeed. Chasing Warwick Banks and Julian Vernaeve, in the Tyrrell-run works cars, Handley caught and passed them and stayed in front to win the class. At the end of the year, he finished fourth overall in the European Championship and took the class. While still being run as a private team, Broadspeed managed to attract some trade support to help defray the costs and Eddie Maher also helped out with some special BMC engine bits.

## John Fitzpatrick

John Fitzpatrick had driven his road Mini in the usual round of hillclimbs, sprints and rallies before using it for his first-ever race, with the BRSCC at Snetterton, in 1962. It was one of four races he did that year. Fitzpatrick busied himself with modifying the car with bits from Speedwell and Alexander Engineering.

Fitzpatrick first met Ralph Broad later that year and, following an under-bonnet inspection of the Fitzpatrick Mini, Broad suggested the inlet manifold for the twin SUs was not right and offered to improve it. Although he had never heard of him

before, Fitzpatrick was so impressed with Broad's enthusiasm that he took him up on his offer. The car's increased performance, combined with Fitzpatrick's preference for racing over other disciplines of the sport, made him determined to do a full season in 1963. That year, he competed in about thirty club races in his Broadspeed Mini and won the BRSCC 500 Trophy.

Intending to move to the 1964 British Saloon Car Championship with a Broadspeed Cooper, Fitzpatrick's true aspirations to join the Cooper Team were realized after a meeting at Surbiton and a test drive at Goodwood. He moved there to replace Ford-bound John Whitmore.

During the early part of the season, Fitzpatrick won the class on several occasions, but, as the private teams caught up, he was sometimes struggling. Ironically, he found his works Mini trailing those of the team for which he had previously driven. After a few races, Downton asked him to drive one of their Mini Coopers in some non-championship events. One Saturday at Mallory, in the Downton car, Fitzpatrick beat John Handley's Broadspeed car. However, the next day, Handley beat Fitzpatrick, who was now at the wheel of the Cooper Car Company vehicle. As a result, Fitzpatrick pestered John Cooper and Ginger Devlin to do a back-to-back test, with a view to getting Downton to prepare their engines. Eventually, Cooper agreed and a test was set up at Goodwood. The morning was a wash-out; to pass the time, John Rhodes took Fitzpatrick round in his Mk2 Jag and scared him to death. In the afternoon, the circuit began to dry and Fitzpatrick went out in the Downton car to set some times. On the third lap he hit a damp patch going into Madgwick, clouted the bank and wrote the car off. Next morning, he came to in the hospital, suffering from bad concussion and convinced that it

*John Terry and Andrew Hedges with their Broadspeed S, BOP 242C, celebrate a class victory in the 1965 Spa 24-Hour race. The car finished eighth overall.*

was the run in the Jaguar that had put him there. It took a long time to convince him that he had had his own accident. Obviously, the test was never completed.

Downton rebuilt the car and entered it in a championship race for Rob Slotemaker to drive. The car was quicker in a straight line than the Cooper Team cars, which proved the point. The advent of the 1275 engines gave the team an advantage, as they were the only ones to have them for a couple of races. John Fitzpatrick finished second in the championship, to Jim Clark's Lotus Cortina. When dates did not clash, he also joined Warwick Banks in the Tyrrell-run car for some of the two-driver races in the European series.

At the end of the season, BMC decided to send a team of Minis to compete in the Sandown Six-Hour Race in Melbourne, Australia. As the result of the flip of a coin, John Fitzpatrick got the fourth seat to join

Paddy Hopkirk, Rauno Aaltonen and Timo Makinen for the two-week trip. Before the race they toured the country demonstrating the driveability of the Minis before arriving at Melbourne for the race. Fitzpatrick and Hopkirk led at one stage, but were put out by a broken alternator.

Fitzpatrick returned to Broadspeed in 1965, to join John Handley and John Terry for a crack at the European crown. However, the Cooper team also put their cars out for the more prestigious rounds in Europe, so Broad succumbed to the temptation of running his cars at home as well. At the Oulton Park round of the British Saloon Car Championship, John Fitzpatrick was under strict orders not to take points off John Rhodes. Fitzpatrick pulled away from Rhodes during the race but, as he passed the pits on the last lap, he saw Broad waving frantically at him to slow down and allow Rhodes to pass. Having proved his point, Fitzpatrick slowed and began to look in his mirror for Rhodes; he intended to allow him past just before the line. He was not really concentrating as he went into Druids, got onto the 'marbles' and lost it. The car mounted the bank and rolled end-over-end along the top. As Rhodes passed by, he witnessed the entertaining sight of his rival crawling from beneath the wrecked car. Ralph Broad was less amused.

## Broadspeed's Final Mini Year

The Broadspeed team was so impressive that, in 1965, they became the works-backed team for the European series. John Handley and John Terry won their class in the Monza 4 Hours on 19 March and the Nurburgring 6 Hours on 13 June, with Terry taking class victory in the Zandvoort race, on 29 August. They also had an emphatic victory at the Spa 24-Hour event. Andrew Hedges and John Terry

There is something extremely satisfactory about this device because the customers can watch the dials and see the improvements in output produced by adjustments to the ignition and carburettor settings. It is this visual satisfaction, perhaps, coupled with the fact that no parts are required, that appeals to the northerners' slightly more down-to-earth attitude towards cash. Whatever the cause,

*Jeff Goodliff and Harry Ratcliffe used this drawing of their rolling road in a publicity leaflet. Left to right, a customer, Goodliff (in car), Alan Clegg, Brian Gillibrand, Ratcliffe, Nobby Clarke, another customer. 890 DMR was Goodliff's hillclimb car.*

won the 1000cc class by no less than six laps and finished eighth overall. Andrew describes it as 'a fantastic race that went like clockwork, just as planned'.

Like many who drove for Ralph Broad, Hedges confirms that Broad was noted for 'stretching the regulations to the maximum, in order to get the best performance from his cars'. Spa might have been a double, but the 1300 car, driven by John Handley and Ralph Broad, was forced to retire with engine failure after thirteen hours, while two laps in front.

Contrary to instructions, Broadspeed did occasionally take points off the Cooper Team. At about the time of the Spa event in 1965, Ralph Broad was banned from entering Eddie Maher's works engine department at Coventry, despite previously having lent him a Broadspeed engine. Unhappy with his treatment at the hands of BMC, Broad defected to Ford for the 1966 season, and John Fitzpatrick went with him as driver.

In 1976, Ralph Broad sold Broadspeed

to John Handley, who needed larger premises for an Opel project at his Tong Park Automotive business. Unfortunately, his acquisition coincided with a recession in the car market and the Opel project, along with two existing Broadspeed development projects, was cancelled. After using part of the premises as a car dealership, Handley sold the building in 1979 for a light industrial redevelopment scheme. Meanwhile, Ralph Broad was finding his new home in Portugal a bit chilly on winter evenings. He used his engineering expertise to design a special wood-burning stove and established Fogo Montanha, now the largest manufacturer of such stoves in Portugal.

## VITA, AUTOVITA AND THE VITAMINS

### BRT

British Vita Racing took its name from

British Vitafoam, the company that, among other interests, sold seat diaphragms, upholstery foam and rubber mouldings to motor manufacturers. The preparation of cars entered by the team was carried out by Harry Ratcliffe and Jeff Goodliff, who ran their own company, BRT, in Littleborough. Ratcliffe was fully conversant with the 'A' Series engine, having raced his own Morris 1000 since 1959. He was no mean Mini driver himself, but his real interest was in preparing the cars.

The three original partners of BRT were Jim Barham, Harry Ratcliffe and John Taylor, who set it up as a part-time business tuning their own and other people's cars. Harry Ratcliffe's father was a motor engineer and allowed them to use his Rochdale premises on evenings and weekends, when they were free from their day jobs.

After a while, the constant late-night noise made them unpopular with the neighbours and they had to move to more remote premises. Finally, they acquired a suitable building at Littleborough and, as business built up, they were able to employ one mechanic. As time went on, two of the partners left and Harry Ratcliffe was joined by Jeff Goodliff from Midsomer Norton; they had met when they were both apprentices at A.V. Roe. Eventually, they both went into the venture full time, keeping the now-familiar name. In autumn 1962, they were one of the first firms in the area to install a Crypton Road-Load chassis dyno. They were setting up three or four cars a night, and the workshop took on something of a club atmosphere as customers and enthusiasts gathered round the workshop stove to watch the pair at work and talk motor racing.

Although they continued to compete, Goodliff and Ratcliffe set themselves a strict rule: they would work on customers'

cars during the day, to pay the bills, and would turn to their own cars only after tea.

## The Reverend Rupert Jones

Along with Derek Astle, Neville Hodkin, Rupert Jones and Brian Redman, Goodliff and Ratcliffe raced as 'Team Red Rose'. British Vitafoam's involvement began when it stepped in to help out the 'Motorsporting Clergyman', the Reverend Rupert Jones, vicar of All Saints, Hamer, near Rochdale. He was an 850 Mini racer, but he was to become better known for his rallying exploits in an array of cars. However, like John Aley, he had Cambridge Racing connections and had notched up a formidable set of results in one of the 'team' Austin A35s.

In 1963, Jones was racing an 850 Mini that had been prepared for him by Harry Ratcliffe. He had a habit of naming all his cars and had promised himself six races in 'George', the 850 Mini, during the season. Event five had produced a class win but had also stretched the budget to the limit. Either 'George' or the LHD Bentley, which was used as a tow barge, had to go. If the Bentley went, then the Mini would have to revert to being the 'parish hack'. Faced with this unenviable choice, Reverend Jones was drowning his sorrows in Oulton Park's Pit Bar and ended up talking to a reporter from the *Manchester Evening News*. The story appeared under the headline 'Curate to quit circuits', and the article was brought to the attention of Norman Grimshaw, managing director of local company Vitafoam. In view of their connection with the British car industry, Grimshaw felt that sponsoring someone like Jones with a proven track record in a British car would be good for Vitafoam. Because of his ecclesiastical background, Jones always received a great deal of press coverage for his exploits.

*Racing clergyman Rupert Jones with 'George', the Team Red Rose 850 Mini, outside his church, All Saints' at Hamer near Rochdale, in 1963. Following an article in the* Manchester Evening News *reporting Jones' enforced retirement due to lack of funds, Norman Grimshaw of Vitafoam stepped in with sponsorship. This heralded the start of British Vita Racing.*

The nub of the deal was that Vitafoam acquired 'George', along with spares and the pit-signalling and timing equipment: a small blackboard, two pieces of chalk and an ex-Army stopwatch. The 850 car was retained and a new 1071 Cooper S was acquired for Reverend Jones. This was run in, then taken to Harry Ratcliffe for preparation for its first outing, on 14 September 1963, at Rufforth, a circuit marked out on the airfield. The new S, known as 'Vita-D', was light blue with a dark blue roof and a matching stripe down the centre of the

bonnet. By the time his sponsors arrived for the race, Jones had qualified fourth-fastest and was on the outside of the front row. He decided to impress them with a good start, and recalls the race as follows:

> The Vitafoam hierarchy took post behind the ropes on the outside of the first corner, marked out by oil drums. I determined to come out of that bend in a good position. Flag down, a good start, second, third, sideways early and keep foot down, don't let them push you out, keep it there. Ping, one oil drum away. Ping, a second, the back end was just collecting them and in the mirror I saw one of them sailing towards the chairman. The situation was saved by a good race result.

Rupert Jones finished third.

The Reverend's remaining outings of the year were suitably impressive and, for 1964, Vitafoam promised a larger budget along with the use of a 27ft (8m) company lorry as transporter. Driver Nobby Clarke would double as mechanic. In addition, Jones' parish youth leader, Geoff Dyson, was taken on part-time as team manager. With this backing, International events became a possibility and the team entered the 1964 Spa 24-Hour Race, with Harry Ratcliffe as the second driver. The newly acquired 1275S travelled across the Channel in the transporter on the ferry with Dyson, Ratcliffe and mechanics Brian Gillibrand and Alan Clegg (who would later spanner for Jackie Stewart), while Jones and his fiancée drove to Southend Airport and flew to Ostend.

The car handled well during practice, the drivers finding that, once they got to know their way round, they could take it nearly all flat out, at about 110mph (175kph). The practice times led them to hope they might be in with a chance of a class win. The start was Le Mans-style and, having decided there was little merit in a rapid departure, Jones took it easy, when the flag dropped, and was last away. It turned out to be a fortuitous decision; the cars running third and fourth touched, bringing down a telegraph pole, which virtually blocked the track. This caused minor comings together further down the field, but when Jones arrived on the scene, he was able to gauge the situation and squeeze through a gap in the debris.

His good work was to no avail however; on lap seven, the engine let go in the biggest possible way. Jones describes the remains as 'like one of those cutaway things you saw at the Earls Court Motor Show'. Subsequent inspection back home would reveal it had been caused by a con-rod failure.

The team also did the 1964 Targa Florio in the 1275 Cooper S, with Harry Ratcliffe and Rupert Jones again sharing the driving. A good start was marred by the car losing a front wheel, which damaged the suspension, resulting in a retirement. Geoff Dyson then retired as team manager, and his place was taken by Brian Gillibrand, Harry Ratcliffe's work colleague, who gave up his job. At the same time, Ratcliffe went full-time in his tuning business, BRT. After leaving Vita, Geoff Dyson had a few 850 races in 'George', including an outing at Brands on 10 May, when he came second in class.

Later in the season, Harry Ratcliffe won the *Daily Mirror* Trophy at the BRSCC Rufforth meeting, in true Mini style, beating larger and more powerful cars. The team also notched up a 1, 2, 3 at Mallory on 10 August. 'The Vitamins' continued to be in the public eye and the company was happy to carry on with its involvement. Rupert Jones continued to race and rally a wide selection of machinery while the Minis saw various drivers behind the wheel.

## Vita D + BRT = Autovita

When it first became involved, Vita took the view that if the motor sport side – Vita Developments, known as 'Vita D' – made a small loss, that was OK. However, it eventually became an integral part of the company business. In 1968, British Vita (which had become a public company in 1966) took a 50 per cent stake in BRT and the company became BVRT. About eighteen months later, it bought the rest and the resulting business, known as Autovita, moved to larger premises in Smitherfield, complete with offices for Brian Gillibrand, Jeff Goodliff and Harry Ratcliffe. It became a stand-alone company within the group and was expected to make a profit every year. Its intention in the long term was to move into motor accessories.

During 1966, John Rhodes had used his motor sport background to establish John Rhodes Autospeed in Wolverhampton. Autovita purchased the business from him in 1970 and it was run as a satellite to the main branch. In 1973, the economic climate had changed radically and British Vita took the decision to stick to their core business selling Autovita back to Goodliff and Ratcliffe. They returned to their original premises down the road, where Jeff Goodliff operates to this day as Goodliff Racing.

### 1964 to 1968

Harry Ratcliffe had a good year in 1965, taking thirteen wins, breaking many lap records and setting the first 100mph (160kph) lap of Silverstone in a Mini. At the Silverstone British Grand Prix meeting, he drove a virtually standard Group 2 Cooper S to third place in the Saloon Car Race against stiff opposition. Two cars were prepared for the 1966 British Saloon Car Championship, a 999cc and a 1293cc

*Harry Ratcliffe (146) in an early Vita Mini, identifiable by the sticker on the front wing, goes for the gap at Shaws Hairpin during the 1964 Mallory Park Boxing Day meeting.*

Cooper; one was to be driven by Harry Ratcliffe, while the other ended up in the hands of various drivers. The competition was hot that year and, while the team got some top three finishes, they did not feature in the championship results.

They also campaigned two more Cooper S cars in club racing spec. Harry Ratcliffe drove one in the Northern Saloon Car Championship. He used this experience to develop his innovative rear beam axle, which not only reduced weight by getting rid of the rear subframe but also allowed a much more precise rear suspension. He won the championship in 1968.

Meanwhile, Jeff Goodliff raced a 1200cc car in the Spring Grove Laundry sponsored series, nicknamed the 'Bagwash Trophy Races' by the team. This championship was unusual in that one of the classes had a cut-off at 1200cc. Goodliff therefore built a special engine, by using an 1100 crank in a 998 block, in order to arrive at the correct capacity. He regularly finished in the points and took class wins at Aintree, Castle Combe, Mallory Park (twice) and Oulton Park (twice). He won the series in 1967.

On one occasion, the team had a particularly fraught meeting at Mallory Park. Jeff Goodliff qualified on the middle of the front row, while Harry Ratcliffe, who had entered his 1000cc car to take points from other competitors, was towards the back. Goodliff shared the front row with fellow Mini men Bill McGovern and Ken Costello. When the flag dropped, McGovern and Costello tried to squeeze Goodliff out but he was having none of it and kept going, spinning the other cars out of the way. He was first into Gerrards but there was mayhem behind him. About a dozen cars were involved, with the Mini of Mac Ross leaping the barriers and crashing through the wall of the ladies toilets, much to the shock of those who were using them at the time. Ratcliffe was also involved and did his car no good at all. Half-way round Gerrards, one of Goodliff's tyres deflated, so he was out too. The race was red-flagged and there was acrimony in the paddock afterwards.

Considering himself a better hillclimber than racing driver, Goodliff's real claim to racing fame came on 30 August 1964, when he was the first 1000cc saloon driver to do the Brands club circuit in under a minute. He went round in 59.8, winning the class and setting a new lap record. The Minis that he drove in sprints and hill-climbs were developed gradually. In 1965, he had a 1000cc five-port engine, which he next upgraded to 1300cc; both used a small cabin-blower supercharger. He won the 1967 BARC Hillclimb Championship in the 1300 Cooper S.

Stuart Turner of BMC had asked the team to represent them at the 1966 Kalemagden Motor Race on 8 May in Yugoslavia, the venue for that year's Motor Trade Show. Brian Gillibrand and a mechanic trailered the car to the event, and Harry Ratcliffe flew out the day before the race to drive it. During practice, round the cobbled-street circuit, Ratcliffe was by far the quickest driver – most of the other competitors were in Yugos and Zastavas. In an attempt to redress the balance, the organizers gave the other drivers virtually a one-lap start.

As it was a two-hour race and his stop-watch was only good for 60 minutes, Gillibrand set his old-fashioned alarm clock for two hours when the flag dropped, calculating that when the bell rang, the race was over. Ratcliffe had lapped the whole field twice when the organizers asked Gillibrand how much longer there was to run. He secretly put the clock forward, making the bell ring after just an hour and three-quarters, to save further humiliation of the home-built cars.

The locals were so impressed with Ratcliffe's performance that they wanted to carry him shoulder-high through the town square before he had even got out of the car! He was terrified as the Mini swayed from side to side as the crowds tried to lift it up; eventually, the officials persuaded them to stop. The winning Vita car had pride of place at the trade show, still bearing the scars – a pair of dented doors – of its treatment at the hands of the over-enthusiastic crowd.

It was not unknown for Harry Ratcliffe to join Jeff Goodliff on the hills. He had good results on the mammoth 3.6-mile (5.75-km) climb at Tholt-y-Will on the Isle of Man in September 1967. To minimize traffic congestion, all mainland competitors, including those in single-seaters, were obliged to leave their tow cars and trailers at their English port of embarkation. This meant driving off the ferry at the other end and making the 16-mile (26-km) journey on public roads from Douglas to Ramsey for scrutineering.

The hill was on closed public roads and, this year, it rained for Saturday practice and was damp and misty for the Sunday timed runs. Such conditions undoubtedly favoured the Vita Minis. Harry Ratcliffe, driving his 1.3 Cooper S, was third-fastest overall (154.69), taking the class by over 12 seconds. Jeff Goodliff, in his usual mount, was third in class.

Ratcliffe had a particularly good outing at the Aosta-Pila hillclimb in the Italian Alps. Having set a record-breaking class-winning time of 7:27.8 in his Morris Cooper S, he came back down in the cable car for a another run in his GT Spec S, which netted him a second in this class. The Italian newspaper made a point of reporting that, one month before, Ratcliffe had smashed Jim Clark's GT record at Oulton Park.

## Paddy Hopkirk, Brian Redman and John Rhodes

Other drivers also had outings in the Vitamins. Paddy Hopkirk was originally signed to do the 1966 British Saloon Car Championship, but he had to fit drives in with his works rally commitments. As a result, he only went out on a few occasions. In his debut outing at Oulton Park, on

2 April, he was fourth-fastest in practice, but the meeting was eventually cancelled due to worsening weather conditions. On 29 August, he took one of the cars to a third place at Brands Hatch. He was out again for the last race of the season at Brands on 30 October. After a real ding-dong with John Handley in one of the works Coopers, he finished fourth.

Through the Red Rose connection, Brian Redman also had occasional Vita outings. He was showing well at Snetterton on 10 April 1965, but his engine cried 'enough' within sight of the finishing line, while he was in second place. He had better luck at Oulton Park on 20 June, where he was third.

When his Cooper Car Company commitments allowed, John Rhodes took a turn, winning races for Vita at Silverstone on 9 July and Croft on 14 August 1966, with Harry Ratcliffe close behind on both occasions, finishing third and second. Rhodes

also drove the Vita Rallycross Mini. He always insisted that the cars should be set up to give him maximum oversteer. This was achieved by having one degree of negative camber all round and using the strongest rear bump stops they could find. When it was Ratcliffe in the Vita Mini versus Rhodes in the Cooper Team car, Rhodes usually won and Ratcliffe came second. Ratcliffe remembers one time when he got ahead of his rival, at Goodwood; on the last lap, he was overtaken by Rhodes, steering with one hand and waving out of the window at him with the other, disappearing to take the win.

## European Touring Car Champions 1968

Peter Browning had a high regard for the British Vita Team and kept them supplied with all the latest tuning bits and information. In 1968, he asked them to run a

*Paddy Hopkirk, more noted for his rally successes, had many Mini race outings with various teams, including Vita. Here, in a Cooper Car Company version, he fends off the attentions of two more powerful saloons at Snetterton on 10 April 1965, to prove that, in the wet, a Mini reigns supreme.*

pair of 970S Coopers in the European Touring Car Championship. Abingdon supplied the cars, KDK 319F and KDK 320F, complete with eight-port heads built by Eddie Maher's team at Coventry. The team also had a spare car, HDK 443E. Two had Lucas and one had TJ fuel injection. John Handley and Alec Poole were appointed as the team drivers. John Handley enthuses about his season with Vita. The 970 engines were known to rev and he was regularly using 10,000rpm; in his view, the cars were not far off the 1275S pace and he thoroughly enjoyed driving them.

After a hectic season of ten races in Austria, Czechoslovakia, England, Germany, Holland, Hungary, Italy, Spain and Yugoslavia and a hillclimb in Switzerland, drivers counted their best seven scores towards their end-of-year total. Handley's tally of two wins, at Brno and Zandvoort, and five seconds saw him emerge not only as the Division One Champion, but also as the driver with the highest overall points honours.

Aware of the benefits of 'tows' during qualifying, Handley arranged for Escort driver John Fitzpatrick to give him one at the Nurburgring. They found, however, that Handley's vision was dangerously impaired when he was driving behind the bigger car, so they came up with another plan. The Ford circulated close behind the Mini, punching an Escort-sized hole in the air. Round the back of the circuit, where the 970 usually ran out of breath, the rev counter went off the clock. The other Mini competitors were amazed when Handley out-qualified them by 23 seconds! The race resulted in the Fiats only just beating him. The Czechoslovakian round, at Brno, nearly had an unexpected sting in the tail. After the race, the team packed up and drove the transporter to the Austrian border; in the meantime, Handley, who was

*1968 European Touring Car Champion John Handley with his British Vita Mini.*

due to fly home the next day, returned to his hotel. On checking his tickets, he discovered that his visa expired at midnight that night. To avoid having to queue at the embassy to extend it, he rang the airport and booked himself on the first available flight. At 10pm he boarded a plane bound for Copenhagen via East Berlin. In the early hours of the very next morning, the Soviet tanks rolled in.

The championship was secured at the last round, a three-hour race at the Jarama Circuit in Spain. The team discovered that the entries in their class were down so, as points scored depended on the number of entries in the class, they drafted in Barrie Williams and Harry Ratcliffe to make up the numbers. The team nearly did not make it at all; on the way to Spain from the Swiss hillclimb, the transporter broke down in the Zaragoza Mountains. The mechanics stripped the engine and, discovering a blown piston, removed the offending item with its rod and put the

*The men behind the 1968 British Vita hat-trick of championships: (left to right) Alan Clegg, Nobby Clarke, team manager Brian Gillibrand and Norman Grimshaw. Jeff Goodliff was BARC Sprint Champion, John Handley won the ETC and Harry Ratcliffe was Northern Saloon Car Champion.*

engine back together as a straight five. It made only another 200 yards before the pressure in the empty bore pumped all the oil out of the sump.

Phoning Brian Gillibrand at the hotel, the mechanics were instructed to load one car with as many spares as possible and drive the remaining 100 miles (160km) to the circuit. This enabled the drivers to use that car to qualify. Meanwhile, Brian organized a heavy recovery truck to tow the stricken transporter to the track. Barrie Williams' car, which had done all the qualifying, broke down, but everything else went well, with John Handley taking class second to secure the championship. The transporter was loaded up and sent to the Madrid BMC dealers for an engine rebuild and the team flew home.

To maximize publicity, BMC invited the team to a reception at the Grosvenor House Hotel in London attended by about 200 dealers. Lord Stokes re-presented the trophy to John Handley, and Brian Gillibrand made a short speech. As they

were leaving, Stokes pulled Gillibrand to one side and said, 'You've done well and I am glad to see you here, but there will be no more motor sport coming out of BMC.' Gillibrand was surprised and disappointed, but the writing was on the wall. Soon afterwards, he negotiated a deal with Ford.

## Vita: The Final Mini Years

The withdrawal of works sponsorship led to a scaled-down Mini programme in 1969. Harry Ratcliffe retained the Northern Saloon Car Championship in his 1293 club car and the company also backed Geoff Wood, who was second in the Redex Championship. Ratcliffe hung up his helmet at the end of the season, having notched up over 200 class and outright wins. When Vita changed its allegiance to Ford, in 1970, they continued to run Wood, from Grimsby, in his 1300S. It now had Ratcliffe's 1969-season engine and Wood chalked up thirty wins in it.

*The ultimate Vitamin: Jeff Goodliff with his 180bhp, super-charged, fuel-injection Mini Sprint, in which he successfully defended the 1969 Castrol BARC Sprint Championship.*

In 1969, Goodliff decided to move up to the GT category by turning his Cooper S into a Mini Sprint with a difference. As well as having the usual chopped roof, to reduce wind resistance, the car was powered by a 1300cc eight-port Mini engine that not only boasted a large Rootes supercharger, but also had Tecalemit fuel injection. It ran a compression ratio of 6:1 and used 3bar boost. This power unit produced around 180bhp at the flywheel and normally reached 105mph (170kph) on the hills, in second gear! Goodliff again won the Castrol BARC Hillclimb Championship and Corgi made a model of the Mini Sprint.

## ARDEN

### Jim Whitehouse

Engineer Jim Whitehouse, from Tanworth in Arden, first developed an interest in motor sport when the 500 movement came along. He progressed to an 8-litre Bentley and, when that became too expensive, he built a 750 Formula Austin 7 that was much smaller and more economic. He called his first 750 car an 'Arden', at the suggestion of racing pal Jack Moore, who lived in another part of Arden, and the name stuck. He founded a company called Arden Engineering and Sports Cars in

1955 and graduated from general repairs to preparing competition cars for customers. The business was run from buildings on the farm where he lived. After a while, he became the victim of his own success – at the end of the season, work would dry up but, at the start of the following season, he was deluged with requests. 'It got so hectic, I was looking after ten people's competition cars and every one of them wanted their car worked on first. It was impossible.'

Whitehouse started to use the quiet winter months to make tuning kits. Their sales eventually became the mainstay of the business and the company changed its name to Arden Conversions. He got involved with 'A' series engines and, when the Minis came along, it was a natural progression. He ended up supplying bolt-on tuning kits to club competitors such as John Handley and Steve Neal, who used them in the rallies, sprints and hillclimbs organized by the local Hagley and District Car Club. Included in Whitehouse's catalogue were 'Formula Junior type' cylinder head, £28 10s (£28.50); reprofiled camshaft, £12 10s (£12.50); and straight-through silencer, £1 15s (£1.75).

## Arden Eight-Port Head

The Arden secret weapon was the eight-port cross-flow head designed by Jim Whitehouse and cast in alloy. His prototype was cast by Birmid. He then machined it up and fitted it with BMC Special Tuning valves, guides and standard-ratio rocker gear. The casting turned out to be slightly faulty and a blow hole in one of the exhaust ports had to be Araldited. First time out, Whitehouse was worried that the temporary repair might not last and told his driver Steve Neal to do only five laps of practice. He had even used the old remedy of cracking an egg

*Arden 1300 throttle bodied T.J. injection engine.*

into the radiator. Neal was enjoying himself so much, appreciating the extra power, that he stayed out for longer. In the race, he was leading two laps from home when the Araldite finally melted, forcing him to retire.

The design was a winner, but, in order to race it in Group 5, it had to be homologated. This meant that the factory had to order 500, the minimum quantity to qualify. Birmid, which cast the heads, made many parts for BMC, including the Mini gearbox casings. Five hundred was a small quantity compared with their usual runs, but a word in the right ear ensured that Whitehouse got a reasonable price for his batch. They were delivered to Arden twenty-five at a time and Whitehouse was kept pretty busy machining them up before sending the heads to the special tuning department at BMC for final assembly.

Jim Whitehouse also had to have the name on the castings altered from 'Arden' to 'Mowog' – for Morris Works Garages – the name that appeared on BMC castings.

At the time, there was some rivalry at BMC between the competitions department ('Comps'), responsible for running cars in competitive events, and special tuning (ST), which sold tuning parts to private competitors and to members of the motoring public who wanted to make their road cars go faster. Peter Browning in Comps wanted the eight-port heads, but all negotiations had to be done through Basil Wales at ST, as the heads would be sold as a Special Tuning item.

Jim Whitehouse has fond memories of his time racing Minis: 'It was more fun in those days, as the politics were only just starting to creep in.' He recalls one wet meeting at Silverstone when Gordon Spice was driving for him. Whitehouse wanted to know exactly how the car handled in the rain, so Spice took him round for a couple of laps. Whitehouse could not believe how much grip there was: 'Gordon was driving just like it was dry. I was waiting for him to spin, or worse. I was petrified.'

## Equipe Arden

Quite early on, Jim Whitehouse's customers began to enter their cars informally under the 'Equipe Arden' banner. Gradually, he decided to form a little racing team as a separate entity and the name was formalized. The team comprised Whitehouse as engineer, Norman Seeney as mechanic and Alan Edis as team manager. Apart from a small amount of sponsorship from BMC, the team relied on prize money and manufacturers bonuses to run the cars.

Peter Browning supplied Arden with a Mini 970S for the 1968 British Saloon Car Championship. His arm had been twisted somewhat, with the team suggesting that, if they did not get support, they would run Gordon Spice in their own 1300 Mini against the works-backed 1275 Coopers. The deal proved beneficial to both parties.

*Equipe Arden: (left to right) Norman Seeney, Gordon Spice, Jim Whitehouse and Alan Edis with Arden 1300 injection Mini Cooper S, which took a class win in the Saloon Car Championship.*

*Steve Neal leaves the following Cortina in a haze of tyre smoke through Cascades at Oulton Park.*

## Steve Neal

Local driver and Arden customer Steve Neal hillclimbed his first self-prepared Mini, 551 BUY, in 1959. Having swapped that car for a Kieft single-seater, modified by Whitehouse, Neal did some Libre races and had outings in his own 1071 Cooper S before reverting to 551 BUY. His first race in the car, which had now received the Arden treatment, was at Llandow at the start of 1963. Having qualified on pole, Neal was blown into the weeds by the Broadspeed cars driven by the more experienced Ralph Broad and John Handley.

Steve Neal went on to race his own 1071S in Group 2 events and the modified car in club races. Using a 1071 crank, off-set bores and modified rockers, Whitehouse built a really quick 1400 engine, which made the car extremely competitive.

By 1966, Neal was driving a 1275S with Arden eight-port head in Group 5 events and still campaigning the 1400 club car. He really came to everyone's notice when he beat the works Group 5 cars at the British GP meeting at Silverstone on 15 July. It was close run; the works cars were using Dunlop CR 65s while Neal was still making do with Green Spots. These went off towards the end and he was having to ease up for Woodcote; he just held on to beat Rhodes by 3ft (1m).

## Gordon Spice

A £12-a-week job as Downton Engineering's Sales Manager enabled Gordon Spice to enter the Mini fray in his former Radford road car. The other part of his employment package was the use of development engines for racing, provided he did not beat the works cars. At the first race of the season, at Brands, the works Minis experienced teething problems with their new cross-flow heads and Gordon Spice got in front. On the last tour, he let one works car past, but the other was going so slowly that Spice could not avoid finishing second.

Funds were tight, so Spice went to Dunlop, pointing out that, although he was not allowed to, he could beat the works boys. On the strength of his Brands position, he persuaded them to pay him first-place bonus money if he finished third to a works 1, 2. For the remainder of the season he was consistently the best of the rest.

Spice was soon approached by Ginger Devlin from Coopers, who asked him if he knew Nurburgring. 'Of course,' he answered, meaning that he knew of it, as everybody did. Devlin told him he was looking for a driver to partner John Rhodes in the six-hour race, as John Handley was due to be in hospital. A figure of £200 was mentioned. Spice, thinking that was the amount he would have to pay for the drive, asked, *'How* much?' Devlin said, 'Well, OK, we can go to £300.' Spice had just secured his first paid International drive.

Spice went out a week early and learnt all the road circuit's bends in a BMW hire car. When the rest of the team arrived, he told them he had just got an earlier flight that day. They were impressed when he was 20 seconds a lap quicker than Rhodes, to whom he eventually confessed his secret. The race was not quite such a success, as the team kept hanging out pit signals with minus figures on them. Spice felt that they were trying to make the point that he was only the guest driver.

In 1968, Gordon Spice joined Equipe Arden. He had a good year, taking many places and winning the one-litre class in the Saloon Car Championship. He raced for them again in 1970.

## Alec Poole

Alec Poole's early years in racing were in a Frogeye. In 1966, Poole, an Abingdon apprentice, moved on to race a Wolseley Hornet. His theory was that his Frog seemed to get more press than the more mundane Mk 2 Sprites and Midgets, so a Hornet should get noticed more than a straightforward Mini. It also helped that the family BMC dealership in Ireland was a Wolseley agent and this connection justified a certain amount of sponsorship by way of the advertising budget. The car had been well tweaked, courtesy of help and parts from Abingdon, and could pull 8,000rpm in top, which equated to 120mph (190kph). On 10 July 1966, he won Oulton's Alan Brown Trophy Race for saloons.

Poole (in his own words, 'a bit of an "A" Series Steptoe') recalls with some amusement one of his visits to the BMC competitions department to get parts. He was abruptly interrupted by Stuart Turner, the boss of 'Comps', and told, 'Before you acquire anything else, let's see if this car is really as good as your results seem to suggest.' Basil Wales was instructed to run the Hornet on the rolling road and report back with his findings. An embarrassed Wales revealed that the results exceeded their own best-ever figures, so Turner suggested to Poole that it might be in everyone's best interest if he wrote down details of all modifications and parts used, regardless of where they came from! Poole's exploits in this car, picking up many wins and lap records, proved he was equally competitive with front-wheel drive as he was in the Sprite.

With this background, and his year as number two to Handley at British Vita where he had scored two early season fourths, Alec Poole was asked to drive for Equipe Arden in the 1969 British Saloon

*Alec Poole keeps the Laurie Hickman Escort at bay as he rounds Old Hall at Oulton Park, to secure the 1969 British Saloon Car Championship.*

Car Championship. Jim Whitehouse had a Group 5 1000cc Mini that was fast and reliable, like the driver. Facilities were second to none, given Whitehouse's machine-shop and engineering expertise, but money was not so straightforward. It was calculated by the team that they had enough to do the first four rounds but, after that, they would have to rely on any prize money won in the first four races to be able to compete in the rest.

The Mini was now using a very sophisticated top end: a light-alloy, eight-port, cross-flow head developed by Whitehouse, as well as Tecalemit-Jackson fuel injection (a standard kit). This enabled the 1000cc engine to produce 115bhp at 9,500rpm. Such a power increase helped to compensate for the fact that many of the lighter bits found on the Ss were not homologated for use on a 1000cc example. In fact, it weighed about 1cwt (50kg) more than a 1275 version on the grid. The configurations of the eight-porter with injection resulted in the car sacrificing mid-range torque for top-end power. It also meant having to run one of Jack Knight's special five-speed gearboxes.

Arden was one of the few teams at the time to use wet suspension, other than the hydrolastic units; the majority of the other suspension parts were manufactured in-house. Everything was rose-jointed and adjustable, including the rear anti-roll bar. Brakes were Girling discs with alloy callipers at the front and finned alloy rear drums, the system having a servo. The subframes were bolted direct to the shell, dispensing with the usual rubber bushes. This comprehensive specification was backed up by meticulous preparation, the car having a strip-down and rebuild between every race. This involved new valve springs every meeting, a new oil pump every other, with crankshaft dampers and big-end bolts changed every three events.

The team's budget fears were ill-founded. Alec Poole won the first four rounds, at Brands Hatch, Silverstone, Snetterton and Thruxton and the resulting prize money enabled them to complete the season and take the championship. It was not all plain sailing and even that first-round victory had its dramas. Poole had not driven the car until official practice and, as he sat on the grid for the race, he suddenly noticed that the oil-pressure gauge was reading zero. He pointed this out to Whitehouse just as the grid was being cleared of officials, so there was no time to check it out. When the flag dropped, Poole dropped the clutch and hoped, while in the pits Whitehouse put his hands over his ears. Despite all the worries, Poole made a perfect getaway and won; the team subsequently found that the oil gauge was faulty.

Ford provided a lot of opposition in the shape of the Broadspeed Escorts and they also backed Laurie Hickman in a 1000cc version to try to keep Alec Poole down. It worked for two races, with Poole coming second at Mallory and Crystal Palace. At Croft, he took fourth place after a penalty for applying a wrong slot, but Hickman's engine gave up during the British Grand Prix support race at Silverstone on 19 July and Poole chalked up another win.

The International Gold Cup meeting at Oulton Park in August was the fourth-last round of the series and, if the Team Arden car won, the championship was in the bag. Whitehouse had established that the Escorts' fatter tyres enabled them to outbrake his Mini, so he got hold of some new lightweight alloy Girling callipers and adjusted the pedal ratio, confident that this would give his driver the edge. Poole quietly tried the new set-up out in practice and agreed that it felt good. Prior to the race, he warmed the car up and drove it to the assembly area, where Whitehouse would change the plugs to the harder ones. He managed to cross-thread one and remembers Poole, strapped in the car, going purple in the face at the thought of not making it on to the grid.

The agreed strategy was that Poole would not utilize the new modification in the race until he absolutely had to. He tailed the Escort for eighteen of the nineteen laps and, on the final tour, utilized his new-found braking power to outbrake his rival into Esso, to take victory and secure the championship. Poole won seven out of his ten races and posted fastest lap in eight of them.

A regulation change made the car ineligible to race in the 1970 championship, so, after a rebuild and subsequent track test by *Motor*, it was sold to New Zealander Mary Donald to race on the other side of the world. At the last minute, Arden managed to squeeze one final year's support out of Leyland but the delay meant that they did not manage to get the new 1275cc car out till after Easter. Missing the early rounds meant that Gordon Spice would not have a fair crack at the title, despite the 128bhp they had managed to screw out of the engine. However, he still took sixth place in the 1970 British Saloon Car Championship.

## DON MOORE

Don Moore's workshop in Cambridge Place, Cambridge, was housed in a modest lock-up between a chapel and a waste-paper merchants, rented from a Mr Banham. Pen Wills, who worked with Moore for fifteen years, remembers that, when they worked at weekends, they 'could hear them chanting next door in the chapel'. Located at the bottom of Mr Banham's garden, Moore was obliged to leave sufficient space overnight for his landlord to garage his pre-war Morris Ten. It was quite a tall order as there was only just enough space for four cars anyway. 'Don Moore' was painted on the brickwork above the pair of sliding doors at the front. When the waste-paper merchants moved, they offered Moore their premises. Glad of the extra space, he took them on and was able to purchase a much-needed dyno to improve his tuning facilities.

Moore was regarded by his contemporaries as a 'brilliant engineer', but he was also no mean driver, gaining many awards in his MG PA. He always drove to the event with either Pen Wills or wife Babs in the passenger seat. This car has recently surfaced and is now being restored by Andrew Bradshaw. Among Moore's satisfied customers were Brian Lister, of Lister Jaguar fame, and Doc Sheppard, as well as some of the better-heeled Cambridge undergraduates with their exotic sports cars. Having carried out modifications to Sheppard's A40 'A' Series engine and then his Mini, Moore went on to do a great deal of work on little cars. Sir John Whitmore, Christabel Carlisle, John Aley and Rob Mason were among his better-known drivers.

Moore was often to be found working at his bench at the rear of the workshop and, whatever he was doing, he always had his 2lb (900g) ball pein hammer standing on the edge. If any visitor tried to get up behind him to see what he was doing when he was working on something special, the curious victim would usually rapidly exit the workshop, nursing a bruised toe. It seems he rarely missed and no one ever saw the hammer move. As well as his flying hammer, Moore's trademark was turquoise blue and he painted all of his engines in this colour.

Don Moore always liked to have a laugh. Cambridge Place was also home to a local auction house whose main trade was in Indian rugs. Sometimes, they would be unrolled in the lane to allow prospective bidders to inspect the pattern. It was not unknown for Moore to drive a car up the lane to 'test the brakes', halt with the drive wheels on the edge of the rug, rev the engine and drop the clutch. The rug would be rolled up rather rapidly!

## MIKE CAMPBELL COLE

Having had his first taste of racing in a Motor Racing Stables Formula Junior in 1962, Mike Campbell Cole had his first club race in his own, Don Moore-prepared 997cc Mini Cooper in August the same year. As a result of problems in practice, he started at the back of the grid but finished a creditable seventh overall. After coming third in an up-to-two-litre Saloon Car race at Cadwell Park in June 1963, he took his first outright win at the Brands Hatch Easter Monday meeting in 1964. The laurels were presented by singer Dusty Springfield. Campbell Cole's two class wins and three class seconds in the 1965 British Saloon Car Championship were good enough to net him class second in the series.

On leaving college, Campbell Cole accepted a job with Don Moore, working in the workshop during the week and racing for him at the weekends. He competed in the British Saloon Car Championship and also drove Moore's modified Minis in club events. Although retaining a fairly standard shell, these cars were very light, with glass-fibre bonnet and boot lid and alloy-skinned doors. Moore also carried out various carburettor modifications, which were not allowed in the championship cars. Mike Campbell Cole continued to enjoy success in both classes.

In 1967, Esso, Don Moore's sponsors, asked him to enter two cars in the RAC Tourist Trophy at Oulton Park on 29 May. Denny Hulme and Paul Hawkins were to be the two drivers, but at the last minute one of them dropped out and Campbell Cole found himself taking part in his first International event. He won the *Daily Express* Trophy, for being the first British driver home in a British car.

John Shaw, one of Moore's customers, wanted to do the 1967 Nurburgring 6-Hour race in his S and it was agreed that Campbell Cole would go with him as co-driver. Unfortunately, the bumps in the circuit made Shaw car-sick every time he tried to practise, so Campbell Cole had to find another driver to share the car with him. The pair took a class fifth. While John Shaw was pleased that his car was placed, he was bitterly disappointed that he did not get to drive it.

## ROGER ENEVER: THE JCB MINI

The son of Syd Enever, head of development at Abingdon, Roger Enever, also employed at Abingdon, raced a diverse range of BMC cars. His Cooper S, which he assembled in a friend's garage in Worcester during 1969, was based on an ex-works rally shell and powered by a 1275cc engine with eight-port head, Lucas

fuel injection and megaphone exhaust, in which his father had a hand.

Roger Enever raced the car in the British Saloon Car round at Silverstone in June 1969, finishing sixth overall after a good dice with Jonathan Buncombe. After further outings, he recalls crashing the car at Brands and subsequently selling the repaired vehicle to someone in Germany.

## ABINGDON TEST DAYS

From time to time, BMC's competition department would book a test day at Silverstone to evaluate and compare drivers. On Thursday 1 September 1966, the following vehicles were to be driven: Cooper Team Mini (GPH 2C), Vitafoam Mini, Don Moore Mini (1394 ND) and works Mini (CRX 90B). Two Sprites and two MGBs were also present. Drivers attending were Roger Enever, Tony Fall, Roger Heavens, Geoff Mabbs, Ian Mitchell, Alec Poole, Harry Ratcliffe, Brian Redman, John Rhodes, Gordon Spice and Barrie Williams.

Also on hand was 'Comps' boss Peter Browning, who arrived in an Austin Westminster complete with signs, spares and a nurse from BMC, and a Castrol transporter with tea- and coffee-making facilities. Various team managers and other Abingdon personnel were present, and they were stationed at each corner to observe the drivers at work. Wise to the fact that braking for corners did not impress, each time one of the Vita drivers went out Harry Ratcliffe disconnected the wire from the brake-light switch. He then told his man to left-foot brake, if he had to, keeping the right foot full on the throttle. In this way, the observers were under the impression that each corner was being taken flat out.

# THE FACTORY ENTRIES

The factory usually only entered long-distance races. One such outing was the Marathon de la Route, an event with an unusual format. It started at Liège in Belgium, where the competing cars assembled and drove to the famous Nurburgring in Germany for an 84-hour race, at the conclusion of which the surviving cars drove back to Liège for the awards ceremony. In effect, it replaced the former Spa-Sofia-Liège Rally. The regulations were complicated and contained provisions as to periods of the race when cars were allowed to visit their pit; stopping at other times incurred additional penalties.

In 1967, two 970S Minis were entered. Tony Fall, Andrew Hedges and Julian Vernaeve were in GRX 5D, while Clive Baker, Roger Enever and Alec Poole drove LRX 830E. (The previous year, Hedges and Vernaeve had won the event outright in an MGB and had been duly presented with their winners' medals by the King of Belgium.) All went according to plan with the Minis in the early stages, but Baker experienced a broken throttle cable, which cost valuable time. Poole was then instructed to go for it, in order to catch up, and lost it in the misty conditions. Meanwhile, the drivers of the other car were revelling in it and, at one stage, when the leading Porsche pitted, actually headed the field.

Despite a pit stop, to replace a wheel bearing and a seized hub wasting more valuable minutes, the audacious little Mini finished second overall and won the class. It was a great achievement, considering the might of some of the other machinery it was up against.

Not all the works entries were so successful. On 25 and 26 July 1970, a team of two Minis was entered in the 24-hour event at Spa, which started at 15.04 on the 25th.

After seven hours, the cars were running in seventeenth and twenty-fourth places, from fifty-nine starters, but pounding round the 8.36-mile circuit eventually took its toll. At 1.30am, the John Rhodes/Geoff Mabbs car retired with a broken cylinder head and at around 3am LBL 606D, driven by Alec Poole and John Handley, cried 'enough', and put a rod through the side of the block. At the end of the year, these two cars, which had been used in British races by Rhodes and Handley during 1969, were sold to Jim Whitehouse.

## 1969: THE END OF AN ERA

When Lord Stokes took over the reins, he very soon made it clear that he did not believe that motor sport success sold cars. In 1969, he pruned the budget and decreed that everything had to be run in-house. The racing contracts for all outside teams were cancelled and the competitions department was told to set up a two-car Mini Cooper S outfit to contest British races. The old Cooper pairing of John Handley and John Rhodes were retained as the drivers.

Reflecting on that year, Handley and Rhodes feel that the factory boys did quite well, under the circumstances. After all, they were really geared up for long distances and had to adapt to the concept of making a car go flat out for thirty minutes. The first test session was most disheartening; the cars would neither go, stop nor handle right. After modifications and further tests, they began to come good but the first outing at Brands saw John Rhodes' car written off and John Handley spinning out of contention. Handley's season was punctuated by mechanical retirements, including a failed engine during the last hour of the Spa 24-Hour, while running fourth overall.

*John Handley, in the factory Mini Cooper S, fends off the attention of Gordon Spice's Britax-Cooper Downton example at the Silverstone British Grand Prix support race, 19 July 1969.*

Handley had managed fourth overall in the Brands Six Hours earlier in the season, but that had really been the only high spot of the year. The most disappointing moment was when he misheard a call from his co-driver Paul Easter on the final day of the Tour de France. They were leading the class in this hybrid race/rally by a good margin and were sixth overall. On the final hillclimb, Handley bounced the car off a parapet and that was the end of the event. Fortunately, the car did not go over the sheer 800ft (245m) drop!

John Rhodes found the change from 10in (25cm) to 12in (30cm) wheels and tyres a mixed blessing, although the tyres lasted better as they were now running at a lower temperature. This also helped the handling. However, they were less well suited to his driving style. 'It just wasn't the same, somehow,' he recalls. During that final Leyland year, despite bigger wheels, overhead cam and injection, the Minis could not really keep up with the Ford Escorts, which were becoming the cars to beat. Rhodes did not score one class win all season. He found it harder racing against fellow Brits, whose ice-cool atti-

tude made it difficult to psyche them into making a mistake. The Germans seemed to get rattled easily and the Italians were too excitable.

Rhodes sums up his time in Minis by saying, 'Single-seaters were thinking man's driving, but Minis were fun.'

*Reunion of prominent members of the 1960s Mini racing fraternity, with Pete Flanagan's replica Vitamin on the Cooper Register stand at Donington Park in March 1996: (left to right) John Handley, John Rhodes, Barrie Williams, Bill Price and Warwick Banks.*

# 4 The Mini Se7en Challenge

In 1966, the Mini 7 Club and the 750 Motor Club conceived a formula to provide cheap entry-level racing for the club competitor. The first race was at Brands Hatch on 17 April, contested by twelve drivers. It was not an auspicious occasion, given that after the presentation of the trophy and lap of honour, it was discovered that Terry Harmer, the first man over the line, was in fact driving a 998 Cooper, rather than an 850cc car. The organizer's mistake was eventually righted and the win was credited to Bob Fox, from Gordon Line and Richard Bromley.

At the time, the 750 Motor Club was primarily running races for self-built single-seaters, so, when a Mini appeared on the front cover of the club magazine in 1966, the letters column in the December issue included a communication from Mr F.H. Crosse, objecting to the 'Min Bin' intrusion. However, the majority seemed to welcome the new formula and the recipe must have been right as, thirty-three years later, Mini Se7ens still have their own, very successful, championship.

In 1968, the Mini Se7en Racing Club took over, and BMC provided some back-

Bob Fox (272) in the pack rounding the hairpin in the Mini Se7en race at Brands Hatch on 29 June 1966. Fox won five out of the six championship races, to be the inaugural Mini Se7en Champion.

ing and office facilities at Abingdon. This was withdrawn at the end of 1969 as part of the Stokes' cutbacks.

# BOB FOX

Bob Fox went on to win four out of the remaining five rounds in that opening year. He retired at Snetterton with a bent rear suspension arm, following running wide at Sear and became the first-ever Mini Se7en Champion. Richard Bromley established the lap record at Silverstone, Snetterton was down to Fox and the pair shared the honours at Castle Combe with 1:27.4.

In 1967, Bill Blydenstein decided to hang up his helmet and offered Bob Fox the use of his 850 engine. Fox accepted and retained the title despite missing the last rounds, having been hospitalized for a month after a 100mph (160kph) bank-clobbering accident at Mallory. He went off at Gerrards when the front nearside wheel came off, after cracking round the nuts. He recalls it was the stronger Cooper S version, which should have withstood the rigours of racing but had probably been over-tightened.

He took seven wins from twelve races, broke the lap record at Castle Combe and established one at Brands. (In the confusion over Harmer's 'win' the previous year, a fastest lap had not been recorded in the results.) His end-of-year score was 88. It was equalled by Mick Walker, but Fox got the crown by virtue of the greater number of wins. He also won the prestigious Issigonis Trophy at Brands, receiving his award from the man himself.

A great motor-racing fan, apprentice motor mechanic Bob Fox had started racing a Free Formula 850 Mini in Special Saloons. Unlike many would-be racers, he was encouraged by his mother who

*Bob Fox receiving the Issigonis Trophy from Alec Issigonis at Brands Hatch in 1967. Fox had seven wins and three second places from his ten outings, to win the championship.*

donated her own Mini as the basis for his car. It seems that the family was tired of him continually talking about racing and felt that if he actually took part they would get some peace! However, there were very few other 850s running in the series and he found he had to race mainly at Snetterton where John Aley usually ensured there was a suitable class. When Mini Se7en was announced, Fox jumped at the chance to compete in the new championship.

In 1968, he went back to Special Saloons and, the following year, upgraded to a 1300 engine. Initially, he felt the bigger engine was too quick, after being used to Se7en power, but he was soon looking for more bhp. During an outing north of the border, he had an accident in practice at Ingliston. He went off backwards into a timber-framed building and came out forwards, the building collapsing as a result of the impact.

Bob Fox is also one of a select band of drivers who have put a car in the lake at

Mallory. He was driving the 1300 Mini in a very wet race and a large puddle had developed on the exit of Gerrards. Part-way through the race the rear wheels aquaplaned, putting him onto the grass. This too was water-logged and he kept going, at a reduced speed, towards the lake. Unable to stop the car in time, he dropped into the edge of the water, about half-way up the wheels. He got out and a tow truck soon had the Mini back on dry land with no harm done, except wet feet and injured pride.

Fox continued to race until the mid-1970s, taking the 1300 class of the Hepolite Glacier Championship in 1972.

## CLIVE TRICKEY

The name of Clive Trickey was well known to Mini tuners and Mini Se7en racers in the late 1960s, but his rise to fame came about in a somewhat unusual way. The March 1965 issue of *Cars and Car Conversions* carried an article on Mini tuning and the following month's issue contained a letter from an anonymous reader correcting the article. He wrote again in May and this time put the name of Clive Trickey to the letter. By the July issue, Mr Trickey, a chemistry teacher, had taken up the magazine's offer to write for them and his first column appeared.

Having already raced his virtually Group 2 850 Mini, 526 COW, in 1963, Trickey now decided to build a Mini Se7en. Naturally, the construction of KTR 223E featured in *Cars and Car Conversions*. On 12 June 1967, the car had its first race at Brands Hatch. The twenty-four hours leading up to this first outing were, to say the least, hectic (but probably not unique). Starting work around 10am at his friend George Lawrence's Ridgeway Road Garage premises in Farnham, the suspension was

set up, wheels tracked, auxiliary instrument panel made, steering column adjusted, the Moto-Lita wheel fitted and many final touches completed. By tea-time the car was almost complete but still had to be run in and had no bonnet mountings, safety harness or instruments fitted. Trickey set off to start running in but only got 100 yards before the car spluttered to a halt with dirt in the fuel tank.

The second attempt resulted in a blown head gasket after 10 miles (16km). The gasket was changed; would it be third-time lucky? No, there was a lack of power above 3,000rpm. The friends adjourned to the pub, got their brains working and at closing time tried harder plugs. With N3s fitted, Trickey finally drove from Farnham to Southampton and back, to start the running in. At 1am on race day he retired to bed. At 5am he got up, made bonnet brackets and installed the instruments, only to discover that the rev counter did not work anyway.

*Clive Trickey (139) leads the final round of the 1967 Mini Se7en Championship at Brands Hatch on 10 December; he was eventually beaten to the line by Richard Ferris. Despite only finishing in eight of the thirteen rounds, Trickey still managed fifth in the series.*

At 8am, Clive Trickey with friend John and respective wives set off in convoy for Brands, with Trickey driving the Mini to complete the running in. John followed in the Trickey Mini Traveller, complete with tools and spares. After 20 miles (30km), the racer stopped, out of petrol; at 12mpg, Trickey realized he had to be rather careful driving the car on the road. The convoy arrived at the circuit at 10.40am after a further fuel stop and the Mini was driven straight into the scrutineering bay. It passed, to amazement all round.

Fifteen minutes remained before practice and Clive Trickey changed the exhaust for the racing system, while John did battle with the safety harness. The final preparation was not complete until 12.30pm, an hour after the finish of the official practice session. All was not lost, as George Lawrence arranged for Trickey to complete his qualification laps during the lunch break, by which time it was raining. On the first lap, Trickey waved a Simca by, and it spun in front of him, causing the Mini to spin in sympathy. Trickey then discovered that the car was misfiring on right-handers and had to pit to add more fuel. The session was over.

Starting the race from the back of the grid, Trickey was determined to make up as many places as possible. A good start saw him on his way and, by the end of the first lap, he was up to sixth place. Despite a little too much understeer, he managed to close on the men in fourth and fifth places; they were so engrossed in their battle, he was able to sneak by on lap 8 and claim fourth for himself.

On Trickey's next outing at Brands, he had a good practice, setting pole despite a hairy moment at Paddock when one of the circuit guard dogs got on to the track and ran in front of his car.

Trickey's budget could not run to a trailer and he had to tow the Mini behind his road car with a rigid bar. One night, he managed to spin the whole lot through 180 degrees on a wet journey home from Castle Combe. Having no trailer posed other problems: he had to carry out some crude temporary repairs to enable him to get the car home after his only damaging accident of the season.

As the season progressed, Clive Trickey's fortunes improved and, despite only completing seven championship races, he came fifth in the series. He had retired from one race while leading, when the coil failed, and was punted off once, also while in the lead. He also took part in a number of non-championship and Free Formula races and his end-of-year tally was two wins, two seconds, three thirds, four fourths, one fifth place and three fastest laps. In addition, George Lawrence, who had provided a great deal of help and expertise with Trickey's car, was third in one Brands Winter Clubbie.

Trickey's end-of-season accounts showed that building the car had cost him £694, and that spares/repairs, entry fees, petrol for racer and tow car and hotel bills had come to £72, or £62 deducting the £10 prize money he had won during the year. It was cheap motor sport, even at 1967 prices.

The next year, Trickey took the laurels with his first overall win at Castle Combe on 10 August, but was deeply embarrassed next time out at Snetterton on 25 August, when he spun on his own oil during practice. He had forgotten to tighten the sump plug after a rebuild!

Clive Trickey was second in the 1969 championship, his results including a win at Mallory on 12 October and five second places. In 1970, he upgraded his car for a Mini Miglia and in this guise the car also sprouted a one-piece Clubman front. In his only year of racing Miglias he finished the year in the top five.

## RON GRAHAM

When Clive Trickey decided to give up Minis at the end of 1970, his Mini was refurbished and sold to *Cars and Car Conversions*, who offered it as a competition prize in the February and March 1971 issues of the magazine. For 6d a go, readers had to put a list of pre-race checks in order of importance, then complete a tie-breaker question, 'I like *Cars and Car Conversions* because...'. The car was won by Dennis Bissell who competed in it during 1972, before selling it to Malcolm Quickfall in March the following year.

American airman Ron Graham, a great friend of Clive Trickey's, acquired the well-known Mini in May 1985, using it to come second, two years running, in the local club Autocross between 1986 and 1990.

Ron Graham then returned the car to the circuits, running it in the Miglia Championship from 1990 to 1994 and coming twelfth in 1993, before shipping it back to the USA at the end of his tour of duty. Graham still competes in events in the USA and won awards for fastest car at the East Coast Mini Meets in 1995 and 1996. He now runs a Mini business trading as Se7en Enterprises.

*Geoff Gilkes heads the Se7ens of Mike Smith and Gerry Allen through Woodcote at Silverstone on 2 September 1968.*

## GEOFF GILKES

Another driver who joined the Se7en brigade from the outset was Geoff Gilkes. He had a new Mini as a road car, went to Oselli for a Stage 1 head and joined the championship in 1966, when he was fourth. In 1967, he was only able to do half the races, but from those he secured three top-three finishes and finished the year in ninth place.

The following year, Geoff Gilkes became part of the Oselli Engineering Mini Se7en Racing Team. The drivers were Gilkes, Mark Shaw and Peter Shepherd, running cars with the notional registration numbers OE 1, OE 2 and OE 3. Gilkes was joint seventh with John Digby, while the other two only managed to take part in a limited number of races.

In 1969, David Oldham of Oselli decided that they should race-prove their 1300 Mini engines and Gilkes and Peter Shepherd mounted a class challenge in Special Saloons, driving OE 1 and OE 2. Gilkes built an all-new car using the last set of aluminium doors, bonnet and boot lid to come out of Abingdon. During his debut race at Silverstone he had problems getting used to the limited slip diff and was trying too hard to make up for a poor start. Catching one of the Jags through Maggots, he eased off, the diff snatched and he was in the bank at about 90mph (145kph), destroying the car. Although it was re-shelled in six weeks, Gilkes was never really happy with it, sold it at the end of 1971, and then took a year off.

Gilkes was out again in 1973 mounted in a Lotus Elan but it would not be long before he was back on a Se7en grid. Brian Lawrence had been building a Mini up and asked Gilkes to accompany him to Silverstone for its maiden test. After a few cautious exploratory laps, the owner returned to the pit and asked Gilkes if he would like a go. After driving it and getting within a second of the lap record, Gilkes told the owner that he thought the car was a race winner. Lawrence offered Gilkes the drive, commenting that he had derived his satisfaction from building the car. Gilkes was happy to agree in principle, but pointed out that he could not afford to repair the car in the event of an accident, unless he sold the Elan. Lawrence agreed to accept the risk and pay for any damage himself.

The first outing was at Snetterton and, on the opening practice lap, the engine did not feel right, so Gilkes decided to coast back to the pits. A big-end bolt had let go, taking the block and gearbox casing with it. Fortunately, a second-hand engine was found and Oselli came to the rescue with the machining.

Fitting the Mini drives around his Elan outings, Gilkes decided to concentrate on the 1973 TEAC Se7en Championship, which paid prize money, but he also managed to do four National Championship rounds as well. The year ended well. He won the TEAC and, despite his limited appearances, came twelfth in the National, with three race second places. Brian Lawrence was itching to build a Mini-Imp Special Saloon, so Gilkes sold the Elan and bought the Se7en for 1974, when five wins helped him achieve third place.

The Mini Imp was not finished in time for the beginning of the 1975 season, but, despite the late start, Geoff Gilkes took his class in the Esso Uniflo Championship. The following year, much to Brian Lawrence's delight, the car usually finished in the top three and established new lap records at Mallory, Oulton and both Silverstone circuits. Geoff Gilkes took the championship outright and concluded that was a good note on which to retire.

# CHRIS TYRRELL

With such a surname, it is hardly surprising that Chris Tyrrell should get involved in racing, although he is not related to Ken. He had his first race at the Monoposto Racing Club Castle Combe meeting on 10 August 1968, when he shared a Free Formula 850 with Dennis Fernie. He achieved a class fifth. The pair continued to campaign the car between them until 1971, when Tyrrell got one second and two third places in the Brands winter clubbies.

From 1972 to 1982, Tyrrell competed in the Mini Se7en Championship, never finishing the year outside the top five and winning it in 1974. He lists 1980 as his most disappointing year; despite winning six races, he lost out on the championship and the prize of a brand-new Mini.

In April 1976, Chris Tyrrell chalked up one of his most memorable wins, having been part of a four-car race-long dice for the lead at Brands. His adversaries were Graham Wenham, Terry Pudwell and Graham Woskett. He managed to stay in front – just – until lap 9, when Woskett inadvertently punted him up the boot at Clearways. As a result, Tyrrell was fourth into Paddock. Pudwell and Woskett were busy baulking each other along the Bottom Straight, which allowed Tyrrell to pass them both on the left. At Clearways he caught Wenham, who played right into his hands and missed a gear, allowing him to get by and win by a bonnet's length. Less than one second separated the four cars at the finish.

Having been offered a sponsored drive in the 1981 Metro Challenge, Chris Tyrrell took part in this series as well as the Minis until 1983, when he intended to concentrate on the Metro. In his own words, 'My time in the Metro is probably best forgotten. We were running with a very limited budget in a championship that was very competitive and really semi-professional.' The car was written off at the end of 1981, and he missed the first half of the 1982 season.

Tyrrell did not fare much better in 1983; in a big accident at Silverstone on Thursday 14 July, during practice for the British GP support race, he went into the barriers at 90mph (145kph). He was in hospital for weeks with a broken skull and kept out of the cockpit until the start of 1985, when he returned to the Se7ens. Despite the 1983 accident, Tyrrell was soon back to his old form. He was runner up that year and winner in 1986 and 1987, when the prize was £1,000.

Tyrrell always raced on the proverbial shoestring and got to know which second-hand parts he could get away with while retaining reasonable reliability. He built up quite a reputation for modifying cylinder heads, a skill learned from Dennis Rowland. From 1970 on, he built his own engines and modified cylinder heads, as

*Chris Tyrrell demonstrates his hard cornering technique in a Mini Se7en. He competed in the series for fifteen years, winning it three times and rarely finishing outside the top five at the end of the season.*

*Where am I going? Chris Tyrrell heads the leading bunch into Woodcote at Silverstone on the last lap of what Jeffrey Parish describes as the best Miglia race he ever saw, at Silverstone on July 9 1978. Tyrrell shot from sixth to first by not braking for this final corner and slamming it into second, dislodging the bonnet. Graham Wenham (1) went on to win, with Tyrrell finishing fourth behind Tristan Batch (34) and John Price (29).*

well as machined bottom-end components for many other racers. Doing a quick 'A' series head properly was not an effective way of making a living – it would take about twenty-four hours' hard work to complete one properly.

Like most drivers, although not all will admit to it, Chris Tyrrell has had his silly moments. He vividly recalls a race at Silverstone when, from the outside of the front row, he was passed by at least half the field before he had rounded the first corner. He finished the race in tenth place and only discovered on his return to the paddock he had left the handbrake on!

During a two-class race at a wet Oulton Park, Tyrrell set the Se7en pole, but tangled with a Miglia car. As a result, he had to sit facing the wrong way while the whole field streamed by. Determined still to win the class, he drove like a man possessed for the remaining five laps. At Druids on lap 6, he got by third and fourth on entry and, with two wheels on the grass, got second on the exit of the bend. He was soon on the boot of second-placed Malcolm Joyce and got by when the other driver understeered on to the grass on the exit of Old Hall. When the official results were published, he was amazed not to have set the fastest lap and still cannot understand to this day what happened.

For his final two years, 1988 and 1989, Chris Tyrrell moved up to Miglias, but found that his limited budget and his problems with the quality of Four Star not being conducive to running 13:1 compression ratio meant that he was not as competitive as he had been in the Se7ens. So he retired, having competed in around 300 races. As well as being National Mini Se7en Champion three times, he was Cadwell Park Champion in 1978 and won the Sevenoaks Cup in 1978 (Se7en) and 1989 (Miglia). He also held the lap record at Cadwell, Croft, Llandow, Oulton, Silverstone and Snetterton, set when the class ran 850cc engines and therefore standing in perpetuity.

What was the secret to his success? Tyrrell considers that it was useful to 'cultivate the reputation of being a hard (though not dirty) driver, perhaps even a bit of a nutter, never appearing to look. Once someone has chickened out, you've got them beaten for all time.' Every driver knows that the start is all-important and that getting into that first corner ahead of everyone else is a good basis for a race win. Tyrrell discovered, almost by accident,

that if he dropped the clutch at 8,000, the front wheels would spin and the drivers on the row behind would begin to go by; but, if he kept his foot down, when his wheels stopped spinning he would be faster than anybody else and would reach that first corner first!

Having lost the use of his workshop in 1990, when the estate was demolished, he ran down his cylinder-head business and now lives in Spain.

## STEVE, GARY AND JAMES HALL

Steve Hall was another driver who, after formative years in Autocross, became disillusioned at the cost of keeping his Mini competitive in Special Saloons, where he competed from 1974 to 1976. He joined the Mini Se7en Racing Club in 1977 after watching a race in which the cars went four abreast into Paddock nearly every lap and thinking 'this is for me'. Converting his car to Se7en spec, he won the inaugural Graham Hill Championship, taking victory in the final round at Brands on

*Steve Hall heads Jim McDougall at Druids, Brands, 11 August 1979. The pair finished second and third behind Patrick Watts.*

*Patrick Watts (5) is the meat in the Hall sandwich, between Steve (1) and Gary (22), at the final round of 1979 at Silverstone on 20 October. Watts won the race and championship from Gary, who was runner-up in both.*

27 November 1977 by 24 seconds, despite the snow.

In 1978, Steve Hall took the National Se7en Championship, achieving his first National race win at Mallory on 2 July. His third win came after making the long journey to Croft on 8 October; the prize, a black and white TV, blew up the first time he used it! His old car went on to win two more championships in the hands of Gerald Dale and Barbara Cowell. After a brief foray into Formula Ford, Steve Hall moved to Miglias in 1980. He was third to Chris Lewis and Mike Fry in the 1983 National and won the Sevenoaks Cup. He now sprints the Red Hot Mini with his brother Gary.

Gary Hall followed his brother into Se7ens for the same reasons. His first race was on 18 June 1978, and he ended the year thirteenth in the National series and eighth in the Graham Hill. In 1979, wins at Brands, Donington and Mallory helped him on his way to second in the championship, just seven points behind Patrick

Watts. Following spasmodic outings, Gary Hall did a full season again in 1986, missing out on the National Championship to Chris Tyrrell by just two points. He had four wins, five seconds and two thirds to his credit, to end the year second again.

In 1998, Steve Hall's son James did the last four rounds of the winter series, finishing tenth in his first-ever race and ending up fourteenth in the series with a car that was well down on power. With Steve and Gary engineering the car, James could well follow in their footsteps.

## JULIAN CUTLER

Julian Cutler had shared an Autocross/sprint Mini with his brother Lawrence. In 1975, when Lawrence bought a Modsports Midget, Julian read his Clive Trickey book and converted the Mini into a Se7en. Local engine-builder Chris Tyrrell had just won the championship and seemed the right person to approach for the power unit. After three exploratory TEAC outings, Julian Cutler played himself in with three National rounds at Snetterton and Brands, which produced two fifths and a sixth, before embarking on a full season in 1976.

The first round at Silverstone saw Cutler on the front row, getting fellow competitors wondering. Each race, Graham Woskett would say, 'Cutler's not been here before, he'll qualify well down.' Most times, Cutler would prove them wrong. Eventually, Woskett, who now regarded Cutler as a bit of a menace, asked him how he learnt circuits so quickly. He replied that it was not so much learning as 'just going for it'.

Despite rolling at the last Oulton Park round, Cutler's points score was good enough to end the year sixth, but he felt rather eclipsed by seventeenth-placed Chris Lewis, who won the best newcomer award. Top-ten finishers were not eligible. Cutler claims that, despite his cars always having excellent Tyrrell engines and looking smart, underneath they were not all they seemed. He had a succession of £25 shells, as it was easier to put sills on a rusty body than to straighten a bent one. Once, when he could not find a replace-

ment, he retrieved the previous example from Banstead Woods and was forced to straighten it.

As a hater of understeer, Cutler probably should not have raced Minis at all. To combat the problem he would accelerate into the corner, back off sharply to bring the rear round, then floor it, going through in what he called a 'banzai drift'. This got results but was hard on his tyre budget.

At this time, Graham Woskett would transport his racer to the circuits in the back of a converted 1950s St Trinian's-style coach. This became something of a social club and Cutler and the other drivers would often repair there on their return from the local pub, enjoying coffee and warmth before retiring to their tents in the early hours.

In 1978, Julian Cutler and his helper Graham Greaves planned a two-week Irish holiday to incorporate championship races at Donington and Snetterton with a Phoenix Park event in the middle. Donington saw Cutler with another destroyed shell and a badly bruised leg. Not to worry, suggested Chris Lewis who was also going to Phoenix Park, they could borrow his spare chassis. They drove back to North Yorkshire and Chris Lewis, his

*The Esses, Snetterton 1977: Patrick Watts (100) looks to see just how close Viv Church (38) is. Meanwhile, Julian Cutler (6) might be having problems on his very tight line. This was Watts' third-ever race, and he soon went on to get a works drive in Touring Cars.*

brother Jonathan and Graham Greaves swapped over engine transmission, wheels and other items. Cutler, who could hardly walk, helped by passing spanners.

Lewis and Cutler came first and second in the Phoenix race; it would not have been the done thing to beat Lewis in his own spare car. The return trip was detoured via Yorkshire to swap the bits back, before returning to Surrey via Snetterton to watch the race he should have been in. The 1979 Donington round resulted in yet another re-shell, none of it Cutler's fault. Dicing with Woskett through Craner Curves, he noticed a blue haze from his old adversary's exhaust. The next thing he knew, he had spun on the oil and was on the grass at Old Hairpin with a dead engine.

Realizing his car was in an extremely vulnerable place, Cutler tried to restart his hot engine, but to no avail. Before he could get out, he was hit in the driver's door by Chris Gould, who also found himself helpless on the oil. Just as Cutler scrambled on to the bank, another Mini ploughed into his own and turned it round, ready for race leader Ben Buckton to shorten the back end by eighteen inches. Cutler had to cut the shell open with a cold chisel to re-use the cage and was so fed up that he sat out the rest of the season. He left Minis in 1981 and went on to win the Grandstand Ford 2000 Championship.

## THE 1981 ANGLO-IRISH SE7EN CHALLENGE

Following his first trip across the water to Ireland, Julian Cutler was asked to get together a team for the 1981 Anglo-Irish Se7en Challenge at Mondello Park. He was joined by Gerald Dale, Gary Hall, John Harvey, Chris Lewis, Dick Robinson, Graham Woskett and two others. Leaving their tow cars and trailers at Holyhead, as they were required to do, the drivers embarked on the late-night ferry, getting what sleep they could in the lounges. As soon as the captain announced arrival at Dun Laoghaire, the nine drivers were on

*Waltzing Se7ens: Jim Mancey (66) and Chris Winter tangle at Paddock Bend, Brands November 1974. Mancey began racing after his wife saw him reading Clive Trickey's articles and persuaded him to build the car, to give him a hobby!*

*Martin Goodall (58) follows Chris Tyrrell and Bob Addison (65) at Thruxton on 8 May 1977. Tony Styles won the race from Addison, Tyrrell and Goodall, but this was to be Goodall's championship year.*

the car deck, changing plugs and filling the air with noise and fumes from their unsilenced cars. When the ramps were lowered, they screeched off the boat in a cloud of tyre smoke.

As part of the foot-and-mouth disease precautions, all cars were directed to drive through disinfectant spray. Woskett had spent the previous day polishing his car, so he drove round it, incurring the wrath of the customs men, and had to go back again. It had been arranged for the English drivers to be trailered straight to the Mondello to learn the circuit. The surface was bumpy and there were no straw bales or tyres to protect walls, railings or park benches. Within three laps, three of them were already below the record and the Irish boys knew they had a fight on. At the Sunday practice, the locals upped their game.

Despite a hangover brought on by the previous night's excessive hospitality, Gerald Dale put his car on pole. On seeing the time sheet, his face apparently changed from green to white and he said, 'That'll do.' Dale, Hall and Cutler headed the field and trounced the home team on a points basis after a hectic but enjoyable weekend.

## 'MARTIN'S MARVELLOUS MINI'

After completing National Service in 1958, Martin Goodall held various garage management positions before joining Downton Engineering in 1968 as works manager, later becoming sales manager. In 1972, he joined former Downton colleagues at Richard Longman and Company as sales manager, leaving there in 1977 to become sales manager at Weber Concessionaires at Sunbury. Working for such an array of tuning companies, it was inevitable that he would become involved in motor sport. From 1969 to 1972, he drove an 850 Mini in Special Saloons.

Following a short break, he first appeared in Mini Se7en during 1974 in his self-built car, still taking in the odd Special Saloon event as well. With backing from his good friend Dieter Dahlemann, he enjoyed good results, usually finishing mid-field. After two years in the series, he pulled off a unique sponsorship deal, obtaining backing from a children's comic.

*Tiger* comic featured a weekly strip called 'Martin's Marvellous Mini', chronicling the adventures of Martin Baker and Tiny Hill and their racing Mini 'George'.

Goodall painted his car the colours of the Mini in the comic, using his artistic flair to cut the graphics out of Fablon. He then contacted the publishers, with a photograph and a self-drawn cartoon. He told them his name was Martin, that he had a marvellous Mini, and that he was looking for sponsorship. It worked. From 1976 to 1979, his yellow and red car was entered as 'Martin's Marvellous Mini' and bore the name 'George'. At meetings, Martin Goodall's children, Sally, Cherie and Tim, were roped in to give away back issues of *Tiger* to any race-goers who had children, and 'Martin's Marvellous Mini' soon had an army of little followers. The publishers even produced 'Tiger Mini Challenge Team' stickers to adorn bedroom walls.

Invariably in the thick of it, Goodall always enjoyed a fine dice. His sense of humour was legendary. The 13 January 1977 issue of *Autosport* carried a picture of 'George' attacking four water-filled plastic drums used to mark a corner at Rufforth. The following week the magazine published Goodall's letter thanking them for including the photograph of 'my liquid suspension experiment for racing Minis'.

Goodall finished fifth at the end of 1976, but the following year, after an appalling start, with a blow-up in practice at Thruxton, was to be his best in the series. He won five championship races with his rebuilt engine and took the 1977 crown. In 1980, he sold 'George' to Adrian Standing.

After a brief foray into the 750 Formula, Martin Goodall turned his interest to motorcycles and, in 1986, was to be found racing on two wheels. Sadly, in 1991 he was killed riding on the M25.

## PATRICK WATTS

Seventeen-year-old Patrick Watts was excited to learn that his brother Graham

*Often on the receiving end when it came to awards, Martin Goodall (left) presents a Weber trophy to Rally driver Mike Stuart in 1980.*

and their father had bought the ex-Mick Osborne Miglia to run as a hillclimb car. It soon became apparent that it was Patrick who had the mechanical aptitude, and he ended up doing most of the preparation work. Apart from a couple of events in which Graham competed, Patrick did most of the driving. The car was gradually developed with coil-sprung rear and a limited-slip diff. He also took the tin snips and angle grinder to it, in order to get the weight down.

Despite running on a shoestring early on in his career, Patrick Watts enjoyed some sprint and hillclimb success, including a class second at Gurston Down in May 1975. The car finally met its end at Loton Park towards the end of the 1976 season. The front tyres were down to the canvas, so he decided that, for his second run, he would put them on the back in order to have better rubber on the driven wheels. This induced too much oversteer and he lost it on turn two, a downhill left-hander. The car hit a tree stump and rolled, before ending up on its roof in a pond. As the cockpit filled with brown water, Watts thought that the radiator had burst and that the water was getting into the cockpit. Then he got a whiff of it and finally realized what had happened. The marshals were less than impressed, as they had to wade into the mud to rescue him.

Having found a second-hand shell, Watts decided to rebuild the car to Mini Se7en regulations, on the basis that racing would get him more miles for his money. It took until the middle of the season to complete the car and he had his first outing at Brands on 12 June, where, despite a coming-together with Steve Hall, he finished the race. Although he only did half the races, he finished tenth in the 1977 championship. The following year he enjoyed a full season and, with £250 sponsorship from Whitepost Garage, ended up fifth, his first race win coming at Castle Combe on 28 August.

For 1979, Patrick Watts went to Richard Longman for an engine and attracted £250 sponsorship from Nick Whiting at All Car Equipe. That year, he secured the Se7en Championship, taking victories at eight of the thirteen rounds, and nearly won the brand-new Mini for the highest score in all three Mini series. He took pole at the penultimate round at Mallory Park but, for some reason, in the race there were men with Union flags on both the inside and outside of the circuit. Watts watched the wrong one! He was fifteenth into the first corner but, suitably charged with adrenalin, was up to second by the end of the first lap and hit the front soon after. However, his problems were far from over. A couple of laps later the bonnet started to flap and was soon coming right up in front of the screen, slowing the car and obstructing his vision. He dropped back to fourth and, next time round, he noticed the black flag and his number displayed at the start line. He thought that was it; by the time he had stopped in the pits and fixed it, he would have no chance.

*Patrick Watts leads Jim McDougall at Castle Combe on 7 May 1979. Despite heading the field here, they tangled later in the race and both finished out of the points.*

Then the other bonnet catch broke and the offending panel sailed over the roof. Watts was soon back in front again and took the chequered flag.

As was customary, series scrutineer Mike Garton checked the three placed cars and, for the first time ever, asked Patrick to remove the carburettor so that he could check the restrictor plate. As expected, the no-go plate would not pass through the inch and a half hole, but then Garton got his feeler gauges out and established that the aperture was oval. The car was excluded, ten points were deducted and the win was awarded to second-placed Gary Hall! Patrick Watts could not believe it; he had bought the whole carb assembly from an advertisement and had never had cause to check it. Furthermore, he had borrowed up to his eyeballs in order to race and was depending on selling the new Mini to pay off his debts. He was one driver who wore a credit-card shaped patch on his overalls carrying the legend 'Live now, pay later'.

Later, in the paddock, Gary Hall came up to Watts to give him the winner's trophy. His view was that, as the hole in the plate was oval, the area was no bigger and, as such, Watts had derived no advantage. Watts had a new restrictor made for the final round at Silverstone and won, proving the point and exiting the series on a high.

With a car and engine prepared by Richard Longman, Patrick Watts spent his final year in Minis contesting the 1980 1275GT Championship, with backing from Harold Bloom Signs. Having won six races, he and Steve Harris were very close on points when it came to the deciding round at Mallory Park. After getting pole, Watts noticed that his engine was smoking a bit; further investigation revealed that one of the rings had packed up. All he could do was put a road plug in that cylinder, to prevent it oiling and hope for the best. He slipstreamed Harris for nine and a half laps and made his move at The Esses on the last tour. Contact was made, and Watts ended up in the barriers.

## Leyland Sponsorship

During the 1977 season, the cars in both the Mini Se7en and Miglia championships were beginning to look more like Special Saloons than road-based cars competing in one-make formulae. In 1978, Leyland asked the club to administer the new 1275GT Challenge. As part of the package, the company agreed to sponsor the Se7ens and Miglias as well, with the proviso that the cars would retain bumpers and radiator grilles so that they would more closely resemble everyday Minis. Manufacturer backing immediately increased the status and credibility of both championships. A brand-new Mini was offered to the driver scoring most overall points in the three championships.

Despite repairing the car and winning the final race, Patrick Watts was second in the championship. After a spell in Metros, he got a works drive and became a leading British Touring Car contender.

## NIGEL GAYMER

Following in brother Paul's footsteps, Nigel Gaymer appeared in the championship from 1978 to 1982. After a couple of years in Metros, he came out again in 1985, kicking off his season with two second places. Gaymer was a constant sparring partner of Julian Cutler and remembers the pair of them having many a fine dice.

Always in the top ten drivers at the end of the year, Nigel Gaymer came second in the 1981 National Championship and, the following season, second in both National and TEAC series. If he had concentrated on the main series, perhaps he might have won it; doing twenty-five races for both series had somewhat diluted his challenge.

## JIM McDOUGAL

£500 was the price Jim McDougal paid for his first Se7en, in 1977. He recalls that he could not get any race tyres for his debut race at Brands, so he had to use a set from a road car. To keep costs down, he concentrated on the southern-based TEAC Championship in 1978, which he won, as well as coming fourth in the Graham Hill Memorial Trophy. He was ninth in the National series on the strength of nine outings. In the next year, he finished sixth in the National before leaving Se7ens on a high with a race win at Brands on 30 March 1980.

Jim McDougal became friends with fellow racer Patrick Watts. One day, the pair shared the front row at Castle Combe, and took turns at slipstreaming each other round the circuit, bumpers touching, to set times two seconds inside the lap record. After practice, Julian Cutler complained that they had been circulating so fast that he had been unable to get behind to 'catch a tow'. Their efforts were to no avail; in the race, they both got taken out, having tangled with each other in the early stages as a gaggle of cars tried to get through Quarry six abreast.

Progression to Miglias was more expensive. £2,000 was the going rate for a decent car for the 1982 season, with Jim McDougal entering races where and when he could. During one heated dice for the lead with Chris Lewis, McDougal felt a strange vibration. Glancing at the rev counter, he realized he was pulling just over 9,000rpm. The prescribed standard cranks had to be changed every six races for fear that fatigue would lead to a big detonation.

Having ended 1983 in seventh place, McDougal managed to secure some sponsorship for 1984. He was lying third in the championship with two races to go, but a blown engine in the last race meant that he had to settle for third in his final Mini season.

## MIKE AND ALAN JACKSON

Most drivers who start racing with the Mini Se7en Racing Club tend to compete for a significant number of years. Mike Jackson, Membership Secretary since 1992, is one such person. He bought his first car in 1976, for £450, and did two races at the end of the season, before starting in earnest in 1978. He had his first race win at Thruxton on 12 November 1983 and then regularly competed in the

*Barbara Cowell leads this bumper-to-bumper trio at Brands Hatch in March 1983. She always prepared her own car and was second in the 1983 and 1984 National Championships.*

National Championship until 1995, finishing second in 1989.

Mike Jackson and his brother Alan built their best-ever Se7en from a new Rover shell and Mike used it to good effect, winning the series in 1992 and 1995. Alan raced the car for two seasons; in 1986, he was ninth, and he finished seventh the following year. Having converted the Se7en to a Miglia for 1996 and 1997, they then put together a purpose-built Miglia that Mike used the next season, when he was fifth, to sort out it for 1999 when he intended to be a serious championship contender.

## BARBARA COWELL

Having competed in Mini Rods since the age of 14, Barbara Cowell came to the notice of former Brands Hatch supremo John Webb in 1981, when she won the National, European and World Mini Rod championships. He put her through the circuit's racing school and she had her first race in Peter Lawton's Se7en at Snetterton on 25 October 1981. Convinced this was for her, Barbara set to and built her own car in a shed at the bottom of her aunt's garden.

When she debuted the car at the start of the 1982 season, the other drivers told her to 'go back to bangers' but Barbara soon commanded their respect when they discovered that she did her own preparation. She and mechanic Roger Gunnell saw their efforts rewarded – the car had a 100 per cent finish record, with Barbara coming eleventh in the championship. She took the Mini Se7en and BWDC Novice awards and the BWDC voted her Number One Race Driver.

The circuit-racing learning curve continued in 1983, four seconds and two thirds helping her on the way to second in the National Championship. She was also second in the Southern Series and took the award for the best-prepared car. The following year, the fight for the championship was between Barbara and Chris Gould; Barbara needed to beat Russell Grady at the last round at Brands Hatch to keep her second place. She passed him on the last bend of the last lap to keep the runner-up slot.

It was always reputed that Miss Cowell loved racing in the wet. In fact, early in her career, she had been advised to try to psyche out the opposition, so she built up a false myth that she enjoyed wet races. As a result, she did well in them. In her view, if the driver in front was looking in the mirror at the driver behind, that driver had them beat.

After an introduction to Gerry Marshall led to a Fiat drive in Uniroyal Production Saloons, Barbara Cowell hasn't looked back. However, she maintains that, when it comes to fun, the Se7ens were still the best.

## SE7ENS GO 1000CC

In 1991, the formula changed from 850cc to 1000cc engines. The reduction in the ratio between 850cc and 1000cc Minis on the road was leading to a shortage of unmachined blocks and cranks. This, combined with the most popular racing piston no longer being available, led to the change in the regulations. Over the years, the specified cam had been getting wilder and, by 1990, most drivers were constantly revving to 9,500. Along with the increased capacity, the cam was changed to the standard Metro profile, thus giving an engine that revved less, produced the same power, and was therefore much more reliable.

## TINA COOPER

The first-ever 1000cc Mini Se7en Championship race was held at Lydden on 10 March 1991. Front-row qualifier Tina Cooper won the race, beating Bill Sollis into second place, helped by the wet conditions in which she always excelled. Perhaps her liking for slippery conditions went back to her days of racing in junior Autocross at the age of 14.

Tina had started in Se7ens in 1985, after an initial circuit-racing season in Fiestas. Despite a front-row grid position with the car 'straight out of the box', her first Mini outing did not prove to be a good race. It ended in the barriers on lap one. Undeterred, she was soon on the pace again but managed a bigger accident at Mallory later in the year, this time destroying the car. Determined not to miss the next outing, her faithful road car 'Boopie' was commandeered for circuit duty, the family working flat out to turn it into a racer in just two weeks.

Over the next three years, Tina Cooper honed her smooth driving style, continuing to excel in the wet. She was fourth in 1987 and fifth the following year. A fully sponsored 'turn up and drive' deal tempted her back to Fiestas for 1989 and then a season in Metro Turbos. For 1991, she returned to the Se7ens, making her presence felt on the front row once more and winning the first 1000cc race. In what would be the last season for the rather tired Boopie-based racer, results included two wins and three fourth places. David Sharp took the other events on board.

Peter Vickers was called upon to do the initial work on the new shell before the Cooper team – father Derek and panel-beater brother Steve (1989 Se7en Champion) – completed the car ready for 1992. Part-way through the season, which had been planned as the development year, illness forced Tina out of the cockpit; she still came tenth, however. David Sharp was persuaded to see the year out and complete the development of the car. In 1993, Tina was back in the hot seat with renewed determination. She won four out of the twelve races, finishing in the top four eleven times; her worst result was sixth and the car had a 100 per cent finishing record. Tina took the championship.

While the Fiesta and Metro Turbos ostensibly had a higher profile than the Se7ens, Tina particularly enjoyed the atmosphere with the Mini crowd: 'Racing Se7ens was very friendly, sheer 100 per cent fun, and if you won a race it was a bonus.'

## STEVE BELL

Two brothers who raced Minis and ten years of acting as mechanic for Chris Tyrrell at circuits all over the UK, led Steve Bell to try his hand at racing a Mini Se7en himself. In 1990, he and Mickey Bray took a year to build the car that they shared for the 1991 season. Tyrrell prepared the engine, in return for occasionally using space in Bell's workshop premises in Epsom. From his share of the season's

outings, Bell managed four top-four finishes, which made him determined to do a full season next time.

To facilitate this, a second car was built for Bray. A chance meeting with the buyer of famous coach-builders Wood and Pickett led to sponsorship, with the Bell Se7en now appearing in the company's black livery. The team was noted for its immaculate turn-out at every meeting and Bell was awarded the trophy for the best-prepared car from 1992 to 1997.

The original car was sold at the end of 1993 and one of a higher specification was built for 1994 and 1995, the year Steve Bell had his first race win. The night before, he and fellow competitors Dave Banwell and Dave Braggins had been at a Karaoke club till the early hours. Surprisingly, the race saw the three drivers hotly contesting the lead. Bell hit the front four laps from the end and stayed ahead to take the flag. It is most unusual for any driver to head the field for so many consecutive laps, so close to the end of the race, and still win. The same year, Bell got in the top ten, finishing seventh in the championship.

Bell was seventh again at the end of the next season, having achieved places but no wins. In 1997, Roy Griffiths joined Bell and long-time friend Russell Billison to build what they regarded as the ultimate Mini Se7en. Their aim was a serious assault on the championship, backed by Moss. The car lived up to expectations, and seven poles, seven wins, two seconds and one third place won Steve Bell the crown. Defending it was not easy – as Bell remarked, 'With the title comes a great big target on your boot lid.' Although at some stage he led every 1998 round bar two, he only managed ten top-five places from his five poles, to come third at the end of the year, missing second by just one point. Miglia beckons for 1999.

## DENISE MANDERSCHEID

Moving to the Se7ens after two years in a Super Coupe Renault 5 Turbo, Denise Manderscheid was told that she would surely sacrifice power, speed and fun. What she actually found was that, while speed was down, the racing was much more competitive; this was what had attracted her to motor sport in the first place. Her first race was at Silverstone on 15 March 1997, where she finished twelfth.

The 1998 Donington round, on 2 August, sticks in her mind as an illustration of the way Mini Se7en racing clouds have a silver lining. Arriving late after a puncture on the motorway, Denise had minutes to complete scrutineering, attend the drivers' briefing and get in her car to qualify on a circuit she had never driven before. In the race, she spun off at Redgate on the first lap and then the red mist descended. She fought her way back through the field, despite taking to the gravel to avoid another competitor's spin. Coming home twenty-third from thirty-two starters, Denise knocked another second off her lap time and really enjoyed herself.

## MATT HAYMAN

A top-ten finish in his first-ever race led Matt Hayman's fellow competitors to ask if he had done much racing before. Hayman had to admit that he had been competing in Autograss since the age of 14. The family found moving into Se7ens a steep learning curve, as the suspension on the Autograss Mini had been far from sophisticated. For the first half of the season Hayman would finish around twelfth but, having qualified a lowly twenty-fifth at Mallory, he was determined to do better.

That, he reckons, was the day it all came together; he came home sixth and never looked back. He won the 1993 novice award, came sixteenth in the National and third in the winter series.

For 1994, they built a new car, with seam-welded shell and multi-point cage. First time out, Hayman was second and took the lap record. That year he was joint winner of the winter series with Kelly Rogers and was seventh in the National Championship. A radical Se7en was built for 1995, but it needed a lot of sorting during the early part of the season. Hayman worked extra hard in the better second half to catch up on points, and finished the year sixth.

They stuck with the same car for 1996 and this paid dividends, as Hayman moved up to fourth in the points. In 1997, they invested in the first brand-new shell, which was given the Hayman treatment. However, while the car was brilliant, Hayman was convinced that his home-built engine was down on power. After borrowing an engine, he found that he was right – he was relieved to discover that it was the engine and not him – again, he was fourth. In 1998, the combination of racecraft, last year's car and a Swiftune engine saw Hayman win the Championship.

It was not all plain sailing. After an incorrect tyre choice for the practice session at Oulton, Hayman was an unaccustomed seventeenth on the grid. The Se7ens were the last race and, as result of delays, it looked as if they might be cancelled due to the circuit's strict 6.30pm Sunday curfew. This would have suited Hayman fine, but somehow the organizers caught up and the race started at 6.10pm; the competitors were told the chequered flag would be hung out at 6.30pm. Swamped off the line, Hayman dropped down to about twentieth, then fought his way up through the field. He hit the front coming through the hairpin on lap five; the digital read-out displayed 6.29pm. The flag was out and he had won his most satisfying victory.

Hayman always enjoyed racing at Spa. In 1998, his visit was made more enjoyable thanks to the antics of Miglia driver Ian Curley. Practice on the first day was dry and both drivers secured fastest lap in their respective class. For the following day's session the track was damp and, after venturing out for an exploratory lap and deciding there was no point, Hayman passed the pit lane, overtaking Curley as he joined the circuit. The next thing he knew, Hayman's rev counter was going off the clock. Looking in his mirror, he saw Curley right behind, grinning from ear to ear and giving him the thumbs up.

Curley's 1300cc car virtually pushed Hayman's 1000cc round the circuit, backing off through the twisty bits and at the end of the lap as they passed the start-line officials. Other Se7en teams in the pit lane looked on with disbelief as the screen displayed a time that was two seconds better than Hayman had done in the dry. The escapade cost each of them a bumper and Curley had to change his oil cooler, which was rather bent.

## NATIONAL MINI SE7EN CHAMPIONS

| | |
|---|---|
| 1966 Bob Fox | 1983 Chris Gould |
| 1967 Bob Fox | 1984 Chris Gould |
| 1968 Mick Osborne | 1985 Russell Grady |
| 1969 Paul Gaymer | 1986 Chris Tyrrell |
| 1970 Len Brammer | 1987 Chris Tyrrell |
| 1971 Graham Wenham | 1988 Malcolm Joyce |
| 1972 Reg Armstrong | 1989 Steve Cooper |
| 1973 Mick Moss | 1990 Bill Sollis |
| 1974 Chris Tyrrell | 1991 Bill Sollis |
| 1975 Graham Wenham | 1992 Mike Jackson |
| 1976 Graham Wenham | 1993 Tina Cooper |
| 1977 Martin Goodall | 1994 Ian Curley |
| 1978 Steve Hall | 1995 Mike Jackson |
| 1979 Patrick Watts | 1996 Phil Manser |
| 1980 Jonathan Lewis | 1997 Steve Bell |
| 1981 Gary Hall | 1998 Matt Hayman |
| 1982 Gerald Dale | |

# 5  Mini Miglia

Introduced in 1969, the Miglia series was a natural progression from Mini Se7en, allowing drivers more mechanical freedom to develop their cars. The main differences were 1000cc engines and wider alloy wheels shod with CR81 racing tyres. As few cars were ready in the first year, the series was run as a class within Special Saloon events. Mick Osborne emerged as the first champion and won again in 1970 (regarded by some as the first proper year of the series). His main rivals were Clive Trickey and Ron Mason, father of leading Special Saloon exponent Rob Mason.

In 1976, when Leyland took over sponsorship, the name was changed to the Mini 1000 Challenge. Leyland insisted that all cars had grilles and bumpers, which made them look more like the showroom item. By now they were using slicks. Manufacturer backing continued until 1981, when Leyland switched allegiance to the new Metro series and the Mini Se7en Racing Club was again left to its own devices. The Miglias continued with reduced grids, but the racing was closer than ever. The manufacturer, now part of Rover, stepped in again in 1989, backing the championship under its Unipart brand.

In 1994, the engine capacity was increased to 1300cc. Over the years, the cars have become increasingly sophisticated and today a front-running Miglia, with multi-point roll cage, intelligent ignition, and so on, can cost up to £25,000 to build. The racing is still very close.

*Phil Spurling looks happy to be in front at Silverstone in 1978, the year he won the championship for the second time in succession.*

# PHIL SPURLING

Deciding that he would like to get involved in Mini racing in 1970, Phil Spurling got a set of the previous year's regulations and set about building a car. Unfortunately, no one told him that the regs for 1970 were due to change. When he turned up part-way through the season, his car, basically a Se7en with Dunlop CR70s, running a 998 engine, was rather out-classed by the new-spec 1000s with wide wheels and racing tyres. A set of alloys and new tyres soon put him back on an even footing and, in 1971, he came third in the series.

Spurling remembers 1972 as the year of Firestone 1B 19 slicks; if you wanted to be on the pace, this was the rubber to have. Although his budget could run to the tyres, he could not afford the proper race pistons and had to use the machined Cooper item, which, in the interest of reliability, had to be changed every six races. He disputed the lead in nearly every race that year with Mick Osborne or Jim Burrows, who were both running split 45s. This meant that Spurling could stay in their slipstream at Mallory's Gerrards Bend but, once he pulled out, it was very difficult to pass. If the boot was on the other foot, they seemed to sail past him.

Spurling enjoyed a game of football for his local club at the weekend and decided to miss morning practice at the Brands

*Charles Hill (69) spins his car in the middle of the pack during a 1980 TEAC championship round, despite running the widest slicks available, off a Tyrrell six-wheel Formula 1 car. Such modifications were not allowed in the National series regulations. Peter Calver (28) heads the pack from Dennis Jellett (54), while Keith Calver (50) and Tim Cockle (30) are about to pass Hill.*

*Thruxton,
29 August 1976,
Alan Curnow (1),
with down-draught
Weber on his Miglia,
leads Steve Harris
(57), Ian Briggs (54)
and Mike Curnow,
who won the
championship that
year, noted for its
Longman V Harris
engine battle.*

Hatch round, then start the afternoon's race from the back of the grid. The regulations were different in those days. His normal helpers trailered the Mini to the track for scrutineering and a friend, apparently noted for his speedy progress around the Hertfordshire lanes, willingly offered to drive him down to Kent in his A35 for the race. The friend's reputation proved to be unfounded and Spurling only arrived just as the race was starting! Mick Osborne emerged as champion, Spurling was second and Jim Burrows third.

New driver Peter Major joined the championship in 1972. Although never a front-runner, he enjoyed eighteen years of shoestring racing and became the longest-serving driver in the series.

Oselli Engineering had agreed to sponsor Spurling's car by building an engine for 1973 and supplying forged pistons and a split 45 Weber set-up. Spurling looked forward to the new season with anticipation, expecting to turn the tables on Osborne and Burrows. In the end, they both defected to other formulae and Spurling had a fairly trouble-free season, save for a few dices with Dudley Fisher. He duly became champion, winning ten of the thirteen rounds, with Fisher second and Eric Groves third.

Mallory Park was one of Phil Spurling's favourite circuits and he always seemed to go well there. Having put the car on pole for the 1973 Mallory round, he decided that he would deliberately fluff the start and make a bit of a race of it. When the flag dropped, he was slow off the line but, as the other cars streamed by, he lost his concentration and missed a gear. He buzzed the engine, which allowed a push rod to pop out. The result was that he had to retire and that he never tried that trick again!

Fancying a change, Spurling sold the championship-winning car and built up a Hornet-based Free Formula 1000 for 1974. In hindsight, it was too innovative and never realized its potential. He did the final ten Mini 1000 races of the 1974 season, the year that split 45s were banned, in a friend's car and came second in the series. The following year was disappointing. He had built his own car around a rolling shell that turned out to flex too much, although he did win one race and was still fifth at the end of the year.

An all-new car was built for 1976. Spurling was third and continued to use this car to good effect until 1979. He was second in 1977 and took the championship two years in a row to bow out in fine style in 1979, before selling the car. After an interim year in 1275GTs, Spurling moved into the Metro Challenge; like many former Mini pilots before him, he found the going intensely costly.

## THE CURNOW BROTHERS

After cutting his teeth in Autocross during 1968, Alan Curnow did Special Saloons with a 998 Cooper from 1969 to 1971 and 1973 to 1974. He drove the Downton-prepared Green Leaves Watercress S in the 1972 Production Saloon Car series and regularly diced with the Firenza and Avenger of Marshall and Unett. Capitalizing on his experience, Curnow entered and won the 1975 Miglia Championship in his Longman-engined car and was victorious in nine out of the twelve rounds he started. The next year he concentrated on 1275GTs. In 1975, John Hazell was also the first to successfully dry-sump a Mini Miglia.

Mike Curnow, another former Special Saloon exponent, joined his brother Alan in the series, coming tenth in 1975 from just five outings. He emerged as champion the following year when he won eight races, again using Longman power. They were the only brothers to take the series in consecutive years. Other commitments permitting, Alan brought out his Miglia to back up Mike, who won the new Mini after achieving the highest score in all three Mini championships.

## MIKE FRY

Mike Fry joined the Mini Se7en Racing Club in 1973 and shared a car with his neighbour and friend Paul Allen for two seasons in Se7ens. He remembers his first race at Castle Combe, when he was second-fastest Se7en in practice for the mixed-class race. At the start, he had been swamped by Miglias on the run-up to Quarry and began to wonder what he was doing there at all. In 1975, the pair converted their Mini to a 1300 Special Saloon and had some good outings in the car.

Towards the end of the 1977 season, Fry appeared in the ex-Steve Harris Miglia and took his first win at Castle Combe on 1 October, beating established drivers Mike Curnow and Paul Gaymer who were second and third. He had arrived! During a full season in 1978, Fry came fourth in the National series and from then until 1985, when he retired as the result of an accident, he only finished outside the top ten once – he was eleventh in 1980.

Fry's most successful years were 1984 and 1985. He won the opening race of each season and went on to take two consecutive championships. He had nine race wins in 1984 and seven the following year, beating, respectively, Chris Lewis and David Carvell for the championship. He is now vice president of the Mini Se7en Racing Club, whose president is John Cooper.

## CHRIS AND JONATHAN LEWIS

Yorkshire brothers Chris and Jonathan Lewis have enjoyed a long association with the Mini Se7en Racing Club championships. Chris first appeared in a Se7en towards the end of the 1976 season and, after just four races, scooped the Best Novice award. He was fifth in the 1977 championship and sixth the following year. Meanwhile, Jonathan was twelfth in 1979, his first year, and became Mini Se7en Champion in 1980.

Both brothers moved up to Miglias in 1981 but, at the same time, Chris was concentrating more on the Metro series, while Jonathan was seriously into Formula Ford. From their limited outings, Chris was twelfth and Jonathan eighteenth in the Miglia series. This year the racing was close up front, but drivers at the back of the field had some pretty lonely outings. Chris mounted a serious assault on the 1982 Miglia crown with a choice of two cars, benefiting from innovative Howley Engines development and backing from Findus. He won nine out of the fifteen races, never finished outside the top six all season and notched up a 100 per cent reliability record. Needless to say, he won the championship; Jonathan, who only did half the races, was tenth.

The next year, Chris recorded ten race wins to retain the title, while Jonathan took five top-four places from five outings to finish sixth. In 1985, Chris once more turned his attentions to Metros but, having fitted in eight Miglia rounds, still finished the year fourth. In 1986, both brothers were in the top four, Chris losing the championship to Russell Grady by one point. Graham Chivers was third, four points ahead of Jonathan, who did the first three races in his car, coming second to his brother twice and finishing third on the other occasion. Jonathan then sat out the next nine races but was back for the last three, which he won in Chris's car.

The pair then went off to do other things, but Chris returned to take the Miglia crown again for two consecutive years in 1994 and 1995. Jonathan, by now running his own single-seater team, raced for close-season fun in the 1997 and 1998 winter series, finishing second in 1998. No longer tied to a single-seater team, he intends to do a full Miglia season in 1999. Having raced Minis and various single-seaters, he says that, given the choice between a race in a Miglia or one in a Formula 1 car, he would choose the Miglia every time. They are just 'so much fun'.

*Jonathan Lewis leads Peter Baldwin in a Winter Series round at Snetterton on 15 November 1998.*

*Richard Wager (500) used to drive Hot Rod Minis, but a Miglia race in a borrowed car soon converted him. Here, complete with tinted windows, he keeps another competitor at bay.*

## RICHARD WAGER

Richard Wager spent eleven and a half years driving 1293 and 1500cc Minis in Hot Rods. In 1979, a former employee of his, Miglia racer John Meale, teased him by saying that he would never make the cut in circuit racing; Wager rose to the bait. Meale agreed to lend his boss the car and began to eat his words when Wager put it on the front row alongside Peter Baldwin's 1275GT. Having gone on to win the race at Brands on 2 December, Wager decided that this was the sport for him.

He was still Hot Rodding in 1980, but he also bought a rather tired Miglia car of his own and rebuilt it during the year. He has competed in Miglias every year since and, at one time or another, has held lap records at most of the circuits. His best-ever race was the Castle Combe round on 15 September 1996, when no less than eight cars broke away and battled for the lead. It could have been anyone's race, but Wager was the one who was able to take great satisfaction in winning.

Richard Wager has driven Minis competitively every season since 1969. He has not finished outside the top ten in the championship in his last ten years of competing and was fourth in 1991, 1994 and 1996. Martin Wager, his son, intends to carry on the tradition. He had his first race in his father's car on 27 October 1996, at Snetterton; just like dad, he won. Martin had two outings in his own car in 1998, winning one, and setting himself up for a full season in 1999.

## JIM BURROWS

In 1971, his first season, Jim Burrows had one win and three thirds. The following year, he improved the car's form and produced four wins, three seconds, three thirds, set five fastest laps and four lap records, finishing third in the 1972 Miglia championship. He remembers 1972 as the year of the fluorescent cars – his was green, Mick Osborne's was pink and Roger Colson's was blue.

At Snetterton on 18 June 1972, Burrows put his car on pole, sharing the front row with Mick Osborne, to whom he had already finished second twice that season. At the start of the race, it looked as if Osborne would make it a hat-trick as he led the field off the line. Burrows had other ideas, however, and the lead changed constantly throughout the first six laps. On the penultimate tour, Burrows just got the inside line at Riches and managed to stay in front to the finish, winning by half a lap. To rub it in, during the course of the dice, Burrows sliced 2.2 seconds off Osborne's lap record. Phil Spurling was third, ahead of another battle between Ian French and Dennis Bissell, who crossed the line together, although a penalty eventually gave the verdict to French.

Group 2 was the next guise for Jim Burrows' game little car and the results for 1973 produced two firsts, three seconds

*At Druids Hairpin, Brands Hatch 1971, Jim Burrows (124) takes a tight line, while Phil Spurling (122) takes to the kerbs in an attempt to find a gap that is not really there. In these early years of the championship, cars looked like Special Saloons.*

(one at Ingliston, where he was forced to take to the grass to allow Frank Gardiner's race-winning Camaro to lap him) and three thirds. Burrows' Mini was the only one that year to beat the all-conquering George Bevan Imps of Bill McGovern and Ivor Goodwin. It happened at Thruxton on 28 May 1973, and afterwards Goodwin's sponsors protested Burrows' Mini, saying there was no way the 1000cc car could beat an Imp. The Mini was found to be totally legal.

Jim Burrows moved on, but the car still graced the Mini Se7en Racing Club grids in the hands of new owner Alan Seekings, who raced it in both Se7en and Miglia forms between 1974 and 1976. In 1976, the Mini found its way back on to the public highway as Seekings' road car. In 1982,

Burrows, who had done a 1275GT season in 1976, spotted his old car languishing in the front garden of a subsequent owner; the temptation was too much and he bought it back. It was a convenient purchase, as he was just about to stop driving for Toyota in the British Saloon Car Championship. The idea of doing Mini Se7ens again for fun was an appealing one.

In 1984, Jim Burrows' name was back on the Mini entry lists. When time permitted, he did a total of sixteen races in his old car, the last in 1989. These outings produced four wins, seven seconds and two thirds, to add to his tally. For 1991, a new car was built. That marked the end of Burrows' Se7en racing era, but it was not the end of the original car.

## RUSSELL DELL

In 1972, Russell Dell did two sprints in his own Cox GTM and, having enjoyed himself, decided to race a Mini Saloon the following year. He built up a Miglia car and engine, with sponsorship from Ripspeed. His first motor sport outing had been a shared drive in Keith Ripp's Autocross Mini, in return for helping with the car. He enjoyed a good year's racing in 1974, competing against the likes of Phil Spurling and Alex Boyle. His results included three wins, three seconds and one third.

Dell's season nearly ended in tears after he was injured in an accident at Snetterton's Esses. The accident was so serious that the corner was realigned after the incident, but three weeks later he was back to win the 12 October round at Lydden, thus securing the championship.

The competition was hotter in 1974, as the series got more professional. Dell found himself frequently dicing and occasionally tangling with Alan Curnow and Steve Harris. After a particularly fraught encounter with the pair at Silverstone, he sold his car and transferred his affections to Formula Ford, still finishing fourth in the Miglias, despite not doing all the rounds. Subsequently, he remained involved with things 'A' Series by going to work for Keith Ripp at Ripspeed for fourteen years as a technician and buyer.

## CHRIS DOBSON

Having started his racing in the ex-Steve Hall 1000cc Special Saloon Mini in 1975, Chris Dobson fancied his chances in Formula Ford and swapped the Mini back with Hall for the Merlyn that had replaced it. Like Hall, Dobson was soon disillusioned with single-seaters and went into Miglias in 1977, taking his new sponsors

Pearce Signs with him. In his first year, driving the ex-Mike Curnow car, he came seventh in the series, his best race positions being a second, two thirds and two fourths. He also took two race wins in the Graham Hill Championship, in which he was fourth. He was sixth in the National at the end of 1978, after achieving seven top-five finishes.

For his final season, Chris Dobson persuaded his sponsors to commission Boopspeed to build him an all-new Miglia. Last year's model would be retained as a spare, or show car. A concerted effort, with lots of mid-week testing, led to Dobson's first National win at Mallory Park on 16 April 1979. Despite this good start and six other top-three places, Dobson came fourth in the championship after Roly Nix and Richard Belcher had tied for second spot.

*Chris Dobson (7) leads Mike Fry (14), who is obviously trying hard, at the Cadwell Hairpin on 25 June 1978. At the end of the season, Dobson was sixth and Fry was fourth in the championship.*

*Like many other drivers, John Davies defected from Special Saloons to Miglias, which offered closer racing at a more reasonable cost. Here, John keeps his Transpeed car ahead of Grant Munday through the Devils Elbow at his local circuit, Lydden Hill, in 1984.*

## JOHN DAVIES

John Davies had a father who competed in the same Mini Cooper for many years and a brother who was well known in his Special Saloon Firenza, so it was not surprising that he himself would become involved in motor racing. He passed his driving test on the morning of his seventeenth birthday, and came home to be told by his father Jack that he was taking him off to Lydden for a test day with the Cooper. After Jack had done some laps, he came back to the paddock and asked John if he wanted a go.

John Davies followed his brother Tony into Special Saloons, buying a Mini that he saw for sale in the paddock at Bodiam Hillclimb in 1971. He persevered with this for ten years, alternating between class wins or places and retirements as a result of mechanical problems. After three consecutive gearbox failures, he took a deep breath and bought a Jack Knight dog box, which he describes as the best investment he ever made. However, as increasing numbers of drivers began to opt for the BDA route to power, he began to realize that racing was moving beyond his reach. He began to look around the one-make formulae and decided that Miglias were a good bet.

To start with, he effectively borrowed a spare engine from Roland Nix and took the car to Steve Harris who, to the best of his ability, converted the Special Saloon to comply with the Mini 1000 regs and put the engine in. Davies retained the Knight box and kept quiet about it. Although legal, they were not being used by many other competitors in the series, on the grounds of cost. Davies derived great confidence from the knowledge that it was virtually bullet-proof.

Davies' first race was at Thruxton on 11 October 1980. Steve Harris had told him to keep it nice and smooth, because he no longer had a limited slip diff to rev the nuts off it. He did just that and planted it on the front row. He had also been advised to keep out of Steve Hampshire's way, as the outcome of the championship depend-

ed on this, the penultimate race in the series. Davies enjoyed a good dice with Hampshire, Rick Cutting and David Carvell and eventually came in fourth, after Hampshire had outbraked him at the chicane on the last tour.

Davies also remembers the first race of the 1981 season, again at Thruxton, as being another particularly exciting outing. An oil-cooler pipe let go on the first lap of practice; having repaired it and qualified out of session, he had to start from the

*Roly Nix leads a train of five Miglias at Snetterton in July 1979. He was second in the championship in 1978 and again in 1979.*

back of the grid. Determined to make amends, Davies made a demon start and, although he does not recall exact details, remembers working his way through the field, from nineteenth to third. At the end of the year, Davies was sixth in the championship. He continued to race until 1992, often finishing in the National top fifteen, despite not doing all rounds.

## ROLY NIX

Roly Nix, 1977 750 Formula Champion, was great friends with Steve Harris. In 1978, he built his Miglia in Harris' workshop, equipped, of course, with a Harris engine. Nix adapted well to the tin-top category and enjoyed the close racing. He came second in the 1978 championship, winning four out of the last five races of the season, and was second again in1979. He had a hectic race with Phil Spurling and Paul Gaymer at Mallory in 1979. He and Spurling were neck and neck along the main straight, when Gaymer tried to drive between them. He touched the back of one of the cars, which half-spun them nose to nose, then his car rode up over the bonnets of both of them.

In his view, Nix's best-ever race was the one that he had with Richard Belcher at Snetterton in 1980, the year he won the title. Belcher led off the line, with Nix slip-streaming him. They both straight-lined the old Russell at the end of lap one and Nix managed to pull out half a lap from his rival along the straight, before dropping back. Shadowing the other car for the next eight tours, Nix made the same move at Russell on lap ten and beat Belcher to the line.

*Paul Gaymer (36) heads Phil Spurling (3) at Cadwell Park on 22 May 1977. It was a close race – Spurling's flailing bumper and missing wheel-arch section are visible. The pair finished both the race and the 1977 championship in this order. Gaymer won ten races, never coming outside the top three all season.*

## Mini Racing in New Zealand

The very active Se7en and Miglia racing championship in New Zealand has been running since 1970. There, the Se7ens run on Hoosier slicks and the carburation is different. The formula for the 1300 cars is called Super Minis, which are very similar to the British Miglias. The cars run mixed grids and races usually attract a total of 35 drivers.

Angus Fogg has raced in the series since 1989 and has won four Se7en championships. Jonathan Lewis often leaves the British winter to race in New Zealand. In 1998, he got pole and had a really hard time from the locals, who were determined that no Pom was going to win one of their races.

## JONATHAN LLOYD

Following in the tyre tracks of father Graham Lloyd's Minis, Jonathan Lloyd had his first Mini Se7en race in 1992. The following year, he joined the Miglias and has been a regular contender ever since. He took the 1993 novice award and was also fourth in the winter series. Graham considers his son to be a natural driver and faster than he himself ever was. Jonathan's best showing was in 1998, when eight top-five race finishes gave him fourth place in the championship.

## BILL SOLLIS

Having won the Mini Se7en Championship in 1990 and 1991 after seven years in the series (four others in the top ten), Bill Sollis moved to Miglias in 1992. He won at Brands on 22 March first time out and only finished outside the top four twice that season, losing the championship to Myck Cable by just three points. Sollis' 1993 season started with two wins but, despite seven other top-four placings, he was again second in the championship.

At the end of the following season Sollis was third, with Chris Lewis as champion. In 1995, Sollis tied at the top of the points table with Lewis, who got the verdict by virtue of one more race win. Stewart Drake had won two races and Ian Curley had won one and between them Lewis and Sollis had won all the others. Sollis was third, by one point, to Peter Baldwin in 1996. Drake had narrowly beaten both of them, to take the crown by three points.

In 1997, the Sollis challenge finally came good – eight wins added to his other points gave him the Unipart-DCM National Mini Miglia Challenge.

## IAN CURLEY

At the age of fifteen, Ian Curley had a racing poster of Peter Baldwin over his bench, but he never dreamed that he would later race against him and even beat him. After a start in karts, Curley joined the Se7ens in July 1992 and found his karting racecraft was good enough to make him runner-up in the winter series. He finished seventh in the 1993 National Championship in an all-new car, built by himself and mechanic Dave Older, and the following year he took the crown in yet another new car.

In 1995, Ian Curley moved to Miglias in a purpose-built Mini utilizing many components made by the family business Curley Mouldings. His father, a noted 1960s motorcycle racer, had always made his own fairings and doing panels for his son's Minis was a natural progression from this. Nowadays, 90 per cent of the cars on a Miglia grid will have at least one Curley part on it, although racing bits are only a small part of the business. In that first season, Curley took eight top-three finishes to end the year in fourth spot. As 1994 Se7en Champion, he was allowed to run as zero.

Peter Vickers did the fabrication for the 1996 car, but the rear wheel-arch modifications, which were also featured on the Bill Sollis car, were deemed to be contrary to the spirit of the regulations. Both drivers were obliged to withdraw from the first round. After that, the year became an uphill struggle; things broke that had never broken before and new ideas did not always work. Curley was eighth in the 1996 championship.

In 1997, Sollis and Curley were head to head. Curley had rebuilt last year's car, which had languished unloved in his

Steve Neal off to a good start from the middle of the front row, beating the sideways Anglia off the line at Mallory Park.

Julian Cutler leads Russell Grady through the Devil's Elbow at Mallory Park on 10 May 1981. The pair were disputing second place which, after a close race, eventually fell to Grady with Cutler third.

Mini Se7en races are always close. Here, Tina Cooper leads Dave Braggins (2), Mike Jackson (1) and Tim Simms (3) at Quarry, Castle Combe, 3 May 1993. Tina won, beating Simms by 0.49 seconds, who was 0.94 seconds ahead of Jackson.

Denise Manderscheid (36) heads Paul Rogers (34), Phil Harvey (13) and Paul Brown (67) at Thruxton in 1998.

Matt Hayman heads the pack on his way to one of the six wins that helped him secure the 1998 Mini Se7en Championship.

The Mini Miglias always provide close racing. Mike Fry at Donington on 11 April 1982 leads 1981 champion Chris Hampshire.

Engine builder Bryan Slark tried things at the sharp end when he raced Miglias himself. Here, he rounds Druids at a snowy Brands Hatch meeting in 1981, fending off the attentions of the nearly sideways Marco del Pizzo (21). Behind, Hugh Ward (87) and Patricia Ingold (27) avoid novice driver Peter Tisdale, who is pointing in the wrong direction.

Mini Se7en Racing Club Membership Secretary Mike Jackson's beautifully prepared Miglia, sponsored by Manders Paints, proves that standards have improved considerably since the early years.

*Ian Curley takes a tight line at Cadwell Park with Peter Baldwin in pursuit. Ian took nine wins from eleven races to become 1998 Champion, with Baldwin second.*

*Adam Lesniewski at speed in the Chamings-built Mini in 1989.*

Dave Forster on his way to third place in the Fastest Mini in the World Race at Silverstone on 29 August 1994. His best lap was 86.72mph (139.57kph).

Bill Cole's Mini was based on an ex-works rally shell and at 1556cc had probably the largest-capacity 'A' Series transverse engine ever built. The power unit was the work of Graham Cooper.

Steve Soper won the 1275GT championship in 1977 and 1979, and was third in 1978.

Peter Burnham's Mini Jem lifts a rear wheel on the way to a class win at Prescott Hillclimb in 1984. Burnham recorded sixteen class wins, thirty-eight seconds and thirty-one third places with his self-built car and 1293cc engine.

In 1981, Steven Roberts moved on to a Mini-engined Davrian. Here, he lifts a wheel while in front of Richard Ward's more powerful Elan at Thruxton, 1983.

Jon Mowatt at Brands' Paddock Bend in his faithful 1275GT. He raced the car in many national and international events from 1978 to 1984. The car's new owner regularly competes in Germany.

*Bryan Slark in the FIA Historic 1071S he shares with Klaus Reineck, fighting off the powerful little Fiat Abarth. Slark and Reineck have scored many class wins and the car has an excellent reliability record.*

*In the thick of it, just as it always was in the 1960s, the Cooper S is a major force to be reckoned with in FIA Historic Racing. Norman Grimshaw in BFO 541D takes a tight inside line at Silverstone in 1998.*

*Classic Touring Car racing at its best: Nick Swift's Mini leads through the bends while two other Minis are also ahead of the more powerful cars at the back of the pack.*

*Paul Stanworth's beautifully rebuilt Broadspeed Austin Mini Cooper S, BOP 243C, in the paddock at the Goodwood Revival Meeting, September 1998.*

*John Brigden at the Nurburgring Karussel in 1995.*

garage until after Christmas. Knowing he was down on power against his rival, he did all he could to maximize his chassis, frustrated that, on most occasions when he passed Sollis, his rival usually had the top end to drive by on the straights. Curley still notched up three victories – his win at Silverstone on 5 October was his most satisfying Miglia win ever. He won the dash to the first corner and there then followed nine laps of the kind of side-by-side racing for which the Miglias are famous. Sollis

got ahead at the end of lap nine, but Curley retrieved the place, with Sollis' engine letting go at the start of the final tour, as he tried to get back on terms Curley took the championship runner-up spot.

Ian Curley became Miglia Champion in 1998 with the same car, incorporating further modifications. He took nine wins, one second and one eleventh place from eleven outings.

## National Mini Miglia Champions

| | |
|---|---|
| 1969 Mick Osborne | 1984 Mike Fry |
| 1970 Mick Osborne | 1985 Mike Fry |
| 1971 Len Brammer | 1986 Russell Grady |
| 1972 Mick Osborne | 1987 Russell Grady |
| 1973 Phil Spurling | 1988 Russell Grady |
| 1974 Russell Dell | 1989 Myck Cable |
| 1975 Alan Curnow | 1990 Owen Hall |
| 1976 Mike Curnow | 1991 Myck Cable |
| 1977 Paul Gaymer | 1992 Myck Cable |
| 1978 Phil Spurling | 1993 Ian Gunn |
| 1979 Phil Spurling | 1994 Chris Lewis |
| 1980 Roland Nix | 1995 Chris Lewis |
| 1981 Chris Hampshire | 1996 Stewart Drake |
| 1982 Chris Lewis | 1997 Bill Sollis |
| 1983 Mike Fry | 1998 Ian Curley |

# 6  Very Special Saloons

Special Saloons provided very fast, close racing and, over the years, the regulations governing just how 'special' the cars were allowed to be have varied enormously. Eventually, the category became the victim of its own success, when many drivers bailed out because of prohibitive costs. This chapter is devoted to racing Minis that ended up with something other than the ubiquitous BMC 'A' Series engine under the bonnet, or, in some cases, under the boot lid! Some of the cars were radical in other ways.

## JOHN HOPKISS AND GRAHAM LLOYD

In 1962, John Hopkiss and Graham Lloyd modified a 997 Cooper to build their first Special Saloon. It had a five-port head fed by a pair of down-draught Webers, with trumpets that stuck up through the bonnet, just in front of the windscreen. The pair shared the driving and were quite successful, but a quest for more power led them to buy one of the first iron eight-port heads from BMC. Now the twin side-draught Webers protruded beyond the front line of the bonnet. After trying various self-made air boxes, they were glad to utilize the Clubman front as soon as it became available.

While the car remained competitive, Hopkiss and Lloyd found they were being regularly beaten in the class by Laurie Hickman's Anglia so, when the Angle-box came up for sale, they bought it. Graham Lloyd raced it twice and hated it; he was a front-wheel-drive man. One day, after

*Special Saloon Minis were always in the thick of the action: Geoff Gilkes (19) in his Brian Lawrence-built Mini Imp takes the lead from Charles Bernstein (22). Behind, David Enderby and Bill Barrett dispute third place.*

Lloyd's son's christening, a group of guests ended up in his garage looking at the two racing saloons. When Lloyd said that he liked the Mini handling and the Anglia's power, one of his friends suggested, tongue in cheek, that they could always put the Ford's engine in the Mini.

This got Hopkiss and Lloyd thinking and they decided that that was what they would do. First, they bought a piece of EN 40B steel and had it machined as an adapter between the Ford crank and the Mini gearbox. It had a great big dowel which fitted in the end of the crank where the spigot bush should have been. To join the Ford block to the Mini gearbox casing, they got some alloy box-section and welded it up to create a sandwich plate. They also had to alter the shape of the Mini casing by cutting out sections and fabricating replacements, again using aluminium. After perfecting the shape, they made wooden moulds and had the finished articles cast in alloy.

The unit was then bolted together and installed in the Mini. Having run it on Harry Ratcliffe's rolling road they were delighted with the power. It was dry-sumped and the boot-mounted tank was fed by pipes running through the car. The first time Graham Lloyd drove it in the wet, the heat from the hot oil steamed up the windows and he could not see a thing. Insulating the pipes cured the problem.

The car was a regular class winner and Hopkiss and Lloyd found that they were beating much more powerful machinery in the wet. So that they would both get a race, one would enter the up to 1000cc class and the other would drive in the event for cars above one litre.

Hopkiss and Lloyd then decided to build an engine for the up-to-850 class. By sleeving down a Ford block and using rally-spec Triumph 2000 pistons, they had an 850cc Ford MAE unit, which they believed to be unique. Having two engines meant they really needed two cars, so they built a second Mini. In 1972, they contested two classes in the Hepolite Glacier Championship. Lloyd came second in the up-to-850s, while Hopkiss won the 1300 crown. They nearly made the double, but Lloyd was just beaten by Mike Evans in his eight-port 850.

During practice for an Oulton Park round, in which he claimed pole, John Hopkiss holed a piston. Determined not to throw away his grid position, he borrowed some welding bottles and, using strips of aluminium cut from his air scoop, welded up the hole with the piston, *in situ*. As it was a Hepolite round, technical staff from the piston company were in attendance and they soon came to see what was going on. They started taking bets as to whether the Mini would even make it to the assembly area under its own power, let alone the grid. Hopkiss stormed off the line and won the race. Hepolite asked if they could have the piston and he sent it to them. At the end-of-season awards ceremony, it was presented to him, duly polished and mounted, as an additional trophy.

The second car was sold to fund Hopkiss and Lloyd's next idea. Inevitably, the next stage of development would be to go for BDA power. To keep costs realistic, they went to Bob Rawlings, a Manchester dealer who specialized in selling single-seater parts. They bought a couple of blown-up Formula 3 engines and made one good engine from the two. With suitable modifications, the BDA was grafted on to the Mini gearbox; sixteen valves and F1 cams meant that they were nearing the limit of what the Mini gears could take. This, combined with the fact that the engines were second-hand to start with, led to some reliability problems. Again they ended up with two engines, changing them over in the one car that they shared, to suit each

131

*David Enderby (92) pursues Peter Day (88) in March 1977. The pair were constant sparring partners in the Hitachi and Esso Uniflo Championships.*

particular race. As well as Cosworths, they were also buying second-hand Holbays; Roger Dunnell, a well-known Holbay builder, was amazed to see one of his old engines in a Mini.

Oulton Park seems to have been the regular place for the pair to come up with a bizarre scheme to cure a major problem. Once, a camshaft broke during practice, so Hopkiss drove to Withers of Winsford for a replacement, while Lloyd fathomed out how to take the old one out without dismantling the engine. Having enlisted some helpers, he tipped the Mini on its side to stop the cam followers from falling into the gearbox. He then turned the remains of the cam, to make sure the followers stayed at the top, and pulled it out. When Hopkiss returned with the replacement, they slipped it in, put the car back on its wheels, replaced the belts and were ready to race.

Like many Mini drivers, Hopkiss and Lloyd found 10in (25cm) wheels limiting. Changing to 13in (32.5cm) ones allowed them to move on to the new breed of Firestone slicks. The first time Lloyd used them, at Mallory Park, he amazed Peter Baldwin by driving round him at Gerrards, nearly every lap.

Hopkiss and Lloyd left Special Saloons in 1973, although Lloyd kept up his involvement with his company, Manders Paints, sponsoring Mike Jackson's Miglia. In recent years, his son, Jonathan Lloyd, has also become a regular competitor.

## DAVID ENDERBY

Anaesthetist Dr David Enderby spent his formative motor sport years in Minis. In 1964, he campaigned his road 850 Mini in autotests, sprints and hillclimbs. As a result of this first taste, he bought a Cooper S in 1968 and got Ken Costello to rebuild the engine. The following year he used the S, which he still owns to this day, to win the ACSMC Sprint Championship.

He now wanted to go into serious motor racing. In 1970, he paid David Hipperson £373 for his Special Saloon 850 Mini. This odd amount took into account the additional price of various spares, which he bought with the car, along with a can of purple cellulose. Hipperson and his brother raced the car in a green livery and Enderby decided that he did not like the colour, so the purple paint was added to the package. The car was resprayed and

Enderby made his debut in it in 1972, running in five Free Formula 850 events, from which he took what was to be the first of many race wins. The next year he recorded five wins from nineteen outings.

During those early days, he had some good dices with friend and arch rival David Canicott. Canicott, who owned a car-spares business in Shoeburyness, retired from racing after rolling down Brands' Paddock Hill Bend and banging his head rather badly. To keep an interest in racing he decided to sponsor Enderby. The Mini was painted in his colours – green with purple stripes – in the hope that, when a competitor came up behind the car, they would think 'yuk' and instinctively brake.

After twenty-seven races in 1974, Enderby came second in class in the Simoniz Special Saloon Car Championship and fourth overall in the TEAC Drivers Championship. Now he was getting into his stride and 1975 gave him championship-class wins in the Simoniz and BRSCC East Anglian Series, from twenty-six outings. Next year, he did twenty-seven races, taking class wins in the Forward Trust and Hitachi Championships and also coming in as joint class winner in the BRSCC Series. In 1977, thirty outings brought him class wins in the Esso Uniflo and Hitachi Series.

Being involved in two championships often meant competing at two different circuits in a weekend and Enderby vividly remembers one Bank Holiday weekend when all his plans almost went wrong. Racing at Oulton Park on the Saturday, he had a coming-together with Charles Bernstein, resulting in a bent subframe. He went back to the house of long-time friend and racing crew member Anthony Rigby, where he always stayed when racing at Oulton. In his garage, Rigby had 'a

Mini that wasn't doing anything'. They removed the subframe and, as the Enderby cars were always noted for their immaculate presentation, decided to clean it up and paint it. The only can of paint in the garage was white and the shops were shut. The repaired car duly appeared on the grid at Mallory on Bank Holiday Monday, pristine and complete with white subframe.

Over the years, David Enderby ran the car with various engine configurations but always sticking to the 850cc class. After using a home-built unit, which proved to be no better than the engine the car came with, he got Peter Vickers to do him a semi short-stroke – an overbored 850 block with a 970 crank. By now he had grafted lightweight panels on to the car and it was going well. The big break on power came when he bought a short-stroker from Neil Dineen, Richard Longman's cousin, which had a special 52mm Gordon Allen crank and revved to 10,000rpm. Enderby remembers going to see Gordon Allen, who had a superb workshop at the time in the cellar of his house. After selling his business, Allen Crankshafts, in about 1980, Allen continued to work from the cellar until his death in 1984.

David Enderby's ultimate engine was this bottom end with an Arden eight-port head, which he rebuilt with the help of Jim Whitehouse. It had MAE valve springs (which occasionally broke) with titanium caps. This 850cc engine produced well over 100bhp at the flywheel and enabled Enderby to beat the all-conquering Imps.

During the six years he ran the Mini, David Enderby did 147 races, taking fifty-one class or overall wins and thirty-eight class or overall second places. At the end of the 1977 season, he sold the shell to Bev Comber and his engine to Bill Richards and continued in Special Saloons, driving various Hillman Imp derivatives. If

*Ingliston 1970: Sedric Bell leads Andy Barton, Jim Bowden and Ken Allen, while the rest of the field follow.*

Enderby's Mini record sounds impressive, consider his career in his VW Karmann-Ghia Special Saloon: eighty-three class or overall wins from ninety-nine outings. He still owns this car, so he may one day chalk up that one-hundredth outing.

## SEDRIC BELL

Twice winner of the Scottish Saloon Car Championship, in 1972 and 1974, Sedric Bell raced 1000cc Minis from 1966. Despite the proliferation of rose-jointed suspension on his fellow competitors' cars, Bell always used rubber bushes, feeling that the rose joints made a Mini much too rigid. He proved his point by securing ten lap records; on his first visit to Brands, he took 2.7 seconds off Bill McGovern's time. His car ran on 13in (32.5cm) wheels, which allowed a wider tyre choice and gave room for Ford $9^1/_2$in (23.75cm) disc brakes.

In 1968, he entered a saloon car race at Oulton Park, where the prize was a holiday for two in Tunisia. Having received his final instructions late, he missed his practice session and qualified with the large-capacity saloons, setting pole time for his own race. However, the other drivers objected, claiming that his time had only been possible because he had been slip-streaming the bigger cars. They wanted him on the back of the grid with a ten-second penalty. In the end, a compromise was reached; Bell started from the back, but the penalty was waived. Despite some bumping, he hit the front on lap three, won the race and had an enjoyable holiday. Having progressed via a BMC unit, which had an Arden head with four Amals and Lucas sliding throttle injection, then TJ injection, Bell built himself a Holbay Mini-Ford engine. This incorporated a casting made by Graham Lloyd. Bell machined the Mini crown wheel and pinion to fit a Ford LSD and welded Ford drive shafts to the BMC flanges. It ran a dry-sump system with a 2-gallon (9-litre) oil tank in the boot and pulled to about 9,750rpm.

In September 1971, Sedric Bell and Imp driver Alec Clacher were hotly disputing second place in the Special Saloon race at Croft. On one lap, Clacher squeezed Bell out along the main straight; he was forced to go down the pit lane, a manoeuvre which he executed at unabated speed. He rejoined the circuit to continue the battle; his adversary had not even missed him. The clerk of the course was not impressed and had Bell black-flagged on the next lap. Up before the committee after the race, he apologized, but pointed out that he had nowhere else to go and that, if he had braked, he could have skidded into some of the officials. No further action was taken, but Bell had lost his race anyway.

Bell was third overall in the Triplex Saloon Car Race at Silverstone on

*The engine bay of Sedric Bell's 'A' Series-powered Mini, sporting Arden eight-port head and four Amal carburettors. Note the large oil cooler and extra radiator to help keep the power unit cool. Bell did not believe in rose joints and always used rubber bushes in his suspension.*

22 October 1972. The 1000cc Mini had a race-long duel with Jeffrey Parish's two-litre Escort and was only beaten by 0.4 seconds, in what he describes as 'one hell of a good race'. Bell also set a new class record for the Grand Prix circuit and secured the BP Driver of the Day award. Having had many other successes with this engine, he eventually sold it to Peter Baldwin after a race at Mallory in 1973.

Sedric Bell then came up with his ultimate power unit: a 997cc BDA, based on an Allen block with a Cosworth cylinder head, which he had ported himself. It breathed through choked-down twin 45s, again proving his rivals wrong. He was often lapping more quickly than drivers with 1300 Mini-Ford power. The engine revved to 13,000rpm and put out 125bhp. The acceleration rate meant that the tacho needle was always behind the true figure, so the driver had to remember to change up when it was reading about 9,500rpm.

Sedric Bell's racing career was curtailed when he emigrated to Canada in 1975.

## MONTY GUILDFORD: MINI-CLIMAX

An accomplished class-winner and series runner-up in the Courier Autocross Championship, Kent builder Monty Guildford had a year in Rallycross, again in a Mini, before turning his attentions to circuit racing in 1970. He bought and repaired the shell written off by Nick Cole in 1968, and used it as a basis for his own Free Formula 850. He took pole and won (by 24.2 seconds) with it at Lydden, first time out. He continued to run the car with 850 and 970 engines until 1972 but, behind the scenes, he was working on a unique way of getting more out of it.

Monty Guildford was the first driver to opt for Imp power in a Mini, calling his

*Monty Guildford's Mini Climax. The only way he could get the engine to produce power was to use a really short exhaust pipe, which exited behind the front nearside wheel; strictly speaking, this was contrary to the regulations. To prevent the scrutineers objecting, Guildford's wife would stand in front of the pipe while the car was being checked.*

project, based around a very straight 1959 shell, the Mini-Climax, as the Imp block was akin to the Coventry Climax. He and his brother Roy used two scrap Imp engines and his Mini gearbox to create a mock-up. They cut bits off here and there and when they were satisfied that the concept would work, they sought the assistance of Peter Wise of Goodland Engineering. Intrigued by the scheme, Wise cut the Imp block in half, removed a small section, then welded it together again. A flange was welded on the bottom to enable the Mini gearbox casing to be bolted in place. The flange was carefully machined to allow the primary gear to mesh correctly.

Monty Guildford had cut the nose off the Mini crank and attacked the Imp shaft in similar fashion until he established the correct length, ultimately dowelling the two pieces together. Using this as a pattern, he paid a visit to Gordon Allen ('a lovely man to deal with') and got him to make one from a steel billet. It cost £250. Allen was most impressed with the presentation of the pattern – customers usually turned up with their requirements on oily pieces of scrap paper. As a dry-lined Imp block had a capacity of 875cc, Allen shortened the stroke of the new crank by a couple of millimetres to bring the capacity back to the required 850cc. The new engine, which always had Bevan cams, was dropped into the car in a vertical position. Guildford managed to mount it low in the shell – impossible in the Imp – and retained subframes front and rear.

The cooling was carefully considered, as Imps were prone to overheating. A special radiator was commissioned and a washing-machine pump, direct driven by a Mini heater motor, was utilized as a remote water pump. It was thermostatically controlled and mounted on the bell housing, saving both weight and motive power.

*The all-aluminium Mini Climax power unit, an Imp block mated to a Mini gearbox casing. Much of the preliminary work was done in the small riverside shed adjacent to engineer Peter Wise's houseboat on the River Medway.*

Guildford calculated that the new engine weighed about 1cwt (50kg) less than the BMC item; this, combined with the lower centre of gravity, greatly improved the car's handling. Power output, on George Bevan's dyno, was measured at 102bhp.

The Mini-Climax, which had taken eighteen months to complete, made its debut at Lydden on Good Friday 1973. Monty Guildford describes the car as amazing in the wet, which he loved anyway, but particularly remembers returning to the paddock after a dry race, and noticing the rev counter showing 11,200. He did not recall any drop in power – no wonder it was deafening in the cockpit. He broke the lap record at Lydden and remembers a hell of a race at Silverstone, when he beat Mick Odell by less than an inch. He successfully ran the car until 1976, when he sold it to John Flack and built himself a lightweight Imp.

## GINGER MARSHALL

From humble beginnings with two fairly heavy 850 Special Saloons, built in 1967 and 1968, Ginger Marshall and his brother David, team manager and co-builder, went on to become legends of the unusual in Special Saloons. For 1969, they came up with the first of their lightweight cars – a Mini shell with everything possible replaced in aluminium, no boot floor and a roll cage that went down to support the subframe. It was powered by an 850 short-stroker, based on an 1100 Sprite block with 970S crank and Norton Dominator pistons.

The Mini tipped the scales at about 9.25cwt (460kg) and Ginger Marshall won the class in the 1969 BARC Special Saloon Car Championship, although it went to the last round at Thruxton. This car was sold to Graeme Janzen, who continued the

137

*The Marshall & Fraser lightweight Mini 850 Special Saloon, with alloy sides, floor and roof, it tipped the scales at 9.5cwt (480kg). The car won the class and was second overall in the 1976 BARC Osram Championship.*

success story and won three more championships in it.

David Marshall considered that the car was too heavy and, in 1971, they began to formulate plans for the ultimate in Special Saloons. They were also looking for something unusual. During this period they founded a business, so it was not until the end of the 1976 season that the space-frame, aluminium-bodied Mini Traveller, which weighed just 8cwt (400kg), appeared on the track. Powered by a 970S with a five-port head, it was quick and successful, but Ginger Marshall found that, on occasions, he was outrun by the Imps. However, he still managed one 1978 championship win.

Although they were satisfied with the car for the time being, they decided to come up with a new engine for 1978, concluding that it would have to be Imp-based and would obviously need a special crank. The car was entered in the Forward Trust Special Saloon Car Championship, which produced some serious racing. After an excellent season and many dices with the likes of Imp drivers John Homewood and Rupert Long, Ginger Marshall took the championship.

The innovative Marshall brains were looking for a new challenge for 1979, perhaps something with a smaller frontal

*David and Ginger Marshall were looking to reduce weight to a bare minimum when they conceived their unique Traveller. This photograph, taken during construction, shows how they got it down to 8cwt (400kg).*

area. It would also need bodywork that could accommodate 13in (32.5cm) wheels to allow use of bigger brakes (one small failing of the Traveller). The Traveller body was sold to hillclimber John Meredith, who got John Maguire to fabricate a space-frame chassis, while Brian Lawrence built another Imp-based power unit. This enabled what had become known in the racing circuit paddocks as 'that bloody van' to continue its distinguished career, this time on the hills.

The unlikely answer to the new bodywork question was a Reliant Kitten! Reliant sold the Marshalls a surplus left-hand drive body, but told them they really wanted nothing to do with the project. Their view was that the idea of a Reliant Kitten that could do 130mph (210kph) would lead to the sort of publicity they could do without. The body was cut about and used to make patterns for the racer body, which was 5in (12.5cm) narrower across the top of the screen than that of a Mini.

The car emerged in 1983 and swept all before it. Ginger Marshall won the Special

Saloon Championship in 1983, 1985, 1987, 1988 and 1989, was second in 1984 and took a class win from just four outings in 1990. During 1986, he had an enforced lay-off due to lack of funds. The car was eventually retired at the end of 1991.

## THE ALUMINIUM MINI

This stillborn project was conceived in 1964 by Steve Neal, who had the idea of putting a Lotus twin-cam engine in a Mini. He considered that he would need more room under the bonnet in order to accommodate the engine and decided that he might as well build a shell from scratch. In a pub he had met a Suttons of Oldbury coach-builder who specialized in making hearses and asked him if it was possible to make an aluminium copy. Suttons took the job on and were supplied with a BMC floor pan, a car to copy and the brief to make it 4in (10cm) longer and 4in (10cm) wider.

Hand-rolling the panels, Suttons produced a seamless shell with no gutters, which was quite good, although Steve

Neal admits that it did droop a bit in the snoop. Almost as soon as the job was finished, the 1275S was announced and the exercise became pointless. Neal sold the shell to a local lorry driver who took it away on the back of his truck and it was never to be seen or heard of again.

# TONY CHAMINGS

## Hi-Lo Suspension

Most Mini racers would agree that their car's handling was revolutionized by the introduction of the Hi-Lo suspension system. Conceived in 1970 by Tony Chamings, who hillclimbed his own Mini, the set-up enabled the ride height of a Mini with dry suspension to be adjusted quickly by using a long Allen key to increase or decrease the length of the central shaft.

Chamings had the parts machined up by a local engineering shop and they were sold through the Leyland dealership, Hawkhurst Service Station, of his friend Bob Kemp. The all-round kit was marketed at £26.50, plus 50p postage, and was sold all over the world. In 1978, Chamings sold the patent to Ripspeed. The kits are still available today, but they now cost £110.46 including VAT (which was not a problem when they were first introduced).

## The First Space-Frame Mini

Tony Chamings also built one of the first (if not *the* first) space-frame Minis. After an off into the Rhododendrons at the Valance Hill Climb, in his home county of Kent, he was left pondering how to repair the badly bent shell of his Mini. He was impressed by the strength of the engine/gearbox unit and formulated the idea that, by bolting a large Dural plate to the gearbox, it could be used as an integral part of a special chassis, as in a single-seater. Chamings was no stranger to building things from scratch; in 1961, he had constructed his own racing kart with all-round independent suspension.

Tony Chamings had met the Gomshall Motor Company's driver Bernard Bird by chance at Crystal Palace. Through him, the Surrey company commissioned Chamings to build the car for them. He used a Mini repair jig, scrounged from another local Leyland dealer, to set his chassis out on. The car was built in his basement workshop, below his father-in-law's shop on the outskirts of Tunbridge Wells and took 15 months to complete.

Gomshall announced the car in the *Daily Express* on Friday 26 July 1974, claiming it would do 155mph (250kph). It appeared on the *Cars and Car Conversions* stand at the Racing Car Show later that year. It had a space-frame chassis with an aluminium and glass-fibre body and was powered by a 1293cc engine with eight-port cross-flow head split Webers, straight-cut gearbox and Jack Knight diff. It was originally photographed with a dummy Gordon Allen Ford power unit, but Peter Vickers built the 'A' series engine actually used for racing.

*Cars and Car Conversions* organized a photo shoot for an article in their December 1974 issue. Fred Game and Phil Whitehead volunteered to collect the dummy engine the day before and Game removed the front seat from his Mini Clubman in order to get it in. On the way back down the M1, the Clubman's oil pump broke and the pair had to call on Keith Ripp to rescue them. The next morning they set off bright and early in a second car, but only just got the 'engine' installed in time.

Tipping the scales at 8.5cwt (425kg), complete with engine and box, the car had

*Exploded view of
the Chamings
space-frame Mini.
The car was never
actually raced with
a Ford engine but
utilized a Peter
Vickers-built 1293cc
'A' Series unit.*

a significantly lower ride height and centre of gravity than a standard Mini. Removing the door sills completely gave a ground clearance of $4^1/_2$in (11.25cm) and reduced the overall height to 47in (117.5cm). It featured fully adjustable rose-jointed suspension and naturally retained Hi-Lo suspension with the Spax shockers mounted inboard. Among the other items fabricated by Chamings were the very special gear linkage and mounting plates for the engine. Solid engine mountings facilitated a mechanical clutch, thus doing away with heavy slave and master cylinders. The car ran on 7 x 13in (17.5 x 32.5cm) Revolutions with Firestone slicks. The cost of the rolling shell? £4,000, at 1974 prices!

In 1975, Chamings built a second car in a Speldhurst barn, which he sold, part completed, to Bob Kemp, who had competed in Minis since 1969. This car, with an all glass-fibre body from a mould made for the manufacture of fibreglass road Minis in India, has never seen the light of day. After Brands Hatch test sessions, Bernard Bird raced the Gomshall Mini during the latter part of 1974 season, but it changed hands at the turn of the year. The new owner, who had bought it for his son, was a bit in awe of the sophisticated set-up of the car, so he swapped it for Gary Streat's 1500cc Rallycross Mini. Having re-assembled the space-frame Mini, Streat had his maiden outing at Brands Hatch, where he made an impressive showing. Owing to problems during practice, he had to start from the back of the grid but a Rallycross-honed demon start, combined with the car's amazing traction, meant that he was third by Paddock on the opening lap! He did not get any higher but, given that this was his first-ever circuit race, it had to be a sign of things to come.

Streat ran the Chamings Mini for four seasons and was always competitive. He won his second race at Lydden Hill, went on to break the class lap record at both Mallory and Lydden and took a number of other wins and places in it. It was then acquired by Adam Lesniewski and Tony Whibley. Lesniewski brought it out again in Special Saloons during the 1989 and 1990 seasons. He did several Lydden events in it but, regrettably, an accident called a temporary halt to the car's competition history. It is now due to be repaired.

## THE TRIPLE C LIGHTWEIGHT MINI

The conception of the Triple C Lightweight Mini featured in *Cars and Car Conversions*. This unusual racing example was built in 1974 by Technical Editor Fred Game, with assistance from Phil Whitehead, who answered the magazine's 'A' Series queries. The car was based on a 1959 shell with alloy-skinned doors, glass-fibre front and a grained leather-effect glass-fibre roof. One of the most unusual features was a lightweight rear end, also in glass fibre.

Everything behind the rear seam, including the boot floor, was cut off and the replacement section pop-riveted then bonded with matting to strengthen the join. The new rear end was made by Four F Sprint, who ran a pair of Rallycross Minis with the same modification, although Fred Game believes that his car was the only circuit racer to have one. Obviously, the rear subframe had to go; it was replaced by an alloy beam axle, which carried the suspension. The car started with a set of special tuning negative camber lower arms, but these were soon replaced with a rose-jointed set, which were sent to the magazine for appraisal.

Phil Whitehead came up with a 970S lump, complete with patch over the tappet chest, where a cam follower had previously escaped, to power the car. It was decided to use 7 x 13in (17.5 x 32.5cm) Revolution wheels and the pair managed to find a set of elusive Firestone B33 slicks for £100. These were really Formula 3 fronts, but all the successful Mini drivers were using them.

The pair tested the car at Brands late in 1974 and, frankly, were disappointed by its handling. David Enderby was persuaded to have a pedal; he returned to the pits ashen-faced after just three laps and agreed that the handling was horrible. He lent the pair a set of his tens and these transformed the car. It later turned out that the Firestones were B18s, made of a rock-hard compound that required a much heavier car to get heat into it. As the tyres were marked with a code rather than the compound number, they had been unable to tell.

Originally, they utilized a Weber 45 IDA down-draught carburettor, which stuck through the bonnet just in front of the windscreen. However, it tended to spit all over the screen. Fred Game found that, at Brands in the late afternoon, the fuel deposited on the screen combined with the setting sun to give a marvellous colour effect, but that it did nothing for the driver's vision. Opting for a 45 side-draught on a long manifold improved performance, and the driver's view of the track.

Fred Game raced the Mini on and off during 1975, with Whitehead also doing a few events, and in 1977 Game did selected rounds of the Special Saloon Championship, achieving a fourth at Mallory, a circuit where the car always went well. He also won his class at the Valance Hillclimb two years running. In 1978, Whitehead did Valance, clipped the bank and broke the rose-jointed suspension, which rolled the car. Although the car was repaired, this was its last outing. Fred Game stresses that it was shoestring racing for fun and that the car was never intended to be a serious championship contender. Phil Whitehead later used the 970 engine in a more conventional Special Saloon Mini, which he raced.

## JOHN MAGUIRE

Helping a friend at the circuits with a Miglia car was John Maguire's first involvement with racing and, after building up another Miglia, his interest in constructing cars grew. Around the late 1970s, one or two mid-engined Imps were appearing on the Special Saloon grids. Close inspection revealed that they were, in fact, old formula car chassis that had been modified to take glass-fibre Imp bodywork. This got John Maguire thinking.

In 1978, Maguire and Tom Shephard built the first Maguire space-frame Mini for Mike Parkes; he soon realized the car's potential, winning that year's British Fusegear Championship 'straight out of the box'. Subsequently, from premises in Stoneystanton Road in Coventry, Maguire and Shephard produced between fifty-five and sixty of their very special Minis, as well as some Imps built along the same lines. Maguire cars were being raced throughout the UK and Europe and Maguire even remembers sending one to Denmark. The cars were built in the winter, so that Maguire and Shephard could go to the circuits as race engineers to the customers' cars during the season.

The cars had been designed to take a power unit that produced between 160 and 170bhp. The Danish owner dropped in a 2-litre Hart engine, which gave about 300bhp. It was his custom to put the car up on stands and warm it up by revving it in gear and then applying the brakes. During this procedure, the trained eye could spot the whole chassis flexing.

One year, Maguire-built cars won every British Special Saloon Championship. Later, John Maguire decided that touring cars were the way to go and he took the decision to stop producing the space-frame cars and go back to building more conventional tin-tops. He is now Technical Commissioner for the British Touring Car Championship.

## DAVE FORSTER

Carlisle joiner Dave Forster started racing in 1982 in a 1000cc Maguire Mini, which had a brief previous history on the hills and put out about 76bhp. He contested the BARC North Western GT Championship, then, having decided against the Cosworth MAE route to more power, bought an eight-port 1000cc 'A' Series engine, which ran on carburettors, from Viv Wallace. He used this to come second overall in the 1985 championship. He won the up-to-1500cc class and missed out on the championship by one and a half points. Over the winter, he returned the engine to Wallace to be converted to injection, with mechanical slide throttles.

Competing in the up-to-one-litre class, Forster won the first race of the season at Cadwell Park. Protested as too fast, the car was put in the two-litre category for the rest of the season. Despite this handicap, Forster still picked up wins and three lap records and finished the season winning the class and coming second overall in the championship, this time by just half a point. If a tappet had not broken on the warm-up lap of the final race, he would have won. While the power output had only increased from 112bhp on carbs to 114bhp with injection, the torque showed a marked increase, immediately good for two seconds a lap round Cadwell.

By the end of the season, having begun to modify the suspension, Forster began to think about improving the whole car. In 1987, he decided that he would build his own space-frame Mini. He redesigned the layout of the tubes, to feed the loads in what he felt would be a better way, and also designed and fabricated a space-frame front with rose-jointed top and bottom uprights. Meanwhile, a boat-builder was found to make glass-fibre body moulds with deeper window reveals to get the rubbers out of the air stream. A local jeweller engraved six chassis plates – F6201 to F6206 – to identify the cars.

After seeing just the front half of the car, laid up on the jigs, Phil Hepworth of Howley Racing was sufficiently impressed to order one from Forster to race himself. Not wanting to have the first of the batch, Hepworth chose to have chassis number 02; Forster later built up 01 for himself. He continued his job as a joiner, working on the space-frame Minis in the evenings and at weekends when he was not racing. He reckons he was working till 10pm seven days a week! All the work was done in the double garage beside his end-of-terrace house in Carlisle – it did, however, boast three-phase supply and a Harrison digital lathe among its equipment!

David Leslie was a great friend, whose team helped David Forster with some of the geometry and setting up. Forster built Minis for, among others, Dino Belvedere, the Kittle brothers, who won a major Irish hillclimb championship in their car, and Jersey hill expert Paul James, who not only took the local Bouley Bay course record but also took outright records at Prescott and Valance on consecutive weekends. Two Forster cars also went to

*The bare space frame of one of Dave Forster's cars; at this stage, it is hard to believe it will end up as a Mini.*

Japanese customers. First time out, one new owner got pole by three seconds and won the race by a significant margin. In all, Forster built ten cars - eight Minis and two Metros - each evolving slightly from its predecessor.

In 1990, Dave Forster finally went full time in motor sport, taking a job as race engineer in Formula Vauxhall Junior with David Leslie Racing. He also found time to complete what he regarded as the ultimate

*A complete Forster-built car showing the 16-valve engine, suspension and aerodynamic aids.*

space-frame Mini for himself. He got Phil Hepworth, from Race Spec, to screw together a 1300 engine, with a KAD 16-valve head. The car weighed 8.75cwt (445kg). At testing at Knockhill in 1994, fuel-pressure problems prevented a fair appraisal, but a run at Silverstone proved that the car was, in Forster's words, 'a projectile, even with a rev limit of 7,200'. Failure to find a more suitable crown wheel and pinion for Silverstone resulted in the engine going back to Hepworth, who altered the settings to allow it to rev to 9,000.

All this preparation meant that Forster was able to take part in the Fastest Mini in the World Race, which formed part of the Mini's thirty-fifth birthday celebrations at Silverstone, on 29 August 1994. Forster qualified on the second row and, after a hectic race, during which he made contact with Ben Edwards three laps from home, he finished third. His car was sold to a Japanese buyer at the end of 1994 to finance the purchase of a Formula Vauxhall Junior, which enabled him to

establish his own team in that series. In 1995, he ran Craig Murray who finished runner-up in the junior category of the series. The Mini jigs and body moulds went to Graham Delouze, to continue the line. Forster now runs Team DFR with his partner Craig Dixon.

## REG WARD

Following some races in Se7ens during 1972, Dorset engineer Reg Ward progressed to a modified, steel-shelled Free Formula 850 Mini. In 1974, he was third in class, behind Charles Bernstein and Richard Belcher in the Esso Uniflo, and fourth in the Simoniz, which was won by Neil Dineen. Continual development of the car made him realize that, to be really competitive, he must have a Mini that was both lighter and lower. He built his own space-frame car in 1976, which still utilized a Mini front subframe to carry the 850 engine. Ward made his own moulds for the all-fibreglass body. In 1977, he had

*Deirdre Ward drives the Mk 1 Ward space-frame Mini at Silverstone on 29 May 1977.*

*After 688 hours' building work, Reg Ward's Imp-engined Mk 2 space-frame Mini was destroyed in its second race, at Thruxton on 24 May 1980, rolling end over end three times at Church. Unable to face the rebuild, Ward retired from racing.*

thirteen wins. He took the BRSCC Championship outright, was fourth in class in the Uniflo and fifth in the Hitachi Championships.

In 1978, a hectic year, Reg and his wife Deirdre campaigned the Mini in different series. Deirdre did the Castle Combe-based BRSCC SW Championship, which she led prior to the double-points final round. Lying second overall and leading the class, she was forced by gearbox gremlins to slow down. Fourteenth overall salvaged her championship second in class and the club presented her with the Driver of the Year award.

Meanwhile, Reg chalked up thirteen wins and six other top-three places to take class victory in both the Hitachi and Wendy Wools Championships. His best dice was with Ginger Marshall at Oulton Park on 8 July; they fought for the lead throughout, but Marshall finally got it by 0.4 seconds. The Wards' car held nine lap records.

Brian Prebble's Imp was based on a Ward space frame and Reg Ward also built

Minis for Richard Hemming and the son-in-law of a Malaysian prince. Ward sold his space-frame car to Peter Baldwin, who installed a Mini Ford engine in it.

In 1979, Reg Ward started working on his idea of the ultimate space-frame Mini, which did away with the subframe, was fully coil sprung and took 688 hours to build. He debuted it at Donington on 25 May 1980. The following day, at Thruxton, a front strut broke in practice, the car rolled end over end three times and his masterpiece was destroyed. Reg Ward retired from motor sport and returned to his previous hobby of scuba diving. It was less expensive and, perhaps, less dangerous.

## GORDON ALLEN, ROGER BUNTING, ROD EMBLEY AND PETER KITCHEN

While precision-tool manufacturer Gordon Allen was best known for his individual crankshafts, he also had a hand in build-

*Gordon Allen (left) and his driver Rod Embley (right) with 620 AXE in what became known as its 'Twin Jag Mini' form. While it had twin engines with modified Jaguar heads, the power units were based on blocks cast to Allen's own design.*

ing several one-off Special Saloon Minis. Indeed, he always maintained that 'playing with engines appeals to my sense of humour'. After competing on motorcycles, he had started racing in his wife's Mini, 620 AXE, fitted with a modified Formula Junior engine, in 1961. Fellow driver Roger Bunting recalls meeting him for the first time when he and Peter Kitchen helped Allen load the car onto the trailer after it had rolled down Paddock Hill Bend at Brands and had briefly caught alight. They joked about what his wife would say – apparently, she had no idea that her husband was using her car on the tracks.

While they were manhandling the Mini, the conversation turned to the main caps on Peter Kitchen's racing A35 van, which kept breaking. Allen told him he had perfected the system of making replacements in steel and then line-boring the block and caps. Although Gordon Allen enjoyed driving, his greatest pleasure was always in engineering the unusual.

Mrs Allen's Mini was re-shelled and Gordon Allen set to and built an 1100cc power unit, completed with forged pistons and a long-throw Cooper crank. This car was pretty invincible until, in 1962, he was beaten by a certain black Mini at Silverstone. The car in question belonged to accountant Rod Embley.

Having sprinted a road Mini, Embley had built up his racing version from a bare shell in 1961, running it with a 1000cc engine for the first season. For 1962, Downton had built him an 1132 unit and Daniel Richmond told him he should drive the car to Goodwood for the first race, in order to run it in. Goodwood was an important meeting for Downton, as former employee Jan Odor, who had just started up on his own, was in Embley's race; obviously, Richmond wanted the Downton car to win. Embley managed to oblige and went on to have a good year with the car. He was learning all the time. He once confided in another driver that his back brakes kept locking up, to be told that efficient rear brakes were a distinct disadvantage. Acting on the advice, he boot-polished all four linings prior to each outing and experienced no further braking problems.

Having beaten Gordon Allen once, Rod Embley repeated the feat next time out. Allen admitted that, although he had the better car, Embley was the better driver and always made a demon start. When they competed against each other again at the autumn Clubman meeting at Silverstone a good dice was developing, but Embley's blown engine resulted in an Allen victory.

In January 1963, Embley put the car up for sale in order to raise the deposit for a house. On seeing the advertisement, Gordon Allen rang and asked if he would like to drive for him. Embley, who was only hanging up his helmet for financial reasons, jumped at the chance. The pair decided that they should come up with

something with, in Allen's words, 'a little more muscle'. This led to Allen's first venture into a special Mini. In 1963, 620 AXE was converted to run a 1498cc Ford pushrod engine, which Allen grafted on to a Mini gear casing. Based on a Ford Classic block, it had a shorter stroke, forged 85mm pistons and an alloy head with three valves per cylinder. The original 8in (20cm) Austin A40 drum brakes only lasted one race, so they were replaced with Cooper S discs.

Rod Embley's first outing in the car – always referred to by Gordon Allen as 'that unsanitary thing' – was at the West Essex CC Snetterton meeting early in 1963. He posted a sub two-minute time in a wet practice, which saw him on the front row with the Anglias of Chris Craft and Alan Peer. Peer beat him off the line but, despite the continuing rain, Embley was in front before the end of the straight and long gone. Gordon Allen won in the car at Silverstone on 13 July and Embley had

*The ultimate back-seat driver: the second engine in the Allen Mini hybrid sits where the rear seat should be. Ducts in the side windows supply air to the boot-mounted radiator and the carburettors are just inches from the driver's left ear!*

two tremendous races at Mallory Park on 22 September, dicing with John Adams in his Team Tourist Trophy 3.8 Jaguar. The pair circulated inches apart and, in both events, the Mini finished a very close second.

## THE ALLEN TWINI-MINIS

For 1965, Gordon Allen built his 'Twini-Mini', still based on 620 AXE, now modified to take very special Allen engines front and rear. He designed a special block, had two cast in alloy at a local foundry and then used the con rods and cylinder heads from two 6-cylinder 2.4 Jaguar engines he had bought. He cut out numbers 4 and 5 combustion chambers, welded the head back together, ending up with 1, 2, 3 and 6. The engines were built up and each mounted transversely on modified Mini front subframes, the one at the rear having a specially locked track rod.

The two gearboxes were linked electromechanically, front operating as normal, rear being shifted by push/pull overdrive solenoids, operated by micro-switches. One clutch pedal controlled two master cylinders and, as well as the normal accelerator pedal, to operate both throttles there was a separate one to the left of the clutch, for the rear engine only. This helped to get the back round on tight corners. The engines ran cams ground to Coventry Climax racing profiles, pistons from a Vincent Black Lightning motorcycle and 1500 Ford steel cranks, built up to take the Jag rods.

Roger Bunting did frequent Silverstone testing in this very fast car; even initially, each 1475cc engine, running on twin Webers, produced 118bhp at 6,000rpm. To help get the power down, Gordon Allen commissioned some special split-rim mag-

nesium-alloy wheels. First time out, Rod Embley lapped a damp Silverstone to set a time of 1:19.

Embley led throughout the early part of the car's first race, but an ominous rattle from the cockpit turned out to be a stray nut in the footwell. Unsure whether this meant a serious problem or not, he decided it was safer to pit and retire. Inspection revealed that it was of no consequence; while Gordon Allen may have been disappointed that the car had missed out on a maiden win, he certainly did not show it, and told Embley that he had done the right thing. Second time out, Rod trounced the field in a saloon car race at RAF Debden in Essex. He also drove the car at other circuits, including Goodwood and Mallory, probably on the car's last outing.

The next of Gordon Allen's hybrids was a long-wheelbase twin-engined Mini, constructed by welding the back of a Mini van to the front of a saloon. The result was equipped with a 997cc engine in the front and a 1275cc unit in the rear. Allen used hydraulic solenoids to link the two gear selectors and installed a compressor to run them. Roger Bunting tested the car at Silverstone, managing to lose it in a big way at Maggots and flat-spotting all four tyres. Allen was just getting over a mild heart attack and watching all his hours of work almost being destroyed was the last thing he needed. However, after the acquisition of some new tyres, Bunting raced it the next weekend. One of the engines went on to three cylinders, the car was retired, and Gordon Allen decided that he would have no more to do with building cars and would stick to crankshafts.

In 1973, he relented and came up with a semi space-frame Mini. He cast his own alloy block, fitted thick wet liners and grafted a BDA head on to it, building a space frame to take the place of the front subframe and support the engine. Peter

149

Kitchen raced the car a few times during the 1973 season. He took pole by two seconds at a wet Silverstone qualifying session, sharing the front row with Frank Gardiner's Camaro and Gerry Marshall in Baby Bertha. Conditions dried for the race and the car finished sixth.

## ERIC SMITH

After five years of developing his own five-port 1293, Eric Smith felt he had gone as far as he could. His view was that the injected eight-port option did not offer a very good pound-per-horsepower ratio, and he began to think in terms of Ford. He cleared his bench and set up a Ford iron block on a Mini gearbox and then concluded that this alternative presented insurmountable problems. However, a conversation with Gordon Allen, on an unrelated matter, changed his mind.

Eric Smith became another of Allen's satisfied customers, using the Allen block, crank and gearbox case extension, along with a BDA head, to build his own 1.3-litre engine. From 1973 Smith chalked up many wins utilizing this power unit. He particularly remembers one Ingliston outing in August 1973, when Allen flew to Scotland to see how the engine performed. The trip was worthwhile, as Smith won the Special Saloon race outright.

After early teething problems with tortional vibration, reliability was good. During the five seasons he ran BDA, Smith broke only two nearside drive shafts, despite the engine (which produced an estimated 170bhp) pulling all the way to 10,000rpm. He put this down to his ZF diff and the fact that all the parts were already turning quickly when the real torque came in.

Eventually, when some competitors started hanging glass-fibre Skoda bodies on Chevron chassis, Eric Smith decided it

*Eric Smith leads a field in a large-capacity saloon-car race at Ingliston.*

*Beautifully engineered, Eric Smith's 1300cc Mini-Ford engine revved to 10,000rpm and produced about 170bhp.*

was time to quit. He retired from racing in 1977.

## JEFF GOODLIFF + HARRY RATCLIFFE = V8 MINI

The V8 Mini project came about in 1964, after Jeff Goodliff and Harry Ratcliffe went to look at a V8 engine that had been advertised. It was a Buick alloy unit, which tipped the scales at a tempting 200lb (90kg). They decided that they just had to buy it and put it in a Mini.

As spares were scarce, the engine was rebuilt with reliability in mind and the car incorporated maximum cooling. A large front-mounted radiator for the water and two floor-mounted oil coolers with scoops kept the lubricant at the right temperature. To eliminate fuel surge, a four-choke

Carter carburettor was used, fed by a twin-barrel SU pump from a 7-gallon (32-litre) tank mounted in the original engine bay. The 10in (25cm) Mini wheels were replaced by a set of Sprite 13in (32.5cm); subsequently, the car would be run with various permutations, including Sprite front and Minilite 10in (25cm) rears, and Minilites all round.

The configuration of this unique car was rear-engine front-wheel drive, achieved by mounting the engine in the boot on a strengthened Mini subframe. This was connected to a Jaguar gearbox, with over-drive and strong prop shaft, which drove the wheels via an E Type diff mounted on a modified front subframe. To prevent the body twisting, the rear floor was beefed up round the suspension mounting points. Initial power output was 155bhp at 4,400rpm but the goal was 220bhp at 5,800rpm!

The completed car weighed in at 12cwt (610kg) and, as the weight distribution differed from that on a standard Mini, the rear suspension was stiffened and the front softened. The car was found to stop adequately with standard Cooper S brakes and, to comply with regulations, it was a four-seater, with two small seats in the rear either side of the engine bulge. The total cost of the project was £1,300.

Brian Gillibrand vividly remembers the first time Harry Ratcliffe drove the car on the road, using trade plates, because he was in the passenger seat. On leaving the workshop, Ratcliffe pootled down the road, got up to 15mph (25kph), and dipped the clutch to change into second. The car turned sharp left, went across the pavement, scattering people in a bus queue, ploughed through a hedge and came to rest in the middle of someone's lawn. A shopping basket, belonging to a lady in the bus queue, was wedged on the bonnet. Harry Ratcliffe was bemused and sat in

*Peter Day lifts a wheel in his two-cylinder Allen BDA Mini.*

the driver's seat puffing on his pipe. The owner of the lawn knocked on the window and asked what was going on. Ratcliffe slid the window back and said, 'Would you mind buggering off? I'm trying to work out why it's done this.'

The problem turned out to be the power lock diff. When this was removed, it made the car slightly better-mannered. Some time later, Brian Redman did some demonstration laps round Oulton Park for BBC North Television. When he returned the car, he apparently said, 'Harry, if you keep driving this thing, we'll be burying you next week.'

Although magazine journalists doing road tests at the time were complimentary about the car, it never really achieved much racing success in the few northern circuit outings it had in Harry Ratcliffe's hands. The rear engine caused the car to go into violent understeer as it entered a corner, and then it would go into violent oversteer half-way round. The team was invited to enter it at the Shelsley Walsh Hillclimb, on 12 June 1965. When the clutch was dropped on the line, the whole car shuddered and the wheels spun for ten seconds before finding grip. Concrete blocks were lashed down in the original

engine bay to get some weight over the driven wheels. Despite the ballast, the car achieved a fourth place.

The car had about six coats of paint and gleamed like a Rolls Royce and, despite its racing shortcomings, one or two people expressed an interest in buying it. The car went to someone from Dover, about as far away as possible from its Littleborough HQ, and was never heard of again.

## PETER DAY 850 BDA

At the other end of the spectrum from the V8 was Peter Day's straight 2. It was based on an Allen block that Peter Baldwin had ventilated; Gordon Allen had later cut it in half and then made special crank, head, cams and manifolds. First run on a dyno, it produced a disappointing 63bhp and Allen sold it to Peter Day, another of his Mini racing customers. Day decided that it needed to breathe better and made a larger-bore exhaust before taking the car to the rolling road. Peter Baldwin discovered that the output had only increased to 73bhp. It was decided to reduce the length of the exhaust pipe and the discovery was made that the shorter the pipe, the greater the power. By the time the exhaust stopped right under the engine bay, the 850cc engine (bore 83.5mm, stroke 73.1mm) produced 115bhp and an amazing 112lb/ft torque.

The car's first race was at Brands on 9 November 1975, when it was retired with loss of oil pressure. Despite winter testing, the Mini was dogged by oil-surge problems, which, over the coming months, would destroy two cranks. Despite these setbacks, Peter Day chalked up his first win at Snetterton on 6 March 1976.

On 26 March at Silverstone, the car collided with the bank. During the re-shell, Day dry-sumped it and, at last, found reliability. The car was so tractable, he could enter a corner in the wrong gear and still get away with it. To remove the exhaust fumes, Day fabricated a Dural duct below the floor, which, because of the resonance, would vibrate to bits if it was not replaced every three races. The transmission had a problem coping with the power but a Jack Knight dog box and changing drive shafts every meeting cured this.

The car was out in its new form on 19 April and by the end of the season Peter Day had amassed nine wins, two seconds and four thirds, with four retirements. For getting the car on the grid for most of his races, despite all the problems, Day was awarded a special 'E for Effort' trophy. It was an enjoyable season, which provided many dices, particularly with David Enderby. Day also won the Champion of Brands, an event for saloons up to 850cc. Before qualifying, other drivers would come and ask, 'Why only two cylinders?' When the times came out and Peter Day was on pole, they would scratch their heads. As the car was further developed, Day got Gordon Allen to make him a traditional webbed crank to replace the original motorcycle-style one, and he would change crank and cylinder heads accord-

*The unique two-cylinder 850cc engine in Peter Day's car was based on the two good bores from a blown-up BDA. Gordon Allen helped with the engineering and, when sorted, the engine produced 115bhp.*

ing to the circuit. He was able to buy blown-up cylinder heads very cheaply, as he only needed two out of the four chambers.

In 1977, Day was even more successful, with nine wins, eight seconds, four thirds and three fourths, with just two retirements. In its heyday, the car would often lap half the field. For 1978, the regulations changed concerning front-exit exhausts, so Day built up a Fiat 500 and installed the 850BDA. This car became known as 'The Mighty Mouse'. Occasionally, the BDA was transferred back to the Mini, for the few events in which it was still eligible, but, eventually, it blew up.

## MINI SCA

### Jan Odor

Jan Odor's Mini SCA was another car built as a design exercise, this time by Janspeed. In 1967, Odor came up with the idea of using a 1966 ex-Formula 2 Ford SCA 1000cc engine and shoe-horning it into a Mini. He enlisted the help of Gordon Allen, who made a new alloy block and crank to mate the power unit to a Mini gear casing, fitted with a BMC close-ratio set. The standard head was utilized after further fettling and the timing cover required slight modification. There was no space for a radiator in the standard posi-

tion, so a specially built one filled the whole of the grille aperture. The engine was dry-sumped, utilizing one of the Mini's twin fuel tanks for the oil, a drip feed lubricating the gearbox.

Geoff Mabbs drove the car, which had lowered hydrolastic suspension with special valves to allow independent adjustment of pressure at each corner, and a rear anti-roll bar. The alloy block produced a saving of 100lb (45.5kg), making the Mini SCA light to steer. During the final round of the 1967 BARC Saloon Car Championship at Silverstone, Mabbs enjoyed a battle royal for the lead with Alan Peer's Anglia. Mabbs established a new lap record at 1:10.4, but, as the result

*Geoff Mabbs in the Janspeed Mini SCA (80) begins to get the tyres smoking as he holds off Alistair McHardy's Hillman Imp and Terry Harmer's Mini (82) at Brands Hatch, 1968.*

*Peter Hawthorne's Mini SCA leads an 'A' Series-powered Mini with down-draught carbs at Copse, Silverstone, 12 May 1968.*

of a slipping clutch contaminated by oil from a leaking main bearing seal, victory eluded him. The engine produced 94bhp at the front wheels and pulled 9,800rpm down the Club Straight! Mabbs also broke the Castle Combe lap record and his time stood for a long while.

## Paul Ivey, Peter Hawthorne and Bob Fox

Long-time tuner and development engineer Paul Ivey, who carried out a great deal of work for BMC, subsequently became involved in the Mini SCA. He did a significant amount of work for Odor who revealed his intention to sell the car. Ivey brokered a deal for Peter Hawthorne to purchase it, on the basis that Ivey's company, Speedsport Conversions, would run it for the 1968 season.

Peter Hawthorne had started doing club events in 1963, driving an ex-Rod Embley circuit Mini. One weekend, he had no trailer available to get his car to a sprint at nearby Church Lawford so, anxious to sample the car, a friend offered to drive it there for him. The friend got a bit carried

away and drove through a radar trap rather faster than he should have. Hawthorne, who was following behind in his road car, was horrified, totting up in his head the fines for no tax, no insurance, no number plates, no speedo, and no horn or lights, let alone the speeding offence. He need not have worried. The police were apparently so interested in the Mini that they let the driver off without even a caution.

Hawthorne's first outing with the SCA was at Silverstone on 24 March 1968. He was forced to retire while leading, although he did set the fastest lap at 1:18.6. Next time out, again at Silverstone, on 15 April, he won. The next three outings in the car all resulted in retirements due to a broken rotor arm, puncture and, at Mallory on 19 May, failed timing gear. Unhappy with the reliability record, Paul Ivey built up a 1293 'A' Series engine for the rest of the season.

Three wins, three lap records and two fastest laps from four outings was a good tally, but it was rather spoilt when Hawthorne wrote the car off at Mallory on 28 July. Following this enforced early end

*Andy Barton's Mini SCA heads Sedric Bell and Alec Clacher's Imp at the Croft Chicane in 1972.*

to the season, the car was re-shelled for 1969. Ivey's 1293 again produced the goods: eleven wins, ten fastest laps, nine seconds, a third, and three new lap records. He had a good day at the final Redex Championship round at Brands Hatch, too, where he won the first heat in the wet, beating Gerry Marshall's Blydenstein Viva. He briefly led in the final, but had to give best to Marshall who had got to grips with the tricky conditions. The car was sold at the end of the season. In 1972/3, Paul Ivey ran a Ford Twin Cam

1300-engined Mini for former Se7en stalwart Bob Fox, Ivey supplying the engine and Fox the car. Reliability problems delayed the initial development; it seems the alloy block used to expand and this would distort the steel timing gears. Cosworth came up with a modification that stopped the timing gears moving and this cured the problem. Bob Fox always considered that they were never able to get the car to handle as well as it might. However, if it finished it usually won. Fox took the class lap record for the

Silverstone Club Circuit, the power circuit at the time.

## Andy Barton Tames the SCA

Long-time Mini racer Andy Barton does not remember exactly how he came to buy the SCA engine from Paul Ivey, but he was certainly the driver who finally realized its full potential. Modifications to the original block gave better reliability for 1969, but, for 1970, Barton decided to start again. Allen supplied another block and crank and Barton purchased a 'swirlpot head' direct from Cosworth, which came with the latest cam-drive gearing and fuel injection. The most significant change was mounting the bottom gear on the crank using a torsion bar. This eradicated the periodic harmonics that had caused all the cam-gear problems.

The other problem had been the lack of a low enough BMC final drive. Barton had to rev so much to get the car off the line that, on one occasion, he dropped the clutch and blew the diff out the back of the engine. He got a Jack Knight 4.8, which, combined with a reduction in the drop gear, gave him a ratio of 5.3:1. Pulling all the way to 10,500rpm and peaking at around 12,000, it really flew. The car had modified front suspension with rear beam axle, having parallel links and 'A' frame, running on specially made Mamba 10in (25cm) wheels, 6in (15cm) wide at the front and 7½in (18.75cm) rears.

The car was a regular 1000cc winner and Barton enjoyed epic dices at his local Croft circuit with Sedric Bell and Alec Clacher. He also took the class in several northern championships.

*'It's like this, Sedric.' Andy Barton points out to Sedric Bell the oil slick that his car (82) laid on the Ingliston circuit when a pipe burst. Bell, standing next to him, knows full well, as both of them skidded off on it. Barton's car seems to have come off worst.*

## BILL NEEDHAM: MINI TWIN CAM

Bill Needham's Mini Twin Cam was just that: a Mini with a 1000cc 'A' Series block with a Ford twin-cam head. He had built two very fast Lotus Elites and, on the strength of their results, set himself up as Coldwell Engineering in Sheffield. He then raced a Mini Cooper and an S with good results and was looking for something a little quicker for the 1967 season. His project necessitated considerable modification to the head as well as getting special pistons cast for the bottom end.

Having originally run the unit with Weber 40 DFAs from a Ford Zephyr, Needham upgraded to Lucas fuel injection. Teething troubles meant the project did not come good until the closing stages of the year, when he had a good race at Oulton Park.

## BILL COLE AND GRAHAM COOPER

The 1971 Curborough sprint programmes might lead the reader to believe that Bill Cole's 1556cc Mini was yet another engine-transplant victim, but this was not the case. Cole's engine was still built around an 'A' Series transverse block by the big-bore maestro of the time, Graham Cooper, who worked from a former Baptist chapel at the bottom of his garden in Sedgley. A former car breaker, Cooper started tuning 'A' Series engines for a hobby and ended up turning it into a full-time business.

The block used was, in fact, a 970S, as this gave the right compression height. At the time, the engine was unique; Laystall, who machined the crank from a standard blank forging, refused to do another because of the difficulties they had encountered in producing it. The required 170 thou oversize pistons were sand-cast by a Birmingham firm. Having found out that the engine smoked using just two rings to minimize friction, Cooper settled for three, albeit very thin ones (Plate 12).

Bill Cole had started sprinting his road Mini in the late 1960s, and soon started using Cooper's engineering expertise, resulting in a purpose-built racer. The car-breaking side of the Cooper business, now run by Graham's brother, had a contract to clear scrap from Abingdon. Sometimes they would be able to get hold of useful items thrown out by the competitions department. Apparently, one of these items was the body shell from the Mini used by Makinen in the 1966 Monte Carlo Rally. When Cole wrote off his first racer, this shell was used to create his mark two version.

This car, purple with a silver roof, was built on a no-compromise basis. While it retained two subframes, the one at the rear had been lightened, leaving just enough meat to support the coil over-shockers. The sheer torque of the 1556 engine gave the car a big appetite for clutch plates, which had to be replaced every four outings, and second gear cogs, which it ate with expensive regularity. More power was obtained from running a pair of inch-and-three-quarter SUs than from the more popular Webers.

During the 1971 season, Bill Cole won eight of the ten rounds of the Midlands Sprint Championship and confessed to using 9,000rpm regularly. Sometimes, he found he was beating fuel-injected 1293 Minis by two and a half seconds. However, Graham Cooper's view was that this large-capacity engine was only suitable for sprint or hillclimb use and was not for racing. In fact, after Cole's first season with it, Cooper expressed surprise that it had lasted at all.

*On location for BBC Television's* Driving Ambition, *Brands Hatch 1983. Peter Baldwin's Mini was given a new livery for the drama series, with Ken Lark Motors as his mythical garage. Shown with the car are Rosemary Martin, Ann Carroll and Gavin Martin from the programme, along with racing consultant Stirling Moss.*

Bill Cole moved on to competing in an E Type and, in 1972, sold the car to local builder John Taylor who also used it for sprints and hillclimbs. It was subsequently sold again and then split up and Cole then lost track of it.

## THE BBC'S *DRIVING AMBITION*

In 1983, the writers at the BBC came up with an eight-part television drama serial about a girl who wanted to break into motor sport. It was built around two characters – Donna Heniti, who drove a Mini, and her racing adversary Alan Hershner, who had a Vauxhall Firenza. Both were supposedly competing in Special Saloons. While the drivers were played by actors, the two cars were real and the driving shots were executed by their owners – Peter Baldwin in the Mini and Tony Davies in the Firenza. Peter Bray's Mini was also used in some sequences. Much of the filming was done on the former West Malling Airfield sprint circuit.

The cars were given new paint jobs and raced for real in their TV livery through-

out the season. To Davies' amusement, Baldwin was required by the director to wear a blond wig under his helmet during the driving sequences so that, from a distance, he looked like 'Donna'.

In the concluding episode, 'Donna' came good and beat 'Alan' on the track. To create this race, the BBC filmed a ten-lap Wendy Wools Special Saloon race at Brands. Obviously, a proper race would not necessarily finish according to the script, so the director used the first five laps of the real race, then worked out a sequence of manoeuvres for the final five. In this way, 'Donna' would take the chequered flag. All the competitors were paid to return to Brands on the following Tuesday, to film the scripted laps.

Tony Davies recalls each driver doing the 'closing laps' with a script taped to the steering wheel. This told them where and when each car should overtake and also called for one or two of them to 'have a moment' by hanging the back out, or locking up a wheel. To the director's amazement the drivers did it in one take, proving the superior driving skills of the Wendy Wools competitors of the time.

Maybe the script was a bit corny, but

*Will it fit? Andrew Cannings proved you can shoe-horn a Ford 2.8i engine and four-wheel drive train into a Mini.*

*Driving Ambition* certainly did much to increase public awareness of club-level motor sport.

## ANDREW CANNINGS' MINI HL 2.8I 4x4

Andrew Cannings started his Mini project in 1992, with the basic aim of proving that it could be done. The object was to fit a Ford 2.8V6 4x4 engine and drive-train into a steel Mini shell. He had friends who owned both types of car, so he was able to take detailed measurements to satisfy himself it was feasible before purchasing the necessary hardware. Breakers' yards yielded a stolen, recovered X-registered Mini, a Sierra drive train and the more powerful engine from a Granada 2.8 EFI. Work then commenced in Cannings' single garage, supplied with electricity via an extension lead from the kitchen window.

The stripped-out shell was on stands at one end, with the engine and transmission at the other, then the floor pan was chopped to take the prop shaft. Next, Cannings cut a hole in the bulkhead. Over a period of about forty hours this was enlarged, bit by bit, until, by a process of trial and error, the drive shafts were lined up with the front wheels. Then it was a question of welding it all up, using 2mm steel. Cannings opted for strength and the car is no lightweight. The engine is quite well back into the cockpit and he wanted something substantial between his body and the moving parts.

Although the drive shafts had to be specially made, the car utilizes standard 1500 Allegro outer and Ford inner CVs. There are Metro Turbo brakes behind the 13in (32.5cm) wheels but the suspension is Leda with adjustable ride height, spring and damper rating. Two years after work started, the car emerged from the garage and passed its MOT first time. Amazingly, this hillclimb car is fully street legal, which allows unlimited testing. The only teething trouble was the engine's inability to idle properly. The ECU supplied with the engine turned out to be the wrong one; once it had been replaced, all was well.

Power output is 150bhp and the car tips the scales at 2,332lb (1,060kg) all up, which means that a normal 1,100lb (500kg) competition Mini only has to produce 75bhp to be on an equal footing.

However, the four-wheel drive is a great advantage for Cannings' chosen application. He has been competing on the hills in his hybrid since 1995 and finds that, if he drops the clutch at 6,500rpm, he is off the line without any wheel spin. The car has class wins, one FTD and a fifth overall to its credit.

*As well as using his Ford-powered Mini for hillclimbs and sprints, Andrew Cannings' car is street legal and can occasionally be seen on the roads of Kent.*

# 7 The Leyland 1275GT Challenge

Obviously impressed by the impact of the Renault 5 Challenge, in the mid-1970s Leyland took the decision to instigate their own one-make series. In 1976, they introduced the 1275GT Challenge, using the non-Cooper-badged replacement for the S. It ran until 1980, when it was superseded by the Metro Challenge. The 1275GT regulations prescribed that the cars should basically race in Group 1 trim with limited engine, suspension and brake modifications.

The first-ever 1275GT event took place at Snetterton in March 1976. It was won by Alan Curnow, although Roger Saunders emerged as the first champion in the series.

During the first season, Leyland ran a celebrity car, although their guest drivers were ineligible for any championship points. Works rally driver Tony Pond took part in the first three races, coming third at Llandow on 11 April. For the remaining events, the car was driven by Mike Smith, Guenda Eadie, Andrew Shanks, Rex Greenslade, Clive Richardson, Andrew Craig and Terry Grimwood, who was fifth at the Brands season-closer on 17 October.

*In the early rounds of the 1275GT Challenge, drivers found the original steel wheels, as specified in the regulations, were not strong enough. Paul Taft watches one of his bounce into the distance at Llandow. In 1977, the rules were changed and everyone had to run on a special alloy wheel.*

*Alan Curnow, using all the kerb, keeps Glyn Swift at bay during one of the 1976 rounds.*

## ALAN CURNOW

Despite having raced all kinds of Minis, Alan Curnow is probably best known for his 1275GT exploits. He remembers that, in the championship's first year, the cars had to appear standard and therefore ran on the original steel wheels. Drivers found they were repeatedly breaking, so Leyland invited Curnow and Steve Soper to thrash two factory 1275s around Llandow Circuit, in order to monitor the rims. After the introduction of a reinforced-steel version, Leyland eventually relented and allowed special alloys, which proved stronger.

Curnow came second in the 1976 challenge, after winning the first three races and adding four seconds and three thirds to his tally. From 1977 to 1979, he joined Richard Longman's team, successfully driving a Longman 1275GT in the British Saloon Car Championship.

*Alan Curnow's Patrick Motor Group, Richard Longman-built 1275GT in a round of the 1977 British Saloon Car Championship.*

*Steve Soper and Paul Taft tangled in the biggest possible way at Brands Hatch on 16 April 1978, both cars bouncing off the armco before ending up on the verge.*

## STEVE SOPER

Having competed in a few Harrow Car Club Sprints in Minis during 1971, Steve Soper spent five years running an Imp and various Minis in Special Saloons. These were enjoyable times, with mixed results, although the budget sometimes ran out before the end of the season. The financial difficulties made Soper decide that he would be better off in a one-make formula, where he felt that his results would not be so directly proportionate to the amount of money spent on the car.

Soper joined the 1275GT Challenge in 1976. Having purchased a second-hand 1275GT road car, he prepared it in accordance with the championship regulations. He did the suspension himself and got Richard Longman to build the engine. In his first season he won the Mallory and

Brands Hatch rounds, and amassed enough points in other races to come fifth in the championship.

For 1977, the car was re-shelled and Soper got the overall weight right down to the limit. The season gave him some exciting racing, with Paul Taft emerging as the main opposition. Nine race wins gave Soper the championship from Roger Saunders, with 'Tafty' third. Taft's car proved to be extremely rapid in a straight line and a few other drivers in the series, including Soper, began to wonder whether the rules were perhaps being bent. At one meeting, he spent the entire time between practice and the race in the back of his van on one side of the circuit, using binoculars to observe Taft's every move on the other side. Scrutineer Mike Garton subsequently checked the Taft car and found everything to be above board.

In the following season, the competition was even closer and, despite five race wins, a couple of non-finishes saw Soper end up third overall. One of the non-finishes was as a result of a huge accident with Paul Taft at Brands' Paddock bend. The two cars made contact and both ploughed into the barriers; the drivers were extracted and carted off to the medical centre in an ambulance. Soper had concussion, while Taft sustained three broken ribs. They were given adjacent beds, separated by a thin nylon curtain. Soper lay there gradually coming to his senses and realizing how lucky he had been. The nurse, rather less than glamorous, came into the cubicle, announced the doctor would see him shortly and then left. Next door, Taft was in considerable pain, moaning in discomfort. Soper decided that his rival needed cheering up. 'Tafty,' he called, 'what's your nurse like? Mine's gorgeous.' The groans gradually became louder, until the curtain was pulled aside and Taft's pale face appeared. There was no sign of any nurse, let alone a gorgeous one. Far from amused, he struggled back to his bed, nursing his injured ribs. He claims that his rib cage is deformed to this day because of the experience.

In 1979, Steve Soper took seven race wins and four seconds to secure the championship once more. Having won the Fiesta and Metro Challenges in 1980 and 1981, he made his way into touring cars as a professional racing driver and later made his mark in FIA GTs.

*Paul Taft two-wheels through the bend, trailing his chrome trim, while Steve Soper waits for a gap, keeping a wary eye on the progress of Roger Saunders, Donington Park, 16 October 1977.*

*The finalists in the 1978 BBC Driver of the Year award all took part in a race driving identical 1275GTs, prepared to Challenge spec by Leyland. Afterwards, they were sold at a very reasonable price to boost the flagging championship grids. Wendy Markey (left) and Georgie Shaw (right), each bought a car and raced in 1978 as the British Women Racing Drivers Club Team.*

## PAUL TAFT

Eight years of scrambling taught Paul Taft his racecraft and, in 1974, he took to the circuits on four wheels in a Special Saloon Cooper S. He entered six races and won two. The following year, his car became one of two identical 'Taft Motor Services' cars, the other driven by his brother Greg. Paul is pleased to say he never let his brother beat him – true, he came close, but he never pulled it off. Thirteen wins from sixteen races gave Paul Taft a class win in

the 1976 Simoniz Special Saloon Car Championship. Deciding that staying in the same series, having won it, was putting your head on the chopping block, he assessed the alternatives before concluding that the 1275GTs looked to be competitive and would probably be cheaper.

From the outset, it was very close racing and he remembers well the mammoth dices with Soper. It provided a good learning experience, with the leading contenders all bringing each other on. Taft's driving style was to go into the quick corners just that little bit faster, which usually gave him half a car's length advantage on exit. He reckons that he had a quicker engine than Soper, but that Soper's chassis was set up better than his. Over a two-year period, he put considerable effort into fine tuning his own suspension and this paid dividends. It needed to, because Soper's engines were getting stronger.

Taft has vivid memories of the old Woodcote at Silverstone. In one race, he was one of a group of drivers who entered the bend five abreast, not once, but almost every other lap. He was sixth in the 1976 championship; he would have won it, but for a penalty incurred early in the season. The regulations stated that the charging system was free, so he changed the dynamo pulley. However, the scrutineer decided that the dynamo pulley was not part of the charging system and, as such, should remain standard. Taft was docked twenty points, more than he had amassed,

and consequently ran with a minus score for the next three rounds. The penalty was even more galling when the regs were eventually changed to allow a different pulley.

Taft was third in 1977 and fifth in 1978 and made occasional appearances in the final two seasons of the challenge.

## THE END OF THE SERIES

In 1981, most drivers took advantage of the factory deal to move on to the replacement Metro series, but there was a move to keep the 1275GTs going as a club formula. There were so few registrations that it did not continue and the remaining cars changed hands, some appearing in other saloon formulae. John Hopwood's old car even ended up back on the road. Steve Gardiner, my former race mechanic, was the last driver to run it as everyday transport.

*Another of the former Driver of the Year cars about to come to a sticky end at Quarry, Castle Combe, 28 July 1979. Robert Mayo-Bignell prepares to nose-dive the tarmac, while Melvyn Johnson continues on his way. Mayo-Bignell did not appear for the rest of the season, but was out again in 1980.*

*Peter Baldwin (5) and Patrick Watts (00) climb the Mountain at Cadwell Park, 1 June 1980. Watts was second in the championship that year, with Baldwin two points behind him in third.*

## Leyland 1275GT Challenge Champions

1976 Roger Saunders
1977 Steve Soper
1978 Jeremy Hampshire

1979 Steve Soper
1980 Steve Harris

*Paul Gaymer tries the Donington chicane on two wheels, 11 June 1978. This allowed Jeremy Hampshire (8) to get through and win the race, Gaymer recovering to take second. Geoff Till (22) is following.*

# 8   Mini-Based GT Cars

A book about Mini racing would not be complete without a chapter on the Mini-based GT cars. Although they all had very different styling, they had one thing in common: they were all based on the mechanical components of the Mini. Those examples that appeared on the tracks did not race in Saloon Car categories, however, but in Modsports or GT classes. Several models even took on the might of Ferrari and the like in the classic endurance races such as the Le Mans 24-Hour and the Nurburgring 1,000km.

## BIOTA

Of the many and various Mini-based GT cars, the Biota is unique in having been designed, by John Houghton, specifically for hillclimbing. Although it first appeared in public at the 1969 Racing Car Show, production proper did not start until 1970,

when Specialised Mouldings, who had a hand in many glass-fibre bodies for Mini derivatives, were brought in to sort out the body. The car was based on a space-frame chassis to which the body was bonded and ran Mini engine and running gear.

John Houghton ran a specially built Biota in the 1972 Castrol BARC Hillclimb Championship. The unique features of the 'works car' were a beam axle and the fact that it had only two pedals – a normal clutch and a combined brake and accelerator. This pedal was cantilevered; to open the throttle, the driver pushed the toe down, to brake, the whole pedal was pushed forward. Chris Seaman, in his ex-Fred Whitaker 1293cc Midget, was one of Houghton's class rivals in the series.

Part-way through the season, Chris Seaman found himself without a car after an errant lorry had demolished his garage and crushed the MG under a pile of rubble the night before he was due out at the next

*Chris Seaman in John Houghton's Biota at the Harewood Speed Hillclimb Championship Finals, September 1972. Seaman won the championship.*

169

round. Houghton sportingly asked Seaman if he would like to share his car for the balance of the season. The only proviso was that Seaman had to prove he was quick in the Biota. A mid-week test was arranged at Sandcroft, a sprint circuit near Doncaster.

After a few laps, Seaman got to grips with the car, mastering the pedals and the reversed 'H' gear-change gate, and was setting some good times. As he entered the fastest right-hand bend on the circuit, a rear wheel tucked under and the car stood on its nose. Seaman remembers thinking, 'Oh dear, this is going to hurt!' The situation was worsened by the fact that the wheel had snapped the brake pipe and applying pressure to the right-hand pedal, with the car tilting forward, gave him full throttle. Fortunately, the expected roll did not happen and the Biota crashed back on to its rear wheels, with a few bits dropping off. It later transpired that a weld on the beam axle had given way, probably because Seaman weighed more than Houghton, for whom the car was designed. Despite this incident, Chris Seaman was deemed fast enough and the two drivers shared the car. Seaman took the championship, Brian Kenyon was second and Houghton, the car's owner, was third.

## BROADSPEED GT 2 + 2

Broadspeed introduced their own GT version of the Mini but, unlike most other Mini-based GTs, theirs was based on the standard body shell. It was modified by cutting off the rear section of the roof together with the back window and the rear panel and reducing the door pillars in height to lower the roof line. A fastback, made in glass fibre, was then bonded on to give the car its unique, modified rear end, complete with spoiler. De-seaming the

*After a preview of the Mini Marcos, Broadspeed designed its own GT car, with sales manager Tony Blore drawing something out on his blotter. The prototype was to be given away in a newspaper competition after being displayed at the 1966 Racing Car Show, but the winner opted for the cash alternative, a bad long-term investment, as the cars are now extremely rare. EOP 89D, shown here, was raced by John Fitzpatrick and Tony Blore.*

remaining front body panels increased the top speed. The engine and running gear were modified to Broad's spec and the interior was re-trimmed and fitted out to a very high standard. The 1275-powered racer was reckoned to have a top speed of 145mph (230kph), some 20mph (35kph) faster than the road model.

The Broadspeed GT 2 + 2 was aimed at the luxury market rather than the racing enthusiast, although a few racing versions, with glass-fibre doors and Perspex windows, were built. John Fitzpatrick drove EOP 89D in its inaugural race at Brands Hatch, on 23 January 1966, immediately after it had been displayed at the Racing Car Show. Another competitor spun in front of him at Paddock during the early stages of the race; he collected him and was forced to retire.

EOP 89D was repaired and then Broadspeed director Tony Blore had about six race outings in it, running a 1340cc engine with a 48 IDA Weber. He remembers delighting the crowd at Oulton Park, when he overtook an AC Cobra. EOP 89D was then sold to a competitor in Holland.

The GT project was effectively killed off when Broadspeed switched to racing Fords and the company wanted them to drop all connections with BMC. When Broadspeed's factory was demolished to make way for a ring road, enforcing a move to a new location, it was the end of the road for the GT. However, it is being made again today by another company.

# COX GTM

## Design and Launch

Designed by Jack Hosker, the Cox GTM – Grand Touring Mini – was originally put into production by Bernard Cox at his garage, Cox and Co., Hazel Grove, Cheshire. Hosker, who worked as service manager at one of Cox's garages, initially made a model chassis from pieces of Cornflake packets. Bernard Cox, who himself raced Elvas, backed the idea and allocated Hosker a disused lubrication bay to build the prototype. This Hosker did, single-handed, in about fourteen months.

Racer Howard Heerey was working in his father Brian's garage next door and was brought in to add his expertise by track-testing the car. The resulting vehicle was almost certainly the first mid-engined kit car. The public liked what they saw and were soon asking the company when they could order one. The original car was bodied in aluminium but a mould was taken from this and subsequent versions were in glass fibre. The hope was that customers would buy GTMs as weekend racers but few were used for this purpose.

Launched at the 1967 Racing Car Show,

the Cox GTM was hailed by *Cars and Car Conversions* as 'just about the most fun yet in the Mini-based GT car line'. They road-tested a 1293cc example, JDB 260E and reported a 0–60 time of 6.4 seconds (despite a slipping clutch), and a top speed of 115.5mph (184.8kph). The glass-fibre body was bolted and bonded to a semi-monocoque chassis made of sheet steel. A Mini front subframe, fitted to the rear, took a Mini engine of any capacity. Up front, in what would normally be the engine bay, was another subframe, a standard Mini fuel tank and a radiator, mounted on its side to fit in the nose.

## Howard Heerey

In road trim, the Cox GTM weighed 10.5cwt (535kg) but the later racing version was pared down to just below 10cwt (510kg); about 50lb (23kg) of this saving was made in the lightweight bodywork. Howard Heerey, well known for his exploits in a Chevron, in which he won the Clubmans Championship, competed in about six races in the aluminium prototype GTM in 1967. He ran a 1293cc engine on SUs, in the over 1150cc class.

For 1968, Cox built a glass fibre-bodied car, using a lighter-gauge steel for the chassis. They decided they would be more competitive in the smaller class, so this version was powered by an 1150cc unit with a Weber. The car had a striking paint job – the top was dark blue, merging to purple, with silver at the bottom. (Howard Heerey had a double-decker trailer and, when he graduated to Formula 3, if there was an available class for the GTM, he would compete in both cars.) He did about twelve events in the 1150cc version, under the name of the 'Hazelgrove Racing Syndicate', and took several class places.

Howard Heerey recalls sitting on the grid at Brands before a race and the driver

*One minute to go: Howard Heerey, Cox GTM, behind two Chevrons on the starting grid at Oulton Park in 1968. Note the Webers poking through the engine cover.*

of a Mini Marcos on the row behind approaching to warn him that, once the flag dropped, he would be coming through so he should watch out for him! This was said despite the fact that Heerey had set a much faster practice time and only served to make Heerey more determined. He was the first Mini derivative home.

During the GT race qualifying session, at his local circuit, Oulton Park, Howard Heerey practised in the dry, while some of the august machinery, such as Lola T70s, GT40s and Chevrons, set their times in the wet. The GTM ended up on the outside of the front row. Heerey was determined to capitalize on this once-in-a-lifetime grid position for the little car. He revved the engine to 7,000rpm and, as soon as the starter's hand twitched, dumped the clutch and got his nose ahead as the pack

streamed toward Old Hall. The getaway proved too much for the top engine steady bar, which broke, allowing the block to rotate, snapping the radiator hoses. The car retired in a cloud of steam at the first corner. Subsequently, steady-bar brackets were welded rather than brazed.

Oulton Park was unkind to Heerey on another occasion. He lost it at Esso Bend, going right through the advertising hoarding and coming to rest with the driver's side wedged against one of the supporting timbers. To make matters worse, the hole in the sign closed up behind him and, for a while, the bemused officials could not work out where the car was.

Hosker repaired the heavily damaged GTM and it was sold.

Having manufactured fifty-five kits, Gordon Cox gave up his garages in 1968. He transferred the project to Howard Heerey and his father, who incorporated a few design changes. These included replacing the subframe at the rear with a purpose-built space frame, which allowed the car to have different ride heights front and rear. Heerey found that producing the GTM precluded time for racing it.

## Richard Hudson-Evans

In 1970, Richard Hudson-Evans, then editor of *Cars and Car Conversions*, built up a yellow car in his garage at home, with the help of some friends, including Colin Hine and Alan Maxwell. The build was featured in a number of articles in the magazine. The cockpit sported an original pair of seats given to Hudson-Evans by Howard Heerey and the car had long-range fuel tanks. Subsequently, the GTM was painted red with CCC chequers, and Hudson-Evans himself raced it at a number of club events around the UK. He certainly made a good start, winning his class first time out at Snetterton.

*Howard Heerey's Cox GTM holds the line at Druids, Brands Hatch, 1968. On the grid, the driver of the Mini Marcos on the row behind warned him to watch out as he would be coming through.*

In September, he entered the car in the 1970 Nurburgring 500km. During the scrutineering, the officials had a field day – the team was asked to get a larger fire extinguisher, change some suspension bolts, fabricate rear wheel-arch spats and re-weld the steering column. The last two items were taken on board by the support vans that BP and Esso sent to such events, to help private entrants. Despite being relatively unsorted for such a bumpy circuit, the GTM qualified with a best lap time of 11:59.2, set during the second practice session.

Drivers of the faster cars such as Chris Craft and Brian Redman, in the Chevrons, nicknamed the car the 'Clockwork Mouse', because they kept lapping it during the

*Richard Hudson-Evans lines up for his first race in the yellow Cox GTM, in 1970.*

race. The club-spec 999cc engine had to work very hard. Hudson-Evans remembers occasions when he was lapped by two cars, one on either side. It was an awesome experience, given the vast size and speed differential.

The GTM eventually suffered sump-gasket failure. Despite pitting every two laps to top up with oil, the bearings went on lap ten and Hudson-Evans was forced to retire while lying third in class.

Richard Hudson-Evans' other major outings were the Seven Fifty Motor Club Silverstone Six-Hour Relay Races in 1970 and 1971, when he was a member of the Triple C Mini Team. By now the GTM was fully sorted and had modified cooling. The suspension had been adjusted by drilling holes in the rubber cones to improve the damping and the ride height had been adjusted by inserting washers under the trumpets.

In the first year the other team members were Clive Trickey (Mini Miglia), Colin Hine (1293 Clubman) and John Francis (1293S). John Foden was drafted in as team manager. Hudson-Evans did some ninety laps during his stints and the GTM cruised round, very understretched.

Some of the other drivers were not so lucky. Trickey had oil-pressure problems, while Hine's car also lost some oil, as well as sucking in a Weber 'O' ring, leaving John Francis to do most of the driving during the closing stages. They came eighth equal on scratch.

In 1971, Richard Hudson-Evans and the GTM were joined by John Rhodes, driving Clive Trickey's car, John Francis and Eric Cook (each in a 1293S), and Colin Hine, now sponsored by Dents glove company. *Cars and Car Conversions* had established an excellent rapport with Jan Odor of Janspeed, who acted as team manager on this occasion.

Things did not go exactly to plan. Both the Coopers soon retired, then Hudson-Evans was forced to bring the Cox in as a result of a cockpit full of oil fumes, diagnosed as a leak in the diff area. John Rhodes got stuck in and recorded some sub lap record times in Trickey's car, but this eventually cried 'enough' when the bottom pulley worked loose. Colin Hine soldiered on alone for the last three hours. Pitting regularly for fuel and oil, he saved the day, and the team recorded a respectable twelfth on scratch.

*By the time he took his GTM to race in the 1970 Nurburgring 500, Richard Hudson-Evans had painted it in full Triple C livery. He was the editor of the magazine at the time.*

In recent years, Richard Hudson-Evans' GTM surfaced in a Devon barn and has now been restored, resplendent in its CCC livery, by Mini enthusiast Derek Wilkins, who is considering racing it in historic events.

## Geoff Bird

In 1986, Geoff Bird, who was regularly competing on the hills in his Mini Saloon, purchased a Cox GTM as a road car. It had been built up using a 1968 Cooper S as the donor vehicle. It soon occurred to Bird he would be better off hillclimbing the Cox and, having installed his competition engine, began campaigning it to good effect at venues in the south-west. Over the years, the car was gradually developed and now runs in the modified category.

It has a full race, big-valve 1380cc engine with split Weber 45s, Jack Knight dog box, Sintered clutch, rose-jointed suspension with Hi-Los, and runs on 6in (15cm) slicks. However, it retains stan-dard Cooper S drive shafts, on the basis that it is cheaper and easier to break one of those rather than something else. Every ounce of power is utilized to the full, the engine has no fan belt, fan or charging system and even has an electric water pump, producing a total saving of 5bhp.

The car is specifically geared for the hills. Bird calculates that it pulls 11.75mph (28kph) per 1,000rpm and thus has a top speed of about 85mph (135kph). With its tall first gear it pulls about 14G off the start line. He has campaigned the car since 1988 and, during that time, has scored thirty wins, twenty-six seconds, twenty-two thirds and fourteen fourth places. He took FTD at Pestalozzi in 1995 and 1996, and has held hill records at five venues. His GTM also won the 1991 *Cars and Car Conversions* Converted Car of the Year award.

# DEEP SANDERSON 301GT

About twenty 301GTs were built, of which probably three remain in existence. Designed by Chris Lawrence, a successful engine tuner and racing driver, the original open prototype was built with an aluminium body in 1961. It was not until 1963 that the 301GT, which had a drag figure of about 3, appeared. Moulds had been taken from an aluminium prototype for the production versions. One of the car's trademarks was the 'Lawrence Link' trailing arm rear suspension, while power came from rear-mounted 997 Cooper engines. Its name was derived from 'Deep Henderson', a jazz tune recorded by Lawrence's father in 1926; Sanderson was the maiden name of his mother, who backed the project.

Lawrence himself had previously competed at Le Mans in a Morgan, so it was no surprise that Deep Sandersons were raced

*Geoff Bird's Cox GTM has been a regular award winner on the hills over the past ten years. Here, he rounds turn four at Oddicombe on 11 October 1992.*

in long-distance events. The original prototype was campaigned by Len Bridge, culminating in the Nurburgring 1,000km, where he retired after hitting a tree. The prototype was eventually cut up.

The 301GT appeared at Le Mans in 1963 and again in 1964. In 1963, Lawrence entered one car, to be co-driven by himself and Chris Spender. It ran well, and on Sunday morning was leading the up to 1000cc class. However, the team's euphoria was to be short-lived. At 10am, an official arrived at the Deep Sanderson pit with the news that, on going through the night's lap times, the organizers had discovered that at midnight the car had been behind on minimum average. As such, it was in breach of the regulations, and Lawrence was asked to retire it. As it was still leading the class, he declined to do so, so it was excluded.

For 1964, a two-car team was assembled. Chris Lawrence was to be partnered by Gordon Spice, with a second car for Jim Donnelly and Hugh Braithwaite. Downtons were too busy to build the engines, so Lawrence got the BMC competition department to do them. Unfortunately, the 1300 power units were not delivered until the day the team was due to leave for France and they had to be installed in a rush. It transpired that they came with Weber carburettors on long manifolds; the bulkheads had to be cut and boxed in order to accommodate them. At the circuit, Chris Lawrence discovered that the carbs had not been properly jetted, so he spent the first part of the Friday afternoon practice session going out for a couple of laps, coming in, changing jets and chokes, then going out again. After three attempts, he got it about right.

Donnelly, who had been circulating in his very off-song car, pitted for his carb to be reset. He went back out, found that he was going about 60mph (95kph) faster, entered White House too quickly and went straight over the wall into retirement. Lawrence and Spice went on to qualify for the race, after going through the Mulsanne Straight speed trap at over 150mph (240kph). In the race, the oil pump broke after ingesting a broken idler gear bearing.

*Chris Lawrence driving his 1000cc Deep Sanderson 301GT through the Esses at Le Mans in 1963. The car was very quick through the corners. Lawrence's suspension design gave 100% camber compensation, so the wheels always stayed upright.*

Around this time, Daniel Richmond contacted Chris Lawrence. He had been approached by Reg Harris, a successful racing cyclist who, getting a little long in the tooth for pedal power, was looking to diversify into motor sport. He had asked Richmond to build him a 'Twini Mini' racing car to use in sprints. Richmond had decided that such a project would be in breach of his development contract with BMC. George Harriman had banned the building of any more twin-engined Minis following John Cooper's terrible accident in one.

Lawrence agreed to take the job on and called it the 401. He asked Richmond to build the two engines but, when the project was half completed, the customer withdrew. By then, however, Lawrence had got his teeth into it and decided to complete the car anyway. One took particular care selecting the gears, as a rushed change would see one engine in second and the other in third. He debuted the 401 in a Libre race at 1963 Boxing Day Brands and also did a Mallory Park event in spring 1964. On both occasions, a tyre burst after about seven laps, the heat from the brakes, three-quarters of an inch (18mm) from the tyre, causing a tube to fail.

In the 1960s, Sydney Allard ran a series of six sprints on three consecutive weekends at venues such as Blackbushe and Kimble. He would invite many eminent drivers to these events. Chris Lawrence asked Tony Kynch, the local service-station proprietor's son, to drive the 401 in the 1965 series. Being very light and having four-wheel drive meant that the car was very quick off the line and was invariably faster than the V8-engined cars over the first eighth of a mile, but it would lose out on the second half of the run. Setting eleven second times for the standing quarter-mile, it always got through the morning eliminator into the afternoon finals.

On one occasion, it nearly won, much to the alarm of Allard, who did not want his American guest drivers humiliated.

## FLETCHER

Based on the Ogle SX1000, the Fletcher was built by the boat-making concern of the same name. The company bought the Ogle moulds with a view to filling the winter gap in their production schedule by building a few for racing. The styling varied from the original Ogle. The first car was built in 1966 and there was an immediate demand for a road version. Unfortunately, difficulty in obtaining parts from BMC resulted in just three more being put together.

John Handley raced a Fletcher entered by prominent local businessman G.R. Baird, which first appeared on a grid in the British Eagle Trophy Race at Brands Hatch on 27 December 1966. The race was won by John Miles in the Lotus 47 (Europa), in that car's first-ever public appearance. Needless to say, this achievement gained most column inches in the race reports. Having qualified sixth, Handley and the Fletcher ran fourth overall. The car was entered for the 1967 Nurburgring 500 and Handley made an excellent showing, qualifying the car third fastest. In the race, he got it up to second and then the engine let go. Subsequently, Handley also drove the car in some other British club races.

## LANDAR

The Landar, first produced in 1963 by cycle-component maker A.E. Randall, is probably one of the most unusual of the Mini-based cars – an open two-seater that was designed as a racing car. Some described it as a miniature Can-Am car. It was only 30in (75cm) high and its original aluminium bodywork was made by Williams and Pritchard, well known for their work in this medium.

John Handley was involved in the project, carrying out development work and then racing the car a few times. He describes it as 'beautifully built, totally in proportion to the small wheels'. It had independent front suspension but used a modified Mini front subframe in the rear, which he found gave the car understeer. It went off the line like a rocket, then the other competitors would catch up and the driver would do his best to fend them off for the rest of the race. While other examples were raced in the UK, the car enjoyed its greatest success in the USA where it won the Sports Car Club of America Under 1300cc Sports Car Championship. Because the Landar was good at getting the power down, it also found favour with the British hillclimb fraternity.

Chris Lawrence was working in the USA in 1988 and, because of his vast experience with British sports cars, was appointed as a scrutineer. One day he looked up from his clipboard to see that the next car was a Landar; its owner was pleased and surprised to find out that someone else knew what it was.

## CAMBER/MAYA GT

Originally named after the place where it was made, this vehicle was the brainchild of George Holmes, who had a business at Camber Sands, and Derek Bishop. Following a parting of the ways, Holmes took over production and the car's name was changed to 'Maya GT', apparently after Holmes' wife's horse. Holmes' company, W. West (Engineers) Ltd, was involved in agricultural engineering and continued to do this kind of work, including the maintenance of the mowers for the nearby golf course. Alongside this activity, the company also manufactured Formula Vee racing cars as well as the Maya.

The Maya had a glass-fibre coupé body mounted on a tubular chassis, which had mountings to accept standard front and

*The Camber GT takes its name from the place in Sussex where it was first built. After six were made, the name was changed to Maya, but the tragic death of designer George Holmes curtailed production and the projected full racing programme.*

rear Mini subframes. Extra strength was provided by a sheet of steel bonded into the roof. One of the cars was built as a lightweight racer, but seems to have spent much of its time in a shed at the back of the factory. It was later purchased by a local person who used it on the road. Max Le Grand, motoring journalist and photographer, knew Holmes well and enjoyed road-testing a Maya for one of the car magazines of the time.

Six examples were made under each guise; the Cambers had low round headlights, while the Maya had the headlights higher in the body, in order to comply with regulations. A very striking example, specially sprayed in blue metal flake by Autospray in Lydd, had been exhibited at the 1967 Racing Car Show. After the show, it was discovered that the headlights were lower than the regulations allowed, so the final six cars were given a modified nose that set the lights higher. The show car was sold with a new nose cone loose in the boot. In 1992, Len Bosshard 'discovered' this car in a very sorry state, complete with the new nose, which had never been fitted. He restored it and was able to leave the front in its original guise, as it now complies to adopted European regulations. The first racing outing of a Camber was probably at the Brands Hatch Boxing Day meeting in 1966, when John Green drove an 1148cc example in the British Eagle Trophy Race, for Special Grand Touring cars. He finished fourth in class, narrowly beaten by P. Anslow's Mini Marcos. Next time out, at Brands on 26 February 1967, Green was forced to retire the car.

There was clearly some intention to embark on a comprehensive racing programme with the Maya. Holmes' stepdaughter Sally Aspinall remembers a meeting at the local pub to discuss the car's racing future. Around the table were the family, Gerald Le Sells from

Checkpoint (the appointed distributors for the Maya), John Green and a pirate radio disc jockey, who had been brought in to help with the publicity. Tragically, however, Holmes was killed while out in his own Maya. He had stopped to rescue an injured bird and was run over by a delivery van. Only twelve Mayas were ever made and the racing programme never took off.

## MINI JEM

Like the Mini Marcos, the Mini Jem was based on Dizzy Addicott's one-off Dart, an aluminium-bodied sports car built on the floor pan of a Mini van. The fibreglass-bodied Jem took its name from its builder Jeremy Delmar-Morgan, who commenced production in late 1966. Two examples were raced at Brands on 16 October, driven by Russell Cassidy and R. Parkes. Delmar-Morgan himself raced a 999cc example in the Special GT Race at the Boxing Day Brands meeting, on 27 December.

Rob Statham took the project over for the following year, introducing the Mark 2 at the 1969 Racing Car Show and racing a supercharged 1275cc version in GT events. When his company Fellpoint closed, production passed to High Performance Mouldings.

### Ian Hall

In 1972, former Modsports Sprite driver Ian Hall decided that he wanted to race something different. He went to see High Performance Mouldings, where Statham's racing Jem was being stored for the receivers. Hall viewed it in a barn, where it stood on 10in (25cm) Revolutions with a brand-new set of four inside. He decided to try a silly offer of £400, which was accepted. There remained one problem: the Jem had never been homologated for Modsports, in which Hall wanted to compete. He applied to the RAC and got the car accepted in time for the 1973 season.

The supercharged engine proved unreliable, so Hall built an 1150. It went well, but he feared he could not get to grips with front-wheel drive. A wet race at Castle Combe, in which he finished fourth from twenty-second on the grid, encouraged him to persevere. A new set of suspension arms changed the castor angle from negative to positive; this transformed the handling and the results started to come. Later, Hall modified the car to run on 13in (32.5cm) Revolutions with Ensign F1 discs and four-pot callipers all round. The front suspension had Mini cones with Spax dampers, while the rear was coil-sprung with fabricated trailing arms. Transmission had Special Tuning SCCR gears and Salisbury Power-Lok diff. Hall won the class in the 1975 BARC Modsports Championship.

The following year, running a Richard Longman 1360cc race engine with twin 45 DCOE Webers and LCB exhaust manifold, Ian Hall amassed fifteen victories on his way to second in the BARC Championship, again taking his class. The car nearly broke in half following a bad accident, but Hall strapped the two halves back together with a rope tourniquet and bonded it. This increased the rigidity and further improved the handling.

In 1978, Hall moved on to an 'A' Series-powered Davrian, in which he had his first outright championship win in 1980. The Mini Jem was sold to John Moore and later written off at Thruxton.

## Peter Burnham

Rob Statham had laid up another light-weight racing shell, which, in 1971, was sold to Peter Burnham, who built it up himself for sprints and hillclimbs. The 1293cc car utilized a modified trailing arm rear suspension set-up from Fellpoint's Mini Bug beach buggy. Burnham competed in the car from 1972 to 1992, taking many class awards. He was 1985 ACSMC

*Mini Jem on the limit: Ian Hall cornering hard at Silverstone's Woodcote in 1977. Hall was noted for making maximum use of the kerbs when going through corners. Sidney Offord of the BARC picked him up on it so many times that, in the end, Hall sold the car. He had become too set in his ways.*

*Ian Hall replaced his Jem with a Mk 7A Davrian with a difference. Most ran Imp-based engines, but his was the first to use a Mini power unit. He won the 1980 BRSCC Modsports Championship outright in this car. Here, with a supercharged 1071 at Prescott in 1982, the Davrian proved more successful on the hills with a blown 1330 S engine.*

class champion and took the class in the 1991 BARC Motorola Sprint Championship. Phil Henshaw and Phil Wadsley also competed in Mini Jems.

## MINI MARCOS

The Mini Marcos, built by Jem Marsh and Frank Costin (hence the name 'Mar-Cos'), was introduced in 1965, as the small brother to the Marcos GT. Tipping the scales at about 10cwt (510kg), the car was regarded by many as a bit of an ugly duckling.

The model's first race was at Castle Combe in September 1965, when a pre-production version, built for the Janspeed team, was driven by Geoff Mabbs in the Grand Touring Car race. The car, which had a Group 2 1293 engine, was only finished the night before the race and Jem Marsh told people not to expect too much of it. It went so well that Mabbs, a Mini expert, put it on pole and won the wet race in fine style. He lapped virtually the whole field, except George Gould's second-placed Ginetta G4 1500cc, which he beat by one and a half minutes. Of course, the subsequent press coverage helped to create a market for the new model. Apparently, another competitor at the meeting had been so impressed that he phoned up on Monday morning and ordered one himself.

### Le Mans 24-Hour Race

Professional deep-sea diver turned Paris Mini Cooper preparation expert, Jean-Claude Hrubon, had always promised himself a visit to the London Racing Car Show. He got there in 1966 and, after many hours walking round the stands, had ordered a Mini Marcos shell in which to compete at Le Mans. Together with Claude Pillson, he built the car, powered by a 1287cc Cooper S engine. It was shaken down at Montlhéry on 2 April, but the engine overheated and then blew. After returning to the workshop for a quick engine change, the team were off to Le Mans for the 'Essals' on 4 April. A best lap

*Marshals at the ready, as Andy Barton rejoins the circuit by the Shell Bridge at Croft in 1966. His Mini Marcos was one from the first batch. Barton had a more spectacular off at Rufforth later in the season, in a roll that destroyed the racer.*

of 5:08, fast enough to qualify for the race, was achieved before the engine again overheated and blew, despite the fact that extra cooling holes had been drilled in the bodywork.

As a result of the team's 5.08 lap, the Automobile Club of Milan offered Hrubon start money to compete in the Monza 1,000km on 23 May. Jean-Louis Marnet and Jean-Pierre Jabouille qualified well, but, because of the appalling weather conditions, despite taking the chequered flag, the team was not recorded as finishing. Having perhaps taken too long over the routine pit stops, they were outside the permitted time. Nevertheless, they did come in twentieth out of the fifty-five starters, averaging 92mph (147kph).

Only three British cars entered the 1966 24-hour classic on 18 June and just one finished: Hrubon's Mini Marcos, driven by well-known Swiss rally driver Claude Ballot-Lena and Jean-Louis Marnat. The car, blue with yellow stripes, ran according to plan, lapping consistently at 5:15. Being such a small car, it also won the hearts of the crowd. There were routine stops for fuel, driver changes and two front tyres. The only unplanned stop was to fix a loose mirror. At 4am, Ballot-Lena pitted for a driver change, concerned that the temperature gauge was stuck on hot. Had the overheating problem come back to haunt them? Inspection revealed that tired suspension had broken the gauge needle.

In the closing stages it began to rain, and the drivers' laps became more and more erratic. Determined that the car must finish having got this far, Jem Marsh, who was spectating as a guest of *Autosport*, visited the pit and persuaded the team to signal their driver to slow down. He did so and the car crossed the line fifteenth, the last competitor to qualify as a finisher. On his return to England, Marsh was told by *Autosport* editor Gregor Grant that, as a result of his intervention, the team had nearly failed to qualify. Because of poor lap charting they had almost reduced their speed too much. To score a finish, every entry had to do a certain percentage of the winning car's distance and the Mini Marcos had scraped through by just half a mile. The car, which averaged 89.7mph (143.5kph) over the twenty-four hours, was subsequently put on display in Paris and stolen.

## Jem Marsh at Le Mans

On 11 June 1967, Jem Marsh entered a car for himself, with co-driver Chris Lawrence. It was nearly excluded even before it had turned a wheel. Having got the car scrutineered, the drivers went off for their medicals only to return to find one of the Le Mans officials deleting their number from the list of starters. It seems that a French driver who was first reserve had protested the roof line, in the hopes of getting a race himself. Determined not to lose his entry, Marsh took his car back to the chateau where they were staying and worked through the night, cutting the roof and moving the windscreen forward, pop-riveting a sheet of alloy over the hole and making good the repair with an aerosol.

To the amazement of the officials, the Mini Marcos was re-presented for scrutineering at 7am the next morning; try as they might, they could find no further deviations from the regulations. In practice, the car was clocked at 141mph (225kph) down the Mulsanne Straight, the revised shape costing just 5mph (8kph), and duly qualified for the race. Chris Lawrence took the start but, during his first stint, the timing gear on the rally-

*The Ballo-Lena / Marnat Mini Marcos in full flight at the 1966 Le Mans 24-Hour Race. It crossed the line fifteenth, the last car to qualify as a finisher.*

*Steven Roberts'
TransXL Mini
Marcos competing
in STP Modsports
Finals at Thruxton
in 1979.*

spec engine broke and he was forced to retire.

During 1967, Jem Marsh himself competed in other long-distance events in the car. In August he was tenth in the Coppa Citta di Enna, scored a class fifth in the Nurburgring 500km and, with co-driver Tim Lalonde, came fifth on handicap at Phoenix Park. He completed the season with a fifteenth overall in the Nine-Hour Race at Kyalami in South Africa. In this race, his co-driver Brian Raubenheimer became so exhausted after his two-hour stint that Marsh ended up driving for seven hours.

## FLIRT

Formed in March 1967, FLIRT, the First Ladies International Racing Team – Jackie Smith, Jacquie Bond-Smith and Joey Cook – intended to compete at Le Mans, but the organizers refused the entry. Undeterred, Bond-Smith and Cook did the Nurburgring 1,000km on 28 May 1967, when a broken con-rod bolt forced their retirement. They came fifth in class at Mugello on 23 July. Their entry at the Ring was as part of a three-car team; Mike Garton and Paddy McNally finished eighteenth, winning the 1300 prototype class,

while Guy Edwards and Peter Anslow were second in class and twenty-third overall. Garton, partnered by Tim Lalonde, also took part at Mugello.

## Steven Roberts

During the 1970s, a few highly modified Mini Marcos examples were to be found racing in Modsports trim on the British club scene, in the STP, STS and McVities Championships. Steven Roberts, of Merlin Motor Sport at Castle Combe, was the most successful competitor during this period. He raced two cars from 1976 to 1982. His first was bought in 1968 from Marcos for use as a road car and later converted for Modsports. Between 1971 and 1976, he did forty-one races and his best year was 1976, when he won the class in the BRSCC Modsports Championship.

The second car, based on a special Mk4 shell, was built for him by Harold Dermott, of D and H Fibreglass Techniques, who had taken over the Mini Marcos. It was specially designed for the track, being both lighter and stronger. The car was debuted at Thruxton on 13 March 1977 with a 1293cc engine modified by Bill Baker of Chosen Engineering (who prepared all

Roberts' engines) and enthusiastically sponsored by Jack Napper, of Swindon company Trans XL. Roberts' final outing in the Mini Marcos was at Mallory Park on 13 April 1980, equipped with a 1460cc engine.

During this period, Roberts did ninety-eight races, achieving class positions of thirty-six firsts, twenty-seven seconds and eleven thirds and set forty-five fastest laps. He took the class in the 1977 BRSCC Modsports Championship and won the series outright the following year, along with the class in the BARC Modsports Championship. In 1979, he concentrated on the BARC Championship, winning it outright, but also won the class in the BRSCC for good measure.

Driving his Mini Marcos, Steven Roberts also set two British land-speed records that have stood for more than twenty years. He has to his credit two records for Class F (1100cc to 1500cc), set at Elvington in 1978: the 1-km Standing Start, set on 29 July, and the 1-mile Flying Start, on 30 July. The car was sold to Neil Roscoe in 1980, who campaigned it in the BRSCC Castle Combe GT Championship. After a disappearance, it has recently surfaced again.

In the 1980s, Steven Roberts moved on to a Davrian Mk 7. The rear-engined Davrian was introduced in 1967 by Adrian Evans. It was originally based on Hillman Imp running gear and power but, by 1963, kits were available to enable it to take a Beetle or Mini lump. Roberts dropped in his 1460 and first raced the car at Thruxton on 27 April 1980. He did seventy-nine events, the last at Castle Combe in October 1984. A second place in the 1981 BARC Modsports Championship was followed up by outright wins in the 1983 and 1984 Castle Combe GT Championship. By now, the 1460 was dry-sumped and had an eight-port head.

## Other Mini Marcos Successes

In 1981, John Moore, another prolific Modsports racer who also drove a Turner, campaigned his Mini Marcos in the 750 MC Garelli Sports Car Championship, finishing the season second. At about the same time, Doug Mitchinson raced a 1380cc version. Today, examples of the Mini Marcos continue to be raced throughout the world. Dean Robertson is probably the quickest man on the UK hills, while Antonella Muscat competes regularly in the Malta Hillclimb Championship. Thomas Hall and Henrik Hanson race in Sweden, while German driver Thomas Hauck has been out in a Marcos at the Nurburgring.

On 6 October 1990, the Mini Marcos team was fourth on handicap in the Birkett 6-Hour Relay Race. Ian Head won the 1992 Phoenix Kit Car Series, in the same year that Phil Wadsley won the Cleanways Filters Sports Series.

## NIMBUS

Long-time motor sport competitor Donald Parker was involved in the development of the GSM Delta kit car and used one of the first bodies to come out of the mould in South Africa as the basis for his own special. He cut it about to suit his requirements and ran it in South African events, powered by a Riley engine. Returning to England with the car, he changed over to Ford Ten power, ever popular with the special builders of the time. He never liked the hassle of selling cars and invariably used the old as the basis for the new.

In 1965, Parker bought a race-spec 1275S engine and straight-cut gearbox unit from BMC and set about further modifying his car to take it. The configuration was to be rear-engine, rear-wheel drive. The Nimbus emerged in a relatively short time, with Parker doing his own welding and needing little outside assistance with the project. It soon started taking awards on the hills.

In its initial set-up, the S unit produced around 100bhp, but obviously the owner was looking to improve on this. After meeting Harry Ratcliffe, Parker was convinced that supercharging was the way to go. Ratcliffe advised him on the full technical details of what would be required to extract 150bhp from his engine. He got a 1.5-litre Shorrock blower and tried various pulley sizes and experimented with different SUs and a Weber carburettor, until he found the right combination to give the required power output.

Awards, including FTDs, kept coming but, having turned his attention to flying, Parker gave the Nimbus to his brother-in-law Mike Hentall. Soon, despite regular maintenance, the Shorrock cried 'enough'; not surprising, since it had consistently been run 2,000rpm above the recommended figure. It was replaced with a much larger supercharger and, after teething problems, continued its winning ways.

## OGLE SX1000

Created in 1961, the SX1000 was constructed by bonding the glass-fibre body onto the customer's existing Mini floor pan, giving tremendous road-holding. David Ogle had hoped to follow in Donald Healey's footsteps by getting BMC to take over production. Despite reports to the contrary, however, John Whitmore is adamant that he never raced an SX1000, stating that it would have been incompatible with the model's upmarket image.

Tragically, David Ogle was killed while driving one of his cars to Brands. Fletcher eventually bought the moulds for the SX1000.

## TERRAPIN

Conceived during the winter of 1964 by Allan Staniforth and Richard Blackmore, the Terrapin was originally intended to be a sports car, but the cost of making a glass-fibre body ruled this out. Instead, they opted for an aluminium-bodied single-seater racing car. The square tube chassis utilized four Mini front uprights and hubs with rear-wheel drive from a rear-mounted Mini engine and box. Staniforth completed the first example in time for the start of the 1965 season and Richard Blackmore built the Mk 2 soon after.

The basic design for the car was featured in Staniforth's first book *High Speed, Low Cost* and readers could buy a set of plans by filling in the tear-out card and sending off £4.50. Staniforth knows of about seventy Terrapins built from the plans by individuals. Some examples were raced in the Monoposto series, while many found their way on to the hills. (According to Staniforth, hillclimb organizers at the time were swamped with entries and favoured single-seaters over saloons.) Staniforth won the Shelsley Bolster award in his example quite early on. He ran a hybrid 1060cc engine with an Arnott supercharger; initially, he could run in the up to 1100cc class, but the organizers soon introduced a percentage loading to take account of the benefits of the supercharger.

As part of the development of the Terrapin, Allan Staniforth was among the first to make his own wide wheels. He used a hacksaw to cut four standard Mini wheels in half, then had specially made steel bands welded in the middle to increase the width. Staniforth wrote to BMC suggesting that they should instigate a series for racing cars powered by Mini engines. They declined and a few years later Formula Ford was introduced!

## TIMEIRE

The Timeire was literally a one-off, created in 1970 by former Speedwell employee Tim Conroy, of Canons Park Motors, Edgware. Conroy's brother Jim raced a Mini Cooper and they also ran one for John Cannadine, in which Rob Mason had a few outings.

The Timeire was based on a Mini, which had the back cut off and an alloy fastback grafted on in its place. There were no drawings and the work was done by two panel beaters who usually made bodies for AC Cobras.

The lone example, 2 BMK, was driven in two GT races at Brands Hatch by Rob Mason and then Gerry Marshall took it over to the Isle of Man for a hillclimb. That was the end of the car's brief racing career and it was sold off in 1973, minus its distinctive number plate.

## THE UNIPOWER GT

Conceived in 1963, by Ernest Unger and racing enthusiast Val Dare-Bryan, the Unipower weighed 10.25 cwt (520kg) and was a natural for racing, given its overall height of between 38 and 39in (95–97.5cm), depending on the size of wheels and tyres fitted. A full space-frame chassis, fabricated from square-section steel

*Allan Staniforth takes the tight hairpin at Baitings Dam Hillclimb, Yorkshire, in 1965. He is driving the first Terrapin. To help the gearing, he ran 10in (25cm) Mini wheels on the front and Vauxhall Viva 12in (30cm) on the rear.*

*Conceived in 1972, by Tim Conroy, the Timeire was raced in Special GT events by Rob Mason.*

tube, to which the glass-fibre body was bonded, carried the independent suspension. The transverse engine was mounted at the rear, driving the rear wheels.

An aluminium-bodied prototype was constructed in 1964 and, after being fitted with a Janspeed engine, the car was shaken down at Brands Hatch by Tony Lanfranchi. At the time, he was working as an instructor for the racing school and would do a couple of laps in the Unipower between lessons. While Lanfranchi was teaching the next pupil, Unger and Dare-Bryan would carry out the suggested adjustments, then Lanfranchi would do another two laps in it, before moving on to the next lesson.

The car was put into production in 1966 by Universal Power Drives, a company run by car enthusiast Tim Powell, whose main business was making heavy forestry equipment. Powell's great friend Andrew Hedges, a BMC works driver, was also a director of the company.

In total, about seventy-five Unipowers were built, of which approximately twenty had more sophisticated engines and sus-

pension for competition use. One of these was also sent to the USA for Group 6 driver Paul Richards, who was well known for his exploits in an Abarth.

Val Dare-Bryan's objective was to build an 850cc-engined car that would do 100mph (160kph), and he achieved this with an 850 Unipower. However, only one of this capacity was built, as customers all wanted the 1275 version.

## Geoff Mabbs

Three Unipowers were built by the factory as full-blown racers, with special bodies. Just one survives today, in the hands of Gerry Hulford, the long-time secretary of the Unipower Register. Janspeed and Unipower jointly developed the first, which was white and had a Janspeed 1071 engine and transmission.

On the weekend of 23 July 1967, Geoff Mabbs drove the first car in the GT race at the European Formula 2 meeting at Spain's Jarama circuit. He finished an excellent sixth overall, despite brake problems in the closing stages. He also competed with his usual verve during the Castle Combe GT race on 24 August, having cheekily dived round the outside of a Ford Mustang whose driver presumably did not see the low car coming. He finished the race third in the 1150 class. The following day, again at Combe, he took class win and fastest lap, despite a spin in the early stages of the race.

### John Miles

Emlyn Newman owned the EN Tool and Jig Company at Slough and was a great friend of Gordon Allen, whose firm Allen Crankshafts, noted for specialist cranks, was in the adjoining premises. Em, as Newman was known, and Allen went together to the Racing Car Show intending to buy a Ginetta to race. However, as a result of Allen's interest in the 'A' Series engine, they came away having ordered a Unipower.

Gordon Allen got Richard Longman to build up a 1300 engine which put out about 120bhp and the car was then tested by Roy Pike. John (Turner) Miles was also invited by Newman and Allen to a test drive at Silverstone and did about half a dozen races in the car. During this time, the Unipower went back to the factory for updating modifications. There was even talk that the pair had plans to drop a Ford Cosworth MA engine in the back of it but there is no proof that this ever happened.

Miles debuted the car in June 1967, recording fourth and fifth places in his two events. On his next outing he came home second behind a Ginetta G12. Miles was again at the wheel on 19 October for a race at Brands Hatch, where, notwithstanding the unfavourable class structure of the event, he managed second in the up-to-1500 category. He recalls that the car did not, in his opinion, handle too well and also remembers racing against the Janspeed version at Brands and Snetterton.

## Brian Harvey

In 1968, Brian Harvey, of *Cars and Car Conversions*, visited Janspeed to write an article about one of their tuning modifications and saw their Unipower standing in

*John Miles driving the Gordon Allen and Em Newman Unipower.*

the corner of the workshop. He was immediately attracted by the shape and asked Jan Odor how much was wanted for the car. A figure was mentioned and, after a week of haggling over the telephone, Harvey became the proud owner. The car was soon painted in Triple C livery and was campaigned in sprints, hillclimbs and slalom events during the 1968 season. (Sometimes, Harvey shared the driving with his wife Rachael, who was occasionally quicker than him.) The Unipower was also used as a promotional vehicle for the magazine, appearing at various functions and receptions.

Harvey had a lot of fun in the little car, but found that it could be a bit of a handful at times. Indeed, he had seen the resulting flat spots on the tyres when he bought the car. The competition handbrake was not really effective, so he resorted to carrying half a brick in the cockpit, which he would wedge under the offside rear wheel when he reached the start line. It was a difficult manoeuvre to execute when strapped in the car.

Harvey and the car recorded one win, two seconds and two fifth places, although it had been difficult to acclimatize to the right-hand gear change – because the gearbox was behind the driver, the gate was the 'wrong' way round. Breaking throttle cables was the car's weakness. Harvey recalls getting stranded at Druids during the Cambridge Motor Club Sprint at Brands, but he managed to fix it at the side of the track.

One evening, Brian Harvey answered the door to an unknown caller who stated that he wanted to buy the competition Unipower. His intention, he said, was to enter it for the Le Mans 24-Hour Race. He offered an amount 25 per cent higher than the price Harvey had paid for the car a few months before and Harvey was sorely tempted. He suggested that the man should come back with the cash and a trailer to transport the car. This happened and the car changed hands. The buyer was Piers Weld-Forrester, who later became the new owner of the company that made the cars.

## Piers Weld-Forrester

Piers Weld-Forrester took over in 1968, and began to trade as Unipower Cars. He immediately wanted to begin a programme of long-distance events. Chief Engineer Nick Ouroussoff and Ernest

*Brian Harvey with his ex-Janspeed Unipower GT, which he later sold to Piers Weld-Forrester, who subsequenly took over the manufacture of the car.*

Unger suggested that he should wait for a couple of years, until the new company was well established, but this fell on deaf ears. So the team set to and built a car for the 1969 Targa Florio, held in June. Andrew Hedges tested it for two days at Silverstone, concentrating on getting the cornering right, given the number of bends on the bumpy 44-mile (70-km) Targa road circuit.

Despite fuel problems, Hedges, who co-drove with Weld-Forrester, qualified the car fourth. After practice, the mechanic set about sorting out the problems and, thinking he had achieved this, took the car for a test drive in the early hours. He crashed a few miles from the circuit and the team were unable to start. Weld-Forrester was apparently not amused and promptly set off home with Hedges, after handing the errant spanner-man the keys to the Transit with a parting 'See you back in England!' The mechanic was forced to scrounge money and petrol to get the damaged racer back to the factory in Willesden.

Next, the Le Mans 24-Hours again beckoned and it was decided that, in order to capitalize on the Unipower's slippery shape on the long Mulsanne Straight, a new ultra-light car should be built. Peter Jackson at Specialised Mouldings, where all the Unipower bodies were produced, made a streamlined version using epoxy scrim reinforced with a $2^1/_2$in mesh of carbon fibre, which had only just come into use. At speed, the outline of the mesh could just be seen as the wind compressed the body. Meanwhile, Weld-Forrester came to an arrangement with BMC for the supply of a special engine.

This special Unipower was entered for Weld-Forrester to co-drive with customer Stan Robinson, who had bought the car. The engine eventually arrived on the evening the team was due to catch the midnight ferry and was hastily installed in the factory with the mechanics carrying out the finishing touches on the boat. The power unit had been supplied with twin $1^1/_2$in SUs but it was decided to use the Weber from the Targa engine, which had been taken out as a spare, as it was felt it would give more power.

Initially, practice did not go well. The car had been fitted with a brand-new set of JAP alloy wheels. Unfortunately, when one of the rims was bolted on, the paint cracked and the torque was not re-checked. This resulted in, firstly, the washer then the wheel nut working loose and the car lost a wheel towards the end of the Mulsanne Straight. Two distraught German race officials later described how they ran and ducked to avoid the errant wheel as it bounced off the trees, likening the incident to being trapped inside a giant pinball machine. Surprisingly, the wheel and tyre survived and were reunited with the car, which, owing to its lightness, had only suffered superficial damage to a front wishbone.

Piers Weld-Forrester subsequently set a practice time of 5:15, which compared favourably with the Renault Alpines at 5:12. During qualifying, the car had reached 140mph (225kph) down the Mulsanne Straight. The French, impressed with the Unipower's performance, christened it the 'Yellow Flea', in reference to its colour, size and nimbleness. However, the car failed to qualify.

The drivers of the larger cars at Le Mans were not entirely happy about having to share the circuit with smaller vehicles such as the Unipowers. During practice, Weld-Forrester cut one of them up. When he was in the pits after his stint, he noticed two heavyweight officials marching down the pit lane in a menacing manner. He commented to his mechanic, 'Someone's for it'; when they stopped at the Unipower pit, he discovered that that 'someone' was him. He was told, 'You have committed a crime, a serious crime.' The driver he had cut up had complained to the organizers.

In July, Piers Weld-Forrester was joined by his friend Dominic Martin for a crack at the Gran Premio de Mugello, an eight-lap race round a very demanding 41-mile (65.5-km) road circuit, for cars conforming to Groups 2, 3, 4 and 6. The pair qualified, but do not appear in the list of finishers. Weld-Forrester qualified for the GP of Denmark on 24 August. This was actually three fifteen-lap sprints round the Jyllandsring in Jutland.

A three-car team was mustered for the Nurburgring 500km on 7 September 1969, each fitted with a 1300cc engine. Weld-Forrester in the Targa Unipower and Stan Robinson in the Le Mans car were joined by Robert Hurst, who trailered out an incomplete car, which they were to

attempt to complete at the circuit. Only Robinson made the start. Weld-Forrester came in during practice with engine maladies, while the Hurst car was not finished in time. Robinson qualified and a fresh engine was built up for the race. The result was not recorded.

Weld-Forrester and Hurst took part in a twelve-hour race for Groups 4 and 6 cars at Montjuic Park, Barcelona, on 5 October. The pair had an excellent practice session, out-qualifying the Alan de Cadenet team, noted endurance specialists. During the race, the Unipower was a frequent pit-caller with oil-seal problems but, although it was running when the chequered flag came out, the car had not covered enough laps to qualify as a finisher.

Early in 1970, despite a full order book, production of this, the prettiest Mini-based GT car, ceased. The racing programme had disrupted the cash flow that is so vital for any small business.

*John Blanckley with Stan Robinson's ex-works Unipower prior to departing for the Nurburgring in 1970.*

Piers Weld-Forrester continued to race various machinery including a GT 40, in which he competed at Daytona and still drove his own Unipower, OYF 80F, with a special Jack Knight five-speed gearbox, on the road. He was killed taking part in a motorcycle race at Brands Hatch, on 31 October 1977. The following day's *Daily Mirror*'s headline read 'Princess Anne's former boyfriend killed in racing accident'. Having met the Princess at a weekend house party, he had, apparently, escorted her on occasions.

## John Blanckley

Stan Robinson continued to race the special Unipower and brought John Blanckley into the team for 1970. Following a wasted trip to the Targa Florio, where over-zealous officials would not allow the pair to try and qualify, Blanckley did a seat-of-his-pants lap at Spa and just qualified for the 1,000-km

race. He found the car had tremendous bump steer and, on that best lap, only just made it through one corner. The suspension was sorted for the next 1,000km race at the Ring, where, running the 1300 engine, Blanckley was second in the new up-to-1600cc class. The car really felt good.

As there was no longer to be an up-to-1300cc category, John Blanckley bought a crashed Brabham F2 car and grafted the engine, gearbox and rear suspension into the Unipower. It now had a 1600 Ford FVA engine and the gear lever was in the middle of the car, where Blanckley considered it belonged. Stan Robinson recorded a class win in a 500km race at Spa. Blanckley qualified second-fastest in class in the Nurburgring 500km, but something broke on the warm-up lap, resulting in a roll which wrote off the car. Blanckley later used the FVA and rear suspension in his Scorpion Group 6 car, which he still has to this day.

*Gerry Hulford proves the Unipower's tractability, getting inside an Elan and Porsche at Becketts, Silverstone, on 10 September 1977. The wide tyres were from a Tyrrell six-wheel Grand Prix car.*

## Gerry Hulford

Unipowers continued to appear in competitive events for some years. Peter Henshall sprinted one of the factory-built racers, which he purchased from Unipower distributor Monty and Ward of Edenbridge. This car is now owned by Gerry Hulford, who bought it from Henshall in August 1976. He raced it in his first Modsports event at a Brands Winter Clubbie in November of that year and continued to have good results in it when he was not racing his saloon in the Mini Se7en Championship.

The racing Unipowers were always considered to have been under-tyred. Regulations for the various Mini formulae restricted the rim and tyre width and, as Unipowers ran Mini tyres, they had to make do with what was available. However, during Hulford's time racing the car, Tyrrell launched their six-wheeled Grand Prix car and the small front wheels were the ideal size for a Unipower. Sueron Racing in Horley, who dealt in second-hand racing tyres, obtained a quantity. Hulford was able to get some and, having bought wider rims, ran his car on more suitable rubber.

BWRDC member Denny Hulford drove the car in one Modsports race at Silverstone. Having been persuaded to take part in the Brighton Speed Trials in 1978, Gerry Hulford won the up-to-1300cc class for five years running. In 1983, the class structure was changed to up-to-1600cc and Hulford missed out by just half a second. To ring the changes, the following year he entered his road Unipower.

By now, the Unipower had become eligible for Historic events and was driven in the HSCC championships. In 1986, Hulford managed almost a full season in this series and won the up-to-2 litre class at the end of the year.

Hulford's car was last seen in public at Le Mans in 1994, when it was eligible to take part in the pre-race parade of cars that had competed twenty-five years ago. For this event, it was back in its 'Yellow Flea' livery.

In Hulford's view, the basic car had definite understeer characteristics. In order to create sufficient foot room, an upside-down, left-hand-drive rack, specially modified by Cam Gears, had to be run forward of the hubs, which were also reversed. The angles that resulted from this configuration were not ideal, leading to understeer, so set-up was all critical.

The standard road car had discs on the front and drum brakes on the rear, while the racers had discs all round, with a modified choke cable used to operate a basic handbrake. The Unipower was the first production sports car to have a front air dam. This came about almost by accident. Working on the prototype in the Mira wind tunnel, Val Dare-Bryan was trying to eliminate the front-end lift. Everything had failed and, just to tick another idea off the list, he taped a sheet of card across the car below the grille. Not only did it kill the lift but, when he worked out the figures on the slide rule, he found the drag factor had been reduced to three-point-something. The front shape of the car was designed around the Triumph Spitfire windscreen; the cost of having a special screen made would have been prohibitive.

Peter Nash from Tunbridge Wells also campaigned a Unipower in the late 1970s, before selling the car to Chris Gow who used it on the hills. It is now in Japan. Tim Wright raced a road-going example with the HSCC.

# 9   Tuners and Drivers

Over the years, a number of drivers who have successfully tweaked their own cars, have been asked by other competitors to do work for them and, thus, founded their own tuning business. Similarly, a number of engineers involved in development were sucked in to become Mini competitors.

## DANIEL AND BUNTY RICHMOND

Daniel and Bunty Richmond of Downton Engineering were two of the best-known of those involved in the British racing scene in the 1960s. Bunty, the Honourable Veronica Romer, was author Somerset Maugham's niece and her husband was the son of Sir Daniel Richmond. Not only did Downton do much of the early Mini

engine development work for BMC, but many former members of staff learnt their craft at the company and went on to establish their own tuning firms. They all made a significant contribution to the continued search for more power from the BMC 'A' Series engine.

Having worked on aircraft research during the war, Daniel Richmond acquired the Downton Engineering Works in 1947. The company had originally been run as an agricultural engineers, but the Richmonds changed the emphasis and Downton Engineering was soon repairing and tuning Bentleys, Bugattis and Lagondas. Daniel Richmond became a familiar sight driving his own Lagonda Rapier; it was a very fast car, thanks to its supercharger and the special Downton cams.

*Daniel Richmond had a liking for fine things; his penchant for vintage champagne was well known, but not everyone knew about his prized Ferrari, FX 9. He is pictured outside his Downton Engineering showroom in Wiltshire.*

Daniel Richmond had a hand in setting up what is now one of England's most famous hillclimbs, at Wiscombe. In 1957, he first drove landowner Richard Chichester up what was to be the course in his Lotus 7A. When Chichester had recovered from his fright, he agreed it would make an excellent course. The following year, the West Hants and Dorset Car Club ran the first-ever event there. Richmond regularly competed in the Lotus and, later, in a Venom Formula Junior, both with 'A' Series power. While he was at home on the hills, Daniel Richmond never raced any of his cars because Bunty would not let him. She also hillclimbed, in a V8 Allard.

When the 'A' Series engine was introduced, it just clicked with Richmond and he seemed to form a natural affinity with it. The company's name became synonymous with first placings in all branches of motor sport and it was one of the first to prepare Minis for competition. At about this time, the business outgrew the original premises and moved 100 yards up the road, to a new purpose-built factory and workshop.

Towards the end of 1961, Downton was doing development work for the projected Mini Cooper S and its driver Jimmy Blumer was asked to compete in a race at Clermont-Ferrand in central France. The prototype 1220cc engine that was used did not have the 100-ton steel crank that was a vital ingredient of the production S engine, so his brief was to keep the revs below 6,800 and get a finish; he did it. Afterwards, he and Daniel Richmond prepared a detailed report on the car's performance and Blumer received a letter of thanks from Alec Issigonis.

In the 1962 Targa Florio, Bernard Cahier and Prince Metternich drove a Downton-prepared Austin Mini Cooper, 176 NWL, to second in the up-to-two-litre Prototype Class, setting an impressive 50.04mph (80.06kph) average speed. For half the race the gauge had showed zero oil pressure and the car had lost second and third gears. Apparently, the various tyre manufacturers had been falling over themselves to supply free rubber for this outing. In the same year, Dutchman Rob Slotemaker, driving Daniel Richmond's Cooper 777 MCG, scored a win in the Touring Car race during the Autosport World Cup Meeting at Zandvoort. After the event, Daniel and Bunty used the car, in race trim, to go sightseeing. The following year, Slotemaker won the 1300 Class of the European Touring Car Championship.

Daniel Richmond competed in the early 850 Mini, UHR 850, from 1959 until 1965. During this period he had class wins on the hills; eventually, UHR became Bunty's everyday transport. Daniel, who would put his head on one side when revealing a secret, apparently did so when telling a friend about taking UHR up a hill: 'I always have to hold it in first gear, you know.'

Bunty Richmond had names for some of the company Minis. The green racing S was 'Sophie', the large-engined pick-up used for towing the racers was 'William'; it was also green. Downton Engineering's Mini van was yellow, so that was christened 'Marigold'.

Downton's premises were on the north side of Downton Village, just outside the 30mph limit signs. Daniel Richmond's method of checking a Mini after he had tuned it was to drive out of the doors and gun along the main road flat out; if he was not doing a hundred before he got to the derestriction signs on the south side, he knew that something was wrong! He had to be careful not to use this test too often, for fear of offending locals. On the right-hand side, going into the yard, was the experimental shop, which was strictly out of bounds to customers and all but a select handful of staff.

Downton dealt exclusively with tuning BMC vehicles from 1960 and Daniel Richmond was a consultant to the company, becoming very close to Alec Issigonis who had a Downton-modified Cooper as his personal transport. Downton was the only tuning company to have BLMC approval and, in 1970, it had sixty employees and a turnover in excess of £250,000, with 30 per cent of its production exported. Daniel had a penchant for vintage champagne and the landlord of his local in Downton, the Bull Inn, always had a bottle of Krug on ice for him behind the bar. His other favourite watering hole was the Bat and Ball at nearby Breamore, which he nicknamed the Truncheon and Testicle, where he and Jimmy Blumer would drink many a Lowenbrau.

While amenable Daniel had the technical knowhow, it was Bunty's business acumen that kept the company afloat. According to former employees, she ruled the place with a rod of iron. If her husband spent too much time talking to staff or customers in the factory, it was not unusual for Bunty to grab him by the ear and march him back to his office. Everything had to be paid for before it left the premises, no matter who the customer was. On one occasion, Bill McGovern was short of funds and tried to get a free cylinder head for his very successful racing Cooper S. When Bunty refused, the staff had a whip-round so that McGovern could compete in his next event.

## David Dorrington and David Miller

David Dorrington, now proprietor of Maniflow, joined Downton as an apprentice aged 16. Bunty was perhaps slightly more amenable to someone like him,

whom she had seen grow up with the company, but this did not stop her taking him to task over his time-keeping. After constant references to his late arrival, she called him into the office and warned him that, if it looked like he was going to be late the next day, he should not bother to come in at all.

Dorrington decided to call her bluff and stayed at home, but returned the day after. The expected summons to the office came at about 10.30am. Following the lecture, Bunty put a brown envelope and a cardboard box on her desk, telling David that choosing one of these items would determine his future with the company. He pondered the two packages and decided that the box looked more interesting. Inside was an alarm clock. He never knew whether the envelope contained a calendar, or his cards. Bunty had made her point. Another apprentice was not so lucky. He was sacked on the spot for putting his pie and chips on the roof of a customer's car.

David Miller, another Downton employee, also tried his hand at racing. He started with a car created from the front half of a wrecked Mini van, to which he welded the rear of an 850 saloon. He later graduated to a new maroon 850 De Luxe, which he and fellow employee Peter Hepponstall converted to a racer by building a 999cc engine. This car was raced complete with full interior trim and bumpers and scored some decent results, which led to Miller having a few drives in Downton 1275 cars.

## The Downton Twin-Engined Mini

Encouraged and assisted by Alec Issigonis, Daniel Richmond conceived a twin-engined car for the 1963 Targa Florio in Sicily. The Mini, 931 RFC, had one engine in the orthodox position, which drove the front wheels, while another in the boot drove the rear. The thinking was that four-wheel drive would be ideal for the twisty mountain-road circuit. Sir John Whitmore and Belgian Paul Frere (whose book *Competition Driving* had just been published in English) were to be the drivers. Whitmore did a 47-minute practice lap around the 44-mile (70-km) road circuit, but, noting how high the tyre wear was, they decided they would have to reduce this to 50 minutes for the race.

On the big day, the radiator header tank for the rear engine split just before the start. Five laps into the race, with pit stops for water after each lap, the offending engine lost all its water. Whitmore was forced to disconnect the gear linkage on the circuit, leaving a two-wheel drive Mini with a spare engine as ballast in the boot. They still finished twenty-fifth from fifty-five starters, fifth in class and both drivers received a cup. The car was then driven home to Longbridge, still on one engine.

## The Tragic End of Downton

When Leyland pulled the plug on racing, Daniel Richmond began to tire of the business and took more interest in trout fishing, a hobby learnt from his mother. He had fishing articles published in *The Field*, and also began to spend a great deal of time at his beloved Beehive Cottage, a sixteenth-century thatched building in Devon, close to the single-bank fishing rights he owned on the River Torr. Later, he bought the opposite bank as well, telling his great fishing companion Dr David Blackridge that BMC had paid for it. His consultancy fee for developing the MG 1300 cylinder head had provided the funds. There was also a rumour that his frequent visits to Devon might have had something to do with a lady friend in the area.

Sadly, in 1974, Daniel Richmond died in hospital, aged just 50. Bunty carried on for a while, further developing one of the ex-Cooper Britax cars but, when this was rolled, she called a halt. The writing was on the wall. The business was not the same without Daniel Richmond's flair and key staff members had started to leave. Despite her blustering manner, Bunty probably missed Daniel more than she realized. Ever-methodical, she started to wind down the business, paid all the bills up to date and finally closed the doors of Downton Engineering, late in 1975.

The death of her dog was the last straw and, in July 1977, Bunty committed suicide. She left a note for the cleaning lady telling her where to find the body. Among other instructions was the wish that her beloved UHR 850 should either go to a museum or be destroyed by fire. Fortunately, it is now in the Heritage Collection at Gaydon.

In this sad way, one of the success stories of the 1960s racing scene came to a tragic end.

## PETER BALDWIN

The rolling-road maestro at the Marshall Motor Group of Cambridge, Peter Baldwin, has been racing BMC/Leyland/Rover vehicles for over thirty seasons. Having read articles about people racing their everyday cars, he saw Julian Vereker's Mini advertised and bought it in 1967. However, after about a week of driving on the road, Baldwin relegated it for circuits only. Following two Duxford Sprints at the end of the season in 1968, he started his twenty-three-year stint in Special Saloons, running in the 850 class.

The following year, he won the Janspeed Championship and, in 1970, took the TEAC Championship and the

Llandow-based Fram Filters series. Part of the prize was a three-day trip to Mallorca. Fram did a film about the series and sent the film crew down to Cambridge to record Baldwin changing a filter for the closing sequence. Baldwin won thirteen out of the twenty races he entered that year.

The car now had a 999cc engine. At Thruxton, Baldwin managed to get hold of two of the newly available 10in (25cm) Firestone slicks, which he put on the front. These gave too much grip and he went off in a big way, destroying the Vereker shell. The car was rebuilt into a new shell and named 'Baby B' by Baldwin's mechanic Paul Herrell. In 1973, Baldwin bought Sedric Bell's one-litre Mini-Ford engine, which proved to be quick but inconsistent in 'Baby B2' over the next three seasons. He took the Esso Uniflo class that year and again in 1974 and 1976. During that period, he also tried an ex-works Group 2 with eight-port 1300 power. The 8-porter eventually went in Baby B2, which became BB3.

In 1975, Peter Baldwin saw Gordon Allen's 1300 Mini-BDA unit at the Racing Car Show and, after two weeks of negotiations, persuaded him he was the driver to realize the project's full potential. This he did, creating Baby B4, but it took three years to get real reliability. At Brands, the ring gear became detached from the lightweight flywheel, sawed its way out of the bell housing and then sliced through the Clubman front, followed by the distributor. At another meeting, a rod went through the side, necessitating yet another new block, which Baldwin had to make from scratch as the pattern had been lost. Despite these setbacks, he recorded some good results.

Baldwin's friend Graham Goode was racing an Escort and had good connections with Cosworth. Through him, Baldwin dis-

covered that he could increase the compression ratio and use bigger valves combined with slide injection; the power output increased to 200bhp. In July 1976, this block had to go in a new shell (BB5) after a big shunt at Mallory. In 1977, Baldwin won the Esso Uniflo, Century Oils and Forward Trust 1000 Championships.

For 1978, Peter Baldwin purchased Reg Ward's original space-frame Mini and fitted the fully sorted BDA. This became the final one of the line. Baldwin beat Nick Whiting's Escort by 50 points to win the Rivet Supply title. In 1979 and 1980, he competed in the 1275GT Challenge and, just to make life interesting, he continued to campaign the Special Saloon too. This resulted in hectic commuting between circuits: if the schedule was tight, he would fly from one track to the other. Roger

*Peter Baldwin works on his car in the paddock prior to the saloon race at the Silverstone International Trophy Meeting on 6 May, 1971.*

Clark had his own plane and airstrip at his house near Mallory and would often fly Baldwin to the next meeting. On one occasion, he came into land at Brands to see his race formed up on the grid and only just made it to his car in time.

On these hectic days, it was not always possible to practise at both circuits. In such cases, provided he had raced at the track within four weeks, the organizing club would allow him to start at the back of the grid with a ten-second penalty. A 1275GT pole at Mallory went to waste when, owing to an adverse weather report, a pilot failed to collect him following the Brands Special Saloon race. Baldwin won the class and was second overall in the 1979 Wendy Wools and Rivet Supply Championships. He came fifth in the 1275GTs. In the next year, he took three outright titles in Special Saloons and was third in the 1275GTs.

Peter Baldwin did his last Special Saloon race in the Mini at Brands on 19 November 1990, where he recorded yet another class win. The car was then sold and later went to Japan. Baldwin then moved on to compete in the Metro and Rover GTi series. From 1968 to 1991, he had taken 320 overall and class wins. He

returned to Minis in 1995, when he did the Miglia series in a borrowed car and was sixth in the championship. The following year, he bought a car and, having only moved the seat, won first time out in it at Donington. He was championship runner up in 1996 and 1998.

Baldwin's best race ever was in the 1275GTs at Aintree on 4 August 1979. He was part of a four-car battle for the lead with Steve Soper, Steve Harris and Chris Lewis. Eventually, he shook off Lewis and then ran neck and neck with the two Steves for the last four laps. All three were giving it 110 per cent. Despite coming 'only' third, Baldwin is adamant that this race was the one that gave him the greatest pleasure.

## BILL BLYDENSTEIN

The oversteering characteristics of his previous racer, a Borgward Isabella, did not prevent Bill Blydenstein from getting to grips with Mini Coopers. He road tested a very early one for John Cooper round the streets of Surbiton and also drove the first racing version at a Brands test session. In 1962, he signed as the fourth driver for the

*Peter Baldwin in 1983, driving his Ford-powered space-frame Mini in a Donington GT round, keeping ahead of Walter Robinson and Mick Hill in his V8 VW Beetle.*

Cooper team, paired with Tony Maggs to drive at selected European and non-championship British races.

Blydenstein's first outing in the 997 Cooper, in April 1962, was the Coupe de Bruxelles, where he and his team-mate, local driver Lucien Bianchi, were quicker than everyone else in practice. It was a Le Mans-style start, which Blydenstein had never experienced before. When the flag dropped, he tripped over a kerb and nearly fell over. He got into the car and pulled away, then realized he had failed to fasten his harness. Having promised his wife he would never race without belts after they had saved his life in a previous accident, he had to slow in order to do them up.

This pause allowed Bianchi in the sister car to get by, but Blydenstein was soon in its slipstream. John Cooper had decreed that, after the start, his drivers should hold station until the last lap, as he did not want them taking each other out. He said that on lap nine he would show them a spare wheel and this was the signal that it was every man for himself. When it became apparent that the signal was not forthcoming, Blydenstein guessed when he was on lap nine, nipped out of the slipstream, and beat his team-mate in the dash to the line.

The Cooper team fielded four Minis at the British GP meeting at Aintree on 21 July. As Bill Blydenstein was not a championship contender, he was allocated a car that had been well used. It was the only time he recalls a Cooper works engine letting go; it went at about the half-way stage and he was able to observe bits of piston following him as he pulled off the circuit.

Things were a lot better at the Oulton Park Gold Cup meeting on 1 September, where Cooper entered Bill Blydenstein, John Love and Denny Hulme. Despite a practice session in which he was four seconds off the pace, Blydenstein finished second in class to Love and shared a new lap record with his team-mate. The improvement was as a result of a chat with Love after practice, when he discovered that his fellow driver did not stick to the prescribed rev limits. In the race, Blydenstein kept it in second a little longer exiting a couple of bends and made up the deficit.

Blydenstein's final race of the year was Boxing Day Brands, where his Mini was fitted with a new, more powerful 997 engine, which put out 76bhp. Practice was a dream and, revelling in the extra power, he set the fastest lap in the class. During the lunch break, he noticed a few stray snowflakes but ignored the team's advice

*Le Mans-style start at Brussels in 1962. Bill Blydenstein stumbles on his way to the car, however, he went on to beat his team-mate and win the race.*

to change his near-bald racing tyres for wets. He was sure that the weather would hold until after the race. Unfortunately, he was wrong and, in what had otherwise been an excellent season, he finished fifth in class.

In 1963, the Blydenstein family moved to Hertfordshire and, while Bill was trying to consolidate his tuning business in a new area, motor racing had to take a back seat. He continued to develop his cylinder heads and did a certain amount of work on the Cooper F1 cars. He soon outgrew the garden shed and built a Marley double garage at the bottom of the garden.

Blydenstein did some work with John Aley, who was also running his business from a garage at home. Indirectly, it was Aley who was to get Blydenstein racing again on a regular basis. He sold him a tired 850 Mini for £150, originally as transport for his wife when he was working away from home. Soon he was trying his latest tuning ideas out on the car and it was not long before he was entering the odd sprint. These went fairly well, so the occasional race was added to the itinerary. At a very wet Snetterton, he got his Blydenstein-tuned 850 in among the Ss. The die was cast and he did a deal with Aley on a lightweight rolling shell. The car was to be entered as an Aley Mini, with Blydenstein driving and doing the development work.

The car started the 1966 season running a 649 cam, Blydenstein head with Weber and Downton manifold, S/C C/R gears and either a 4.6 or 4.9 final drive using a Jack Knight LSD. This configuration gave the power unit tremendous torque. The Mini was lowered by reducing the length of the trumpet links to the cones and it was set up with negative camber all round. At the front this was achieved by stretching the bottom links, while the rear suspension bracket was relocated to give the required effect. The tyres were mounted on $4^{1}/_{2}$in (11.25cm) wheels, but the use of Minifins and spacers vastly improved the cornering.

First time out at Brands, Blydenstein was up against Unett and Lanfranchi in the new Fraser Imps. He finished third behind the pair, well ahead of the next Mini. Next time out, at Snetterton, he was second, just beaten by George Caley in another Aley Mini. Meanwhile, Blydenstein had been working on what he regarded as the ultimate spec 850 engine. A virtually 'square' configuration was needed to keep the revs up. To achieve this, the block was bored to 64.5mm and the stroke of the crank reduced to 65mm, which brought the capacity to just under 850cc. A Cooper S damper and Duplex gear were utilized to help the engine take the expected frequent use of 8,000rpm.

The final pieces of the jigsaw were a specially designed cam profile, which Bill christened the BB 340/320, and a hand-picked 997 head that received the full

*Early days of Blydenstein Engineering: (left to right) Alan Jackson, Blydenstein, Han Arersloot and Don Hagger in the first workshop, a Marley concrete garage erected at the bottom of Blydenstein's garden.*

Blydenstein treatment with lightened S valves and rocker gear. A compression ratio of 12.5:1 and a usable band of 6,000 to 9,000rpm saw the power output of 80bhp. Now it was time to put the theory to the test. At a Woburn hillclimb he achieved a class win by three seconds (an excellent margin for a win on the hills). This was followed by a resounding win at the Mallory Park race meeting on Easter Monday.

At the start of British Summer Time, Blydenstein forgot to put his clock forward on the Saturday night and arrived too late for his practice session on Sunday morning. Qualifying out of session meant starting from the back of the grid and, knowing all eyes would be upon him, he made an inspired start. By Druids on lap one he was up to sixth place, having scythed through the field off the line. Next tour, he overtook Ron Mason for fifth and lap six saw him up to third, which was where he finished. Those Imps again!

The season continued well but, during a hectic dice with John Anstead's Fiat Abarth on the Brands long circuit (Anstead had beaten Blydenstein at Snetterton a couple of weeks before), a con-rod pinch bolt snapped. The engine blew in the biggest possible way, resulting in retirement not only from the race, but also from Mini racing. Funds were sufficient for a rebuild but not for a continued programme and the car was sold to Gerry Marshall towards the end of the season. However, in 1967 Blydenstein helped Bob Fox win the Mini Se7en series (*see* Chapter 4), and his varied development work continues to this day.

## NICK COLE

Service manager at Nerus, 1968 to 1971; Senior Engineer at KAD, 1992 to 1998 –

these are just two extracts from the CV of a man who started his motor sport taking his Smoke Grey Mini, RKM 348, up the hill at Bodiam in East Sussex on 17 October 1964. The young Nick Cole was a bit miffed that he was beaten by a 40-year-old expert by the name of Wally Pratt, but admits the experience was good for the soul.

Nerus – the company name came from the backward spelling of the name of the Suren family – was located at the back of the Rother Ironworks, in Rye. The Surens, from nearby Winchelsea, owned the Rother Ironworks and, like Nerus boss Frank Webb, were huge car enthusiasts. Nick Cole went to Nerus after a first job in nuclear power came to an end after less than a year and alternative employment at Weslakes failed to materialize. Originally destined to work in the drawing office at Weslakes, he arrived at Nerus to find out that Frank Webb had in mind a more hands-on approach to the tuning business. He was put to work in the grinding shop, learning all about gas-flowing cylinder heads. The hours were 9 to 6 Monday to Saturday and the pay 1/9d an hour, but Cole describes it as the finest thing he ever did. In the firm's heyday, twelve men worked in the grinding shop.

After six months, Cole got involved in the research side of the company, working on a two-litre BMW engine to go in a racing Elva. When Keith St John had engine problems with his Radio London-backed Elva, Cole was sent to Silverstone to sort it out. Arriving in the early hours, he soon had the engine stripped down and discovered that it needed a new rod and piston. He was able to replace them from the selection of spares he had taken with him. The problem was how to balance them; someone suggested that the village Post Office might have accurate scales, so, at the crack of dawn, Cole was banging on the door. His knocks were eventually answered by a 'What do you want?', accompanied by two barrels of a shotgun poked through the letterbox. Having persuaded the postmaster it wasn't a robbery, Cole was allowed in to weigh the components and file them off to match. Then he returned to the paddock and put the engine together.

This trip to Silverstone gave Nick Cole the racing bug. After the climb at Bodiam in 1964, he took part in motor sport of all disciplines, enjoying some backing from Nerus. Of course, he modified his own engine and cylinder heads.

During practice for a Lydden sprint in 1965, Cole had problems and assumed he would play no further part in the proceedings. In the paddock, he was approached by a complete stranger who was most insistent that Cole should borrow his car to do the timed runs. They

stripped out the seats and Cole swapped over the cylinder head, carbs, wheels and tyres from his own car. After the event, all the bits were changed back so that the man could drive home. By now, Cole had decided that, if he were to get anywhere, he really needed a proper racing Mini. Fate now took a hand.

A local woman parked her Mini on the bank of the River Rother in Rye and, on returning to the car, started it in reverse. She and the car ended up in the river and both needed to be rescued. Nick Cole bought the salvage for £35, to use as the basis for his racer in a joint project with Tony Barnard. The car was transported back to the garage at Cole's home and built up for the 1966 season, when the learning curve continued. Needing to run in the engine, Cole rang the local constabulary and asked if it would be all right to put some miles on it by driving round the

*Nick Cole rounding Druids Hairpin at Brands Hatch in 1968. This self-built car was considerably developed during his time working for Nerus Engineering in Rye.*

lanes on the Romney Marshes. They agreed, provided he promised not to venture on to the main roads. The car was, of course, not taxed and hardly complied with the Road Traffic Act.

Cole recalls a similar incident when he was working for Trojan McLaren in London. In the early hours, they had driven an unregistered racing car round the block; in view of the late hour, they had omitted to consult the law. They woke up a resident who called the police and who, when asked for the car's registration number, replied, 'It was number 3.' Eventually turning up at the workshop, the police were suitably amused.

Towards the end of 1968, Cole found himself leading the TEAC Drivers Championship. He had also just bent the car rather badly. Determined to go for the title, he bought an early Mini Cooper, CPE 290B, part-stripped it out and transferred over the racing bits from his other car. The championship went to the last round at Lydden and it was between Cole and Turner-driver Geoff Darryn. Each had to win their respective races to take the crown. Cole got to the front of his event on lap 9, with Alan Rogers in second; he eased off for the final lap, thinking that his pal Alan would surely not deny him the championship. Another valuable lesson was learnt as he was beaten in a neck-and-neck dash to the line! He was second in the championship.

The annual televized Boxing Day meeting was also held at Lydden that year and the BBC had engaged none other than Graham Hill to do the commentary. Nick Cole had a good dice for the lead with John Calvert in his Imp and, by chance, his parents, who hitherto disapproved of his racing, happened to be watching at home. Seeing their son's achievement apparently brought them round.

The following year, Nick Cole decided not to do a championship but to compete in selected National and International races, in particular, the saloon events that supported the Bank Holiday F 5000 series rounds. He bought a new 998cc engine for £29 from local BMC dealer Skinners of Rye and, later, a 1275, which cost him £44. A Jack Knight limited slip diff (£32) was also added to the equipment. He now had the option of racing the car in three different classes, swapping engines to suit available races. The season produced good results.

Nick Cole's five years in Minis netted him fifteen wins and many other top-three placings. He enjoyed the wet, believing, like many, that it was a great leveller. He went on to drive in many other formulae and returned to Minis in 1996, when he did three races in a Miglia. His more recent involvement included building the special KAD monocoque Mini that Bill Sollis used to win the Fastest Mini in the World race during the thirty-fifth birthday celebrations at Silverstone on 29 August 1994. The car has now been sold to a Japanese collector and Cole has subsequently made three trips to Japan to check it over, prior to a demonstration run at the Mini Festival there. Both Bill Sollis and Richard Longman have driven it at this event.

## PAUL GAYMER: BOOPSPEED

Clive Trickey's racing Mini was one of the first to be worked on by Paul Gaymer, when he was employed by George Lawrence at Ridgeway Garage. Gaymer remembers testing the racing Minis of both Trickey and Lawrence up and down the Farnham by-pass, with a set of trade plates and a motorcycle bulb horn tied to the window. The stopwatch was set up in the lay-by beside the Bull at Bentley, along with a toolbox for running adjustments. On a good day, the 1300 Mini would reach about 125mph (200kph) – who needed a rolling road?

Inspired by Clive Trickey's success, Paul Gaymer built his own Mini Se7en in 1969, and he used it to take third and first places in two pre-season Free Formula 850 races. Encouraged, he entered the Se7en Championship and won the first round at Thruxton on 27 April. Two more wins and a second place followed and he arrived for the next race at Castle Combe full of expectation. Not only did he boil the car, but he also managed to roll it in the same race. His woes continued as, during the inversion, the battery acid leaked from the boot into the cockpit and burnt holes in his jeans, which had been borrowed from his girlfriend!

By the end of the season, Gaymer had eight wins and two second places to his credit and this won him the 1969 Mini Se7en Championship, ahead of Clive Trickey, no less. His exploits had also put £90 prize money in his pocket. Having conquered the Se7ens, he put a 1300 engine in the same car and, from 1970 to 1972, competed in both the Osram and Triplex Special Saloon Championships. He was class winner in the Osram in 1970 and fourth in the Triplex. He took the Triplex Class in 1971, with a second in the Osram. He only managed eight outings in 1972, and then hung up his helmet until 1977.

Paul Gaymer had set up Boopspeed, his Mini-repairing, building and tuning concern, in 1969. At first, he ran it from a shed at the bottom of his garden, but the council moved him on for operating without planning permission. In 1971, he moved to new premises – the building where his father ran a motorcycle business. Gaymer's trademark was to become the BOOP number plates that appeared on the racing Minis that he built. At the last count, he was up to BOOP 23, the numbers having started in 1978.

The Miglia Championship was the next target and, over the winter of 1976, a car was built ready for the new season. Repeating his previous form, Gaymer chalked up eight wins, six seconds and two thirds, and took the 1977 crown. The car finished every race and the engine was neither rebuilt nor removed from the car all year. He was also the highest points scorer in all three Mini championships and won a brand-new 1275GT.

Feeling he needed a bit more of a challenge for 1978, he did the Miglias in his 1977 car and built another to drive in the 1275GT series as well. The opening round of both series was at Castle Combe on 22 March, when he put both cars on pole in consecutive practice sessions. Throughout the season he often jumped straight out of one car into the next, learning to adjust quickly to the different handling characteristics. He was also persuaded by his brother Nigel, known as 'Boot' Gaymer, to build him a Mini Se7en, based on an ex-Dave Sambell car. The two brothers often ran three cars at a meeting.

Combining three projects was ambitious, but Paul Gaymer still managed second in the GTs and third in the Miglias. He often wonders whether he could have won if he had concentrated on the 1275, and gone down in history as the only driver to take all three Mini championships. The 1979 season started well with a Miglia race win at Thruxton, but a knee injury sustained at the next round, while changing a customer's clutch, put Gaymer out for the rest of the year. He returned in 1980, coming second at the end of the year to Roland Nix, and from 1980–84 he ran in the Metro Challenge.

Gaymer has never employed anyone, and has, single-handed, built all twenty-three Boopspeed Minis, including champi-

*Paul Gaymer of Boopspeed raced mainly in the one-make Mini Se7en Racing Club Series but in 1971 he tried his hand in Special Saloons using this 1300S with an eight-port head. He won the Triplex Special Saloon Car Series that year.*

onship-winning cars for Chris Lewis and Chris Hampshire and the immaculately turned out Pearce Signs cars for Chris Dobson. He has also built many transverse and in-line 'A' Series engines, including several for Sprites. In 1998, he was commissioned to restore George Harrison's custom-built Mini, which was displayed at the first Goodwood Revival Meeting.

## IAN HARGREAVES

According to his mother, Ian Hargreaves was the only child in the district to wear out the tyres on his Mobo scooter, so he was just bound to end up in motor sport. Hargreaves bought his first Mini Cooper for £200 in 1973 and sprinted it on a shoe-string for a couple of years to learn about the car before going racing. He recalls an early event at Blackbushe, when he and his wife Pam drove to the sprint and stripped the seats out before competing in the Modified Saloon class. He had been advised that, despite running on street-legal Rally Specials, the Cooper's Weber and 731 cam meant that he must compete

in the modified category. He was third in class, beating the Cutty Sark Mini, which had a short-stroke engine with split Webers.

By 1977, Ian Hargreaves also had a 1300 short-stroker and was doing about five races a year, which was all his budget would allow. He tended to race at Brands, Castle Combe, Lydden, Thruxton and Silverstone, which were all easily accessed from his home in Surrey, competing in Wendy Wool rounds and also the BOAC 1000. He had a hell of a dice at Castle Combe with John Morgan's 3.8 Jaguar, which had the crowd on their feet for all ten laps; it was real David and Goliath stuff. He finished seventh overall, won the class and set the fastest class lap. Hargreaves also remembers Brands Hatch commentator Brian Jones being quite beside himself when the Hargreaves Mini had a battle with the one-litre Imps of Kevin Law, Bill McGovern and John Mooredit. It was another race that Hargreaves thoroughly enjoyed.

A self-employed qualified engineer, Hargreaves worked as a purchasing agent in the electronics and petrochemical

*Ian Hargreaves' Avonbar Mini in action at Goodwood in 1978, the year he was joint second to Jonathan Palmer in the BARC Drivers Championship.*

industries. When it became apparent that it would be to his financial advantage to set himself up as a limited company, he visited an off-the-shelf company specialist to see what names they could offer him. Towards the top he saw 'Avonbar' and had the name registered to him.

As he became more involved with tuning Minis, he started putting Avonbar decals on the side of his car and set up Avonbar Racing full time in 1975. Chris Hampshire's 1981 Mini Miglia Championship-winning 1000cc engine was built by Avonbar and, as a result, Hargreaves bought himself a Miglia from a customer who was retiring. He rebuilt this and did a few events in it between 1980 and 1982, along with his 1300 car, but obviously found there was a great power difference. In 1982, a friend borrowed it and rolled it into a ball at Cadwell Park. Not having been in the position to do a full championship before, Hargreaves competed in the Metro Challenge in 1983.

Nowadays, Avonbar mainly supplies and manufactures parts for Minis, but still does a certain amount of tuning work for customers.

## STEVE HARRIS

Local resident Steve Harris was an apprentice at Downton Engineering from 1964 to 1971, when he left to go into partnership with Richard Longman and George Toth. In 1973, when Harris was still doing work for Longmans but on a self-employed basis, Bunty Richmond asked if he would go back to Downton. He accepted, partly in order to cut down his daily travelling. Part of the deal was limited sponsorship for Harris to race a Mini Miglia.

When Downton was being wound down following Daniel Richmond's untimely death, Steve Harris bought some of the machinery and, in 1974, set up Steve

*Steve Harris driving his Special Saloon Mini at Castle Combe in May 1978.*

Harris Engineering in Cranbourne, where he continues to trade to this day. In 1976, using the Miglia car with a 1300 engine, and running at quite a weight disadvantage compared with the other competitors, Harris won the BRSCC South Western Special Saloon Car Championship. Next, he built a 1275GT and won the 1978 championship, beating the likes of Peter Baldwin, Jeremy Hampshire, Chris Lewis, Steve Soper and Paul Taft. Harris reckons that, during his time in Minis, he chalked up about forty-five wins. Hampshire also went on to win the series using one of his engines.

Ian Bax bought the 1275GT and, having agreed terms with Harris over the telephone, drove over to collect the car. Unfortunately, Harris had been out at lunch-time with the lads and had 'crashed out' by the time Bax arrived. Harris' friend and fellow Mini racer Roland Nix happened to be driving past at the time and saw Bax peering through the gates. Being a helpful sort of chap, he asked if he could help. He soon opened up, took the money and helped Bax load up before closing the gates and going on his way. When Harris eventually surfaced, he was horrified to find the GT missing. Its disappearance was only explained when Nix rang to tell him he had sold the car and that he had the money for him.

For the following season, Steve Harris moved to Metros, but he was spending so much time doing customers' engines that his own racing had to take a back seat. More recently, he has taken to the hills, driving various customers' cars, and is building a hillclimb Mini for 1999.

## RICHARD LONGMAN

Richard Longman always had an interest in cars but, after a couple of early engineering jobs, one with Gordon Rouse, he ended up as a hospital technician. Bunty Richmond had broken her ankle and, happening to see Longman at the hospital, asked why he was no longer working with cars. She suggested that he should come to see her husband about a job at Downton, and he started there in 1964.

During Longman's four years with the company, Downton strengthened its alliance with BMC. Longman started to race his own 1293 Cooper S in 1966, securing two wins at his first meeting, at Llandow. He worked on customers' vehicles by day and then rushed home to prepare his own racer in the evenings. Jimmy McClements, who worked for Downton's Irish agent, Kane of Comber, used to come to the factory once a year to be updated on the latest innovations. He recalls that most of the local car crowd had Coopers, in various stages of tune and that they frequently met at the Kings Head at Redlynch. He describes the noise after closing time as unbelievable, as all the Coopers were thrashed home across the New Forest.

*Richard Longman's
Special Saloon Mini
Ford competing in a
Simoniz round in
September 1974.*

In 1968, Janspeed persuaded Richard Longman to go and work for them, with a Janspeed-backed drive as part of the job package. He capitalized on this, taking the 1000-to-1300cc class in the Osram-GEC Championship, coming third overall, just two points behind the winner.

Downton wanted him back and tempted him with a sponsorship package that would involve driving one of the ex-Cooper Britax cars. His races in that car produced twenty-seven wins (more than any other club racer), and secured him the Osram-GEC Championship overall. At Thruxton, on 25 May 1969, he won the 100-km race, despite an enforced pit stop for spilling fuel. He had a hell of a dice with Geoff Mabbs having his first outing in the Janspeed car that Longman had driven the previous season.

In 1970, Longman went Group 2 in an ex-Cooper Downton car. He won at the Brands race of the champions round, but the car was written off in its fourth race when the servo failed at Silverstone. Longman found things at Downton were

not as they had been; Daniel Richmond was losing interest and Bunty seemed to be finding it hard to cope.

In 1971, Richard Longman, George Toth and Steve Harris forged a partnership and set up Longman and Company in Christchurch. They continued to do a lot of work on Mini Coopers and picked up most of Downton's old customers when the company finally closed. Inlet manifolds and cylinder heads were further developed, and soon the name Longman was replacing Downton as the winning Mini engine-builder throughout the world.

Richard Longman himself continued to race but, in 1975, he had a serious accident at Thruxton. As a result of complications following a routine operation, he was off work for a year. While recuperating, he gave some thought to his racing future. He had no doubts about going back, but decided that the faithful Cooper S would have to go, as it was running out of homologation. He turned his attentions to the 1275GT. Helped by Ron Elkins at Leyland, Longman managed to get the right bits

*Neck and neck, Richard Longman's Mini 1275GT and Martin Brundle's Toyota Celica GT 1.6 in the Silverstone round of the Tricentrol RAC British Saloon Car Championship, on 29 May 1978. Longman won his class, one of ten such victories that would help him take the overall championship.*

homologated for the car. This turned it into a British Saloon Car Championship winner, opening another chapter in the Mini success story.

In 1977, Longman and Alan Curnow drove a pair of Patrick Motor Group Longman 1275GTs, giving the crowds some thrilling dices as they fought with Bernard Unett's 1300 Hillman Avenger for the class lead. Throughout the year, the cars were constantly developed and, although they had to give best to Unett at the end of the year, Longman and Curnow came second and third in class. The development was to pay handsome dividends in the following two seasons.

Richard Longman won the class ten times in twelve races to take the 1978 crown. In 1979, the team had a clean sweep of victories, Longman taking ten wins and Curnow taking the other two. Longman won the championship and the pair took the team prize. In 1990,

Longman reappeared in a Mini to race FIA Historics. The company still does a great deal of work for Mini competitors.

## JON MOWATT

Although his early career, including a spell at Lotus, had Ford connections, Jon Mowatt was to become another champion of the 'A' Series engine. He had a Mini racing career from 1964, when he made his Mini debut in a road car, to 1984, when he last raced his faithful 1275GT.

In 1965, Mowatt built a lightweight Mini from a write-off that he towed to meetings on the back of an 1100cc Mini pick-up. For the following season, he built a higher-spec 998 car, but it was too heavy, so over the winter he did a 970 engine and reduced the weight of the car. This combination gave him fourteen wins in 1967. Part-way through the season, he bought a

1275S from Brent Greeves and took both cars to a Players No 6 Autocross round. He used the 1275 in the wet heats and brought out the 970 for the final on the drying track and utilized its race engine power to take victory. The cash award was used to buy a new lawnmower!

In 1967, Mowatt got planning permission to build a new workshop which would house his now well-known rolling road, so he concluded that he would have to do less racing in 1968. The building was completed by May and, having squeezed in a few local races, he decided he would like to try a Group 5 Mini in the BTCC. He put his 970 engine in the Barry Walter car but found great difficulty in getting entries as the races were always oversubscribed. Eventually, he got a race at Brands. Having practised as reserve, he finished in fourth place.

Now a points scorer, Mowatt received a phone call from Oulton Park inviting him to compete at the next round. As he was due to visit his sister in Germany he had to decline, saying he would be in Germany that weekend. Much to his embarrassment, the secretary of the meeting, assuming he was an International star racing abroad, wished him good luck.

During the holiday, Mowatt phoned home to make sure that all was well with his business, which he had left in the capable hands of employee Gordon Dawkins. He learnt that Dawkins, who had raced at Brands on Sunday 13 July 1969, had made the front page of the tabloids. He had rolled at Paddock and was pictured in his inverted car, 14ft (4m) in the air. Mowatt abandoned his trip and drove home.

Some weeks later, Mowatt drove his club racing 970S round to visit Dawkins, who was recuperating at home with his knee in plaster. As the patient was obviously bored, Mowatt suggested they go for a drive, bundled him into the S, and told

the family they would be back soon. The pair ended up at Santa Pod, where Dawkins broke the class standing quarter-mile record in Mowatt's Mini. They declined the offer of a certificate for a fee of £14.

In the European round of the championship at Brands, Jon Mowatt ran the 970 engine to come fifth in the two-hour Race on Saturday, then changed the engine overnight for the six-hour event on the Sunday. During this, he was mixing it with all the established Mini teams. At about the half-way mark, the right-hand tank broke loose, shorted on the battery and, eventually, the leaking fuel caught light. He stopped at a marshal's post and the fire was extinguished, enabling him to drive back to the pits. Gordon Dawkins opened the boot to check the damage and the air immediately re-ignited the fire, flames leaping high in the air. The pit-lane marshals quickly dowsed the flames with their new dry-powder extinguishers, admitting that it was the first time they had used them. (Mowatt was so impressed that he immediately got one for the workshop.) Fourteen minutes were lost while the damage was repaired. The scrutineer passed the car as fit to race, but said he was sure that it would never start. It went first pull, to enormous cheers from the grandstand. The team's perseverance got Mowatt another fifth, while John Fitzpatrick got the 1300 GP circuit lap record down to 1:50.2.

Having got the taste for Group 5, Jon Mowatt built his own car to the regs, with aluminium doors, bonnet, boot lid and Perspex windows. Meanwhile, the 970S was used for some Rallycross events. Mowatt also invested in his first set of Minilites, which he found were much kinder to the diff. However, when the car was taken to Brands for the Boxing Day race meeting, he discovered that

*Jon Mowatt on two wheels in his Group 5 Cooper S at Copse Corner, Silverstone, in 1971. The damage to the nearside wheel arch was caused by hitting the Castrol marker cones on the inside of Copse and Becketts.*

Rallycross had ruined it as a circuit car, so the shell was sold.

For 1970 it was decided to concentrate on the British Championship rounds. Places were often achieved, but wins proved elusive against the works-backed cars. As regulations specified that radiator grilles were mandatory, the car tended to overheat in the summer. Finding that running with 25lb cap and the heater full on was a bit of a killer, Mowatt carried out some modifications to the block and radiator to dissipate the heat. He used his rolling road to establish that optimum power came at 70 degrees centigrade; as soon as the temperature went above that, the power dropped dramatically.

Awards in the British Championship rounds were quite good; the organizers paid out to last place – £15 – so it was important to at least take the start and do one lap. Third in class and, say, fourteenth overall would be good for about £110. Roger Weller, competition boss at Castrol, also helped with free oil and fuel, sometimes even wangling some for the tow car, which was booked out for testing the championship Fiestas!

Taking George Bevan's advice, Mowatt did a lot of machining of discs and drive flanges and so on, to reduce the run-out. This resulted in a couple of hundred extra revs down the long straight at Silverstone, which brought the lap times down. Mowatt's outing at Crystal Palace that year was momentous only for the fact that he had his biggest-ever accident. Mowatt's wife Bobbie was helping their daughter up the slide in the children's playground at the time. On being told 'Daddy's just had an accident, we must leave.', young Janine insisted on 'Just one more go, Mummy. Please.'!

In 1970, Tony Bunton of Carlow

Engineering asked Mowatt to drive his recently completed 970S Special Saloon in the Six-Hour Relay. The car was meticulously built and innovative, running on 13in (32.5cm) wheels, with an engine that had all the right bits. Gordon Dawkins (1275S) and Dave Conway (1275 Riley Elf) were the other members of the team. After practice, Mowatt was frankly disappointed, finding the car quirky to drive and the cockpit very fumey. Again, in his stint in the race, he found that the car did not live up to its promise; after several laps, he was mortified to see that it had started raining.

Called into the pits, he handed the sash to Conway. Dawkins took Mowatt to the old galvanized scrutineering bay, where they and the rest of the team descended on the car. The rear screen was removed, the wheels were changed for 10in (25cm) rims with wets and the suspension was adjusted. Back on the track in the refuelled car, Mowatt found that the smaller wheels transformed both the handling and the gearing and he was soon achieving better lap times than he had in the dry. During the fifty-minute wet period, he took the car from twenty-fourth to fifth overall on scratch, lapping one sports car three times. He recalls, 'For fifty minutes I was in heaven.'

In 1971, Mowatt scored his first International win at Mallory Park. In the following year he got an eight-port head as soon as they were homologated. He tried 32mm Amals, the largest generally available, but got more power when Barry Johnson managed to get him a set of four 38mm. Using this set-up, he ran a Cooper with good results until 1973, when a disastrous flirtation with a BMW made him return to his roots in 1974 and go scrambling. From 1975, he ran a club car with Richard Asquith for two years. Mowatt drove and Asquith carried out develop-

ment work in an attempt to reduce the roll centre. Mowatt persevered, but found that the modifications did not necessarily suit his driving style.

In 1978, something significant happened. Barry Johnson arrived for a rolling-road appointment with his newly built 1275GT. Jon Mowatt looked round the car, and approved. Having set up the Steve Harris-built engine, he was even more impressed to record just under 100bhp at the wheels on SUs. Mowatt and Johnson met up again at the British Grand Prix meeting and Johnson asked if he would like to co-drive at the Silverstone TT; Mowatt agreed.

In qualifying, Mowatt was quicker than the car's owner and all was going well in the race until the final half-hour, when the crank let go with Mowatt driving. He had been told it was an S crank, good for 8,000rpm; as it was not his car and he had been using 7,500, Mowatt felt duty-bound to rebuild it.

After a phone call from Barry Johnson's sponsor, a London Leyland dealer, Mowatt drove the car at Oulton Park. He made a good showing, having a good tussle with Richard Longman for the lead but, again, the crank let go. Nevertheless, the sponsors were delighted, because their car had got in front of the championship-leading car. At the end of the season, Johnson offered Mowatt the car and he bought it.

For the 1979 season, Mowatt managed to resolve the crank problem and had a competitive year of National and International events. He continued with the GT on and off until 1984, when the TT at Donington was one of his last races in it. He dusted it off in 1991, for a sprint at North Weald, and was amazed to fall foul of the scrutineers over his rubber-mounted petrol tank. Eventually, they relented; it had, after all, passed muster at several Internationals.

The car then sat in the workshop until 1998, when Nick Swift brokered a deal and Jon Mowatt sold the car to German Helmut Kuhavy, who races it in his home country. The white GT returned to the UK for the very wet Mini World Trophy Race at Lydden on 23 August 1998, where Kuhavy was fourth overall. Jon Mowatt now sprints his historic Morgan.

## BILL RICHARDS

One of the last intake of Abingdon competition department apprentices, Bill Richards found himself out of a job when the Stokes axe fell in 1969. The following year, he decided to use his knowledge to set up Bill Richards Racing in London, specializing in things 'A' Series. In the late 1980s, working in the city was becoming increasingly unappealing, so he took advantage of a local authority grant to move the business to Ashford in Kent, just up the road from Lydden Hill, his local circuit.

Richards started his racing in 1969 with a steel-shelled car, which he called Myrtle. During his learning curve, he bent the car regularly and successive replacements had more glass-fibre panels and holes than the last. His first 850 engine sported a five-port head but, while still working at Abingdon, he managed to get an eight-porter at a reasonable price and was soon running that on the car.

In 1978, he took Myrtle 5 to John Maguire for advice. Maguire's view was that it was so frail that, if he had an off, he could kill himself. Richards therefore bought one of the first John Maguire space frames and raced that with the eight-port 850 engine, which produced 112bhp at the wheels. After a hectic season of dices with Barry Reece, Charles Bernstein and Mike Parkes, Richards won the 850 class in the 1980 Wendy Wools Special Saloon Car Championship. He was runner-up the following year.

Deciding to go BDA, Richards made a modified bonnet to cover the new engine, but was concerned at the lack of aerodynamics offered by the new front end. This coincided with the introduction of the Metro and he immediately realized that this car's shape would more effectively clothe the Ford engine and have less drag. A heavily damaged example was purchased and repaired sufficiently to make a mould. Thus, Richards' BDA Maguire Mini became a Metro and a second body was made for long-time racing friend Viv Wallace to follow suit.

Bill Richards continues to race the Metro and, once a year, he has an Historic Mini outing in Portland, USA. He had a guest drive in the 1998 Mighty Minis series, resulting in a win. Nowadays, he also seems to be brought many of the damaged Maguire space frames to repair.

## RALPH SAUNDERS

Oxfordshire lad Ralph Saunders learnt his trade at Oselli Engineering, where he worked for many years. During one break from racing, he tried his hand at being a publican, but he soon went back to his 'A' series career and established Pitstop.

The company is noted for looking after many of the cars as well as running up to six Mini Se7ens at race meetings all over the UK. They have also run Caterhams, Westfields and so on, in other championships.

Ralph Saunders soon acquired the reputation with his drivers of being a hard taskmaster; his criticisms were frequently countered by mutterings of, 'Could *you* do any better?' Towards the end of the 1998 season, Chris Huck, one of Saunders' cus-

*Bill Richards' Maguire space-frame Mini on the grid at Mallory Park in 1980. He used the 112bhp that his eight-port 850 engine produced to good effect, winning the class in the Wendy Wools Championship that year and taking the runner-up spot in 1981.*

tomers, was unable to do the last race of the winter series and offered Saunders the use of his car. Much to everyone's surprise, Saunders accepted the offer. He did the course to get his licence and, aged 37, turned up at Brands on 22 November to compete in his first-ever race. He qualified fifteenth out of twenty starters, and finished the race in eighth position.

## BRYAN SLARK

Mechanic Bryan Slark, who joined the head shop at Downton Engineering in 1967, was taught cylinder-head modification by George Toth. Slark, in common with most of the Downton employees,

enjoyed his time with the company; if it had not closed, he suggests, many of the former staff would still be there to this day. He remembers the last three years as being very busy. After it became apparent that the firm was likely to close, Slark started working for himself in his spare time. He had the chance to go to Longman, but decided instead to set up Slark Race Engineering in 1974.

Bryan Slark is regarded as the innovator of the big, big valve 'A' Series heads. He says that they were a spin-off from the heads that he did at Downton for Derek Warwick's Hot Rod and Tom Airey's Rallycross Mini. Indeed, many of his early customers were Rallycross drivers. Initially, he shied away from racing himself, for fear that he would spend too much time on his own car and not enough on the customers'. However, in 1979, he gave in and built up a Miglia, which he campaigned until 1981. Once he started, that was it. In his opinion, 'racing is akin to smoking. You have some, you get hooked, and you want more.'

Slark remembers Mike Fry as being very helpful to him as the new boy, even slowing down in practice to allow him to follow his line through corners. In his first season, Slark was eleventh and took the award for Best Newcomer, although he did write his car off at the end of the year. The first time he ever led a race, he took seasoned campaigner Chris Lewis for first place then could not get used to that big empty space in front of him. The glory was short-lived and John Simpson eventually won the race.

As he had feared, Slark found that the demands of his customers did not really leave him enough time for the dedication required for serious racing. Having enjoyed his stint, he sold the car to Mark Jones and continued to look after it for him. Jones won the 1986 Southern and Lydden series and was runner up in the 1987 National Championship.

Bryan Slark can now be found competing in European Historic Saloons in a 1071S, which he shares with Klaus Reineck. His son Neil has joined him in the business, where the latest 'A' series innovation is a chain-free timing-gear set.

## GLYN SWIFT

Although he started in Autocross as early as 1965, with two damaged Minis welded together, Glyn Swift claims to be a better engine-builder than driver. None the less, he enjoyed his motor sport. Having stuck with Autocross until 1967, he moved to Rallycross the following year. He remembers doing a round of the ITV Lydden series. He put a set of R65 road-race tyres on his Mini, which gave it so much grip that the wheel sheared off when he was well placed in the final. He sat in the car fuming until the marshals came and dragged him out; the whole thing was captured by the cameras and he then had to live down the reputation of being a miserable so and so.

Rallycross gave Swift the taste for tarmac and, from 1968 to 1977, he took part in circuit racing in Minis whenever circumstances permitted. The final two seasons saw him doing about eight rounds of the 1275GT Challenge where, despite not being a regular contender, he got four pole positions. At one Silverstone meeting he out-qualified leading front-runner Paul Taft, but a waterway blew in the closing stages of practice. He was in the transporter Aralditing it up when Taft came in. He looked over his shoulder, pointed to the cylinder head and said, 'Look at the ports on that. No wonder the bastard passes me on the straights.'

Swift also has mixed memories of a Brands Hatch round, where, from a good grid position, he got squeezed out going into Paddock and crashed into the concrete marshal's post on the inside of the corner. There was a rending sound of metal, but the engine was still running. He selected reverse and was surprised when he was able to back the car off the obstruction. Putting it in first, he gingerly set off. There was nothing rubbing and he recalls, 'I thought "Sod it", and went tearing off after the rest of them, although they were long gone. I went from last to fifth in ten laps – not bad!'

Swiftune was first started as a part-time business in Essex, with Swift going full time in 1965. He found things a bit tight and so, in 1966, he got a job on the

217

twilight shift at Ford's Dunton research facility. He worked from 5.15pm to 1.45am. During the early hours it was usually very quiet, so he made a point of washing for bed before he knocked off. He would then tear home on the empty roads and be in bed by 2am. Getting up at 10am gave him most of the day to do his own work on heads and engines and by 5pm he was back at Fords. It was not unheard of for a Mini head to find its way into the blue oval premises to be finished off. This pattern lasted two years, by which time Swiftune had really taken off.

In 1982, yearning for a change, Swift sold most of his gear to Jon Mowatt and bought a Devon dairy farm. It was hard to make the dairy herd pay and, after diversifying the farming interests, Swift began to look at ways of using the now-empty milking parlour. He bought a couple of pieces of equipment and soon had a machine shop once again. He made contact with the local motor club and it was not long before the work built up and he was also doing jobs for some of his old customers and delivering it to them.

One local Autocrosser asked him to build a no-expense-spared Ford engine for his car. He debuted it at the same time that Glyn Swift's son Nick, then 17, first came out in his 850 Autocross Mini. After practice, the man was most upset that the young Nick had beaten his time.

Things did not work out in Devon and Bob Monk at Kent Cams was able to persuade Glyn Swift to move back to the south-east in 1985. He was soon in the thick of it with his son Nick on board and building on revived success, Swiftune moved to its present premises in Betheresden in 1989. In 1998, Swiftune Engines won five championships, including the double – both UK Se7en and Miglia Championships – in what must be a first.

*'Never give up' was Glyn Swift's motto after being forced off the track into a concrete marshal's post on the first bend of this Brands Hatch 1275GT race, on 18 April 1976. Swift (16) rounds Clearways in pursuit of Geoff Till (18), on his way from last to fifth place. Despite racing in less than half the qualifying rounds, Swift was eighth in the 1976 championship.*

# 10 Historics

It is said that, if a car stays on the racing scene for long enough, it will end up with an historic category in which to compete, and the illustrious Mini is no exception. Despite having three one-make championships of their own, Minis are now to be found in both the CSCC and FIA Historic Championships. Initially, when the formulae for historic saloons began to evolve, the Minis were excluded, on the premise they might repeat their feat of the 1960s and sweep all before them. But common sense prevailed and they are now eligible.

Not surprisingly, among the current front-runners in the Historic Championships are well-known Mini names from the past. The environment in these races is more relaxed than in the Nationals and Internationals and, perhaps, the emphasis is more on the fun element, but the racing is just as close.

## NORMAN GRIMSHAW

British Vita Racing lives again thanks to Norman Grimshaw, son of the man of the same name who used to be MD of British Vita, continuing his interest in 1960s Minis. His year on the European Championship road in 1969, as mechanic, obviously rubbed off on Norman junior, and he is now in the Vita hot seat himself. While the driver is new, the familiar names of Jeff Goodliff, Brian Gillibrand and Harry Clarke are still on the team, involved in preparation.

Norman Grimshaw bought his historic car from Richard Longman in 1994 and took it back to Goodliff. At one time, Goodliff had banned Minis from his workshop but, as he said, 'I could hardly refuse young Norman, could I?' The car was readied for the 1994 FIA Historic season, which produced a satisfying debut. An enjoyable season ('enjoy' and 'enjoyable' are the new Vita team's watchwords) produced a class win and third overall. For 1995, Norman Grimshaw again claimed the class in his 1966 black and red 1293S. Due to family commitments, there were only occasional outings in 1996 and 1997, but in 1998 the team embarked on long-distance racing, with Barrie Williams, another familiar name in the Vita camp, back on board as second driver.

Another well-known name turned out for Vita in the St Mary's Trophy Race, at the first Goodwood Revival meeting on 20 September 1998. Norman Grimshaw was racing his own car, so his historic rally S was turned out in race trim (although it still had the Haldas on the dash) for John Rhodes to drive. Rhodes proved he had lost none of his flair and finished fifth overall, out of a field of thirty assorted saloons. Grimshaw in the proper race car did not fare so well and a damaged valve forced him out of contention.

## LIONEL DODKINS

There are probably very few one-owner 1965 Cooper Ss, but the car that Lionel Dodkins races in the FIA Historics series is one such vehicle. Having only started racing in 1991, Dodkins did his debut FIA

*Richard Dodkins in brother Lionel's 1965 Cooper S on the way to an outright win in the St Mary's Trophy race at the inaugural Goodwood Revival Meeting on 20 September 1998.*

event at Paul Ricard and has raced regularly ever since. Driving the same car, Lionel's brother Richard won the 1998 Goodwood St Mary's Trophy Race for saloon cars. He took the laurels in true Mini style, beating considerably more powerful cars.

## JIM BURROWS

In 1970, Jim Burrows bought a racing 970S from DNA Shells of Stratford, which dealt in racing cars. The white and gold Mini, MLX 588D, which looked as if it had stood for a while, turned out to be Ken Costello's old car. After a varied history (*see* Chapter 5), the car was rebuilt by Peter Vickers in 1994, and Burrows now races it in the CSCC series, with a 1300 engine. However, he did also manage to buy back the original 970 lump, which he had sold to a grass-tracker in 1972 and which, subsequently, ended up in another

friend's shed. The car, which has raced in five different guises over the last thirty years, is perhaps a unique one.

The car is now finished in Surf Blue and white and won first time out at Silverstone at the start of the 1998 season. This was followed by two more wins, three seconds, one third and four fastest laps. Burrows also set a new lap record on the Brands Indy Circuit, breaking the old one by 1.3 seconds. He came second in class and sixth overall in the championship.

## NICK SWIFT

Nick Swift had a grounding in Autocross, the 1986 Minicross Championship and three years in the Metro Challenge under his belt. When he and his father Glyn were looking for a new vehicle to promote the Swiftune name, they settled on the Classic Touring Car Championship. They built up a car on a Mark 1 shell, which, to comply

*Jim Burrows keeps a GT Cortina at bay in his 1966 Austin Cooper S, the same car raced by Ken Costello thirty years ago.*

with the regulations, had to run on road tyres. This made the car interesting to drive, given the fact that the 1460 engine, running on a single 48, was putting out 152bhp at the flywheel. Nick won the class in 1994, 1995 and 1997, and was also second overall in all three years. A broken suspension link at Brands cost him the 1997 overall crown, by just one point.

In 1995, the series had fourteen rounds at twelve circuits, including two double headers, and Nick Swift took ten lap records. His best-ever race was the dry Oulton Park round, when he finished the race in second position. While he usually expected to be well up the overall pecking order in the wet owing to the Mini's legendary traction, in dry conditions it was another matter. After avoiding a mêlée in the early stages, which had left a lot of oil down, Swift was enjoying a hectic dice for second place with fellow Mini man Graham Churchill. During one of their place-swapping sessions, Swift glanced up

to see if he had room to shut the door and noticed a very out-of-shape Camaro in front of him.

Dennis Clarke had braked for another oil slick on the run up to Lodge and, with the big Yank virtually across the track, Swift had nowhere to go. He was already committed to his line, so he took to the grass and was momentarily airborne as he got through the gap, taking the Camaro's wing mirror with him. He crossed the start line leading the race and the pit lane erupted. He eventually finished third and just 1.5 seconds covered the top six places.

## PAUL STANWORTH

With a father who worked on the prototype Mini, Paul Stanworth was given a lasting interest in the cars. When he heard that one of his dad's former work colleagues was selling a 1965 Mini, that had been in his possession for many years, Stanworth decided to buy it and restore it. The fact that BOP 243C was one of the Broadspeed cars made him even more keen to bring this particular Mini back to its former glory.

The car now encompasses Broadspeed spec with seam-welded shell and sub-frames, incorporating current-day safety equipment, including the all-important full cage. Stanworth prefers to have a car he can really race, rather than a vehicle to polish and look at. Keeping things period, the 1293cc engine was tuned by Jeff Goodliff, who used to drive and prepare the Vitamins.

Following the completion of the work in 1993, Paul Stanworth drove the car in hill-climbs and sprints until 1997, coming third in class in the 1996 MCR Championship. In 1998, the temptation to return the car to its circuit-racing roots proved too much. He entered the 1998 FIA Pre-1965 Historic series and, despite his XSP-based engine being 10bhp down on the opposition, had a good season, with some enjoyable dices. He was also among the select band of Mini drivers who were invited to race their cars at the first Goodwood Revival Meeting, in 1998.

## NURBURGRING 24-HOURS: AT LAST

While the Mini entry in the June 1995 Nurburgring 24-Hour Race was not an official Historic outing, it was a momentous occasion, as it marked the first time a Mini completed a twenty-four-hour race at the Ring. It was masterminded by John Brigden, who shared the driving with Tony Dron and Jeremy Coulter. The car used had originally been prepared under the Brigden Coulter Motorsport banner, for Dron to drive in the 1994 RAC Rally. It

was lent to them by Paul Barrett, who now owned it.

Bill Richards rebuilt the engine and gearbox, while Southern Carburettors produced the management system. Two days before qualifying, the Mini arrived at the Ring in full rally trim. To the amazement of the locals, Richards, with Simon Skelton, Nick Chalkley and Andy Williams, rebuilt the car to race spec in their pit-lane garage. Dron took the start, and returned the overheating car to the pits at the end of lap one. The team concluded that, as some 180 cars had left the line and the Mini had qualified in the middle of the rear group, lack of clean air had caused the problem. It was a correct diagnosis. The drivers each did stints of two and a half hours between fuel stops and, when they handed over, were absolutely wrung out after mastering the circuit's 184 bends.

Brigden took the graveyard shift – 1.30am to 3.30am – when it was really wet. He outbraked six other cars into a corner and then left them for dead. It was a wonderful feeling to have; he gained twenty-five places in his two hours. BMW had only recently taken over Rover, so, in certain sections of the crowd, the drivers would see German spectators simultaneously waving Union Jacks and BMW flags. The Mini was in among Fiat Cinquecentos and the commentators were hyping up this battle for the benefit of the crowd. When he got past one, Brigden could hear the spectators' roaring their approval above the cockpit noise.

Only two sets of Dunlop intermediates were used in the predominantly wet race; the team reckoned that they could have got away with one set if it had been dry. They qualified as finishers, crossing the line seventh in class. John Brigden says it is the most fun he has ever had in a Mini.

# Bibliography

The majority of the information in this book has been obtained by speaking directly to the people involved, but the following publications have been useful for the verification of certain facts.

Barber, David M., *Marcos – The Story of a Great British Sportscar* (Cedar Publishing, 1995)

Bentley, John, with Cooper, John, *The Grand Prix Carpet-Baggers* (Doubleday and Co., 1977)

Brigden, John, *The Sporting Minis* (Motor Racing Publications, 1989)

Golding, Rob, *Mini Thirty Years On* (Osprey, 1979)

Harvey, Chris, *Mighty Minis* (Haynes, 1993)

Kahn, Mark, *Down The Hatch Life & Fast Times of Tony Lanfranchi Motor-Racing's Last Cavalier* (W. Foulsham & Co., 1980)

Price, Bill, *The BMC/BL Competitions Department* (Haynes, 1989)

Walton, Jeremy, *Only Here For The Beer – Gerry Marshall* (Foulis Haynes, 1978)

Wilkins, Jasper, *The Amazing Sports Car Journal* (Brooklands, 1973)

# Index

CU00701337

# Suzuki
# GSX-R600 and 750
## Service and Repair Manual

## by Matthew Coombs

### Models covered

GSX-R600V, W and X. 600cc. 1997 to 1999
GSX-R750T, V, W and X. 749cc. 1996 to 1999

*(3553-1AB1-280)*

ABCDE
FGHIJ
KLMNO

© Haynes Publishing 2002

A book in the **Haynes Service and Repair Manual Series**

**All rights reserved. No part of this book may be reproduced or transmitted in any form or by any means, electronic or mechanical, including photocopying, recording or by any information storage or retrieval system, without permission in writing from the copyright holder.**

ISBN **1 85960 553 2**

**British Library Cataloguing in Publication Data**
A catalogue record for this book is available from the British Library

Library of Congress Catalog Card Number **99-73032**

Printed in the USA

**Haynes Publishing**
Sparkford, Yeovil, Somerset BA22 7JJ, England

**Haynes North America, Inc**
861 Lawrence Drive, Newbury Park, California 91320, USA

**Editions Haynes**
4, Rue de l'Abreuvoir
92415 COURBEVOIE CEDEX, France

**Haynes Publishing Nordiska AB**
Box 1504, 751 45 UPPSALA, Sweden

# Contents

## LIVING WITH YOUR SUZUKI GSX-R

## MAINTENANCE

# Contents

## REPAIRS AND OVERHAUL

## REFERENCE

# Suzuki
# Every Which Way

## by Julian Ryder

### From Textile Machinery to Motorcycles

Suzuki were the second of Japan's Big Four motorcycle manufacturers to enter the business, and like Honda they started by bolting small two-stroke motors to bicycles. Unlike Honda, they had manufactured other products before turning to transportation in the aftermath of World War II. In fact Suzuki has been in business since the first decade of the 20th-Century when Michio Suzuki manufactured textile machinery.

The desperate need for transport in post-war Japan saw Suzuki make their first motorised bicycle in 1952, and the fact that by 1954 the company had changed its name to Suzuki Motor Company shows how quickly the sideline took over the whole company's activities. In their first full manufacturing year, Suzuki made nearly 4500 bikes and rapidly expanded into the world markets with a range of two-strokes.

Suzuki didn't make a four-stroke until 1977 when the GS750 double-overhead-cam across-the-frame four arrived. This was several years after Honda and Kawasaki had established the air-cooled four as the industry standard, but no motorcycle epitomises the era of what came to be known as the Universal

**The T500 two-stroke twin**

50 cc racer won six of the eight world titles chalked up by Suzuki during the 1960s as well as providing Mitsuo Itoh with the distinction of being the only Japanese rider to win an Isle of Man TT. Mr Itoh still works for Suzuki, he's in charge of their racing program.

Europe got the benefit of Suzuki's two-stroke expertise in a succession of air-cooled twins, the six-speed 250 cc Super Six being the most memorable, but the arrival in 1968 of the first of a series of 500 cc twins which were good looking, robust and versatile marked the start of mainstream success.

So confident were Suzuki of their two-stroke expertise that they even applied it to the burgeoning Superbike sector. The GT750 water-cooled triple arrived in 1972. It was big, fast and comfortable although the handling and stopping power did draw some comment. Whatever the drawbacks of the road bike, the engine was immensely successful in Superbike and Formula 750 racing. The roadster has its devotees, though, and is now a sought-after bike on the classic Japanese scene. Do not refer to it as the Water Buffalo in such company. Joking aside, the later disc-braked versions were quite civilised, but the audacious idea of using a big two-stroke motor in what was essentially a touring bike was a surprising success until the fuel crisis of the mid-'70s effectively killed off big strokers.

The same could be said of Suzuki's only real lemon, the RE5. This is still the only mass-produced bike to use the rotary (or Wankel) engine but never sold well. Fuel consumption in the mid-teens allied to frightening complexity and excess weight meant the RE5 was a non-starter in the sales race.

**One of the later GT750 'kettle' models with front disc brakes**

Japanese motorcycle better than the GS. So well engineered were the original fours that you can clearly see their genes in the GS500 twins that are still going strong in the mid-1990s. Suzuki's ability to prolong the life of their products this way means that they are often thought of as a conservative company. This is hardly fair if you look at some of their landmark designs, most of which have been commercial as well as critical successes.

## Two-stroke Success

Early racing efforts were bolstered by the arrival of Ernst Degner who defected from the East German MZ team at the Swedish GP of 1961, bringing with him the rotary-valve secrets of design genius Walter Kaaden. The new Suzuki 50 cc racer won its first GP on the Isle of Man the following year and winning the title easily. Only Honda and Ralph Bryans interrupted Suzuki's run of 50 cc titles from 1962 to 1968.

The arrival of the twin-cylinder 125 racer in 1963 enabled Hugh Anderson to win both 50 and 125 world titles. You may not think 50 cc racing would be exciting - until you learn that the final incarnation of the thing had 14 gears and could do well over 100 mph on fast circuits. Before pulling out of GPs in 1967 the

**Suzuki's GT250X7 was an instant hit in the popular 250 cc 'learner' sector**

The GS400 was the first in a line of four-stroke twins

## Development of the Four-stroke range

When Suzuki got round to building a four-stroke they did a very good job of it. The GS fours were built in 550, 650, 750, 850, 1000 and 1100 cc sizes in sports, custom, roadster and even shaft-driven touring forms over many years. The GS1000 was in on the start of Superbike racing in the early 1970s and the GS850 shaft-driven tourer was around nearly 15 years later. The fours spawned a line of 400, 425, 450 and 500 cc GS twins that were essentially the middle half of the four with all their reliability. If there was ever a criticism of the GS models it was that with the exception of the GS1000S of 1980, colloquially known as the ice-cream van, the range was visually uninspiring.

They nearly made the same mistake when they launched the four-valve-head GSX750 in 1979. Fortunately, the original twin-shock version was soon replaced by the 'E'-model with Full-Floater rear suspension and a full set of all the gadgets the Japanese industry was then keen on and has since forgotten about, like 16-inch front wheels and anti-dive forks. The air-cooled GSX was like the GS built in 550, 750 and 1100 cc versions with a variety of half, full and touring fairings, but the GSX that is best remembered is the Katana that first appeared in 1981. The power was provided by an 1000 or 1100 cc GSX motor, but wrapped around it was the most outrageous styling package to come out of Japan. Designed by Hans Muth of Target

Design, the Katana looked like nothing seen before or since. At the time there was as much anti feeling as praise, but now it is rightly regarded as a classic, a true milestone in motorcycle design. The factory have even started making 250 and 400 cc fours for the home market with the same styling as the 1981 bike.

Just to remind us that they'd still been building two-strokes for the likes of Barry Sheene, in 1986 Suzuki marketed a road-going version of their RG500 square-four racer which had put an end to the era of the four-stroke in 500 GPs when it appeared in 1974. In 1976 Suzuki not only won their first 500 title with Sheene, they sold RG500s over the counter and won every GP with them - with the exception of the Isle of Man TT which the works riders boycotted. Ten years on, the RG500 Gamma gave road riders the nearest experience they'd ever get to riding a GP bike. The fearsome beast could top 140 mph and only weighed 340 lb - the other alleged GP replicas were pussy cats compared to the Gamma's man-eating tiger.

The RG only lasted a few years and is already firmly in the category of collector's item; its four-stroke equivalent, the GSX-R, is still with us and looks like being so for many years. You have to look back to 1985 and its launch to realise just what a revolutionary step the GSX-R750 was: quite simply it was the first race replica. Not a bike dressed up to look like a race bike, but a genuine racer with lights on, a bike that could be taken straight to the track and win.

The first GSX-R, the 750, had a completely new motor cooled by oil rather than water and an aluminium cradle frame. It was sparse, a little twitchy and very, very fast. This time Suzuki got the looks right, blue and white bodywork based on the factory's racing colours and endurance-racer lookalike twin headlights. And then came the 1100 - the big GSX-R got progressively more brutal as it chased the Yamaha EXUP for the heavyweight championship.

The GS750 led the way for a series of four cylinder models

Later four-stroke models, like this GSX1100, were fitted with 16v engines

And alongside all these mould-breaking designs, Suzuki were also making the best looking custom bikes to come out of Japan, the Intruders; the first race replica trail bike, the DR350; the sharpest 250 Supersports, the RGV250; and a bargain-basement 600, the Bandit. The Bandit proved so popular they went on to build 1200 and 750 cc versions of it. I suppose that's predictable, a range of four-stroke fours just like the GS and GSXs. It's just like the company really, sometimes predictable, admittedly - but never boring.

## No Compromise

In the techno wars of super-sports motor-cycling, GSX-R is a name that gets respect. The original 1985 oil-cooled version wasn't just a winner straight out of the crate it was revolutionary. The 1996 version wasn't so obviously path-breaking but it was still a winner. It's just that the twin-beam aluminium frame and water-cooled motor made it look a bit like the competition from Honda (FireBlade) and Kawasaki (ZX-7R). But you couldn't see what made it so different: weight – or rather lack of it. The first of the new-generation 750 Suzukis weighed in at just 179 kg (395 lb) thanks to ultra-thin materials, hollow swinging arm castings, composite-coated cylinders doing away with the need for liners, drilled fasteners, and a host of other detail tweaks. For comparison, a ZX-7R

Suzuki's GSX-R range represented their cutting edge sports bikes

The GSX-R600 model

weighed in at 203 kg and a FireBlade at 183 kg (dry weights).

The big saving on the motor's architecture was the camchain drive on the left end of the crank doing away with the need for one main bearing. Only when you stood it next to other 750s of the day did you realise how small it was and understood what Suzuki meant when they said they'd used lessons learnt from Kevin Schwantz's 500 in building the GSX-R. the relationship goes deeper than the characteristic rounded shape of the seat hump.

Not surprisingly, the GSX-R750 was the nearest thing you could buy to a racer for the roads despite the fact it was half the price of Honda's Superbike homologation special, the RC45. Suzuki didn't have a homologation special, like the RC45 or Yamaha's new R7, the standard, mass-produced roadbike did the job. Which tells you just how much of a racer it is. Not surprisingly, it was quick but it didn't suffer fools gladly, in fact it didn't suffer fools at all. This was a cutting-edge motorcycle in every way demanding concentration and application from its rider.

The only surprise was that this high-tech missile still sported carburettors. We had to wait until 1998 for fuel-injection. It also got a larger airbox and a revised exhaust system to go with the new intake system plus a higher, more bulbous screen and an hydraulic steering damper. It was also one of the first bikes to use

the latest trick bit of automotive electronics, the high-tension coil built into what look like giant spark-plug caps, thus doing away with separate coils bolted to the frame. The result was a cleaner pick-up through the rev-range plus a little more top end, but most road riders

would have been hard pushed to spot the difference. The fuel injection was really there for the World Superbike Championship, but the works bikes didn't use it until 1999. When they did, Suzuki got its first wins since 1989.

The Supersports 600 class got its first

The GSX-R750 model

GSX-R in 1997, and true-to-type it was the lightest, shortest, twitchiest bike in the class and became the hottest 600 on the race track. Jon Crawford won the 1998 British Championship on one and Fabrizio Pirovano won the 1998 World Supersport Series that runs alongside the World Superbike Championship.

On the road the GSX-R600 was just like the 750 only more so, standing out from its competition even more than the 750 did as the raciest bike in its class. It even looked like a scaled down 750 and like its bigger brother breathed through carburettors. On the road its lack of midrange and ultra-sensitive handling made it the hardest bike in its class to live with. Unless, of course, you buy a bike to use at track days.

## Acknowledgements

Our thanks are due to GT Motorcycles of Mudford, Yeovil, who supplied the machines featured in the illustrations throughout this manual. We would also like to thank NGK Spark Plugs (UK) Ltd for supplying the colour spark plug condition photos and the Avon Rubber Company for supplying information on tyre fitting.

The introduction 'Every Which Way' was written by Julian Ryder. Kel Edge supplied the rear cover photograph.

## About this manual

The aim of this manual is to help you get the best value from your motorcycle. It can do so in several ways. It can help you decide what work must be done, even if you choose to have it done by a dealer; it provides information and procedures for routine maintenance and servicing; and it offers diagnostic and repair procedures to follow when trouble occurs.

We hope you use the manual to tackle the work yourself. For many simpler jobs, doing it yourself may be quicker than arranging an appointment to get the motorcycle into a dealer and making the trips to leave it and pick it up. More importantly, a lot of money can be saved by avoiding the expense the shop must pass on to you to cover its labour and overhead costs. An added benefit is the sense of satisfaction and accomplishment that you feel after doing the job yourself.

References to the left or right side of the motorcycle assume you are sitting on the seat, facing forward.

**We take great pride in the accuracy of information given in this manual, but motorcycle manufacturers make alterations and design changes during the production run of a particular motorcycle of which they do not inform us. No liability can be accepted by the authors or publishers for loss, damage or injury caused by any errors in, or omissions from, the information given.**

Professional mechanics are trained in safe working procedures. However enthusiastic you may be about getting on with the job at hand, take the time to ensure that your safety is not put at risk. A moment's lack of attention can result in an accident, as can failure to observe simple precautions.

There will always be new ways of having accidents, and the following is not a comprehensive list of all dangers; it is intended rather to make you aware of the risks and to encourage a safe approach to all work you carry out on your bike.

## Asbestos

● Certain friction, insulating, sealing and other products - such as brake pads, clutch linings, gaskets, etc. - contain asbestos. Extreme care must be taken to avoid inhalation of dust from such products since it is hazardous to health. If in doubt, assume that they do contain asbestos.

## Fire

● Remember at all times that petrol is highly flammable. Never smoke or have any kind of naked flame around, when working on the vehicle. But the risk does not end there - a spark caused by an electrical short-circuit, by two metal surfaces contacting each other, by careless use of tools, or even by static electricity built up in your body under certain conditions, can ignite petrol vapour, which in a confined space is highly explosive. Never use petrol as a cleaning solvent. Use an approved safety solvent.

● Always disconnect the battery earth terminal before working on any part of the fuel or electrical system, and never risk spilling fuel on to a hot engine or exhaust.

● It is recommended that a fire extinguisher of a type suitable for fuel and electrical fires is kept handy in the garage or workplace at all times. Never try to extinguish a fuel or electrical fire with water.

## Fumes

● Certain fumes are highly toxic and can quickly cause unconsciousness and even death if inhaled to any extent. Petrol vapour comes into this category, as do the vapours from certain solvents such as trichloro-ethylene. Any draining or pouring of such volatile fluids should be done in a well ventilated area.

● When using cleaning fluids and solvents, read the instructions carefully. Never use materials from unmarked containers - they may give off poisonous vapours.

● Never run the engine of a motor vehicle in an enclosed space such as a garage. Exhaust fumes contain carbon monoxide which is extremely poisonous; if you need to run the engine, always do so in the open air or at least have the rear of the vehicle outside the workplace.

## The battery

● Never cause a spark, or allow a naked light near the vehicle's battery. It will normally be giving off a certain amount of hydrogen gas, which is highly explosive.

● Always disconnect the battery ground (earth) terminal before working on the fuel or electrical systems (except where noted).

● If possible, loosen the filler plugs or cover when charging the battery from an external source. Do not charge at an excessive rate or the battery may burst.

● Take care when topping up, cleaning or carrying the battery. The acid electrolyte, evenwhen diluted, is very corrosive and should not be allowed to contact the eyes or skin. Always wear rubber gloves and goggles or a face shield. If you ever need to prepare electrolyte yourself, always add the acid slowly to the water; never add the water to the acid.

## Electricity

● When using an electric power tool, inspection light etc., always ensure that the appliance is correctly connected to its plug and that, where necessary, it is properly grounded (earthed). Do not use such appliances in damp conditions and, again, beware of creating a spark or applying excessive heat in the vicinity of fuel or fuel vapour. Also ensure that the appliances meet national safety standards.

● A severe electric shock can result from touching certain parts of the electrical system, such as the spark plug wires (HT leads), when the engine is running or being cranked, particularly if components are damp or the insulation is defective. Where an electronic ignition system is used, the secondary (HT) voltage is much higher and could prove fatal.

# Remember...

✗ **Don't** start the engine without first ascertaining that the transmission is in neutral.

✗ **Don't** suddenly remove the pressure cap from a hot cooling system - cover it with a cloth and release the pressure gradually first, or you may get scalded by escaping coolant.

✗ **Don't** attempt to drain oil until you are sure it has cooled sufficiently to avoid scalding you.

✗ **Don't** grasp any part of the engine or exhaust system without first ascertaining that it is cool enough not to burn you.

✗ **Don't** allow brake fluid or antifreeze to contact the machine's paintwork or plastic components.

✗ **Don't** siphon toxic liquids such as fuel, hydraulic fluid or antifreeze by mouth, or allow them to remain on your skin.

✗ **Don't** inhale dust - it may be injurious to health (see Asbestos heading).

✗ **Don't** allow any spilled oil or grease to remain on the floor - wipe it up right away, before someone slips on it.

✗ **Don't** use ill-fitting spanners or other tools which may slip and cause injury.

✗ **Don't** lift a heavy component which may be beyond your capability - get assistance.

✗ **Don't** rush to finish a job or take unverified short cuts.

✗ **Don't** allow children or animals in or around an unattended vehicle.

✗ **Don't** inflate a tyre above the recommended pressure. Apart from over-stressing the carcass, in extreme cases the tyre may blow off forcibly.

✔ **Do** ensure that the machine is supported securely at all times. This is especially important when the machine is blocked up to aid wheel or fork removal.

✔ **Do** take care when attempting to loosen a stubborn nut or bolt. It is generally better to pull on a spanner, rather than push, so that if you slip, you fall away from the machine rather than onto it.

✔ **Do** wear eye protection when using power tools such as drill, sander, bench grinder etc.

✔ **Do** use a barrier cream on your hands prior to undertaking dirty jobs - it will protect your skin from infection as well as making the dirt easier to remove afterwards; but make sure your hands aren't left slippery. Note that long-term contact with used engine oil can be a health hazard.

✔ **Do** keep loose clothing (cuffs, ties etc. and long hair) well out of the way of moving mechanical parts.

✔ **Do** remove rings, wristwatch etc., before working on the vehicle - especially the electrical system.

✔ **Do** keep your work area tidy - it is only too easy to fall over articles left lying around.

✔ **Do** exercise caution when compressing springs for removal or installation. Ensure that the tension is applied and released in a controlled manner, using suitable tools which preclude the possibility of the spring escaping violently.

✔ **Do** ensure that any lifting tackle used has a safe working load rating adequate for the job.

✔ **Do** get someone to check periodically that all is well, when working alone on the vehicle.

✔ **Do** carry out work in a logical sequence and check that everything is correctly assembled and tightened afterwards.

✔ **Do** remember that your vehicle's safety affects that of yourself and others. If in doubt on any point, get professional advice.

● If in spite of following these precautions, you are unfortunate enough to injure yourself, seek medical attention as soon as possible.

## Identifying model years

The procedures in this manual identify the bikes by model code. The model code (eg GSX-R**V**) is printed on the identification plate or label, which is located on the right-hand frame spar close to the steering head. The model code and production year can also be determined from the frame serial numbers as follows:

**UK models**

| Model, code and year | Frame number | Carburettor number |
| --- | --- | --- |
| GSX-R600V (1997) | JS1AD111400100001 - on | 34EO |
| GSX-R600W (1998) | JS1AD111400101736 - on | 34EO |
| GSX-R600X (1999) | JS1AD111400103985 - on | 34EO |
| GSX-R750T (1996) | JS1GR7DA000500001 - on | 33EO |
| GSX-R750V (1997) | JS1GR7DA000504678 - on | 33EO |
| GSX-R750W (1998) | JS1GR7DA000507570 - on | Not applicable |
| GSX-R750X (1999) | JS1GR7DA000511803 - on | Not applicable |

**US models**

| Model, code and year | Frame number | Carburettor number |
| --- | --- | --- |
| GSX-R600V (1997) | JS1GN78A V2100001 - on | 34E1/34E3 (US/CALIF) |
| GSX-R600W (1998) | JS1GN78A W2100001 - on | 34E1/34E3 (US/CALIF) |
| GSX-R600X (1999) | JS1GN78A X2100001 - on | 34E1/34E3 (US/CALIF) |
| GSX-R750T (1996) | JS1GR7DA T2100001 - on | 33E1/33E7 (US/CALIF) |
| GSX-R750V (1997) | JS1GR7DA V2100001 - on | 33E1/33E7 (US/CALIF) |
| GSX-R750W (1998) | JS1GR7DA W2100001 - on | Not applicable |
| GSX-R750X (1999) | JS1GR7DA X2100001 - on | Not applicable |

The frame serial number or VIN (Vehicle Identification Number) is stamped into the right-hand side of the steering head. The engine number is stamped into the back of the crankcase. Both of these numbers should be recorded and kept in a safe place so they can be furnished to law enforcement officials in the event of a theft. Where applicable, the carburettor number is stamped into the body of each carburettor.

The frame serial number, engine serial number and carburettor identification number should also be kept in a handy place (such as with your driving licence) so they are always available when purchasing or ordering parts for your machine.

## Buying spare parts

Once you have found all the identification numbers, record them for reference when buying parts. Since the manufacturers change specifications, parts and vendors (companies that manufacture various components on the machine), providing the ID numbers is the only way to be reasonably sure that you are buying the correct parts.

Whenever possible, take the worn part to the dealer so direct comparison with the new component can be made. Along the trail from the manufacturer to the parts shelf, there are numerous places that the part can end up with the wrong number or be listed incorrectly.

The two places to purchase new parts for your motorcycle – the accessory store and the franchised dealer – differ in the type of parts they carry. While dealers can obtain virtually every part for your motorcycle, the accessory dealer is usually limited to normal high wear items such as shock absorbers, spark plugs, various engine gaskets, cables, chains, brake parts, etc. Rarely will an accessory outlet have major suspension components, cylinders, transmission gears, or cases.

Used parts can be obtained for roughly half the price of new ones, but you can't always be sure of what you're getting. Once again, take your worn part to the breaker (wrecking yard) for direct comparison.

Whether buying new, used or rebuilt parts, the best course is to deal directly with someone who specialises in parts for your particular make.

**The engine number is stamped into the back of the crankcase**

**The identification plate or label is on the right-hand frame spar close to the steering head**

**The frame number is stamped on the right-hand side of the steering head**

**Note:** *The daily (pre-ride) checks outlined in the owner's manual covers those items which should be inspected on a daily basis.*

# 1 Engine/transmission oil level check

## Before you start:

✔ Start the engine and allow it to reach normal operating temperature.

*Caution: Do not run the engine in an enclosed space such as a garage or workshop.*

✔ Stop the engine and support the motorcycle in an upright position, using an auxiliary stand if required. Allow it to stand undisturbed for a few minutes to allow the oil level to stabilise. Make sure the motorcycle is on level ground.

## The correct oil

● Modern, high-revving engines place great demands on their oil. It is very important that the correct oil for your bike is used.

● Always top up with a good quality oil of the specified type and viscosity and do not overfill the engine.

| Oil type | API grade SF or SG (minimum) motor oil |
|---|---|
| Oil viscosity | SAE 10W40 |

## Bike care:

● If you have to add oil frequently, you should check whether you have any oil leaks. If there is no sign of oil leakage from the joints and gaskets the engine could be burning oil (see *Fault Finding*).

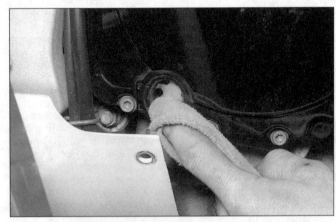

**1** Wipe the oil level window in the clutch cover so that it is clean.

**2** With the motorcycle held vertical, the oil level should lie between the 'F' and 'L' lines.

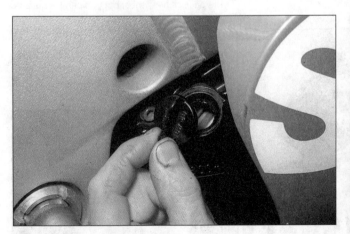

**3** If the level is below the 'L' line, remove the filler cap from the top of the clutch cover.

**4** Top the engine up with the recommended grade and type of oil, to bring the level up to the 'F' line on the window. Do not overfill.

## 2 Coolant level check

**Warning: DO NOT remove the radiator pressure cap to add coolant. Topping up is done via the coolant reservoir tank filler. DO NOT leave open containers of coolant about, as it is poisonous.**

### Before you start:
✔ Make sure you have a supply of coolant available (a mixture of 50% distilled water and 50% corrosion inhibited ethylene glycol anti-freeze is needed).
✔ Support the motorcycle in an upright position, using an auxiliary stand if required, whilst checking the level. Make sure the motorcycle is on level ground.

### Bike care:
● Use only the specified coolant mixture. It is important that anti-freeze is used in the system all year round, and not just in the winter. Do not top the system up using only water, as the system will become too diluted.
● Do not overfill the reservoir tank. If the coolant is significantly above the 'F' level line at any time, the surplus should be siphoned or drained off to prevent the possibility of it being expelled out of the overflow hose.
● If the coolant level falls steadily, check the system for leaks (see Chapter 1). If no leaks are found and the level continues to fall, it is recommended that the machine is taken to a Suzuki dealer for a pressure test.

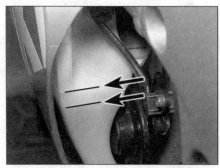

**1** The coolant reservoir is located on the inside of the left-hand fairing side panel. The coolant 'F' and 'L' level lines (arrowed) are on the back of the reservoir.

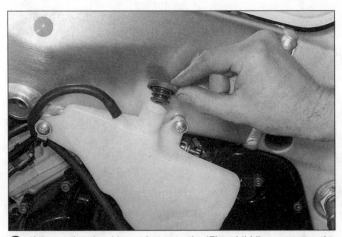

**2** If the coolant level is not between the 'F' and 'L' lines, remove the left-hand fairing side panel (see Chapter 8), then remove the reservoir filler cap.

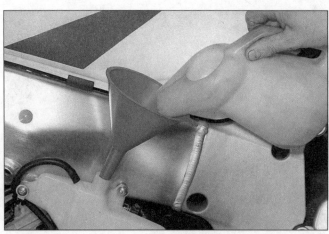

**3** Top the coolant level up with the recommended coolant mixture, using a funnel to avoid spillage. Fit the cap securely, then install the fairing side panel.

## 3 Suspension, steering and final drive checks

### Drive chain
● Check that the drive chain slack isn't excessive, adjust if necessary (see Chapter 1).
● If the chain looks dry, lubricate it (see Chapter 1).

### Suspension and Steering
● Check that the front and rear suspension operates smoothly without binding.
● Check that the suspension is adjusted as required.

● Check that the steering moves smoothly from lock-to-lock.

# 4 Brake fluid level checks

> **Warning:** Brake hydraulic fluid can harm your eyes and damage painted surfaces, so use extreme caution when handling and pouring it and cover surrounding surfaces with rag. Do not use fluid that has been standing open for some time, as it absorbs moisture from the air which can cause a dangerous loss of braking effectiveness.

## Before you start:

✔ Support the motorcycle in an upright position, using an auxiliary stand if required, and turn the handlebars until the top of the front brake master cylinder is as level as possible.

✔ The rear master cylinder reservoir is located behind the seat cowling on the right-hand side of the machine.

✔ If topping up is necessary, make sure you have the correct hydraulic fluid. DOT 4 is recommended.

✔ Wrap a rag around the reservoir being worked on to ensure that any spillage does not come into contact with painted surfaces.

✔ Access to the rear reservoir cap screws is restricted by the seat cowling. Remove the cowling to access the screws (see Chapter 8).

## Bike care:

● The fluid in the front and rear brake master cylinder reservoirs will drop slightly as the brake pads wear down.

● If any fluid reservoir requires repeated topping-up this is an indication of an hydraulic leak somewhere in the system, which should be investigated immediately.

● Check for signs of fluid leakage from the hydraulic hoses and components – if found, rectify immediately.

● Check the operation of both brakes before taking the machine on the road; if there is evidence of air in the system (spongy feel to lever or pedal), it must be bled as described in Chapter 7.

**1** The front brake fluid level is visible through the reservoir body – it must be between the UPPER and LOWER level lines.

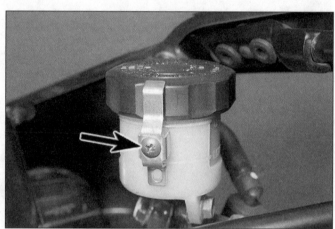

**2** If the level is below the LOWER level line, remove the reservoir cap clamp screw (arrowed), then unscrew the cap and remove the diaphragm plate and the diaphragm.

**3** Top up with new clean DOT 4 brake fluid, until the level is just below the UPPER level line. Do not overfill the reservoir, and take care to avoid spills (see **Warning** above).

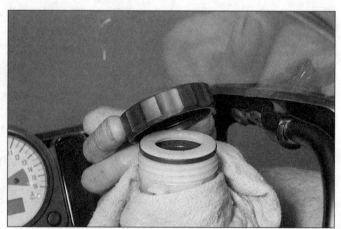

**4** Ensure that the diaphragm is correctly seated before installing the plate and cap. Tighten the cap and the clamp screw securely.

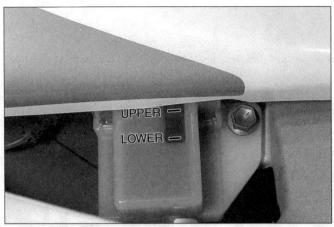

**5** The rear brake fluid level is visible by looking through the translucent body of the reservoir - the fluid level must be between the UPPER and LOWER level lines.

**6** If the level is below the LOWER level line, remove the seat cowling (see Chapter 8). Unscrew the two bolts securing the fuel tank bracket to the frame and swing the bracket upwards.

**7** Unscrew the reservoir cover screws and remove the cover and diaphragm.

**8** Top up with new clean DOT 4 brake fluid, until the level is just below the UPPER level line. Do not overfill the reservoir, and take care to avoid spills (see **Warning** above).

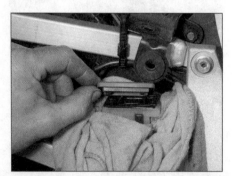

**9** Ensure that the diaphragm is correctly seated before installing the cover. Tighten the cover screws securely, then install the tank bracket and seat cowling (see Chapter 8).

# 5 Legal and safety checks

## Lighting and signalling

● Take a minute to check that the headlight, taillight, brake light, instrument lights and turn signals all work correctly.
● Check that the horn sounds when the switch is operated.
● A working speedometer graduated in mph is a statutory requirement in the UK.

## Safety

● Check that the throttle grip rotates smoothly and snaps shut when released, in all steering positions. Also check for the correct amount of freeplay (see Chapter 1).
● Check that the engine shuts off when the kill switch is operated.
● Check that sidestand return spring holds the stand securely up when retracted.

## Fuel

● This may seem obvious, but check that you have enough fuel to complete your journey. If you notice signs of fuel leakage, rectify the cause immediately.
● Ensure you use the correct grade unleaded fuel – see Chapter 4 Specifications.

# 6 Tyre checks

## The correct pressures

● The tyres must be checked when **cold**, not immediately after riding. Note that low tyre pressures may cause the tyre to slip on the rim or come off. High tyre pressures will cause abnormal tread wear and unsafe handling.

● Use an accurate pressure gauge.

● Proper air pressure will increase tyre life and provide maximum stability and ride comfort.

| Tyre pressures (cold) | |
|---|---|
| Front | 36 psi (2.50 Bar) |
| Rear | 36 psi (2.50 Bar) |

## Tyre care

● Check the tyres carefully for cuts, tears, embedded nails or other sharp objects and excessive wear. Operation of the motorcycle with excessively worn tyres is extremely hazardous, as traction and handling are directly affected.

● Check the condition of the tyre valve and ensure the dust cap is in place.

● Pick out any stones or nails which may have become embedded in the tyre tread. If left, they will eventually penetrate through the casing and cause a puncture.

● If tyre damage is apparent, or unexplained loss of pressure is experienced, seek the advice of a tyre fitting specialist without delay.

1 Check the tyre pressures when the tyres are **cold** and keep them properly inflated.

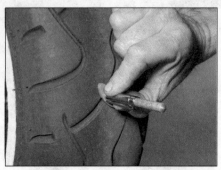

2 Measure tread depth at the centre of the tyre using a tread depth gauge.

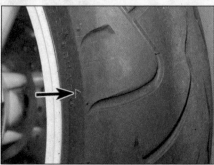

3 Tyre tread wear indicator bar and its location marking (usually either an arrow, a triangle or the letters TWI) on the sidewall (arrowed).

## Tyre tread depth

● At the time of writing UK law requires that tread depth must be at least 1 mm over 3/4 of the tread breadth all the way around the tyre, with no bald patches. Many riders, however, consider 2 mm tread depth minimum to be a safer limit. The manufacturer's recommended minimum tread depth is given below.

● Many tyres now incorporate wear indicators in the tread. Identify the triangular pointer or 'TWI' mark on the tyre sidewall to locate the indicator bar and renew the tyre if the tread has worn down to the bar.

| Minimum tyre tread depths | |
|---|---|
| Front | 1.6 mm |
| Rear | 2.0 mm |

# Chapter 1
# Routine maintenance and Servicing

## Contents

## Degrees of difficulty

| | | | | |
|---|---|---|---|---|
| **Easy,** suitable for novice with little experience  | **Fairly easy,** suitable for beginner with some experience  | **Fairly difficult,** suitable for competent DIY mechanic | **Difficult,** suitable for experienced DIY mechanic | **Very difficult,** suitable for expert DIY or professional |

## Specifications

### Engine/transmission

Valve clearances (COLD engine)
Inlet valves . . . . . . . . . . . . . . . . . . . . . . . . . . . . . . . . . . . . . . . . 0.10 to 0.20 mm
Exhaust valves . . . . . . . . . . . . . . . . . . . . . . . . . . . . . . . . . . . . . 0.20 to 0.30 mm
Spark plugs
Type
    Standard . . . . . . . . . . . . . . . . . . . . . . . . . . . . . . . . . . . . . . NGK CR9E or Nippondenso U27ESR-N
    For cold climate (below 5°C) . . . . . . . . . . . . . . . . . . . . . . . . NGK CR8E or Nippondenso U24ESR-N
    For extended high speed riding . . . . . . . . . . . . . . . . . . . . . . NGK CR10E or Nippondenso U31ESR-N
Electrode gap . . . . . . . . . . . . . . . . . . . . . . . . . . . . . . . . . . . . . 0.7 to 0.8 mm
Engine idle speed
UK GSX-R600 models . . . . . . . . . . . . . . . . . . . . . . . . . . . . . . 1200 ± 100 rpm
US GSX-R600 models . . . . . . . . . . . . . . . . . . . . . . . . . . . . . . 1300 ± 100 rpm
All GSX-R750 models . . . . . . . . . . . . . . . . . . . . . . . . . . . . . . . 1200 ± 100 rpm
Clutch release mechanism screw (see text) . . . . . . . . . . . . . . . . . 1 1/4 turns out
Cylinder compression
Standard . . . . . . . . . . . . . . . . . . . . . . . . . . . . . . . . . . . . . . . . 156 to 213 psi (11 to 15 Bar)*
Minimum . . . . . . . . . . . . . . . . . . . . . . . . . . . . . . . . . . . . . . . . 128 psi (9 Bar)*
Maximum difference between cylinders . . . . . . . . . . . . . . . . . . . 28 psi (2 Bar)*
Oil pressure (with engine warm) . . . . . . . . . . . . . . . . . . . . . . . . . 28 to 71 psi (2.0 to 5.0 Bar) at 3000 rpm, oil at 60°C
*Note: If all cylinders record less than the standard (even if they are above the minimum), or if the difference between any two cylinders is greater than the maximum, or if any one cylinder is less than the minimum, the engine should be overhauled.

## Frame and cycle parts

Drive chain
    Freeplay .......................................... 20 to 30 mm
    Stretch limit (21 pin length – see text) ...................... 319.4 mm
Fuel level
    GSX-R600 ......................................... 15.5 ± 0.5 mm
    GSX-R750T and V ................................... 15.7 ± 0.5 mm
Freeplay adjustments
    Clutch cable
        GSX-R600 models .............................. 10 to 15 mm
        GSX-R750 models .............................. 3 to 13 mm
    Throttle cables
        GSX-R600V models, GSX-R750T and V models
            Accelerator cable ......................... 0.5 to 1.0 mm
            Decelerator cable ......................... 0.5 to 1.0 mm
        GSX-R600W and X models, GSX-R750W and X models
            Accelerator cable ......................... 2 to 4 mm
            Decelerator cable ......................... zero freeplay (see text)
Rear brake pedal height ................................ 55 mm
Tyre pressures (cold) and tread depth ...................... see *Daily (pre-ride) checks*

## Recommended lubricants and fluids

Drive chain lubricant ................................ Heavy engine oil (40 or 50 weight), or aerosol chain lubricant suitable for O-ring chains
Engine/transmission oil type ............................ API grade SF or SG (minimum) motor oil
Engine/transmission oil viscosity ....................... SAE 10W40
Engine/transmission oil capacity
    Oil change .......................................... 2.6 litres
    Oil and filter change ................................. 2.8 litres
    Following engine overhaul – dry engine, new filter .............. 3.5 litres
Coolant type ........................................ 50% distilled water, 50% corrosion inhibited ethylene glycol anti-freeze
Coolant capacity ..................................... 2.55 litres
Brake fluid ......................................... DOT 4

### Miscellaneous

Steering head bearings ................................ Lithium-based multi-purpose grease
Wheel bearings (unsealed) ............................. Lithium-based multi-purpose grease
Swingarm pivot bearings .............................. Lithium-based multi-purpose grease
Suspension linkage bearings ........................... Lithium-based multi-purpose grease
Bearing seal lips .................................... Lithium-based multi-purpose grease
Gearchange lever/rear brake pedal/footrest pivots .............. Lithium-based multi-purpose grease
Front brake lever and clutch lever pivots ..................... 10W40 motor oil
Cables ............................................ Cable lubricant or 10W40 motor oil
Sidestand pivot and spring hook ......................... Lithium-based multi-purpose grease
Throttle grip ....................................... Multi-purpose grease or dry film lubricant

## Torque settings

Rear axle nut ....................................... 100 Nm
Spark plugs ........................................ 12 Nm
Engine/transmission oil drain plug ....................... 28 Nm
Steering stem nut .................................... 90 Nm
Fork clamp bolts .................................... 23 Nm
Exhaust downpipe clamp bolts .......................... 23 Nm
Silencer mounting bolts ............................... 23 Nm
Brake hose banjo bolts ................................ 23 Nm
Main oil gallery plug ................................. 40 Nm

**Note:** *Always perform the pre-ride inspection at every maintenance interval (in addition to the procedures listed). The intervals listed below are the intervals recommended by the manufacturer for each particular operation during the model years covered in this manual. Your owner's manual may have different intervals for your model.*

## Daily (pre-ride)
☐ See *'Daily (pre-ride) checks'* at the beginning of this manual.

## After the initial 600 miles (1000 km)
**Note:** *This check is usually performed by a Suzuki dealer after the first 600 miles (1000 km) from new. Thereafter, maintenance is carried out according to the following intervals of the schedule.*

## Every 600 miles (1000 km)
☐ Check, adjust and lubricate the drive chain (Section 1)

## Every 4000 miles (6000 km) or 6 months
*Carry out all the items under the Daily (pre-ride) checks and the 600 mile (1000 km) check, plus the following:*
☐ Clean the air filter element (Section 2)
☐ Check the spark plugs (Section 3)
☐ Check the fuel hoses, EVAP hoses (California models), and fuel system components (Section 4)
☐ Change the engine oil (Section 5)
☐ Check and adjust the engine idle speed (Section 6)
☐ Check throttle/choke cable operation and freeplay (Section 7)
☐ Check the operation of the clutch (Section 8)
☐ Check the cooling system (Section 9)
☐ Check for drive chain wear and stretch (Section 10)
☐ Check the brake pads for wear (Section 11)
☐ Check the operation of the brakes, and for fluid leakage (Section 12)
☐ Check the tyre and wheel condition, and the tyre tread depth (Section 13)
☐ Check the tightness of all nuts and bolts (Section 14)
☐ Check and lubricate the sidestand, lever pivots and cables (Section 15)

## Every 7500 miles (12,000 km) or 12 months
*Carry out all the items under the 4000 mile (6000 km) check, plus the following:*
☐ Renew the spark plugs (Section 16)
☐ Check carburettor or throttle body synchronisation (Section 17)
☐ Check the steering head bearing freeplay (Section 18)
☐ Check the front and rear suspension (Section 19)
☐ Check the tightness of the exhaust system bolts (Section 20)

## Every 11,000 miles (18,000 km) or 18 months
*Carry out all the items under the 4000 mile (6000 km) check, plus the following:*
☐ Renew the air filter element (Section 21)
☐ Change the engine oil and renew the oil filter (Section 22)

## Every 15,000 miles (24,000 km) or 24 months
*Carry out all the items under the 7500 mile (12,000 km) check, plus the following:*
☐ Check the valve clearances (Section 23)

## Every two years
☐ Change the brake fluid (Section 24)
☐ Change the coolant (Section 25)

## Every four years
☐ Renew the brake hoses (Section 26)
☐ Renew the fuel hoses and EVAP hoses (California models) (Section 27)

## Non-scheduled maintenance
☐ Check the headlight aim (Section 28)
☐ Check the wheel bearings (Section 29)
☐ Change the front fork oil (Section 30)
☐ Check the cylinder compression (Section 31)
☐ Check the engine oil pressure (Section 32)
☐ Re-grease the steering head bearings (Section 33)
☐ Re-grease the swingarm and suspension linkage bearings (Section 34)
☐ Renew the brake master cylinder and caliper seals (Section 35)

1

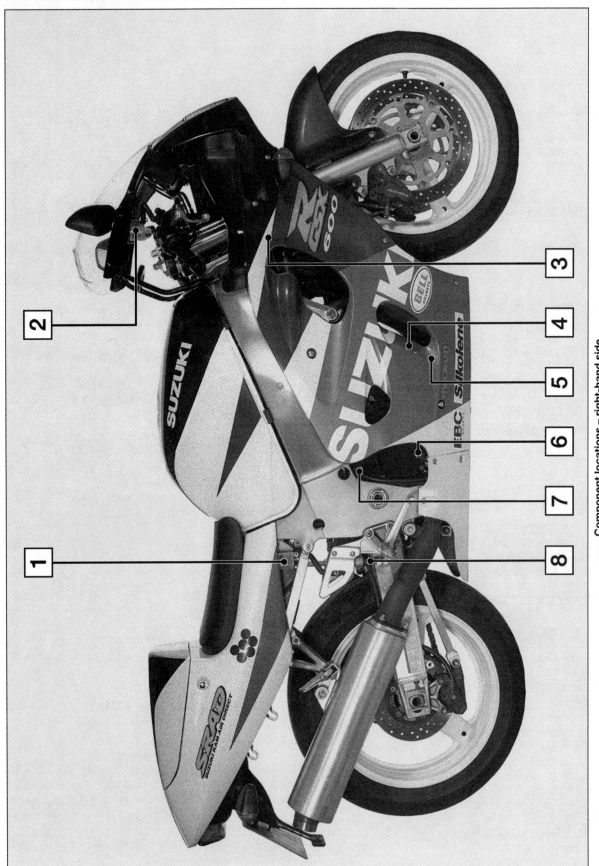

**Component locations – right-hand side**

1   Rear brake fluid reservoir
2   Front brake fluid reservoir
3   Radiator pressure cap
4   Engine/transmission oil filter
5   Engine/transmission oil
    drain plug
6   Engine/transmission oil level sightglass
7   Engine/transmission oil filler
8   Rear brake pedal height adjuster

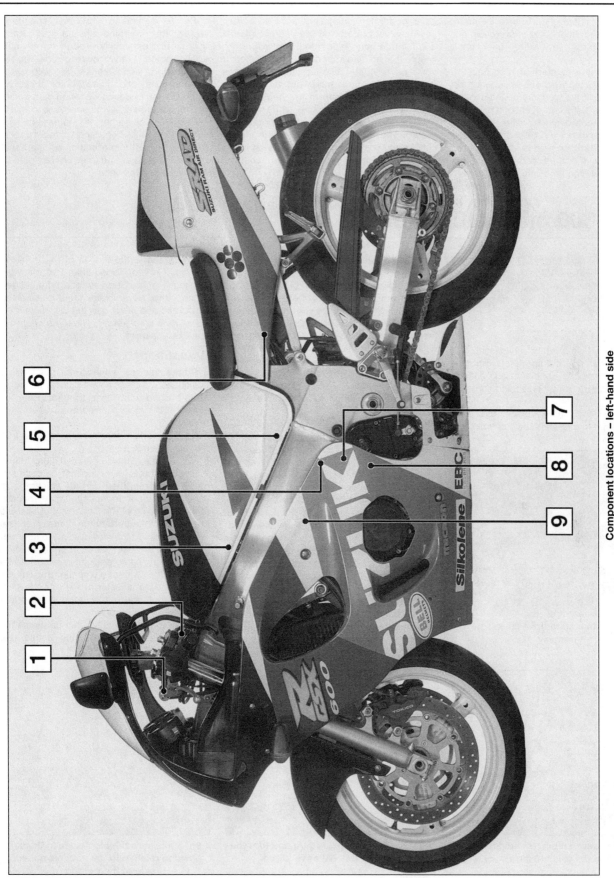

**Component locations – left-hand side**

1  Clutch cable upper adjuster
2  Steering head bearing adjuster
3  Air filter
4  Idle speed adjuster
5  Fuel filter
6  Battery
7  Clutch cable lower adjuster
8  Clutch release mechanism adjuster
9  Coolant reservoir

**1**

**1** This Chapter is designed to help the home mechanic maintain his/her motorcycle for safety, economy, long life and peak performance.

**2** Deciding where to start or plug into the routine maintenance schedule depends on several factors. If the warranty period on your motorcycle has just expired, and if it has been maintained according to the warranty standards, you may want to pick up routine maintenance as it coincides with the next mileage or calendar interval. If you have owned the machine for some time but have never performed any maintenance on it, then you may want to start at the nearest interval and include some additional procedures to ensure that nothing important is overlooked. If you have just had a major engine overhaul, then you may want to start the maintenance routine from the beginning. If you have a used machine and have no knowledge of its history or maintenance record, you may desire to combine all the checks into one large service initially and then settle into the maintenance schedule prescribed.

**3** Before beginning any maintenance or repair, the machine should be cleaned thoroughly, especially around the oil filter, spark plugs, valve cover, side panels, carburettors, etc. Cleaning will help ensure that dirt does not contaminate the engine and will allow you to detect wear and damage that could otherwise easily go unnoticed.

**4** Certain maintenance information is sometimes printed on decals attached to the motorcycle. If the information on the decals differs from that included here, use the information on the decal.

# Every 600 miles (1000 km)

**1   Drive chain** – check, adjustment, cleaning and lubrication

### Check

**1** A neglected drive chain won't last long and can quickly damage the sprockets. Routine chain adjustment and lubrication isn't difficult and will ensure maximum chain and sprocket life.

**2** To check the chain, place the bike on its sidestand and shift the transmission

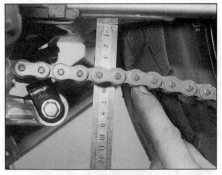

**1.3  Measuring drive chain freeplay**

into neutral. Make sure the ignition switch is OFF.

**3** Push up on the bottom run of the chain and measure the slack midway between the two sprockets, then compare your measurement to that listed in this Chapter's Specifications **(see illustration)**. As the chain stretches with wear, adjustment will periodically be necessary (see below). Since the chain will rarely wear evenly, roll the bike forwards so that another section of chain can be checked; do this several times to check the entire length of chain.

**4** In some cases where lubrication has been neglected, corrosion and galling may cause the links to bind and kink, which effectively shortens the chain's length. Such links should be thoroughly cleaned and worked free. If the chain is tight between the sprockets, rusty or kinked, it's time to fit a new one (see Chapter 6). If you find a tight area, mark it with felt pen or paint, and repeat the measurement after the bike has been ridden. If the chain's still tight in the same area, it may be damaged or worn. Because a tight or kinked chain can damage the transmission output shaft bearing, it's a good idea to renew it.

*Caution: If the machine is ridden with excessive slack in the drive chain, the chain could contact the frame and swingarm, causing severe damage.*

**5** Check the entire length of the chain for damaged rollers, loose links and pins, and missing O-rings. Fit a new chain if damage is found. **Note:** *Never install a new chain on old sprockets, and never use the old chain if you install new sprockets – renew the chain and sprockets as a set.*

### Adjustment

**6** Rotate the rear wheel until the chain is positioned with the tightest point at the centre of its bottom run. If available, raise the rear wheel off the ground using an auxiliary stand or support.

**7** On US models, remove the split pin from the rear axle nut.

**8** Slacken the rear axle nut **(see illustration)**.

**9** Slacken the adjuster locknut on each side of the swingarm, then turn the adjuster bolts evenly until the amount of freeplay specified at the beginning of the Chapter is obtained at the centre of the bottom run of the chain **(see illustration)**. Following chain adjustment, check that the back of each chain adjuster block is in the same position in relation to the marks on the swingarm **(see illustration)**. It is important each adjuster aligns with the same notch; if not, the rear wheel will be out of alignment with the front.

**10** Tighten the axle nut to the torque setting specified at the beginning of the Chapter **(see**

**1.8  Remove the split pin (US models), then slacken the axle nut (arrowed)**

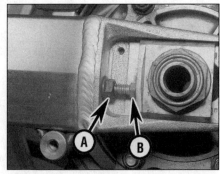

**1.9a  Slacken the locknut (A) and turn the adjuster bolt (B) as required**

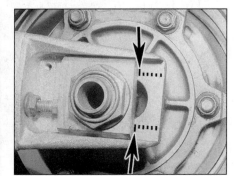

**1.9b  Make sure the blocks are in the same position relative to the notches on each side of the swingarm**

**illustration)**. Tighten the chain adjuster locknuts securely **(see illustration 1.9a)**. On US models, fit a new split pin through the axle nut and bend the ends of the pin securely.

### Cleaning and lubrication

**11** If required, wash the chain in paraffin (kerosene), then wipe it off and allow it to dry, using compressed air if available. If the chain is excessively dirty it should be removed from the machine and allowed to soak in the paraffin (see Chapter 6).
*Caution: Don't use petrol (gasoline), solvent or other cleaning fluids which might damage the internal sealing properties of the chain. Don't use high-pressure water. The entire process shouldn't take longer than ten minutes – if it does, the O-rings in the chain rollers could be damaged.*
**12** For routine lubrication, the best time to lubricate the chain is after the motorcycle has been ridden. When the chain is warm, the lubricant will penetrate the joints between the

**1.10 Tighten the axle nut to the specified torque**

side plates better than when cold. **Note:** *Suzuki specifies heavy engine oil (40 or 50 weight) or an aerosol drive chain lubricant suitable for O-ring chains only; do not use a chain lube which may contain solvents that could damage the O-rings.* Apply the lubricant to the area where the side plates overlap – not the middle of the rollers **(see illustration)**.

**1.12 Applying an aerosol chain lubricant**

**HAYNES HiNT** *Apply the lubricant to the top of the lower chain run, so centrifugal force will work the oil into the chain when the bike is moving. After applying the lubricant, let it soak in a few minutes before wiping off any excess.*

# Every 4000 miles (6000 km) or 6 months

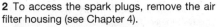

### 2 Air filter – cleaning

*Caution: If the machine is continually ridden in dusty conditions, the filter should be cleaned more frequently.*
**1** Raise the fuel tank (see Chapter 4).
**2** Remove the air filter cover screws and lift off the cover **(see illustration)**. Withdraw the filter from the housing **(see illustration)**.
**3** Tap the filter on a hard surface to dislodge any dirt. If compressed air is available, use it to clean the element, directing the air from the outside **(see illustration)**. If the element is torn or extremely dirty, install a new one.
**4** Install the filter by reversing the removal procedure. Make sure the filter is properly seated, and the O-ring around the underside of the cover is located in its groove. When fitting the cover, locate the tabs at the back in the slots in the housing **(see illustration)**.
**5** Remove the drain cover(s) from the bottom of the air filter housing. Allow any fluid to drain, then install the cover(s).

### 3 Spark plug gaps – check and adjustment

**1** Make sure your spark plug socket is the correct size before attempting to remove the plugs – a suitable one is supplied in the motorcycle's tool kit which is stored under the passenger seat. Make sure the ignition is switched OFF.

**2** To access the spark plugs, remove the air filter housing (see Chapter 4).
**3** Clean the area around the plug caps to prevent any dirt falling into the spark plug channels. Check that the cylinder location is

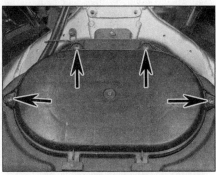

**2.2a Remove the screws (arrowed) and the cover . . .**

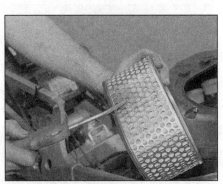

**2.3 Clean the element using compressed air directed from the outside**

marked on each plug lead or connector and mark them accordingly if not.
**4** On GSX-R750T and V models, pull the spark plug cap off each spark plug.
**5** On all other models, disconnect the ignition

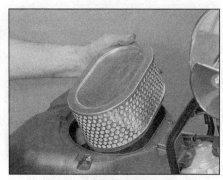

**2.2b . . . and lift out the filter**

**2.4 Locate the tabs on the back of the cover in the slots in the housing**

**1**

3.5a Disconnect the wiring connector . . .

3.5b . . . then pull the coil/plug cap off the spark plug

3.6 Removing a spark plug using the tool supplied in the bike's toolkit

coil/plug cap wiring connectors (see illustration). Pull the coil/cap off each spark plug (see illustration).

6 Clean the area around the base of the plugs to prevent any dirt falling into the engine. Using either the plug removing tool supplied in the bike's toolkit or a deep socket type wrench, unscrew the plugs from the cylinder head (see illustration). Lay each plug out in relation to its cylinder; if any plug shows up a problem it will then be easy to identify the troublesome cylinder.

7 Inspect the electrodes for wear. Both the centre and side electrodes should have square edges and the side electrodes should be of uniform thickness. Look for excessive deposits and evidence of a cracked or

3.10a A wire type gauge is recommended to measure the spark plug electrode gap

chipped insulator around the centre electrode. Compare your spark plugs to the colour spark plug reading chart at the end of this manual. Check the threads, the washer and the ceramic insulator body for cracks and other damage.

8 If the electrodes are not excessively worn, and if the deposits can be easily removed with a wire brush, the plugs can be re-gapped and re-used (if no cracks or chips are visible in the insulator). If in doubt concerning the condition of the plugs, install new ones – the expense is minimal.

9 Cleaning spark plugs by sandblasting is permitted, provided you clean the plugs with a high flash-point solvent afterwards.

10 Before installing the plugs, make sure they are the correct type and heat range and check the gap between the electrodes (see illustrations). Compare the gap to that specified and adjust as necessary. If the gap must be adjusted, bend the side electrodes only and be very careful not to chip or crack the insulator nose (see illustration). Make sure the washer is in place before installing each plug.

11 Since the cylinder head is made of aluminium, which is soft and easily damaged, thread the plugs into the head turning the tool by hand (see illustration). Once the plugs are finger-tight, tighten them to the torque setting specified at the beginning of the Chapter. If a torque wrench is not available, tighten them an extra 1/4 to 1/2 turn. Do not over-tighten them.

**HAYNES HiNT** *As the plugs are quite recessed, slip a short length of hose over the end of the plug to use as a tool to thread it into place. The hose will grip the plug well enough to turn it, but will start to slip if the plug begins to cross-thread in the hole – this will prevent damaged threads.*

12 Reconnect the spark plug caps or coils/caps, making sure they are securely connected to the correct cylinder (see illustration 3.5b). Where appropriate, connect the coil/cap wiring connectors (see illustration 3.5a).

13 Install the air filter housing (see Chapter 4).

**HAYNES HiNT** *Stripped plug threads in the cylinder head can be repaired with a thread insert – see 'Tools and Workshop Tips' in the Reference section.*

4 Fuel system – check

⚠ *Warning: Petrol (gasoline) is extremely flammable, so take extra precautions when you work on any part of the fuel*

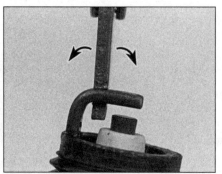

3.10c Adjust the electrode gap by bending the side electrode only, as indicated by the arrows

3.11 Thread the plug as far as possible by hand

3.10b A blade type feeler gauge can also be used

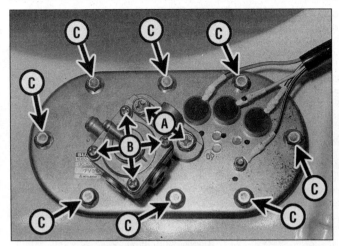

4.2 Fuel valve mounting bolts (A) and assembly screws (B), fuel pump mounting bolts (C)

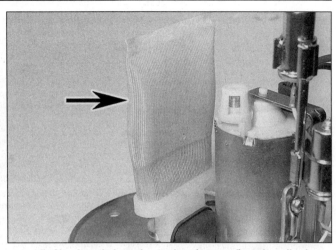

4.7 Check and clean the strainer (arrowed) as described

*system. Don't smoke or allow open flames or bare light bulbs near the work area, and don't work in a garage where a natural gas-type appliance is present. If you spill any fuel on your skin, rinse it off immediately with soap and water. When you perform any kind of work on the fuel system, wear safety glasses and have a fire extinguisher suitable for a Class B type fire (flammable liquids) on hand.*

### Check

**1** Raise the fuel tank (see Chapter 4) and check the tank, the fuel valve or pressure regulator, the fuel hoses, and on California models the EVAP system hoses (see Chapter 4), for signs of leakage, deterioration or damage; in particular check that there is no leakage from the fuel hoses. Renew any hoses which are cracked or deteriorated.

**2** On GSX-R600 and GSX-R750T and V models, if the fuel valve is leaking from between it and the fuel pump mounting plate, tighten the mounting bolts **(see illustration)**. If leakage persists, remove the valve (see Chapter 4) and renew the O-ring. If the valve itself is leaking, tighten the assembly screws. If leakage persists, a new one must be fitted (see Chapter 4). If there is leakage from between the fuel pump mounting plate and the tank, tighten the mounting bolts. If leakage persists, remove the pump and fit a new gasket (see Chapter 4).

**3** On GSX-R750W and X models, if there is leakage from between the fuel pump mounting plate and the tank, tighten the mounting bolts. If leakage persists, remove the pump and fit a new gasket (see Chapter 4).

**4** If the carburettor gaskets are leaking, the carburettors should be disassembled and rebuilt using new gaskets and seals (see Chapter 4).

### Filter renewal

**5** Cleaning and/or renewal of the fuel strainer (GSX-R600 and GSX-R750T and V models) or

strainer and filter (GSX-R750W and X models) is advised after a particularly high mileage has been covered. It is also necessary if fuel starvation is suspected.

**6** Remove the fuel pump (see Chapter 4).

**7** On GSX-R600 and GSX-R750T and V models, clean the strainer and check it for holes **(see illustration)**. Fit a new one if any are found. Blow it through and dry it using compressed air, if available.

**8** On GSX-R750W and X models, remove the screw securing the pump cover and remove it, noting how it fits. Before removing the filter, note which way up it fits and be sure to install the new one the same way round, as the direction of flow is important. Release the clamps securing the hoses to the filter and detach the hoses, then remove the screws securing the filter to the pump, noting how the slit in the bracket locates over the raised section on the mounting. Also clean the strainer and check it for holes. Fit a new one if any are found. Blow it through and dry it using compressed air, if available.

### Fuel level check – GSX-R600 and GSX-R750T and V models,

**9** A check can be made of the fuel level in the carburettors without the need to remove and dismantle the carburettors to measure the float height. To perform the check, a special tool is needed (Pt. No. 09913-10760), which consists of a calibrated gauge and some hose. Alternatively a short length of clear fuel hose and a ruler will suffice.

**10** Make sure the bike is on level ground and place it on an auxiliary stand, but making sure both wheels are on the ground. Adjust the position of the bike as necessary until the carburettors are level. This is fundamental to the accuracy of the test. Use a spirit level to ensure accuracy.

**11** Install the gauge or the fuel hose over the end of the drain nozzle on the bottom of the float chamber of the first carburettor **(see illustration 4.14)**. Unscrew the drain screw on

the bottom of the float chamber a couple of turns or until fuel flows into the hose. Make sure all air is bled from the hose by flicking it at the lowest point.

**12** Start the engine and run it for a few minutes to ensure the float chambers are full of fuel, then leave it idling.

**13** Hold the gauge or hose against the side of the carburettor so that it is vertical.

**14** When the fuel level in the hose has settled, check that the distance between the fuel level and the point shown on the carburettor body is as specified at the beginning of the Chapter **(see illustration)**. Turn off the engine.

**15** On completion, tighten the drain screw. Invert the gauge and drain the fuel into a suitable container, then remove the hose from the nozzle. Check the other carburettors in the same way.

**16** If the fuel level in any carburettor is incorrect, remove the carburettors, then remove the float chambers and adjust the float height as described in Chapter 4.

**1**

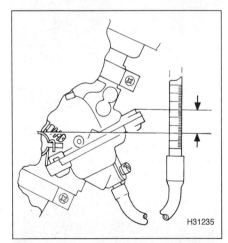

4.14 Check that the distance between the top of the fuel in the tube and the point shown on the carburettors is as specified

## 5 Engine/transmission – oil change

**Warning: Be careful when draining the oil, as the exhaust pipes, the engine, and the oil itself can cause severe burns.**

**1** Consistent routine oil and filter changes are the single most important maintenance procedure you can perform on a motorcycle. The oil not only lubricates the internal parts of the engine, transmission and clutch, but it also acts as a coolant, a cleaner, a sealant, and a protectant. Because of these demands, the oil takes a terrific amount of abuse and should be renewed often with new oil of the recommended grade and type. Saving a little money on the difference in cost between a good oil and a cheap oil won't pay off if the engine is damaged. The oil filter should be changed with every second oil change (see Section 22).

**2** Before changing the oil, warm up the engine so the oil will drain easily.

**3** Put the motorcycle on its sidestand, and position a clean drain tray below the engine. Unscrew the oil filler cap from the clutch cover to vent the crankcase and to act as a reminder that there is no oil in the engine **(see illustration)**.

**4** Next, unscrew the oil drain plug from the sump on the bottom of the engine and allow the oil to flow into the drain tray **(see illustrations)**. Hold the bike upright while the oil is draining. Check the condition of the sealing washer on the drain plug and discard it if it is in any way damaged or worn. To remove the washer from the plug, it will probably be necessary to cut it off **(see illustration)**.

**HAYNES HiNT** *To help determine whether any abnormal or excessive engine wear is occurring, place a strainer between the engine and the drain tray so that any debris in the oil is filtered out and can be examined. If there are flakes or chips of metal in the oil, then something is drastically wrong internally and the engine will have to be disassembled for inspection and repair. If there are pieces of fibre-like material in the oil, the clutch is experiencing excessive wear and should be checked*

**5** When the oil has completely drained, fit the plug into the sump, using a new sealing washer if necessary, and tighten it to the torque setting specified at the beginning of the Chapter **(see illustrations)**. Avoid overtightening, as damage to the sump will result.

**6** Refill the engine to the proper level using the recommended type and amount of oil (see *Daily (pre-ride) checks*). With the motorcycle held vertical, the oil level should lie between the 'F' and 'L' lines on the inspection window (see *Daily (pre-ride) checks*). Install the filler cap **(see illustration 5.3)**. Start the engine and let it run for two or three minutes (make sure that the oil pressure warning display and the warning light extinguish after a few seconds). Shut it off, wait a few minutes, then check the oil level. If necessary, add more oil to bring the level up to the 'F' line on the window. Check around the drain plug for leaks.

**HAYNES HiNT** *Saving a little money on the difference between good and cheap oils won't pay off if the engine is damaged as a result.*

**7** The old oil drained from the engine cannot be re-used and should be disposed of properly. Check with your local refuse disposal company, disposal facility or environmental agency to see whether they will accept the used oil for recycling. Don't pour used oil into drains or onto the ground.

OIL CARE
FOLLOW THE CODE

OIL BANK LINE
**0800 66 33 66**

*Note: It is antisocial and illegal to dump oil down the drain. To find the location of your local oil recycling bank, call this number free.*

*In the USA, note that any oil supplier must accept used oil for recycling.*

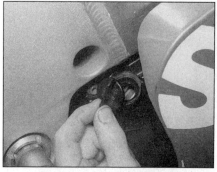

5.3 Unscrew the oil filler cap

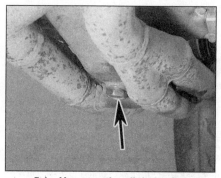

5.4a Unscrew the oil drain plug (arrowed) . . .

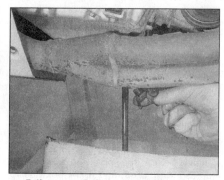

5.4b . . . and allow all the oil to drain

5.4c To remove the old sealing washer, cut it off

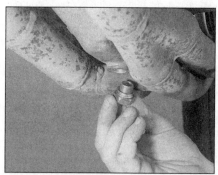

5.5a Install the drain plug, using a new sealing washer if necessary . . .

5.5b . . . and tighten it to the specified torque

**6.3 Idle speed adjuster (arrowed)**

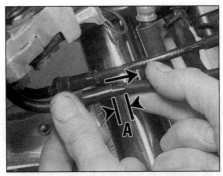

**7.3a On GSX-R600V models and GSX-R750T and V models, pull the cable out of the socket and measure the free travel (A)**

**7.3b On GSX-R600W and X models and GSX-R750W and X models, twist the throttle and measure the amount of free rotation (B)**

## 6  Idle speed – check and adjustment

**1** The idle speed should be checked and adjusted before and after the carburettors or throttle bodies are synchronised (balanced) and when it is obviously too high or too low. Before adjusting the idle speed, make sure the valve clearances and spark plug gaps are correct (see Sections 23 and 3). Also, turn the handlebars back-and-forth and see if the idle speed changes as this is done. If it does, the throttle cables may not be adjusted correctly, or may be worn out. This is a dangerous condition that can cause loss of control of the bike. Be sure to correct this problem before proceeding (see Section 7).

**2** The engine should be at normal operating temperature, which is usually reached after 10 to 15 minutes of stop and go riding. Place the motorcycle on its sidestand, and make sure the transmission is in neutral.

**3** The idle speed adjuster is located inside the left-hand fairing side panel **(see illustration)**. With the engine idling, adjust the idle speed by turning the adjuster screw until the idle speed listed in this Chapter's Specifications is obtained. Turn the screw clockwise to increase idle speed, and anti-clockwise to decrease it.

**4** Snap the throttle open and shut a few times, then recheck the idle speed. If necessary, repeat the adjustment procedure.

**5** If a smooth, steady idle can't be achieved, the fuel/air mixture may be incorrect (see Chapter 4) or the carburettors/throttle bodies may need synchronising (see Section 17).

## 7  Throttle and choke cables – check

### Throttle cables

**1** Make sure the throttle grip rotates easily from fully closed to fully open with the front wheel turned at various angles. The grip should return automatically from fully open to fully closed when released.

**2** If the throttle sticks, this is probably due to a cable fault. Remove the cables (see Chapter 4) and lubricate them (see Section 15). Install the cables, making sure they are correctly routed. If this fails to improve the operation of the throttle, the cables must be renewed. Note that in very rare cases the fault could lie in the carburettors or throttle bodies, rather than the cables, necessitating their removal and inspection of the throttle linkage (see Chapter 4).

**3** With the throttle operating smoothly, check

for a small amount of freeplay before the throttle opens and compare the amount to that listed in this Chapter's Specifications. On GSX-R600V models and GSX-R750T and V models, freeplay is measured in terms of the amount of free movement the outer cables have in their sockets in the adjusters before they become tight **(see illustration)**. On GSX-R600W and X models and GSX-R750W and X models, freeplay is measured in terms of the amount of throttle (twistgrip) rotation before the throttle opens **(see illustration)**. If it's incorrect, adjust the cables to correct it.

**4** To adjust the cables on GSX-R600V models and GSX-R750T and V models, loosen the lockring on the decelerator (throttle closing) cable adjuster, and turn the adjuster until the specified amount of freeplay is obtained (see this Chapter's Specifications) **(see illustration)**. Retighten the lockring. Now repeat the procedure for the accelerator (throttle opening) cable.

**5** To adjust the cables on GSX-R600W and X models and GSX-R750W and X models, loosen the lockring on the decelerator (throttle closing) cable adjuster and turn the adjuster fully in **(see illustration 7.4)**. Now loosen the lockring on the accelerator (throttle opening) cable and turn the adjuster until the specified amount of freeplay is obtained (see this Chapter's Specifications), then retighten the lockring. Now turn the decelerator (throttle closing) cable adjuster out until a resistance can just be felt – at this point all the freeplay has been taken up. Do not turn the adjuster out any further than the point at which the resistance is felt. Tighten the lockring.

**6** If the adjusters have reached their limit, or if major adjustment is required, reset them so that the freeplay is at a maximum (ie the adjusters are fully turned in), then raise the fuel tank and, if required for improved access, remove the air filter housing (see Chapter 4), and adjust the cables at the carburettor/throttle body end. Slacken the adjuster locknuts, then turn the adjusters until the specified amount of freeplay is obtained (see Step 3), then tighten the locknuts **(see illustrations)**. Further adjustments can now

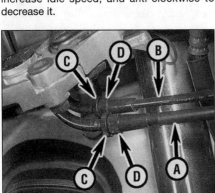

**7.4 Accelerator cable (A), decelerator cable (B). Adjuster locknut (C), adjuster (D)**

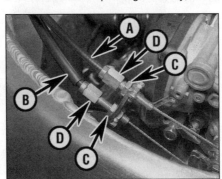

**7.6a Accelerator cable (A), decelerator cable (B). Adjuster locknut (C), adjuster (D) - carburettor models**

**1**

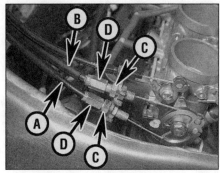

7.6b Accelerator cable (A), decelerator cable (B). Adjuster locknut (C), adjuster (D) - fuel injection models

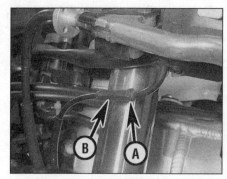

7.9 Choke cable adjuster locknut (A) and adjuster (B)

8.1 Measuring clutch cable freeplay

be made at the throttle end. If the cables cannot be adjusted as specified, install new ones (see Chapter 4).

 **Warning: Turn the handlebars all the way through their travel with the engine idling. Idle speed should not change. If it does, the cable may be routed incorrectly. Correct this condition before riding the bike.**

**7** Check that the throttle twistgrip operates smoothly and snaps shut quickly when released.

## Choke cable

**8** If the choke does not operate smoothly this is probably due to a cable fault. Remove the cable (see Chapter 4) and lubricate it (see Section 15). Install the cable, making sure it is correctly routed.

**9** Check for a small amount of freeplay in the cable before the choke opens and adjust it if necessary using the adjuster at the lever end of the cable. Slacken the locknut, then turn the adjuster as required until a small amount of freeplay is evident, then retighten the locknut **(see illustration)**. If this fails to improve the operation of the choke, the cable must be renewed. Note that in very rare cases the fault could lie in the carburettors rather than the cable, necessitating the removal of the carburettors and inspection of the choke valves (see Chapter 4).

**10** On GSX-R750W and X models, the choke cable is also adjustable at the throttle body end, and is done so in the same way as the throttle cables (see Step 6 and **illustration 7.6b**)

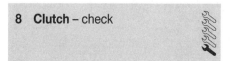

**8 Clutch** – check

## Cable adjustment

**1** Periodic adjustment of the clutch cable is necessary to compensate for wear in the clutch plates and stretch of the cable. Check that the amount of freeplay at the clutch lever end is within the specifications listed at the beginning of the Chapter **(see illustration)**. If adjustment is required, it can be made at either the lever end of the cable or at the clutch end.

**2** To adjust the freeplay at the lever, turn the adjuster in or out until the required amount of freeplay is obtained **(see illustration)**. To increase freeplay, turn the adjuster clockwise (in). To reduce freeplay, turn the adjuster anti-clockwise (out).

**3** If all the adjustment has been taken up at the lever, reset the adjuster (turn it fully in) to give the maximum amount of freeplay, then set the correct amount of freeplay using the

adjuster at the clutch end of the cable (Step 4). Subsequent adjustments can then be made using the lever adjuster only.

**4** To adjust the freeplay at the clutch end of the cable, slacken the locknut on the adjuster on the top of the sprocket cover and turn the adjuster until the specified amount of freeplay is obtained **(see illustration)**. To increase freeplay, turn the adjuster clockwise (in). To reduce freeplay, turn the adjuster anti-clockwise (out). Tighten the locknut securely. To improve access to the adjuster, remove the left-hand fairing side panel (see Chapter 8) and displace the coolant reservoir (see Chapter 3).

## Release mechanism adjustment

**Note:** *Clutch plate wear can be compensated for by adjusting the release mechanism set in the sprocket cover. If it is impossible to eliminate clutch drag or slip with cable adjustment, set the release mechanism freeplay as follows.*

**5** Turn the adjuster at the lever end of the cable fully in **(see illustration 8.2)**. This creates slack in the cable.

**6** Remove the left-hand fairing side panel (see Chapter 8) and displace the coolant reservoir (see Chapter 3). Remove the rubber cover from the clutch release mechanism set in the engine sprocket cover **(see illustration)**.

**7** Slacken the locknut on the release mechanism adjuster screw, then unscrew the

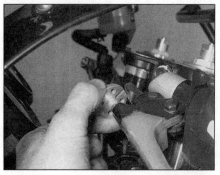

8.2 Turn the adjuster as required

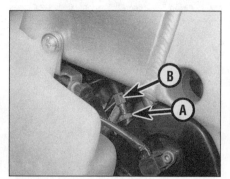

8.4 Slacken the locknut (A) and turn the adjuster (B) as required

8.6 Remove the rubber cover . . .

**8.7 . . . then slacken the locknut and turn the adjuster screw as described**

**9.6 Remove the radiator pressure cap as described**

adjuster screw a few turns **(see illustration)**. Now turn the adjuster screw in until resistance is felt, then back it off 1/4 turn. When doing this, counter-hold the locknut as shown to prevent it from tightening and locking the adjuster.

**8** Now counter-hold the adjuster screw to prevent it turning and tighten the locknut. Refit the rubber cover.

**9** Slacken the locknut on the adjuster on the top of the sprocket cover and turn the adjuster until the specified amount of freeplay is obtained **(see illustration 8.4)**. To increase freeplay, turn the adjuster clockwise (in). To reduce freeplay, turn the adjuster anti-clockwise (out). Tighten the locknut securely.

**10** Set the correct amount of freeplay at the lever by adjusting the cable as described in Steps 1 to 4.

## 9  Cooling system – check

**Warning: The engine must be cool before beginning this procedure.**

**1** Check the coolant level (see *Daily (pre-ride) checks*).

**2** Remove the fairing side panels (see Chapter 8). The entire cooling system should be checked for evidence of leakage. Examine each rubber coolant hose along its entire length. Look for cracks, abrasions and other damage. Squeeze each hose at various points. They should feel firm, yet pliable, and return to their original shape when released. If they are damaged, dried out, cracked or hard, renew them (see Chapter 3).

**3** Check for evidence of leaks at each cooling system joint and around the bottom of the water pump, which is on the left-hand side of the engine. Tighten the hose clips carefully to prevent future leaks. If the pump is leaking, refer to Chapter 3 and check it.

**4** Check the radiator for leaks and other damage. Leaks in the radiator leave tell-tale scale deposits or coolant stains on the outside of the core below the leak. If leaks are noted, remove the radiator (see Chapter 3) and have it repaired or renew it.

*Caution: Do not use a liquid leak stopping compound to try to repair leaks.*

**5** Check the radiator fins for mud, dirt and insects, which may impede the flow of air through the radiator. If the fins are dirty, remove the radiator (see Chapter 3) and clean it using water or low pressure compressed air directed through the fins from the backside. If the fins are bent or distorted, straighten them carefully with a screwdriver. If the air flow is restricted by bent or damaged fins over more than 30% of the radiator's surface area, renew the radiator.

**6** Remove the pressure cap from the radiator filler neck by turning it anti-clockwise until it reaches a stop. If you hear a hissing sound (indicating there is still pressure in the system), wait until it stops. Now press down on the cap and continue turning the cap until it can be removed **(see illustration)**. Check the condition of the coolant in the system. If it is rust-coloured or if accumulations of scale are visible, drain, flush and refill the system with new coolant (See Section 25). Check the cap seal for cracks and other damage. If in doubt about the pressure cap's condition, have it tested by a Suzuki dealer or renew it with a new one. Install the cap by turning it clockwise until it reaches the first stop then push down on the cap and continue turning until it can turn no further.

**7** Check the antifreeze content of the coolant with an antifreeze hydrometer. Sometimes coolant looks like it's in good condition, but might be too weak to offer adequate

protection. If the hydrometer indicates a weak mixture, drain, flush and refill the system (see Section 25).

**8** Start the engine and let it reach normal operating temperature, then check for leaks again. As the coolant temperature increases, the fan should come on automatically and the temperature should begin to drop. If it does not, refer to Chapter 3 and check the fan, the fan switch and fan circuit carefully.

**9** If the coolant level is consistently low, and no evidence of leaks can be found, have the entire system pressure checked by a Suzuki dealer.

## 10  Drive chain – wear and stretch check

**1** Check the entire length of the chain for damaged rollers, loose links and pins, and missing O-rings. Fit a new chain if damage is found. **Note:** *Never install a new chain on old sprockets, and never use the old chain if you install new sprockets – renew the chain and sprockets as a set.*

**2** The amount of chain stretch be measured and compared to the stretch limit specified at the beginning of the Chapter. On US models, remove the split pin from the rear axle nut, then on all models slacken the axle nut **(see illustration 1.8)**. Slacken the adjuster locknut on each side of the swingarm, then turn the adjuster bolts evenly until the chain is tight **(see illustration 1.9a)**. Measure along the bottom run the length of 21 pins (from the centre of the 1st pin to the centre of the 21st pin) and compare the result with the service limit specified at the beginning of the Chapter **(see illustration)**. Rotate the rear wheel so that several sections of the chain are measured, then calculate the average. If the chain exceeds the service limit it must be renewed (see Chapter 5). **Note:** *Never install a new chain on old sprockets, and never use the old chain if you install new sprockets – renew the chain and sprockets as a set.* Refer to Section 1 and reset the correct amount of chain freeplay, then tighten the axle nut and adjuster bolt nuts and on US models install a

**1**

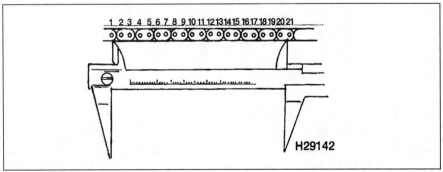

**10.2 Measure the distance between the 1st and 21st pins to determine chain stretch**

new split pin to secure the axle nut (bend the split pin ends securely).

**3** Remove the front sprocket cover (see Chapter 6). Check the teeth on the front and rear sprockets for wear **(see illustration)**.

**4** Inspect the drive chain slider on the swingarm for excessive wear and renew it if worn (see Chapter 6).

## 11 Brake pads – wear check

**1** Each brake pad has wear indicator cutouts or a line that can be viewed without removing the pads from the caliper. On the front brake caliper, unscrew the two bolts securing the pad spring and remove the spring – the pad wear indicator cutouts are visible by looking at the top edge of the pads **(see illustrations)**. On the rear brake caliper, remove the caliper cover by levering it off with a screwdriver – the pad wear lines are visible by looking up at the bottom edge of the pads from under the caliper **(see illustrations)**.

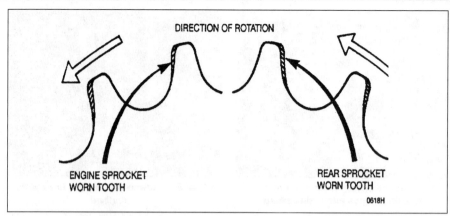

10.3 Check the sprockets in the areas indicated to see if they are worn excessively

 **TOOL TiP** *Checking the rear brake pads is much easier if you use a mirror.*

**2** If the pads are worn to or beyond the base of the grooves, new ones must be installed. If the pads are dirty or if you are in doubt as to

the amount of friction material remaining, remove them for inspection (see Chapter 7). **Note:** *Some after-market pads may use different indicators to those on the original equipment as shown.*

**3** Refer to Chapter 7 for details of fitting new pads.

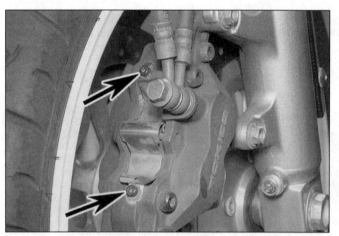

11.1a  Unscrew the bolts (arrowed) and remove the pad spring

11.1b  Front brake pad wear cutouts (arrowed)

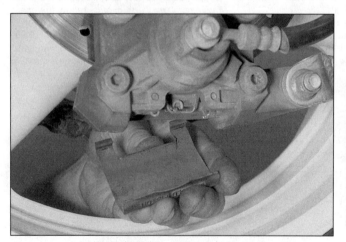

11.1c  Remove the rear caliper's cover

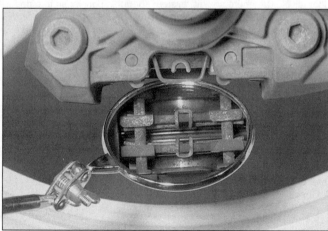

11.1d  Using a mirror to check the rear brake pad wear – these pads are worn down to the wear indicator lines

12.3 Flex the brake hoses and check for cracks, bulges and leaking fluid

12.5 Rear brake light switch (arrowed)

12.6 Adjusting the front brake lever span

## 12 Brake system – check

1 A routine general check of the brake system will ensure that any problems are discovered and remedied before the rider's safety is jeopardised.

2 Check the brake lever and pedal for loose connections, improper or rough action, excessive play, bends, and other damage. Renew any damaged parts with new ones (see Chapter 6).

3 Make sure all brake fasteners are tight. Check the brake pads for wear (see Section 11) and make sure the fluid level in the reservoirs is correct (see *Daily (pre-ride) checks*). Look for leaks at the hose connections and check for cracks in the hoses **(see illustration)**. If the lever or pedal is spongy, bleed the brakes (see Chapter 7).

4 Make sure the brake light operates when the front brake lever is pulled in. The front brake light switch is not adjustable. If it fails to operate properly, check it (see Chapter 9).

5 Make sure the brake light is activated just before the rear brake takes effect. The switch is mounted on the inside of the frame on the right-hand side, above the brake pedal. If

adjustment is necessary, hold the switch and turn the adjuster nut on the switch body until the brake light is activated when required **(see illustration)**. If the brake light comes on too late, turn the ring clockwise. If the brake light comes on too soon or is permanently on, turn the ring anti-clockwise. If the switch doesn't operate the brake light, check it (see Chapter 9).

6 The front brake lever has a span adjuster which alters the distance of the lever from the handlebar **(see illustration)**. Pull the lever away from the handlebar and turn the adjuster dial until the setting which best suits the rider is obtained. Align the setting number with the arrow on the lever.

7 Check the position of the rear brake pedal. The distance between the top of the end of the brake pedal and the top of the rider's footrest should be as specified at the beginning of the Chapter **(see illustration)**. If the pedal height is incorrect, or if you want to adjust it to suit your own preference, slacken the locknut on the master cylinder pushrod, then turn the pushrod using a spanner on the hex at the top of the rod until the pedal is at the correct height **(see illustration)**. Tighten the locknut securely. Adjust the rear brake light switch after adjusting the pedal height (see Step 5).

## 13 Wheels and tyres – general check

### Wheels

1 Cast wheels are virtually maintenance free, but they should be kept clean and checked periodically for cracks and other damage. Also check the wheel runout and alignment (see Chapter 7). Never attempt to repair damaged cast wheels; they must be renewed if damaged.

### Tyres

2 Check the tyre condition and tread depth thoroughly – see *Daily (pre-ride) checks*. Check the valve rubber for signs of damage or deterioration and have it renewed if necessary by a tyre fitting specialist. Also, make sure the valve stem cap is in place and tight.

## 14 Nuts and bolts – tightness check

1 Since vibration of the machine tends to loosen fasteners, all nuts, bolts, screws, etc.

**1**

12.7a Rear brake pedal height measurement

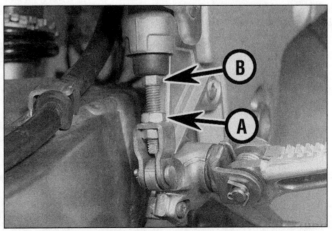

12.7b Slacken the pushrod locknut (A) and turn the pushrod as required using the hex (B)

should be periodically checked for proper tightness.

2 Pay particular attention to the following:
*Spark plugs*
*Engine oil drain plug*
*Gearchange pedal bolt*
*Footrest, footrest bracket and stand bolts*
*Engine mounting bolts*
*Shock absorber mounting bolts and*
*suspension linkage bolts*
*Handlebar bolts*
*Front axle nut and clamp bolt*
*Front fork clamp bolts (top and bottom*
*yoke)*
*Rear axle nut*
*Swingarm pivot nut*
*Brake caliper mounting bolts*
*Brake hose banjo bolts and caliper bleed*
*valves*
*Brake disc bolts and rear sprocket nuts*
*Exhaust system bolts/nuts (see Section 20)*

3 If a torque wrench is available, use it along with the torque specifications at the beginning of this, or other, Chapters.

## 15 Stand, lever pivots and cables – lubrication

### Pivot points

1 Since the controls, cables and various other components of a motorcycle are exposed to the elements, they should be lubricated

**15.3a  Lubricating a cable with a cable oiler clamp. Make sure the tool seals around the inner cable**

periodically to ensure safe and trouble-free operation.

2 The footrests, clutch and brake levers, brake pedal, gearchange lever linkage and sidestand pivots should be lubricated frequently. In order for the lubricant to be applied where it will do the most good, the component should be disassembled (see Chapter 6). However, if an aerosol chain lubricant is being used, it can be applied to the pivot joint gaps and will usually work its way into the areas where friction occurs. If motor oil or light grease is being used, apply it sparingly as it may attract dirt (which could cause the controls to bind or wear at an accelerated rate). **Note:** *One of the best lubricants for the control lever pivots is a dry-film lubricant (available from many sources by different names).*

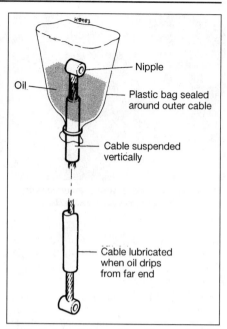

**15.3b  Lubricating a cable with a makeshift funnel and motor oil**

### Cables

3 To lubricate the cables, disconnect the relevant cable at its upper end, then lubricate the cable with a cable oiler clamp, or if one is not available, using the set-up shown **(see illustrations)**. See Chapter 4 for the choke and throttle cable removal procedures, and Chapter 2 for the clutch cable.

# Every 7500 miles (12,000 km) or 12 months

*Carry out all the items under the 4000 mile (6000 km) check, plus the following:*

## 16 Spark plugs – renewal

1 Remove the old spark plugs as described in Section 3 and install new ones.

## 17 Carburettors/throttle bodies – synchronisation

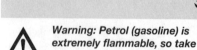

⚠ *Warning: Petrol (gasoline) is extremely flammable, so take extra precautions when you work on any part of the fuel system. Don't smoke or allow open flames or bare light bulbs near the work area, and don't work in a garage where a natural gas-type appliance is present. If you spill any fuel on your skin, rinse it off immediately with soap and water. When you perform any kind of work on the fuel system, wear safety glasses and have a*

*fire extinguisher suitable for a Class B type fire (flammable liquids) on hand.*
*Warning: Take great care not to burn your hand on the hot engine unit when accessing the gauge take-off points on the inlet manifolds. Do not allow exhaust gases to build up in the work area; either perform the check outside or use an exhaust gas extraction system.*

1 Carburettor or throttle body synchronisation is simply the process of adjusting the carburettors or throttle bodies so they pass the same amount of fuel/air mixture to each cylinder. This is done by measuring the vacuum produced in each cylinder. Carburettors or throttle bodies that are out of synchronisation will result in decreased fuel mileage, increased engine temperature, less than ideal throttle response and higher vibration levels. Before synchronising the carburettors or throttle bodies, make sure the valve clearances are correct.

2 To properly synchronise the carburettors or throttle bodies, you will need a set of vacuum gauges or calibrated tubes to indicate engine vacuum. The equipment used should be suitable for a four cylinder engine and come

complete with the necessary adapters and hoses to fit the take off points. **Note:** *Because of the nature of the synchronisation procedure and the need for special instruments, most owners leave the task to a Suzuki dealer.*

3 Start the engine and let it run until it reaches normal operating temperature, then shut it off.

4 On GSX-R600 models, remove the fuel tank (see Chapter 4). On W and X models, displace the solenoid mounting bracket from the bottom of the No. 1 carburettor **(see illustration)**.

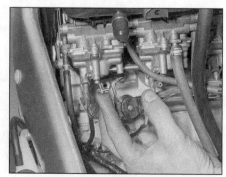

**17.4a  Remove the screws securing its bracket and displace the solenoid**

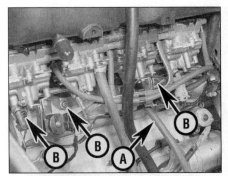

**17.4b Disconnect the fuel valve vacuum hose (A) and remove the blanking screws (B)**

**17.4c Fit the adapters . . .**

**17.4d . . . and connect the hoses to them**

Disconnect the fuel valve vacuum hose from the take-off stub on no. 3 inlet manifold and remove the blanking screws from the take-off points of the remaining manifolds **(see illustration)**. Thread the vacuum gauge hose adapters into the take-off points, then connect the gauge hoses to the adapters **(see illustrations)**. Make sure they are a good fit because any air leaks will result in false readings.

**5** On GSX-R750T and V models, remove the air filter housing and displace the carburettors from the inlet manifolds – there is no need to disconnect any cables or hoses (see Chapter 4). Disconnect the vacuum hose from the take-off stub on no. 4 carburettor body and remove the blanking caps from the take-off points on the remaining carburettors. The take-off points are located on the engine side of the carburettors, and are positioned at about the 10 o'clock position (when viewed from the front), just behind the rims where the carburettors fit into the inlet manifolds on the cylinder head. Connect the gauge hoses to the take-off stubs. Make sure they are a good fit because any air leaks will result in false readings. Fit the carburettors back into the manifolds and tighten the clamp screws (see Chapter 4).

*Caution: On GSX-R750 models, the carburettors/throttle bodies are synchronised with the air filter housing removed. To negate the possibility of drawing dirt into the engine, it is advisable to cut up an old pair of stockings and fit a circle of the material over each inlet and secure it with an elastic band or cable tie. The material acts as a filter.*

**6** On GSX-R750W and X models, disconnect the IAT (inlet air temperature) sensor wiring connector, then remove the sensor from the air filter housing and reconnect the wiring **(see illustration)**. Also remove the screw securing the IAP (inlet air pressure) sensor to the housing and displace the sensor **(see illustration)**. Remove the air filter housing (see Chapter 4). Disconnect the vacuum hose from the take-off stub on no. 4 throttle body and plug its end **(see**

**illustration)**. Also remove the blanking caps from the take-off stubs of the remaining throttle bodies. Connect the gauge hoses to the take-off stubs. Make sure they are a good fit because any air leaks will result in false readings.

**7** Arrange a temporary fuel supply, either by using a small temporary tank or by using extra long fuel pipes to the now remote fuel tank. Alternatively, position the tank on a suitable base on the motorcycle, taking care not to scratch any paintwork, and making sure that the tank is safely and securely supported. Start the engine and increase the idle speed to 1750 rpm on carburettor models and

1200 rpm on fuel injected models, using the idle speed adjuster screw **(see illustration 6.3)**. If using vacuum gauges fitted with damping adjustment, set this so that the needle flutter is just eliminated but so that they can still respond to small changes in pressure.

**8** The vacuum readings for all of the cylinders should be the same **(see illustration)**. If the vacuum readings vary, proceed as follows.

**9** On GSX-R600 and 750T and V models, the carburettors are balanced by turning the synchronising screws situated in-between each carburettor, in the throttle linkage **(see**

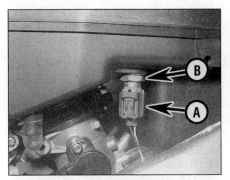

**17.6a Disconnect the wiring connector (A), then slacken the nut (B) and unscrew the IAT sensor**

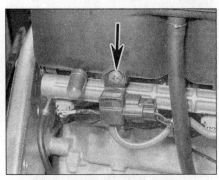

**17.6b Remove the screw (arrowed) and displace the sensor, leaving it connected**

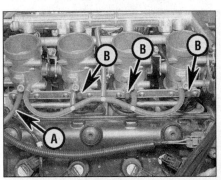

**17.6c Disconnect the vacuum hose (A) and remove the blanking caps (B)**

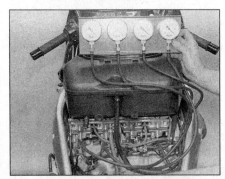

**17.8 Carburettor/throttle body synchronisation gauge set-up**

1

17.9 Carburettor synchronising screws (arrowed) – air filter housing shown removed for clarity

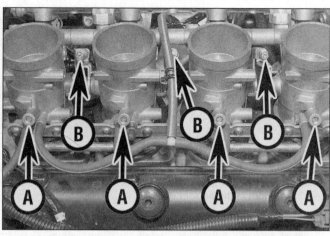

17.10 Throttle body air screws (A), synchronising screws (B)

illustration). **Note:** *Do not press on the screws whilst adjusting them, otherwise a false reading will be obtained.* First synchronise no. 3 carburettor to no. 4 using the right-hand synchronising screw until the readings are the same. Then synchronise no. 1 carburettor to no. 2 using the left-hand screw. Finally synchronise nos. 1 and 2 carburettors to nos. 3 and 4 using the centre screw. When all the carburettors are synchronised, open and close the throttle quickly to settle the linkage, and recheck the gauge readings, readjusting if necessary.

**10** On GSX-R750W and X models, if the vacuum difference between the throttle bodies is less than 20 mmHg, use the air screws located above the take-off point on each throttle body for fine adjustment – each air screw should be set at about 1/2 a turn out from its seat **(see illustration)**. If the vacuum difference is greater than 20 mmHg, check that each air screw is correctly set at about 1/2 turn out, then balance the throttle bodies by turning the synchronising screws situated in-between each body, in the throttle linkage. **Note:** *Do not press on the screws whilst adjusting them, otherwise a false reading will be obtained.* When using the synchronising screws, first synchronise no. 3 body to no. 4 using the left-hand synchronising screw (as shown in the illustration) until the readings are the same. Then synchronise no. 1 body to no. 2 using the right-hand screw. Finally synchronise nos. 1 and 2 bodies to nos. 3 and 4 using the centre screw. When all the bodies are synchronised, open and close the throttle quickly to settle the linkage, and recheck the gauge readings, readjusting if necessary.

**11** When the adjustment is complete, recheck the vacuum readings, then adjust the idle speed by turning the adjuster screw until the idle speed listed in this Chapter's Specifications is obtained. Stop the engine.

**12** On GSX-R750T and V models, displace the carburettors from the inlet manifolds. On all models remove the gauge hoses, and on GSX-R600 models the adapters, then fit the fuel valve vacuum hose onto no. 3 inlet manifold (600 models) or the vacuum hose onto no. 4 carburettor/throttle body (750 models) and the take-off blanking screws or caps onto the others.

**13** On GSX-R600 models, detach the temporary fuel supply. Install the carburettors, air filter housing and fuel tank as required by your model, in a reverse of the removal procedure.

## 18 Steering head bearings – freeplay check and adjustment

**1** Steering head bearings can become dented, rough or loose during normal use of the machine. In extreme cases, worn or loose steering head bearings can cause steering wobble – a condition that is potentially dangerous.

### Check

**2** Support the motorcycle in an upright position using an auxiliary stand. Raise the front wheel off the ground either by having an assistant push down on the rear or by placing a support under the engine (first remove the fairing side panels (see Chapter 8)). On models equipped with a steering damper,

18.4 Checking for play in the steering head bearings

disconnect one end to allow free movement of the steering.

**3** Point the front wheel straight-ahead and slowly move the handlebars from side-to-side. Any dents or roughness in the bearing races will be felt and the bars will not move smoothly and freely.

**4** Next, grasp the fork sliders and try to move them forward and backward **(see illustration)**. Any looseness in the steering head bearings will be felt as front-to-rear movement of the forks. If play is felt in the bearings, adjust the steering head as follows. Reconnect the steering damper, where applicable.

**HAYNES HiNT** *Freeplay in the fork due to worn fork bushes can be misinterpreted for steering head bearing play – do not confuse the two.*

### Adjustment

**5** Although not essential, it is wise to raise the fuel tank to avoid the possibility of damage should a tool slip while adjustment is being made (see Chapter 4).

**6** Slacken the steering stem nut, then slacken the fork clamp bolts in the bottom yoke **(see illustrations)**.

18.6a Slacken the steering stem nut (arrowed) . . .

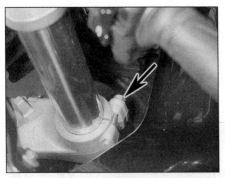

18.6b ... and the clamp bolt (arrowed) for each fork in the bottom yoke

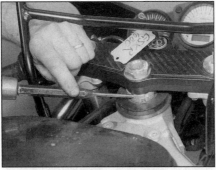

18.7a Slacken the locknut ..

18.7b ... then turn the adjuster nut as described until the bearings are correctly set

7 Using a slim C-spanner or a suitable drift located in one of the notches, slacken the adjuster locknut **(see illustration)**. Now, slacken the adjuster nut slightly by tapping the drift with a hammer, until pressure is just released, then tighten it until all freeplay in the forks is removed, yet the steering is able to move freely from side to side **(see illustration)**. The object is to set the adjuster nut so that the bearings are under a very light loading, just enough to remove any freeplay.
*Caution: Take great care not to apply excessive pressure because this will cause premature failure of the bearings.*
8 If the bearings cannot be set up properly, or if there is any binding, roughness or notchiness, they will have to be removed for inspection or renewal (see Chapter 6).
9 With the bearings correctly adjusted, tighten the locknut securely against the adjuster ring, making sure the adjuster does not turn as you do so. Now tighten the steering stem nut and the fork clamp bolts in the bottom yoke to the torque settings specified at the beginning of the Chapter.
10 Check the bearing adjustment as described above and re-adjust if necessary.

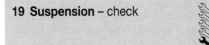

## 19 Suspension – check

1 The suspension components must be maintained in top operating condition to ensure rider safety. Loose, worn or damaged suspension parts decrease the motorcycle's stability and control.

### Front suspension

2 While standing alongside the motorcycle, apply the front brake and push on the handlebars to compress the forks several times. See if they move up-and-down smoothly without binding. If binding is felt, the forks should be disassembled and inspected (see Chapter 6).
3 Inspect the area above (GSX-R600) or below (GSX-R750) the dust seal for signs of oil leakage, then carefully lever off the dust seal using a flat-bladed screwdriver and

inspect the area around the fork seal **(see illustrations)**. If leakage is evident, the seals must be renewed (see Chapter 6).
4 Check the tightness of all suspension nuts and bolts to be sure none have worked loose, referring to the torque settings specified at the beginning of Chapter 6.

### Rear suspension

5 Inspect the rear shock for fluid leakage and tightness of its mountings. If leakage is found, a new shock must be installed (see Chapter 6).
6 With the aid of an assistant to support the bike, compress the rear suspension several times. It should move up and down freely without binding. If any binding is felt, the worn or faulty component must be identified and

renewed. The problem could be due to either the shock absorber, the suspension linkage components or the swingarm components.
7 Support the motorcycle using an auxiliary stand so that the rear wheel is off the ground. Grab the swingarm and rock it from side to side – there should be no discernible movement at the rear **(see illustration)**. If there's a little movement or a slight clicking can be heard, check the tightness of all the rear suspension mounting bolts and nuts, referring to the torque settings specified at the beginning of Chapter 6, and re-check for movement. Next, grasp the top of the rear wheel and pull it upwards – there should be no discernible freeplay before the shock absorber begins to compress **(see illustration)**. Any freeplay felt in either check

19.3a Lever up the dust seal ...

19.3b ... and check for signs of oil leakage

19.7a Checking for play in the swingarm bearings

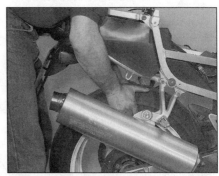

19.7b Checking for play in the suspension linkage bearings

**1**

indicates worn bearings in the suspension linkage or swingarm, or worn shock absorber mountings. The worn components must be renewed (see Chapter 6).

**8** To make a more accurate assessment of the swingarm bearings, remove the rear wheel (see Chapter 7) and the bolt securing the suspension linkage rods to the linkage arm (see Chapter 6). Grasp the rear of the swingarm with one hand and place your other hand at the junction of the swingarm and the frame. Try to move the rear of the swingarm from side-to-side. Any wear (play) in the bearings should be felt as movement between the swingarm and the frame at the front. If there is any play, the swingarm will be felt to move forward and backward at the front (not from side-to-side). Next, move the swingarm up and down through its full travel. It should move freely, without any binding or rough spots. If any play in the swingarm is noted or if the swingarm does not move freely, the bearings must be removed for inspection or renewal (see Chapter 6).

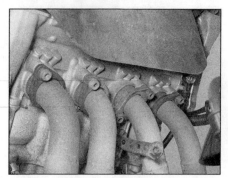

20.2a Tighten the downpipe bolts . . .

20.2b . . . and the middle and rear mounting bolts (arrowed) to the specified torque

### 20 Exhaust system bolts – tightness check

**1** Remove the fairing side panels (see Chapter 8). Refer to Chapter 3 and remove the radiator mounting bolts, then displace the radiator to improve access to the exhaust downpipe bolts. It should not be necessary to disconnect any hoses or wiring, but check that no strain is placed on them. If required, remove the radiator completely.

**2** Using a torque wrench, check that the exhaust downpipe clamp bolts and the silencer mounting bolts are tightened to the torque settings specified at the beginning of the Chapter **(see illustrations)**.

# Every 11,000 miles (18,000 km) or 18 months

*Carry out all the items under the 4000 mile (6000 km) check:*

### 21 Air filter – renewal

**1** Remove the old air filter as described in Section 2 and install a new one.

### 22 Engine/transmission – oil and oil filter change

⚠️ *Warning: Be careful when draining the oil, as the exhaust pipes, the engine, and the oil itself can cause severe burns.*

**1** Remove the right-hand fairing side panel (see Chapter 8).

**2** Drain the engine oil as described in Section 5, Steps 2 to 5.

**3** Now place the drain tray below the oil filter, which is on the right-hand side of the engine at the front. Unscrew the oil filter using a filter adapter, chain wrench or strap wrench and tip any residue oil into the drain tray **(see illustrations)**. Wipe any oil off the exhaust pipes to prevent too much smoke when you start it.

**4** Smear clean engine oil onto the rubber seal of the new filter, then manoeuvre it into position and screw it onto the engine by hand until the seal just seats **(see illustrations)**.

22.3a Unscrew the filter . . .

22.3b . . . and drain it into the tray

22.4a Smear some clean oil onto the seal . . .

22.4b . . . then thread the filter onto the cooler . . .

Now tighten it a further two whole turns using a filter adapter, or if one is not available, tighten the filter by hand **(see illustration)**. **Note:** *Although Suzuki specify two whole turns, on the models we stripped down the filter became very tight well before this, and tightening it further would possibly have* damaged the filter. *It is best to use your own judgement should the filter become very tight - the most important consideration is that the filter does not leak.*

5 Refill the engine with oil as described in Section 5, Step 6.

**22.4c . . . and tighten it as described**

# Every 15,000 miles (24,000 km) or 24 months

*Carry out all the items under the 7500 mile (12,000 km) check:*

## 23 Valve clearances – check and adjustment

### Check

1 The engine must be completely cool for this maintenance procedure, so let the machine sit overnight before beginning.
2 Remove the spark plugs (see Section 3).
3 Remove the valve cover (see Chapter 2). The cylinders are identified by number, and are numbered 1 to 4 from left to right.
4 Make a chart or sketch of all valve positions so that a note of each clearance can be made against the relevant valve.
5 Unscrew the timing inspection plug and the centre plug from the starter clutch cover on the right-hand side of the engine **(see illustration)**. Discard the plug O-rings as new ones should be used. The engine can be turned using a 14 mm socket on the starter clutch bolt and turning it in a clockwise direction only **(see illustration 23.6a)**. Alternatively, place the motorcycle on an auxiliary stand so that the rear wheel is off the ground, select a high gear and rotate the rear wheel by hand in its normal direction of rotation.
6 Turn the engine until the scribe line on the starter clutch aligns with the notch in the timing inspection hole **(see illustration)**. **Note:** *Turn the engine in the normal direction of rotation (clockwise) only, viewed from the right-hand end of the engine.* Now, check the position of the notch in the left-hand end of each camshaft. If the notch in the inlet camshaft is facing down and the notch on the exhaust camshaft is at 8 o'clock, then no. 1 cylinder is at TDC on the compression stroke **(see illustration)**. If the notch on the inlet camshaft is facing up and the notch on the exhaust camshaft is at 2 o'clock, then no. 4 cylinder is at TDC on the compression stroke **(see**

**illustration)**. If the marks are not positioned as required for the cylinders being checked, turn the crankshaft through 360° (one complete turn).
7 With no. 1 cylinder at TDC on the compression stroke, the following valves can be checked:
 a) No. 1, inlet and exhaust
 b) No. 2, exhaust
 c) No. 3, inlet

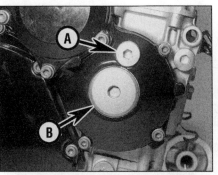

**23.5 Remove the timing inspection plug (A) and the centre plug (B)**

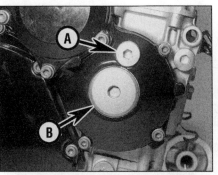

8 With no. 4 cylinder at TDC on the compression stroke, the following valves can be checked:
 a) No. 2, inlet
 b) No. 3, exhaust
 c) No. 4, inlet and exhaust
9 Insert a feeler gauge of the same thickness as the correct valve clearance (see Specifications) between the base of the camshaft lobe and the follower of each valve

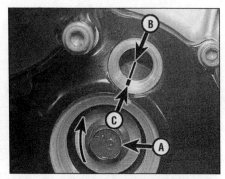

**23.6a Turn the engine clockwise using the bolt (A), until the timing mark (B) aligns with the notch (C)**

**23.6b When the notch (A) on the inlet camshaft is down and the notch (B) on the exhaust camshaft is at 8 o'clock, No. 1 cylinder is at TDC on the compression stroke**

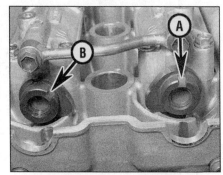

**23.6c When the notch (A) on the inlet camshaft is up and the notch (B) on the exhaust camshaft is at 2 o'clock, No. 4 cylinder is at TDC on the compression stroke**

1

**23.9 Insert the feeler gauge as shown (arrowed) and measure the clearance**

**23.13a Lift out the follower . . .**

**23.13b . . . and retrieve the shim, which will probably be inside the follower**

**23.14 Measure the shim thickness using a micrometer**

and check that it is a firm sliding fit – you should feel a slight drag when the you pull the gauge out **(see illustration)**. If not, use the feeler gauges to obtain the exact clearance. **Note:** *The inlet and exhaust valve clearances are different.* Record the measured clearance on the chart.

**10** Rotate the engine so that the timing rotor turns through 360° and measure the valve clearance of the remaining valves using the method described in Step 9. **Note:** *Turn the engine in the normal direction of rotation (clockwise) only, viewed from the right-hand end of the engine.*

## Adjustment

**11** When all clearances have been measured and charted, identify whether the clearance on any valve falls outside that specified. If it does, the shim between the follower and the valve must be replaced with one of a thickness which will restore the correct clearance.

**12** Shim renewal requires removal of the camshafts (see Chapter 2). There is no need to remove both camshafts if shims from only one side of the engine need replacing.

**13** With the camshaft removed, remove the cam follower of the valve in question using either a magnet or a pair of pliers **(see illustration)**. Retrieve the shim from either the inside of the follower **(see illustration)**, or pick it out of the top of the valve, using either a magnet, a small screwdriver with a dab of grease on it (the shim will stick to the grease), or a pair of pliers **(see illustration 23.17a)**. Do not allow the shim to fall into the engine.

**14** The shim size should be stamped on its face, however, it is recommended that the shim is measured to check that it has not worn **(see illustration)**. The size marking is in the form of a three figure number, e.g. 180 indicating that the shim is 1.800 mm thick.

| MEASURED TAPPET CLEARANCE (mm) | PRESENT SHIM SIZE (mm) | | | | | | | | | | | | | | | | | | | | |
|---|---|---|---|---|---|---|---|---|---|---|---|---|---|---|---|---|---|---|---|---|---|
| | 1.20 | 1.25 | 1.30 | 1.35 | 1.40 | 1.45 | 1.50 | 1.55 | 1.60 | 1.65 | 1.70 | 1.75 | 1.80 | 1.85 | 1.90 | 1.95 | 2.00 | 2.05 | 2.10 | 2.15 | 2.20 |
| 0.00-0.04 | | | 1.20 | 1.25 | 1.30 | 1.35 | 1.40 | 1.45 | 1.50 | 1.55 | 1.60 | 1.65 | 1.70 | 1.75 | 1.80 | 1.85 | 1.90 | 1.95 | 2.00 | 2.05 | 2.10 |
| 0.05-0.09 | | 1.20 | 1.25 | 1.30 | 1.35 | 1.40 | 1.45 | 1.50 | 1.55 | 1.60 | 1.65 | 1.70 | 1.75 | 1.80 | 1.85 | 1.90 | 1.95 | 2.00 | 2.05 | 2.10 | 2.15 |
| 0.10-0.20 | SPECIFIED CLEARANCE/NO ADJUSTMENT REQUIRED | | | | | | | | | | | | | | | | | | | | |
| 0.21-0.25 | 1.30 | 1.35 | 1.40 | 1.45 | 1.50 | 1.55 | 1.60 | 1.65 | 1.70 | 1.75 | 1.80 | 1.85 | 1.90 | 1.95 | 2.00 | 2.05 | 2.10 | 2.15 | 2.20 | 2.20 | |
| 0.26-0.30 | 1.35 | 1.40 | 1.45 | 1.50 | 1.55 | 1.60 | 1.65 | 1.70 | 1.75 | 1.80 | 1.85 | 1.90 | 1.95 | 2.00 | 2.05 | 2.10 | 2.15 | 2.20 | | | |
| 0.31-0.35 | 1.40 | 1.45 | 1.50 | 1.55 | 1.60 | 1.65 | 1.70 | 1.75 | 1.80 | 1.85 | 1.90 | 1.95 | 2.00 | 2.05 | 2.10 | 2.15 | 2.20 | | | | |
| 0.36-0.40 | 1.45 | 1.50 | 1.55 | 1.60 | 1.65 | 1.70 | 1.75 | 1.80 | 1.85 | 1.90 | 1.95 | 2.00 | 2.05 | 2.10 | 2.15 | 2.20 | | | | | |
| 0.41-0.45 | 1.50 | 1.55 | 1.60 | 1.65 | 1.70 | 1.75 | 1.80 | 1.85 | 1.90 | 1.95 | 2.00 | 2.05 | 2.10 | 2.15 | 2.20 | | | | | | |
| 0.46-0.50 | 1.55 | 1.60 | 1.65 | 1.70 | 1.75 | 1.80 | 1.85 | 1.90 | 1.95 | 2.00 | 2.05 | 2.10 | 2.15 | 2.20 | | | | | | | |
| 0.51-0.55 | 1.60 | 1.65 | 1.70 | 1.75 | 1.80 | 1.85 | 1.90 | 1.95 | 2.00 | 2.05 | 2.10 | 2.15 | 2.20 | | | | | | | | |
| 0.56-0.60 | 1.65 | 1.70 | 1.75 | 1.80 | 1.85 | 1.90 | 1.95 | 2.00 | 2.05 | 2.10 | 2.15 | 2.20 | | | | | | | | | |
| 0.61-0.65 | 1.70 | 1.75 | 1.80 | 1.85 | 1.90 | 1.95 | 2.00 | 2.05 | 2.10 | 2.15 | 2.20 | | | | | | | | | | |
| 0.66-0.70 | 1.75 | 1.80 | 1.85 | 1.90 | 1.95 | 2.00 | 2.05 | 2.10 | 2.15 | 2.20 | | | | | | | | | | | |
| 0.71-0.75 | 1.80 | 1.85 | 1.90 | 1.95 | 2.00 | 2.05 | 2.10 | 2.15 | 2.20 | | | | | | | | | | | | |
| 0.76-0.80 | 1.85 | 1.90 | 1.95 | 2.00 | 2.05 | 2.10 | 2.15 | 2.20 | | | | | | | | | | | | | |
| 0.81-0.85 | 1.90 | 1.95 | 2.00 | 2.05 | 2.10 | 2.15 | 2.20 | | | | | | | | | | | | | | |
| 0.86-0.90 | 1.95 | 2.00 | 2.05 | 2.10 | 2.15 | 2.20 | | | | | | | | | | | | | | | |
| 0.91-0.95 | 2.00 | 2.05 | 2.10 | 2.15 | 2.20 | | | | | | | | | | | | | | | | |
| 0.96-1.00 | 2.05 | 2.10 | 2.15 | 2.20 | | | | | | | | | | | | | | | | | |
| 1.01-1.05 | 2.10 | 2.15 | 2.20 | | | | | | | | | | | | | | | | | | |
| 1.06-1.10 | 2.15 | 2.20 | | | | | | | | | | | | | | | | | | | |
| 1.11-1.15 | 2.20 | | | | | | | | | | | | | | | | | | | | |

H31236

**23.15a Shim selection chart – inlet valves**

| MEASURED TAPPET CLEARANCE (mm) | PRESENT SHIM SIZE (mm) | | | | | | | | | | | | | | | | | | | | |
|---|---|---|---|---|---|---|---|---|---|---|---|---|---|---|---|---|---|---|---|---|---|
| | 1.20 | 1.25 | 1.30 | 1.35 | 1.40 | 1.45 | 1.50 | 1.55 | 1.60 | 1.65 | 1.70 | 1.75 | 1.80 | 1.85 | 1.90 | 1.95 | 2.00 | 2.05 | 2.10 | 2.15 | 2.20 |
| 0.05-0.09 | | | | 1.20 | 1.25 | 1.30 | 1.35 | 1.40 | 1.45 | 1.50 | 1.55 | 1.60 | 1.65 | 1.70 | 1.75 | 1.80 | 1.85 | 1.90 | 1.95 | 2.00 | 2.05 |
| 0.10-0.14 | | | 1.20 | 1.25 | 1.30 | 1.35 | 1.40 | 1.45 | 1.50 | 1.55 | 1.60 | 1.65 | 1.70 | 1.75 | 1.80 | 1.85 | 1.90 | 1.95 | 2.00 | 2.05 | 2.10 |
| 0.15-0.19 | | 1.20 | 1.25 | 1.30 | 1.35 | 1.40 | 1.45 | 1.50 | 1.55 | 1.60 | 1.65 | 1.70 | 1.75 | 1.80 | 1.85 | 1.90 | 1.95 | 2.00 | 2.05 | 2.10 | 2.15 |
| 0.20-0.30 | SPECIFIED CLEARANCE/NO ADJUSTMENT REQUIRED | | | | | | | | | | | | | | | | | | | | |
| 0.31-0.35 | 1.30 | 1.35 | 1.40 | 1.45 | 1.50 | 1.55 | 1.60 | 1.65 | 1.70 | 1.75 | 1.80 | 1.85 | 1.90 | 1.95 | 2.00 | 2.05 | 2.10 | 2.15 | 2.20 | 2.20 | |
| 0.36-0.40 | 1.35 | 1.40 | 1.45 | 1.50 | 1.55 | 1.60 | 1.65 | 1.70 | 1.75 | 1.80 | 1.85 | 1.90 | 1.95 | 2.00 | 2.05 | 2.10 | 2.15 | 2.20 | | | |
| 0.41-0.45 | 1.40 | 1.45 | 1.50 | 1.55 | 1.60 | 1.65 | 1.70 | 1.75 | 1.80 | 1.85 | 1.90 | 1.95 | 2.00 | 2.05 | 2.10 | 2.15 | 2.20 | | | | |
| 0.46-0.50 | 1.45 | 1.50 | 1.55 | 1.60 | 1.65 | 1.70 | 1.75 | 1.80 | 1.85 | 1.90 | 1.95 | 2.00 | 2.05 | 2.10 | 2.15 | 2.20 | | | | | |
| 0.51-0.55 | 1.50 | 1.55 | 1.60 | 1.65 | 1.70 | 1.75 | 1.80 | 1.85 | 1.90 | 1.95 | 2.00 | 2.05 | 2.10 | 2.15 | 2.20 | | | | | | |
| 0.56-0.60 | 1.55 | 1.60 | 1.65 | 1.70 | 1.75 | 1.80 | 1.85 | 1.90 | 1.95 | 2.00 | 2.05 | 2.10 | 2.15 | 2.20 | | | | | | | |
| 0.61-0.65 | 1.60 | 1.65 | 1.70 | 1.75 | 1.80 | 1.85 | 1.90 | 1.95 | 2.00 | 2.05 | 2.10 | 2.15 | 2.20 | | | | | | | | |
| 0.66-0.70 | 1.65 | 1.70 | 1.75 | 1.80 | 1.85 | 1.90 | 1.95 | 2.00 | 2.05 | 2.10 | 2.15 | 2.20 | | | | | | | | | |
| 0.71-0.75 | 1.70 | 1.75 | 1.80 | 1.85 | 1.90 | 1.95 | 2.00 | 2.05 | 2.10 | 2.15 | 2.20 | | | | | | | | | | |
| 0.76-0.80 | 1.75 | 1.80 | 1.85 | 1.90 | 1.95 | 2.00 | 2.05 | 2.10 | 2.15 | 2.20 | | | | | | | | | | | |
| 0.81-0.85 | 1.80 | 1.85 | 1.90 | 1.95 | 2.00 | 2.05 | 2.10 | 2.15 | 2.20 | | | | | | | | | | | | |
| 0.86-0.90 | 1.85 | 1.90 | 1.95 | 2.00 | 2.05 | 2.10 | 2.15 | 2.20 | | | | | | | | | | | | | |
| 0.91-0.95 | 1.90 | 1.95 | 2.00 | 2.05 | 2.10 | 2.15 | 2.20 | | | | | | | | | | | | | | |
| 0.96-1.00 | 1.95 | 2.00 | 2.05 | 2.10 | 2.15 | 2.20 | | | | | | | | | | | | | | | |
| 1.01-1.05 | 2.00 | 2.05 | 2.10 | 2.15 | 2.20 | | | | | | | | | | | | | | | | |
| 1.06-1.10 | 2.05 | 2.10 | 2.15 | 2.20 | | | | | | | | | | | | | | | | | |
| 1.11-1.15 | 2.10 | 2.15 | 2.20 | | | | | | | | | | | | | | | | | | |
| 1.16-1.20 | 2.15 | 2.20 | | | | | | | | | | | | | | | | | | | |
| 1.21-1.25 | 2.20 | | | | | | | | | | | | | | | | | | | | |

H31237

**23.15b Shim selection chart – exhaust valves**

Shims are available in 0.05 mm increments from 1.200 to 2.200 mm. If the shim thickness is less than its denomination, this must be taken into account when selecting a new shim.

**15** Using the appropriate shim selection chart, find where the measured valve clearance and existing shim thickness values intersect and read off the shim size required **(see illustrations)**. Note: *If the existing shim is marked with a number not ending in 0 or 5, round it up or down as appropriate to the nearest number ending in 0 or 5 so that the chart can be used.* **Note:** *If the required renewal shim is greater than 2.20 mm (the largest available), the valve is probably not seating correctly due to a build-up of carbon deposits and should be checked and cleaned or resurfaced as required (see Chapter 2).*

**16** Obtain the correct thickness shims from your Suzuki dealer. Where the required thickness is not equal to the available shim thickness, round off the measurement to the nearest available size.

**17** Obtain the replacement shim, then lubricate it with engine oil or molybdenum disulphide oil (a 50/50 mixture of molybdenum disulphide grease and engine oil) and fit it into its recess in the top of the valve, with the size marking on each shim facing down **(see illustration)**. Check that the shim is correctly seated, then lubricate the follower with engine oil or molybdenum disulphide oil and install it onto the valve **(see illustration)**. Repeat the process for any other valves as required, then install the camshafts (see Chapter 2).

**18** Rotate the crankshaft several turns to seat the new shim(s), then check the clearances again.

**19** Install all disturbed components in a reverse of the removal sequence. Use a new O-ring on the centre plug and a new sealing washer on the timing inspection plug and smear the O-ring and the plug threads with engine oil or molybdenum disulphide oil (a 50/50 mixture of molybdenum disulphide grease and engine oil) **(see illustration)**.

**1**

**23.17a Fit the shim into the recess in the top of the valve . . .**

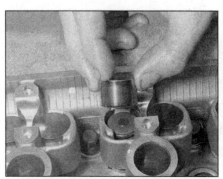

**23.17b . . . then install the follower**

**23.19 Use a new O-ring and sealing washer on the centre and inspection plugs**

# Every two years

### 24 Brakes – fluid change

1 The brake fluid should be changed at the prescribed interval or whenever a master cylinder or caliper overhaul is carried out. Refer to the brake bleeding section in Chapter 7, noting that all old fluid must be pumped from the fluid reservoir and hydraulic line before filling with new fluid.

> **HAYNES HINT** *Old brake fluid is invariably much darker than new fluid, making it easy to see when all old fluid has been expelled from the system.*

### 25 Cooling system – draining, flushing and refilling

> ⚠️ *Warning: Allow the engine to cool completely before performing this maintenance operation. Also, don't allow antifreeze to come into contact with your skin or the painted surfaces of the motorcycle. Rinse off spills immediately with plenty of water. Antifreeze is highly toxic if ingested. Never leave antifreeze lying around in an open container or in puddles on the floor; children and pets are attracted by its sweet smell and may drink it. Check with local authorities (councils) about disposing of antifreeze. Many communities have collection centres which will see that antifreeze is disposed of safely. Antifreeze is also combustible, so don't store it near open flames.*

### Draining

1 Remove the fairing side panels (see Chapter 8). Remove the pressure cap by turning it anti-clockwise until it reaches a stop. If you hear a hissing sound (indicating there is still pressure in the system), wait until it stops. Now press down on the cap and continue turning the cap until it can be removed **(see illustration 9.6)**.
2 Position a suitable container beneath the water pump on the left-hand side of the engine. Slacken the clamp securing the radiator hose to the front of the water pump and release the cable tie, then pull the hose off its union and allow the coolant to completely drain from the system **(see illustrations)**. Also remove the reservoir cap, then detach the hose from the bottom of the reservoir and drain the coolant **(see illustration)**. Reconnect the hose after the reservoir has drained.

### Flushing

3 Flush the radiator with clean tap water by inserting a garden hose in the radiator filler neck. Allow the water to run through until it is clear and flows cleanly out of the drain holes. If the radiator is extremely corroded, remove it (see Chapter 3) and have it cleaned professionally.
4 Now reconnect the radiator hose to the water pump and fill the system with clean water, then drain it again. Reconnect the hose and tighten the clamp.
5 Fill the cooling system with clean water mixed with a flushing compound. Make sure the flushing compound is compatible with aluminium components, and follow the manufacturer's instructions carefully. Fit the pressure cap.
6 Start the engine and allow it to reach normal operating temperature. Let it run for about ten minutes.
7 Stop the engine. Let it cool for a while, then cover the pressure cap with a heavy rag and turn it anti-clockwise to the first stop, releasing any pressure that may be present in the system. Once the hissing stops, push down on the cap and remove it completely.
8 Drain the system once again.
9 Fill the system with clean water, fit the radiator cap and repeat the procedure in Steps 6 to 8.

### Refilling

10 Fit the radiator hose onto the water pump and tighten the clamp securely, then fit the cable tie **(see illustration 25.2a)**.
11 Fill the system with the proper coolant mixture (see this Chapter's Specifications) **(see illustration)**. **Note:** *Pour the coolant in slowly to minimise the amount of air entering the system.*
12 When the system is full (all the way up to the top of the radiator filler neck), install the pressure cap. Also top up the coolant reservoir to the 'F' level line (see *Daily (pre-ride) checks*).
13 Start the engine and allow it to idle for 2 to 3 minutes. Flick the throttle twistgrip part open 3 or 4 times, so that the engine speed rises to approximately 4000 – 5000 rpm, then stop the engine. Any air trapped in the system should have bled back to the radiator filler neck.
14 Let the engine cool then remove the pressure cap as described in Step 1. Check that the coolant level is still up to the radiator filler neck. If it's low, add the specified mixture until it reaches the top of the filler neck. Refit the cap.
15 Check the coolant level in the reservoir and top up if necessary.
16 Check the system for leaks.
17 Do not dispose of the old coolant by pouring it down the drain. Instead pour it into a heavy plastic container, cap it tightly and take it into an authorised disposal site or service station – see **Warning** at the beginning of this Section.

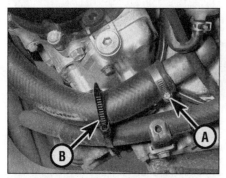

**25.2a Slacken the clamp (A) and release the cable tie (B) . . .**

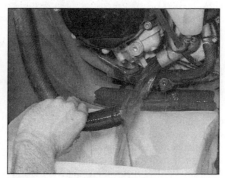

**25.2b . . . then detach the hose and drain the system**

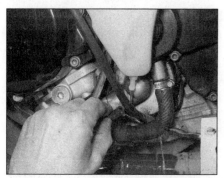

**25.2c Detach the hose and drain the reservoir**

**25.11 Fill the system with the specified coolant mixture**

# Every four years

## 26 Brake hoses – renewal

1 The hoses will in time deteriorate with age and should be renewed regardless of their apparent condition.
2 Refer to Chapter 7 and disconnect the brake hoses from the master cylinders and calipers. Always renew the banjo union sealing washers and tighten the banjo union bolts to the specified torque setting.

## 27 Fuel hoses and EVAP hoses – renewal

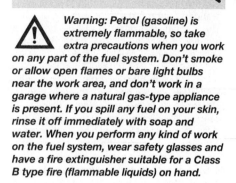 *Warning: Petrol (gasoline) is extremely flammable, so take extra precautions when you work on any part of the fuel system. Don't smoke or allow open flames or bare light bulbs near the work area, and don't work in a garage where a natural gas-type appliance is present. If you spill any fuel on your skin, rinse it off immediately with soap and water. When you perform any kind of work on the fuel system, wear safety glasses and have a fire extinguisher suitable for a Class B type fire (flammable liquids) on hand.*

1 The fuel delivery, return (injection models) and vacuum hoses should be renewed regardless of their condition. On California models, also renew the emission control system hoses (see Chapter 4).
2 Refer to Chapter 4 and raise or remove the fuel tank and remove the air filter housing. Disconnect the fuel hoses from the fuel tank, valve and from the carburettors or injector rail and pressure regulator as appropriate, noting the routing of each hose and where it connects. It is advisable to make a sketch of the various hoses before removing them to ensure they are correctly installed.
3 Secure each new hose to its unions using new clamps. Run the engine and check that there are no leaks before taking the machine out on the road.

# Non-scheduled maintenance

## 28 Headlight aim – check and adjustment

Note: *An improperly adjusted headlight may cause problems for oncoming traffic or provide poor, unsafe illumination of the road ahead. Before adjusting the headlight aim, be sure to consult with local traffic laws and regulations – for UK models refer to MOT Test Checks in the Reference section.*
1 The headlight beam can adjusted both horizontally and vertically. Before making any adjustment, check that the tyre pressures are correct and the suspension is adjusted as required. Make any adjustments to the headlight aim with the machine on level ground, with the fuel tank half full and with an assistant sitting on the seat. If the bike is usually ridden with a passenger on the back, have a second assistant to do this.
2 Horizontal adjustment is made by turning the adjuster screw on the top outer corner of each headlight unit (see illustration). Turn it clockwise to move the beam out (away from the centre of the bike), and anti-clockwise to move it in.
3 Vertical adjustment is made by turning the adjuster screw on the bottom outer corner of each headlight unit (see illustration 28.2). Turn it clockwise to move the beam down, and anti-clockwise to move it up.

## 29 Wheel bearings – check

1 Wheel bearings will wear over a period of time and result in handling problems.

2 Support the motorcycle upright using an auxiliary stand so that the wheel being checked is off the ground. Check for any play in the bearings by pushing and pulling the wheel against the hub (see illustration). Also rotate the wheel and check that it rotates smoothly.
3 If any play is detected in the hub, or if the wheel does not rotate smoothly (and this is not due to brake or transmission drag), the wheel bearings must be removed and inspected for wear or damage (see Chapter 7).

## 30 Front forks – oil change

1 Fork oil degrades over a period of time and loses its damping qualities. Refer to Chapter 6 for front fork removal, oil draining and refilling, following the relevant steps. The forks do not need to be completely disassembled.

28.2 Horizontal beam adjuster (A), vertical beam adjuster (B)

## 31 Cylinder compression – check

1 Among other things, poor engine performance may be caused by leaking valves, incorrect valve clearances, a leaking head gasket, or worn pistons, rings and/or cylinder walls. A cylinder compression check will help pinpoint these conditions and can also indicate the presence of excessive carbon deposits in the cylinder head.
2 The only tools required are a compression gauge (with a threaded adapter to suit the spark plug hole in the cylinder head) and a spark plug wrench. Depending on the outcome of the initial test, a squirt-type oil can may also be needed.
3 Make sure the valve clearances are correctly set (see Section 23) and that the cylinder head bolts are tightened to the correct torque setting (see Chapter 2).
4 Refer to *Fault Finding Equipment* in the

29.2 Checking for play in the wheel bearings

1

Reference section for details of the compression test, and to the Specifications at the beginning of this Chapter for the test data.

## 32 Engine – oil pressure check
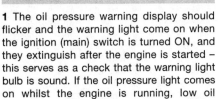

1 The oil pressure warning display should flicker and the warning light come on when the ignition (main) switch is turned ON, and they extinguish after the engine is started – this serves as a check that the warning light bulb is sound. If the oil pressure light comes on whilst the engine is running, low oil pressure is indicated – stop the engine immediately and carry out an oil level check (see *Daily (pre-ride) checks*).

2 An oil pressure check must be carried out if the warning light comes on when the engine is running yet the oil level is good (Step 1). It can also provide useful information about the condition of the engine's lubrication system.

3 To check the oil pressure, a suitable gauge and adapter piece (which screws into the crankcase) will be needed. Suzuki provide a kit (pt nos. 09915-74510 and 09915-74540) for this purpose.

4 Warm the engine up to normal operating temperature then stop it.

5 Place a suitable container below the main oil gallery plug below the starter clutch cover on the right-hand side of the engine to catch any oil. Unscrew the plug and swiftly screw the adapter into the crankcase threads **(see illustration)**. Connect the gauge to the adapter. If much oil is lost, replenish it to the correct level before proceeding (see *Daily (pre-ride) checks*).

6 Start the engine and increase the engine speed to 3000 rpm whilst watching the gauge reading. The oil pressure should be similar to that given in the Specifications at the start of this Chapter.

7 If the pressure is significantly lower than the standard, either the pressure regulator is stuck open, the oil pump is faulty, the oil strainer or filter is blocked, or there is other engine damage. Begin diagnosis by checking the oil filter, strainer and regulator, then the oil pump (see Chapter 2). If those items check out okay, chances are the bearing oil clearances are excessive and the engine needs to be overhauled.

8 If the pressure is too high, either an oil passage is clogged, the regulator is stuck closed or the wrong grade of oil is being used.

9 Stop the engine and unscrew the gauge and adapter from the crankcase.

10 Install the main oil gallery plug using a new sealing washer, and tighten it to the torque setting specified at the beginning of the Chapter. Check the oil level (see *Daily (pre-ride) checks*).

## 33 Steering head bearings – lubrication

1 Over a period of time the grease will harden or may be washed out of the bearings by incorrect use of jet washes.

2 Disassemble the steering head for re-greasing of the bearings. Refer to Chapter 6 for details.

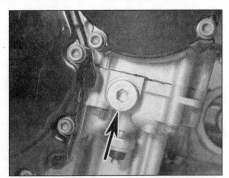
**32.5 Main oil gallery oil plug (arrowed)**

## 34 Rear suspension bearings – lubrication

1 Over a period of time the grease will harden or dirt will penetrate the bearings.

2 The suspension components are not equipped with grease nipples. Remove the swingarm and the suspension linkage as described in Chapter 6 for greasing of the bearings.

## 35 Brake caliper and master cylinder seals – renewal

1 Brake seals will deteriorate over a period of time and lose their effectiveness, leading to sticking operation or fluid loss, or allowing the ingress of air and dirt. Refer to Chapter 7 and dismantle the components for seal renewal.

# Chapter 2
# Engine, clutch and transmission

## Contents

**2**

## Degrees of difficulty

| **Easy,** suitable for novice with little experience |  | **Fairly easy,** suitable for beginner with some experience | | **Fairly difficult,** suitable for competent DIY mechanic |  | **Difficult,** suitable for experienced DIY mechanic | | **Very difficult,** suitable for expert DIY or professional |  |

## Specifications – GSX-R600 models

### General

Type . . . . . . . . . . . . . . . . . . . . . . . . . . . . . . . . . . . . . . . . . . . . . . . Four-stroke in-line four
Capacity . . . . . . . . . . . . . . . . . . . . . . . . . . . . . . . . . . . . . . . . . . . . 600 cc
Bore . . . . . . . . . . . . . . . . . . . . . . . . . . . . . . . . . . . . . . . . . . . . . . . 65.5 mm
Stroke . . . . . . . . . . . . . . . . . . . . . . . . . . . . . . . . . . . . . . . . . . . . . . 44.5 mm
Compression ratio . . . . . . . . . . . . . . . . . . . . . . . . . . . . . . . . . . . . . 12.0 to 1
Clutch . . . . . . . . . . . . . . . . . . . . . . . . . . . . . . . . . . . . . . . . . . . . . . Wet multi-plate
Transmission . . . . . . . . . . . . . . . . . . . . . . . . . . . . . . . . . . . . . . . . . 6-speed constant mesh
Final drive . . . . . . . . . . . . . . . . . . . . . . . . . . . . . . . . . . . . . . . . . . . Chain

## Camshafts – V models

Inlet lobe height
   California models
      Standard . . . . . . . . . . . . . . . . . . . . . . . . . . . . . . . . . . . . . . . . . .   33.992 to 34.048 mm
      Service limit (min) . . . . . . . . . . . . . . . . . . . . . . . . . . . . . . . . . .   33.70 mm
   All other models
      Standard . . . . . . . . . . . . . . . . . . . . . . . . . . . . . . . . . . . . . . . . . .   35.992 to 36.048 mm
      Service limit (min) . . . . . . . . . . . . . . . . . . . . . . . . . . . . . . . . . .   35.70 mm
Exhaust lobe height
   Standard . . . . . . . . . . . . . . . . . . . . . . . . . . . . . . . . . . . . . . . . . .   35.292 to 35.348 mm
   Service limit (min) . . . . . . . . . . . . . . . . . . . . . . . . . . . . . . . . . .   35.00 mm
Journal diameter . . . . . . . . . . . . . . . . . . . . . . . . . . . . . . . . . . . . . . .   23.959 to 23.980 mm
Journal holder diameter . . . . . . . . . . . . . . . . . . . . . . . . . . . . . . . . . .   24.012 to 24.025 mm
Journal oil clearance
   Standard . . . . . . . . . . . . . . . . . . . . . . . . . . . . . . . . . . . . . . . . . .   0.032 to 0.066 mm
   Service limit (max) . . . . . . . . . . . . . . . . . . . . . . . . . . . . . . . . . .   0.15 mm
Runout (max) . . . . . . . . . . . . . . . . . . . . . . . . . . . . . . . . . . . . . . . . . .   0.10 mm

## Camshafts – W and X models

Inlet lobe height
   California models
      Standard . . . . . . . . . . . . . . . . . . . . . . . . . . . . . . . . . . . . . . . . . .   33.980 to 34.048 mm
      Service limit (min) . . . . . . . . . . . . . . . . . . . . . . . . . . . . . . . . . .   33.68 mm
   All other models
      Standard . . . . . . . . . . . . . . . . . . . . . . . . . . . . . . . . . . . . . . . . . .   36.660 to 36.728 mm
      Service limit (min) . . . . . . . . . . . . . . . . . . . . . . . . . . . . . . . . . .   36.36 mm
Exhaust lobe height
   Standard . . . . . . . . . . . . . . . . . . . . . . . . . . . . . . . . . . . . . . . . . .   34.780 to 34.848 mm
   Service limit (min) . . . . . . . . . . . . . . . . . . . . . . . . . . . . . . . . . .   34.48 mm
Journal diameter . . . . . . . . . . . . . . . . . . . . . . . . . . . . . . . . . . . . . . .   23.959 to 23.980 mm
Journal holder diameter . . . . . . . . . . . . . . . . . . . . . . . . . . . . . . . . . .   24.012 to 24.025 mm
Journal oil clearance
   Standard . . . . . . . . . . . . . . . . . . . . . . . . . . . . . . . . . . . . . . . . . .   0.032 to 0.066 mm
   Service limit (max) . . . . . . . . . . . . . . . . . . . . . . . . . . . . . . . . . .   0.15 mm
Runout (max) . . . . . . . . . . . . . . . . . . . . . . . . . . . . . . . . . . . . . . . . . .   0.10 mm

## Valves, guides and springs

Valve clearances . . . . . . . . . . . . . . . . . . . . . . . . . . . . . . . . . . . . . . .   see Chapter 1
Inlet valve
   Head diameter . . . . . . . . . . . . . . . . . . . . . . . . . . . . . . . . . . . . .   26.5 mm
   Stem diameter . . . . . . . . . . . . . . . . . . . . . . . . . . . . . . . . . . . . .   4.475 to 4.490 mm
   Guide bore diameter . . . . . . . . . . . . . . . . . . . . . . . . . . . . . . . . .   4.500 to 4.512 mm
   Stem-to-guide clearance . . . . . . . . . . . . . . . . . . . . . . . . . . . . .   0.010 to 0.037 mm
   Stem deflection (max) – see text . . . . . . . . . . . . . . . . . . . . . . .   0.35 mm
   Margin thickness (min) . . . . . . . . . . . . . . . . . . . . . . . . . . . . . .   0.5 mm
   Seat width . . . . . . . . . . . . . . . . . . . . . . . . . . . . . . . . . . . . . . . .   0.9 to 1.1 mm
   Head runout (max) . . . . . . . . . . . . . . . . . . . . . . . . . . . . . . . . . .   0.03 mm
   Stem runout (max) . . . . . . . . . . . . . . . . . . . . . . . . . . . . . . . . . .   0.05 mm
Exhaust valve
   Head diameter . . . . . . . . . . . . . . . . . . . . . . . . . . . . . . . . . . . . .   22.0 mm
   Stem diameter . . . . . . . . . . . . . . . . . . . . . . . . . . . . . . . . . . . . .   4.455 to 4.470 mm
   Guide bore diameter . . . . . . . . . . . . . . . . . . . . . . . . . . . . . . . . .   4.500 to 4.512 mm
   Stem-to-guide clearance . . . . . . . . . . . . . . . . . . . . . . . . . . . . .   0.030 to 0.057 mm
   Stem deflection (max) – see text . . . . . . . . . . . . . . . . . . . . . . .   0.35 mm
   Margin thickness (min) . . . . . . . . . . . . . . . . . . . . . . . . . . . . . .   0.5 mm
   Seat width . . . . . . . . . . . . . . . . . . . . . . . . . . . . . . . . . . . . . . . .   0.9 to 1.1 mm
   Head runout (max) . . . . . . . . . . . . . . . . . . . . . . . . . . . . . . . . . .   0.03 mm
   Stem runout (max) . . . . . . . . . . . . . . . . . . . . . . . . . . . . . . . . . .   0.05 mm
Valve springs (inlet and exhaust)
   Free length limit (min)
      Inner spring . . . . . . . . . . . . . . . . . . . . . . . . . . . . . . . . . . . . .   36.8 mm
      Outer spring . . . . . . . . . . . . . . . . . . . . . . . . . . . . . . . . . . . . .   38.6 mm
   Spring tension
      Inner spring . . . . . . . . . . . . . . . . . . . . . . . . . . . . . . . . . . . . .   29.9 mm with 4.5 kg load
      Outer spring . . . . . . . . . . . . . . . . . . . . . . . . . . . . . . . . . . . . .   33.4 mm with 15.5 kg load

## Cylinder block

Bore . . . . . . . . . . . . . . . . . . . . . . . . . . . . . . . . . . . . . . . . . . . . . . . .   65.500 to 65.515 mm
Warpage (max) . . . . . . . . . . . . . . . . . . . . . . . . . . . . . . . . . . . . . . . .   0.20 mm
Cylinder compression . . . . . . . . . . . . . . . . . . . . . . . . . . . . . . . . . . .   see Chapter 1

## Cylinder head
Warpage (max) . . . . . . . . . . . . . . . . . . . . . . . . . . . . . . . . . . . . . . .  0.20 mm

## Pistons
Piston diameter (measured 15.0 mm up from skirt, at 90º to piston pin axis)
    Standard . . . . . . . . . . . . . . . . . . . . . . . . . . . . . . . . . . . . . . .  65.470 to 65.485 mm
    Service limit (min) . . . . . . . . . . . . . . . . . . . . . . . . . . . . . . . .  65.380 mm
Piston-to-bore clearance . . . . . . . . . . . . . . . . . . . . . . . . . . . . . . .  0.025 to 0.035 mm
Piston pin diameter
    Standard . . . . . . . . . . . . . . . . . . . . . . . . . . . . . . . . . . . . . . .  14.993 to 15.000 mm
    Service limit (min) . . . . . . . . . . . . . . . . . . . . . . . . . . . . . . . .  14.980 mm
Piston pin bore diameter in piston
    Standard . . . . . . . . . . . . . . . . . . . . . . . . . . . . . . . . . . . . . . .  15.002 to 15.008 mm
    Service limit (max) . . . . . . . . . . . . . . . . . . . . . . . . . . . . . . . .  15.030 mm

## Piston rings
Ring end gap (free)
    Top ring
        Standard
            V models . . . . . . . . . . . . . . . . . . . . . . . . . . . . . . . . . . .  6.90 mm (approx.)
            W models . . . . . . . . . . . . . . . . . . . . . . . . . . . . . . . . . . .  6.20 mm (approx.)
            X models . . . . . . . . . . . . . . . . . . . . . . . . . . . . . . . . . . .  5.40 mm (approx.)
        Service limit (min)
            V models . . . . . . . . . . . . . . . . . . . . . . . . . . . . . . . . . . .  5.50 mm
            W models . . . . . . . . . . . . . . . . . . . . . . . . . . . . . . . . . . .  4.90 mm
            X models . . . . . . . . . . . . . . . . . . . . . . . . . . . . . . . . . . .  4.30 mm
    2nd ring
        Standard
            V models . . . . . . . . . . . . . . . . . . . . . . . . . . . . . . . . . . .  8.70 mm (approx.)
            W models . . . . . . . . . . . . . . . . . . . . . . . . . . . . . . . . . . .  8.00 mm (approx.)
            X models . . . . . . . . . . . . . . . . . . . . . . . . . . . . . . . . . . .  5.90 mm
        Service limit (min)
            V models . . . . . . . . . . . . . . . . . . . . . . . . . . . . . . . . . . .  6.90 mm
            W models . . . . . . . . . . . . . . . . . . . . . . . . . . . . . . . . . . .  6.40 mm
            X models . . . . . . . . . . . . . . . . . . . . . . . . . . . . . . . . . . .  4.70 mm
Ring end gap (installed)
    Top ring
        Standard . . . . . . . . . . . . . . . . . . . . . . . . . . . . . . . . . . .  0.10 to 0.25 mm
        Service limit (max) . . . . . . . . . . . . . . . . . . . . . . . . . . . .  0.50 mm
    2nd ring
        Standard . . . . . . . . . . . . . . . . . . . . . . . . . . . . . . . . . . .  0.10 to 0.25 mm
        Service limit (max) . . . . . . . . . . . . . . . . . . . . . . . . . . . .  0.50 mm
Ring thickness
    Top ring . . . . . . . . . . . . . . . . . . . . . . . . . . . . . . . . . . . . . . .  0.97 to 0.99 mm
    2nd ring . . . . . . . . . . . . . . . . . . . . . . . . . . . . . . . . . . . . . . .  0.77 to 0.79 mm
Ring groove width in piston
    Top ring . . . . . . . . . . . . . . . . . . . . . . . . . . . . . . . . . . . . . . .  1.01 to 1.03 mm
    2nd ring . . . . . . . . . . . . . . . . . . . . . . . . . . . . . . . . . . . . . . .  0.81 to 0.83 mm
    Oil ring . . . . . . . . . . . . . . . . . . . . . . . . . . . . . . . . . . . . . . .  1.51 to 1.53 mm
Ring-to-groove clearance
    Top ring (max) . . . . . . . . . . . . . . . . . . . . . . . . . . . . . . . . . .  0.18 mm
    2nd ring (max) . . . . . . . . . . . . . . . . . . . . . . . . . . . . . . . . . .  0.18 mm

## Clutch
Friction plate
    Quantity . . . . . . . . . . . . . . . . . . . . . . . . . . . . . . . . . . . . . . . .  9
    Thickness . . . . . . . . . . . . . . . . . . . . . . . . . . . . . . . . . . . . . . .  2.92 to 3.08 mm
    Tab width (min) – V models . . . . . . . . . . . . . . . . . . . . . . . . . . .  13.0 mm
    Tab width – W and X models
        Standard . . . . . . . . . . . . . . . . . . . . . . . . . . . . . . . . . . .  13.7 to 13.8 mm
        Service limit (min) . . . . . . . . . . . . . . . . . . . . . . . . . . . . .  12.9 mm
Plain plate
    Quantity . . . . . . . . . . . . . . . . . . . . . . . . . . . . . . . . . . . . . . . .  8 (see text)
    Warpage (max) . . . . . . . . . . . . . . . . . . . . . . . . . . . . . . . . . . .  0.1 mm
Assembled clutch plate thickness
    W models . . . . . . . . . . . . . . . . . . . . . . . . . . . . . . . . . . . . . . .  40.068 to 40.668 mm with 5 kg load (see text)
    X models . . . . . . . . . . . . . . . . . . . . . . . . . . . . . . . . . . . . . . .  45.085 to 45.685 mm with 5 kg load (see text)
Diaphragm spring free height (min) . . . . . . . . . . . . . . . . . . . . . . .  2.9 mm
Release mechanism screw . . . . . . . . . . . . . . . . . . . . . . . . . . . . . .  1/4 turn out

2

## Lubrication system

Oil pressure . . . . . . . . . . . . . . . . . . . . . . . . . . . . . . . . . . . . . . . . . . . . . . . . see Chapter 1

Oil pump       **Standard**    **Service limit (max)**

| | Standard | Service limit (max) |
|---|---|---|
| Inner rotor tip-to-outer rotor clearance . . . . . . . . . . . . . . . . . . . . . . | 0.10 mm | 0.15 mm |
| Outer rotor-to-body clearance . . . . . . . . . . . . . . . . . . . . . . . . . . . | 0.15 to 0.22 mm | 0.35 mm |

## Transmission

Gear ratios (no. of teeth) – V models

| | |
|---|---|
| Primary reduction . . . . . . . . . . . . . . . . . . . . . . . . . . . . . . . . . . . . . . . . . | 1.756 to 1 (72/41T) |
| Final reduction . . . . . . . . . . . . . . . . . . . . . . . . . . . . . . . . . . . . . . . . . . . . | 2.812 to 1 (45/16T) |
| 1st gear . . . . . . . . . . . . . . . . . . . . . . . . . . . . . . . . . . . . . . . . . . . . . . . . . | 2.866 to 1 (43/15T) |
| 2nd gear . . . . . . . . . . . . . . . . . . . . . . . . . . . . . . . . . . . . . . . . . . . . . . . . | 2.058 to 1 (35/17T) |
| 3rd gear . . . . . . . . . . . . . . . . . . . . . . . . . . . . . . . . . . . . . . . . . . . . . . . . . | 1.650 to 1 (33/20T) |
| 4th gear . . . . . . . . . . . . . . . . . . . . . . . . . . . . . . . . . . . . . . . . . . . . . . . . . | 1.428 to 1 (30/21T) |
| 5th gear . . . . . . . . . . . . . . . . . . . . . . . . . . . . . . . . . . . . . . . . . . . . . . . . . | 1.285 to 1 (27/21T) |
| 6th gear . . . . . . . . . . . . . . . . . . . . . . . . . . . . . . . . . . . . . . . . . . . . . . . . . | 1.181 to 1 (26/22T) |

Gear ratios (no. of teeth) – W and X models

| | |
|---|---|
| Primary reduction . . . . . . . . . . . . . . . . . . . . . . . . . . . . . . . . . . . . . . . . . | 1.756 to 1 (72/41T) |
| Final reduction . . . . . . . . . . . . . . . . . . . . . . . . . . . . . . . . . . . . . . . . . . . . | 2.875 to 1 (46/16T) |
| 1st gear . . . . . . . . . . . . . . . . . . . . . . . . . . . . . . . . . . . . . . . . . . . . . . . . . | 2.866 to 1 (43/15T) |
| 2nd gear . . . . . . . . . . . . . . . . . . . . . . . . . . . . . . . . . . . . . . . . . . . . . . . . | 2.052 to 1 (39/19T) |
| 3rd gear . . . . . . . . . . . . . . . . . . . . . . . . . . . . . . . . . . . . . . . . . . . . . . . . . | 1.650 to 1 (33/20T) |
| 4th gear . . . . . . . . . . . . . . . . . . . . . . . . . . . . . . . . . . . . . . . . . . . . . . . . . | 1.428 to 1 (30/21T) |
| 5th gear . . . . . . . . . . . . . . . . . . . . . . . . . . . . . . . . . . . . . . . . . . . . . . . . . | 1.285 to 1 (27/21T) |
| 6th gear . . . . . . . . . . . . . . . . . . . . . . . . . . . . . . . . . . . . . . . . . . . . . . . . . | 1.181 to 1 (26/22T) |

## Selector drum and forks

Selector fork-to-groove clearance

| | |
|---|---|
| Standard . . . . . . . . . . . . . . . . . . . . . . . . . . . . . . . . . . . . . . . . . . . . . . . | 0.1 to 0.3 mm |
| Service limit (max) . . . . . . . . . . . . . . . . . . . . . . . . . . . . . . . . . . . . . . . . | 0.5 mm |
| Selector fork end thickness . . . . . . . . . . . . . . . . . . . . . . . . . . . . . . . . . | 4.8 to 4.9 mm |
| Selector fork groove width . . . . . . . . . . . . . . . . . . . . . . . . . . . . . . . . . . | 5.0 to 5.1 mm |

## Crankshaft and bearings

Journal diameter

| | |
|---|---|
| Code A . . . . . . . . . . . . . . . . . . . . . . . . . . . . . . . . . . . . . . . . . . . . . . . . . | 33.992 to 34.000 mm |
| Code B . . . . . . . . . . . . . . . . . . . . . . . . . . . . . . . . . . . . . . . . . . . . . . . . . | 33.984 to 33.992 mm |
| Code C . . . . . . . . . . . . . . . . . . . . . . . . . . . . . . . . . . . . . . . . . . . . . . . . . | 33.976 to 33.984 mm |

Main bearing oil clearance

| | |
|---|---|
| Standard – V models . . . . . . . . . . . . . . . . . . . . . . . . . . . . . . . . . . . . . | 0.020 to 0.044 mm |
| Standard – W and X models . . . . . . . . . . . . . . . . . . . . . . . . . . . . . . . | 0.016 to 0.040 mm |
| Service limit (max) – all models . . . . . . . . . . . . . . . . . . . . . . . . . . . . . | 0.080 mm |
| Runout (max) . . . . . . . . . . . . . . . . . . . . . . . . . . . . . . . . . . . . . . . . . . . | 0.05 mm |
| Thrust bearing clearance . . . . . . . . . . . . . . . . . . . . . . . . . . . . . . . . . . | 0.055 to 0.110 mm |

Thrust bearing thickness

| | |
|---|---|
| Right-hand side . . . . . . . . . . . . . . . . . . . . . . . . . . . . . . . . . . . . . . . . . . | 2.425 to 2.450 mm |
| Left-hand side . . . . . . . . . . . . . . . . . . . . . . . . . . . . . . . . . . . . . . . . . . . | 2.350 to 2.500 mm |

## Connecting rods

Small-end internal diameter

| | |
|---|---|
| Standard . . . . . . . . . . . . . . . . . . . . . . . . . . . . . . . . . . . . . . . . . . . . . . . | 15.010 to 15.018 mm |
| Service limit (max) . . . . . . . . . . . . . . . . . . . . . . . . . . . . . . . . . . . . . . . . | 15.040 mm |

Big-end side clearance

| | |
|---|---|
| Standard . . . . . . . . . . . . . . . . . . . . . . . . . . . . . . . . . . . . . . . . . . . . . . . | 0.1 to 0.2 mm |
| Service limit (max) . . . . . . . . . . . . . . . . . . . . . . . . . . . . . . . . . . . . . . . . | 0.3 mm |
| Big-end width . . . . . . . . . . . . . . . . . . . . . . . . . . . . . . . . . . . . . . . . . . . | 20.95 to 21.00 mm |
| Crankpin width . . . . . . . . . . . . . . . . . . . . . . . . . . . . . . . . . . . . . . . . . . | 21.10 to 21.15 mm |

Big-end diameter

| | |
|---|---|
| Code 1 . . . . . . . . . . . . . . . . . . . . . . . . . . . . . . . . . . . . . . . . . . . . . . . . . | 35.000 to 35.008 mm |
| Code 2 . . . . . . . . . . . . . . . . . . . . . . . . . . . . . . . . . . . . . . . . . . . . . . . . . | 35.008 to 35.016 mm |

Crankpin diameter

| | |
|---|---|
| Code 1 . . . . . . . . . . . . . . . . . . . . . . . . . . . . . . . . . . . . . . . . . . . . . . . . . | 31.992 to 32.000 mm |
| Code 2 . . . . . . . . . . . . . . . . . . . . . . . . . . . . . . . . . . . . . . . . . . . . . . . . . | 31.984 to 31.992 mm |
| Code 3 . . . . . . . . . . . . . . . . . . . . . . . . . . . . . . . . . . . . . . . . . . . . . . . . . | 31.976 to 31.984 mm |

Big-end oil clearance

| | |
|---|---|
| Standard . . . . . . . . . . . . . . . . . . . . . . . . . . . . . . . . . . . . . . . . . . . . . . . | 0.032 to 0.056 mm |
| Service limit (max) . . . . . . . . . . . . . . . . . . . . . . . . . . . . . . . . . . . . . . . . | 0.08 mm |

## Torque wrench settings – see end of Specifications

# Specifications – GSX-R750 models

## General

Type ............................................. Four-stroke in-line four
Capacity .......................................... 749 cc
Bore .............................................. 72.0 mm
Stroke ............................................ 46.0 mm
Compression ratio ................................. 11.8 to 1
Clutch ............................................ Wet multi-plate
Transmission ...................................... 6-speed constant mesh
Final drive ....................................... Chain

## Camshafts – T and V models

Inlet lobe height
  California models
    Standard ...................................... 33.992 to 34.048 mm
    Service limit (min) ........................... 33.70 mm
  All other models
    Standard ...................................... 36.502 to 36.558 mm
    Service limit (min) ........................... 36.21 mm
Exhaust lobe height
  Standard ...................................... 35.692 to 35.748 mm
  Service limit (min) ........................... 35.40 mm
Journal diameter .................................. 23.959 to 23.980 mm
Journal holder diameter ........................... 24.012 to 24.025 mm
Journal oil clearance
  Standard ...................................... 0.032 to 0.066 mm
  Service limit (max) ........................... 0.15 mm
Runout (max) ...................................... 0.10 mm

## Camshafts – W and X models

Inlet lobe height
  Standard ...................................... 36.660 to 36.728 mm
  Service limit (min) ........................... 36.70 mm
Exhaust lobe height
  Standard ...................................... 35.280 to 35.348 mm
  Service limit (min) ........................... 34.98 mm
Journal diameter .................................. 23.959 to 23.980 mm
Journal holder diameter ........................... 24.012 to 24.025 mm
Journal oil clearance
  Standard ...................................... 0.032 to 0.066 mm
  Service limit (max) ........................... 0.15 mm
Runout (max) ...................................... 0.10 mm

## Cylinder head

Warpage (max) ..................................... 0.20 mm

## Valves, guides and springs

Valve clearances .................................. see Chapter 1
Inlet valve
  Head diameter ................................. 29.0 mm
  Stem diameter ................................. 4.475 to 4.490 mm
  Guide bore diameter ........................... 4.500 to 4.512 mm
  Stem-to-guide clearance ....................... 0.010 to 0.037 mm
  Stem deflection (max) – see text .............. 0.35 mm
  Margin thickness (min) ........................ 0.5 mm
  Seat width .................................... 0.9 to 1.1 mm
  Head runout (max) ............................. 0.03 mm
  Stem runout (max) ............................. 0.05 mm
Exhaust valve
  Head diameter ................................. 24.0 mm
  Stem diameter ................................. 4.455 to 4.470 mm
  Guide bore diameter ........................... 4.500 to 4.512 mm
  Stem-to-guide clearance ....................... 0.030 to 0.057 mm
  Stem deflection (max) – see text .............. 0.35 mm
  Margin thickness (min) ........................ 0.5 mm
  Seat width .................................... 0.9 to 1.1 mm
  Head runout (max) ............................. 0.03 mm
  Stem runout (max) ............................. 0.05 mm

2

## Valves, guides and springs (continued)

Valve springs (inlet and exhaust)
    Free length limit (min)
        Inner spring . . . . . . . . . . . . . . . . . . . . . . . . . . . . . . . . . . . . . . . .   36.8 mm
        Outer spring . . . . . . . . . . . . . . . . . . . . . . . . . . . . . . . . . . . . . . . .   38.6 mm
    Spring tension
        Inner spring . . . . . . . . . . . . . . . . . . . . . . . . . . . . . . . . . . . . . . . .   29.9 mm with 4.5 kg load
        Outer spring – T and V models . . . . . . . . . . . . . . . . . . . . . . . . . .   33.4 mm with 15.5 kg load
        Outer spring – W and X models . . . . . . . . . . . . . . . . . . . . . . . . .   33.4 mm with 18.3 kg load

## Cylinder block

Bore . . . . . . . . . . . . . . . . . . . . . . . . . . . . . . . . . . . . . . . . . . . . . . . . . . .   72.000 to 72.015 mm
Warpage (max) . . . . . . . . . . . . . . . . . . . . . . . . . . . . . . . . . . . . . . . . .   0.20 mm
Cylinder compression . . . . . . . . . . . . . . . . . . . . . . . . . . . . . . . . . . .   see Chapter 1

## Pistons

Piston diameter (measured 15.0 mm up from skirt, at 90° to piston pin axis)
    Standard – T and V models . . . . . . . . . . . . . . . . . . . . . . . . . . . . .   71.955 to 71.970 mm
    Standard – W and X models . . . . . . . . . . . . . . . . . . . . . . . . . . . .   71.970 to 71.985 mm
    Service limit (min) . . . . . . . . . . . . . . . . . . . . . . . . . . . . . . . . . . . .   71.880 mm
Piston-to-bore clearance
    T and V models . . . . . . . . . . . . . . . . . . . . . . . . . . . . . . . . . . . . . .   0.040 to 0.050 mm
    W and X models . . . . . . . . . . . . . . . . . . . . . . . . . . . . . . . . . . . . .   0.025 to 0.035 mm
Piston pin diameter
    Standard . . . . . . . . . . . . . . . . . . . . . . . . . . . . . . . . . . . . . . . . . . .   15.995 to 16.000 mm
    Service limit (min) . . . . . . . . . . . . . . . . . . . . . . . . . . . . . . . . . . . .   15.980 mm
Piston pin bore diameter in piston
    Standard . . . . . . . . . . . . . . . . . . . . . . . . . . . . . . . . . . . . . . . . . . .   16.002 to 16.008 mm
    Service limit (max) . . . . . . . . . . . . . . . . . . . . . . . . . . . . . . . . . . .   16.030 mm

## Piston rings

Ring end gap (free)
    Top ring
        Standard
            T and V models . . . . . . . . . . . . . . . . . . . . . . . . . . . . . . . . .   6.90 mm (approx.)
            W and X models . . . . . . . . . . . . . . . . . . . . . . . . . . . . . . . .   7.20 mm (approx.)
        Service limit (min)
            T and V models . . . . . . . . . . . . . . . . . . . . . . . . . . . . . . . . .   5.50 mm
            W and X models . . . . . . . . . . . . . . . . . . . . . . . . . . . . . . . .   5.70 mm
    2nd ring
        Standard
            T and V models . . . . . . . . . . . . . . . . . . . . . . . . . . . . . . . . .   8.70 mm (approx.)
            W and X models . . . . . . . . . . . . . . . . . . . . . . . . . . . . . . . .   8.50 mm (approx.)
        Service limit (min)
            T and V models . . . . . . . . . . . . . . . . . . . . . . . . . . . . . . . . .   6.90 mm
            W and X models . . . . . . . . . . . . . . . . . . . . . . . . . . . . . . . .   6.80 mm
Ring end gap (installed)
    Top ring
        Standard . . . . . . . . . . . . . . . . . . . . . . . . . . . . . . . . . . . . . . .   0.10 to 0.25 mm
        Service limit (max) . . . . . . . . . . . . . . . . . . . . . . . . . . . . . . . .   0.50 mm
    2nd ring
        Standard . . . . . . . . . . . . . . . . . . . . . . . . . . . . . . . . . . . . . . .   0.10 to 0.25 mm
        Service limit (max) . . . . . . . . . . . . . . . . . . . . . . . . . . . . . . . .   0.50 mm
Ring thickness
    Top ring . . . . . . . . . . . . . . . . . . . . . . . . . . . . . . . . . . . . . . . . . . .   0.97 to 0.99 mm
    2nd ring . . . . . . . . . . . . . . . . . . . . . . . . . . . . . . . . . . . . . . . . . . .   0.77 to 0.79 mm
Ring groove width in piston
    Top ring . . . . . . . . . . . . . . . . . . . . . . . . . . . . . . . . . . . . . . . . . . .   1.01 to 1.03 mm
    2nd ring . . . . . . . . . . . . . . . . . . . . . . . . . . . . . . . . . . . . . . . . . . .   0.81 to 0.83 mm
    Oil ring . . . . . . . . . . . . . . . . . . . . . . . . . . . . . . . . . . . . . . . . . . . .   1.51 to 1.53 mm
Ring-to-groove clearance
    Top ring (max) . . . . . . . . . . . . . . . . . . . . . . . . . . . . . . . . . . . . . .   0.18 mm
    2nd ring (max) . . . . . . . . . . . . . . . . . . . . . . . . . . . . . . . . . . . . . .   0.18 mm

## Clutch

Friction plate
  Quantity . . . . . . . . . . . . . . . . . . . . . . . . . . . . . . . . . . . . . . . . . . .  10
  Thickness . . . . . . . . . . . . . . . . . . . . . . . . . . . . . . . . . . . . . . . .  2.92 to 3.08 mm
  Tab width (min) . . . . . . . . . . . . . . . . . . . . . . . . . . . . . . . . . . . .  13.0 mm
Plain plate
  Quantity . . . . . . . . . . . . . . . . . . . . . . . . . . . . . . . . . . . . . . . . . . .  9
  Warpage (max) . . . . . . . . . . . . . . . . . . . . . . . . . . . . . . . . . . . . .  0.1 mm
Assembled clutch plate thickness (W and X models) . . . . . . . . . . . . .  45.05 to 45.65 mm with 5 kg load (see text)
Diaphragm spring free height (min) . . . . . . . . . . . . . . . . . . . . . . . .  2.9 mm
Release mechanism screw . . . . . . . . . . . . . . . . . . . . . . . . . . . . . . .  1/4 turn out

## Lubrication system

Oil pressure . . . . . . . . . . . . . . . . . . . . . . . . . . . . . . . . . . . . . . . . .  see Chapter 1
Oil pump – T and V models
  Inner rotor tip-to-outer rotor clearance
    Standard . . . . . . . . . . . . . . . . . . . . . . . . . . . . . . . . . . . . . . .  0.10 mm
    Service limit (max) . . . . . . . . . . . . . . . . . . . . . . . . . . . . . . . . .  0.15 mm
  Outer rotor-to-body clearance
    Standard . . . . . . . . . . . . . . . . . . . . . . . . . . . . . . . . . . . . . . .  0.15 to 0.22 mm
    Service limit (max) . . . . . . . . . . . . . . . . . . . . . . . . . . . . . . . . .  0.35 mm
Oil pump – W and X models
  Inner rotor tip-to-outer rotor clearance (max) . . . . . . . . . . . . . . . . .  0.20 mm
  Outer rotor-to-body clearance (max) . . . . . . . . . . . . . . . . . . . . . . .  0.35 mm

## Transmission

Gear ratios (no. of teeth) – T and V models
  Primary reduction . . . . . . . . . . . . . . . . . . . . . . . . . . . . . . . . . . .  1.756 to 1 (72/41T)
  Final reduction . . . . . . . . . . . . . . . . . . . . . . . . . . . . . . . . . . . . .  2.687 to 1 (43/16T)
  1st gear . . . . . . . . . . . . . . . . . . . . . . . . . . . . . . . . . . . . . . . . . .  2.866 to 1 (43/15T)
  2nd gear . . . . . . . . . . . . . . . . . . . . . . . . . . . . . . . . . . . . . . . . . .  2.058 to 1 (35/17T)
  3rd gear . . . . . . . . . . . . . . . . . . . . . . . . . . . . . . . . . . . . . . . . . .  1.650 to 1 (33/20T)
  4th gear . . . . . . . . . . . . . . . . . . . . . . . . . . . . . . . . . . . . . . . . . .  1.428 to 1 (30/21T)
  5th gear . . . . . . . . . . . . . . . . . . . . . . . . . . . . . . . . . . . . . . . . . .  1.260 to 1 (29/23T)
  6th gear . . . . . . . . . . . . . . . . . . . . . . . . . . . . . . . . . . . . . . . . . .  1.120 to 1 (28/25T)
Gear ratios (no. of teeth) – W and X models
  Primary reduction . . . . . . . . . . . . . . . . . . . . . . . . . . . . . . . . . . .  1.756 to 1 (72/41T)
  Final reduction . . . . . . . . . . . . . . . . . . . . . . . . . . . . . . . . . . . . .  2.750 to 1 (44/16T)
  1st gear . . . . . . . . . . . . . . . . . . . . . . . . . . . . . . . . . . . . . . . . . .  2.625 to 1 (42/16T)
  2nd gear . . . . . . . . . . . . . . . . . . . . . . . . . . . . . . . . . . . . . . . . . .  1.950 to 1 (39/20T)
  3rd gear . . . . . . . . . . . . . . . . . . . . . . . . . . . . . . . . . . . . . . . . . .  1.565 to 1 (36/23T)
  4th gear . . . . . . . . . . . . . . . . . . . . . . . . . . . . . . . . . . . . . . . . . .  1.363 to 1 (30/22T)
  5th gear . . . . . . . . . . . . . . . . . . . . . . . . . . . . . . . . . . . . . . . . . .  1.227 to 1 (27/22T)
  6th gear . . . . . . . . . . . . . . . . . . . . . . . . . . . . . . . . . . . . . . . . . .  1.120 to 1 (28/25T)

## Selector drum and forks

Selector fork-to-gear groove clearance
  Standard . . . . . . . . . . . . . . . . . . . . . . . . . . . . . . . . . . . . . . . . .  0.1 to 0.3 mm
  Service limit (max) . . . . . . . . . . . . . . . . . . . . . . . . . . . . . . . . . . .  0.5 mm
Selector fork end thickness . . . . . . . . . . . . . . . . . . . . . . . . . . . . . .  4.8 to 4.9 mm
Selector fork groove width in gears . . . . . . . . . . . . . . . . . . . . . . . . .  5.0 to 5.1 mm

## Crankshaft and bearings

Journal diameter
  Code A . . . . . . . . . . . . . . . . . . . . . . . . . . . . . . . . . . . . . . . . . . .  33.992 to 34.000 mm
  Code B . . . . . . . . . . . . . . . . . . . . . . . . . . . . . . . . . . . . . . . . . . .  33.984 to 33.992 mm
  Code C . . . . . . . . . . . . . . . . . . . . . . . . . . . . . . . . . . . . . . . . . . .  33.976 to 33.984 mm
Main bearing oil clearance
  Standard – T and V models . . . . . . . . . . . . . . . . . . . . . . . . . . . . .  0.020 to 0.044 mm
  Standard – W and X models . . . . . . . . . . . . . . . . . . . . . . . . . . . . .  0.016 to 0.040 mm
  Service limit (max) – all models . . . . . . . . . . . . . . . . . . . . . . . . . .  0.080 mm
Runout (max) . . . . . . . . . . . . . . . . . . . . . . . . . . . . . . . . . . . . . . . .  0.05 mm
Thrust bearing clearance . . . . . . . . . . . . . . . . . . . . . . . . . . . . . . . .  0.055 to 0.110 mm
Thrust bearing thickness
  Right-hand side . . . . . . . . . . . . . . . . . . . . . . . . . . . . . . . . . . . . .  2.425 to 2.450 mm
  Left-hand side . . . . . . . . . . . . . . . . . . . . . . . . . . . . . . . . . . . . . .  2.350 to 2.500 mm

2

## Connecting rods

Small-end internal diameter
    Standard . . . . . . . . . . . . . . . . . . . . . . . . . . . . . . . . . . . . . . . . 16.010 to 16.018 mm
    Service limit (max) . . . . . . . . . . . . . . . . . . . . . . . . . . . . . . . . . . 16.040 mm
Big-end side clearance
    Standard . . . . . . . . . . . . . . . . . . . . . . . . . . . . . . . . . . . . . . . . 0.1 to 0.2 mm
    Service limit (max) . . . . . . . . . . . . . . . . . . . . . . . . . . . . . . . . . . 0.3 mm
Big-end width . . . . . . . . . . . . . . . . . . . . . . . . . . . . . . . . . . . . . . . . 20.95 to 21.00 mm
Crankpin width . . . . . . . . . . . . . . . . . . . . . . . . . . . . . . . . . . . . . . . . 21.10 to 21.15 mm
Big-end diameter
    Code 1 . . . . . . . . . . . . . . . . . . . . . . . . . . . . . . . . . . . . . . . . . . 37.000 to 37.008 mm
    Code 2 . . . . . . . . . . . . . . . . . . . . . . . . . . . . . . . . . . . . . . . . . . 37.008 to 37.016 mm
Crankpin diameter
    Code 1 . . . . . . . . . . . . . . . . . . . . . . . . . . . . . . . . . . . . . . . . . . 33.992 to 34.000 mm
    Code 2 . . . . . . . . . . . . . . . . . . . . . . . . . . . . . . . . . . . . . . . . . . 33.984 to 33.992 mm
    Code 3 . . . . . . . . . . . . . . . . . . . . . . . . . . . . . . . . . . . . . . . . . . 33.976 to 33.984 mm
Big-end oil clearance
    Standard . . . . . . . . . . . . . . . . . . . . . . . . . . . . . . . . . . . . . . . . 0.032 to 0.056 mm
    Service limit (max) . . . . . . . . . . . . . . . . . . . . . . . . . . . . . . . . . . 0.08 mm

# Torque wrench settings (all models)

Engine mountings
    Adjusting bolt . . . . . . . . . . . . . . . . . . . . . . . . . . . . . . . . . . . . . . 10 Nm
    Adjusting bolt locknut . . . . . . . . . . . . . . . . . . . . . . . . . . . . . . . . . 45 Nm
    Upper and lower rear mounting bolt nuts . . . . . . . . . . . . . . . . . . . . 79 Nm
    Right-hand and left-hand front mounting bolts
        GSX-R600 models . . . . . . . . . . . . . . . . . . . . . . . . . . . . . . . . 55 Nm
        GSX-R750 models . . . . . . . . . . . . . . . . . . . . . . . . . . . . . . . . 79 Nm
    Mounting lug pinchbolts . . . . . . . . . . . . . . . . . . . . . . . . . . . . . . . 23 Nm
Oil cooler bolt . . . . . . . . . . . . . . . . . . . . . . . . . . . . . . . . . . . . . . . . 73 Nm
Valve cover bolts . . . . . . . . . . . . . . . . . . . . . . . . . . . . . . . . . . . . . . 14 Nm
Cam chain tensioner mounting bolts . . . . . . . . . . . . . . . . . . . . . . . . 10 Nm
Cam chain tensioner and guide blade pivot bolts . . . . . . . . . . . . . . . 10 Nm
Cam chain top guide bolts . . . . . . . . . . . . . . . . . . . . . . . . . . . . . . 10 Nm
Cam chain stopper bolt . . . . . . . . . . . . . . . . . . . . . . . . . . . . . . . . 14 Nm
Camshaft holder bolts . . . . . . . . . . . . . . . . . . . . . . . . . . . . . . . . . 10 Nm
Oil pipe to camshaft holder banjo bolts . . . . . . . . . . . . . . . . . . . . . . 10 Nm
Cylinder head 10 mm bolts
    Initial setting . . . . . . . . . . . . . . . . . . . . . . . . . . . . . . . . . . . . . . 25 Nm
    Final setting . . . . . . . . . . . . . . . . . . . . . . . . . . . . . . . . . . . . . . . 43 Nm
Cylinder head 6 mm bolts . . . . . . . . . . . . . . . . . . . . . . . . . . . . . . . 10 Nm
Oil hose to cylinder head banjo bolt . . . . . . . . . . . . . . . . . . . . . . . . 20 Nm
Cylinder block nuts . . . . . . . . . . . . . . . . . . . . . . . . . . . . . . . . . . . 10 Nm
Coolant union to cylinder block bolts . . . . . . . . . . . . . . . . . . . . . . . 10 Nm
Clutch nut . . . . . . . . . . . . . . . . . . . . . . . . . . . . . . . . . . . . . . . . . 150 Nm
Gearchange mechanism locating pin in crankcase . . . . . . . . . . . . . . 19 Nm
Starter clutch bolt . . . . . . . . . . . . . . . . . . . . . . . . . . . . . . . . . . . . 54 Nm
Oil pressure regulator . . . . . . . . . . . . . . . . . . . . . . . . . . . . . . . . . . 28 Nm
Oil strainer housing bolts . . . . . . . . . . . . . . . . . . . . . . . . . . . . . . . 12 Nm
Oil pick-up tube bolts . . . . . . . . . . . . . . . . . . . . . . . . . . . . . . . . . . 12 Nm
Oil sump bolts . . . . . . . . . . . . . . . . . . . . . . . . . . . . . . . . . . . . . . 14 Nm
Oil pump bolts . . . . . . . . . . . . . . . . . . . . . . . . . . . . . . . . . . . . . . 10 Nm
Crankshaft journal bolts (9 mm) . . . . . . . . . . . . . . . . . . . . . . . . . . . 32 Nm
Crankcase bolts (8 mm) . . . . . . . . . . . . . . . . . . . . . . . . . . . . . . . . 24 Nm
Crankcase bolts (6 mm) . . . . . . . . . . . . . . . . . . . . . . . . . . . . . . . . 11 Nm
Oil hose banjo bolt to upper crankcase . . . . . . . . . . . . . . . . . . . . . . 20 Nm
Oil pipe banjo bolt to lower crankcase . . . . . . . . . . . . . . . . . . . . . . . 25 Nm
Alternator oil jet . . . . . . . . . . . . . . . . . . . . . . . . . . . . . . . . . . . . . . 5 Nm
Selector drum stopper plate bolt . . . . . . . . . . . . . . . . . . . . . . . . . . . 10 Nm
Connecting rod cap nuts
    Initial setting . . . . . . . . . . . . . . . . . . . . . . . . . . . . . . . . . . . . . . 35 Nm
    Final setting . . . . . . . . . . . . . . . . . . . . . . . . . . . . . . . . . . . . . . . 67 Nm

## 1 General information

The engine/transmission unit is a water-cooled in-line four. The valves are operated by double overhead camshafts which are chain driven off the crankshaft. The engine/transmission assembly is constructed from aluminium alloy. The crankcase divides horizontally into three parts.

The crankcase incorporates a wet sump, pressure-fed lubrication system which uses a gear-driven, dual-rotor oil pump, an oil filter and by-pass valve assembly, a relief valve and an oil pressure switch. The oil is routed around a cooler unit which is fed off the engine's cooling system.

Power from the crankshaft is routed to the transmission via the clutch, which is of the wet, multi-plate type with diaphragm springs, and is cable-operated. The transmission is a six-speed constant-mesh unit. Final drive to the rear wheel is by chain and sprockets.

## 2 Operations possible with the engine in the frame

The components and assemblies listed below can be removed without having to remove the engine/transmission assembly from the frame. If however, a number of areas require attention at the same time, removal of the engine/transmission is recommended.

*Oil cooler*
*Valve cover*
*Cam chain tensioner and cam chain guides*
*Cam chain and cam chain tensioner blade*
*Camshafts*
*Cylinder head*
*Cylinder block, pistons and piston rings*
*Ignition rotor and pulse generator coil*
*  assembly*
*Clutch*
*Gearchange mechanism (external*
*  components)*
*Alternator*
*Starter clutch and idle gear*
*Oil sump, oil strainer and oil pressure relief*
*  valve*
*Oil pump*
*Starter motor*

## 3 Operations requiring engine removal

It is necessary to remove the engine/transmission assembly from the frame and separate the crankcase halves to gain access to the following components.

*Transmission shafts*
*Selector drum and forks*
*Crankshaft and bearings*
*Connecting rods and bearings*

## 4 Major engine repair – general note

1 It is not always easy to determine when or if an engine should be completely overhauled, as a number of factors must be considered.
2 High mileage is not necessarily an indication that an overhaul is needed, while low mileage, on the other hand, does not preclude the need for an overhaul. Frequency of servicing is probably the single most important consideration. An engine that has regular and frequent oil and filter changes, as well as other required maintenance, will most likely give many miles of reliable service. Conversely, a neglected engine, or one which has not been run in properly, may require an overhaul very early in its life.
3 Exhaust smoke and excessive oil consumption are both indications that piston rings and/or valve guides are in need of attention, although make sure that the fault is not due to oil leakage.
4 If the engine is making obvious knocking or rumbling noises, the connecting rod and/or main bearings are probably at fault.
5 Loss of power, rough running, excessive valve train noise and high fuel consumption rates may also point to the need for an overhaul, especially if they are all present at the same time. If a complete tune-up does not remedy the situation, major mechanical work is the only solution.
6 An engine overhaul generally involves restoring the internal parts to the specifications of a new engine. The piston rings and main and connecting rod bearings are usually renewed during a major overhaul. Generally the valve seats are re-ground, since they are usually in less than perfect condition at this point. The end result should be a like new engine that will give as many trouble-free miles as the original.
7 Before beginning the engine overhaul, read through the related procedures to familiarise yourself with the scope and requirements of the job. Overhauling an engine is not all that difficult, but it is time consuming. Plan on the motorcycle being tied up for a minimum of two weeks. Check on the availability of parts and make sure that any necessary special tools, equipment and supplies are obtained in advance.
8 Most work can be done with typical workshop hand tools, although a number of precision measuring tools are required for inspecting parts to determine if they must be renewed. Often a dealer will handle the inspection of parts and offer advice concerning reconditioning and renewal. As a general rule, time is the primary cost of an overhaul so it does not pay to install worn or substandard parts.
9 As a final note, to ensure maximum life and minimum trouble from a rebuilt engine, everything must be assembled with care in a spotlessly clean environment.

## 5 Engine – removal and installation

*Warning: The engine is very heavy. Removal and installation should be carried out with the aid of at least one assistant; personal injury or damage could occur if the engine falls or is dropped. If available, an hydraulic or mechanical floor jack can be used to support and lower or raise the engine.*

Note: *Peg spanners are required to slacken and tighten the locknut and adjuster bolt on the lower rear engine mounting bolts If the Suzuki service tool (pt. no. 09940-14980) or a suitable peg spanner is not available, one will have to be obtained, or fabricated (see* **Tool Tip***).*

Note: *The rear engine mounting bolt nuts are self-locking, and Suzuki advise that they can only be used once, so new ones should be obtained before installing the engine.*

Note: *On GSX-R750 models, the lower rear mounting bolt, adjusting bolt and locknut were upgraded on V (1997) models onwards. Owners of T models should ask their dealer whether they advise fitting the new parts on their model when installing the engine, noting that they must be fitted as a set.*

### Removal

1 Support the bike securely in an upright position using an auxiliary stand. Work can be made easier by raising the machine to a suitable working height on an hydraulic ramp or a suitable platform. Make sure the motorcycle is secure and will not topple over (see *Tools and Workshop Tips* in the Reference section).
2 If the engine is dirty, particularly around its mountings, wash it thoroughly before starting any major dismantling work. This will make work much easier and rule out the possibility of caked on lumps of dirt falling into some vital component.
3 Drain the engine oil and, if required, remove the oil filter (see Chapter 1).
4 Remove the seats, the fairing side panels and the lower fairing (see Chapter 8).
5 Disconnect the negative (-ve) lead from the battery (see Chapter 9). Also disconnect the earth wire and its connector **(see illustration)**.

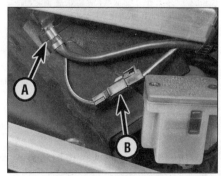

**5.5 Disconnect the earth lead (A) and the earth wire connector (B)**

**2**

5.8a Disconnect the coil/cap wiring connectors . . .

5.8b . . . and on injection models the camshaft position sensor wiring connector (arrowed)

5.11a Coolant temperature sensor wiring connector (A) and hose clamp (B) – carburettor models

Release the earth lead from any clips or ties, then feed it through to the engine and coil it on the crankcase, noting its routing.

6 Remove the fuel tank and the air filter housing (see Chapter 4).

7 Remove the carburettors or throttle bodies according to model (see Chapter 4). Plug the engine inlet manifolds with clean rag.

8 On GSX-R750T and V models, pull the spark plug cap off each spark plug and secure the leads clear of the engine. On all other models, disconnect the ignition coil/plug cap wiring connectors, and on GSX-R750W and X models the camshaft position sensor wiring

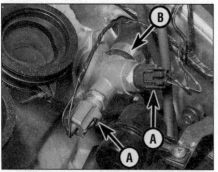

5.11b Coolant temperature sensor wiring connectors (A) and hose clamp (B) – injection models

connector, and secure the wiring clear of the engine (see illustrations).

9 Remove the exhaust system (see Chapter 4).

10 Remove the radiator and the coolant reservoir (see Chapter 3).

11 Disconnect the coolant temperature sensor wiring connector(s) from the sensor(s) in the thermostat housing, then slacken the clamp securing the coolant hose to the housing and detach the hose – there is no need to draw the hose out of its hole in the frame (see illustrations). On fuel injected models, note which connector fits on which sensor (grey – left-facing sensor, brown – rear-facing sensor).

12 Pull back the rubber cover on the starter motor terminal and remove the screw (600 models) or nut (750 models) securing the lead to the motor (see illustration). Secure it clear of the engine.

13 Trace the ignition pulse generator wiring back from the top of the starter clutch cover on the left-hand side of the engine and disconnect it at the 2-pin connector with the black and green wires (see illustration). Release the wiring from any clips or ties, noting its routing, and coil it on top of the crankcase so that it does not impede engine removal.

14 Trace the neutral switch wiring back from

the bottom of the front sprocket cover and disconnect it at the 2-pin connector with the blue and pink wires (GSX-R600V and GSX-R750T and V models) or the 3-pin connector with the blue, pink and black/white wires (GSX-R600 W and X and GSX-R750W and X models) (see illustration 5.13). Release the wiring from any clips or ties, noting its routing, and coil it on top of the crankcase so that it does not impede engine removal.

15 Trace the alternator wiring back from the top of the alternator cover on the left-hand side of the engine and disconnect it at the 3-pin connector with the three black wires (see illustration 5.13). Release the wiring from any clips or ties, noting its routing, and coil it on top of the crankcase so that it does not impede engine removal.

16 Trace the sidestand switch wiring back from the stand and disconnect it at the 2-pin connector with the green and black/white wires (see illustration 5.13). Release the wiring from any clips or ties, noting its routing, and position it clear so that it does not impede engine removal.

17 Trace the oil pressure switch wiring back from the switch on the right-hand side of the engine and disconnect it at the 1-pin connector with the green/yellow wire (see illustration). Coil it on top of the crankcase so that it does not impede engine removal.

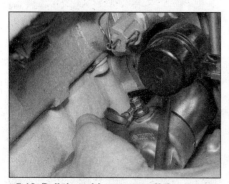

5.12 Pull the rubber cover off the starter motor terminal and disconnect the lead

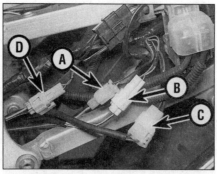

5.13 Pulse generator wiring connector (A), neutral switch wiring connector (B), alternator wiring connector (C), sidestand switch wiring connector (D)

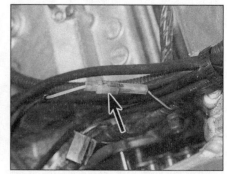

5.17 Oil pressure switch wiring connector (arrowed)

**5.20 Slacken the bolt (A) and swivel the guide to provide clearance to the lower rear mounting bolt (B) components**

**5.21a Unscrew and remove the locknut . . .**

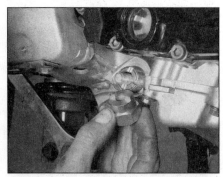

**5.21b . . . and unscrew the adjusting bolt – the tool shown is the MacPherson strut tool**

**18** Remove the front sprocket cover and the sprocket (see Chapter 6). After removing the cover, separate the clutch cable from it (see Section 18).

**19** At this point, position an hydraulic or mechanical jack under the engine with a block of wood between the jack head and sump. Make sure the jack is centrally positioned so the engine will not topple in any direction when the last mounting bolt is removed. Take the weight of the engine on the jack.

**20** Slacken the bolt securing the engine breather hose guide to the underside of the frame on the right-hand side and swivel it round to provide clearance to the lower rear engine mounting bolt **(see illustration)**.

**21** Unscrew the nut on the lower rear engine mounting bolt **(see illustration 5.20)**. Using either the Suzuki service tool *(pt. no. 09940-14980)*, a suitable peg spanner or a fabricated tool (see *Tool Tip*), unscrew the locknut on the adjusting bolt fitted in the right-hand side of the frame **(see illustration)**. Using a similar but smaller tool, slacken the adjusting bolt and unscrew it until it no longer protrudes from the inside of the frame, but do not remove it **(see illustration)**. Do not yet withdraw the mounting bolt.

**22** Slacken the pinchbolt on the mounting lug for the upper rear mounting bolt, then unscrew the nut **(see illustration)**. Do not yet withdraw the mounting bolt.

Holes in the frame provide the best access for a socket extension on the bolt and nut.

**23** Slacken the pinchbolts on the mounting lugs for the right-hand front mounting bolts, then unscrew and remove the bolts **(see illustration)**.

**24** Unscrew and remove the left-hand front mounting bolts **(see illustration)**.

**25** Make sure the engine is properly supported on the jack, and have an assistant support it as well. Withdraw the upper and lower rear engine mounting bolts **(see illustrations)**.

**26** The engine can now be removed from the frame. Check that all wiring, cables and hoses

*For the locknut, a peg spanner can be made by cutting an old 22 mm socket as shown – measure the width and depth of the slots in the locknut to determine the size of the castellations cn the socket. If an old socket is not available, castellations can be welded onto a suitable nut. For the adjusting bolt, a similar tool must be made, though smaller. Alternatively, an automotive suspension strut tool, known as a MacPherson No. 1 Strut tool, can be used. This is available from Sykes Pickavant, pt. no. 08920170, along with other sizes. It is important to use a tool to which a torque wrench can be applied on installation, rather than using a drift to knock the nut and bolt loose.*

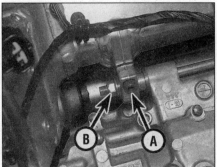

**5.22 Slacken the pinchbolt (A) and unscrew the nut (B)**

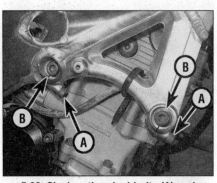

**5.23 Slacken the pinchbolts (A) and unscrew the right-hand front bolts (B)**

2

**5.24 Unscrew the left-hand front bolts (arrowed)**

**5.25a Withdraw the upper and lower rear mounting bolts (arrowed) . . .**

**5.25b ... making sure the engine is properly supported**

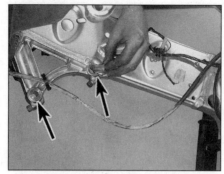

**5.29 Fit the spacers into their sockets (arrowed)**

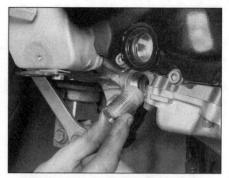

**5.31a Install the adjusting bolt if removed ...**

are disconnected and clear, then manoeuvre the engine out of the frame.

27 Remove the spacers for the right-hand front and upper rear mounting bolts, noting how they fit **(see illustration 5.29)**. If required, thread the adjusting bolt for the lower rear mounting out of the frame **(see illustration 5.31a)**.

28 The engine mounting bolt nuts are self-locking, and Suzuki advise that they can only be used once. Discard all the nuts and obtain new ones for installation.

## Installation

29 Install the spacers for the right-hand front and upper rear mounting bolts, making sure their shouldered ends face the inside **(see illustration)**.

30 With the aid of an assistant place the engine unit on top of the jack and block of wood and carefully raise it into position in the frame, making sure the mounting bolt holes align. Also make sure no wires, cables or hoses become trapped between the engine and the frame.

31 If removed, thread the adjusting bolt for the lower rear mounting bolt into the right-hand side of the frame and tighten it finger-tight against the engine **(see illustration)**. Slide the lower rear mounting bolt through from the left-hand side, but do not yet fit either the adjusting bolt locknut or the new mounting bolt nut **(see illustration)**.

32 Slide the upper rear mounting bolt through from the left-hand side **(see illustration)**. Thread the new nut onto the bolt and tighten it finger-tight.

33 Install the right-hand front mounting bolts (55 mm) and tighten them finger-tight **(see illustration)**.

34 Install the left-hand front mounting bolts (45 mm) and tighten them finger-tight **(see illustration)**.

35 Tighten the adjusting bolt to the torque setting specified at the beginning of the Chapter using the tool as on removal **(see illustration)**. Make a reference mark between the adjusting bolt and the frame as a check against the bolt turning while the locknut is being tightened. Fit the locknut **(see illustration 5.21a)** and tighten it to the specified torque setting using the peg spanner or socket **(see illustration)**. Check that the reference marks still align – if they don't, repeat the installation and tightening

**5.31b ... then slide the lower rear mounting bolt through ...**

**5.32 ... followed by the upper rear bolt**

**5.33 Install the longer bolts into the right-hand side ...**

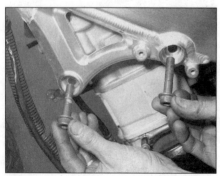

**5.34 ... and the shorter bolts into the left-hand side**

**5.35a Tighten the adjusting bolt ...**

**5.35b ... and then the locknut to the specified torque ...**

5.35c . . . then fit the nut finger-tight

5.36a  Tighten the bolts as described . . .

5.36b  . . . to the specified torque settings

procedure. Thread the nut onto the mounting bolt and tighten it finger-tight (see illustration).

36  Tighten the two nuts on the rear mounting bolts, then the left-hand front bolts, and then the right-hand front bolts, to the torque settings specified at the beginning of the Chapter. Best access to the upper rear bolt is via the holes in the frame, and it will probably be necessary to counter-hold the bolt while the nut is tightened (see illustrations). Now tighten the pinchbolts on the mounting lugs for the upper rear and right-hand front mounting bolts to the specified torque setting (see illustrations 5.22 and 23).

37  The remainder of the installation procedure is the reverse of removal, noting the following points.

a) Make sure all wires, cables and hoses are correctly routed and connected, and secured by the relevant clips or ties.
b) Adjust the throttle and clutch cable freeplay (see Chapter 1).
c) Adjust the drive chain (see Chapter 1).
d) Refill the engine with oil and coolant (see Chapter 1 and 'Daily (pre-ride) checks').
e) Prior to installing the fairing side panels start the engine and check that there is no coolant/oil leakage.

## 6  Engine disassembly and reassembly – general information

### Disassembly

1  Before disassembling the engine, the external surfaces of the unit should be thoroughly cleaned and degreased. This will prevent contamination of the engine internals, and will also make working a lot easier and cleaner. A high flash-point solvent, such as paraffin (kerosene) can be used, or better still, a proprietary engine degreaser such as Gunk. Use old paintbrushes and toothbrushes to work the solvent into the various recesses of the engine casings. Take care to exclude solvent or water from the electrical components and inlet and exhaust ports.

 Warning: The use of petrol (gasoline) as a cleaning agent should be avoided because of the risk of fire.

2  When clean and dry, arrange the unit on the workbench, leaving suitable clear area for working. Gather a selection of small containers and plastic bags so that parts can be grouped together in an easily identifiable manner. Some paper and a pen should be on hand to permit notes to be made and labels attached where necessary. A supply of clean rag is also required.

3  Before commencing work, read through the appropriate section so that some idea of the necessary procedure can be gained. When removing components it should be noted that great force is seldom required, unless specified. In many cases, a component's reluctance to be removed is indicative of an incorrect approach or removal method – if in any doubt, re-check with the text. In cases where fasteners have corroded, have a can of penetrating oil or WD40 available.

4  An engine support stand made from short lengths of 2 x 4 inch wood bolted together into a rectangle will help support the engine (see illustration). The perimeter of the mount should be just big enough to accommodate the sump within it so that the engine rests on its crankcase.

5  When disassembling the engine, keep 'mated' parts together (including gears, cylinders, pistons, connecting rods, valves, etc. that have been in contact with each other

6.4  An engine support made from pieces of 2 x 4 inch wood

during engine operation). These 'mated' parts must be reused or renewed as an assembly.

6  Engine/transmission disassembly should be done in the following general order with reference to the appropriate Sections.

Remove the valve cover
Remove the cam chain tensioner and cam chain guide blades
Remove the camshafts
Remove the cylinder head
Remove the cylinder block
Remove the pistons
Remove the starter clutch
Remove the pulse generator coil assembly (see Chapter 5)
Remove the clutch
Remove the oil pump
Remove the gearchange mechanism
Remove the alternator (see Chapter 9)
Remove the starter motor (see Chapter 9)
Remove the oil sump
Separate the lower crankcase from the middle crankcase
Remove the transmission shafts/gears
Remove the selector drum and forks
Separate the middle and upper crankcases
Remove the crankshaft and connecting rods

### Reassembly

7  Reassembly is accomplished by reversing the general disassembly sequence.

## 7  Oil cooler – removal and installation

Note: The oil cooler can be removed with the engine in the frame. If the engine has been removed, ignore the steps which do not apply.

### Removal

1  Remove the fairing side panels (see Chapter 8).

2  Drain the engine oil and remove the oil filter (see Chapter 1). Drain the cooling system (see Chapter 1), or have some means of blocking or clamping the hoses to avoid excessive loss of coolant.

2

7.3 Slacken the clamps (arrowed) and detach the coolant hoses

7.4 Unscrew the cooler bolt (arrowed) using a 30 mm socket

7.5a Fit the O-ring into the groove in the cooler

7.5b Locate the bracket over the lug (arrowed)

7.5c Tighten the cooler bolt to the specified torque

**3** Slacken the clamp securing each hose to the cooler and detach the hoses **(see illustration)**.

**4** Unscrew the cooler bolt using a 30 mm socket and remove the cooler **(see illustration)**, noting how the cutout in the bracket locates over the lug on the crankcase. Check the condition of the cooler O-ring – if it is in any way damaged, deformed or deteriorated a new one must be used.

### Installation

**5** Installation is the reverse of removal, noting the following:

  a) *Use a new O-ring if necessary, and smear it with clean engine oil. Make sure it seats in its groove (see illustration).*

  b) *Locate the bracket on the cooler over the lug on the crankcase (see illustration). Do not forget the washer with the bolt.*

  c) *Tighten the cooler bolt to the torque setting specified at the beginning of the Chapter (see illustration).*

  d) *Make sure the coolant hoses are pressed fully onto their unions and are secured by the clamps (see illustration 7.3).*

  e) *Fit a new oil filter and fill the engine with oil (see Chapter 1 and 'Daily (pre-ride) checks').*

  f) *Refill the cooling system if it was drained,*

or check the level in both the radiator and the reservoir and top up if necessary (see Chapter 1 and 'Daily (pre-ride) checks').

### 8 Valve cover – removal and installation

**Note:** *The valve cover can be removed with the engine in the frame. If the engine has been removed, ignore the steps which do not apply.*

### Removal

**1** Remove the fairing side panels (see Chapter 8).

**2** Remove the fuel tank, air filter housing, and carburettors or throttle bodies according to model (see Chapter 4). Plug the engine inlet manifolds with clean rag.

**3** On GSX-R750T and V models, pull the spark plug cap off each spark plug and secure the leads clear of the engine. On all other models, disconnect the ignition coil/plug cap wiring connectors and secure the wiring clear of the engine **(see illustration 5.8a)**. On GSX-R750W and X models, also disconnect the camshaft position sensor wiring connector **(see illustration 5.8b)**. Pull the coil/cap off each spark plug and remove them.

**4** Unscrew the valve cover bolts and remove them along with their sealing washers **(see illustration)**. Check the condition of the sealing washers and renew them if necessary. It is a good idea to renew them as a matter of course.

**5** Lift the valve cover off the cylinder head. If it is stuck, do not try to lever it off with a screwdriver. Tap it gently around the sides with a rubber hammer or block of wood to dislodge it. Remove the dowels from the cylinder head or cover if they are loose.

### Installation

**6** Check the valve cover gaskets for signs of

8.4 Valve cover bolts (arrowed)

8.7a Make sure the gaskets sit in their grooves

8.7b Smear some adhesive into the cutouts

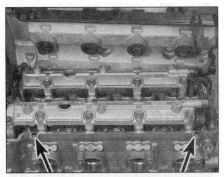

8.8a Make sure the cover locates onto the dowels (arrowed)

damage or deterioration and renew them if necessary.

7 Clean the mating surface of the cylinder head with lacquer thinner, acetone or brake system cleaner. If new gaskets are being fitted, clean all traces of any adhesive from the gasket grooves in the valve cover, then apply a smear of a suitable adhesive (such as Suzuki Bond no. 1207B) into the grooves. Lay the gaskets onto the valve cover, making sure they fit correctly into the grooves (**see illustration**). Also apply the adhesive to the cut-outs in the cylinder head where the gasket half-circles fit (**see illustration**).

8 If removed, fit the dowels into the cylinder head. Position the cover on the cylinder head, making sure the gaskets stay in place and the cover locates correctly onto the dowels (**see illustration**). Install the cover bolts, using new sealing washers if required, and tighten them to the torque setting specified at the beginning of the Chapter (**see illustration**).

9 Install the remaining components in the reverse order of removal.

| 9 | Cam chain, tensioner and blades – removal, inspection and installation |

**Note:** *The cam chain tensioner and guide blades can be removed with the engine in the frame.*

## Cam chain tensioner

*Caution: Once you start to remove the tensioner bolts, you must remove the tensioner all the way and reset it before tightening the bolts. The tensioner extends itself and locks in place, so if you loosen the bolts partway and then retighten them, the tensioner or cam chain will be damaged.*

### Removal

1 On GSX-R600V and W models, and GSX-R750T, V and W models, remove the plug from the centre of the tensioner cap (**see illustration**). On GSX-R600X models and GSX-R750X models, unscrew the tensioner cap bolt.

2 Insert a flat-bladed screwdriver into the slot in the end of the tensioner, and turn it clockwise to lock the plunger (**see illustration**). On GSX-R600X models and GSX-R750X models, a special tool (Pt. No. 09917-62430) is available which keeps the tensioner locked, rather than having to hold the screwdriver to prevent the tensioner unlocking itself.

3 Unscrew the two tensioner mounting bolts and withdraw the tensioner from the back of the cylinder block (**see illustration**).

4 Remove the gasket from the base of the tensioner or from the cylinder block and discard it as a new one must be used.

8.8b Use new sealing washers on the bolts if necessary

### Inspection

5 Examine the tensioner components for signs of wear or damage.

6 Release the tensioner by turning the slotted end anti-clockwise with a screwdriver, or by removing the special tool, and check that the plunger moves freely in and out of the tensioner body (**see illustration 9.9**).

7 If the tensioner or any of its components (except gaskets, screws, bolts etc) are worn or damaged, or if the plunger is seized in the body, a new tensioner must be installed – individual components are not available.

**2**

9.1 Remove the plug or bolt from the tensioner . . .

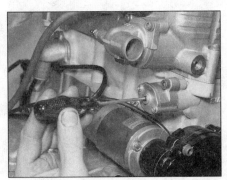

9.2 . . . and turn the slotted end clockwise

9.3 Unscrew the bolts (arrowed) and remove the tensioner

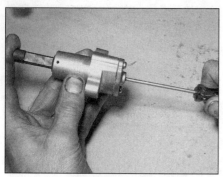

9.9 Release the plunger and push it all the way into the body

9.10a Fit the new gasket . . .

9.10b . . . and install the tensioner

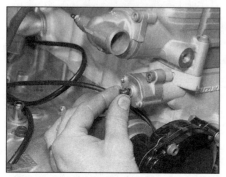

9.12 Fit the plug or bolt and washer into the tensioner

## Installation

8 Unscrew the centre plug from the starter clutch cover on the right-hand side of the engine **(see illustration 10.2)**. Discard the plug O-ring as a new one should be used. Turn the engine in a clockwise direction using a 14 mm socket on the starter clutch bolt **(see illustration 10.3a)**. Alternatively, place the motorcycle on an auxiliary stand so that the rear wheel is off the ground, select a high gear and rotate the rear wheel by hand in its normal direction of rotation. This removes all the slack between the crankshaft and the camshaft in the front run of the chain and transfers it to the back run where it will be taken up by the tensioner.

9 Release the tensioner by turning the slotted end anti-clockwise and press the plunger all the way into the tensioner body, then lock the plunger in this position by turning the slotted end clockwise **(see illustration)**. On GSX-R600X models and GSX-R750X models, a special tool (Pt. No. 09917-62430) is available which keeps the tensioner locked, rather than having to hold the screwdriver to prevent the tensioner unlocking itself.

10 Place a new gasket on the tensioner body, then install it in the engine **(see illustrations)**. Tighten the mounting bolts to the torque setting specified at the beginning of the Chapter.

11 Release the tensioner by turning the slotted end anti-clockwise, or on GSX-R600X models and GSX-R750X models by removing the special tool or screwdriver **(see illustration 9.2)**.

12 On GSX-R600V and W models, and GSX-R750T, V and W models, fit the plug into the centre of the tensioner cap **(see illustration)**. On GSX-R600X models and GSX-R750X models, fit a new sealing washer onto the cap bolt. Install the cap bolt and tighten it securely.

13 It is advisable to remove the valve cover (see Section 8) and check that the cam chain is tensioned. If it is slack, the tensioner plunger did not release.

14 Fit the centre plug into the starter clutch cover using a new O-ring, and smear it and the threads with clean engine oil **(see illustration 10.32)**. If removed, install the valve cover (see Section 8).

## Cam chain guides and tensioner blade

### Removal

15 Remove the valve cover (see Section 8).
16 To remove the top cam chain guide, unscrew the two bolts securing it to the cylinder head **(see illustration)**.
17 To remove the front cam chain guide, first remove the cylinder head (see Section 11). Lift the front cam chain guide out of the front of the cam chain tunnel, noting which way round it fits and how it locates **(see illustration)**.
18 To remove the tensioner blade, first remove the inlet camshaft (see Section 10) and the starter clutch (see Section 20). Unscrew the tensioner blade pivot bolt, noting the washer that fits on the inside of the blade, and on X

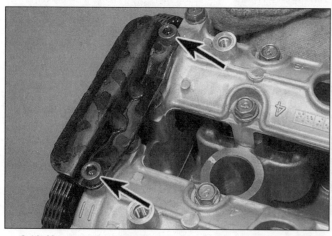

9.16 Unscrew the bolts (arrowed) and remove the top guide

9.17 Lift the front guide out of the tunnel, noting how it hooks onto the pivot bolt (arrowed)

9.18a Unscrew the pivot bolt . . .

9.18b . . . then twist the blade and remove it. Note the washer on the inside

9.21 Make sure the lugs locate in the cutouts (arrowed)

models also on the outside (see illustration). Twist the blade and lift it out of the back of the cam chain tunnel, noting which way round it fits and how it locates (see illustration).

## Inspection

19 Examine the sliding surface of the guides and blade for signs of wear or damage, and renew them if necessary. Check carefully for cracks in the blades and along the edges. Install new blades if necessary.

## Installation

20 Install the tensioner blade into the back of the cam chain tunnel, making sure it is the correct way round. Apply a suitable non-permanent thread locking compound to the pivot bolt threads, making sure none gets on the pivot section, then install the bolt, not forgetting the washer(s) (see illustration 9.18b), and tighten it to the torque setting specified at the beginning of the Chapter. Install the starter clutch (see Section 20) and the inlet camshaft (see Section 10).

21 Install the front guide blade into the front of the cam chain tunnel (see illustration 9.17), making sure it locates correctly onto its pivot bolt seat and its lugs locate in their cut-outs (see illustration). Install the cylinder head (see Section 11).

22 Install the top guide onto the cylinder head and tighten the mounting bolts to the torque setting specified at the beginning of the Chapter (see illustration).

23 Install the valve cover (see Section 8).

## Cam chain

### Removal

24 If the tensioner and front guide blades are also being removed, do that first (see above). If not, remove the camshafts (see Section 10) and the starter clutch (see Section 20).

25 If the blades haven't been removed, unscrew their pivot bolts (see illustrations 9.17 and 9.18a), noting the washers that fit on the inside, and on X models on the outside of the tensioner blade as well, then push the bottom of each blade aside to provide clearance for the chain.

26 Unscrew and remove the cam chain stopper bolt (see illustration). Discard the seal as a new one must be fitted.

9.22 Install the top guide and tighten the bolts to the specified torque

27 Slip the cam chain down the tunnel and off its sprocket on the crankshaft (see illustration). If required, slide the cam chain sprocket/timing rotor off the crankshaft (see illustration).

## Installation

28 If removed, slide the cam chain sprocket/timing rotor onto the crankshaft, aligning the punchmark on the sprocket with that in the end of the shaft (see illustration). Using a piece of wire hooked over at the end, draw the cam chain up the tunnel and slip the bottom onto its sprocket on the crankshaft, making sure it is properly engaged (see illustration 9.27a). Wire the chain to another component to prevent it slipping back down the tunnel.

9.26 Remove the stopper bolt (arrowed) . . .

**2**

9.27a . . . then remove the chain . . .

9.27b . . . and if required, the sprocket/timing rotor

9.28 Make sure the punchmarks on the sprocket and crankshaft (arrowed) are aligned

**9.29 Use a new sealing washer on the stopper bolt**

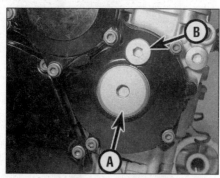

**10.2 Unscrew the centre plug (A) and the timing inspection plug (B)**

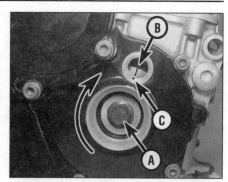

**10.3a Turn the engine clockwise using the bolt (A), until the timing mark (B) aligns with the notch (C)**

**29** Fit a new seal onto the cam chain stopper bolt, making sure its lipped side will face the engine, and smear it with clean oil **(see illustration)**. Install the bolt, making sure the shaft sits between the two runs of chain, and tighten it to the torque setting specified at the beginning of the Chapter.

**30** If the tensioner and guide blades are in situ, apply a suitable non-permanent thread locking compound to the pivot bolt threads, making sure none gets on the pivot section, then install the bolts, not forgetting the washers **(see illustrations 9.17 and 9.18b)**, and tighten them to the torque setting specified at the beginning of the Chapter.

**31** If removed, install the tensioner and guide blades (see above). Otherwise install the camshafts (see Section 10) and the starter clutch (see Section 20).

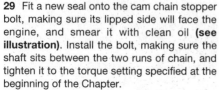

**10 Camshafts** – removal, inspection and installation

**Note:** *The camshafts can be removed with the engine in the frame.*

### Removal

**1** Remove the valve cover (see Section 8).
**2** Unscrew the timing inspection plug and the centre plug from the starter clutch cover on the right-hand side of the engine **(see illustration)**. Discard the plug O-rings as new

ones should be used. The engine can be turned using a 14 mm socket on the starter clutch bolt and turning it in a clockwise direction only **(see illustration 10.3a)**. Alternatively, place the motorcycle on an auxiliary stand so that the rear wheel is off the ground, select a high gear and rotate the rear wheel by hand in its normal direction of rotation.

**3** Turn the engine until the scribe line on the starter clutch aligns with the notch in the timing inspection hole and the number 1 arrow on the exhaust camshaft sprocket points forwards and is level with the top surface on the cylinder head **(see illustrations)**. **Note:** *Turn the engine in the normal direction of rotation (clockwise) only, viewed from the right-hand end of the engine.* If the number 3 arrow is pointing forwards, turn the engine through 360° until the scribe line again aligns with the notch – the number 1 arrow will now be correctly positioned. This is how the camshafts must be positioned for installation later.

**4** Remove the cam chain tensioner and the cam chain top guide (see Section 9).
**5** Unscrew the two oil pipe bolts, noting their different lengths, and remove the pipe, noting which way round it fits **(see illustration)**. Discard the sealing washers as new ones must be fitted.
**6** Before disturbing the camshaft holders, check for identification markings. The inlet camshaft holder is marked IN, and the

**10.3b Make sure the timing marks are as shown with the No. 1 arrow on the exhaust sprocket pointing forwards**

exhaust camshaft holder is marked EX. These markings ensure that the holders can be matched up to their original camshaft on installation. If no markings are visible, mark your own using a felt pen.

**7** Working on one camshaft at a time, unscrew the holder bolts evenly and a little at a time in a reverse of the numerical sequence marked on each holder until they are all loose **(see illustration)**. While slackening the bolts make sure that the holder is lifting squarely away from the cylinder head and is not sticking on the locating dowels. Remove the bolts, then lift off the camshaft holder, noting how it fits **(see illustration)**. Retrieve the dowels from either the holder or the cylinder head if they are loose. Slip the cam chain off

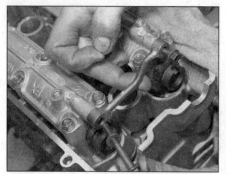

**10.5 Unscrew the bolts and remove the oil pipe**

**10.7a Camshaft holder bolts (arrowed) – note the number cast next to each bolt**

**10.7b Remove the holder . . .**

10.7c . . . then the camshaft

10.7d Note the identification mark on each camshaft

10.9 Remove each camshaft end bearing half ring retainer

the sprocket and lift the shaft out of the head (see illustration). The camshafts are marked for identification. The inlet camshaft is marked 'IN' and the exhaust camshaft is marked 'EX' (see illustration).

*Caution: If the bolts are carelessly loosened and the holder does not come squarely away from the head, the holder is likely to break. If this happens the complete cylinder head assembly must be renewed; the holders are matched to the cylinder head and cannot be renewed separately. Also, a camshaft could break if the holder bolts are not slackened evenly and the pressure from a depressed valve causes the shaft to bend.*

8 While the camshafts are out, either let the chain rest on the stopper bolt shaft, or wire it to another component to prevent it from dropping. Also, cover the top of the cylinder head with a rag to prevent foreign objects from falling into the engine.

9 Remove the two bearing half-ring retainers from the cylinder head or from the bearings on the camshafts, noting how they fit (see illustration).

### Inspection

10 Inspect the bearing surfaces of the head and the holders and the corresponding journals on the camshaft. Look for score marks, deep scratches and evidence of spalling (a pitted appearance) (see illustration).

11 Check the camshaft lobes for heat discoloration (blue appearance), score marks, chipped areas, flat spots and spalling (see illustration). Measure the height of each lobe with a micrometer and compare the results to the minimum lobe height listed in this Chapter's Specifications (see illustration). If damage is noted or wear is excessive, the camshaft must be renewed. Also check the condition of the cam followers in the cylinder head (see Section 13).

12 Check the amount of camshaft runout by supporting each end of the camshaft on V-blocks, and measuring any runout using a dial gauge. If the runout exceeds the specified limit the camshaft must be renewed.

> **HAYNES HINT** *Refer to Tools and Workshop Tips in the Reference section for details of how to read a micrometer and dial gauge.*

13 The camshaft bearing oil clearance should now be checked. There are two possible ways of doing this, either by direct measurement (see Step 14) or by the use of a product known as Plastigauge (see Steps 15 to 18). If the Plastigauge method is used and the oil clearance is excessive, the direct method

will then have to be used to determine whether it is the camshaft or the holder that is worn.

14 If the direct measurement method is to be used, make sure the camshaft holder dowels are in position then fit the holders, making sure they are in their correct location (see Step 6). Tighten the holder bolts evenly and a little at a time in a criss-cross pattern to the torque setting specified at the beginning of the Chapter. Using telescoping gauges and a micrometer (see *Tools and Workshop Tips*), measure the journal holder diameter. Now measure the diameter of the camshaft journal with a micrometer (see illustration 10.18b). To determine the journal oil clearance, subtract the holder diameter from the journal diameter and compare the result to the clearance specified. If the clearance is greater than specified, compare the measurements of the camshaft journal and the holder to those specified and renew whichever component is beyond its limit.

15 If the Plastigauge method is to be used, clean the camshaft and the bearing surfaces in the cylinder head and camshaft holder with a clean lint-free cloth, then lay the camshafts in place in the cylinder head, positioning them so that their lobes face away from the followers, and so will not fully depress the valves when the holder is installed. Work on one camshaft at a time.

**2**

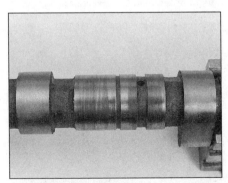

10.10 Check the journal surfaces of the camshaft for scratches or wear

10.11a Check the lobes of the camshaft for wear – here's an example of damage requiring camshaft repair or renewal

10.11b Measure the height of the camshaft lobes with a micrometer

10.16 Place a strip of Plastigauge on each bearing journal, parallel with the centreline

10.18a Compare the width of the crushed Plastigauge to the scale provided with it to obtain the clearance

10.18b Measure the cam bearing journal with a micrometer

**16** Cut strips of Plastigauge and lay one piece on each bearing journal, parallel with the camshaft centreline **(see illustration)**. Make sure the camshaft holder dowels are in position then fit the holder, making sure it is in its correct location (see Step 6). Tighten the holder bolts evenly and a little at a time in the correct numerical sequence as marked on the holder to the torque setting specified at the beginning of the Chapter. While doing this, don't let the camshaft rotate.

**17** Now unscrew the bolts evenly and a little at a time in a criss-cross pattern, and carefully lift off the camshaft holder.

**18** To determine the oil clearance, compare the crushed Plastigauge (at its widest point) on each journal to the scale printed on the Plastigauge container **(see illustration)**. Compare the results to this Chapter's Specifications. If the oil clearance is greater than specified, measure the journal holder diameter using telescoping gauges and a micrometer (see Step 14) (see *Tools and Workshop Tips*). Now measure the diameter of the camshaft journal with a micrometer **(see illustration)**. Compare the measurements of the camshaft holder and the journal to those specified and renew whichever component is beyond its limit.

*Before renewing camshafts or the cylinder head and journal holders because of damage, check with local machine shops specialising in motorcycle engine work. In the case of the camshafts, it may be possible for cam lobes to be welded, reground and hardened, at a cost far lower than that of a new camshaft. If the bearing surfaces in the cylinder head are damaged, it may be possible for them to be bored out to accept bearing inserts. Due to the cost of a new cylinder head it is recommended that all options be explored!*

**19** Check the condition of the end bearing on each camshaft, referring to *Tools and Workshop Tips* (Section 5) in the Reference Section. If the bearings are worn, new camshafts must be installed as the bearings are not available separately.

**20** Except in cases of oil starvation, the cam chain wears very little. If the chain has stretched excessively, which makes it difficult to maintain proper tension, renew it (see Section 9).

**21** Check the sprockets for wear, cracks and other damage. If the sprockets are worn, the chain and the sprocket on the crankshaft are probably worn as well. If wear this severe is apparent, the entire engine should be disassembled for inspection. The camshaft sprockets are integral with the camshafts, while the crankshaft sprocket is available separately (see Section 9).

**22** Check the cam chain guides and tensioner blade for wear or damage (see Section 9). If any is found, the chain may be worn out or improperly tensioned. Check the operation of the cam chain tensioner (see Section 9).

### Installation

**23** Fit each bearing half-ring retainer into its groove in the cylinder head **(see illustration 10.9)**.

**24** Make sure the bearing surfaces in the cylinder head, on the camshafts and in the holders are clean, then liberally apply

10.25 Lay the exhaust camshaft in the head, positioning it as described, and engage the chain with the sprocket

molybdenum disulphide oil (a 50/50 mixture of molybdenum disulphide grease and engine oil) to each of them. Also apply oil to the camshaft lobes and the followers.

**25** Check that the cam chain is engaged around the sprocket teeth on the crankshaft and that the crankshaft is positioned as described in Step 3. Keeping the front run of the cam chain taut, lay the exhaust camshaft (identified by EX) **(see illustration 10.7d)** onto the cylinder head, positioning the camshaft so that the arrow marked 1 on the sprocket points forwards and is flush with the top of the cylinder head mating surface, and the arrow marked 2 points vertically upwards **(see illustration 10.3b)**. Check that the bearing retainer locates into the groove in the bearing, and engage the chain on the sprocket teeth **(see illustration)**.

**26** Starting with the cam chain pin that is directly above the arrow marked 2 on the exhaust camshaft sprocket, count 15 pins along the chain towards the inlet side. Lay the inlet camshaft (identified by IN) onto the cylinder head, making sure the bearing retainer locates into the groove in the bearing, then engage the chain with the sprocket so that the arrow marked 3 on the sprocket aligns with the 15th pin **(see illustrations)**.

**27** Before proceeding further, check that everything aligns as described in Steps 3, 25 and 26. If it doesn't, the valve timing will be

10.26a Install the inlet camshaft as described . . .

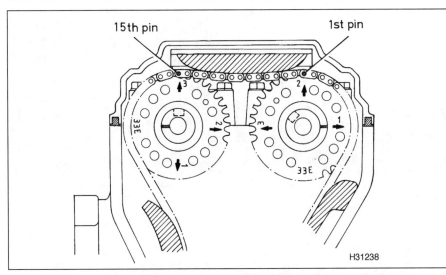

15th pin     1st pin

H31238

**10.26b . . . and check that all the marks and the chain are aligned as shown**

inaccurate and the valves could contact the pistons when the engine is turned over.

**28** Make sure the camshaft holder dowels are in position then fit the holders, making sure they are in their correct locations (see Step 6) **(see illustration)**. Tighten the holder bolts evenly and a little at a time in the numerical sequence marked on each holder to the torque setting specified at the beginning of the Chapter **(see illustrations)**. Whilst tightening the bolts, make sure the holders are being pulled squarely down and

are not binding on the dowels. **Note:** *The camshaft holder bolts are of the high tensile type, indicated by a 9 mark on the bolt head. Don't use any other type of bolt.*
*Caution: The camshaft is likely to break if it is tightened down onto the closed valves before the open valves. The holders are likely to break if they are not tightened down evenly and squarely.*

**29** With all caps tightened down, check that the valve timing marks still align (see Steps 3, 25 and 26). Check that each camshaft is not

pinched by turning the crankshaft a few degrees in each direction with a 14 mm socket on the starter clutch bolt.

**30** Fit the oil pipe using new sealing washers, making sure the white paint mark on the pipe faces up, and tighten the bolts to the specified torque setting – the longer bolt fits on the exhaust side **(see illustration 10.5)**. If the cylinder head has been removed, pour approximately 50 cc of the specified engine oil into the oil pockets in the head.

**31** Install the cam chain top guide and the cam chain tensioner (see Section 9).

**32** Use a new O-ring on the centre plug and a new sealing washer on the timing inspection plug and smear the O-ring and the plug threads with engine oil or molybdenum disulphide oil (a 50/50 mixture of molybdenum disulphide grease and engine oil) **(see illustration)**.

**33** Check the valve clearances and adjust them if necessary (see Chapter 1).

**34** Install the valve cover (see Section 8).

## 11 Cylinder head – removal and installation

**Caution:** *The engine must be completely cool before beginning this procedure or the cylinder head may become warped.*
**Note:** *The cylinder head can be removed with the engine in the frame. If the engine has already been removed, ignore the steps which don't apply.*

### Removal

**1** Remove the exhaust system (see Chapter 4).
**2** Remove the camshafts (see Section 10).
**3** Obtain a container which is divided into sixteen compartments, and label each compartment with the location of its corresponding valve in the cylinder head and whether it belongs with an inlet or an exhaust valve. If a container is not available, use labelled plastic bags. Lift each cam follower out of the cylinder head using either a magnet or a pair of pliers and store it in its corresponding compartment in the container **(see illustration)**. Retrieve the shim from

2

**10.28a Install the holders, making sure the dowels (arrowed) are installed . . .**

**10.28b . . . then install the bolts . . .**

**10.28c . . . and tighten them in sequence to the specified torque**

**10.32 Use a new O-ring and sealing washer on the centre and inspection plugs**

**11.3a Lift out the follower . . .**

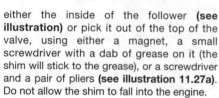

**11.3b . . . and retrieve the shim, which will probably be inside the follower**

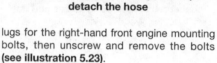

**11.5 Unscrew the banjo bolt (arrowed) and detach the hose**

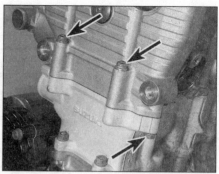

**11.10a Unscrew the 6 mm bolts (arrowed)**

either the inside of the follower **(see illustration)** or pick it out of the top of the valve, using either a magnet, a small screwdriver with a dab of grease on it (the shim will stick to the grease), or a screwdriver and a pair of pliers **(see illustration 11.27a)**. Do not allow the shim to fall into the engine.

**4** Drain the cooling system (see Chapter 1). Either remove the thermostat (see Chapter 3), or disconnect the coolant temperature sensor wiring connector(s) from the sensor(s) in the thermostat housing, then slacken the clamp securing the coolant hose to the housing and detach the hose – there is no need to draw the hose out of its hole in the frame **(see illustrations 5.11a and b)**. On fuel injected models, note which connector fits on which sensor (grey – left-facing sensor, brown – rear-facing sensor).

**5** Unscrew the oil hose banjo bolt and detach the hose from the cylinder head **(see illustration)**. Discard the sealing washers as new ones must be used.

**6** On California models, unscrew the nuts securing the PAIR system pipes to the cylinder head and detach the pipes. Remove the gaskets and discard them as new ones must be fitted.

**7** Slacken the pinchbolts on the mounting

lugs for the right-hand front engine mounting bolts, then unscrew and remove the bolts **(see illustration 5.23)**.

**8** Unscrew and remove the left-hand front engine mounting bolts **(see illustration 5.24)**.

**9** Unscrew and remove the camshaft stopper bolt **(see illustration 9.26)**. Discard the seal as a new one must be fitted.

**10** The cylinder head is secured by three 6 mm bolts and ten 10 mm bolts. First unscrew and remove the 6 mm bolts **(see illustration)**. Now slacken the 10 mm bolts evenly and a little at a time in a **reverse** of their numerical sequence until they are all slack, then remove the bolts and their washers **(see illustration)**.

**11** Lift the head off the block, passing the cam chain down through the tunnel as you do **(see illustration)**. If it is stuck, tap around the joint faces of the cylinder head with a soft-faced mallet to free the head. Do not attempt to free the head by inserting a screwdriver between the head and block – you'll damage the sealing surfaces.

**12** Do not let the cam chain fall into the tunnel – secure it with a piece of wire or metal bar to prevent it from doing so. Remove the old cylinder head gasket and discard it. Stuff a clean rag into the cam chain tunnel to prevent any debris falling into the engine.

**13** If they are loose, remove the dowel from each rear corner of the cylinder block. If either appears to be missing it is probably stuck in the underside of the cylinder head. If the engine is in the frame, also remove the spacers for the right-hand front engine mounting bolts for safekeeping, if required.

**14** Check the cylinder head gasket and the mating surfaces on the cylinder head and block for signs of leakage, which could indicate warpage. Refer to Section 13 and check the flatness of the cylinder head.

**15** Clean all traces of old gasket material from the cylinder head and block. If a scraper is used, take care not to scratch or gouge the soft aluminium. Be careful not to let any of the gasket material fall into the crankcase, the cylinder bores or the oil passages.

### Installation

**16** If removed, install the two dowels onto the cylinder block and, if the engine is in the frame, position the spacers for the right-hand front engine mounting bolts between the frame and the engine, making sure their shouldered ends face the engine. Lubricate the cylinder bores with engine oil.

**17** Ensure both cylinder head and block mating surfaces are clean, then lay the new

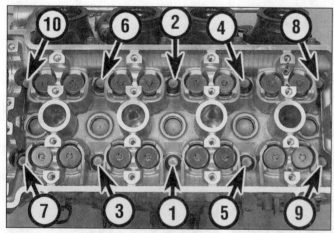

**11.10b Cylinder head 10 mm bolts (arrowed) – slacken them in reverse numerical order, and tighten them in the correct numerical order**

**11.11 Lift the cylinder head up off the block**

11.17 Fit the new gasket, making sure it locates over the dowels (arrowed)

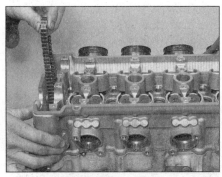

11.18 Install the head, passing the cam chain up through the tunnel as you do

11.19a Do not forget the washers with the cylinder head 10 mm bolts

head gasket in place on the cylinder block, making sure it locates over the dowels and all the holes are correctly aligned **(see illustration)**. Never re-use the old gasket.

**18** Carefully lower the cylinder head onto the block **(see illustration)**. It is helpful to have an assistant to pass the cam chain up through the tunnel and slip a piece of wire through it to prevent it falling back into the engine. Keep the chain taut to prevent it becoming disengaged from the crankshaft sprocket.

**19** Apply clean engine oil to the cylinder head 10 mm bolt washers, then install the bolts and tighten them finger-tight **(see illustration)**. Now tighten the 10 mm bolts in their correct numerical sequence **(see illustration 11.10b)** first to the initial torque setting specified at the

beginning of the Chapter, then tighten them in the same sequence to the final torque setting specified **(see illustration)**.

**20** When the bolts are correctly torqued, install the 6 mm bolts and tighten them to the specified torque setting **(see illustration)**.

**21** Fit a new seal onto the cam chain stopper bolt, making sure its lipped side will face the engine, and smear it with clean oil. Install the bolt, making sure the shaft sits between the two runs of chain, and tighten it to the torque setting specified at the beginning of the Chapter **(see illustration 9.29)**.

**22** Install the left-hand front mounting bolts (45 mm) and tighten them to the specified torque setting **(see illustration 5.34)**.

**23** Install the right-hand front engine

mounting bolts (55 mm) and tighten them to the specified torque setting **(see illustration 5.33)**. Now tighten the pinchbolts on the mounting lugs to the specified torque setting **(see illustration 5.23)**.

**24** On California models, fit a new gasket onto each PAIR system pipe union, then fit the pipes and tighten the nuts securely.

**25** Install the oil hose using new sealing washers on each side of the union and tighten the banjo bolt to the specified torque setting **(see illustration)**.

**26** Either install the thermostat (see Chapter 3), or connect the coolant hose to the thermostat housing and tighten the clamp, then connect the wiring connector(s) to the sensor(s), depending on your removal procedure **(see illustrations 5.11a and b)**.

**27** Lubricate each shim with engine oil or molybdenum disulphide oil (a 50/50 mixture of molybdenum disulphide grease and engine oil) and fit it into its recess in the top of the valve, with the size marking on each shim facing down **(see illustration)**. Check that the shim is correctly seated, then lubricate the follower with engine oil or molybdenum disulphide oil and install it onto the valve **(see illustration)**. **Note:** *It is most important that the shims and followers are returned to their original valves otherwise the valve clearances will be inaccurate.*

**28** Install the camshafts (see Section 10).

**29** Install the exhaust system (see Chapter 4). Fill the cooling system (see Chapter 1).

11.19b Tighten the bolts as described to the specified torque

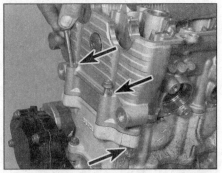

11.20 Install the 6 mm bolts (arrowed) and tighten them to the specified torque

**2**

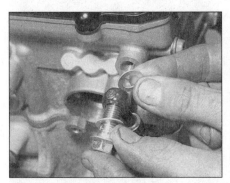

11.25 Use new sealing washers on each side of the hose union

11.27a Fit the shim into the recess in the top of the valve . . .

11.27b . . . then install the follower

## 12 Valves/valve seats/valve guides – servicing

1 Because of the complex nature of this job and the special tools and equipment required, most owners leave servicing of the valves, valve seats and valve guides to a professional.
2 The home mechanic can, however, remove the valves from the cylinder head, clean and check the components for wear and assess the extent of the work needed, and, unless a valve service is required, grind in the valves (see Section 13).
3 The dealer service department will remove the valves and springs, renew the valves and guides, recut the valve seats, check and renew the valve springs, spring retainers and collets (as necessary), renew the valve seals with new ones and reassemble the valve components. **Note**: *Suzuki recommends against grinding in the valves after the seats have been recut. The valve seat must be soft and unpolished in order for final seating to occur when the engine is first run.*
4 After the valve service has been performed, the head will be in like-new condition. When the head is returned, be sure to clean it again very thoroughly before installation on the engine to remove any metal particles or abrasive grit that may still be present from the valve service operations. Use compressed air, if available, to blow out all the holes and passages.

## 13 Cylinder head and valves – disassembly, inspection and reassembly

1 As mentioned in the previous section, valve servicing, valve seat re-cutting and valve guide renewal should be left to a Suzuki dealer. However, disassembly, cleaning and inspection of the valves and related components can be done (if the necessary special tools are available) by the home mechanic. This way no expense is incurred if the inspection reveals that overhaul is not required at this time.
2 To disassemble the valve components without the risk of damaging them, a valve spring compressor is absolutely necessary. This tool can usually be rented, but if it's not available, have a dealer handle the entire process of disassembly, inspection, service or repair (if required) and reassembly of the valves.

### Disassembly

3 Before proceeding, arrange to label and store the valves along with their related components in such a way that they can be returned to their original locations without getting mixed up **(see illustration)**. A good way to do this is to use the same container as the followers and shims are stored in (see

Section 11), or to obtain a separate container which is divided into sixteen compartments, and to label each compartment with the identity of the valve which will be stored in it (ie number of cylinder, inlet or exhaust side, inner or outer valve). Alternatively, labelled plastic bags will do just as well.
4 If not already done, clean all traces of old gasket material from the cylinder head. If a scraper is used, take care not to scratch or gouge the soft aluminium.

HAYNES HiNT *Refer to Tools and Workshop Tips for details of gasket removal methods.*

5 Compress the valve spring on the first valve with a spring compressor, making sure it is correctly located onto each end of the valve assembly **(see illustrations)**. On the underside of the head make sure the plate on the compressor only contacts the valve and not the soft aluminium of the head – if the plate is too big for the valve, use a spacer between them **(see illustration)**. Do not compress the springs any more than is absolutely necessary. Remove the collets, using either needle-nose pliers, tweezers, a magnet or a screwdriver with a dab of grease on it **(see illustration)**. Carefully release the valve spring compressor and remove the spring retainer, noting which way up it fits, the springs, the spring seat, and the valve from the head **(see illustration 13.3)**. If the valve binds in the guide (won't pull through),

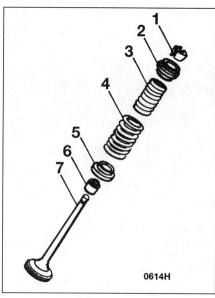

0614H

**13.3 Valve components**

| | |
|---|---|
| 1 Collets | 5 Spring seat |
| 2 Spring retainer | 6 Stem seal |
| 3 Inner spring | 7 Valve |
| 4 Outer spring | |

push it back into the head and deburr the area around the collet groove with a very fine file or whetstone **(see illustration)**.
6 Repeat the procedure for the remaining valves. Remember to keep the parts for each valve together and in order so they can be reinstalled in the same location.

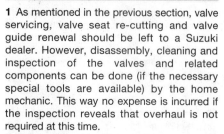

**13.5a Compressing the valves using a valve spring compressor**

**13.5b Make sure the compressor is a good fit both on the top . . .**

**13.5c . . . and the bottom of the valve assembly**

**13.5d Use a spacer between the plate and the valve if the plate is too big**

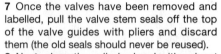

**13.5e Remove the collets with needle-nose pliers, tweezers, a magnet or a screwdriver with a dab of grease on it**

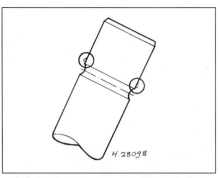

**13.5f If the valve stem won't pull through the guide, deburr the area above the collet groove**

**13.13 Checking the cylinder head gasket face for distortion**

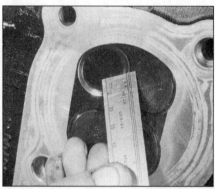

**13.14 Measure the valve seat width with a ruler (or for greater precision use a vernier caliper)**

7 Once the valves have been removed and labelled, pull the valve stem seals off the top of the valve guides with pliers and discard them (the old seals should never be reused).

8 Next, clean the cylinder head with solvent and dry it thoroughly. Compressed air will speed the drying process and ensure that all holes and recessed areas are clean.

9 Clean all of the valve springs, collets, retainers and spring seats with solvent and dry them thoroughly. Do the parts from one valve at a time so that no mixing of parts between valves occurs.

10 Scrape off any deposits that may have formed on the valve, then use a motorised wire brush to remove deposits from the valve heads and stems. Again, make sure the valves do not get mixed up.

## Inspection

11 Inspect the head very carefully for cracks and other damage. If cracks are found, a new head will be required. Check the cam bearing surfaces for wear and evidence of seizure. Check the camshafts for wear as well (see Section 10).

12 Inspect the outer surfaces of the cam followers for evidence of scoring or other damage. If a follower is in poor condition, it is probable that the bore in which it works is also damaged. Check for clearance between the followers and their bores. Whilst no specifications are given, if slack is excessive, renew the followers. If the bores are seriously out-of-round or tapered, the cylinder head and the followers must be renewed.

13 Using a precision straight-edge and a feeler gauge set to the warpage limit listed in the specifications at the beginning of the Chapter, check the head gasket mating surface for warpage (see illustration). Refer to Tools and Workshop Tips in the Reference section for details of how to use the straight-edge.

14 Examine the valve seats in the combustion chamber. If they are pitted, cracked or burned, the head will require work beyond the scope of the home mechanic. Measure the valve seat width and compare it to this Chapter's Specifications (see illustration). If it exceeds the service limit, or if it varies around its circumference, valve overhaul is required. If available, use Prussian blue to determine the

extent of valve seat wear. Uniformly coat the seat with the Prussian blue, then install the valve and rotate it back and forth using a lapping tool. Remove the valve and check whether the ring of blue on the valve is uniform and continuous around the valve, and of the correct width as specified.

15 Clean the valve guides to remove any carbon build-up, then install each valve in its guide in turn so that its face is 10 mm above the seat. Mount a dial gauge against the side of the valve face and measure the amount of side clearance (wobble) between the valve stem and its guide in two perpendicular directions (see illustration). If the clearance exceeds the limit specified, remove the valve and measure the valve stem diameter (see illustration). Also measure the inside

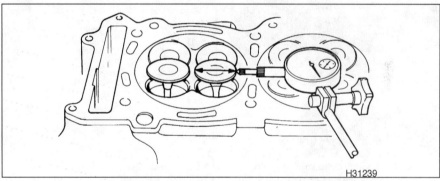

**13.15a Measure the amount of 'wobble' as shown**

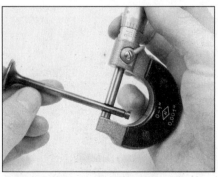

**13.15b Measure the valve stem diameter with a micrometer**

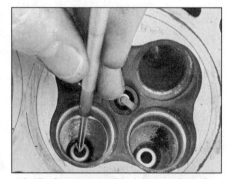

**13.15c Insert a small hole gauge into the valve guide and expand it so there's a slight drag when it's pulled out**

2

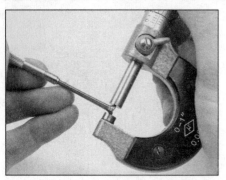

**13.15d Measure the small hole gauge with a micrometer**

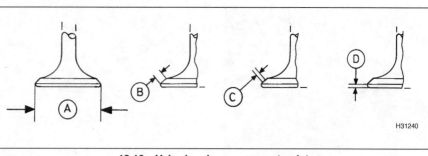

H31240

**13.16a Valve head measurement points**

*A Head diameter*    *B Face width*    *C Seat width*    *D Margin thickness*

diameter of the guide with a small hole gauge and micrometer **(see illustrations)**. Measure the guides at the ends and at the centre to determine if they are worn in a bell-mouth pattern (more wear at the ends). Subtract the stem diameter from the valve guide diameter to obtain the valve stem-to-guide clearance. If the stem-to-guide clearance is greater than listed in this Chapter's Specifications, renew whichever, of the components is worn beyond its specifications. If the valve guide is within specifications, but is worn unevenly, it should be renewed.

**16** Carefully inspect each valve face for cracks, pits and burned spots. Measure the valve margin thickness and compare it to this Chapter's Specifications **(see illustrations)**. If

it exceeds the service limit, or if it varies around its circumference, valve overhaul is required.

**17** Check the valve stem and the collet groove area for cracks **(see illustration)**. Rotate the valve and check for any obvious indication that it is bent. Check the end of the stem for pitting and excessive wear. The presence of any of the above conditions indicates the need for valve servicing. The stem end can be ground down, provided that the amount of stem above the collet groove after grinding is sufficient. When installing a valve whose end has been ground, check that the stem end protrudes above the collets.

**18** Using V-blocks and a dial gauge, measure the valve stem runout and the valve head runout and compare the results to the specifications **(see illustration)**. If either

measurement exceeds the service limit specified, the valve must be discarded.

**19** Check the end of each valve spring for wear and pitting. Measure the spring free length and compare it to that listed in the specifications **(see illustration)**. If any spring is shorter than specified it has sagged and must be renewed. Also place the spring upright on a flat surface and check it for bend by placing a ruler against it **(see illustration)**. If the bend in any spring is excessive, it must be renewed. The spring tension should also be checked by measuring the amount of weight needed to compress each spring to a particular length. If the weight required to compress the spring to the specified length is greater or less than the weight specified, the spring must be renewed.

**20** Check the spring retainers and collets for obvious wear and cracks. Any questionable parts should not be reused, as extensive damage will occur in the event of failure during engine operation.

**21** If the inspection indicates that no overhaul work is required, the valve components can be reinstalled in the head.

### Reassembly

**22** Unless a valve service has been performed, before installing the valves in the head they should be ground in (lapped) to ensure a positive seal between the valves and seats. **Note:** *Suzuki advise against grinding in the valves after the seats have been recut. The valve seat must be soft and unpolished in order for final seating to occur when the engine is first run.* This procedure requires coarse and fine valve grinding compound and

**13.16b Measure the valve margin thickness as shown**

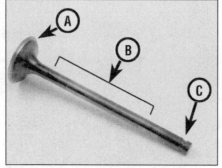

**13.17 Check the valve face (A), stem (B) and collet groove (C) for signs of wear and damage**

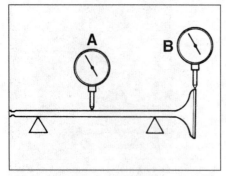

**13.18 Measure the valve stem runout (A) and the valve head runout (B)**

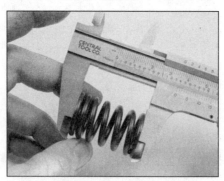

**13.19a Measure the free length of the valve springs**

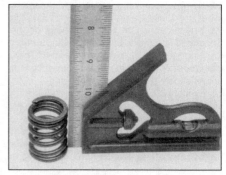

**13.19b Check the valve springs for squareness**

**13.23 Apply the lapping compound very sparingly, in small dabs, to the valve face only**

**13.24a Rotate the valve grinding tool back and forth between the palms of your hands**

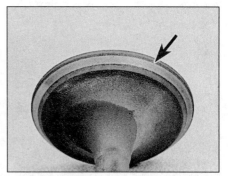

**13.24b The valve face and seat should show a uniform unbroken ring (arrowed) . . .**

a valve grinding tool. If a grinding tool is not available, a piece of rubber or plastic hose can be slipped over the valve stem (after the valve has been installed in the guide) and used to turn the valve.

**23** Apply a small amount of coarse grinding compound to the valve face, then slip the valve into the guide **(see illustration)**. **Note:** *Make sure each valve is installed in its correct guide and be careful not to get any grinding compound on the valve stem.*

**24** Attach the grinding tool (or hose) to the valve and rotate the tool between the palms of your hands. Use a back-and-forth motion (as though rubbing your hands together) rather than a circular motion (ie so that the valve rotates alternately clockwise and anti-clockwise rather than in one direction only) **(see illustration)**. Lift the valve off the seat

and turn it at regular intervals to distribute the grinding compound properly. Continue the grinding procedure until the valve face and seat contact area is of uniform width and unbroken around the entire circumference of the valve face and seat **(see illustrations)**.

**25** Carefully remove the valve from the guide and wipe off all traces of grinding compound. Use solvent to clean the valve and wipe the seat area thoroughly with a solvent soaked cloth.

**26** Repeat the procedure with fine valve grinding compound, then repeat the entire procedure for the remaining valves.

**27** Working on one valve at a time, install a new valve stem seal onto the valve guide. Use an appropriate size deep socket to push the seal over the end of the valve guide until it is felt to clip into place **(see illustration)**. Don't

twist or cock it, or it will not seal properly against the valve stem. Also, don't remove it again or it will be damaged.

**28** Lay the spring seat in place in the cylinder head, with its shouldered side facing up so that it fits into the base of the springs (the spring seat can be identified from the spring retainer by its larger internal diameter – be sure not to mix up the two) **(see illustration 13.3)**.

**29** Coat the valve stem with molybdenum disulphide grease, then install it into its guide, rotating it slowly to avoid damaging the seal **(see illustration)**. Check that the valve moves up and down freely in the guide. Next, install the inner and outer springs, with their closer-wound coils facing down into the cylinder head, followed by the spring retainer, with its shouldered side facing down so that it fits into the top of the springs **(see illustrations)**.

**13.24c . . . and the seat (arrowed) should be the specified width all the way round**

**13.27 Press the valve stem seal into position using a suitable deep socket**

**13.29a Lubricate the valve stem and slide it into its guide**

**2**

**13.29b Fit the inner valve spring . . .**

**13.29c . . . and the outer valve spring, with their closer-wound coils facing down . . .**

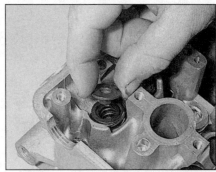

**13.29d . . . then fit the spring retainer**

**13.30a A small dab of grease will help to keep the collets in place on the valve while the spring is released**

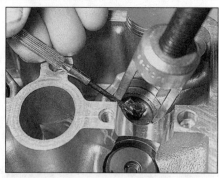

**13.30b Compress the springs and install the collets, making sure they locate in the groove**

**30** Apply a small amount of grease to the collets to help hold them in place **(see illustration)**. Compress the spring with the valve spring compressor and install the collets **(see illustration)**. When compressing the spring, depress it only as far as is absolutely necessary to slip the collets into place. Make certain that the collets are securely locked in the retaining groove.

**31** Repeat the procedure for the remaining valves. Remember to keep the parts for each valve together and separate from the other valves so they can be reinstalled in the same location.

**32** Support the cylinder head on blocks so the valves can't contact the workbench top, then very gently tap each of the valve stems with a soft-faced hammer. This will help seat the collets in their grooves.

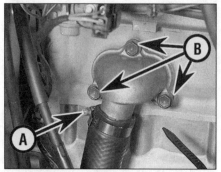

**14.3 Hose clamp (A), union bolts (B)**

**14.4 Unscrew the nuts (arrowed)**

> **HAYNES HiNT**
> *Check for proper sealing of the valves by pouring a small amount of solvent into each of the valve ports. If the solvent leaks past any valve into the combustion chamber area the valve grinding operation on that valve should be repeated.*

## 14 Cylinder block – removal, inspection and installation

**Note:** *The cylinder block can be removed with the engine in the frame.*

### Removal

**1** Remove the cylinder head (see Section 11).
**2** Lift the cam chain front guide out of the front of the cam chain tunnel, noting which way round it fits and how it locates **(see illustration 9.17)**.
**3** Either slacken the clamp securing the coolant hose to the union on the rear of the cylinder block and detach the hose, or unscrew the three bolts securing the coolant union to the block and detach the union, or do both if required **(see illustration)**. If the union is detached, discard the O-ring as a new one must be used. Also unscrew the bolts securing the radiator bracket to the front of the block and detach the bracket.

**14.5 Lift the block up off the crankcase and pistons**

**4** Unscrew the nuts which secure the right-hand side of the block to the crankcase **(see illustration)**.
**5** Hold the cam chain up and lift the cylinder block up off the crankcase, then pass the cam chain down through the tunnel **(see illustration)**. Do not let the chain fall into the crankcase. If the block is stuck, tap around the joint faces of the block with a soft-faced mallet to free it from the crankcase. Don't attempt to free the block by inserting a screwdriver between it and the crankcase – you'll damage the sealing surfaces. When lifting the block off the pistons, try not to let them fall against the crankcase as they become free. When the block is removed, stuff clean rags around the pistons to prevent anything falling into the crankcase.
**6** Remove the dowels from the mating surface of the crankcase or the underside of the block if they are loose; be careful not to let them drop into the engine.
**7** Remove the gasket and clean all traces of old gasket material from the cylinder block and crankcase mating surfaces. If a scraper is used, take care not to scratch or gouge the soft aluminium. Be careful not to let any of the gasket material fall into the crankcase or the oil passages.

### Inspection

**8** Check the cylinder walls carefully for scratches and score marks.
**9** Using a precision straight-edge and a feeler gauge set to the warpage limit listed in the specifications at the beginning of the Chapter, check the block gasket mating surface for warpage. Refer to *Tools and Workshop Tips* in the Reference section for details of how to use the straight-edge. If warpage is excessive the block must be renewed.
**10** Using telescoping gauges and a micrometer (see *Tools and Workshop Tips*), check the dimensions of each cylinder to assess the amount of wear, taper and ovality. Measure near the top (but below the level of the top piston ring at TDC), centre and bottom (but above the level of the oil ring at BDC) of the bore, both parallel to and across the crankshaft axis **(see illustration)**. Compare the results to the specifications at the beginning of the Chapter.

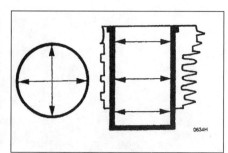

**14.10 Measure the cylinder bore in the directions shown with a telescoping gauge, then measure the gauge with a micrometer**

**14.14 Fit the new gasket, locating it over the dowels (arrowed)**

**14.16 Lower the block and feed in the pistons and rings as described**

**14.18 Fit the nuts and tighten them down**

**11** If the precision measuring tools are not available, take the block to a Suzuki dealer or specialist motorcycle repair shop for assessment and advice.

**12** If the cylinders are worn beyond the service limit, or badly scratched, scuffed or scored, the cylinder block must be renewed. The block material is not suitable for rebore, and thus Suzuki do not supply oversize pistons and rings. The cylinders are coated with Suzuki's SCEM (Suzuki Composite Electrochemical Material), a highly wear resistant nickel-silicon-carbide plating which should last the life of the engine. Note that the cylinder bores should not be honed.

### Installation

**13** Check that the mating surfaces of the cylinder block and crankcase are free from oil or pieces of old gasket. If removed, fit the dowels into the crankcase.

**14** Remove the rags from around the pistons, then lay the new base gasket in place on the crankcase making sure it locates over the dowels and all the holes are correctly aligned **(see illustration)**. Never re-use the old gasket.

**15** If required, install piston ring clamps onto the pistons to ease their entry into the bores as the block is lowered. This is not essential as each cylinder has a good lead-in enabling the piston rings to be hand-fed into the bore. If possible, have an assistant support the block while this is done.

 **HAYNES HiNT** *Rotate the crankshaft until the inner pistons (2 and 3) are uppermost and feed them into the block first. Access to the lower pistons (1 and 4) is easier since they are on the outside.*

**16** Lubricate the cylinder bores, pistons and piston rings, and the connecting rod big- and small-ends, with clean engine oil, then lower the block down until the uppermost piston crowns fit into the bores **(see illustration)**. At this stage feed the cam chain up through the tunnel and secure it in place with a piece of wire to prevent it from falling back down.

**17** Gently push down on the cylinder block, making sure the pistons enter the bores squarely and do not get cocked sideways. If piston ring clamps are not being used, carefully compress and feed each ring into the bore as the block is lowered. If necessary, use a soft mallet to gently tap the block down, but do not use force if the block appears to be stuck as the pistons and/or rings will be damaged. If clamps are used, remove them once the pistons are in the bore.

**18** When the pistons are correctly installed in the cylinders, press the block down onto the base gasket, making sure it locates correctly onto the dowels. Install the two nuts and tighten them to the torque setting specified at the beginning of the Chapter (this will probably have to be done by feel as it is not actually

possible to get a socket and therefore a torque wrench onto the nuts) **(see illustration)**.

**19** If removed, fit a new O-ring into the groove in the coolant union and smear it with grease, then attach the union and tighten the bolts to the specified torque setting **(see illustration 14.3)**. If detached, connect the hose to the union and secure it with the clamp. Also fit the radiator bracket onto the front of the block and tighten its bolts.

**20** Install the front guide blade into the front of the cam chain tunnel **(see illustration 9.17)**, making sure it locates correctly onto its pivot bolt seat and its lugs locate in their cut-outs **(see illustration 9.21)**.

**21** Install the cylinder head (see Section 11).

### 15 Pistons – removal, inspection and installation

*Note: The pistons can be removed with the engine in the frame.*

### Removal

**1** Remove the cylinder block (see Section 14).

**2** Before removing the piston from the connecting rod, and if not already done, stuff a clean rag into the hole around the rod to prevent the circlips or anything else from falling into the crankcase. Use a sharp scriber or felt marker pen to write the cylinder identity on the crown of each piston (or on the inside of the skirt if the piston is dirty and going to be cleaned). Each piston should also have a triangle or punchmark on its crown which should point forwards **(see illustration 15.3b)**. If this is not visible, mark the piston accordingly so that it can be installed the correct way round.

**3** Carefully prise out the circlip on one side of the piston using needle-nose pliers or a small flat-bladed screwdriver inserted into the notch **(see illustration)**. Push the piston pin out from the other side to free the piston from the connecting rod **(see illustration)**. Remove the other circlip and discard them as new ones must be used. When the piston has been removed, install its pin back into its bore so that related parts do not get mixed up. Rotate the crankshaft so that the best access is obtained for each piston.

**15.3a Remove the circlip using pointed-nose pliers or a small screwdriver inserted in the notch . . .**

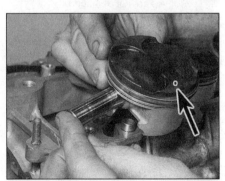

**15.3b . . . then push the pin out from the other side and withdraw it from the piston. Note the punchmark (arrowed) in each piston – it must face forward**

**2**

15.5a Removing the piston rings using a ring removal and installation tool

 *To prevent the circlip from pinging away or from dropping into the crankcase, pass a rod or screwdriver which has a diameter greater than the gap between the circlip ends, through the piston pin. This will trap the circlip if it springs out.*

 *If a piston pin is a tight fit in the piston bosses, soak a rag in boiling water then wring it out and wrap it around the piston – this will expand the alloy piston sufficiently to release its grip on the pin. If the piston pin is particularly stubborn, extract it using a drawbolt tool, but be careful to protect the piston's working surfaces – see Tools and Workshop Tips in the Reference section.*

### Inspection

4 Before the inspection process can be carried out, the pistons must be cleaned and the old piston rings removed.

5 Using your thumbs or a piston ring removal and installation tool, carefully remove the rings from the pistons **(see illustration)**. Do not nick or gouge the pistons in the process. Carefully note which way up each ring fits and in which groove as they must be installed in their original positions if being re-used. The upper surface of each ring is marked at one end **(see illustration)**. The top ring is identified by the letter R, and the second (middle) ring by the letters RN (though after-market rings may be differently marked). The rings can also be identified by their different cross-section shape.

6 Scrape all traces of carbon from the tops of the pistons. A hand-held wire brush or a piece of fine emery cloth can be used once most of the deposits have been scraped away. Do not, under any circumstances, use a wire brush mounted in a drill motor to remove deposits from the pistons; the piston material is soft and will be eroded away by the wire brush.

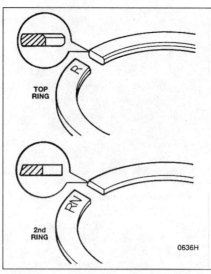

15.5b Note the letters, which must face up, and don't confuse the top ring with the second ring

7 Use a piston ring groove cleaning tool to remove any carbon deposits from the ring grooves. If a tool is not available, a piece broken off an old ring will do the job. Be very careful to remove only the carbon deposits. Do not remove any metal and do not nick or gouge the sides of the ring grooves.

8 Once the deposits have been removed, clean the pistons with solvent and dry them thoroughly. If the identification previously marked on the piston is cleaned off, be sure to re-mark it with the correct identity. Make sure the oil return holes below the oil ring groove are clear.

9 Carefully inspect each piston for cracks around the skirt, at the pin bosses and at the ring lands. Normal piston wear appears as even, vertical wear on the thrust surfaces of the piston and slight looseness of the top ring in its groove. If the skirt is scored or scuffed, the engine may have been suffering from overheating and/or abnormal combustion, which caused excessively high operating temperatures. The oil pump should be checked thoroughly. Also check that the circlip grooves are not damaged.

15.12 Measure the piston diameter with a micrometer at the specified distance from the bottom of the skirt

15.11 Measure the piston ring-to-groove clearance with a feeler gauge

10 A hole in the piston crown, an extreme to be sure, is an indication that abnormal combustion (pre-ignition) was occurring. Burned areas at the edge of the piston crown are usually evidence of spark knock (detonation). If any of the above problems exist, the causes must be corrected or the damage will occur again.

11 Measure the piston ring-to-groove clearance by laying each piston ring in its groove and slipping a feeler gauge in beside it **(see illustration)**. Make sure you have the correct ring for the groove (see Step 5). Check the clearance at three or four locations around the groove. If the clearance is greater than specified, renew both the piston and rings as a set. If new rings are being used, measure the clearance using the new rings. If the clearance is greater than that specified, the piston is worn and must be renewed.

12 Check the piston-to-bore clearance by measuring the bore (see Section 14) and the piston diameter. Make sure each piston is matched to its correct cylinder. Measure the piston 15.0 mm up from the bottom of the skirt and at 90° to the piston pin axis **(see illustration)**. Subtract the piston diameter from the bore diameter to obtain the clearance. If it is greater than the specified figure, the piston must be renewed (assuming the bore itself is within limits, otherwise a new cylinder block must be fitted).

13 Apply clean engine oil to the piston pin, insert it into the piston and check for any freeplay between the two **(see illustration)**.

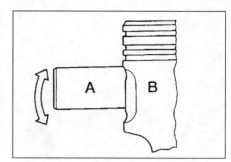

15.13a Slip the pin (A) into the piston (B) and try to rock it back and forth. If it's loose, renew the piston and pin

Measure the pin external diameter and the pin bore in the piston and compare the measurements to the specifications at the beginning of the Chapter **(see illustrations)**. Repeat the measurements between the pin and the connecting rod small-end **(see illustration)**. Renew components that are worn beyond the specified limits.

### Installation

**14** Inspect and install the piston rings (see Section 16).

**15** Lubricate the piston pin, the piston pin bore and the connecting rod small-end bore with clean engine oil or molybdenum disulphide oil (a 50/50 mixture of molybdenum disulphide grease and clean engine oil).

**16** Install a new circlip in one side of the piston (do not re-use old circlips) **(see illustration)**. Line up the piston on its correct connecting rod, making sure the triangle or punchmark on the piston crown faces forwards, and insert the piston pin from the other side **(see illustration 15.3b)**. Secure the pin with the other new circlip. When installing the circlips, compress them only just enough to fit them in the piston, and make sure they are properly seated in their grooves with the open end away from the removal notch.

## 16 Piston rings –
inspection and installation

**1** It is good practice to renew the piston rings when an engine is being overhauled. Before installing the new piston rings, the ring end gaps must be checked, both free and installed.

**2** Lay out the pistons and the new ring sets so the rings will be matched with the same piston and cylinder during the end gap measurement procedure and engine assembly.

**3** To measure the free end gap of each ring, lay the ring on a flat surface and measure the gap between the ends using a vernier caliper **(see illustration)**. Compare the results to the specifications at the beginning of the Chapter and renew any ring that is outside its service limit.

**15.13b  Measure the external diameter of the pin . . .**

**15.13d  . . . and the internal diameter of the connecting rod small-end**

**4** To measure the installed end gap, insert the top ring into the top of the first cylinder and square it up with the cylinder walls by pushing it in with the top of the piston. The ring should be about 20 mm below the top edge of the cylinder. Slip a feeler gauge between the ends of the ring and compare the measurement to the specifications at the beginning of the Chapter **(see illustration)**.

**5** If the gap is larger or smaller than specified, double check to make sure that you have the correct ring before proceeding.

**6** If the gap is too small, it must be enlarged or the ring ends may come in contact with each other during engine operation, which can cause serious damage. The end gap can be increased by filing the ring ends very carefully with a fine file. When performing this

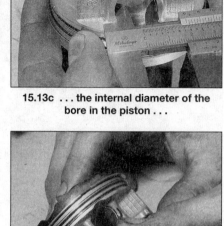

**15.13c  . . . the internal diameter of the bore in the piston . . .**

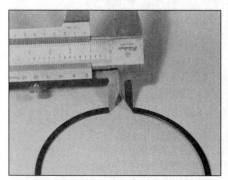

**15.16  Install the circlip, making sure it is properly seated in its groove, with the open end away from the notch**

operation, file only from the outside in **(see illustration)**.

**7** Excess end gap is not critical unless it exceeds the service limit. Again, double-check to make sure you have the correct rings for your engine and check that the bore is not worn.

**8** Repeat the procedure for each ring that will be installed in the cylinders. Remember to keep the rings, pistons and cylinders matched up.

**9** Once the ring end gaps have been checked/corrected, the rings can be installed on the pistons.

**10** The oil control ring (lowest on the piston) is installed first. It is composed of three separate components, namely the expander and the upper and lower side rails. Slip the

**2**

**16.3  Measuring piston ring free end gap**

**16.4  Measuring piston ring installed end gap**

**16.6  Ring end gap can be enlarged by clamping a file in a vice and filing the ring ends**

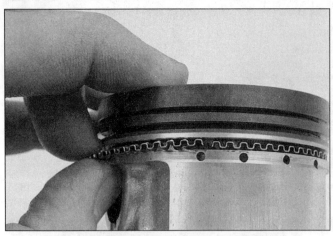

16.10a Install the oil ring expander in its groove . . .

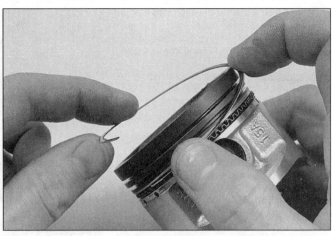

16.10b . . . and fit the side rails each side of it

expander into the groove, then install the upper side rail **(see illustration)**. Do not use a piston ring installation tool on the oil ring side rails as they may be damaged. Instead, place one end of the side rail into the groove between the expander and the ring land **(see illustration)**. Hold it firmly in place and slide a finger around the piston while pushing the rail into the groove. Next, install the lower side rail

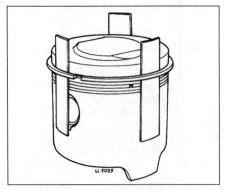

16.12 Old pieces of feeler gauge blade can be used to guide the ring over the piston

in the same manner. Make sure the ends of the expander do not overlap.

11 After the three oil ring components have been installed, check to make sure that both the upper and lower side rails can be turned smoothly in the ring groove.

12 The upper surface of each compression ring is marked at one end **(see illustration 15.5b)**. The top ring is identified by the letter R, and the second (middle) ring by the letters RN (though after-market rings may be differently marked). The rings can also be identified by their different cross-section shape. Install the second (middle) ring next. Make sure that the identification letter near the end gap is facing up. Fit the ring into the middle groove in the piston. Do not expand the ring any more than is necessary to slide it into place. To avoid breaking the ring, use a piston ring installation tool **(see illustration 15.5a)** or old pieces of feeler gauge blades **(see illustration)**.

13 Finally, install the top ring in the same manner into the top groove in the piston. Make sure the identification letter near the end gap is facing up.

14 Once the rings are correctly installed, check they move freely without snagging and stagger their end gaps as shown **(see illustration)**.

## 17 Clutch – removal, inspection and installation

**Note:** *The clutch can be removed with the engine in the frame.*

### Removal

**Note:** *It is advisable to order new diaphragm spring holder screws in advance of disassembling the clutch and renew them as a matter of course, as their size means they are easily damaged or stressed, even though it may not be apparent.*

1 Remove the fairing side panels (see Chapter 8). Drain the engine oil (see Chapter 1).

2 Working in a criss-cross pattern, evenly slacken the clutch cover bolts **(see illustration)**. Note which size bolts fit where, and that some bolts are fitted with sealing

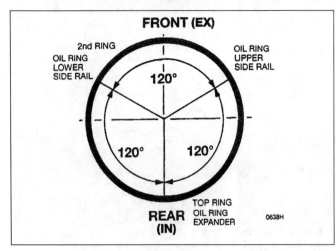

16.14 When installing the rings, stagger their end gaps as shown

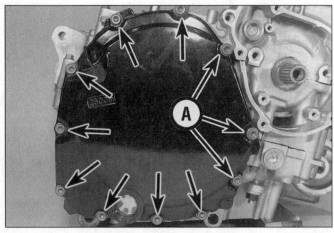

17.2 Clutch cover bolts (arrowed) – note the positions of the bolts with sealing washers (A)

17.3a Remove the circlip using a pair of internal circlip pliers . . .

17.3b . . . then remove the pressure plate lifter

17.4a Withdraw the pushrod end-piece along with the thrust washer and release bearing . . .

washers. Discard these washers as new ones should be used. Lift the cover away from the engine, being prepared to catch any residual oil which may be released as the cover is removed. Remove the gasket and discard it. Note the positions of the two locating dowels fitted to the crankcase and remove them for safe-keeping if they are loose.

**3** Remove the circlip securing the pressure plate lifter inside the pressure plate and remove the lifter **(see illustrations)**.

**4** Remove the thrust washer, release bearing and pushrod end-piece from either the back of the pressure plate or the end of the input shaft **(see illustration)**. If required, withdraw the clutch pushrod right-hand half from the input shaft **(see illustration)** – if a magnet is not available, it will have to be poked through from the other side using the left-hand half of the pushrod, requiring removal of the front sprocket cover, or the engine will have to be tipped on its side (if it is out of the frame).

**5** Unstake the clutch nut using a suitable drift **(see illustration)**. To remove the clutch nut the input shaft must be locked using one of the following two methods:
a) *If the engine is in the frame, engage 1st gear and have an assistant hold the rear brake on hard with the rear tyre in firm contact with the ground.*
b) *Use the Suzuki service tool (Pt. No. 09920-34820).*
c) *If the engine is out of the frame, fit a suitable ring spanner around the*

*transmission output shaft end (where the front sprocket fits) and counter-hold the shaft while slackening the nut.*
d) *If the engine has been, or is going to be, disassembled, use piston holders, or blocks of wood under the pistons and a metal bar through the pistons pins, to prevent the engine turning.*

Unscrew the nut and remove the dished washer from the input shaft, noting which way round it fits **(see illustration)**.

**6** Remove the three screws securing the diaphragm spring holder and remove the holder, noting how it fits **(see illustration)**. Take care to use the correct size screwdriver when removing these screws as the heads are easily rounded off. Also make sure that the

screws are removed immediately after the clutch nut, as they are not strong enough to hold the pressure of the diaphragm springs without the nut and will stretch. It is advisable to order new screws in advance of disassembling the clutch and renew them as a matter of course, as their small size means they are easily damaged or stressed, even though it may not be apparent.

**7** Remove the two diaphragm springs, noting how they fit, followed by the pressure plate **(see illustrations 17.29c and b)**. If required, remove the spring seat from inside the pressure plate **(see illustration 17.29a)**.

**8** Pull the clutch centre and the clutch friction and plain plates off the shaft as an assembly **(see illustration)**. If required, screw two M6

17.4b . . . and if required the right-hand half of the pushrod

17.5a Unstake the clutch nut using a suitable drift . . .

**2**

17.5b . . . then unscrew it, using one of the locking methods described, and remove the washer

17.6 Remove the three screws (arrowed) and withdraw the diaphragm spring holder

17.8 Grasp the clutch centre and pull it off with the plates

**17.9 Withdraw the needle bearing and spacer from the centre of the housing . . .**

**17.10 . . . then remove the housing, noting how it engages with the primary drive gear**

**7.12 Turn the gear so the drive pin (A) is horizontal, then remove the circlip (B) and slide the gear and its washer(s) off the shaft**

**17.13a Measure the thickness of the friction plates . . .**

**17.13b . . . and the width of their tabs**

bolts into the threaded holes in the clutch centre and use them to pull the assembly off. Also remove the outer thrust washer from behind the clutch centre **(see illustration 17.24d)**.

**9** Withdraw the needle roller bearing and spacer from the centre of the clutch housing **(see illustration)**. It may be necessary to pull the clutch housing part-way out and then push it back in order to expose the bearing and spacer.

**10** Remove the clutch housing from the shaft, then remove the inner thrust washer **(see illustration and 17.23a)**. If required, the oil pump drive gear can be separated from the clutch housing by lifting it off the back of the primary driven gear **(see illustration 17.23b)**.

**11** If required for either inspection or renewal, remove the clutch friction and plain plates from the clutch centre, followed by the anti-

judder spring and spring seat, noting which way round they fit **(see illustrations 17.25a)**. Keep the friction and plain plates in their original order (there are different types of each plate – keeping them in order will avoid confusion on reassembly).

**12** If the engine is being completely disassembled or if the oil pump is being removed, turn the oil pump drive gear so that its drive pin is horizontal (this will prevent it from dropping out) **(see illustration)**. Remove the circlip from the end of the oil pump drive shaft, then remove the outer washer (where fitted) and the driven gear. Also remove the drive pin from the shaft, noting how it fits into the slot in the back of the gear, and the inner washer.

### Inspection

**13** After an extended period of service the clutch friction plates will wear and promote clutch slip. Measure the thickness of each friction plate and the width of their tabs using a vernier caliper **(see illustrations)**. If any plate has worn to or beyond the service limits given in the Specifications at the beginning of the Chapter, the friction plates must be renewed as a set. Also, if any of the plates smell burnt or are glazed, they must be renewed as a set.

**14** The plain plates should not show any signs of excess heating (bluing). Check for warpage using a surface plate and feeler gauges **(see illustration)**. If any plate exceeds the maximum permissible amount of warpage, or shows signs of bluing, all plain plates must be renewed as a set.

**15** On W and X models (600 and 750), the total thickness of the assembled friction and plain plates should be measured. Wipe the oil off the plates, then assemble them in order on a surface plate (or a piece of plate glass). Place a 5 kg weight on the assembled plates, then measure their thickness **(see illustration)**. If it is less (or greater) than specified, and the thickness of each individual friction plate and warpage of each plain plate is within specifications, some of the No. 1 plain plates must be replaced with No. 2

**17.14 Check the plain plates for warpage**

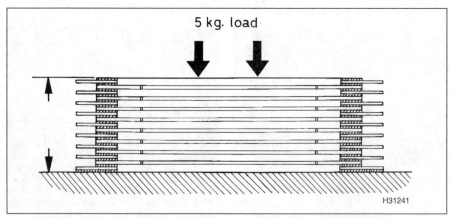

5 kg. load

H31241

**17.15 Measure the total thickness of the assembled and weighted plates as shown**

17.16 Measure the height of the inner edge of each diaphragm spring

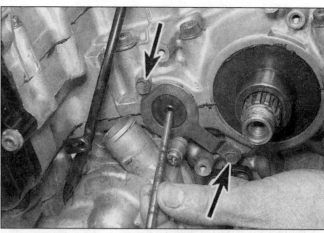

17.19 Withdraw the pushrod and check it is straight. The oil seal retainer plate is secured by two bolts (arrowed)

plates (which are slightly thicker), or vice versa if the total is too thick – (on 600X models, a No. 3 plain plate, which is thinner than the No. 1 plate, is available) to bring the overall thickness to that specified. Up to four (750W and X models) or three (600W models) of the thicker plain plates can be used, and they should be the third to seventh (750) or third to sixth (600) plain plates fitted as counted from the outside (see Table). On 600X models, one of the thicker plates can be used, and it should be the sixth or seventh plate as counted from the outside, and one of the thinner plates can be used, and it should be the first or second plate as counted from the outside.

16 Lay each diaphragm spring in turn on a surface plate (or a piece of plate glass) and measure the height of the inner edge of the spring (see illustration). Renew the spring if the height measured is less than the limit specified at the beginning of the Chapter.

17 Inspect the clutch assembly for burrs and indentations on the edges of the protruding tangs of the friction plates and/or slots in the edge of the housing with which they engage. Similarly check for wear between the inner tongues of the plain plates and the slots in the clutch centre. Wear of this nature will cause clutch drag and slow disengagement during gear changes, since the plates will snag when the pressure plate is lifted. With care, a small amount of wear can be corrected by dressing with a fine file, but if this is excessive the worn components should be renewed.

18 Check the pressure plate, release bearing, pushrod end piece and thrust washer for signs of roughness, wear or damage, and renew any parts necessary as necessary. Check that the pushrod is straight by rolling it on a flat surface.

19 To access the pushrod oil seal, remove the left-hand fairing side panel (see Chapter 8) and displace the coolant reservoir (see Chapter 3). Unscrew the gearchange lever linkage arm pinch bolt and remove the arm from the shaft, noting any alignment marks (see illustration 18.2). If no marks are visible, make your own before removing the arm so that it can be correctly aligned with the shaft on installation. Disconnect the speedometer sensor wiring connector (see illustration 18.3). Unscrew the bolts securing the front sprocket cover and remove the cover (see illustration 18.4). Note the position of the dowels and remove them if loose. Withdraw the clutch pushrod left-hand half and check it for straightness by rolling it on a surface plate (see illustration). Check the pushrod oil seal for signs of leakage and renew it if necessary. Unscrew the bolts securing the oil seal retainer plate and remove the plate (on T and V models, first remove the front sprocket (see Chapter 6). On W and X models, it may also be necessary to remove the sprocket, depending on whether your tools allow you to access the lower bolt which is partially obscured by the chain). Lever out the old seal using a screwdriver, then drive a new seal squarely into place. Install the retainer plate and where removed, the engine sprocket (see Chapter 6).

20 Inspect the clutch release mechanism whilst the engine sprocket cover is removed (see illustration). Check the mechanism for smooth operation and any signs of wear or damage. Unscrew the two bolts securing the mechanism to the cover and remove it for cleaning and re-greasing if required (see illustration). Apply a dab of grease to the pushrod end (see illustration 18.7b).

### Installation

21 Remove all traces of old gasket from the crankcase and clutch cover surfaces.

22 If removed, slide the inner washer onto the oil pump drive shaft, then fit the drive pin into its hole in the shaft, making sure it is

| | No. 1 plain plate | No. 2 plain plate | No. 3 plain plate | Total plates |
|---|---|---|---|---|
| GSX-R600W | 5 to 8 plates | 3 to 0 plates | | 8 |
| GSX-R600X | 7 or 8 plates | 1 or 0 plates | 1 or 0 plates | 8 |
| GSX-R750W | 5 to 8 plates | 4 to 1 plates | | 9 |
| GSX-R750X | 5 to 8 plates | 4 to 1 plates | | 9 |

17.20a Check the release mechanism for damage and smooth operation

17.20b The mechanism is secured in the cover by the two bolts (arrowed)

2

**17.22a Fit the inner washer . . .**

**17.22b . . . and slide the drive pin into the shaft . . .**

**17.22c . . . then fit the gear onto the drive pin . . .**

**17.22d . . . and secure the assembly with the circlip**

**17.23a Slide the inner thrust washer onto the shaft with its flat side facing out**

central **(see illustrations)**. Locate the oil pump driven gear onto the shaft so that the drive pin locates into the slot in the back of the gear, then install the outer washer (where fitted) and secure the assembly with the circlip, making sure it is properly seated in its groove **(see illustrations)**.

**23** Slide the inner thrust washer, with its flat surface facing out, onto the end of the input shaft **(see illustration)**. If removed, fit the oil pump drive gear onto the primary driven gear on the back of the clutch housing, making sure the shouldered inner section faces the housing and the flat side faces the engine **(see illustrations)**.

**24** Lubricate the needle roller bearing and spacer with clean engine oil. Slide the clutch housing onto the shaft, making sure it engages correctly with the teeth on the primary drive gear and the oil pump driven gear, then support it in position and slide the spacer and needle roller bearing onto the shaft and into the middle of the housing **(see illustrations)**. Slide the outer thrust washer onto the shaft **(see illustration)**.

**25** Install the spring seat and anti-judder spring onto the clutch centre **(see illustration)**, noting that the anti-judder spring must be fitted the correct way round, with its outer edge raised off the spring seat **(see illustration)**. Slide the clutch centre onto the shaft splines **(see illustration)**.

**26** On T and V models, before building up the plates in the clutch housing, identify the single

**17.23b Fit the oil pump drive gear onto the back of the housing . . .**

**17.23c . . . making sure it is the correct way round**

**17.24a Engage the clutch housing with the primary drive and oil pump driven gears . . .**

**17.24b . . . then slide the spacer . . .**

**17.24c . . . and the needle bearing into the centre of the housing . . .**

17.24d ... followed by the outer thrust washer

17.25a Install the spring seat and the spring ...

17.25b ... making sure they are correctly fitted ...

friction plate that has a larger internal diameter than the rest, and the one (600 models) or two (750 models) plain plates that are slightly thicker than the rest. The friction plate with the larger internal diameter is fitted first and locates over the anti-judder spring and seat. The thicker plain plate(s) is fourth out of eight to be fitted on 600 models, and are fifth and sixth out of nine to be fitted on 750 models.

27 On W and X models, before building up the plates in the clutch housing, identify the single friction plate that has a larger internal diameter than the rest, and on 600X models the friction plate that has a green paint mark on it (original equipment only). The friction plate with the larger internal diameter is fitted first and locates over the anti-judder spring and seat. On 600X models, the painted friction plate fits last, and its tabs locate in the shallow slots in the housing, rather than in the deep slots with the rest of the friction plates. Also refer to Step 15 and identify the different plain plates and fit them as described.

28 Coat each clutch plate with clean engine, then build up the plates in the clutch housing, starting with the friction plate (with the larger internal diameter), then a plain plate and alternating friction and plain plates (not forgetting the order) until all are installed (see illustrations).

29 If removed, install the diaphragm spring seat into the pressure plate (see illustration). Fit the pressure plate into the clutch centre, then install the two diaphragm springs, making sure their higher inner edges face out (see illustrations).

17.25c ... then slide the clutch centre on the shaft

17.28a Install the first friction plate with the larger internal diameter ...

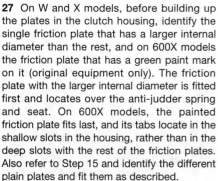

17.28b ... followed by a plain plate ...

17.28c ... followed by a standard friction plate

**2**

17.29a Fit the diaphragm spring seat into the pressure plate if removed ...

17.29b ... then fit the pressure plate into the clutch centre

17.29c Fit the two diaphragm springs with their raised inner edges facing out

17.30a Fit the spring holder into the pressure plate . . .

17.30b . . . and secure it with the new screws

17.31a Install the dished washer with its raised inner edge facing out . . .

17.31b . . . then fit the clutch nut . . .

17.31c . . . and tighten it to the specified torque setting

**30** Install the diaphragm spring holder and secure it with the three screws, preferably using new ones **(see illustrations)**. Tighten the screws evenly, taking care not to strip their threads as the screws are very small. Proceed to the next step immediately, as the screws are not strong enough to secure the spring holder against the pressure of the springs without the clutch nut, and consequently will stretch.

**31** Fit the dished washer, with its raised inner edge facing out, onto the shaft, then install the clutch nut and, using the method employed on removal to lock the input shaft, tighten the nut to the torque setting specified at the beginning of the Chapter **(see illustrations)**. Stake the nut against the shaft using a punch to secure it **(see illustration)**.

**32** If removed, lubricate the pushrod right-hand half and slide it into the end of the input shaft **(see illustration)**. Lubricate both sides of the release bearing and thrust washer with clean engine oil, then fit them onto the end of the pushrod end-piece and slide the assembly into the shaft as well **(see illustrations)**.

**33** Install the pressure plate lifter and secure it with the circlip, making sure it is properly seated in its groove and that its sharper edge faces out **(see illustrations)**.

**34** Apply a smear of sealant (Suzuki Bond 1207B or equivalent) to the area around the

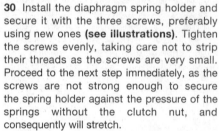
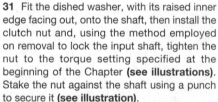

17.31d Stake the nut against the shaft using a punch

17.32a Slide in the pushrod if removed . . .

17.32b . . . then fit the release bearing and thrust washer onto the pushrod end-piece . . .

17.32c . . . and slide that into the shaft

17.33a Install the pressure plate lifter . . .

17.33b . . . and secure it with its circlip

17.34a Apply the sealant to the crankcase joints (arrowed)

17.34b Make sure the gasket locates correctly over the dowels (arrowed)

crankcase joints as shown (see illustration). If removed, insert the clutch cover dowels into the crankcase, then place a new gasket onto the crankcase, making sure it locates correctly over the dowels (see illustration).

35 Install the clutch cover and tighten its bolts evenly in a criss-cross sequence, making sure that new sealing washers are used on the front three bolts (see illustration 17.2).

36 Refill the engine with oil (see Chapter 1). Install the fairing side panels (see Chapter 8).

37 Adjust the clutch release mechanism, followed by the clutch cable as described in Chapter 1.

## 18 Clutch cable – removal and installation

### Removal

1 Remove the left-hand fairing side panel (see Chapter 8) and displace the coolant reservoir (see Chapter 3).

2 Unscrew the gearchange linkage arm pinch bolt and remove the arm from the shaft, noting any alignment marks (see illustration). If no marks are visible, make your own before removing the arm so that it can be correctly aligned with the shaft on installation.

3 Trace the wiring from the speedometer

sensor on the front sprocket cover and disconnect it at the connector (see illustration).

4 Unscrew the bolts securing the sprocket cover to the crankcase and move the cover aside (see illustration). On W and X models, note the rubber bushing for the gearchange shaft and remove it from the cover if required.

5 Bend out the tab in the cable retainer on the end of the release mechanism arm, then lift the arm and slip the cable end out of the retainer, noting how it fits (see illustrations). Slacken the cable adjuster locknut on the top of the cover, then unscrew the adjuster and withdraw the cable from the cover (see illustration).

6 Thread the clutch adjuster at the lever end fully into the lever bracket, then back it off

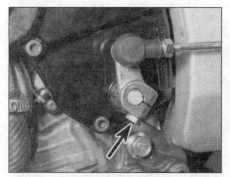

18.2 Unscrew the bolt (arrowed) and slide the arm off the shaft

18.3 Disconnect the speedometer sensor wiring connector

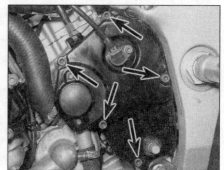

18.4 Sprocket cover bolts (arrowed)

18.5a Bend out the tab on the retainer . . .

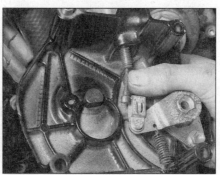

18.5b . . . and free the cable end from the arm

18.5c Slacken the locknut (arrowed), then thread the adjuster out of the cover and withdraw the cable

2

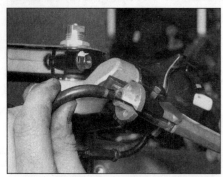

**18.6a With the slots in the adjuster and bracket aligned, pull the outer cable out of the adjuster, . . .**

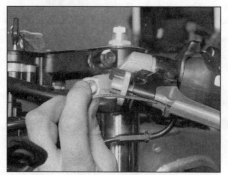

**18.6b . . . the inner cable out of the bracket . . .**

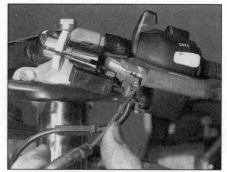

**18.6c . . . and the cable end out of the lever**

until its slot aligns with that in the lever bracket **(see illustration)**. Pull the outer cable end from the socket in the adjuster and release the inner cable from the lever **(see illustrations)**. Remove the cable from the machine, noting its routing.

> **HAYNES HiNT** *Before removing the cable from the bike, tape the lower end of the new cable to the upper end of the old cable. Slowly pull the lower end of the old cable out, guiding the new cable down into position. Using this method will ensure the cable is routed correctly.*

### Installation

**7** Installation is the reverse of removal, making sure the cable is correctly routed. Bend in the retainer to secure the cable end **(see illustration)**. Before installing the cover, check the clutch release actuating mechanism for smooth operation and any signs of wear or damage **(see illustration 17.20a)**. Unscrew the two bolts securing the mechanism to the cover and remove it for cleaning and re-greasing if required **(see illustration 17.20b)**. Apply a dab of grease to the pushrod end **(see illustration)**.
**8** Make sure the dowels are either in the crankcase or the sprocket cover. Install the cover, making sure the speedometer

rotor fits properly into the sensor and the dowels locate correctly, and tighten its bolts **(see illustration)**. On W and X models, if removed, fit the rubber bushing for the gearchange shaft into the cover **(see illustration)**.
**9** Slide the gearchange linkage arm onto the shaft, aligning the marks, and tighten the pinch bolt **(see illustration 18.2)**.
**10** Reconnect the speedometer sensor wiring connector **(see illustration 18.3)**.
**11** Adjust the amount of clutch lever freeplay (see Chapter 1).

---

### 19 Gearchange mechanism – removal, inspection and installation

**Note:** *The gearchange mechanism can be removed with the engine in the frame.*

### Removal

**1** Remove the fairing side panels (see Chapter 8) and the clutch (see Section 17). Displace the coolant reservoir (see Chapter 3).
**2** Shift the transmission into neutral. Unscrew the gearchange linkage arm pinch bolt and remove the arm from the shaft, noting any alignment marks **(see illustration 18.2)**. If no marks are visible, make your own before removing the arm so that it can be correctly aligned with the shaft on installation.
**3** Trace the wiring from the speedometer sensor on the front sprocket cover and disconnect it at the connector **(see illustration 18.3)**.
**4** Unscrew the bolts securing the sprocket cover to the crankcase and move the cover aside **(see illustration 18.4)**. On W and X models, note the rubber bushing for the gearchange shaft and remove it from the cover if required. The cover can be secured out of the way with the clutch cable still connected.
**5** Remove the circlip from the left-hand end

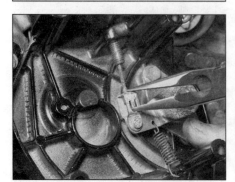

**18.7a Bend up the tab on the retainer to secure the cable end**

**18.7b Smear some grease onto the end of the pushrod**

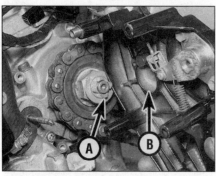

**18.8a Make sure the rotor (A) fits correctly into the sensor (B)**

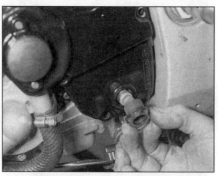

**18.8b Where fitted and if removed, fit the rubber bush for the gearchange shaft**

19.5 Remove the circlip and washer

19.6 Withdraw the gearchange shaft from the engine, noting how it fits

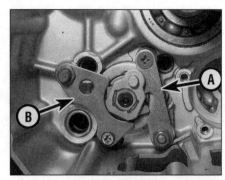

19.7 Front cam guide plate (A), rear guide plate (B)

of the gearchange shaft and slide off the washer (see illustration).
6 Working on the right-hand side of the engine, note how the gearchange shaft centralising spring ends fit on each side of the locating pin in the crankcase, and how the eye in the shaft arm locates over the roller on the selector cam, then withdraw the gearchange shaft from the right-hand side of the engine (see illustration). If the washer does not come with the shaft, retrieve it from the engine. Remove the roller from the pin on the cam for safekeeping (see illustration 19.18b).
7 Remove the screw and the nut securing the front cam guide plate and the screw and locating pin securing the rear guide plate to the crankcase and remove them along with the spacers (one for each plate) (see illustration). A thread-locking compound is used on these screws during assembly, which may necessitate the use of an impact driver for removal.
8 The pawls are spring-loaded in the selector cam. Before withdrawing the cam, place a finger over each pawl to prevent them from springing out when the cam is withdrawn (see illustration). Remove the cam along with the pawls. Place the cam on a bench and carefully release the pawls, noting how they and their pins and springs fit in the cam.

9 Note how the stopper arm roller locates in the neutral detent in the stopper plate. If the selector drum is to be removed, or if required, remove the stopper arm return spring, noting how it fits, then unscrew the stopper arm stud and remove the arm and washer (see illustrations).

## Inspection

10 Inspect the shaft centralising spring for fatigue, wear or damage. If any is found, it must be renewed. It is retained on the shaft by a circlip (see illustration 19.18a). Similarly check the stopper arm return spring.

11 Check the gearchange shaft for straightness and damage to the splines, and check for wear on the eye in the arm and the roller on the selector cam pin. If the shaft is bent you can attempt to straighten it, but if the splines or eye are damaged or worn the shaft must be renewed.
12 Check the condition of the shaft oil seal in the left-hand side of the crankcase. If it is damaged or deteriorated it must be renewed. Lever out the old seal and press or drive the new one squarely into place, with its lip facing inward, using a seal driver or suitable socket (see illustrations).
13 Check that the gearchange shaft needle bearings rotate freely and have no sign of

19.8 Press each pawl in and carefully withdraw the cam

19.9a Remove the return spring (arrowed), noting how it fits . . .

19.9b . . . then unscrew the stud (arrowed) and remove the arm

19.12a Lever out the old seal . . .

19.12b . . . and press the new one into place

**19.13 Check the bearings (arrowed) – there is another one behind the oil seal (see illustration 19.12a)**

**19.15a Slide the arm and washer onto the stud and install the assembly . . .**

**19.15b . . . then fit the return spring**

freeplay between them and the crankcase **(see illustration)**. Renew the bearings if necessary. To renew them, first remove the oil seal (see Step 12), then draw them out of the crankcase, noting that once removed they cannot be re-used. Drive the new bearings into place, making sure they enter squarely. Refer to *Tools and Workshop Tips* in the Reference Section for more information on bearings and how to remove and install them.

**14** Check the selector cam, pawls, pins and springs for wear and damage. Renew them if defects are found. Also check the stopper arm roller and the detents in the stopper plate for wear or damage. Check that the arm is a light fit on the bolt with no appreciable freeplay between them.

### Installation

**15** Slide the stopper arm and its washer onto the stopper arm bolt, making sure the cutout in the arm will face the front when installed **(see illustration)**. Apply a suitable non-permanent thread locking compound to the bolt threads and tighten it securely **(see illustration 19.9b)**. Fit the return spring, making sure the ends locate correctly against the cutout in the arm and the crankcase **(see illustration)**, and locate the roller onto the neutral detent in the stopper plate **(see illustration 19.9a)**.

**16** Install the springs, pins and pawls in the selector cam as shown **(see illustrations)**. Make sure the rounded end of each pawl fits into the rounded cut-out in the cam, and that

the pins locate correctly in the cut-outs in the pawls, with the wider edge of the cut-out on the outside. It will be necessary to hold each pawl assembly in place while the cam is installed in the end of the selector drum **(see illustration)**. Install the selector cam with its roller pin positioned as shown so it will align with the eye in the gearchange shaft arm when it is installed **(see illustration 19.19a)**.

**17** Apply a suitable non-permanent thread locking compound to the front and rear cam guide plate screws, nut and locating pin, then install the plates, not forgetting the spacers between the plates and the engine on the screw mountings, and tighten the screws and nut securely, and the locating pin to the torque setting specified at the beginning of the Chapter **(see illustrations)**.

**19.16a Fit the spring into the hole . . .**

**19.16b . . . and the pin onto the spring . . .**

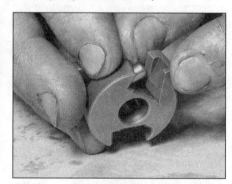

**19.16c . . . then locate the rounded end of the pawl in the cutout**

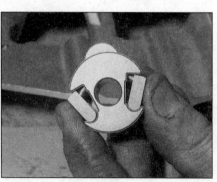

**19.16d Press the pawls in against the pins when installing the cam**

**19.17a Locate the spacer for the front plate . . .**

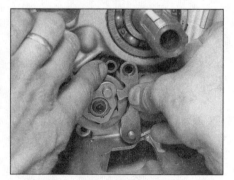

**19.17b . . . then position the plate . . .**

19.17c ... and fit the screw and nut

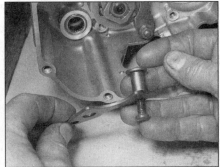

19.17d Fit the screw into the rear plate and slide the spacer on it ...

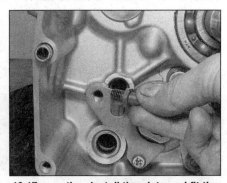

19.17e ... then install the plate and fit the locating pin

**18** If removed, slide the centralising spring onto the gearchange shaft and locate the spring ends each side of the tab on the arm. Fit the circlip, making sure it locates in its groove, then slide on the washer **(see illustration)**. Fit the roller onto the pin on the selector cam **(see illustration)**.

**19** Apply a smear of grease to the lip of the gearchange shaft seal in the left-hand side of the crankcase and smear clean engine oil over the gearchange shaft. Carefully guide the gearchange shaft into place, making sure the centralising spring ends locate correctly on each side of the pin in the crankcase, and locate the eye in the shaft arm over the roller on the selector cam **(see illustrations)**.

**20** Install the washer and circlip onto the left-

hand end of the gearchange shaft **(see illustrations)**.

**21** Make sure the dowels are either in the crankcase or the sprocket cover. Install the cover, making sure the speedometer rotor fits properly into the sensor and the dowels locate correctly, and tighten its bolts **(see illustration 18.8a)**. On W and X models, if removed, fit the rubber bushing for the gearchange shaft into the cover **(see illustration 18.8b)**.

**22** Slide the gearchange linkage arm onto the shaft, aligning the marks, and tighten the pinch bolt **(see illustration 18.2)**. Check that the mechanism works correctly

**23** Reconnect the speedometer sensor wiring connector **(see illustration 18.3)**.

**24** Install the clutch (see Section 17), the coolant reservoir (see Chapter 3) and the fairing side panels (see Chapter 8).

## 20 Starter clutch and idle/ reduction gear – removal, inspection and installation

**Note:** *The starter clutch and idle/reduction gear assembly can be removed with the engine in the frame.*

### Removal

**1** Remove the right-hand fairing side panel (see Chapter 8).

**2** Unscrew the bolts securing the

19.18a Make sure the return spring is correctly fitted and secured by the circlip

19.18b Fit the roller on the cam pin

19.19a Slide the shaft through ...

**2**

19.19b ... and locate the eye and return spring ends as shown

19.20a Slide on the washer ...

19.20b ... and fit the circlip

20.2 Idle/reduction gear cover bolts (arrowed) – note the bolt with the sealing washer (A)

20.3a Starter clutch cover bolts (arrowed) (W and X models shown) – note the bolt with the sealing washer (A)

idle/reduction gear cover to the starter clutch cover, noting the sealing washer fitted on the lower front bolt, and remove the cover **(see illustration)**. Remove the gasket and discard it. Note the position of the locating dowels and remove them for safe-keeping if loose. Remove the wave washer and outer thrust washer from the starter No. 1 idle/reduction gear shaft, then remove the gear with its bearing, noting which way round the gear fits, the inner thrust washer and the shaft **(see illustrations 20.16d, c, b and a)**.

3 Now unscrew the bolts securing the starter clutch cover, noting the sealing washer fitted on the upper front bolt **(see illustration)**. On T and V models, the cover has four bolts and one locating dowel, while on W and X models the cover has five bolts and two dowels. Remove the cover, being prepared to catch any residual oil. Remove the gasket and discard it. Note the position of the dowel(s) and remove it/them for safe-keeping if loose. Remove the wave washer from the starter No. 2 idle/reduction gear shaft, then withdraw the shaft and remove the gear, noting which way round it fits **(see illustration)**.

4 Before proceeding further, the operation of the starter clutch can be checked while it is in situ. Check that the gear on the back of the clutch is able to rotate freely anti-clockwise as you look at it, but locks when rotated clockwise.

5 To remove the starter clutch bolt it is necessary to stop the starter clutch and crankshaft from turning using one of the following methods, then unscrew the bolt and slide the starter clutch and its thrust washer off the end of the crankshaft.

  a) *If the engine is in the frame, engage 1st gear and have an assistant hold the rear brake on hard with the rear tyre in firm contact with the ground.*

  b) *If the cylinder block has been removed, use a con-rod stopper or block of wood under the pistons.*

  c) *The Suzuki service tool (Pt. No. 09920-34830), or a home-made equivalent made from two strips of steel, with a bolt through one end of each strip, and bolted together in the middle, can be used (by inserting the bolts into the holes in the starter clutch) to stop the clutch from*

turning*(see illustration). On some W models, the starter clutch design was changed, as was the special tool, however its part number has remained the same, so it is necessary to quote your engine number if ordering the tool. The engine numbers affected are R731-100043 to 101067, and R732-100007 to 100700. The tool for these models also requires spacers, Pt. No. 09180-08140.*

6 Clean all old gasket and sealant from the cover and crankcase.

### Inspection

7 With the clutch face down on a workbench, check that the gear rotates freely in a clockwise direction and locks against the rotor in an anti-clockwise direction **(see illustration)**. If it doesn't, renew the starter clutch.

8 Withdraw the starter driven gear from the starter clutch. If it appears stuck, rotate it clockwise as you withdraw it to free it from the starter clutch.

9 Check the bearing surface of the starter driven gear hub and the condition of the

20.3b Remove the No. 2 idle/reduction gear assembly

20.5 Unscrewing the starter clutch bolt using the home-made tool described

20.7 With the clutch face down, the gear should rotate freely clockwise and should lock when turned anti-clockwise

**20.9 Check the condition of the rollers (arrowed) and the corresponding surface on the gear hub**

**20.12 Fit the bearing and gear into the clutch**

**20.13a Slide on the thrust washer and clutch . . .**

rollers inside the clutch body **(see illustration)**. If the bearing surface shows signs of excessive wear or the rollers are damaged, marked or flattened at any point, they should be renewed.

**10** Remove the needle roller bearing from the centre of the starter clutch and from the centre of the No. 1 idle/reduction gear. Check the condition of the rollers and the cages and renew the bearing if any wear or damage is found, or if any roughness or stiffness is detected when the components are assembled and turned.

**11** Examine the teeth of the starter idle/reduction gears and the corresponding teeth of the starter driven gear and starter motor drive shaft. Renew the gears and/or starter motor if worn or chipped teeth are discovered on related gears. Also check the idle/reduction gear shafts for damage, and check that the gears are not a loose fit on the shafts. Renew the shafts if necessary.

### Installation

**12** Lubricate the needle bearing and the hub of the starter driven gear with clean engine oil, then install the bearing and the gear into the clutch, rotating the gear clockwise as you do

**20.13b . . . making sure the scribe line aligns with the punchmark . . .**

so to spread the rollers and allow the hub of the gear to enter **(see illustration)**.

**13** Slide the thrust washer and the starter clutch assembly onto the end of the crankshaft, aligning the scribe line on the clutch with the punchmark on the crankshaft end **(see illustrations)**. Apply a little clean engine oil to the starter clutch bolt and its washer, then install the bolt **(see illustration)**. Using the method employed on removal to stop the clutch from turning, tighten the bolt to the torque setting specified

**20.13c . . . then install the bolt with its washer . . .**

at the beginning of the Chapter **(see illustration)**.

**14** Lubricate the No. 2 idle/reduction gear shaft with clean engine oil and slide it through the gear. Install the idle/reduction gear, making sure the smaller (14T) pinion faces inwards and meshes correctly with the teeth of the starter driven gear, and fit the wave washer onto the end of the shaft **(see illustration)**.

**15** Apply a smear of sealant (Suzuki Bond 1207B or equivalent) to the area around the

**2**

**20.13d . . . and tighten it to the specified torque**

**20.14 Install the No. 2 idle/reduction gear and shaft, not forgetting the wave washer (arrowed)**

20.15a  Apply some sealant to the crankcase joints (arrowed) . . .

20.15b . . . then locate the gasket onto the dowels (arrowed) . . .

20.15c . . . and install the cover

crankcase joints as shown **(see illustration)**. If removed, insert the dowel(s) in the crankcase, then install the starter clutch cover using a new gasket, making sure it locates correctly onto the dowel(s) **(see illustrations)**. Tighten the cover bolts evenly in a criss-cross sequence, making sure the sealing washer is installed on the upper front bolt **(see illustration 20.3a)**.

**16** Lubricate the No. 1 idle/reduction gear shaft with clean engine oil and fit it into its bore in the crankcase, then slide on the inner thrust washer **(see illustrations)**. Lubricate the needle bearing and slide it into the gear, then slide the gear onto the shaft, making sure the smaller (14T) pinion faces inwards and meshes correctly with the teeth of the No. 2 gear outer pinion, and the larger pinion

meshes with the starter motor drive shaft **(see illustration)**. Fit the outer thrust washer followed by the wave washer onto the end of the shaft **(see illustration)**.

**17** If removed, insert the dowels in the crankcase, then install the idle/reduction gear cover using a new gasket, making sure it locates correctly onto the dowels **(see illustrations)**. Tighten the cover bolts evenly in a criss-cross sequence, making sure the sealing washer is installed on the lower front bolt **(see illustration 20.2)**.

**18** Check the engine/transmission oil level and top up if necessary (see *Daily (pre-ride) checks*).

**19** Install the right-hand fairing side panel (see Chapter 8).

## 21 Oil sump, strainer and pressure regulator – removal, inspection and installation

**Note:** *The oil sump, strainer and pressure regulator can be removed with the engine in the frame. If work is being carried out with the engine removed ignore the preliminary steps.*

### Removal

**1** Remove the exhaust system (see Chapter 4).

**2** Drain the engine oil (see Chapter 1).

**3** Unscrew the sump bolts, slackening them evenly in a criss-cross sequence to prevent

20.16a  Fit the shaft into its bore . . .

20.16b . . . then slide on the inner thrust washer

20.16c  Fit the bearing into the gear and the gear onto the shaft . . .

20.16d . . . then fit the outer thrust washer and the wave washer

20.17a  Locate the gasket onto the dowels (arrowed) . . .

20.17b . . . then install the cover

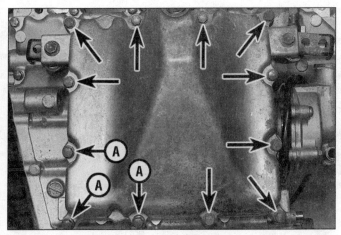

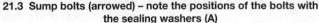

21.3 Sump bolts (arrowed) – note the positions of the bolts with the sealing washers (A)

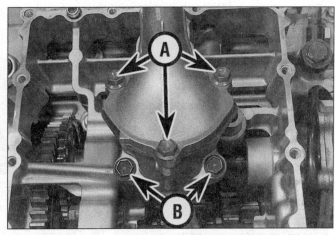

21.4 Pick-up tube bolts (A), strainer housing bolts (B)

distortion, and remove the sump (see illustration). Note the position of the bolts with the sealing washers. Discard the gasket as a new one must be used. Remove the two locating dowels from either the sump or the crankcase, if loose.

4 To access the oil strainer, unscrew the three bolts securing the oil pick-up tube to the strainer housing and remove the tube, the gasket and the strainer (see illustration). Discard the gasket as a new one must be used.

5 To remove the complete strainer housing, unscrew the two bolts securing the housing to the underside of the crankcase (see illustration 21.4). Discard the O-ring as a new one must be used.

6 If required, unscrew the oil pressure regulator from inside the sump and remove it (see illustration).

7 Remove all traces of gasket from the sump and crankcase mating surfaces.

### Inspection

8 Clean the sump, making sure all the oil passages are free of any debris.

9 Make sure the oil strainer is clean and remove any debris caught in the mesh, using compressed air if available. Inspect the strainer for any signs of wear or damage and renew it if necessary.

10 Clean the pressure regulator, and check that the plunger moves freely in its body. Inspect the pressure regulator for signs of wear or damage and renew it if necessary.

### Installation

11 Install the oil pressure regulator and tighten it to the torque setting specified at the beginning of the Chapter (see illustration 21.6).

12 To install the strainer housing, use a new O-ring and smear it with clean engine oil, then tighten the bolts to the specified torque setting (see illustrations). If the engine is in the frame, it may be easier to locate the O-ring on the housing, rather than hope it will stay in place on the engine while the housing is fitted (though the oil should help it stick).

13 To install the strainer, position it on the housing, then install the pick-up tube using a

new gasket and tighten its bolts to the specified torque setting (see illustrations). If the engine is in the frame, it may be easier to locate the gasket and the strainer on the pick-up tube, rather than hope they will stay in place on the housing while the tube is fitted.

14 If removed, fit the two locating dowels into the crankcase (if the engine has been removed and is positioned upside down on the work surface) or into the sump (if the

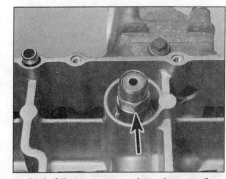

21.6 Oil pressure regulator (arrowed)

2

21.12a Fit a new O-ring into the groove . . .

21.12b . . . then install the housing and tighten the bolts to the specified torque

21.13a Fit the strainer . . .

21.13b . . . the gasket . . .

21.13c . . . and the pick-up tube

engine is in the frame). Lay a new gasket onto the crankcase or sump, making sure the holes in the gasket align correctly with the bolt holes, and that the gasket locates correctly onto the dowels **(see illustration)**.

**15** Position the sump on the crankcase and install the bolts, using new sealing washers on the three right-hand rear corner bolts **(see illustration and 21.3)**. Tighten the bolts evenly in a criss-cross pattern to the specified torque setting.

**16** Install the exhaust system (see Chapter 4), but do not yet fit the fairing side panels.

**17** Fill the engine with the correct type and quantity of oil as described in Chapter 1. Start the engine and check that there are no leaks around the sump, then install the fairing side panels (see Chapter 8).

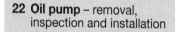

**22 Oil pump** – removal, inspection and installation

**Note:** *The oil pump can be removed with the engine in the frame.*

### Removal

**1** Remove the clutch (see Section 17). If not already done, turn the oil pump driven gear so that its drive pin is horizontal (this will prevent it from dropping out) **(see illustration 17.12)**. Remove the circlip from the end of the oil pump drive shaft, then remove the outer washer (where fitted) and the oil pump driven gear. Also remove the drive pin from the shaft, noting how it fits into the slot in the back of

the oil pump driven gear, and the inner washer.

**2** Unscrew the three bolts securing the pump to the crankcase, then remove the pump **(see illustrations)**. Remove the O-ring and discard it as a new one must be used.

### Inspection

**3** Inspect the pump body for any obvious damage such as cracks or distortion, and check that the shaft rotates freely and without any side-to-side play or excessive endfloat.

**4** Remove the screw on the inside of the pump cover and remove the cover **(see illustrations)**.

**5** Withdraw the pump drive shaft along with the inner rotor, then remove the outer rotor from the

21.14 Locate the gasket onto the dowels (arrowed) . . .

21.15 . . . then install the sump

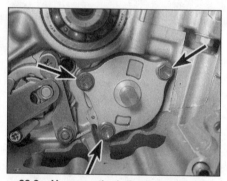

22.2a Unscrew the bolts (arrowed) . . .

22.2b . . . and withdraw the pump

22.4a Remove the screw (arrowed) . . .

22.4b . . . and lift off the cover

22.5 Withdraw the shaft and inner rotor, then remove the outer rotor

22.6 Look for scoring and wear, such as on this outer rotor

22.7 Measuring inner rotor tip-to-outer rotor clearance

pump body (see illustration). Note how the pin locates through the shaft and in the notches in the inner rotor, and how the punchmarks on the rotors face out towards the pump cover. Clean all the components in solvent.

6 Inspect the pump body and rotors for scoring and wear (see illustration). If any damage, scoring or uneven or excessive wear is evident, renew the pump (individual components are not available).

7 Measure the clearance between the inner rotor tip and the outer rotor with a feeler gauge and compare it to the maximum clearance listed in the specifications at the beginning of the Chapter (see illustration). If the clearance measured is greater than the maximum listed, renew the pump.

8 Measure the clearance between the outer rotor and the pump body with a feeler gauge and compare it to the maximum clearance listed in the specifications at the beginning of the Chapter (see illustration). If the clearance measured is greater than the maximum listed, renew the pump.

9 Check the pump drive and driven gears for wear or damage, and renew them as a set if necessary.

10 If the pump is good, make sure all the components are clean, then lubricate them with new engine oil.

11 Install the outer rotor into the pump body with the punchmark facing out towards the pump cover (see illustration).

12 Fit the drive pin into the pump drive shaft,

then slide the inner rotor onto the round end of the shaft, making sure the drive pin ends fit into the notches in the inside of the rotor, and therefore the punchmark faces out (see illustrations). Fit the shaft and inner rotor into the pump body (see illustration).

13 Install the cover (see illustration 22.4b), then apply a suitable non-permanent thread locking compound to the screw and tighten it securely (see illustration).

### Installation

14 Align the tabbed end of the pump drive shaft so that it will fit easily into the slot in the water pump shaft on installation. Fit a new O-ring onto the oil pump, then install the pump, wiggling the shaft if necessary to make it

22.8 Measuring outer rotor-to-body clearance

22.11 Fit the outer rotor into the body with the punchmark facing out

22.12a Fit the drive pin into the shaft . . .

**2**

22.12b . . . then slide the inner rotor onto the pin, locating the pin ends into the slots . . .

22.12c . . . then slide the shaft through the pump and fit the inner rotor in the outer rotor

22.13 Apply thread-lock to the cover screw

22.14a Fit the new O-ring into the grooves . . .

22.14b . . . then install the pump, making sure the tabbed end of the shaft is aligned as described

22.14c Apply a thread-lock to the pump bolts . . .

22.14d . . . and tighten them to the specified torque

locate in the water pump (see illustrations). Apply a suitable non-permanent thread locking compound to the threads of the pump bolts and tighten them to the torque setting specified at the beginning of the Chapter (see illustrations).

15 Slide the inner washer onto the oil pump drive shaft, then fit the drive pin into its hole in the shaft, making sure it is central (see illustrations 17.22a and b). Locate the oil pump driven gear onto the shaft so that the drive pin locates into the slot in the back of the gear, then install the outer washer (where fitted) and secure the assembly with the circlip, making sure it is properly seated in its groove (see illustrations 17.22c and d).

16 Install the clutch (see Section 17).

## 23 Crankcases – separation and reassembly

Note: *When the engine is upside down, referrals to the right and left-hand ends or sides of the transmission shafts or components are made as though the engine is the correct way up. Therefore the right-hand end of a shaft or side of a crankcase will actually be on your left as you look down onto the underside of the crankcase assembly.*

### Separation

1 To access the transmission shafts and selector drum and forks, the lower crankcase must be separated from the middle crankcase. To access the crankshaft, connecting rods and bearings, the lower crankcase must be separated from the middle crankcase and the transmission shafts removed, then the middle crankcase must be separated from upper the crankcase.

2 To enable the crankcases to be separated, the engine must be removed from the frame (see Section 5).

### Lower crankcase

3 Before the lower crankcase can be separated, remove the oil sump and the oil strainer housing (see Section 21). If the lower crankcase is being separated for removal of the transmission shafts, remove the clutch (see Section 17). If it is being separated to access

the selector drum and forks, the clutch can be left in situ, though the cover must be removed, and it is advisable to remove the clutch itself for ease of installation. If the selector drum and forks are being removed, first remove the gearchange mechanism (see Section 19) and the neutral switch (see Chapter 9).

4 If the lower crankcase is being separated as part of a complete engine overhaul, remove the oil cooler, then unscrew the bolts securing the cooler base and detach it from the crankcase. Discard the gasket as a new one must be used. Also remove the oil and water pumps (see Section 22 and Chapter 3 respectively), the oil pressure regulator (see Section 21), the gearchange mechanism (see Section 19), and the neutral and oil pressure switches (see Chapter 9). Note: *If required, all those components can be removed after the lower crankcase has been separated.* After separation, remove the selector drum and forks (see Section 27).

5 Slacken the clamp securing the coolant hose to the top of the water pump and detach the hose.

6 Unscrew the banjo bolts securing the oil pipe to the lower and upper crankcases and detach the hose (see illustration). Discard the sealing washers as new ones must be used.

7 Unscrew the bolts securing the oil seal retainer plate and remove the plate (see illustration).

8 Unscrew the seven bolts in the upper crankcase, noting the positions of the bolts with sealing washers (see illustration). Note:

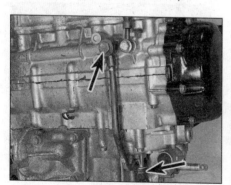

23.6 Unscrew the banjo bolts (arrowed) and remove the oil pipe

23.7 Unscrew the bolts (arrowed) and remove the plate

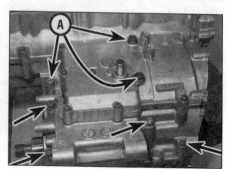

23.8 Unscrew the bolts (arrowed) in the upper and middle crankcase. The bolts (A) have copper sealing washers

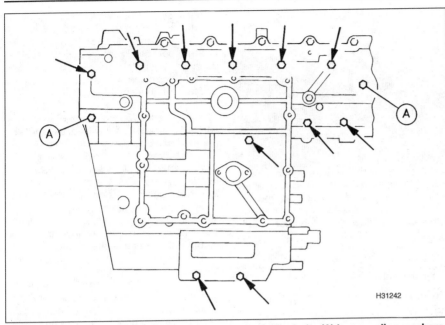

23.10 Unscrew the lower crankcase bolts (arrowed). The bolts (A) have sealing washers

23.11 Lift the lower crankcase up off the middle case

As each bolt is removed, store it in its relative position in a cardboard template of the crankcase halves. This will ensure all bolts are installed in the correct location on reassembly. Also note the washers fitted with certain bolts, and keep them with their bolts as different washers are used in different places.

**9** Turn the engine upside down. Support it on wood blocks if required.

**10** Unscrew the thirteen lower crankcase bolts, noting the positions of the bolts with sealing washers **(see illustration)**.

**11** Carefully lift the lower crankcase off the middle, using a soft-faced hammer to tap around the joint to initially separate the halves if necessary **(see illustration)**. **Note:** *If the halves do not separate easily, make sure all fasteners have been removed. Do not try and separate the halves by levering against the crankcase mating surfaces as they are easily scored and will leak oil.* The lower crankcase half will come away with the oil pump, water pump and gearchange mechanism (unless

previously removed), and the selector drum and forks, leaving the transmission shafts in the middle crankcase.

**12** Remove the three locating dowels from the crankcase if they are loose (they could be in either case), noting their locations **(see illustration 23.36)**. Also remove the five oil passage O-rings from the middle crankcase **(see illustration 23.37)**. Discard these as new ones must be used.

**Middle crankcase**

**13** Before the middle crankcase can be separated, remove the starter clutch cover (see Section 20), the alternator cover (see Chapter 9), the lower crankcase (see above) and the transmission shafts (see Section 25). If the engine is being completely overhauled, remove the following components:

a) Cam chain tensioner, cam chain and tensioner blade (Section 9).
b) Camshafts (Section 10).

c) Cylinder head and cam chain front blade (Section 11).
d) Cylinder block (Section 14).
e) Pistons (Section 15).
f) Starter clutch and starter idle/reduction gear assembly (Section 20).
g) Ignition pulse generator coil (Chapter 5).
h) Alternator (Chapter 9).
i) Starter motor (Chapter 9).

**Note:** *If the crankcases are being separated to remove the crankshaft leaving the connecting rods in place, the cylinder head and cylinder block can remain in situ. If this is the case, the connecting rods must be separated from the crankshaft before removing the crankshaft. However, if removal of the crankshaft with the connecting rod assemblies is intended, the cylinder head, cylinder block and pistons must be removed.*

**14** Unscrew the nine upper crankcase bolts **(see illustration)**. Note the position of the earth (ground) cable and the bolt with sealing washer.

**15** Turn the engine upside down. Support it on wood blocks if required.

**16** Unscrew the six middle crankcase bolts, noting the positions of the bolts with wiring clips **(see illustration)**.

**17** Working in a **reverse** of the tightening sequence shown and as cast into the casing **(see illustration)**, slacken each crankshaft journal bolt a little a time until they are all finger-tight, then remove the bolts. **Note:** *As*

**2**

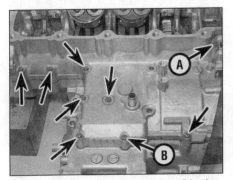

23.14 Unscrew the bolts (arrowed) in the upper crankcase. The bolt (A) has a sealing washer and (B) holds the earth lead

23.16 Unscrew the middle crankcase bolts (arrowed), noting the wiring clips (A) for the oil pressure switch

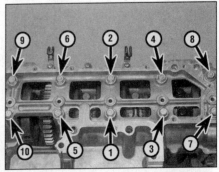

23.17 Crankshaft journal bolt TIGHTENING sequence. Slacken them in REVERSE order

23.18 Lift the middle crankcase up off the upper case

23.24 Make sure the dowels (arrowed) are installed in one of the cases. W and X models shown here – on T and V models the rearmost dowel is at the back of the case

each bolt is removed, store it in its relative position in a cardboard template of the crankcase halves. This will ensure all bolts are installed in the correct location on reassembly.
18 Carefully lift the middle crankcase off the upper, using a soft-faced hammer to tap around the joint to initially separate the halves if necessary (see illustration). Note: If the halves do not separate easily, make sure all fasteners have been removed. Do not try and separate the halves by levering against the crankcase mating surfaces as they are easily scored and will leak oil. The middle crankcase will come away by itself, leaving the crankshaft in the upper crankcase.
19 Remove the three locating dowels from the crankcase if they are loose (they could be in either case), noting their locations (see illustration 23.24).
20 Refer to Sections 24 to 30 for the removal and installation of the components housed within the crankcases.

### Reassembly

#### Middle crankcase

21 Remove all traces of sealant from the middle and upper crankcase mating surfaces.
22 Ensure that all components and their bearings are in place in the upper crankcase. Check that the crankshaft thrust bearings are correctly located, and that all oil jets have been installed, if removed.
23 Generously lubricate the crankshaft, particularly around the bearings, with clean engine oil, then use a rag soaked in high flash-point solvent to wipe over the gasket surfaces of both cases to remove all traces of oil.
24 If removed, fit the three locating dowels into the upper crankcase (see illustration).
25 Apply a small amount of suitable sealant (such as Suzuki Bond 1207B) to the mating surface of the middle crankcase (see illustration).
Caution: Do not apply an excessive amount of sealant as it will ooze out when the case halves are assembled and may obstruct oil passages. Do not apply the sealant on or too close to any of the bearing inserts or surfaces.
26 Check again that all components are in position, particularly that the bearing shells are still correctly located in the middle crankcase. Carefully fit the middle crankcase onto the upper crankcase, making sure the dowels all locate correctly into the middle crankcase (see illustration 23.18).
27 Check that the middle crankcase is correctly seated. Note: The crankcase halves should fit together without being forced. If the casings are not correctly seated, remove the middle crankcase and investigate the problem. Do not attempt to pull them together using the crankcase bolts as the casing will crack and be ruined.
28 Clean the threads of the 9 mm crankshaft journal bolts and insert them in their original locations (see illustration). Secure all bolts finger-tight at first, then tighten the bolts a little at a time and in the numerical sequence shown, and as marked on the casing, to the torque setting specified at the beginning of the Chapter (see illustration 23.17).
29 Turn the engine over. Install the nine upper crankcase bolts, not forgetting the sealing washer with the right-hand front bolt and the earth (ground) cable with the middle rear bolt (clean the terminal first) (see illustration 23.14). Tighten the bolts evenly and a little at a time to the specified torque setting, working from the middle outwards.
30 Turn the engine over. Clean the threads of the six middle crankcase bolts and insert them in their original locations, not forgetting the wiring clips (see illustration 23.16). Tighten the bolts evenly and a little at a time

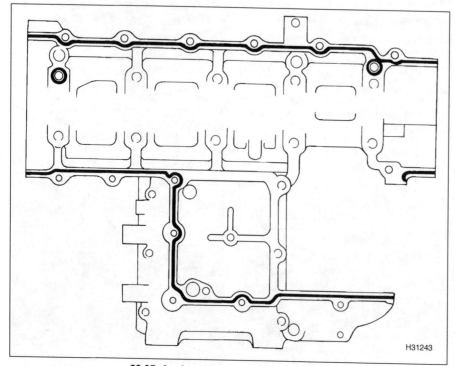

23.25 Apply sealant to the shaded areas

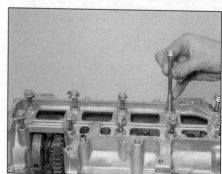

23.28 Install the crankshaft journal bolts

to the specified torque setting, working from the middle outwards.

**31** With all crankcase fasteners tightened, check that the crankshaft rotates smoothly and easily. If there are any signs of undue stiffness, tight or rough spots, or of any other problem, the fault must be rectified before proceeding further.

**32** Install all other removed assemblies according to Step 13.

### Lower crankcase

**33** Remove all traces of sealant from the crankcase mating surfaces.

**34** Ensure that all components and their bearings are in place in the middle and lower crankcases. Check that the transmission bearing locating pins and half-ring retainers are correctly located, and that the oil jet has been installed, if removed.

**35** Generously lubricate the transmission shafts and the selector drum and forks, particularly around the bearings, with clean engine oil, then use a rag soaked in high flash-point solvent to wipe over the gasket surfaces of both cases to remove all traces of oil.

**36** If removed, fit the three locating dowels into the middle crankcase **(see illustration)**. Make sure that the selector drum is in the neutral position.

**37** Fit new O-rings into the oil passage holes in the middle crankcase **(see illustration)**.

**38** Apply a small amount of suitable sealant (such as Suzuki Bond 1207B) to the mating surface of the lower crankcase **(see illustration)**.

23.36 Make sure the dowels (arrowed) are installed in one of the cases

23.37 Fit a new O-ring around each oil passage (arrowed)

*Caution: Do not apply an excessive amount of sealant as it will ooze out when the case halves are assembled and may obstruct oil passages. Do not apply the sealant on or too close to any of the bearing inserts or surfaces.*

**39** Check again that all components are in position. Carefully fit the lower crankcase onto the middle crankcase, making sure the selector forks locate correctly into their grooves in the transmission shaft gears **(see illustration)**. Make sure the dowels all locate correctly into the lower crankcase.

**40** Check that the lower crankcase is correctly seated. **Note:** *The crankcase halves should fit together without being forced. If the casings are not correctly seated, remove the lower crankcase and investigate the problem.*

*Do not attempt to pull them together using the crankcase bolts as the casing will crack and be ruined.*

**41** Check that the transmission shafts rotate freely and independently in neutral.

**42** Clean the threads of the thirteen lower crankcase bolts and insert them in their original locations, not forgetting the sealing washers with the specified bolts **(see illustration 23.10)**. Secure all bolts finger-tight only.

**43** Turn the engine over. Clean the threads of the seven upper crankcase bolts and insert them in their original locations, not forgetting the copper sealing washers with the specified bolts **(see illustration 23.8)**. Tighten all the bolts evenly and a little at a time to the specified torque setting, working from the middle outwards.

**44** Turn the engine over. Tighten the thirteen lower crankcase bolts evenly and a little at a time to the specified torque setting, working from the middle outwards **(see illustration 23.10)**.

**45** With all crankcase fasteners tightened, check that the crankshaft and transmission shafts rotate smoothly and easily. Rotate the selector drum by hand and select each gear in turn whilst rotating the input shaft. Check that all gears can be selected and that the shafts rotate freely in every gear. If there are any signs of undue stiffness, tight or rough spots, or of any other problem, the fault must be rectified before proceeding further.

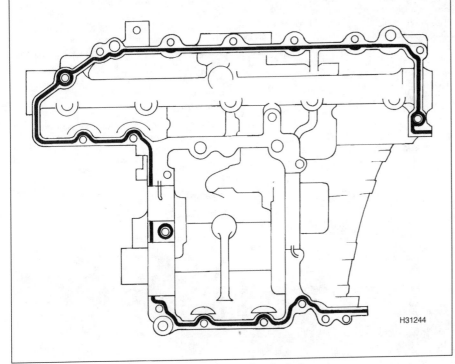

23.38 Apply sealant to the shaded areas

23.39 Make sure each selector fork locates in the groove in its gear pinion

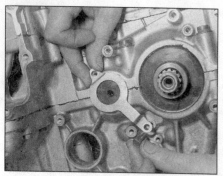

**23.46 Fit the retainer plate and tighten the bolts**

**23.47 Use new sealing washers on each side of each union**

**46** Install the oil seal retainer plate and tighten the bolts securely **(see illustration)**.
**47** Fit the oil pipe onto the lower and upper crankcases, using new sealing washers on each side of the unions, and tighten the banjo bolts to the specified torque settings **(see illustration)**.
**48** Install all other removed assemblies in the reverse of the sequence given in Steps 3 and 4. Use a new gasket on the oil cooler base.
**49** Fit the coolant hose from the cylinder block onto the top union on the water pump and tighten the clamp securely.

## 24 Crankcases – inspection and servicing

**1** After the crankcases have been separated, remove all the components housed within them (if not already done), referring to the relevant Sections of this Chapter and to Chapter 9 for the oil pressure and neutral switches. Remove the transmission oil jet from the lower crankcase using a flat-bladed screwdriver **(see illustration)**. Remove the alternator oil jet from the upper crankcase using a suitable socket or spanner **(see illustration)**. Unscrew the bolts securing the piston oil jets in the upper crankcase and remove the jets, noting how

they fit – there are four of them. Remove the O-rings and discard them as new ones should be used.
**2** The crankcases should be cleaned thoroughly with new solvent and dried with compressed air. All oil passages and oil jets should be blown out with compressed air.
**3** All traces of old gasket sealant should be removed from the mating surfaces. Minor damage to the surfaces can be cleaned up with a fine sharpening stone or grindstone.
*Caution: Be very careful not to nick or gouge the crankcase mating surfaces or oil leaks will result. Check the crankcases very carefully for cracks and other damage.*
**4** Small cracks or holes in aluminium castings may be repaired with an epoxy resin adhesive as a temporary measure. Permanent repairs can only be effected by argon-arc welding, and only a specialist in this process is in a position to advise on the economy or practical aspect of such a repair. If any damage is found that can't be repaired, renew the crankcase halves as a set.
**5** Damaged threads can be economically reclaimed by using a diamond section wire insert, of the Heli-Coil type, which is easily fitted after drilling and re-tapping the affected thread.
**6** Sheared studs or screws can usually be removed with screw extractors, which consist

of a tapered, left thread screw of very hard steel. These are inserted into a pre-drilled hole in the stud, and usually succeed in dislodging the most stubborn stud or screw.

**HAYNES HiNT** *Refer to Tools and Workshop Tips for details of installing a thread insert and using screw extractors.*

**7** Fit a new O-ring onto the base of each piston oil jet and smear it with clean engine oil. Push each jet into its bore in the upper crankcase, making sure the oil nozzle points up. Apply a suitable non-permanent thread locking compound to the jet bolts and tighten them securely. Fit the alternator oil jet in the upper crankcase and tighten it to the torque setting specified at the beginning of the Chapter. Screw the transmission oil jet into the lower crankcase.
**8** Install all other components and assemblies, referring to the relevant Sections of this Chapter and to Chapter 9, before reassembling the crankcase halves.

## 25 Transmission shafts – removal and installation

**Note:** *To remove the transmission shafts the engine must be removed from the frame and the lower crankcase separated.*
**Note:** *Referrals to the right and left-hand ends of the transmission shafts are made as though the engine is the correct way up, even though throughout this procedure it is upside down. Therefore the right-hand end of a shaft will actually be on your left as you look down onto the underside of the upper crankcase assembly.*

### Removal

**1** Separate the lower crankcase from the middle crankcase (see Section 23).
**2** Remove the clutch pushrod oil seal from the left-hand end of the input shaft **(see**

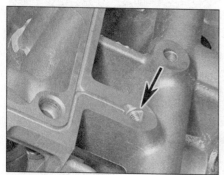

**24.1a Transmission oil jet location (arrowed)**

**24.1b Alternator oil jet**

**25.2a Remove the clutch pushrod oil seal . . .**

**25.2b** . . . and if required, the output shaft oil seal

**25.3  Lift each shaft out of the casing**

**25.4  Remove the half ring retainers (A) and the dowel pins (B)**

illustration). If required, remove the oil seal from the left-hand end of the output shaft, noting how it fits **(see illustration)**.

**3** Lift the output shaft and input shaft out of the crankcase, noting their relative positions in the crankcase and how they fit together **(see illustration)**. If they are stuck, use a soft-faced hammer and gently tap on the ends of the shafts to free them.

**4** Remove the ball bearing half-ring retainers and the needle bearing dowel pins from the middle crankcase, noting how they fit **(see illustration)**. If they are not in their slot or hole

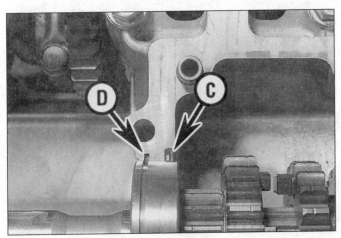

**25.7a  Locate the pin (A) in the hole (B),** . . .

**25.7b** . . . the bearing pin in its cutout (C), and the retainer in the groove (D)

in the crankcase, remove them from the bearings themselves on the shafts.

**5** If required, the shafts can be disassembled and inspected for wear or damage (see Section 26).

### Installation

**6** Install the ball bearing half-ring retainers into their slots in the upper crankcase half, and install the needle bearing dowels into their holes **(see illustration 25.4)**.

**7** Lower the input shaft into position in the middle crankcase, making sure the hole in the needle bearing engages correctly with the dowel, the ball bearing locating pin faces forward and locates in its recess, and the groove in the bearing engages correctly with the half-ring retainer **(see illustrations)**.

**8** Lower the output shaft into position in the middle crankcase, making sure the hole in the needle bearing engages correctly with the dowel, the ball bearing locating pin faces back and locates in its recess, and the groove in the bearing engages correctly with the half-ring retainer **(see illustration)**.

**9** Smear the lips of the new output shaft oil seal with grease. Slide the oil seal onto the left-hand end of the output shaft **(see illustration 25.2b)**. Smear the lips of the new clutch pushrod oil seal with grease. Fit the

seal against the left-hand end of the shaft **(see illustration 25.2a)**.

**10** Make sure both transmission shafts are correctly seated and their related pinions are correctly engaged.

*Caution: If the ball bearing locating pins and half-ring retainers or needle bearing dowel pins are not correctly engaged, the crankcase halves will not seat correctly.*

**11** Position the gears in the neutral position and check the shafts are free to rotate easily and independently (ie the input shaft can turn whilst the output shaft is held stationary) before proceeding further.

**12** Install the lower crankcase (see Section 23).

### 26  Transmission shafts – disassembly, inspection and reassembly

**Note:** *References to the right- and left-hand ends of the transmission shafts are made as though they are installed in the engine and the engine is the correct way up.*

**1** Remove the transmission shafts from the middle crankcase (see Section 25). Always

**25.8  Locate the bearing pin in its cutout (A) and the retainer in the groove (B)**

**2**

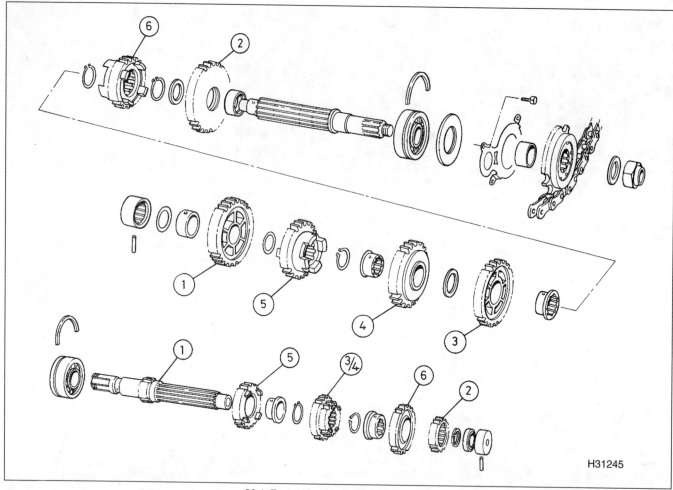

**26.1 Transmission shaft components**
*Numbers indicate gears*

disassemble the transmission shafts separately to avoid mixing up the components **(see illustration)**.

### Input shaft disassembly

 *When disassembling the transmission shafts, place the parts on a long rod or thread a wire through them to keep them in order and facing the proper direction.*

**2** Remove the needle bearing and oil seal from the left-hand end of the shaft **(see illustrations 26.20b and a)**.
**3** Reach behind the 6th gear pinion with circlip pliers, spread the circlip and slide it toward the 3rd/4th gear pinion **(see illustration 26.19e and d)**. Slide the 6th and 2nd gear pinions back to expose the snapring on the end of the shaft, then remove it and slide the 2nd and 6th gear pinions and the bush off the shaft **(see illustrations 26.19c, b and a, and 26.18b and a)**.

**4** Remove the circlip securing the combined 3rd/4th gear pinion, then slide the pinion off the shaft **(see illustration 26.17b and a)**.
**5** Remove the circlip securing the 5th gear pinion, then slide the 5th gear pinion and its bush off the shaft **(see illustrations 26.16c, b and a)**.
**6** The 1st gear pinion is integral with the shaft.

### Input shaft inspection

**7** Wash all of the components in clean solvent and dry them off.
**8** Check the gear teeth for cracking chipping, pitting and other obvious wear or damage. Any pinion that is damaged as such must be renewed.
**9** Inspect the dogs and the dog holes in the gears for cracks, chips, and excessive wear especially in the form of rounded edges. Make sure mating gears engage properly. Renew the paired gears as a set if necessary.
**10** Check for signs of scoring or bluing on the pinions, bushes and shaft. This could be caused by overheating due to inadequate

lubrication. Check that all the oil holes and passages are clear. Renew any damaged pinions or bushes.
**11** Check that each pinion moves freely on the shaft or bush but without undue freeplay. Check that each bush moves freely on the shaft but without undue freeplay.
**12** The shaft is unlikely to sustain damage unless the engine has seized, placing an unusually high loading on the transmission, or the machine has covered a very high mileage. Check the surface of the shaft, especially where a pinion turns on it, and renew the shaft if it has scored or picked up, or if there are any cracks. Damage of any kind can only be cured by renewal.
**13** Check the ball bearing for play or roughness, and that it is a tight fit on the shaft. Renew the bearing if it is worn, loose or damaged, using a bearing puller to remove it. Install the bearing using a press or a length of tubing which bears only on the bearing's inner race. Install the needle roller bearing onto the shaft, and check it for play or roughness. Renew the bearing if it is worn or damaged.

26.16a Slide on the 5th gear pinion . . .

26.16b . . . and its bush . . .

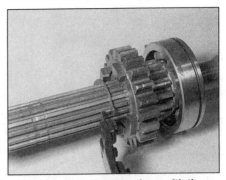

26.16c . . . and secure them with the circlip

26.17a Slide on the 3rd/4th gear pinion . . .

26.17b . . . and its circlip, positioning it beyond its groove toward the 3rd/4th gear pinion

26.18a Slide on the bush, aligning the oil holes . . .

**14** Check the needle bearing oil seal and renew it if it is damaged or deteriorated. Discard all the circlips and the snap-ring as new ones must be used.

## Input shaft reassembly

**15** During reassembly, apply molybdenum disulphide oil (a 50/50 mixture of molybdenum disulphide paste or grease and clean engine oil) to the mating surfaces of the shaft, pinions and bushes. When installing the circlips, do not expand the ends any further than is necessary. Install the stamped circlips so that their chamfered side faces the pinion it secures, ie so that its sharp edge faces the

direction of thrust load (see *correct fitting of a stamped circlip* illustration in Tools and Workshop Tips of the Reference section).
**16** Slide the 5th gear pinion, with its dogs facing away from the integral 1st gear, onto the left-hand end of the shaft **(see illustration)**. Slide the 5th gear bush onto the shaft so that it fits into the pinion **(see illustration)**. Install the circlip, making sure that it locates correctly in the groove in the shaft **(see illustration)**.
**17** Slide the combined 3rd/4th gear pinion onto the shaft, so that the larger (4th gear) pinion faces the 5th gear pinion dogs **(see illustration)**. Fit the circlip onto the shaft but

do not locate it in its groove – slide it past the groove and as far towards the 3rd/4th gear pinion as possible **(see illustration)**.
**18** Slide the 6th gear pinion splined bush onto the shaft, with its shouldered end facing the circlip and aligning the oil hole in the bush with that in the shaft **(see illustration)**. Slide the 6th gear pinion onto the bush, with its dogs facing the dogs on the 3rd gear pinion **(see illustration)**.
**19** Slide the 2nd gear pinion onto the shaft and secure it with the snap-ring, making sure it is properly seated in its groove **(see illustrations)**. Now slide the 6th and 2nd gear pinions along to expose the groove for the

**2**

26.18b . . . and slide the 6th gear pinion onto the bush

26.19a Slide on the 2nd gear pinion . . .

26.19b . . . and fit the snap-ring into its groove

26.19c Slide the 6th and 2nd gear pinions along . . .

26.19d . . . followed by the circlip . . .

26.19e . . . and fit it into its groove

26.20a Fit the oil seal . . .

26.20b . . . and the bearing

26.20c Check that the assembled shaft is as shown

3rd/4th gear pinion circlip, then move the circlip along the shaft and fit it into the groove **(see illustrations)**.

**20** Apply some grease to the needle bearing oil seal. Slide the oil seal and the needle bearing onto the shaft end **(see illustrations)**. Check that all components have been correctly installed **(see illustration)**.

### Output shaft disassembly

**21** Remove the needle bearing and the thrust washer from the right-hand end of the shaft **(see illustration 26.1)**.

**22** Slide the 1st gear pinion and its bush off the shaft, followed by the thrust washer and the 5th gear pinion.

**23** Remove the circlip securing the 4th gear pinion, then slide the pinion and its splined bush off the shaft, followed by the thrust washer, the 3rd gear pinion and its bush.

**24** Remove the circlip securing the 6th gear pinion, then slide the pinion off the shaft.

**25** Remove the circlip securing the 2nd gear pinion, then slide the thrust washer, the 2nd gear pinion and its bush off the shaft.

### Output shaft inspection

**26** Refer to Steps 7 to 14 above.

### Output shaft reassembly

**27** During reassembly, apply molybdenum disulphide oil (a 50/50 mixture of molyb-denum disulphide paste or grease and clean

engine oil) to the mating surfaces of the shaft, pinions and bushes. When installing the circlips, do not expand the ends any further than is necessary. Install the stamped circlips so that their chamfered side faces the pinion it secures, ie so that its sharp edge faces the direction of thrust load (see *correct fitting of a stamped circlip* illustration in Tools and Workshop Tips of the Reference section) **(see illustration 26.1)**.

**28** Slide the 2nd gear pinion (flat faces towards the bearing) and its bush onto the shaft, followed by the thrust washer, and secure them in place with the circlip, making sure it is properly seated in its groove.

**29** Slide the 6th gear pinion onto the shaft with its selector fork groove facing away from the 2nd gear pinion, and secure it in place with the circlip, making sure it is properly seated in its groove.

**30** Slide the 3rd gear pinion splined bush onto the shaft, with its shouldered side facing the circlip and aligning the oil hole in the bush with that in the shaft. Slide the 3rd gear pinion onto the bush so that its open side faces the 6th gear pinion.

**31** Slide the thrust washer and the 4th gear pinion (open side facing away from the 3rd gear pinion) onto the shaft, then fit the 4th gear pinion bush into the pinion, aligning the oil hole in the bush with that in the shaft. Secure them in place with the circlip, making sure it is properly seated in its groove.

**32** Slide the 5th gear pinion onto the shaft with its selector fork groove facing the 4th gear pinion, followed by the thrust washer.

**33** Slide the 1st gear pinion (with its open side facing the 5th gear pinion) and its bush onto the shaft, followed by the thrust washer.

**34** Slide the needle bearing onto the shaft end. Check that all components have been correctly installed.

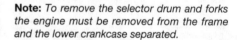

**27 Selector drum and forks** – removal, inspection and installation

**Note:** *To remove the selector drum and forks the engine must be removed from the frame and the lower crankcase separated.*

### Removal

**1** Separate the lower crankcase from the middle crankcase (see Section 23). The selector drum and forks are housed inside the lower case. If not already done, remove the gearchange mechanism (see Section 19).

**2** Before removing the selector forks, mark each fork for identification using a felt pen and note which way round they fit, as an aid to installation.

**3** Supporting the selector forks, withdraw the fork shafts from the right-hand side of the crankcase and remove the forks **(see**

27.3 Withdraw the shafts and remove the forks

27.6 Withdraw the selector drum

illustration). Once removed from the crankcase, slide the forks back onto the shafts in their correct order and way round.

4 If not already done, remove the neutral switch (see Chapter 9).

5 If required, counter-hold the selector drum using a spanner on the flats on its left-hand end, then unscrew the stopper plate bolt and remove the plate, the washer and the two locating pins.

6 Slide the drum out of the right-hand side of the case (see illustration).

### Inspection

7 Inspect the selector forks for any signs of wear or damage, especially around the fork ends where they engage with the groove in the pinion. Check that each fork fits correctly in its pinion groove. Check closely to see if the forks are bent. If the forks are in any way damaged they must be renewed.

8 With the fork engaged with its gear pinion groove, measure the fork-to-groove clearance using a feeler gauge, and compare the result to the specifications at the beginning of the Chapter (see illustration). If the clearance exceeds the service limit specified, measure the thickness of the fork ends and the width of the groove and compare the readings to the specifications (see illustrations). Renew whichever components are worn beyond their specifications.

9 Check that the forks fit correctly on their shaft. They should move freely with a light fit but no appreciable freeplay. Check that the fork shaft holes in the crankcases are not worn or damaged.

10 The selector fork shafts can be checked for trueness by rolling them along a flat surface. A bent rod will cause difficulty in selecting gears and make the gearshift action heavy. Renew the shafts if bent.

11 Inspect the selector drum grooves and selector fork guide pins for signs of wear or damage. If either components show signs of wear or damage they must be renewed.

12 Check that the selector drum bearings

rotate freely and have no sign of freeplay between them and the crankcase. A needle bearing is on the left-hand end (in the crankcase) and a caged ball bearing is on the right-hand end (on the selector drum). Renew the bearings if necessary. To renew the ball bearing, remove the stopper plate (if not already done – see Step 5) and slide it off the end of the selector drum. To renew the needle bearing, drift it out of the crankcase, noting that once it has been removed it cannot be re-used (see illustration). Draw or drive the new bearing into place, making sure it enters squarely. Refer to Tools and Workshop Tips in

the Reference Section for more information on bearings and how to remove and install them.

### Installation

13 Slide the drum into position in the crankcase (see illustration 27.6).

14 If removed, fit the stopper plate locating pins into the end of the drum. Slide the washer and stopper plate onto the selector drum, making sure the holes in the plate locate onto the pins in the drum. Apply a suitable non-permanent thread locking compound to the stopper plate bolt threads, then tighten it to the torque setting specified

27.8a Measure the fork-to-groove clearance using a feeler gauge

27.8b Measure the thickness of the fork end . . .

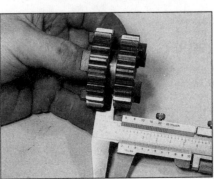

27.8c . . . and the width of the groove

27.12 The needle bearing is in the crankcase

2

**27.16a Position the front fork with its pin in the centre groove in the selector drum and slide the shaft through**

**27.16b Similarly install the rear forks**

**29.2 Measure the clearance between the outer thrust bearing and the crankshaft as shown**

at the beginning of the Chapter, using a spanner on the selector drum flats to counter-hold it as on removal. Position the selector drum so that the neutral detent in the stopper plate, identifiable by its different outline to the other detents, is roughly aligned at the 2 o'clock position, so that the stopper arm locates onto it when it is later installed.

15  Install the neutral switch (see Chapter 9).

16  Lubricate each selector fork shaft with clean engine oil and slide them into the bores in the crankcase (see illustrations). As each shaft is installed, fit each selector fork in turn, making sure it is in its correct location and the right way round (see Step 2), and that its guide pin locates in its track in the selector drum.

17  Install the gearchange mechanism (see Section 19).

18  Install the lower crankcase (see Section 23).

## 28 Main and connecting rod bearings – general information

1  Even though main and connecting rod bearings are generally renewed with new ones during the engine overhaul, the old bearings should be retained for close examination as they may reveal valuable information about the condition of the engine.

2  Bearing failure occurs mainly because of lack of lubrication, the presence of dirt or other foreign particles, overloading the engine and/or corrosion. Regardless of the cause of bearing failure, it must be corrected before the engine is reassembled to prevent it from happening again.

3  When examining the connecting rod bearings, remove them from the connecting rods and caps and lay them out on a clean surface in the same general position as their location on the crankshaft journals. This will enable you to match any noted bearing problems with the corresponding crankshaft journal.

4  Dirt and other foreign particles get into the engine in a variety of ways. It may be left in

the engine during assembly or it may pass through filters or breathers. It may get into the oil and from there into the bearings. Metal chips from machining operations and normal engine wear are often present. Abrasives are sometimes left in engine components after reconditioning operations, especially when parts are not thoroughly cleaned using the proper cleaning methods. Whatever the source, these foreign objects often end up embedded in the soft bearing material and are easily recognised. Large particles will not embed in the bearing and will score or gouge the bearing and journal. The best prevention for this cause of bearing failure is to clean all parts thoroughly and keep everything spotlessly clean during engine reassembly. Frequent and regular oil and filter changes are also recommended.

5  Lack of lubrication or lubrication breakdown has a number of interrelated causes. Excessive heat (which thins the oil), overloading (which squeezes the oil from the bearing face) and oil leakage or throw off (from excessive bearing clearances, worn oil pump or high engine speeds) all contribute to lubrication breakdown. Blocked oil passages will also starve a bearing and destroy it. When lack of lubrication is the cause of bearing failure, the bearing material is wiped or extruded from the steel backing of the bearing. Temperatures may increase to the point where the steel backing and the journal turn blue from overheating.

**HAYNES HiNT** *Refer to Tools and Workshop Tips for bearing fault finding.*

6  Riding habits can have a definite effect on bearing life. Full throttle low speed operation, or labouring the engine, puts very high loads on bearings, which tend to squeeze out the oil film. These loads cause the bearings to flex, which produces fine cracks in the bearing face (fatigue failure). Eventually the bearing material will loosen in pieces and tear away from the steel backing. Short trip riding leads to corrosion of bearings, as insufficient engine

heat is produced to drive off the condensed water and corrosive gases produced. These products collect in the engine oil, forming acid and sludge. As the oil is carried to the engine bearings, the acid attacks and corrodes the bearing material.

7  Incorrect bearing installation during engine assembly will lead to bearing failure as well. Tight fitting bearings which leave insufficient bearing oil clearances result in oil starvation. Dirt or foreign particles trapped behind a bearing insert result in high spots on the bearing which lead to failure.

8  To avoid bearing problems, clean all parts thoroughly before reassembly, double check all bearing clearance measurements and lubricate the new bearings with clean engine oil during installation.

## 29 Crankshaft and main bearings – removal, inspection and installation

**Note:** *To remove the crankshaft the engine must be removed from the frame and the crankcases separated.*

### Removal

1  Separate the middle crankcase from the upper crankcase (see Section 23).

2  Before removing the crankshaft check the thrust bearing clearance. The thrust bearings are located between the crank webs and the main bearing housing between cylinder Nos. 1 and 2. Push the crankshaft as far as it will go toward the left-hand (alternator) end (this eliminates play in the inner bearing). Insert a feeler gauge between the crankshaft and the outer thrust bearing and record the clearance (see illustration). Compare the measurement with this Chapter's Specifications. If the clearance is excessive, refer to Steps 11 and 12 for selection of new bearings.

3  If the crankshaft only is being removed and the piston/connecting rod assemblies are staying in the engine, separate the connecting rods from the crankshaft (see Section 30) and gently push them to the top of the bores.

4  Remove the thrust bearings, noting how

**29.4 Remove each thrust bearing, and do not mix them up**

**29.5 To remove a main bearing shell, push it sideways and lift it out**

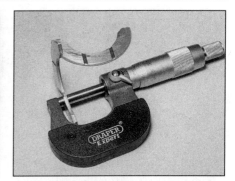

**29.11 Measure the thickness of the inner thrust bearing**

and where they fit – do not get the inner and outer bearings mixed up (note their different coloured ends) **(see illustration)**.

Lift the crankshaft, together with the connecting rods if they haven't been separated, out of the upper crankcase. If the crankshaft appears stuck, tap it gently on each end using a soft-faced mallet.

**5** The main bearing shells can be removed from their cut-outs by pushing their centres to the side, then lifting them out **(see illustration)**. Keep the bearing shells in order.

**6** If required and not already done, separate the connecting rods from the crankshaft (see Section 30).

### Inspection

**7** Clean the crankshaft with solvent, using a rifle-cleaning brush to scrub out the oil passages. If available, blow the crank dry with compressed air, and also blow through the oil passages. Check the cam chain sprocket for wear or damage. If any of the sprocket teeth are excessively worn, chipped or broken, the sprocket must be renewed. Similarly check the primary drive gear.

**8** Refer to Section 28 and examine the main bearing shells. If they are scored, badly scuffed or appear to have been seized, new bearings must be installed. Always renew the main bearings as a set. If they are badly damaged, check the corresponding crankshaft journals. Evidence of extreme heat, such as discoloration, indicates that

lubrication failure has occurred. Be sure to thoroughly check the oil pump and pressure regulator as well as all oil holes and passages before reassembling the engine.

**9** The crankshaft journals should be given a close visual examination, paying particular attention where damaged bearings have been discovered. If the journals are scored or pitted in any way a new crankshaft will be required. Note that undersizes are not available, precluding the option of re-grinding the crankshaft.

**10** Place the crankshaft on V-blocks and check the runout at the main bearing journals using a dial gauge. Compare the reading to the maximum specified at the beginning of the Chapter. If the runout exceeds the limit, a new crankshaft must be installed.

### Thrust bearing selection

**11** If the thrust bearing clearance was excessive (see Step 2), measure the thickness of the inner thrust bearing, and compare the result to the specifications at the beginning of the Chapter **(see illustration)**. If the thickness measured is below the service limit specified, the inner thrust bearing must be renewed. There is only one size of replacement inner bearing. Install the new inner bearing and check the clearance again (see Step 2). If the clearance is still excessive, or if the inner bearing was within specifications, select a new outer bearing as follows:

**12** Remove the outer thrust bearing. Install

the inner bearing and push the crankshaft as far as it will go toward the left-hand (alternator) end to eliminate any clearance. Insert a feeler gauge between the crankshaft and the main bearing housing where the outer bearing fits, and record the clearance **(see illustration)**. Using the table below, select a replacement outer thrust bearing according to the clearance measured. For example, if the clearance recorded was 2.495 mm, the bearing colour-code required is blue. Re-check the clearance with the new bearings (see Step 2).

| Outer bearing clearance (bearing removed) | Bearing colour-code required |
|---|---|
| 2.430 to 2.460 mm | Red |
| 2.460 to 2.485 mm | Black |
| 2.485 to 2.510 mm | Blue |
| 2.510 to 2.535 mm | Green |
| 2.535 to 2.560 mm | Yellow |
| 2.560 to 2.585 mm | White |

### Main bearing shell selection

**13** New bearing shells for the main bearings are supplied on a selected fit basis. Code numbers stamped on various components are used to identify the correct replacement bearings. The crankshaft main bearing journal size letters, one letter for each journal (either an A, B or C), are stamped on the outside of the crankshaft left-hand web **(see illustration)**. The corresponding main bearing housing size letters (either an A or B), are

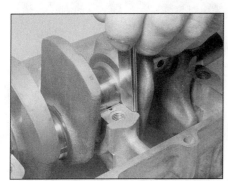

**29.12 Measure the clearance between the crankshaft and the main bearing housing**

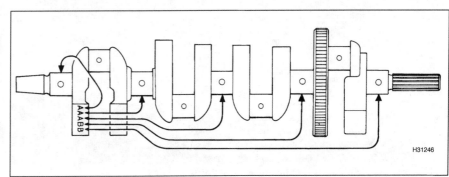

**29.13a Crankshaft journal size letters**

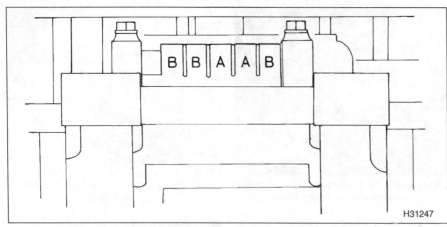

29.13b **Bearing housing size letters**

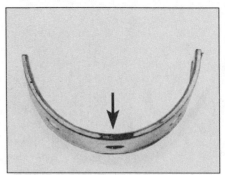

29.14 **The colour code is marked on the side of the shell**

stamped into the rear of the upper crankcase (see illustration). The first letter of each set of five is for the outer left-hand journal, the second for the inner left-hand, the third for the middle, the fourth for the inner right-hand, and the fifth for the outer right-hand journal. **Note:** *Referrals to left- and right-hand are made as though the engine is the correct way up. Do not confuse the two if the engine is upside down.*

14 A range of bearing shells is available. To select the correct bearing for a particular journal, using the table below cross-refer the main bearing journal size letter (stamped on the crank web) with the main bearing housing size letter (stamped on the crankcase) to determine the colour code of the bearing required. For example, if the journal code is C, and the housing code is B, then the bearing required is Yellow. The colour is marked on the side of the shell (see illustration).

| Crankcase housing code | Crankshaft journal code | | |
| --- | --- | --- | --- |
| | A | B | C |
| A | Green | Black | Brown |
| B | Black | Brown | Yellow |

### Oil clearance check

15 Whether new bearing shells are being fitted or the original ones are being re-used,

the main bearing oil clearance should be checked before the engine is reassembled. Main bearing oil clearance is measured with a product known as Plastigauge.

16 Clean the backs of the bearing shells and the bearing housings in both crankcase halves.

17 Press the bearing shells into their cut-outs, ensuring that the tab on each shell engages in the notch in the crankcase (see illustration). Make sure the bearings are fitted in the correct locations and take care not to touch any shell's bearing surface with your fingers.

18 Ensure the shells and crankshaft are clean and dry. Lay the crankshaft in position in the upper crankcase.

19 Cut several lengths of the appropriate size Plastigauge (they should be slightly shorter than the width of the crankshaft journals). Place a strand of Plastigauge on each (cleaned) journal (see illustration). Make sure the crankshaft is not rotated.

20 Carefully lower the middle crankcase onto the upper, making sure it seats correctly (see illustration 23.18). **Note:** *Do not tighten the crankcase bolts if the casing is not correctly seated.* Clean the threads of the 9 mm crankshaft journal bolts and insert them in their original locations (see illustration 23.28). Secure all bolts finger-tight at first, then

tighten the bolts a little at a time and in the numerical sequence shown to the torque setting specified at the beginning of the Chapter (see illustration 23.17). Make sure that the crankshaft is not rotated as the bolts are tightened.

21 Slacken each bolt in reverse sequence starting at number 10 and working backwards to number 1. Slacken each bolt a little at a time until they are all finger-tight, then remove the bolts. Carefully lift off the middle crankcase, making sure the Plastigauge is not disturbed.

22 Compare the width of the crushed Plastigauge on each crankshaft journal to the scale printed on the Plastigauge envelope to obtain the main bearing oil clearance (see illustration). Compare the reading to the specifications at the beginning of the Chapter.

23 On completion carefully scrape away all traces of the Plastigauge material from the crankshaft journal and bearing shells; use a fingernail or other object which is unlikely to score them.

24 If the oil clearance falls into the specified range, no bearing shell replacement is required (provided they are in good condition). If the clearance is more than the standard range, but within the service limit, refer to the marks on the case and the marks on the crankshaft and select new bearing shells (see Steps 13 and 14). Install the new shells and check the oil clearance once again (the new shells may bring bearing clearance within the

29.17 **Make sure the tabs on the shells locate in the notches in the bearing housings**

29.19 **Lay a strip of Plastigauge on each journal parallel to the crankshaft centreline**

29.22 **Measure the width of the crushed Plastigauge (be sure to use the correct scale – metric and imperial are included)**

29.25 Measure the diameter of each crankshaft journal

29.30 Install the thrust bearings with their grooves toward the crankshaft web

30.2 Slip a feeler gauge between the connecting rod and the crank web to check side clearance

specified range). Always renew all of the shells at the same time.

25 If the clearance is still greater than the service limit listed in this Chapter's Specifications (even with new shells), the crankshaft journal is worn and the crankshaft should be renewed. Measure the diameter of each journal and compare the measurements to the specifications to confirm **(see illustration)**. By measuring the diameter at a number of points around each journal's circumference, you'll be able to determine whether or not the journal is out-of-round. Also take a measurement at each end of the journal, near the crank throws, as well as in the middle, to determine if the journal is tapered.

### Installation

26 If removed with the crankshaft and separated from it, fit the connecting rods onto the crankshaft (see Section 30).

27 Clean the backs of the bearing shells and the bearing cut-outs in the upper and middle crankcases. If new shells are being fitted, ensure that all traces of the protective grease are cleaned off using paraffin (kerosene). Wipe the shells and crankcases dry with a lint-free cloth. Make sure all the oil passages and holes are clear, and blow them through with compressed air if it is available.

28 Lubricate each shell, preferably with molybdenum paste, molybdenum disulphide oil (a 50/50 mixture of molybdenum disulphide

paste or grease and clean engine oil), or if not available then with clean engine oil. Press the bearing shells into their locations. Make sure the tab on each shell engages in the notch in the casing **(see illustration 29.17)**. Make sure the bearings are fitted in the correct locations and take care not to touch any shell's bearing surface with your fingers.

29 Lower the crankshaft into position in the upper crankcase.

30 Install the thrust bearings into their correct locations (do not mix up the inner with the outer) between the crank webs and the main bearing housing between cylinder Nos. 1 and 2, making sure that the oil grooves face towards the crankshaft web **(see illustration)**.

31 If the crankshaft only was removed and the piston/connecting rod assemblies are in the engine, draw each connecting rod/piston down its bore and fit them onto the crankshaft (see Section 30).

32 Reassemble the crankcases (see Section 23).

### 30 Connecting rods – removal, inspection and installation

**Note:** *To remove the connecting rods the engine must be removed from the frame and the crankcases separated.*

### Removal

1 Remove the cylinder block (see Section 14)

and, if required, the pistons (see Section 15), then separate the middle crankcase from the upper crankcase (see Section 23). **Note:** *If the crankshaft is being removed with the connecting rods attached, the pistons must be removed. If the crankshaft is being left in place, the pistons can remain on the connecting rods if no work is being carried out on them or the small ends.*

2 Before separating the rods from the crankshaft, measure the big-end side clearance on each rod with a feeler gauge **(see illustration)**. If the clearance on any rod is greater than the service limit listed in this Chapter's Specifications, measure the big-end and crankpin widths as described in Step 7.

3 Using paint or a felt marker pen, mark the relevant cylinder identity on each connecting rod and cap. Mark across the cap-to-connecting rod join and note which side of the rod faces the front of the engine to ensure that the cap and rod are fitted the correct way around on reassembly. Note that the number already across the rod and cap indicates size grade, not cylinder number, and that this number faces the rear of the engine **(see illustration)**.

4 Unscrew the cap bolts and separate the connecting rod, cap and both bearing shells from the crankpin **(see illustration)**. There are locating pins between each rod and cap. To help separation, before the bolts are fully unscrewed tap on the bolt heads to push the rod off the crank **(see illustration)**. Keep the

30.3 This number indicates the connecting rod bearing size and faces back – make your own marks to indicate cylinder number

30.4a Slacken and partially unscrew the cap bolts . . .

30.4b . . . then tap on the bolt heads to separate the rod from the crank

2

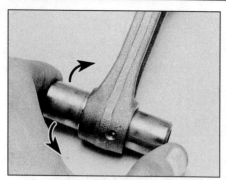

**30.6 Slip the piston pin into the rod's small-end and check for freeplay between them**

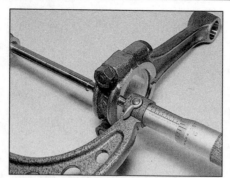

**30.7a Measure the width of the connecting rod . . .**

**30.7b . . . and of the corresponding crankpin**

rod, cap, bolts and (if they are to be reused) the bearing shells together in their correct positions to ensure correct installation.

## Inspection

**5** Check the connecting rods for cracks and other obvious damage.

**6** If not already done (see Section 15), apply clean engine oil to the piston pin, insert it into the connecting rod small-end and check for any freeplay between the two **(see illustration)**. Measure the pin external diameter and the small-end bore diameter and compare the measurements to the specifications at the beginning of the Chapter **(see illustrations 15.13b and 15.13d)**. Renew components that are worn beyond the specified limits.

**7** If the side clearance measured in Step 2 exceeds the service limit specified, measure the width of the connecting rod big-end and the width of the crankpin **(see illustrations)**. Compare the results to the specifications at the beginning of the Chapter, and renew whichever component exceeds those specifications.

**8** Refer to Section 28 and examine the connecting rod bearing shells. If they are scored, badly scuffed or appear to have seized, new shells must be installed. Always renew the shells in the connecting rods as a set. If they are badly damaged, check the corresponding crankpin. Evidence of extreme heat, such as discoloration, indicates that

lubrication failure has occurred. Be sure to thoroughly check the oil pump and pressure regulator as well as all oil holes and passages before reassembling the engine.

**9** Have the rods checked for twist and bend by a Suzuki dealer if you are in doubt about their straightness.

## Bearing shell selection

**10** New bearing shells for the big-end bearings are supplied on a selected fit basis. Codes stamped on various components are used to identify the correct replacement bearings. The crankpin journal size numbers are stamped on the crankshaft inner left web and will be either a 1, 2 or 3 **(see illustration)**. The number coming immediately after the L is for the outer left-hand big-end (cyl No. 1), the next number is for the inner left-hand big-end (cyl No. 2), the next for the inner right-hand (cyl No. 3) and the number coming before the R is for the outer right-hand big-end (cyl No. 4). The connecting rod size code is marked on the flat face of the connecting rod and cap and will be either a 1 or a 2 **(see illustration 30.3)**.

**11** A range of bearing shells is available. To select the correct bearing for a particular big-end, using the table below cross-refer the crankpin journal size number (stamped on the web) with the connecting rod size letter (stamped on the rod) to determine the colour code of the bearing required. For example, if the connecting rod size is 2, and the crankpin

size is 3, then the bearing required is Yellow. The colour is marked on the side of the shell **(see illustration 29.14)**.

| Connecting rod code | Crankpin code | | |
|---|---|---|---|
| | **1** | **2** | **3** |
| 1 | Green | Black | Brown |
| 2 | Black | Brown | Yellow |

## Oil clearance check

**12** Whether new bearing shells are being fitted or the original ones are being re-used, the connecting rod bearing oil clearance should be checked prior to reassembly.

**13** Clean the backs of the bearing shells and the bearing locations in both the connecting rod and cap.

**14** Press the bearing shells into their locations, ensuring that the tab on each shell engages the notch in the connecting rod/cap **(see illustration)**. Make sure the bearings are fitted in the correct locations and take care not to touch any shell's bearing surface with your fingers.

**15** Cut a length of the appropriate size Plastigauge (it should be slightly shorter than the width of the crankpin). Place a strand of Plastigauge on the (cleaned) crankpin journal and fit the (clean) connecting rod, shells and cap **(see illustration 30.22)**. Make sure the cap is fitted the correct way around so the previously made markings align, and that the rod is facing the right way, and tighten the cap bolts in two stages, first to the initial torque setting specified at the beginning of the

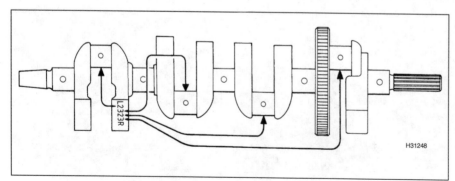

**30.10 Crankpin journal size numbers**

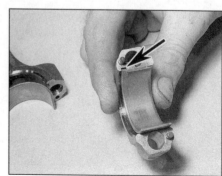

**30.14 Make sure the tab locates in the notch (arrowed)**

30.19 Measure the width of the crankpin

30.22 Fit the caps onto the rods, making sure the pins locate correctly

30.23 Tighten the cap bolts as described to the specified torque settings

Chapter, and then to the final torque setting specified, whilst ensuring that the connecting rod does not rotate. Slacken the cap bolts and remove the connecting rod, again taking great care not to rotate the crankshaft.

**16** Compare the width of the crushed Plastigauge on the crankpin to the scale printed on the Plastigauge envelope to obtain the connecting rod bearing oil clearance **(see illustration 29.22)**. Compare the reading to the specifications at the beginning of the Chapter.

**17** On completion carefully scrape away all traces of the Plastigauge material from the crankpin and bearing shells using a fingernail or other object which is unlikely to score the shells.

**18** If the clearance is within the range listed in this Chapter's Specifications and the bearings are in perfect condition, they can be reused. If the clearance is beyond the service limit, renew the bearing shells with new ones (see Steps 10 and 11). Check the oil clearance once again (the new shells may be thick enough to bring bearing clearance within the specified range). Always renew all of the shells at the same time.

**19** If the clearance is still greater than the service limit listed in this Chapter's Specifications, measure the diameter of the crankpin journal with a micrometer and compare your findings with this Chapter's Specifications **(see illustration)**. Also, by measuring the diameter at a number of points around the journal's circumference, you'll be able to determine whether or not the journal is out-of-round. Also take a measurement at each end of the journal, near the crank throws, as well as in the middle, to determine if the journal is tapered.

**20** If any journal has worn down past the limit, renew the crankshaft.

**21** Repeat the bearing selection procedure for the remaining connecting rods.

### Installation

**22** Fit the bearing shells in the connecting rods and caps, aligning the notch in the bearing with the groove in the rod or cap **(see illustration 30.14)**. Lubricate the shells, preferably with molybdenum paste, molybdenum disulphide oil (a 50/50 mixture of molybdenum disulphide paste or grease and clean engine oil), or if not available

then with clean engine oil, and assemble each connecting rod on its correct crankpin so that the previously made matchmarks align and the connecting rod size letter is facing the rear of the engine **(see illustration)**. Tighten the bolts finger-tight at this stage. Check to make sure that all components have been returned to their original locations using the marks made on disassembly.

**23** Tighten the bearing cap bolts in two stages, first to the initial torque setting specified at the beginning of the Chapter, and then to the final torque setting specified **(see illustration)**.

**24** Check that the rods rotate smoothly and freely on the crankpin. If there are any signs of roughness or tightness, remove the rods and re-check the bearing clearance. Sometimes tapping the connecting rod cap bolts will relieve tightness, but if in doubt, recheck the clearances.

**25** Install the remaining components and assemble the crankcases.

## 31 Initial start-up after overhaul

**1** Make sure the engine oil level and coolant level are correct (see *Daily (pre-ride) checks*).

**2** Pull the plug caps off the spark plugs and insert a spare spark plug into each cap. Position the spare plugs so that their bodies are earthed (grounded) against the engine. Turn on the ignition switch and crank the engine over with the starter until the oil pressure warning LED goes off (which indicates that oil pressure exists). Turn off the ignition. Remove the spare spark plugs and reconnect the plug caps.

**3** Make sure there is fuel in the tank, then turn the fuel tap to the ON position and operate the choke.

**4** Start the engine and allow it to run at a moderately fast idle until it reaches operating temperature.

 *Warning: If the oil pressure warning LED doesn't go off, or it comes on while the engine is running, stop the engine immediately.*

**5** Check carefully for oil leaks and make sure the transmission and controls, especially the brakes, function properly before road testing the machine. Refer to Section 32 for the recommended running-in procedure.

**6** Upon completion of the road test, and after the engine has cooled down completely, recheck the valve clearances (Chapter 1) and check the engine oil level (see *Daily (pre-ride) checks*).

## 32 Recommended running-in procedure

**1** Treat the machine gently for the first few miles to make sure oil has circulated throughout the engine and any new parts installed have started to seat.

**2** Even greater care is necessary if a new cylinder block or crankshaft has been installed. In the case of a new cylinder block, the bike will have to be run in as when new. This means greater use of the transmission and a restraining hand on the throttle until at least 500 miles (800 km) have been covered. There's no point in keeping to any set speed limit – the main idea is to keep from labouring the engine and to gradually increase performance up to the 500 mile (800 km) mark. These recommendations can be lessened to an extent when only a new crankshaft is installed. Experience is the best guide, since it's easy to tell when an engine is running freely. The maximum engine speed limitations in the table below, which Suzuki provide for new motorcycles, can be used as a guide.

**3** If a lubrication failure is suspected, stop the engine immediately and try to find the cause. If an engine is run without oil, even for a short period of time, severe damage will occur.

| | | |
|---|---|---|
| Up to 500 miles (800 km) | 6500 rpm max | Vary throttle position/speed |
| 500 to 1000 miles (800 to 1600 km) | 10,000 rpm max | Vary throttle position/speed. Use full throttle for short bursts |
| Over 1000 miles (1600 km) | 13,500 rpm max | Do not exceed tachometer red line |

2

**Notes**

# Chapter 3
## Cooling system

## Contents

## Degrees of difficulty

| Easy, suitable for novice with little experience | Fairly easy, suitable for beginner with some experience | Fairly difficult, suitable for competent DIY mechanic | Difficult, suitable for experienced DIY mechanic | Very difficult, suitable for expert DIY or professional |
|---|---|---|---|---|

## Specifications

**Coolant**
Mixture type and capacity . . . . . . . . . . . . . . . . . . . . . . . . . . . . . . . . . . . . . see Chapter 1

**Pressure cap**
Cap valve opening pressure . . . . . . . . . . . . . . . . . . . . . . . . . . . . . . . 13.5 to 17.7 psi (0.95 to 1.25 Bar)

**Fan switch**
Cooling fan cut-in temperature . . . . . . . . . . . . . . . . . . . . . . . . . . . . approx. 105°C
Cooling fan cut-out temperature . . . . . . . . . . . . . . . . . . . . . . . . . . . approx. 100°C

**Coolant temperature sensor**
Resistance
GSX-R600 and GSX-R750T and V models
  @ 50°C . . . . . . . . . . . . . . . . . . . . . . . . . . . . . . . . . . . . . . . . . . . approx. 9.56 K-ohms
  @ 100°C . . . . . . . . . . . . . . . . . . . . . . . . . . . . . . . . . . . . . . . . . . . approx. 2.78 K-ohms
  @ 120°C . . . . . . . . . . . . . . . . . . . . . . . . . . . . . . . . . . . . . . . . . . . approx. 0.69 K-ohms
  @ 130°C . . . . . . . . . . . . . . . . . . . . . . . . . . . . . . . . . . . . . . . . . . . approx. 0.50 K-ohms
GSX-R750W and X models
  @ 20°C . . . . . . . . . . . . . . . . . . . . . . . . . . . . . . . . . . . . . . . . . . . approx. 2.450 K-ohms
  @ 50°C . . . . . . . . . . . . . . . . . . . . . . . . . . . . . . . . . . . . . . . . . . . approx. 0.811 K-ohms
  @ 80°C . . . . . . . . . . . . . . . . . . . . . . . . . . . . . . . . . . . . . . . . . . . approx. 0.318 K-ohms
  @ 110°C . . . . . . . . . . . . . . . . . . . . . . . . . . . . . . . . . . . . . . . . . . . approx. 0.142 K-ohms
  @ 130°C . . . . . . . . . . . . . . . . . . . . . . . . . . . . . . . . . . . . . . . . . . . approx. 0.088 K-ohms

**Thermostat**
Opening temperature . . . . . . . . . . . . . . . . . . . . . . . . . . . . . . . . . . . 74.5 to 78.5°C
Valve lift . . . . . . . . . . . . . . . . . . . . . . . . . . . . . . . . . . . . . . . . . . . . . 7 mm (min) @ 90°C

## Torque settings

Cooling fan bolts . . . . . . . . . . . . . . . . . . . . . . . . . . . . . . . . . . . . . . . . 6 Nm
Cooling fan switch
   GSX-R600 and GSX-R750T and V models . . . . . . . . . . . . . . . . . . . . 17 Nm
   GSX-R750W and X models . . . . . . . . . . . . . . . . . . . . . . . . . . . . . . 18 Nm
Coolant temperature gauge sensor
   GSX-R600 and GSX-R750T and V models . . . . . . . . . . . . . . . . . . . . 9 Nm
   GSX-R750W and X models . . . . . . . . . . . . . . . . . . . . . . . . . . . . . . 18 Nm
Thermostat cover bolts . . . . . . . . . . . . . . . . . . . . . . . . . . . . . . . . . . . 10 Nm
Radiator mounting bolts . . . . . . . . . . . . . . . . . . . . . . . . . . . . . . . . . . . 6 Nm
Water pump impeller bolt . . . . . . . . . . . . . . . . . . . . . . . . . . . . . . . . . . 8 Nm
Water pump mounting bolts . . . . . . . . . . . . . . . . . . . . . . . . . . . . . . . . 6 Nm
Water pump cover screws . . . . . . . . . . . . . . . . . . . . . . . . . . . . . . . . . 6 Nm
Coolant union to cylinder block bolts . . . . . . . . . . . . . . . . . . . . . . . . . 10 Nm

## 1 General information

The cooling system uses a water/antifreeze coolant to carry away excess energy in the form of heat. The cylinders are surrounded by a water jacket from which the heated coolant is circulated by thermo-syphonic action in conjunction with a water pump, driven by the oil pump. The hot coolant from the engine flows via the thermostat to the radiator. The coolant then flows across the radiator core, where it is cooled by the passing air, to the water pump and back to the engine where the cycle is repeated.

A thermostat is fitted in the system to prevent the coolant flowing through the radiator when the engine is cold, therefore accelerating the speed at which the engine reaches normal operating temperature. A coolant temperature sensor mounted in the thermostat housing transmits to the temperature gauge on the instrument panel. A thermostatically-controlled cooling fan is also fitted to aid cooling in extreme conditions.

The complete cooling system is partially sealed and pressurised, the pressure being controlled by a valve contained in the spring-loaded pressure cap. By pressurising the coolant the boiling point is raised, preventing premature boiling in adverse conditions. The overflow pipe from the system is connected to a reservoir into which excess coolant is expelled under pressure. The discharged coolant automatically returns to the radiator when the engine cools.

⚠️ *Warning: Do not remove the pressure cap from the radiator when the engine is hot. Scalding hot coolant and steam may be blown out under pressure, which could cause serious injury. When the engine has cooled, place a thick rag, like a towel over the pressure cap; slowly rotate the cap anti-clockwise to the first stop. This procedure allows any residual pressure to escape. When the steam has stopped escaping, press down on the cap while turning it anti-clockwise and remove it. Do not allow antifreeze to come in contact with your skin or painted surfaces of the motorcycle. Rinse off any spills immediately with plenty of water. Antifreeze is highly toxic if ingested. Never leave antifreeze lying around in an open container or in puddles on the floor; children and pets are attracted by its sweet smell and may drink it. Check with the local authorities about disposing of used antifreeze. Many communities will have collection centres which will see that antifreeze is disposed of safely.*

*Caution: At all times use the specified type of antifreeze, and always mix it with distilled water in the correct proportion. The antifreeze contains corrosion inhibitors which are essential to avoid damage to the cooling system. A lack of these inhibitors could lead to a build-up of corrosion which would block the coolant passages, resulting in overheating and severe engine damage. Distilled water must be used as opposed to tap water to avoid a build-up of scale which would also block the passages.*

## 2 Pressure cap – check

1 If problems such as overheating or loss of coolant occur, check the entire system as

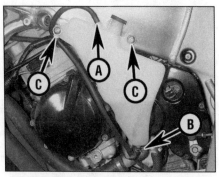

**3.2 Detach the breather hose (A) and the radiator hose (B) and drain the reservoir, then unscrew the bolts (C) and remove the reservoir**

described in Chapter 1. The radiator cap opening pressure should be checked by a Suzuki dealer with the special tester required to do the job. If the cap is defective, renew it.

## 3 Coolant reservoir – removal and installation

### Removal

1 The coolant reservoir is located on the inside of the left-hand fairing side panel. Remove the panel (see Chapter 8) for access.
2 Detach the breather/overflow hose from the top of the reservoir **(see illustration)**.
3 Place a suitable container underneath the reservoir, then release the clamp securing the radiator overflow hose to the base of the reservoir. Detach the hose and allow the coolant to drain into the container **(see illustration 3.2)**.
4 Unscrew the reservoir mounting screws, noting how the rear one secures the idle speed adjuster, and remove the reservoir **(see illustration 3.2)**.

### Installation

5 Installation is the reverse of removal. Make sure the hoses are correctly installed and secured with their clamps. On completion refill the reservoir as described in *Daily (pre-ride) checks*.

## 4 Cooling fan and cooling fan switch – check and renewal

### Cooling fan

#### Check

1 If the engine is overheating and the cooling fan isn't coming on, first check the cooling fan circuit fuse (see Chapter 9) and then the fan switch as described in Steps 9 to 16 below.
2 If the fan does not come on, (and the fan switch is good), the fault lies in either the cooling fan motor or the relevant wiring. Test all the wiring and connections as described in Chapter 9.
3 To test the cooling fan motor, remove the

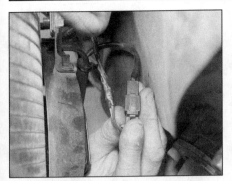

**4.3a It may be possible to access the connector from behind the radiator . . .**

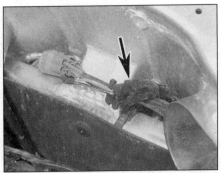

**4.3b . . . although you may have to remove the air filter housing to access it (arrowed)**

**4.5 The fan assembly is secured by three bolts (arrowed)**

fairing side panels (see Chapter 8). Disconnect the fan wiring connector **(see illustration)**. It may be possible to reach behind the radiator and access the connector by drawing the wiring down (removing the radiator mounting bolts and shifting it forward will help – see Section 7) **(see illustration)**, although if the connector is positioned behind the steering head under the air filter housing, it may be necessary to remove the air filter housing for access (see Chapter 4) **(see illustration)**. Using a 12 volt battery and two jumper wires, connect the battery to the terminals on the fan side of the wiring connector. Once connected the fan should operate. If it does not, and the wiring is all good, then the fan is faulty.

### Renewal

 *Warning: The engine must be completely cool before carrying out this procedure.*

**4** Remove the radiator (see Section 7).
**5** Unscrew the three bolts securing the fan shroud and fan assembly to the radiator and remove the fan **(see illustration)**.
**6** If required, remove the three screws on the front and separate the fan from the shroud.
**7** Installation is the reverse of removal. Tighten the cooling fan bolts to the torque setting specified at the beginning of the Chapter.
**8** Install the radiator (see Section 7).

## *Cooling fan switch*

### Check

**9** If the engine is overheating and the cooling fan isn't coming on, first check the cooling fan circuit fuse (see Chapter 9). If the fuse is blown, check the fan circuit for a short to earth (see the wiring diagrams at the end of this book). If the fuse is good, proceed as follows.
**10** On GSX-R600 and GSX-R750T and V models, remove the right-hand fairing side panel (see Chapter 8), and disconnect the wiring connector from the fan switch on the right-hand side of the radiator **(see illustration)**.
**11** On GSX-R750W and X models, raise the fuel tank (see Chapter 4). Disconnect the

wiring connector from the fan switch on the thermostat cover **(see illustration)**.
**12** Using a jumper wire, connect across the two terminals on the wiring connector. The fan should come on. If it does, the fan switch is defective and must be renewed. If it does not come on, the fan motor should be tested (see Step 3).
**13** If the fan is on the whole time, disconnect the wiring connector. The fan should stop. If it does, the switch is defective and must be renewed. If it doesn't, check the wiring between the switch and the fan for a short to earth, and the fan itself.
**14** If the fan works but is suspected of cutting in at the wrong temperature, a more comprehensive test of the switch can be made as follows.
**15** Remove the switch (see Steps 17 to 20). Fill a small heatproof container with oil and place it on a stove. Connect the positive (+ve) probe of an ohmmeter to one terminal of the switch and the negative (-ve) probe to the other, and using some wire or other support suspend the switch in the oil so that just the sensing portion and the threads are submerged **(see illustration 5.2)**. Also place a thermometer capable of reading temperatures up to 110°C in the oil so that its bulb is close to the switch. **Note:** *None of the components should be allowed to directly touch the container.*
**16** Initially the ohmmeter reading should be very high indicating that the switch is open (OFF). Heat the oil, stirring it gently.

**4.10 Disconnect the fan switch wiring connector (arrowed)**

 *Warning: This must be done very carefully to avoid the risk of personal injury.*

When the temperature reaches around 105°C the meter reading should drop to around zero ohms, indicating that the switch has closed (ON). Now turn the heat off. As the temperature falls below 100°C the meter reading should show infinite (very high) resistance, indicating that the switch has opened (OFF). If the meter readings obtained are different, or they are obtained at different temperatures, then the switch is faulty and must be renewed.

### Renewal

 *Warning: The engine must be completely cool before carrying out this procedure.*

**17** Drain the cooling system (see Chapter 1).
**18** On GSX-R600 and GSX-R750T and V models, remove the right-hand fairing side panel (see Chapter 8), and disconnect the wiring connector from the fan switch on the right-hand side of the radiator **(see illustration 4.10)**.
**19** On GSX-R750W and X models, raise the fuel tank (see Chapter 4). Disconnect the wiring connector from the fan switch on the thermostat cover **(see illustration 4.11)**.
**20** Unscrew the switch and withdraw it.
**21** Apply some grease to the O-ring. Install the switch and tighten it to the torque setting specified at the beginning of the Chapter. Take care not to overtighten the switch.

**3**

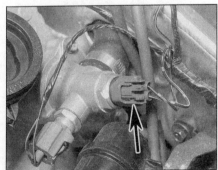

**4.11 Disconnect the fan switch wiring connector (arrowed)**

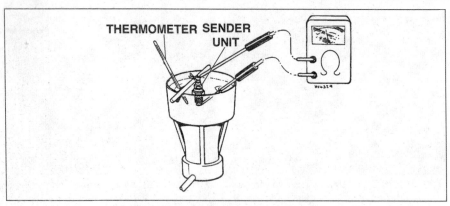

THERMOMETER SENDER UNIT

5.2 Coolant temperature sensor testing set-up

**22** Reconnect the switch wiring and refill the cooling system (see *Daily (pre-ride) checks*). Lower the fuel tank and tighten its bolts securely.

## 5 Coolant temperature sensor – check and renewal

### Check

**1** Raise the fuel tank (see Chapter 4). The sensor is mounted in the thermostat housing, which is on the back of the cylinder head on the right-hand side.

**2** Remove the sensor (see Steps 4 and 5 below). Fill a small heatproof container with oil and place it on a stove. Using an ohmmeter, on GSX-R600 and GSX-R750T and V models, connect the positive (+ve) probe of the meter to the terminal on the sensor, and the negative (-ve) probe to the body of the sensor. On GSX-R750W and X models, connect the positive (+ve) probe of the meter one terminal on the sensor, and the negative (-ve) probe to the other terminal. Using some wire or other support suspend the sensor in the oil so that just the sensing portion and the threads are submerged. Also place a thermometer capable of reading temperatures up to 140°C in the oil so that its bulb is close to the sensor **(see illustration)**. **Note:** *None of the components should be allowed to directly touch the container.*

**3** Heat the oil, stirring it gently.

 *Warning: This must be done very carefully to avoid the risk of personal injury.*

As the temperature of the oil rises, the resistance of the sensor will fall. Check that the specified resistance is obtained at the correct temperature, as specified at the beginning of the Chapter. If the meter readings obtained are different, or they are obtained at different temperatures, then the sensor is faulty and must be renewed. If the readings are as specified, the fault could lie in the coolant temperature display circuit in the instrument cluster (see Chapter 9).

### Renewal

 *Warning: The engine must be completely cool before carrying out this procedure.*

**4** Drain the cooling system (see Chapter 1). Raise the fuel tank (see Chapter 4). The sensor is mounted in the thermostat housing, which is on the back of the cylinder head on the right-hand side.

**5** Disconnect the sensor wiring connector **(see illustrations)**. Unscrew the sensor and remove it from the thermostat housing.

**6** On GSX-R600 and GSX-R750T and V models, apply a smear of sealant to the threads of the sensor. On GSX-R750W and X models, make sure the washer is fitted and is in good condition. Thread the sensor into the thermostat housing and tighten it to the torque setting specified at the beginning of the Chapter. Connect the sensor wiring.

**7** Refill the cooling system (see Chapter 1).

**8** Lower the fuel tank and tighten its bolts securely.

## 6 Thermostat – removal, check and installation

### Removal

 *Warning: The engine must be completely cool before carrying out this procedure.*

**1** The thermostat is automatic in operation and should give many years service without requiring attention. In the event of a failure, the valve will probably jam open, in which case the engine will take much longer than normal to warm up. Conversely, if the valve jams shut, the coolant will be unable to circulate and the engine will overheat. Neither condition is acceptable, and the fault must be investigated promptly.

**2** Drain the cooling system (see Chapter 1). Raise the fuel tank (see Chapter 4).

**3** The thermostat is located in the thermostat housing, which is on the back of the cylinder head on the right-hand side. Disconnect the temperature sensor wiring connector, and on GSX-R750W and X models the fan switch wiring connector **(see illustrations 5.5a and b and 4.11)**.

**4** Unscrew the two bolts securing the cover

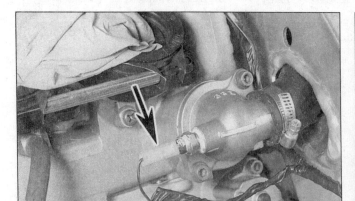

5.5a Temperature sensor wiring connector (arrowed) – GSX-R600 and GSX-R750T and V models

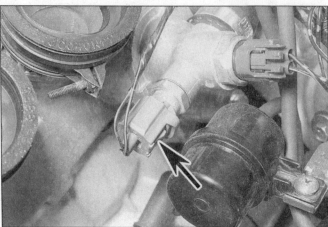

5.5b Temperature sensor wiring connector (arrowed) – GSX-R750W and X models

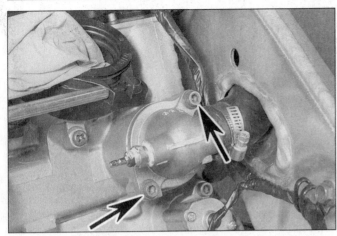

6.4a Unscrew the bolts (arrowed) and detach the cover . . .

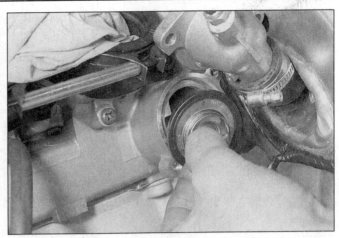

6.4b . . . and remove the thermostat

and detach it (see illustration). Withdraw the thermostat, noting how it fits (see illustration).

### Check

5 Examine the thermostat visually before carrying out the test. If it remains in the open position at room temperature, it should be renewed.

6 Suspend the thermostat by a piece of wire in a container of cold water, making sure it does not touch the bottom or sides. Place a thermometer in the water so that the bulb is close to the thermostat (see illustration). Heat the water, noting the temperature when the thermostat opens, and compare the result with the specifications given at the beginning of the Chapter. Also check the amount the valve opens after it has been heated at 90°C for a few minutes and compare the measurement to the specifications. If the readings obtained differ from those given, the thermostat is faulty and must be renewed.

7 In the event of thermostat failure, as an emergency measure only, it can be removed

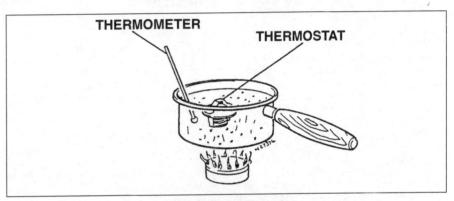

6.6 Thermostat testing set-up

and the machine used without it. Note: Take care when starting the engine from cold as it will take much longer than usual to warm up. Ensure that a new unit is installed as soon as possible.

### Installation

8 Installation is the reverse of removal. Apply a smear of grease to the rubber seal on the thermostat and install it with the bleed hole at the top (see illustration). Make sure the thermostat seats correctly. Tighten the cover bolts to the torque setting specified at the beginning of the Chapter (see illustration). Connect the wiring connector(s).

9 Refill the cooling system (see Chapter 1).

10 Lower the fuel tank and tighten its bolts securely.

3

6.8a Fit the thermostat with the hole at the top . . .

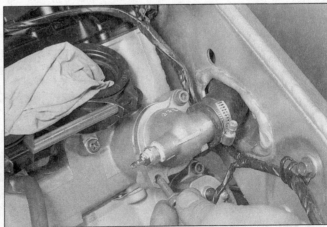

6.8b . . . refit and tighten the bolts to the specified torque

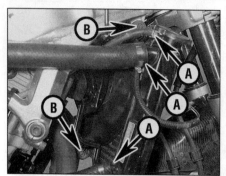

7.2a Radiator hoses (A) and mounting bolts (B) – right-hand side

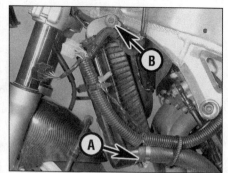

7.2b Radiator hose (A) and mounting bolt (B) – left-hand side

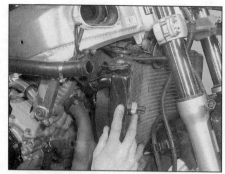

7.3 Remove the radiator

## 7 Radiator – removal and installation

### Removal

⚠️ **Warning: The engine must be completely cool before carrying out this procedure.**

**1** Remove the fairing side panels (see Chapter 8) and drain the cooling system (see Chapter 1).
**2** Slacken the clamps securing the main hoses to the top and bottom right-hand side and bottom left-hand side of the radiator and detach the hoses **(see illustrations)**. Also detach the reservoir hose from the filler neck. On GSX-R600 and GSX-R750T and V models, disconnect the fan switch wiring connector **(see illustration 4.10)**.
**3** Unscrew the radiator mounting bolts and disconnect the fan wiring connector as it becomes accessible **(see illustration 4.3a)**; note that on GSX-R750W and X models the horn will be freed as the radiator top left-hand mounting bolt is removed. Remove the radiator **(see illustration)**.
**4** If necessary, separate the cooling fan from the radiator (see Section 4).
**5** Check the radiator for signs of damage and clear any dirt or debris that might obstruct air flow and inhibit cooling. If the radiator fins are badly damaged or broken the radiator must

be renewed. Also check the rubber mounting grommets, and renew them if necessary.

### Installation

**6** Installation is the reverse of removal, noting the following.
a) *Make sure the rubber grommets and collars are correctly installed with the mounting bolts* **(see illustration)**.
b) *Make sure that the fan and fan switch (where applicable) wiring is correctly connected.*
c) *Ensure the coolant hoses are in good condition (see Chapter 1), and are securely retained by their clamps, using new ones if necessary.*
d) *On completion refill the cooling system as described in Chapter 1.*

## 8 Water pump – check, removal and installation

### Check

**1** The water pump is located on the lower left side of the engine. Visually check the area around the pump for signs of leakage.
**2** To prevent leakage of water from the cooling system to the lubrication system and vice versa, two seals are fitted on the pump shaft. The seal on the water pump side is of the mechanical type which bears on the rear

face of the impeller. The second seal, which is mounted behind the mechanical seal is of the normal feathered lip type. If on inspection there are signs of leakage, the seals must be removed and new ones installed. If you are not sure about their condition, remove the pump and check them visually, looking for signs of damage and leakage.
**3** Remove the pump cover (see Step 10). Wiggle the water pump impeller back-and-forth and in-and-out, and spin it by hand. If there is excessive movement, or the pump is noisy or rough when turned, the drive shaft bearings must be renewed. If you are not sure about their condition, remove the pump and check them visually and mechanically, referring to *Tools and Workshop Tips* in the reference Section. Also check for corrosion or a build-up of scale in the pump body and clean or renew the pump as necessary.

### Removal

**4** Drain the coolant and the engine oil (see Chapter 1).
**5** Remove the coolant reservoir (see Section 3).
**6** Unscrew the gearchange linkage arm pinch bolt and remove the arm from the shaft, noting any alignment marks **(see illustration)**. If no marks are visible, make your own before removing the arm so that it can be correctly aligned with the shaft on installation.
**7** Trace the wiring from the speedometer sensor on the front sprocket cover and disconnect it at the connector **(see illustration)**.

7.6 Make sure the grommets are in good condition and the collars are installed

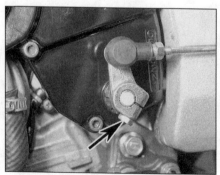

8.6 Unscrew the bolt and slide the arm off the shaft

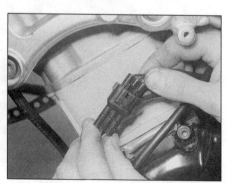

8.7 Disconnect the speedometer sensor wiring connector

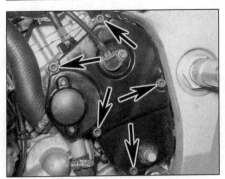

8.8 Sprocket cover bolts (arrowed)

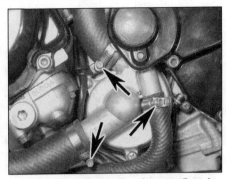

8.9 Slacken the clamps (arrowed) and detach the hoses

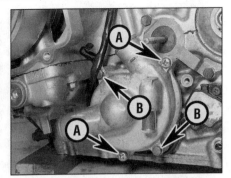

8.10 Pump screws (A), pump bolts (B)

**8** Unscrew the bolts securing the sprocket cover to the crankcase and move the cover aside **(see illustration)**. On W and X models, note the rubber bushing for the gearchange shaft and remove it from the cover if required. The cover can be secured out of the way with the clutch cable still connected.

**9** Slacken the clamps securing the coolant hoses to the pump cover and detach the hoses, noting which fits where **(see illustration)**.

**10** To remove the pump cover, remove the two screws and the two bolts, noting the wiring clamp with the top bolt, and remove the cover **(see illustration)**. Discard the cover O-ring as a new one must be used.

**11** To remove the pump body after removing the cover, carefully draw it out of the

crankcase, noting how it fits **(see illustration)**. Remove the O-ring from the rear of the pump body and discard it as a new one must be used **(see illustration)**.

**12** To remove the whole pump as an assembly, unscrew the two bolts securing the pump assembly to the crankcase **(see illustration 8.10)** and carefully draw the pump out, noting how it fits **(see illustration)**. Remove the O-ring from the rear of the pump body and discard it as a new one must be used **(see illustration 8.11b)**. Separate the cover from the pump by removing the two screws if required.

### Seal and bearing renewal

**13** Remove the pump cover, then remove the pump (see above).

**14** Counter-hold the impeller or pump drive shaft to prevent it from turning, then unscrew the impeller bolt, noting the washers, and remove the impeller **(see illustration)**. Remove the seal ring from the back of the impeller, and draw out the drive shaft from the rear of the pump body.

**15** To renew the bearings, use a bearing puller (see *Tools and Workshop Tips* in the reference Section), and draw out the two bearings from the rear of the body. Once the bearings have been removed, they cannot be reused – new ones must be fitted.

**16** To renew the seals, first remove the bearings (see above). Using a suitable socket

inserted into the rear of the pump body, drive out the seals together, noting which way round the oil seal fits. Discard them as new ones must be fitted.

**17** Press or carefully drive the new mechanical seal into the front of the pump body using a suitable sized socket or seal driver.

**18** Apply a smear of grease to the lips of the new oil seal. Press or carefully drive the new oil seal into the rear of the pump body so that it fits against the back of the mechanical seal – use a suitable sized socket or seal driver and make sure the seal is the correct way round. Take care not dislodge the mechanical seal by driving the oil seal too far in.

**19** Press or drive the new bearings into the rear of the pump body, using a suitable sized socket or bearing driver. The smaller diameter bearing fits on the inside, and the larger one is on the outside. Drive the bearings in until they are properly seated.

**20** Slide the narrow end of the drive shaft into the rear of the pump body and push it through until the shouldered sections are properly seated against their bearings. Fit the seal ring onto the back of the impeller, making sure the marked side of the ring faces the impeller, then fit the impeller onto the shaft. Counter-hold the impeller or shaft as before and tighten the impeller bolt (not forgetting its washers) to the torque setting specified at the beginning of the Chapter **(see illustration 8.14)**.

8.11a Draw the pump out of the crankcase

8.11b Remove and discard the O-ring

8.12 Unscrew the bolts and withdraw the pump

8.14 Counter-hold the shaft and unscrew the bolt

**3**

8.21 Fit a new O-ring into the groove in the pump body

8.22 Grease the O-ring and fit it into the cover

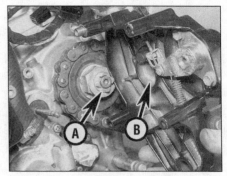

8.25a Make sure the rotor (A) fits correctly into the sensor (B)

## Installation

**21** Apply a smear of grease to the new pump body O-ring and fit it into the groove in the body **(see illustration)**. Slide the pump into the crankcase, aligning the slot in the impeller shaft with the tab on the oil pump shaft **(see illustration 8.11a)**.

**22** To fit the cover, smear the new O-ring with grease and fit it into its groove in the cover **(see illustration)**.

**23** Fit the cover onto the pump, then install the two bolts, not forgetting the wiring clamp with the top bolt, and the two screws and tighten them to the torque setting specified at the beginning of the Chapter **(see illustration 8.10)**.

**24** If detached, attach the coolant hoses to the pump cover and secure them with their clamps **(see illustrations 8.9)**.

**25** Make sure the dowels are either in the crankcase or the sprocket cover. Install the cover, making sure the speedometer rotor fits properly into the sensor and the dowels locate

correctly, and tighten its bolts **(see illustration)**. On W and X models, if removed, fit the rubber bushing for the gearchange shaft into the cover **(see illustration)**.

**26** Slide the gearchange linkage arm onto the shaft, aligning the marks, and tighten the pinch bolt **(see illustration 8.6)**. Check that the mechanism works correctly

**27** Reconnect the speedometer sensor wiring connector **(see illustration 8.7)**.

**28** Install the coolant reservoir (see Section 3). Refill the cooling system and the engine oil (see Chapter 1).

## 9 Coolant hoses – removal and installation

### Removal

**1** Before removing a hose, drain the coolant (see Chapter 1).

**2** Use a screwdriver to slacken the larger-bore hose clamps, then slide them back along the hose and clear of the union spigot. The smaller-bore hoses are secured by spring clamps which can be expanded by squeezing their ears together with pliers.

*Caution: The radiator unions are fragile. Do not use excessive force when attempting to remove the hoses.*

**3** If a hose proves stubborn, release it by rotating it on its union before working it off. If all else fails, cut the hose with a sharp knife then slit it at each union so that it can be peeled off in two pieces. Whilst this means renewing the hose, it is preferable to buying a new radiator.

**4** The coolant inlet hose union on the cylinder block can be removed by unscrewing its bolts **(see illustration)**. If the union is removed, the O-ring must be renewed.

### Installation

**5** Slide the clips onto the hose and then work it on to its respective union.

> **HAYNES HiNT**
> *If the hose is difficult to push on its union, it can be softened by soaking it in very hot water, or alternatively a little soapy water can be used as a lubricant.*

**6** Rotate the hose on its unions to settle it in position before sliding the clamps into place and tightening them securely.

**7** If the inlet union to the cylinder block has been removed, fit a new O-ring, then install the union and tighten the mounting bolts to the torque setting specified at the beginning of the Chapter **(see illustration 9.4)**.

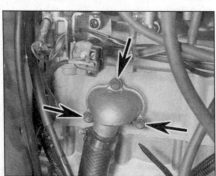

8.25b Where fitted and if removed, fit the rubber bush for the gearchange shaft

9.4 The union is secured by three bolts (arrowed)

# Chapter 4
# Fuel and exhaust systems

## Contents

## Degrees of difficulty

| | | | | |
|---|---|---|---|---|
| **Easy,** suitable for novice with little experience |  **Fairly easy,** suitable for beginner with some experience |  **Fairly difficult,** suitable for competent DIY mechanic | **Difficult,** suitable for experienced DIY mechanic | **Very difficult,** suitable for expert DIY or professional 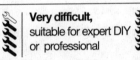 |

## Specifications

**Fuel**

| | |
|---|---|
| Grade . . . . . . . . . . . . . . . . . . . . . . . . . . . . . . . . . . . . . . . . . . . . . . | Unleaded, minimum 91 RON (Research Octane Number) |
| Fuel tank capacity (including reserve) . . . . . . . . . . . . . . . . . . . . . . . | 18 litres |

**Carburettors – GSX-R600V**

| | |
|---|---|
| Type . . . . . . . . . . . . . . . . . . . . . . . . . . . . . . . . . . . . . . . . . . . . . . . | Mikuni BDSR36 |
| Bore . . . . . . . . . . . . . . . . . . . . . . . . . . . . . . . . . . . . . . . . . . . . . . . | 36.5 mm |
| I.D. no. | |
|     UK . . . . . . . . . . . . . . . . . . . . . . . . . . . . . . . . . . . . . . . . . . . . | 34E0 |
|     US . . . . . . . . . . . . . . . . . . . . . . . . . . . . . . . . . . . . . . . . . . . . | 34E1 |
|     California . . . . . . . . . . . . . . . . . . . . . . . . . . . . . . . . . . . . . . . | 34E3 |
| Pilot jet . . . . . . . . . . . . . . . . . . . . . . . . . . . . . . . . . . . . . . . . . . . . . | 12.5 |
| Needle jet | |
|     UK . . . . . . . . . . . . . . . . . . . . . . . . . . . . . . . . . . . . . . . . . . . . | P-O |
|     US and California . . . . . . . . . . . . . . . . . . . . . . . . . . . . . . . . . | P-OM |
| Jet needle | |
|     UK . . . . . . . . . . . . . . . . . . . . . . . . . . . . . . . . . . . . . . . . . . . . | 5DH18-52-3 |
|     US and California . . . . . . . . . . . . . . . . . . . . . . . . . . . . . . . . . | 5DH20-53 |
| Main jet | |
|     Cylinder 1 . . . . . . . . . . . . . . . . . . . . . . . . . . . . . . . . . . . . . . . | 125 |
|     Cylinders 2, 3 and 4 . . . . . . . . . . . . . . . . . . . . . . . . . . . . . . . | 122.5 |
| Pilot screw setting (turns out) | |
|     UK | |
|         Cylinders 1 and 4 . . . . . . . . . . . . . . . . . . . . . . . . . . . . . . | 3 1/2 turns out |
|         Cylinders 2 and 3 . . . . . . . . . . . . . . . . . . . . . . . . . . . . . . | 2 1/2 turns out |
|     US and California . . . . . . . . . . . . . . . . . . . . . . . . . . . . . . . . . | Pre-set |

**4**

## Carburettors – GSX-R600V (continued)

| | |
|---|---|
| Float height | 7.0 ± 1.0 mm |
| Fuel level | 15.5 ± 0.5 mm |
| Idle speed | see Chapter 1 |
| Throttle position sensor resistance | 3.5 to 6.5 K-ohms |
| Heater system resistance (UK models) | 12 to 18 ohms |

## Carburettors – GSX-R600W

| | |
|---|---|
| Type | Mikuni BDSR36 |
| Bore | 36.5 mm |
| I.D. no. | |
|   UK | 34E6 |
|   US | 34E7 |
|   California | 34E9 |
| Pilot jet | 12.5 |
| Needle jet | |
|   UK | P-O |
|   US and California | P-OM |
| Jet needle | |
|   UK | 5DHZ31-3 |
|   US | 5DHZ32 |
|   California | 5DH20-53 |
| Main jet | |
|   Cylinders 1 and 4 | 135 |
|   Cylinders 2 and 3 | 132.5 |
| Pilot screw setting (turns out) | |
|   UK | |
|     Cylinders 1 and 4 | 3 turns out |
|     Cylinders 2 and 3 | 2 3/4 turns out |
|   US and California | Pre-set |
| Float height | 7.0 ± 1.0 mm |
| Fuel level | 15.5 ± 0.5 mm |
| Idle speed | see Chapter 1 |
| Throttle position sensor resistance | 3.5 to 6.5 K-ohms |
| Heater system resistance (UK models) | 12 to 18 ohms |

## Carburettors – GSX-R600X

| | |
|---|---|
| Type | Mikuni BDSR36 |
| Bore | 36.5 mm |
| I.D. no. | |
|   UK | 34E6 |
|   US | 34EC |
|   California | 34EE |
| Pilot jet | 12.5 |
| Needle jet | |
|   UK | P-O |
|   US and California | P-OM |
| Jet needle | |
|   UK | 5DHZ31-3 |
|   US | 5DH20-53 |
|   California | 5DH20-53 |
| Main jet | |
|   UK | |
|     Cylinders 1 and 4 | 135 |
|     Cylinders 2 and 3 | 132.5 |
|   US and California | |
|     Cylinders 1 and 4 | 132.5 |
|     Cylinders 2 and 3 | 130 |
| Pilot screw setting (turns out) | |
|   UK | |
|     Cylinders 1 and 4 | 3 turns out |
|     Cylinders 2 and 3 | 2 3/4 turns out |
|   US and California | Pre-set |
| Float height | 7.0 ± 1.0 mm |
| Fuel level | 15.5 ± 0.5 mm |
| Idle speed | see Chapter 1 |
| Throttle position sensor resistance | 3.5 to 6.5 K-ohms |
| Heater system resistance (UK models) | 12 to 18 ohms |

## Carburettors – GSX-R750T and V

| | |
|---|---|
| Type . . . . . . . . . . . . . . . . . . . . . . . . . . . . . . . . . . . . . . . . . . . . . . . . | Mikuni BDSR39 |
| Bore . . . . . . . . . . . . . . . . . . . . . . . . . . . . . . . . . . . . . . . . . . . . . . . . . | 39 mm |
| I.D. no. | |
|   UK . . . . . . . . . . . . . . . . . . . . . . . . . . . . . . . . . . . . . . . . . . . . . | 33EO |
|   US . . . . . . . . . . . . . . . . . . . . . . . . . . . . . . . . . . . . . . . . . . . . . | 33E1 |
|   California . . . . . . . . . . . . . . . . . . . . . . . . . . . . . . . . . . . . . . . | 33E7 |
| Pilot jet . . . . . . . . . . . . . . . . . . . . . . . . . . . . . . . . . . . . . . . . . . . . . . | 12.5 |
| Needle jet | |
|   UK . . . . . . . . . . . . . . . . . . . . . . . . . . . . . . . . . . . . . . . . . . . . . | P-O |
|   US and California . . . . . . . . . . . . . . . . . . . . . . . . . . . . . . . . . | P-OM |
| Jet needle | |
|   UK . . . . . . . . . . . . . . . . . . . . . . . . . . . . . . . . . . . . . . . . . . . . . | 6E38-54-3 |
|   US . . . . . . . . . . . . . . . . . . . . . . . . . . . . . . . . . . . . . . . . . . . . . | 6E41-55 |
|   California . . . . . . . . . . . . . . . . . . . . . . . . . . . . . . . . . . . . . . . | 6E39-55 |
| Main jet | |
|   UK | |
|     Cylinders 1 and 4 . . . . . . . . . . . . . . . . . . . . . . . . . . . . . . | 127.5 |
|     Cylinders 2 and 3 . . . . . . . . . . . . . . . . . . . . . . . . . . . . . . | 125 |
|   US and California | |
|     Cylinders 1 and 4 . . . . . . . . . . . . . . . . . . . . . . . . . . . . . . | 127.5 |
|     Cylinders 2 and 3 . . . . . . . . . . . . . . . . . . . . . . . . . . . . . . | 125 |
| Pilot screw setting (turns out) | |
|   UK | |
|     Cylinders 1 and 4 . . . . . . . . . . . . . . . . . . . . . . . . . . . . . . | 2 turns out |
|     Cylinders 2 and 3 . . . . . . . . . . . . . . . . . . . . . . . . . . . . . . | 2 turns out |
|   US and California . . . . . . . . . . . . . . . . . . . . . . . . . . . . . . . | Pre-set |
| Float height . . . . . . . . . . . . . . . . . . . . . . . . . . . . . . . . . . . . . . . . . | 7.0 ± 1.0 mm |
| Idle speed . . . . . . . . . . . . . . . . . . . . . . . . . . . . . . . . . . . . . . . . . . | see Chapter 1 |
| Throttle position sensor resistance . . . . . . . . . . . . . . . . . . . . . | 3.5 to 6.5 K-ohms |
| Heater system resistance (UK models) . . . . . . . . . . . . . . . . . . | 12 to 18 ohms |

## Fuel injection system – GSX-R750W and X models

| | |
|---|---|
| Operating pressure . . . . . . . . . . . . . . . . . . . . . . . . . . . . . . . . . . | 41 psi |
| Inlet air control valve operating rpm | |
|   Open . . . . . . . . . . . . . . . . . . . . . . . . . . . . . . . . . . . . . . . . . . . | above 5400 rpm |
|   Closed . . . . . . . . . . . . . . . . . . . . . . . . . . . . . . . . . . . . . . . . . | below 5200 rpm |
| Inlet air control solenoid valve resistance . . . . . . . . . . . . . . . . | 36 to 44 ohms |
| Fuel injector resistance . . . . . . . . . . . . . . . . . . . . . . . . . . . . . . . | 11 to 16 ohms @ 20°C |
| Air screw setting . . . . . . . . . . . . . . . . . . . . . . . . . . . . . . . . . . . . | 1/2 turn out |
| Camshaft position (CMP) sensor resistance . . . . . . . . . . . . . . | 0.9 to 1.3 K-ohms |
| Camshaft position (CMP) sensor peak voltage . . . . . . . . . . . . | min. 0.8 V |
| Crankshaft position (CKP) sensor resistance . . . . . . . . . . . . . . | 50 to 200 ohms |
| Crankshaft position (CKP) sensor peak voltage . . . . . . . . . . . . | min 0.5 V |
| Inlet air pressure (IAP) sensor input voltage . . . . . . . . . . . . . . | 4.5 to 5.5 V |
| Inlet air pressure (IAP) sensor output voltage . . . . . . . . . . . . . | approx. 2.85 V at idle |
| Throttle position (TP) sensor input voltage . . . . . . . . . . . . . . . | 4.5 to 5.5 V |
| Throttle position (TP) sensor resistance | |
|   Closed . . . . . . . . . . . . . . . . . . . . . . . . . . . . . . . . . . . . . . . . . | approx. 1.2 K-ohms |
|   Open . . . . . . . . . . . . . . . . . . . . . . . . . . . . . . . . . . . . . . . . . . . | approx. 4.4 K-ohms |
| Throttle position (TP) sensor output voltage | |
|   Closed . . . . . . . . . . . . . . . . . . . . . . . . . . . . . . . . . . . . . . . . . | approx. 1.1 V |
|   Open . . . . . . . . . . . . . . . . . . . . . . . . . . . . . . . . . . . . . . . . . . . | approx. 4.2 V |
| Engine coolant temperature (ECT) sensor input voltage . . . . . . . . . . | 4.5 to 5.5 V |
| Engine coolant temperature (ECT) sensor resistance . . . . . . . . . . . . | 2.3 to 2.6 K-ohms @ 20°C |
| Inlet air temperature (IAT) sensor input voltage . . . . . . . . . . . | 4.5 to 5.5 V |
| Inlet air temperature (IAT) sensor resistance . . . . . . . . . . . . . . | 2.2 to 2.7 K-ohms @ 20°C |
| Atmospheric pressure (AP) sensor input voltage . . . . . . . . . . . | 4.5 to 5.5 V |
| Atmospheric pressure (AP) sensor output voltage . . . . . . . . . . | approx. 3.6 V @ 760 mmHg |
| Tip-over (TO) sensor resistance . . . . . . . . . . . . . . . . . . . . . . . . | 60 to 64 K-ohms |
| Tip-over (TO) sensor voltage . . . . . . . . . . . . . . . . . . . . . . . . . . . | approx. 2.5 V |
| Gear position (GP) sensor voltage . . . . . . . . . . . . . . . . . . . . . . | min. 0.6 V |
| Injector voltage . . . . . . . . . . . . . . . . . . . . . . . . . . . . . . . . . . . . . | Battery voltage |

## Fuel pump

| | |
|---|---|
| Discharge rate | |
|   GSX-R600 and GSX-R750T and V models . . . . . . . . . . . . . . . . . . . . | min. 1.0 litre per minute |
|   GSX-R750W and X models . . . . . . . . . . . . . . . . . . . . . . . . . . . . . . . | 26 to 30 cc per 3 secs. |

**4**

## Torque settings

| | |
|---|---|
| Carburettor heaters (UK models) | 3 Nm |
| Throttle position sensor screws | 3.5 Nm |
| Fuel pressure check bolt | 10 Nm |
| Fuel supply union screws | 3 Nm |
| Fuel pressure regulator bolts | 5 Nm |
| Fuel rail bolts | 13 Nm |
| Silencer to downpipe assembly nuts | 26 Nm |
| Silencer mounting nut/bolt | 23 Nm |
| Downpipe assembly bolts | 23 Nm |

### 1 General information and precautions

#### General information

The fuel system consists of the fuel tank, the fuel pump and its relay, the strainer and/or filter, the fuel valve (carburettor models), the fuel hoses and control cables. All GSX-R600 models and GSX-R750T and V models have carburettors, while GSX-R750W and X models have a fuel injection system controlled by various sensors which feed information to the electronic management system.

The fuel pump is housed inside the tank. On models with carburettors, the pump incorporates a strainer. On fuel injected models, the pump incorporates a strainer and a filter, and fuel pressure is controlled by a regulator.

The fuel valve is opened by a vacuum sourced from the inlet manifold and created when the engine is turned over.

The carburettors used are CV types, and there is a carburettor for each cylinder. A throttle position sensor mounted on the carburettors feeds information to the electronic ignition system.

Fuel injected models have an injector for each cylinder, housed in the throttle body.

For cold starting, a choke lever is incorporated in the left-handlebar switch housing and is connected by a cable.

The fuel warning circuit is operated by a level sensor inside the tank.

Air is drawn into the carburettors or throttle bodies via an air filter which is housed under the fuel tank.

The exhaust system is a two piece four-into-one design.

Many of the fuel system service procedures are considered routine maintenance items and for that reason are included in Chapter 1.

#### Precautions

 **Warning: Petrol (gasoline) is extremely flammable, so take extra precautions when you work on any part of the fuel system. Don't smoke or allow open flames or bare light bulbs near the work area, and don't work in a garage where a natural gas-type appliance is present. If you spill any fuel on your skin, rinse it off immediately with soap and water. When you perform any kind of work on the fuel system, wear safety glasses and have a fire extinguisher suitable for a class B type fire (flammable liquids) on hand.**

Always perform service procedures in a well-ventilated area to prevent a build-up of fumes.

Never work in a building containing a gas appliance with a pilot light, or any other form of naked flame. Ensure that there are no naked light bulbs or any sources of flame or sparks nearby.

Do not smoke (or allow anyone else to smoke) while in the vicinity of petrol (gasoline) or of components containing it. Remember the possible presence of vapour from these sources and move well clear before smoking.

Check all electrical equipment belonging to the house, garage or workshop where work is being undertaken (see the Safety first! section of this manual). Remember that certain electrical appliances such as drills, cutters etc. create sparks in the normal course of operation and must not be used near petrol (gasoline) or any component containing it. Again, remember the possible presence of fumes before using electrical equipment.

Always mop up any spilt fuel and safely dispose of the rag used.

Any stored fuel that is drained off during servicing work must be kept in sealed containers that are suitable for holding petrol (gasoline), and clearly marked as such; the containers themselves should be kept in a safe place. Note that this last point applies equally to the fuel tank if it is removed from the machine; also remember to keep its filler cap closed at all times.

Read the Safety first! section of this manual carefully before starting work.

Owners of machines used in the US, particularly California, should note that their machines must comply at all times with Federal or State legislation governing the permissible levels of noise and of pollutants such as unburnt hydrocarbons, carbon monoxide etc. that can be emitted by those machines. All vehicles offered for sale must comply with legislation in force at the date of manufacture and must not subsequently be altered in any way which will affect their emission of noise or of pollutants.

In practice, this means that adjustments may not be made to any part of the fuel, ignition or exhaust systems by anyone who is not authorised or mechanically qualified to do so, or who does not have the tools, equipment and data necessary to properly carry out the task. Also if any part of these systems is to be renewed it must be renewed with only genuine Suzuki components or by components which are approved under the relevant legislation. The machine must never be used with any part of these systems removed, modified or damaged.

### 2 Fuel tank – removal and installation

 **Warning: Refer to the precautions given in Section 1 before starting work.**

#### Raise

**1** Make sure the fuel cap is secure.

**2** Remove the rider's and passenger seats (see Chapter 8). Remove the fuel tank support bar from the storage space.

**3** Unscrew the two bolts securing the front of the fuel tank to the frame (see illustration). Lift up the front of the tank and place the support between it and the steering head nut, locating the very angled end of the support through the hole in the nut and the straighter

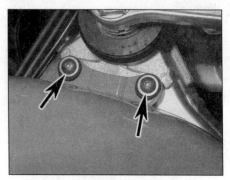

**2.3a Unscrew the bolts (arrowed) . . .**

2.3b . . . then raise the tank and position the support bar as described

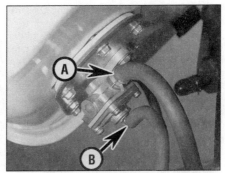

2.8a Detach the fuel hose (A) and the vacuum hose (B) . . .

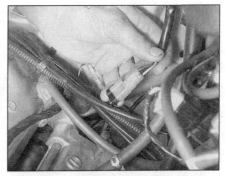

2.8b . . . and disconnect the wiring connector

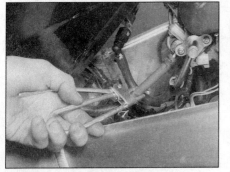

2.9a Attach a clamp to the return hose . . .

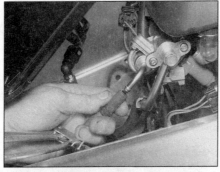

2.9b . . . and detach it from the regulator

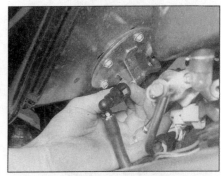

2.9c Press in the clip ears . . .

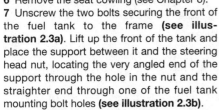

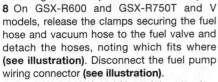

end through one of the fuel tank mounting bolt holes **(see illustration)**.

### Removal

**4** Make sure the fuel cap is secure.
**5** Remove the rider's and passenger seats (see Chapter 8). Remove the fuel tank support bar from the storage space.
**6** Remove the seat cowling (see Chapter 8).
**7** Unscrew the two bolts securing the front of the fuel tank to the frame **(see illustration 2.3a)**. Lift up the front of the tank and place the support between it and the steering head nut, locating the very angled end of the support through the hole in the nut and the straighter end through one of the fuel tank mounting bolt holes **(see illustration 2.3b)**.
**8** On GSX-R600 and GSX-R750T and V models, release the clamps securing the fuel hose and vacuum hose to the fuel valve and detach the hoses, noting which fits where **(see illustration)**. Disconnect the fuel pump wiring connector **(see illustration)**.
**9** On GSX-R750W and X models, attach a hose clamp (see *Tools and Workshop Tips*) to the fuel return hose which runs from the pressure regulator to the fuel tank **(see illustration)**. Have a rag handy to catch any residue fuel, then detach the hose from the regulator **(see illustration)**. Fit a suitable plug into the end of the hose as a back-up to the clamp. Press in the clip ears on the fuel supply hose from the outlet on the fuel tank and detach the hose **(see illustrations)**. Disconnect the fuel pump wiring connector **(see illustration)**.

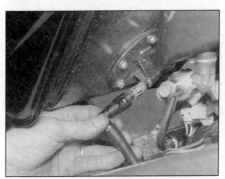

2.9d . . . and detach the fuel supply hose from the tank

**10** Unscrew the bolts securing the fuel tank bracket to the frame **(see illustration)**. Remove the tank support, then carefully lift the tank off the bike, drawing the drain and breather hoses with it, noting their routing and

2.10a Unscrew the tank bracket bolts . . .

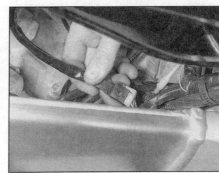

2.9e Disconnect the wiring connector

making sure they do not snag **(see illustration)**. Take care not to lose the mounting rubbers from between the sides of the tank and the frame, noting how they fit.
**11** Inspect the tank mounting rubbers for

2.10b . . . and remove the tank

**4**

**2.14 Route the hoses as described and through the guide (arrowed)**

signs of damage or deterioration and renew them if necessary. Also inspect the rubbers on the fuel tank mounting brackets. Renew the rubbers if necessary.

### Installation

**12** Check that the front and side tank rubbers are fitted, then carefully lower the fuel tank into position, making sure the rubbers remain in place.
**13** Install the tank rear bracket bolts to locate the bracket, but leave the bolts loose **(see illustration 2.10a)**. ¹se the tank up onto its support bar **(see illustration 2.3b)**.
**14** Route the drain and breather hoses down the right-hand side of the shock absorber, between the frame and the swingarm and the frame and the engine, and through the hose guide at the bottom **(see illustration)**. Make sure the breather hose does not become kinked or pinched as this could prevent a full flow of fuel.
**15** On GSX-R600 and GSX-R750T and V models, attach the fuel hose to the union on the side of the fuel valve, and the vacuum hose to the union on the bottom of the valve, and secure them with their clamps **(see illustration 2.8a)**. Connect the fuel pump wiring connector **(see illustration 2.8b)**.
**16** On GSX-R750W and X models, make sure the hose clamp on the fuel return hose is secure. Remove the plug from the end of the hose and attach the hose to the union on the fuel pressure regulator **(see illustration 2.9b)**. Also attach the fuel supply hose to the outlet on the fuel tank, making sure the clip ears lock into the cutouts **(see illustration 2.9d)**.

**4.7 Fuel valve bolts (arrowed)**

Connect the fuel pump wiring connector **(see illustration 2.9e)**.
**17** Remove the support from the front of the tank, then lower the tank. Install the front tank bolts and tighten them securely **(see illustration 2.3a)**. Now tighten the tank bracket bolts.
**18** Start the engine and check that there is no sign of fuel leakage, then shut if off.
**19** Install the seat cowling (if the tank was removed) and the seats (see Chapter 8).

### 3 Fuel tank – cleaning and repair

**1** All repairs to the fuel tank should be carried out by a professional who has experience in this critical and potentially dangerous work. Even after cleaning and flushing of the fuel system, explosive fumes can remain and ignite during repair of the tank.
**2** If the fuel tank is removed from the bike, it should not be placed in an area where sparks or open flames could ignite the fumes coming out of the tank. Be especially careful inside garages where a natural gas-type appliance is located, because the pilot light could cause an explosion.

### 4 Fuel valve (GSX-R600 and GSX-R750T and V models) – check, removal and installation

> ⚠ **Warning: Refer to the precautions given in Section 1 before starting work.**

### Check

**1** Raise the fuel tank (see Section 2).
**2** Release the clamp securing the fuel hose to the outlet union on the fuel valve and detach the hose **(see illustration 2.8a)**. Obtain an auxiliary length of hose and attach one end to the outlet union on the valve. Place the open end of the hose in a container suitable for holding fuel.
**3** Switch the ignition ON and turn the engine over on the starter motor. Fuel should flow into the container as soon as the engine is turned. If it doesn't (and there is fuel in the tank), first

**5.4a Fuel pump relay (arrowed)**

check that the vacuum hose from the inlet manifold is secure at both ends and is not split or cracked. Fit a new hose if in doubt.
**4** If there is still no flow, remove the valve (see below) and apply a vacuum (negative pressure) of -1.89 psi to the vacuum union using a vacuum pump and gauge. With the vacuum applied and held, blow through the fuel outlet union. If air flows through the valve when you blow into the outlet, the valve is good. If no air flows, a new valve must be fitted – no internal parts are available.
**5** If the valve is good, check the fuel pump, strainer and filter.

### Removal

**6** Remove the fuel tank (see Section 2). Connect a drain hose to the fuel outlet union and insert its end in a container suitable for holding fuel. Also connect a hose to the vacuum union. Apply a vacuum to the hose and allow the fuel to drain from the tank.
**7** Turn the tank upside down and rest it on some rags. Unscrew the two bolts securing the valve to the tank and remove the valve **(see illustration)**. Discard the O-ring and the bolt sealing washers as new ones must be used.

### Installation

**8** Fit the valve onto the tank, using a new O-ring. Fit new sealing washers onto the bolts and tighten the bolts securely.
**9** Install the fuel tank (see Section 2).

### 5 Fuel pump, relay and fuel level sensor – check, removal and installation

> ⚠ **Warning: Refer to the precautions given in Section 1 before starting work.**

### Check

#### Fuel pump and relay

**1** The fuel pump is located inside the fuel tank.
**2** On GSX-R600 and GSX-R750T and V models, it should be possible to hear the fuel pump running whenever the engine is turning over – remove the rider's seat (see Chapter 8) and place your ear close to the rear of the tank. If you can't hear anything, check the relay (see Step 4).
**3** On GSX-R750W and X models, the fuel pump runs for three seconds when the ignition is switched ON, then cuts out when the system is up to operating pressure, until the engine is started. If you can't hear anything, first check the fuse (see Chapter 9), then check the relay (see Step 4). If they are good, renew the pump.
**4** To access the relay, remove the seat cowling (see Chapter 8). The relay is on the left-hand side of the rear sub-frame **(see illustration)**. Disconnect the relay wiring connector. Using a continuity tester, check for continuity between terminals 1 and 2 on the relay side of the

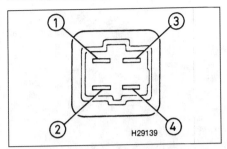

**5.4b Fuel pump relay terminal identification (see text)**

connector (**see illustration**). There should be no continuity. If there is, renew the relay. Using a fully charged 12 volt battery and two insulated jumper wires, connect the battery positive (+ve) terminal to terminal 3 on the connector, and the battery negative (-ve) terminal to terminal 4 on the connector. Now check again for continuity between terminals 1 and 2 on the connector. There should be continuity with the battery connected. If not, renew the relay. If the fuse and relay are good, check the wiring and terminals for physical damage or loose or corroded connections and rectify as necessary (see the *Wiring Diagrams* at the end of Chapter 9).

**5** On GSX-R600 and GSX-R750T and V models, if the pump still does not work, raise the fuel tank (see Section 2) and disconnect the fuel pump wiring connector (**see illustration 2.8b**). Using a fully charged 12 volt battery and two insulated jumper wires, connect the battery positive (+ve) terminal to the pump's yellow/red wire terminal, and the battery negative (-ve) terminal to the pump's black/white wire terminal. The pump should operate. If the pump does not operate, renew it.

**6** If the pump operates but is thought to be delivering an insufficient amount of fuel, first check that the fuel tank breather hose is unobstructed, that all fuel hoses are in good condition and not pinched or trapped. Check that the fuel strainer or filter is not blocked. On GSX-R600 and GSX-R750T and V models, check the fuel valve (see Section 4). On GSX-R750W and X models, check the fuel injection system (see Section 16).

**7** The fuel pump's output can be checked as follows: make sure there is at least 5 litres of

fuel in the tank, the battery is fully charged and the ignition switch is OFF. Raise the fuel tank (see Section 2).

**8** On GSX-R600 and GSX-R750T and V models, release the clamp securing the fuel hose to the outlet union on the fuel valve and detach the hose (**see illustration 2.8a**). Obtain an auxiliary length of hose and attach one end to the outlet union on the valve. Place the other end into a graduated beaker. Also detach the vacuum hose from the fuel valve and apply a vacuum (negative pressure) of -1.89 psi to the union using a vacuum pump and gauge. Disconnect the fuel pump wiring connector (**see illustration 2.8b**). Using a fully charged 12 volt battery and two insulated jumper wires, connect the battery positive (+ve) terminal to the pump's yellow/red wire terminal, and the battery negative (-ve) terminal to the pump's black/white wire terminal. Let fuel flow from the pump into the beaker for 1 minute, then disconnect the battery.

**9** On GSX-R750W and X models, attach a hose clamp (see *Tools and Workshop Tips*) to the fuel return hose which runs from the pressure regulator to the fuel tank (**see illustration 2.9a**). Have a rag handy to catch

any residue fuel, then detach the hose from the regulator (**see illustration 2.9b**). Fit a suitable plug into the end of the hose as a back-up to the clamp. Obtain an auxiliary length of hose and attach one end to the outlet union on the regulator. Place the other end into a graduated beaker. Turn the ignition switch ON and let fuel flow from the pump into the beaker for 3 seconds, then switch the ignition OFF.

**10** Measure the amount of fuel that has flowed into the beaker, then compare it to the amount specified at the beginning of the Chapter. If the flow rate recorded is below the minimum required, the fuel pump must be renewed. On GSX-R750W and X models, if the pump is good but the system is still suspect, perform a fuel pressure check (see Section 17).

**Fuel level sensor**

**11** Remove the fuel pump/level sensor assembly (see below).

**12** Unscrew the nuts securing the sensor wires to their terminals on the mounting plate and detach the wires (**see illustration**). Remove the screws securing the fuel level sensor to the fuel pump and remove the sensor, noting how it fits.

**13** Connect a test light as shown in the four separate tests (**see illustration**). Give the light

**5.12 Unscrew the nuts (A) and detach the wires, then remove the screws (B) and remove the sensor**

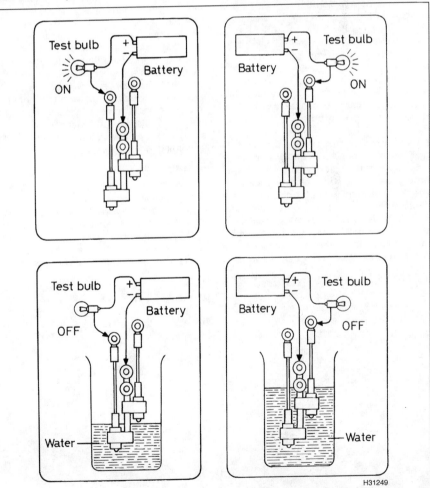

**5.13 Fuel level sensor test set-ups**

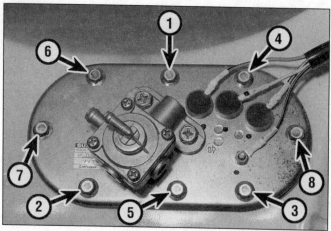

5.15a Unscrew the bolts (arrowed) – numbers indicate tightening sequence . . .

5.15b . . . and remove the pump assembly

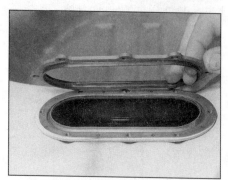

5.15c Discard the gasket and fit a new one

a few seconds to react in each case, and stir the sensor around in the water when submerged. If the test results are as shown, the level sensor is good, which means there is a fault elsewhere in the circuit, or in the display in the instrument cluster (see Chapter 9). If the test results are not as described, a new fuel pump and level sensor assembly must be installed – the level sensor is not available separately. Take care to wipe all water off the sensor before installing it in the fuel tank.

### Removal

14 Make sure the ignition is switched OFF. Remove the fuel tank and drain it (see Section 2). Turn the tank upside down and rest it on some clean rag.
15 Unscrew the bolts securing the fuel pump mounting plate to the tank, then withdraw the pump assembly **(see illustrations)**. Discard the gasket as a new one must be used. If a new fuel pump/level sensor is being installed it comes as an assembly with the mounting plate, so there is no need to dismantle the old assembly. It is wise to order the new pump along with a new strainer and/or filter (according to model).

### Installation

16 Installation is the reverse of removal, noting the following:
a) Check the condition of the strainer and/or filter on the fuel pump and clean or renew as required (see Chapter 1).
b) Make sure the wires are correctly and securely fitted to the pump and sensor.
c) Install the pump assembly using a new gasket and tighten the cover bolts evenly and a little at a time in the numerical sequence shown to the torque setting specified at the beginning of the Chapter **(see illustrations 5.15c and a)**.
d) On completion, start the engine and look carefully for any signs of leaks around the pump mounting plate and at the hose connections.

## 6 Air filter housing – removal and installation

### Removal

1 Raise the fuel tank (see Section 2). If required for improved access, remove the tank completely.
2 Unscrew the bolt securing the front of the airbox to the frame **(see illustration)**.
3 Release the clamp securing the crankcase breather hose to the back of the housing and detach the hose from its union **(see illustration)**.

6.2 Unscrew the bolt (arrowed)

6.3 Detach the breather hose

6.4a  Detach the IAT sensor wiring connector (arrowed) . . .

6.4b  . . . and remove the screw (arrowed) securing the IAP sensor

6.5a  On carburettor models, slacken the screw on each clamp (arrowed)

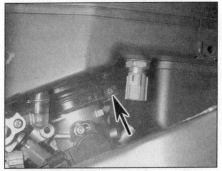

6.5b  On injection models, slacken the double-clamp screw (arrowed) on each side

6.5c  On carburettor models, detach the vent hose

6.5d  On injection models detach the vacuum hose

4  On GSX-R750W and X models, disconnect the IAT sensor wiring connector from the right-hand side of the housing, and remove the screw securing the IAP sensor to the back of the housing (see illustrations).

5  Slacken the clamp screws securing the housing to the carburettors or throttle bodies; on carburettor models, there is a clamp screw for each clamp, while on injection models double-clamps are used, whereby one screw acts on two clamps (see illustrations). Carefully lift the housing up, on GSX-R600 and GSX-R750T and V models, detaching the carburettor vent hose from the front of the housing (see illustration), and on GSX-R750W and X models detaching the vacuum hose from the inlet air control system diaphragm on the underside of the housing (see illustration), and remove the housing.

### Installation

6  Installation is the reverse of removal. Make sure the inlets in the housing locate correctly against the ducts in the frame – there should be no gaps between them.

## 7  Idle fuel/air mixture adjustment (carburettor models) – general information

1  Due to the increased emphasis on controlling motorcycle exhaust emissions, certain governmental regulations have been formulated which directly affect the carburation of this machine. In order to comply with the regulations, the carburettors on US models are sealed so they can't be tampered with. The pilot screws on other models are accessible, but the use of an exhaust gas analyser is the only accurate way to adjust the idle fuel/air mixture and be sure the machine doesn't exceed the emissions regulations.

2  The pilot screws are set to their correct position by the manufacturer and should not be adjusted unless it is necessary to do so for a carburettor overhaul. If the screws are adjusted they should be reset to the settings specified at the beginning of the Chapter.

3  If the engine runs extremely rough at idle or continually stalls, and if a carburettor overhaul does not cure the problem, take the motorcycle to a Suzuki dealer equipped with an exhaust gas analyser. They will be able to properly adjust the idle fuel/air mixture to achieve a smooth idle and restore low speed performance.

## 8  Carburettor overhaul – general information

1  Poor engine performance, hesitation, hard starting, stalling, flooding and backfiring are all signs that major carburettor maintenance may be required.

2  Keep in mind that many so-called carburettor problems are really not carburettor problems at all, but mechanical problems within the engine or ignition system malfunctions. Try to establish for certain that the carburettors are in need of maintenance before beginning a major overhaul.

3  Check the fuel filter, the fuel hoses, the inlet manifold joint clamps, the air filter, the ignition system, the spark plugs and carburettor synchronisation before assuming that a carburettor overhaul is required.

4  Most carburettor problems are caused by dirt particles, varnish and other deposits which build up in and block the fuel and air passages. Also, in time, gaskets and O-rings shrink or deteriorate and cause fuel and air leaks which lead to poor performance.

5  When overhauling the carburettors, disassemble them completely and clean the parts thoroughly with a carburettor cleaning solvent and dry them with filtered, unlubricated compressed air. Blow through the fuel and air passages with compressed air to force out any dirt that may have been loosened but not removed by the solvent. Once the cleaning process is complete, reassemble the carburettor using new gaskets and O-rings.

6  Before disassembling the carburettors, make sure you have all necessary O-rings and other parts, some carburettor cleaner, a supply of clean rags, some means of blowing out the carburettor passages and a clean

**4**

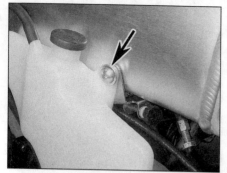

**9.3 Remove the screw (arrowed) and detach the idle speed adjuster**

**9.4 Disconnect the TPS wiring connector (arrowed)**

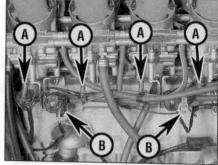

**9.5 Disconnect the carburettor heater wiring connectors (A), and where fitted the solenoid valve wiring connector(s) (B)**

place to work. It is recommended that only one carburettor be overhauled at a time to avoid mixing up parts.

## 9 Carburettors – removal and installation

**Warning: Refer to the precautions given in Section 1 before starting work.**

### Removal

**1** Remove the air filter housing (see Section 6).
**2** If the fuel tank was raised rather than removed, release the clamp securing the fuel hose to the fuel valve and detach the hose **(see illustration 2.8a)**.
**3** Remove the left-hand fairing side panel. Remove the coolant reservoir screw which retains the idle speed adjuster and release the adjuster **(see illustration)**. Feed it through to the carburettors.
**4** Disconnect the throttle position sensor wiring connector **(see illustration)**.
**5** On UK models, disconnect the carburettor heater wiring connectors from the carburettors **(see illustration)**. On GSX-R600W and X models, disconnect the two solenoid valve wiring connectors, and on GSX-R750T and V models disconnect the single solenoid valve wiring connector.
**6** On California models disconnect the two

EVAP system purge hoses from their T-piece unions under the carburettors.
**7** Detach the throttle cables and the choke cable from the carburettors (see Sections 22 and 23). If access is too restricted with the carburettors in situ, detach them after the carburettors have been displaced and lifted.
**8** Remove the blanking plug from the access hole in each side of the frame. Using a long screwdriver inserted through the hole, slacken the clamp screws securing the carburettors to the inlets – one screw on each side secures both carburettors for that side **(see illustration)**. Ease the carburettors up off the inlets and remove them, noting the routing of the various hoses **(see illustration)**.
**9** Place a suitable container below the float chambers then slacken the drain screw on the bottom of each carburettor and drain all the fuel from them **(see illustration)**. Once all the fuel has been drained, tighten the drain screws securely.
**10** If required, remove the screws securing the inlet adapters to the cylinder head and remove the adapters and O-rings, noting how they fit. Discard the O-rings as new ones must be used. Also note the UP mark which must be at the top.

### Installation

**11** Installation is the reverse of removal, noting the following.
 a) Check for cracks or splits in the cylinder head inlet adapters and the air filter

housing rubbers, and renew them if necessary.
 b) If removed, make sure the inlet adapters are installed correctly using new O-rings (see Step 10).
 c) Make sure the air filter housing and the cylinder head inlet adapters are fully engaged with the carburettors and their retaining clamps are securely tightened.
 d) Make sure all hoses are correctly routed and secured and not trapped or kinked.
 e) Do not forget to connect the throttle position sensor wiring connector, the carburettor heater wiring connectors, and the solenoid valve wiring connector (s), as appropriate to your model.
 f) Check the operation of the choke and throttle cables and adjust them as necessary (see Chapter 1).
 g) Check idle speed and carburettor synchronisation and adjust as necessary (see Chapter 1).

## 10 Carburettors – disassembly, cleaning and inspection

**Warning: Refer to the precautions given in Section 1 before starting work.**

### Disassembly

**1** Remove the carburettors from the machine as described in the previous Section. **Note:**

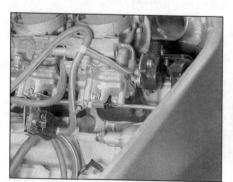

**9.8a Slacken the clamp screws using a long screwdriver as shown . . .**

**9.8b . . . then remove the carburettors**

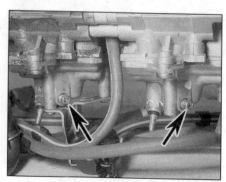

**9.9 Carburettor drain screws (arrowed)**

10.2a Remove the screws (arrowed) and lift off the cover . . .

10.2b . . . then remove the spring . . .

10.2c . . . and the O-ring

*Do not separate the carburettors unless absolutely necessary; each carburettor can be dismantled sufficiently for all normal cleaning and adjustments while in place on the mounting brackets. Dismantle the carburettors separately to avoid interchanging parts.*

**2** On GSX-R750 models, disconnect the air hose from the top cover. Unscrew and remove the top cover retaining screws **(see illustration)**. Lift off the cover and remove the spring from inside the piston **(see illustration)**. Also remove the small O-ring from around the air passage **(see illustration)**.

**3** Carefully peel the diaphragm away from its sealing groove in the carburettor and withdraw the diaphragm and piston assembly, noting which way round it fits **(see illustration)**.

*Caution: Do not use a sharp instrument to displace the diaphragm as it is easily damaged.*

**4** Grasp the needle holder using a pair of pliers and carefully draw it out of the piston **(see illustration)**. Push the jet needle up from the bottom of the piston and withdraw it from the top **(see illustration)**. Take care not to lose the washer on the top of the needle and the spring in the holder **(see illustrations 12.10a and c)**.

**5** On UK models, if required, remove the carburettor heater (see Section 13). On GSX-R750 models, disconnect the solenoid valve system air hoses from the float chamber, noting which fits where **(see illustration 14.10)**.

**6** Remove the screws securing the float chamber to the base of the carburettor and remove the float chamber, noting how it fits **(see illustration)**. Remove the rubber gasket

and discard it as a new one must be used. Depending on your model and which carburettor is being worked on, it may be necessary to displace the solenoid valve from its bracket to access the screws.

**7** Using a pair of thin-nose pliers, carefully withdraw the float pivot pin **(see illustration)**. If necessary, carefully displace the pin using a small punch or a nail. Remove the float assembly, noting how it fits **(see illustration 12.6d)**. Unhook the needle valve from the tab on the float, noting how it fits **(see illustration 12.6c)**. If required, remove the screw securing the needle valve seat and draw out the seat **(see illustrations 12.6b and a)**. Discard its O-ring as a new one must be used.

**8** Unscrew and remove the main jet from the base of the needle jet **(see illustration)**.

10.3 Carefully remove the diaphragm and piston assembly

10.4a Grasp the needle holder and pull it out . . .

10.4b . . . then push the needle up from the bottom and remove it

10.6 Remove the float chamber screws (arrowed)

10.7 Withdraw the float pivot pin (arrowed) and remove the float assembly

10.8 Unscrew and remove the main jet (arrowed)

10.9  Unscrew and remove the needle jet (arrowed)

10.10  Unscrew and remove the pilot jet (arrowed)

10.11  Unscrew and remove the pilot screw (arrowed)

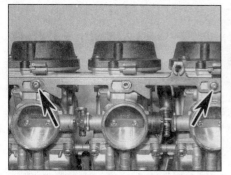

10.12a  Remove the screws (arrowed) securing the linkage bar and remove the bar

10.12b  Unscrew the choke plunger nut using thin-nosed pliers

9  Unscrew and remove the needle jet (see illustration).

10  Unscrew and remove the pilot jet (see illustration).

11  The pilot screw can be removed if required, but note that its setting will be disturbed (see **Haynes Hint**). On UK models unscrew and remove the pilot screw along with its spring, washer and O-ring (see illustration). Discard the O-ring as a new one must be used. Pilot screw removal is the same for US models, except that the screw head is sealed off with a blanking plug. Carefully drill or punch a hole in the plug and prise it out using a hooked tool, or by threading in a self-tapping screw and grasping that with a pair of pliers. If drilling

through, do not drill further than a depth of 6 mm.

> **HAYNES HiNT**  *To record the pilot screw's current setting, turn the screw in until it seats lightly, counting the number of turns necessary to achieve this, then fully unscrew it. On installation, the screw is simply backed out the number of turns you've recorded.*

12  Remove the screws securing the choke linkage bar to the carburettors, noting the plastic washers (see illustration). Lift off the bar, noting how it fits (see illustration 12.1b). Unscrew the choke plunger nut, using a pair

of thin nosed pliers as access is too restricted for a spanner, and withdraw the plunger and spring from the carburettor body, noting how they fit (see illustration). Take care not to lose the spring when removing the nut.

13  If required, remove the bolts securing the inlet funnel and remove the funnel, noting how it fits (see illustration). Discard the O-ring as a new one must be used.

14  If required, remove the throttle position sensor from the right-hand (no. 4) carburettor (see Section 15).

*Caution: Suzuki advise against removing the sensor from the carburettors unless absolutely necessary.*

### Cleaning

*Caution: Use only a petroleum based solvent or dedicated carburettor cleaner for carburettor cleaning. Don't use caustic cleaners.*

15  Submerge the metal components in the solvent for approximately thirty minutes (or longer, if the directions recommend it).

16  After the carburettor has soaked long enough for the cleaner to loosen and dissolve most of the varnish and other deposits, use a nylon-bristled brush to remove the stubborn deposits. Rinse it again, then dry it with compressed air.

17  Use a jet of compressed air to blow out all of the fuel and air passages in the main and upper body, not forgetting the air jets in the carburettor inlet (see illustration).

10.13  Inlet funnel bolts (arrowed)

10.17  Do not forget the small air passages (arrowed) in the inlet

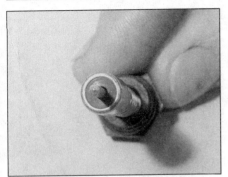

10.18 Check the choke plunger as described

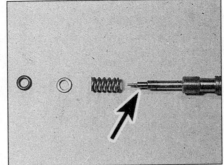

10.19 Check the tapered portion of the pilot screw (arrowed) for wear

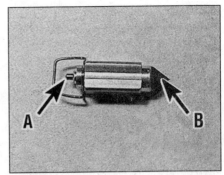

10.24 Check the valve's spring loaded rod (A) and tip (B) for wear or damage

*Caution: Never clean the jets or passages with a piece of wire or a drill bit, as they will be enlarged, causing the fuel and air metering rates to be upset.*

## Inspection

18 Check the operation of each choke plunger. If the plunger doesn't move smoothly, inspect the needle and seat on the end of the choke plunger, the spring and the plunger linkage bar **(see illustration)**. Renew any component that is worn, damaged or bent.

19 If removed from the carburettor, check the tapered portion of the pilot screw and the spring and O-ring for wear or damage **(see illustration)**. Renew them if necessary.

20 Check the carburettor body, float chamber and top cover for cracks, distorted sealing surfaces and other damage. If any defects are found, renew the faulty component, although renewal of the entire carburettor will probably be necessary (check with a Suzuki dealer on the availability of separate components).

21 Check the piston diaphragm for splits, holes and general deterioration. Holding it up to a light will help to reveal problems of this nature.

22 Insert the piston guide and piston in the carburettor body and check that the piston moves up-and-down smoothly. Check the surface of the piston for wear. If it's worn excessively or doesn't move smoothly in the guide, renew the components as necessary.

23 Check the jet needle for straightness by

rolling it on a flat surface such as a piece of glass (having first removed the E-clip and spacer, noting which notch the E-clip fits into) **(see illustration 12.10a)**. Renew it if it's bent or if the tip is worn.

24 Check the tip of the float needle valve and the valve seat **(see illustration)**. If either has grooves or scratches in it, or is in any way worn, they must be renewed as a set.

25 Operate the throttle shaft to make sure the throttle butterfly valves open and close smoothly. If they do not, cleaning the throttle linkage may help. Otherwise, renew the carburettors.

26 Check the float for damage. This will usually be apparent by the presence of fuel inside one of the floats. If the float is damaged, it must be renewed.

## 11 Carburettors – separation and joining

⚠️ **Warning: Refer to the precautions given in Section 1 before proceeding**

### Separation

1 The carburettors do not need to be separated for normal overhaul. If you need to separate them (to renew a carburettor body, for example), refer to the following procedure.

2 Remove the carburettors from the machine (see Section 9). Mark the body of each

carburettor with its cylinder location to ensure that it is positioned correctly on reassembly.

3 Remove the screws securing the choke linkage bar to the carburettors, noting the plastic washers **(see illustrations 10.12a)**. Lift off the bar, noting how it fits **(see illustration 12.1b)**.

4 Make a note of how the throttle return springs, linkage assembly and carburettor synchronisation springs are arranged to ensure that they are fitted correctly on reassembly **(see illustration)**. Also note carefully the arrangement of the various hoses and their unions, and make drawings as an aid if required **(see illustrations)**. Refer to Section 14 and remove the solenoid valve system components if required.

5 Unscrew and withdraw the two long bolts which hold the carburettors together **(see illustration)**.

11.4a Note carefully how the linkage assembly . . .

4

11.4b . . . the synchronisation springs . . .

11.4c . . . and the hoses and unions fit

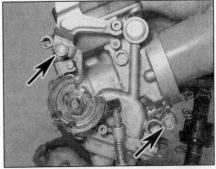

11.5 Unscrew the bolts (arrowed) and carefully separate the carburettors

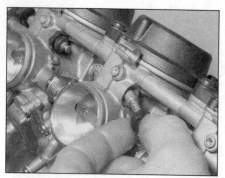

12.1a  Fit the plunger into the carburettor and tighten the nut ...

12.1b  ... then locate the linkage bar onto the plungers ...

12.1c  ... and install the screws with their plastic washers

**6** Carefully separate the carburettors. Retrieve the synchronisation springs and note the fitting of the various fuel hose T-pieces and O-rings or seals, and the vent hose T-pieces, and the solenoid valve system hoses connections (see Section 14) as they are separated. Discard the O-rings or seals as new ones must be used.

## Joining

**7** Assembly is the reverse of the disassembly procedure, noting the following.

a) *Make sure the fuel hose T-pieces and O-rings or seals and the air vent hose T-pieces are correctly and securely inserted into the carburettors (see illustration 11.4c).*

b) *Install the synchronisation springs after the carburettors are joined together. Make* sure they are correctly and squarely seated *(see illustration 11.4b).*

c) *Check the operation of both the choke and throttle linkages ensuring that both operate smoothly and return quickly under spring pressure before installing the carburettors on the machine (see illustration 11.4a).*

d) *Install the carburettors (see Section 9) and check carburettor synchronisation and idle speed (see Chapter 1).*

## 12 Carburettors – reassembly and float height check

⚠️ *Warning: Refer to the precautions given in Section 1 before proceeding.*

**Note:** *When reassembling the carburettors, be sure to use new O-rings and seals. Do not overtighten the carburettor jets and screws as they are easily damaged.*

**1** Install the choke plunger and spring into the carburettor body and tighten the nut to secure it **(see illustration)**. Fit the choke linkage bar onto the plungers, making sure the slots locate correctly behind the nipple on the end of each choke plunger **(see illustration)**. Fit the plastic washers and secure the linkage bar in place with the screws **(see illustration)**.

**2** Install the pilot screw (if removed) along with its spring, washer and O-ring, turning it in until it seats lightly **(see illustration 10.11)**. Now, turn the screw out the number of turns previously recorded, or as specified at the beginning of the Chapter. If the pilot screw was disturbed on US models, read the notes in Sections 1 and 7 concerning maladjustment and emissions; the pilot screw housing should be sealed by fitting a new blanking plug.

**3** Install the pilot jet **(see illustration)**.

**4** Install the needle jet **(see illustration)**.

**5** Install the main jet into the needle jet **(see illustration)**.

**6** If removed, fit a new O-ring onto the needle valve seat, then press it into place and secure it with the screw **(see illustrations)**. Hook the float needle valve onto the tab on the float assembly, then position the float assembly in the carburettor, making sure the needle valve

12.3  Install the pilot jet ...

12.4  ... the needle jet ...

12.5  ... and the main jet

12.6a  Press the needle valve seat in ...

12.6b  ... and secure it with the screw

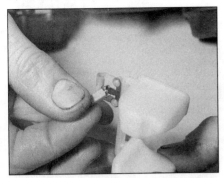

**12.6c  Fit the needle valve onto the float tab . . .**

**12.6d  . . . then install the float assembly . . .**

**12.6e  . . . and slide in the pin**

locates in the seat, and install the pin, making sure it is secure **(see illustrations)**.

**7** To check the float height, hold the carburettor so the float hangs down, then tilt it back until the needle valve is just seated, but not so far that the needle's spring-loaded tip is compressed (the float chamber mating surface will be at approx. 45°). Measure the height from the top of the float to the mating surface with an accurate ruler **(see illustration)**. The correct setting should be as given in the Specifications at the beginning of the Chapter. If it is incorrect, adjust the float height by carefully bending the float tab a little at a time until the correct height is obtained.

**8** With the float height checked, fit a new sealing ring into the float chamber, making sure it is seated properly in its groove, then install the chamber and tighten its screws securely **(see illustration)**. Where appropriate, locate the solenoid valve onto its bracket. On GSX-R750 models, connect the solenoid valve system air hoses to the chamber, referring to Section 14 for the system diagram **(see illustration 14.10)**.

**9** If removed, install the carburettor heater (see Section 13).

**10** Fit the washer onto the jet needle, then fit the needle into the piston **(see illustrations)**. Fit a new O-ring onto the retainer and check that the spring is correctly fitted, then locate the holder onto the top of the needle and press it down until the O-ring is felt to locate **(see illustrations)**.

**11** Insert the piston/diaphragm assembly into

**12.7  Check the float height as described**

**12.8  Install the float chamber using a new gasket**

**12.10a  Make sure the washer, E-clip and seat are fitted on the needle . . .**

**12.10b  . . . then insert it in the piston**

the carburettor **(see illustration)**. Lightly push the piston down, ensuring the needle is correctly aligned with the needle jet. Press the

diaphragm outer edge into its groove, making sure it is correctly seated **(see illustration 10.3)**. Check the diaphragm is not

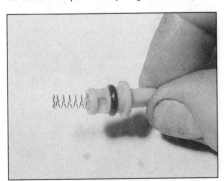

**12.10c  Fit the O-ring and spring onto the holder . . .**

**12.10d  . . . then press it into position**

**12.11a  Fit the piston into the carburettor and seat the diaphragm**

12.11b Fit the O-ring around the air passage

12.12a Install the spring and fit the top cover lug into it . . .

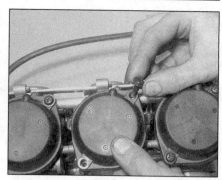

12.12b . . . then fit the cover screws

creased, and that the piston moves smoothly up and down in the guide. Fit a new O-ring around the air passage (see illustration).

**12** Install the spring into the piston assembly, making sure it locates correctly, then fit the top cover, making sure the top of the spring fits over the lug in the middle of the cover, and that the protrusion in the cover locates over the O-ring and air passage, and tighten its screws securely (see illustrations). On GSX-R750 models, connect the air hose from the diaphragm assembly on the float chamber to the top cover.

**13** If removed, install the inlet funnel using a new O-ring and apply a suitable non-permanent thread locking compound to the bolts (see illustration 10.13). Do not overtighten them.

**14** If removed, install the throttle position sensor (see Section 15).

**15** Install the carburettors (see Section 9).

## 13 Carburettor heater system (UK models) – check

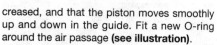

 *Warning: Refer to the precautions given in Section 1 before starting work.*

**1** On all GSX-R600 models and on GSX-R750T and V models, each carburettor has a heater unit threaded into its float chamber. The heaters are controlled by a thermo-switch, housed in the fairing.

**2** Raise the fuel tank (see Section 2), and disconnect the wiring connectors from the heaters (see illustration 9.5).

**3** Using an ohmmeter or multimeter set to the ohms x 1 scale, connect the positive (+ve) probe to the tip of the heater and the negative (-ve) probe to the spade terminal on No. 1 carburettor or to the hex on the base of each heater on the other carburettors (see illustration). The resistance of each heater should be as specified at the beginning of the Chapter.

**4** If a meter is not available, connect a fully charged 12 volt battery to each heater in turn, using the terminals as described above. After about five minutes, the float chamber should be felt to be warm.

**5** If any heater does not perform as described, unscrew it from the carburettor. Apply a smear of thermo-grease to the new heater, then thread it into the carburettor and tighten it to the torque setting specified at the beginning of the Chapter.

**6** To check the thermo switch, remove the inner panel from the left-hand fairing side panel (see Chapter 8). Locate the thermo-switch and unplug it from the wiring loom (see illustration). Using a continuity tester or multimeter, insert the probes into the switch wiring connector and check for continuity. In normal or warm conditions, there should be no continuity. Now immerse the switch into a bowl of ice. After a few minutes the switch should close and continuity should be shown. If not, the switch is faulty.

**7** If the heaters and the switch are all good, turn the ignition switch ON and check for battery voltage at each heater wiring connector, and at the switch wiring connector in the loom. If there is none, refer to the wiring diagrams at the end of Chapter 9 and check the circuits for damaged or broken wiring.

## 14 Carburettor solenoid valve system – check

 *Warning: Refer to the precautions given in Section 1 before starting work.*

### GSX-R600W and X models

**1** The solenoid valves are controlled electronically by the ignition control unit, and when open allow an extra amount of air via an air jet in the hose into the carburettor to weaken the mixture. Information fed to the ECU concerning engine speed determines when it is necessary for the valve to open and close. There is one valve for carburettors 1 and 4, and one for carburettors 2 and 3.

**2** Raise the fuel tank (see Section 2), and disconnect the wiring connector from each solenoid valve (see illustration 9.5). Release the clip and slip the valve off its mounting bracket, then disconnect the hoses, noting which fits where (see illustration).

**3** Using jumper wires, connect the positive (+ve) lead from a fully charged 12 volt battery

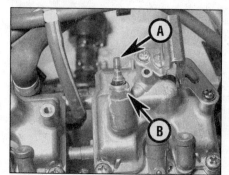

13.3 Measure the resistance between the tip (A) and the base (B)

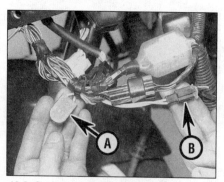

13.6 Carburettor heater thermo switch (A) and its wiring connector (B)

14.2 Release the clip, detach the hoses and remove the solenoid

to the orange/white wire terminal of the solenoid valve. Now connect the negative (-ve) lead to the other terminal on the valve. At the moment of contact of the negative lead, the valve should be heard to click. Now disconnect the negative lead – the valve should again be heard to click. If the valve does not click when it is connected and disconnected, it is faulty, and a new one must be installed. If the valve is good, reconnect the hoses, then fit the valve onto its bracket and connect the wiring connector. The valve for carburettors 1 and 4 is mounted on the bracket on No. 3 carburettor, and has the white wiring connector. The valve for carburettors 2 and 3 is mounted on the bracket on No. 1 carburettor, and has the black wiring connector.

4 To check that each valve is switching ON (open) and OFF (closed) at the correct time, insert the positive (+ve) probe of a voltmeter into the orange/white socket of the wiring connector, which must remain connected to the valve, and the negative (-ve) probe into the light green socket (when testing the valve with the white connector for Nos. 1 and 4 carburettors) or the dark green socket (when testing the valve with the black connector for Nos. 2 and 3 carburettors). Start the engine and slowly increase its speed. Referring to the tables, check that each valve switches at the specified engine speed. When the valve is closed, the meter should read zero volts. When the valve is open, the meter should read battery voltage (a little over 12 volts).

### GSX-R600W (all markets) and GSX-R600X (UK)

| Valve for Nos. 1 and 4 carburettors | Engine speed/rpm (approx.) |
| --- | --- |
| OPEN | 2700 |
| CLOSED | 4200 |
| OPEN | 5700 |
| CLOSED | 8800 |

| Valve for Nos. 2 and 3 carburettors | Engine speed/rpm (approx.) |
| --- | --- |
| OPEN | 2700 |
| CLOSED | 5000 |
| OPEN | 7300 |
| CLOSED | 10,000 |

### GSX-R600X – US and California

| Valve for Nos. 1 and 4 carburettors | Engine speed/rpm (approx.) |
| --- | --- |
| OPEN | 2700 |
| CLOSED | 4050 |
| OPEN | 5800 |
| CLOSED | 9100 |

| Valve for Nos. 2 and 3 carburettors | Engine speed/rpm (approx.) |
| --- | --- |
| OPEN | 2700 |
| CLOSED | 4950 |
| OPEN | 7650 |
| CLOSED | 10,550 |

5 If either valve does not operate at all (but is heard to click when tested in Step 3), or opens and closes at the wrong engine speeds, refer to the wiring diagrams at the end of Chapter 9 and check the circuit for faulty wiring and connectors. If the wiring is good, it is possible that the ignition control unit is faulty (see Chapter 5).

### GSX-R750T and V

6 The solenoid valve is controlled electronically by the ignition control unit, and is activated when the throttle is opened quickly from the closed position. Information on engine speed, throttle position and gear position is fed to the ECU, which determines when it is necessary for the valve to open and close. When open, the valve allows a vacuum from the inlet manifold of No. 4 carburettor to act on a diaphragm mounted on the float chamber of each carburettor, which opens an airway from the air filter housing to the top cover of the carburettor. This affects the rate at which the piston lifts, thereby compensating the fuel/air mixture, so that the sudden opening of the throttle does not upset carburation.

7 Raise the fuel tank (see Section 2), and disconnect the wiring connector from the solenoid valve. Slip the valve off its mounting bracket and disconnect the hoses, noting which fits where.

8 Using jumper wires, connect the positive (+ve) lead from a fully charged 12 volt battery to the orange/white terminal of the solenoid valve. Now connect the negative (-ve) lead to the other terminal on the valve. At the moment of contact of the negative lead, the valve should be heard to click. Now disconnect the negative lead – the valve should again be heard to click. If the valve does not click when it is connected and disconnected, it is faulty, and a new one must be installed. If the valve is good, reconnect the hoses, then fit the valve onto its bracket and connect the wiring connector.

9 To check that the valve is switching ON (open) at the correct time, insert the positive (+ve) probe of a voltmeter into the orange/white socket of the wiring connector, which must remain connected to the valve, and the negative (-ve) probe into the light green socket. Start the engine and allow it to idle. When the engine is idling, the valve is closed and the meter should read zero volts. Now open the throttle quickly and suddenly, then shut it off again. The meter should deflect to read battery voltage (a little over 12 volts) as the valve opens, then drop back to zero as the throttle is closed.

10 If the solenoid is good, but the system is thought to be malfunctioning, for example if the engine stalls when the throttle is snapped open from the fully closed position, then it is likely that the vacuum side of the system is faulty. First check that all the hoses, including the larger bore ones from the air filter housing, are securely connected, that they are in good condition without any signs of cracks or splits, and are not kinked or trapped (see illustration). Next disconnect the hoses from the vacuum valve, fitted in the hose between the vacuum take-off point and the solenoid valve. Note which way round the valve fits – its brown side should face away from the solenoid valve, and its black side should face towards it. Apply a vacuum to the union on the brown side – the valve should be open and allow air to be sucked through it. Now apply a vacuum to the union on the black side – the valve should close and no air should pass. If either of the conditions are not as described, the valve is faulty and a new one must be installed. Make sure it is fitted with the coloured sides facing as described.

11 If the valve is good, remove the carburettors (see Section 9) and check the diaphragm in the base of each float chamber. Remove the screws securing the diaphragm cover, then carefully lift off the cover, noting that it is under spring pressure. Remove the spring, spring seat, spacer and diaphragm, noting how they fit. Hold the diaphragm up to the light and check for splits and holes. Also check the rim for evidence of wear or damage that will not allow it to seat properly. If the diaphragm is damaged, the whole float chamber must be renewed as individual components are not available.

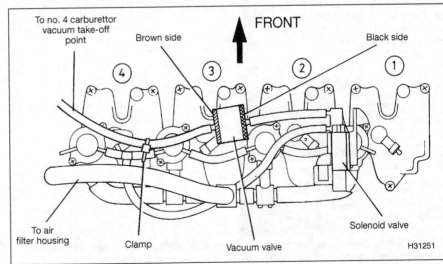

**14.10 Solenoid valve system – GSX-R750T and V**

## 15 Throttle position sensor –
check, removal and installation

⚠ **Warning: Refer to the precautions given in Section 1 before starting work.**

### Check

#### GSX-R600 and GSX-R750T and V models

1 The throttle position sensor is mounted on the outside of the right-hand (No. 4) carburettor. Raise the fuel tank for access (see Section 2).

2 Disconnect the wiring connector from the top of the sensor **(see illustration 9.4)**. Using a multimeter set to the K-ohm scale, connect the probes to the two outer terminals on the sensor. If the resistance reading obtained is not within the range specified at the beginning of the Chapter, take the sensor to a Suzuki dealer for testing. If it is confirmed to be faulty, a new one must be installed; the sensor is a sealed unit and cannot therefore be repaired.

3 Check the sensor visually for cracks and other damage.

4 Using a multimeter set to resistance or a continuity tester, check for continuity between the terminals of the sensor wiring connector and the corresponding terminals on the ignition control module connector. There should be continuity between each terminal. If not, this is probably due to a damaged or broken wire between the connectors; pinched or broken wires can usually be repaired.

#### GSX-R750W and X models

5 Refer to Section 16.

### Removal

**Caution: Suzuki advise against removing the sensor from the carburettors or throttle bodies unless absolutely necessary.**

6 The throttle position sensor is mounted on the outside of the right-hand (No. 4) carburettor or throttle body. Raise the fuel tank for access (see Section 2). Disconnect

**15.7 Throttle position sensor screws (arrowed) – mark their position relative to the switch before removing them**

the wiring connector from the top of the sensor **(see illustration 9.4)**.

7 Before removing the mounting screws, mark or scribe lines on the sensor to indicate the exact position of the screws in relation to it **(see illustration)**. Remove the screws and remove the sensor, noting how it fits.

### Installation

8 If the original sensor is being installed, and its set-up is not suspected of being incorrect, fit the sensor onto the carburettor or throttle body and install the screws, aligning them exactly with the marks made on removal. On GSX-R750W and X models smear some grease onto the seal around the throttle shaft end before installing the sensor. Tighten the screws to the torque setting specified at the beginning of the Chapter, making sure the position of the sensor is not disturbed.

9 On GSX-R600 and GSX-R750T and V models, if a new sensor is being installed, or if you want to check the set-up is correct, fit the sensor onto the carburettor and install the screws, but do not tighten them, so that the sensor can be turned. Using two ohmmeters set to the K-ohm scale, and set up as shown, and with the throttle held open, check the reading on meter 1, then adjust the sensor until the reading on meter 2 is 76% of the reading on meter 1 **(see illustration)**. For example (see graph), if meter 1 reads 5 K-ohms, meter 2 must read 3.8 K-ohms. When it is correctly adjusted, tighten the screws to the torque setting specified at the beginning of

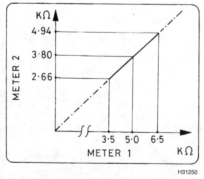

**15.9 Throttle position sensor test set-up – carburettor models**

the Chapter, making sure the position of the sensor is not disturbed.

10 On GSX-R750W and X models, if a new sensor is being installed, or if you want to check the set-up is correct, smear some grease onto the seal around the throttle shaft end before installing the sensor, then fit the sensor onto the carburettor and install the screws, but do not tighten them, so that the sensor can be turned. Using an ohmmeter or multimeter set to the K-ohms scale, measure the resistance between the blue and black/brown wire terminals on the sensor itself, first with the throttle closed, then with it fully open. Adjust the position until the readings are as specified at the beginning of the Chapter. When it is correctly adjusted, tighten the screws to the torque setting specified at the beginning of the Chapter, making sure the position of the sensor is not disturbed. If the sensor cannot be set-up properly, take the motorcycle to a dealer with the special fault code reader – it has a specific function on it for setting up the sensor.

11 Connect the wiring connector to the top of the sensor and lower the fuel tank.

## 16 Fuel injection system –
general description and fault diagnosis

⚠ **Warning: Refer to the precautions given in Section 1 before starting work.**

### General description

1 The electronic fuel injection system consists of two main component groups, namely the fuel circuit and the electronic control circuit.

2 The fuel circuit consists of the tank, pump, filter, pressure regulator and injectors. Fuel is supplied from the tank and pumped by an electric pump through a filter to the fuel distributor rail, from which the individual injectors are fed. Operating pressure is generated by the pump and is maintained and controlled by the pressure regulator. Excess fuel released by the regulator flows back to the tank.

3 The electronic control circuit consists of the electronic control unit which assesses information which it receives form various sensors in the engine. These sensors provide information on engine load (air flow into the engine), engine speed, crankshaft position, air temperature, engine temperature, throttle position and air density. The control unit uses this information to calculate the required opening time of the fuel injectors and thus the quantity of fuel required, and sends the equivalent electrical pulse to each injector. As the injector opens, pressurised fuel is sprayed around the inlet valve, where it mixes with air and vaporises, before entering the cylinder where it is compressed and ignited.

4 The system incorporates two safety

circuits. When the ignition is switched ON, the fuel pump runs for three seconds and pressurises the system. Thereafter the pump automatically switches off until the engine is started. The second circuit incorporates a tip-over sensor, which automatically switches off the fuel pump and cuts the ignition and injection circuits if the motorcycle falls over.

### Fault diagnosis

5 The system incorporates a self-diagnostic function, whereby any faults are detected by the electronic control unit. In the event of a sensor failing, the unit will determine whether the engine can still be run. If it can, the fail-safe set-up means that the bike can be ridden home or to a dealer. When this occurs, the LCD display in the instrument cluster will indicate the letters FI every two seconds (alternating with the coolant temperature reading), and the LED lamp will come on. If the unit decides that the fault is too serious, it will be impossible to start the engine. When this occurs, the LCD display in the instrument cluster will indicate the letters FI continuously, and the LED lamp will flash.

6 To diagnose the exact cause of a failure in the system, a fault code reader, specifically designed for this system, is essential. Special meters are also required to test the individual sensors. Hence if a problem occurs, the motorcycle should be taken to a Suzuki dealer.

7 However the system is not completely untouchable, and the components that can be checked or worked on at home are covered in this and the next few sections. Also, if a fault is indicated, first check the wiring and connectors from the electronic control unit to the various sensors – it may well be that a connector has come loose or a wire has become pinched and is shorting out. A continuity test of all wires will locate such a problem – refer to the Wiring Diagrams at the end of Chapter 9. Where appropriate, also check that any air hoses attached to the sensors are secure, and are not cracked or split, blocked, kinked or trapped.

8 It is also possible to check all of the sensors individually using a multimeter and referring to the tests below and the specifications given at the beginning of the Chapter, but note that different meters could well give slightly different results to those specified even though the sensor being tested is not faulty – so do not consign a sensor to the bin before having it double-checked. Also, the tests given are those which can be carried out at home using only a multimeter and may only cover one aspect of a sensor's function. Therefore a correct resistance reading does not necessarily mean that the sensor will perform correctly in all circumstances. Peak voltage adapters and other testing equipment are needed to make a full check. This is why it is best to leave it to a dealer. Also, the problem may lie in the ignition control unit rather than any of the other components in the system (see Chapter 5).

### Camshaft position (CMP) sensor

9 Make sure the ignition is switched OFF. Remove the air filter housing (see Section 6). The CMP sensor is on the left-hand end of valve cover (see illustration). Disconnect the wiring connector and check the resistance between the terminals is as specified. Also check that there is no continuity between each terminal and earth.

### Crankshaft position (CKP) sensor (pulse generator coil)

10 Make sure the ignition is switched OFF. The CKP sensor is on the right-hand end of the crankshaft. Remove the seat cowling (see Chapter 8). Trace the wiring from the end cover and disconnect it at the wiring connector with the green and black wires (see illustration). Check the resistance between the terminals is as specified. Also check that there is no continuity between each terminal and earth.

### Inlet air pressure (IAP) sensor

11 Make sure the ignition is switched OFF. Raise the fuel tank (see Section 2). The IAP sensor is on the back of the air filter housing (see illustration). Disconnect the wiring connector from the sensor and turn the ignition switch ON. Connect the positive (+ve) probe of a voltmeter to the red wire terminal on the loom side of the wiring connector and the negative (-ve) probe first to ground, then to the black/brown wire terminal – in each case the input voltage should be as specified. If not, check the connector and the wiring.

12 Connect the wiring to the sensor, then start the engine and allow it idle. Check the output voltage by inserting the positive (+ve) probe of a voltmeter into the dark brown wire terminal and the negative (-ve) probe to the black/brown wire – it may be necessary to insert short pieces of wire into the connector to make contact, and attach crocodile clips to these, if your meter probes are too thick. If the reading is not as specified, and the wiring and vacuum hose are good, the sensor is faulty. If the reading is good, and the wiring and vacuum hose are good, take the sensor to a dealer for further testing.

### Throttle position (TP) sensor

13 Make sure the ignition is switched OFF. Raise the fuel tank (see Section 2). The TP sensor is on the right-hand end of the throttle bodies. Disconnect the wiring connector from the sensor and turn the ignition switch ON (see illustration 19.4b). Connect the positive (+ve) probe of a voltmeter to the red wire terminal on the loom side of the wiring connector and the negative (-ve) probe first to ground, then to the black/brown wire terminal – in each case the input voltage should be as specified. If not, check the connector and the wiring.

14 Now check for continuity between the blue wire terminal in the connector and ground – there should be no continuity.

15 Using an ohmmeter or multimeter set to the K-ohms scale, measure the resistance between the blue and black/brown wire terminals on the sensor itself, first with the throttle closed, then with it fully open. If the readings are not as specified, but are close to them, slacken the sensor mounting screws and adjust its position until the readings are as specified. If the sensor cannot be adjusted to the range, or if no readings are obtained, the sensor is faulty.

16 Connect the wiring to the sensor, then switch the ignition ON. Check the output voltage by inserting the positive (+ve) probe of a voltmeter into the blue wire terminal and the negative (-ve) probe to the black/brown wire –

**4**

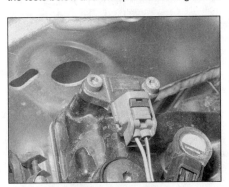

16.9 Camshaft position (CMP) sensor

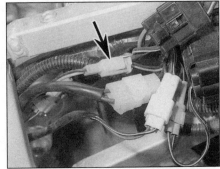

16.10 Crankshaft position (CKP) sensor wiring connector (arrowed)

16.11 Inlet air pressure (IAP) sensor (arrowed)

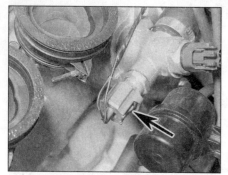

**16.17 Engine coolant temperature (ECT) sensor (arrowed)**

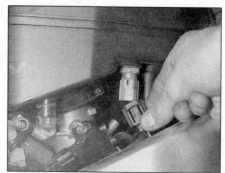

**16.19 Disconnect the inlet air temperature (IAT) sensor wiring connector**

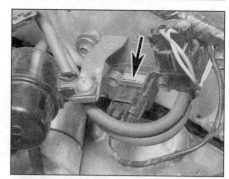

**16.21 Atmospheric pressure (AP) sensor (arrowed)**

it may be necessary to insert short pieces of wire into the connector to make contact, and attach crocodile clips to these, if your meter probes are too thick. Measure the voltage first with the throttle closed, then with it fully open. If the readings are not as specified, the sensor is faulty.

### Engine coolant temperature (ECT) sensor

**17** Make sure the ignition is switched OFF. Remove the air filter housing (see Section 6). The ECT sensor is in the thermostat housing on the right-hand side of the engine **(see illustration)**. Disconnect the wiring connector from the sensor and turn the ignition switch ON. Connect the positive (+ve) probe of a voltmeter to the black/green wire terminal on the loom side of the wiring connector and the negative (-ve) probe first to ground, then to the black/brown wire terminal – in each case the input voltage should be as specified. If not, check the connector and the wiring.

**18** Using an ohmmeter or multimeter set to the K-ohms scale, measure the resistance between the terminals on the sensor itself. If the reading is not as specified, the sensor is faulty.

### Inlet air temperature (IAT) sensor

**19** Make sure the ignition is switched OFF. Raise the fuel tank (see Section 2). The IAT sensor is on the right-hand side of the air filter housing. Disconnect the wiring connector from the sensor and turn the ignition switch ON **(see illustration)**. Connect the positive

(+ve) probe of a voltmeter to the light blue wire terminal on the loom side of the wiring connector and the negative (-ve) probe first to ground, then to the black/brown wire terminal – in each case the input voltage should be as specified. If not, check the connector and the wiring.

**20** Using an ohmmeter or multimeter set to the K-ohms scale, measure the resistance between the terminals on the sensor itself. If the reading is not as specified, the sensor is faulty.

### Atmospheric pressure (AP) sensor

**21** Make sure the ignition is switched OFF. Raise the fuel tank (see Section 2). The AP sensor is on the inside of the right-hand frame spar **(see illustration)**. Disconnect the wiring connector from the sensor and turn the ignition switch ON. Connect the positive (+ve) probe of a voltmeter to the red wire terminal on the loom side of the wiring connector and the negative (-ve) probe first to ground, then to the black/brown wire terminal – in each case the input voltage should be as specified. If not, check the connector and the wiring.

**22** Connect the wiring to the sensor, then turn the ignition switch ON. Check the output voltage by inserting the positive (+ve) probe of a voltmeter into the blue/black wire terminal and the negative (-ve) probe to the black/brown wire – it may be necessary to insert short pieces of wire into the connector to make contact, and attach crocodile clips to these, if your meter probes are too thick. If the reading is not as specified, and the wiring and

vacuum hose are good, the sensor is faulty. If the reading is good, and the wiring and vacuum hose are good, take the sensor to a dealer for further testing.

### Tip-over (TO) sensor

**23** Make sure the ignition is switched OFF. The TO sensor is behind the seat cowling on the left-hand side – remove the cowling for access (see Chapter 8). Disconnect the sensor wiring connector **(see illustration)**. Using an ohmmeter or multimeter set to the K-ohms scale, measure the resistance between the terminals on the sensor side of the connector. If the reading is not as specified, the sensor is faulty.

**24** Reconnect the wiring connector and turn the ignition switch ON. Connect the positive (+ve) probe of a voltmeter into the black wire terminal on the loom side of the wiring connector and the negative (-ve) probe into the black/brown wire terminal – it may be necessary to insert short pieces of wire into the connector to make contact, and attach crocodile clips to these, if your meter probes are too thick. If the reading is not as specified, and the wiring and connector are good, the sensor is faulty. If the reading is good, with the aid of an assistant carefully lean the motorcycle to an angle of 43°, first on one side and then on the other – at each point the reading should drop to zero. If not the sensor is faulty.

### Gear position (GP) switch

**25** Place the motorcycle on an auxiliary stand and raise the sidestand. Remove the seat cowling (see Chapter 8). Trace the gear position switch wiring from the left-hand side of the engine to the white connector with the blue, pink and black/white wires, and leave it connected **(see illustration)**. Turn the ignition switch ON and make sure the engine kill switch is in the RUN position.

**26** Connect the positive (+ve) probe of a voltmeter into the pink wire terminal on the loom side of the wiring connector and the negative (-ve) probe to ground – it may be necessary to insert a short piece of wire into the connector to make contact, and attach a crocodile clip to it, if your meter probe is too thick. Select each gear in turn and check that

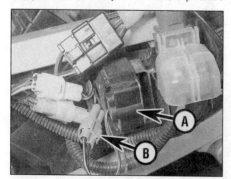

**16.23 Tip-over (TO) sensor (A) and its wiring connector (B)**

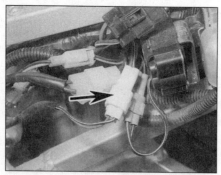

**16.25 Gear position (GP) sensor wiring connector (arrowed)**

the voltage in each gear is as specified (the voltage will be different for each gear selected, but they must all be above the specified minimum). If not, and the wiring and connector are good, the switch is faulty.

## 17 Fuel pressure and pressure regulator (GSX-R750W and X models) – check

⚠ *Warning: Refer to the precautions given in Section 1 before starting work.*

1 To check the fuel pressure, a suitable gauge and adapter piece (which screws into the end of the fuel rail) will be needed. Suzuki provide a kit (Pt. Nos. 09915-74520, 09915-77330 and 09940-40210) for this purpose.
2 Raise the fuel tank (see Section 2).
3 Place a container suitable for holding petrol (gasoline) under the right-hand end of the fuel rail, then slacken the pressure check bolt and allow the residual fuel to drain **(see illustration)**. Unscrew the bolt and thread the adapter in its place. Connect the gauge to the adapter.
4 Turn the ignition switch ON and check the pressure reading on the gauge. The pressure should as specified at the start of this Chapter.
5 Turn the ignition OFF and unscrew the gauge and adapter from the crankcase, being prepared to catch the residual fuel as before.
6 Install the pressure check bolt using a new sealing washer, and tighten it to the torque setting specified at the beginning of the Chapter.
7 If the pressure is too low, either the pressure regulator is stuck open, the fuel pump is faulty, the strainer or filter is blocked, or there is a leak in the system, probably from a hose joint.
8 If the pressure is too high, either the return hose is pinched or clogged, the regulator is stuck closed or the fuel pump check valve is faulty.
9 Refer to the relevant Sections of this Chapter and Chapter 1 and check the possible problems according to whether the pressure was too low or too high. Suzuki provide no test procedure for the pressure regulator. However, if it is stuck open, it will be possible to blow through it with a low pressure air source. If it is stuck closed, then a high pressure air source with a gauge can be used to check the pressure at which it does open, if at all. Alternatively, substitute the suspect one with a known good one and repeat the fuel pressure check.
10 To remove the pressure regulator, unscrew the two bolts securing it to the fuel rail and pull it out of its socket **(see illustration)**. Discard the O-ring as a new one must be used. Fit a new O-ring, then press the regulator into the rail and tighten the bolts to the specified torque setting.

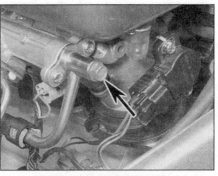

17.3 Fuel pressure check bolt (arrowed)

17.10 Fuel pressure regulator bolts (arrowed)

## 18 Inlet air control valve system (GSX-R750W and X models) – check

1 The system operates a flap in the air filter housing which regulates the air flow into it according to engine speed. At low to medium engine speeds, the flap is closed. At medium to high engine speeds, the flap is open. The flap is activated by a rod connected to a diaphragm, which itself is activated by a vacuum taken from the inlet manifold. The vacuum to the diaphragm is controlled by a solenoid valve, which is controlled by the ECU. At low to medium engine speeds, the solenoid valve is open so the vacuum acts on the diaphragm and closes the flap. At medium to high engine speeds, the solenoid valve is closed so the vacuum is cut off and the flap opens. A one-way valve and a damper are incorporated in the vacuum hose between the manifold and the solenoid valve.
2 To check that the system is operating correctly, remove the air filter (see Chapter 1). Start the engine and slowly open the throttle while looking inside the filter housing at the flap in its base. The flap should open at 5400 rpm and stay open at engine speeds above that. Slowly close the throttle – the flap should close at 5200 rpm and remain closed at engine speeds below that. If the flap does not open and close as described,

check the system components as described below.
3 First check that all the hoses are securely connected, that they are in good condition without any signs of cracks or splits, and are not kinked or trapped. It will be necessary to displace the air filter housing to check the hose from the solenoid valve to the diaphragm on the underside of the housing (see Section 6).
4 To check the solenoid valve, located on the inside of the right-hand frame spar, first disconnect the wiring connector from the solenoid **(see illustration)**. Using an ohmmeter or multimeter set to the ohms x 10 scale, measure the resistance between the terminals on the solenoid and compare the reading to that specified at the beginning of the Chapter. If the reading obtained is not within the specified range, a new solenoid valve must be installed.
5 To check the one-way valve, located at the right-hand end of the throttle bodies, disconnect the valve hoses **(see illustration)**. Blow through the valve from the orange side – the valve should be open and allow air to pass through. Now reverse the valve and blow through from the other side – the valve should be closed and not allow air to pass through. If either of the conditions are not as described, the valve is faulty and a new one must be installed. Make sure it is fitted with the orange side facing back towards the solenoid valve.

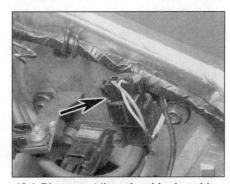

18.4 Disconnect the solenoid valve wiring connector (arrowed)

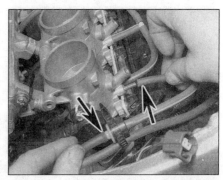

18.5 Disconnect the valve hoses (arrowed)

**4**

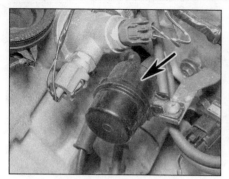

18.6 Damper (arrowed)

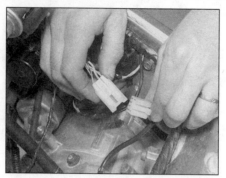

19.4a Disconnect the fuel injector loom wiring connector . . .

19.4b . . . the throttle position sensor wiring connector . . .

**6** Visually check the damper, located on the inside of the right-hand frame spar, for cracks, dents or any other damage and renew it if any are found **(see illustration)**.

**7** To check the diaphragm, remove the air filter and first check that the connecting rod between it and the flap has not come away. Now trace the vacuum hose from the diaphragm on the underside of the filter housing and disconnect it from the solenoid. Using a hand-operated vacuum pump, apply a vacuum through the hose and check whether the flap closes when the vacuum is applied and opens when it is released. Do not apply more than -180 mmHg of vacuum (negative pressure) to avoid damaging the diaphragm. If the flap does not open and close, a new diaphragm must be installed.

### 19 Throttle bodies (GSX-R750W and X models) – removal and installation

> ⚠ **Warning: Refer to the precautions given in Section 1 before starting work.**

### Removal

**1** Remove the air filter housing (see Section 6).
**2** Place a container suitable for holding petrol (gasoline) under the right-hand end of the fuel rail, then slacken the pressure check bolt and allow the residual fuel to drain **(see illustration 17.3)**. When the fuel has drained, tighten the bolt to the torque setting specified at the beginning of the Chapter, using a new sealing washer if necessary.

**3** If the fuel tank was raised rather than removed, attach a hose clamp (see *Tools and Workshop Tips*) to the fuel return hose which runs from the pressure regulator to the fuel tank **(see illustration 2.9a)**. Have a rag handy to catch any residue fuel, then detach the hose from the regulator **(see illustration 2.9b)**. Fit a suitable plug into the end of the hose as a back-up to the clamp. Also detach the fuel supply hose from either the fuel tank or the inlet union on the fuel rail **(see illustrations 2.9c and d)**.
**4** Disconnect the common wiring connector for all the fuel injectors (as opposed to the connector on each individual injector) **(see illustration)**. Also disconnect the throttle position sensor wiring connector **(see illustration)**, and the inlet air pressure sensor wiring connector **(see illustration)**.
**5** Remove the left-hand fairing side panel. Remove the coolant reservoir screw which retains the idle speed adjuster and release the adjuster **(see illustration 9.3)**. Feed it through to the carburettors.
**6** Detach the throttle cables and the choke cable from the throttle bodies (see Sections 22 and 23). Also disconnect the vacuum hose from its union on the No. 4 throttle body **(see illustration)**.
**7** Remove the blanking plug from the access hole in each side of the frame **(see illustration)**. Using a long screwdriver inserted through the hole, slacken the clamp screws securing the throttle bodies to the inlets – one screw on each side secures both bodies for that side **(see illustration)**. Ease the bodies up off the inlets and remove them **(see illustration)**.

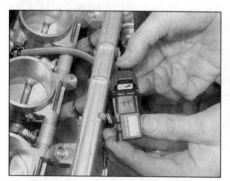

19.4c . . . and the IAP wiring connector

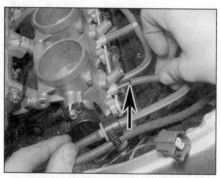

19.6 Pull the vacuum hose off its union (arrowed)

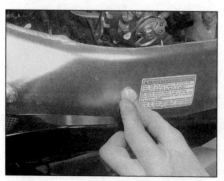

19.7a Remove the blanking caps . . .

19.7b . . . then slacken the clamp screws . . .

19.7c . . . and remove the throttle bodies

## Installation

8 Installation is the reverse of removal, noting the following.
  a) *Make sure the throttle bodies are fully engaged with the inlet manifolds on the cylinder heads.*
  b) *Make sure the throttle body retaining clamps are secure, but take care not to overtighten them.*
  c) *Make sure all the wiring connectors are reconnected.*
  d) *Make sure the hose clamp on the fuel return hose is secure, then remove the plug from the end of the hose and attach the hose to the union on the bottom of the fuel pressure regulator. Also make sure the fuel supply hose clicks properly onto its union and is secure.*
  e) *Check the operation of the choke and throttle cables and adjust them as necessary (see Chapter 1).*
  f) *Check idle speed and throttle synchronisation and adjust as necessary (see Chapter 1).*

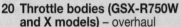
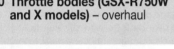

## 20 Throttle bodies (GSX-R750W and X models) – overhaul

**Warning: Refer to the precautions given in Section 1 before starting work.**

## Disassembly

1 Remove the fuel injectors (see section 21).
2 If required, remove the throttle position sensor, but only do so if absolutely necessary (see Section 15).
3 If required, disconnect the vacuum hoses from the throttle bodies and the pressure regulator and release them from the clip, but leave the hoses connected to each other (unless they need renewing) **(see illustration)**.
4 The pilot air screws, located just ahead of the vacuum hose unions, can be removed if required, but note that their setting will be disturbed (see **Haynes Hint**). On UK models unscrew and remove the pilot screw along with its spring, washer and O-ring. Discard the O-ring as a new one must be used. Pilot screw removal is the same for US models, except that the screw head is sealed off with a blanking plug. Carefully drill or punch a hole in the plug and prise it out using a hooked tool, or by threading in a self-tapping screw and grasping that with a pair of pliers. If drilling, do not drill further than a depth of 6 mm.

**HAYNES HiNT** *To record the air screw's current setting, turn the screw in until it seats lightly, counting the number of turns necessary to achieve this, then fully unscrew it. On installation, the screw is simply backed out the number of turns you've recorded.*

**20.3 Pull the hoses off the unions on the throttle bodies (A) and the pressure regulator (B)**

## Cleaning

**Caution: Use only a petroleum based solvent or dedicated carburettor cleaner for throttle body cleaning. Don't use caustic cleaners.**
5 Submerge the metal components in the solvent for approximately thirty minutes (or longer, if the directions recommend it). If a spray cleaner is used, direct the spray into all passages.
6 After the components have soaked long enough for the cleaner to loosen and dissolve most of the varnish and other deposits, use a nylon-bristled brush to remove the stubborn deposits. Rinse them again, then dry them with compressed air.
7 Use a jet of compressed air to blow out all of the fuel and air passages.
**Caution: Never clean the jets or passages with a piece of wire or a drill bit, as they will be enlarged, causing the fuel and air metering rates to be upset.**

## Inspection

8 Check the throttle bodies for cracks or any other damage which may result in air getting in.
9 Check that the throttle butterflies move smoothly and freely in the bodies, and make sure that the inside of each body is completely clean.
10 Check that the throttle and choke cable cams move smoothly and freely, taking into

**20.14 Carefully note the arrangement of the linkage assembly and synchronisation springs (arrowed)**

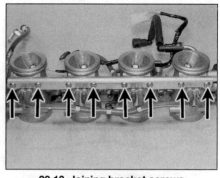

**20.13 Joining bracket screws (arrowed)**

account spring pressure. Clean any grit and dirt from around the cams.

## Separation and joining

11 The throttle bodies do not need to be separated for normal overhaul. If you need to separate them (to renew a body, for example), refer to the following procedure:
12 Mark each body with its cylinder location to ensure that it is positioned correctly on reassembly.
13 Remove the screws securing the joining bracket and remove the bracket, noting how it fits **(see illustration)**.
14 Make a note of how the throttle return springs, linkage assembly and synchronisation springs are arranged to ensure that they are fitted correctly on reassembly **(see illustration)**. Also note carefully the arrangement of the various hoses and their unions, and make drawings as an aid if required.
15 Unscrew and withdraw the long bolt which holds the bodies together **(see illustration)**.
16 Carefully separate the bodies. Retrieve the synchronisation springs and note the fitting of the joining spacers.
17 Joining is the reverse of the separation procedure. Install the synchronisation springs after the carburettors are joined together. Make sure they are correctly and squarely seated. Check the operation of the throttle linkage ensuring it operates smoothly and

**20.15 Unscrew and withdraw the bolt (arrowed)**

**4**

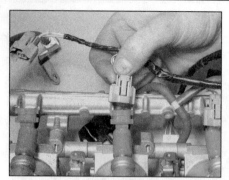

**21.2 Disconnect the injector wiring connector**

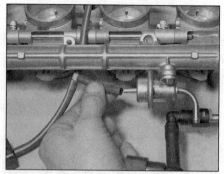

**21.6 Pull the vacuum hose off the pressure regulator**

**21.8a Unscrew the bolts (arrowed) . . .**

returns quickly under spring pressure. Check carburettor synchronisation and idle speed (see Chapter 1) after installation.

### Reassembly

**18** Install the pilot air screw (if removed) along with its spring, washer and using a new O-ring, turning it in until it seats lightly. Now, turn the screw out the number of turns previously recorded, or as specified at the beginning of the Chapter. If the pilot screw was disturbed on US models, read the notes in Sections 1 and 7 concerning maladjustment and emissions; the pilot screw housing should be sealed by fitting a new blanking plug.
**19** If disconnected, attach the vacuum hoses to the throttle bodies (see illustration 20.3).
**20** If removed, install the throttle position sensor (see Section 15).
**21** Install the fuel injectors (see section 21).

### 21 Fuel injectors (GSX-R750W and X models) – check, removal and installation

> ⚠ **Warning: Refer to the precautions given in Section 1 before proceeding.**

### Check

**1** Raise the fuel tank (see Section 2).
**2** Make sure the ignition is switched OFF. Disconnect the wiring connector from the

injector being tested (see illustration). Using an ohmmeter or multimeter, check that the resistance between the terminals on the injector is as specified. Also check that there is no continuity between each terminal and ground. If the readings are not as specified, install a new injector.
**3** If the readings are good, set the meter to read dc volts and check that battery voltage exists between the yellow/red wire terminal on the injector wiring connector and ground, with the ignition switched ON, noting that after it is switched ON you only have 3 seconds to take the reading before the ECU automatically cuts the voltage. If no voltage exists, check the connector and the wiring for faults. If voltage exists, it is likely that there is a fault elsewhere in the system or in the ECU itself (see Section 16).

### Removal

**4** Remove the air filter housing (see Section 6). The fuel injectors can be removed with the throttle bodies in situ. If the bodies have been removed, ignore the Steps which do not apply.
**5** Place a container suitable for holding petrol (gasoline) under the right-hand end of the fuel rail, then slacken the pressure check bolt and allow the residual fuel to drain (see illustration 17.3). When the fuel has drained, tighten the bolt to the torque setting specified at the beginning of the Chapter, using a new sealing washer if necessary.

**6** If the fuel tank was raised rather than removed, attach a hose clamp (see Tools and Workshop Tips) to the fuel return hose which runs from the pressure regulator to the fuel tank (see illustration 2.9a). Have a rag handy to catch any residue fuel, then detach the hose from the regulator (see illustration 2.9b). Fit a suitable plug into the end of the hose as a back-up to the clamp. Also detach the fuel supply hose from either the fuel tank or the inlet union on the fuel rail (see illustrations 2.9c and d). Pull the vacuum hose off its union on the pressure regulator (see illustration).
**7** Disconnect the common wiring connector for all the fuel injectors (as opposed to the connector on each individual injector) (see illustration 19.4a).
**8** Unscrew the bolts securing the fuel rail and lift the rail off the throttle bodies – the injectors will come away with the rail (see illustrations).
**9** To separate the injectors from the fuel rail, release the clip on the injector wiring connector and detach the connector (see illustration 21.2). Carefully pull the injector out of the fuel rail, noting how it fits (see illustration). Discard the injector seals and O-ring as new ones must be used (see illustration).
**10** If required, unscrew the bolts or screws securing the pressure regulator and/or the fuel inlet union to the fuel rail and detach them

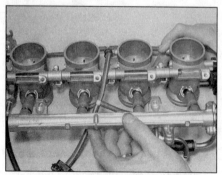

**21.8b . . . and remove the fuel rail and injectors**

**21.9a Carefully pull the injector out of the rail**

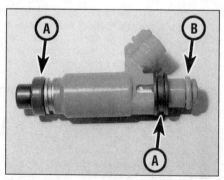

**21.9b Discard the seals (A) and O-ring (B)**

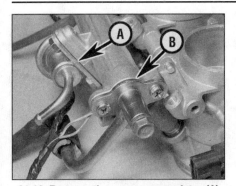

21.10 Remove the pressure regulator (A) and inlet union (B) if required

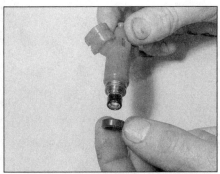

21.13a Fit a new bottom seal . . .

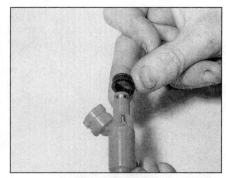

21.13b . . . top seal . . .

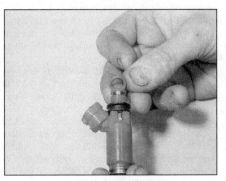

21.13c . . . and O-ring

21.14a Install the bolts . . .

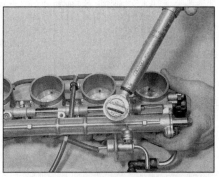

21.14b . . . and tighten them to the specified torque

(see illustration). Discard the O-rings as new ones must be used.

11 Modern fuels contain detergents which should keep the injectors clean and free of gum or varnish from residue fuel. If the injector is suspected of being blocked, clean it through with injector cleaner. If the injector is clean but its performance is suspect, take it to a Suzuki dealer for assessment.

### Installation

12 If removed, fit a new O-ring onto the fuel supply union and the pressure regulator and smear them with clean engine oil. Press each component into the fuel rail and tighten its screws or bolts to the torque settings specified at the beginning of the Chapter.

13 Fit new seals and O-ring onto each injector (see illustrations). Push the injector into the fuel rail, making sure you do not turn it whilst doing so, and that it is properly seated (see illustration 21.9a).

14 Fit the fuel rail and injectors onto the throttle bodies, making sure each injector seats correctly (see illustration 21.8b). Install the fuel rail bolts and tighten them to the specified torque setting (see illustrations). Connect the individual injector wiring connectors (see illustration 21.2), and the common connector into the wiring loom (see illustration 19.4a).

15 If the fuel tank was raised rather than removed, make sure the hose clamp on the fuel return hose is secure, then remove the

plug from the end of the hose and attach the hose to the union on the bottom of the fuel pressure regulator (see illustration 2.9b). Also connect the fuel supply hose to either the tank or the inlet union according to your removal procedure, making sure it clicks properly onto its union and is secure (see illustration 2.9d). Attach the vacuum hose to its union on the pressure regulator (see illustration 21.6).

16 Install the air filter housing (see Section 6).

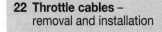

## 22 Throttle cables – removal and installation

 Warning: Refer to the precautions given in Section 1 before proceeding.

### Removal

1 Raise the fuel tank (see Section 2).

2 Slacken the top locknut on one of the cables, then unscrew the adjuster until the bottom locknut is clear of the bracket (see illustration). Free the adjuster from its mounting bracket, then rotate the cam using your finger and detach the inner cable from the throttle cam (see illustrations). Repeat for the other cable.

3 Remove the screw securing the front (accelerator) cable retaining plate to the

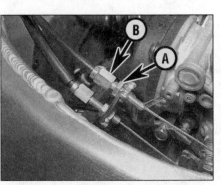

22.2a Slacken the top locknut (A) and unscrew the adjuster (B) . . .

22.2b . . . then free it from the bracket . . .

4

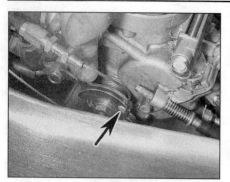

22.2c . . . and detach the cable end (arrowed) from the throttle cam

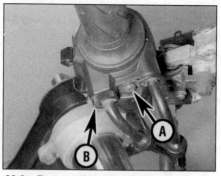

22.3a Remove the retainer plate screw (A) and unscrew the ring (B)

22.3b Remove the housing screws (arrowed) and separate the halves

handlebar switch/throttle pulley housing, and unscrew the rear (decelerator) cable retaining ring (see illustration). Remove the handlebar switch/throttle pulley housing screws and separate the halves (see illustration). Hook the cable ends out of the pulley and remove the cable elbows from the housing (see illustrations). Mark each cable to ensure it is connected correctly on installation.

4 Slacken the bolt securing the cable guide to the frame (see illustration). Remove the cables from the machine noting the correct routing of each cable.

## Installation

5 Install the cables making sure they are correctly routed – tighten the guide bolt after fitting the cables into it (see illustration 22.4).

22.3c Detach the cable ends from the pulley . . .

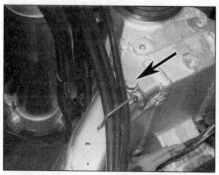

22.4 Slacken the bolt (arrowed) and free the cables from the guide

The cables must not interfere with any other component and should not be kinked or bent sharply. Note that on carburettor models, the top cable is the accelerator (throttle opening cable) and the bottom cable is the decelerator (throttle closing) cable. On fuel injected models, it is the other way around (not counting the choke cable).

6 Install the cables into the throttle pulley housing, making sure the accelerator cable is at the front and the decelerator is at the back. Secure the accelerator cable elbow with the retainer plate (see illustration), and thread the decelerator cable retaining ring into the housing. Lubricate the end of each inner cable with multi-purpose grease, then locate the lower half of the housing and attach them to the pulley (see illustration 22.3c).

22.3d . . . and draw them out of the housing

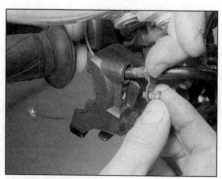

22.6 Fit the cable elbows into the housing

7 Assemble the housing, aligning its locating pin with the hole in the top of the handlebar (see illustration). Install the retaining screws, and tighten them securely (see illustration 22.3b).

8 Lubricate the lower end of each inner cable with multi-purpose grease and attach them to the carburettor throttle cam (see illustration 22.2c).

9 Make sure the cables are correctly connected and locate the outer cable adjusters in the mounting brackets (see illustration 22.2b). Set the adjuster locknuts so that the slack in the inner cable is taken up, but not so that it is tight (see illustration 22.2a). Tighten the top locknut securely.

10 Lower the fuel tank (see Section 2).

11 Adjust the cables as described in Chapter 1. Turn the handlebars back and forth to make sure the cables don't cause the steering to bind.

12 Install the fuel tank (see Section 2).

13 Start the engine and check that the idle speed does not rise as the handlebars are turned. If it does, correct the problem before riding the motorcycle.

## 23 Choke cable –
removal and installation

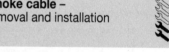

### Removal

1 Raise the fuel tank (see Section 2).

2 On GSX-R600 and GSX-R750T and V

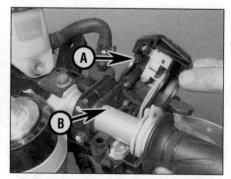

22.7 Locate the pin (A) into the hole (B)

23.2a Pull the outer cable out of its bracket . . .

23.2b . . . and detach the inner cable from the bar

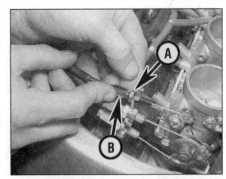

23.3a Slacken the top locknut (A) and unscrew the adjuster (B) . . .

models, free the choke outer cable from its bracket on the carburettor by pulling it out, then free the inner cable from the choke linkage bar (see illustrations).

3 On GSX-R750W and X models, slacken the top locknut on the cable, then unscrew the adjuster until the bottom locknut is clear of the bracket (see illustration). Free the adjuster from its mounting bracket and detach the inner cable from the choke cam (see illustrations).

4 Slacken the choke lever clamp screw, then unscrew the two handlebar switch/choke lever housing screws, one of which secures the choke cable elbow via a retainer plate, and separate the two halves; open the choke lever fully as you separate the halves, noting how it fits into the housing (see illustrations). Detach the cable nipple from the choke lever,

23.3b . . . then free it from the bracket . . .

then withdraw the cable and elbow from the housing (see illustrations).

5 Slacken the bolt securing the cable guide to

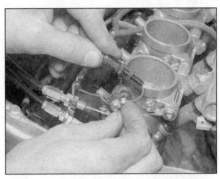

23.3c . . . and detach the cable end from the throttle cam

the frame (see illustration 22.4). Remove the cable from the machine noting its correct routing.

### Installation

6 Install the cable making sure it is correctly routed – tighten the guide bolt after fitting the cable into it (see illustration 22.4). The cable must not interfere with any other component and should not be kinked or bent sharply.

7 Lubricate the upper cable nipple with multi-purpose grease. Install the cable in the switch/choke lever housing and attach the nipple to the choke lever (see illustrations 23.4d and c). Fit the two halves of the housing onto the handlebar, again with the choke lever in the fully open position, making sure the lever fits correctly, and the pin in the upper half locates in the hole in the top of the handlebar (see illustration and 23.4b). Install

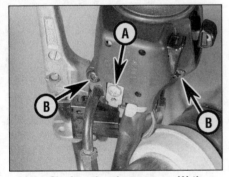

23.4a Slacken the clamp screw (A) then remove the housing screws (B)

23.4b Push the lever fully open as you separate the housing

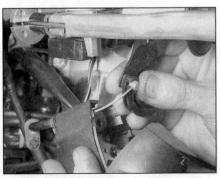

23.4c Detach the cable end from the lever . . .

23.4d . . . and draw it out of the housing

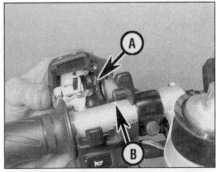

23.7 Locate the pin (A) into the hole (B)

4

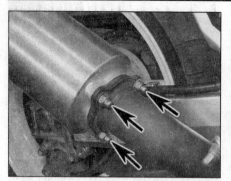

24.1 Silencer-to-downpipe nuts (arrowed)

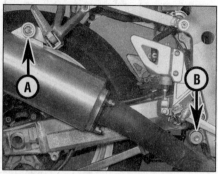

24.2 Silencer mounting (A), downpipe rear mounting (B)

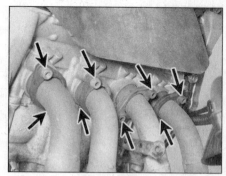

24.10 Downpipe clamp bolts (arrowed)

the screws, making sure the elbow retainer is correctly positioned, and tighten them securely, then tighten the spring clamp screw (see illustration 23.4a).

8 On GSX-R600 and GSX-R750T and V models, lubricate the lower cable nipple with multi-purpose grease and attach it to the choke linkage bar on the carburettor (see illustration 23.2b). Fit the outer cable into its bracket (see illustration 23.2a).

9 On GSX-R750W and X models, lubricate the lower cable nipple with multi-purpose grease and attach it to the choke cam (see illustration 23.3c). Locate the outer cable adjuster in the mounting bracket (see illustration 23.3b). Set the adjuster locknuts so that the slack in the inner cable is taken up, but not so that it is tight (see illustration 23.3a). Tighten the top locknut securely.

10 Check the operation of the choke cable (see Chapter 1).

11 Lower the fuel tank (see Section 2).

## 24 Exhaust system – removal and installation

**Warning: If the engine has been running the exhaust system will be very hot. Allow the system to cool before carrying out any work.**

### Silencer

#### Removal

1 Unscrew the nuts and remove the washers securing the silencer to the downpipe assembly (see illustration).

2 Unscrew and remove the silencer mounting nut and bolt, then release the silencer from the exhaust downpipe assembly (see illustration).

3 Remove the sealing ring from the end of the downpipe assembly and discard it as a new one should be used.

#### Installation

4 Fit the new sealing ring onto the end of the downpipe assembly.

5 Fit the silencer onto the downpipe assembly, making sure it is pushed fully home. Align the silencer mounting bracket at the rear and install the bolt, but do not yet tighten the nut.

6 Install the silencer nuts with their washers and tighten them to the torque setting specified at the beginning of the Chapter, then tighten the silencer mounting bolt to the specified torque.

7 Run the engine and check the system for leaks.

### Complete system

#### Removal

8 Remove the fairing side panels and the lower fairing (see Chapter 8).

9 Unscrew the silencer mounting nut but do not yet remove the bolt (see illustration 24.2). Unscrew the bolt securing the rear of the downpipe assembly to the frame (see illustration 24.2).

10 Unscrew the eight downpipe clamp retaining bolts from the cylinder head (see illustration).

11 Supporting the system, remove the silencer mounting bolt, then lower the system from the machine (see illustration 24.14).

12 Remove the gasket from each port in the cylinder head and discard them as new ones must be fitted.

#### Installation

13 Fit a new gasket into each of the cylinder head ports with the tabs on each gasket facing inwards (see illustration). Apply a smear of grease to the gaskets to keep them in place whilst fitting the downpipe if necessary.

14 Manoeuvre the assembly into position so that the head of each downpipe is located in its port in the cylinder head, then install the silencer mounting bolt and the rear bolt for the downpipe assembly, but do not yet tighten them (see illustration).

15 Install the downpipe clamp bolts and tighten them to the torque setting specified at the beginning of the Chapter (see illustration). Now tighten the other bolts to the specified torque.

16 Run the engine and check that there are no air leaks from the exhaust system.

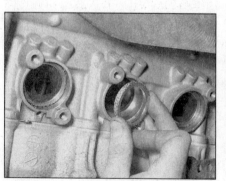

24.13 Fit a new gasket into each port

24.14 Manoeuvre the system into position and locate the rear bolts to support it

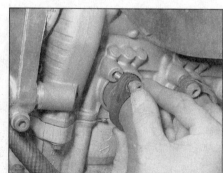

24.15 Install the downpipe clamp bolts and tighten them to the specified torque

## 25 EVAP and PAIR systems
(California models)

### Evaporative emission control system (EVAP)

#### General information

**1** This system prevents the escape of fuel vapour into the atmosphere by storing it in a charcoal-filled canister located on the frame right-hand side at the rear **(see illustration)**.

**2** When the engine is stopped, fuel vapour from the tank is directed into the canister where it is absorbed and stored whilst the motorcycle is standing. When the engine is started, inlet manifold depression opens the purge control valves, thus drawing vapours which are stored in the canister into the carburettors to be burned during the normal combustion process.

**3** The tank vent pipe also incorporates a roll-over valve which closes and prevents any fuel from escaping through it in the event of the bike falling over. The tank filler cap has a one way valve which allows air into the tank as the volume of fuel decreases, but prevents any fuel vapour from escaping.

**4** The system is not adjustable and can be properly tested only by a Suzuki dealer. However the owner can check that all the hoses are in good condition and are securely connected at each end. Renew any hoses that are cracked, split or generally deteriorated.

**5** The purge control valves can be checked by disconnecting their hoses (noting which way round they fit) and blowing through them. If the valve is working correctly, air should pass through when blowing into the union on the narrower side of the valve, but should not pass through when blowing into the union on the fatter side. When installing the valves, make sure the union on the narrower side is connected to the hose that goes to the canister, and the union on the fatter side is connected to the hose that comes from the carburettor or throttle body.

#### Removal and installation

**6** To access the canister remove the seat cowling (see Chapter 8). Label and disconnect the hoses, remove the clamp screw and take the canister out. Make sure the hoses are correctly reconnected on installation.

**7** The two purge control valves and the roll-over valve are mounted under the fuel tank.

### Pulse secondary air injection system (PAIR)

#### General information

**8** When the engine is running, the depression present in the inlet manifold of No. 2 or No. 3 cylinder (whichever cylinder the hose connects to) acts on a diaphragm in the PAIR control valve, opening the valve. With the control valve open, whenever there is a negative pulse in the exhaust system, filtered fresh air is drawn from the PAIR air cleaner, through the reed valves and into the exhaust ports in the front of the cylinder head.

**9** This fresh air promotes the burning of any excess fuel present in the exhaust gases, so reducing the amount of harmful hydrocarbons emitted into the atmosphere via the exhaust gases. Exhaust gases are prevented from passing back into the PAIR system by the reed valves.

**10** The system is not adjustable and requires no maintenance, except to ensure that the hoses are in good condition and are securely connected at each end. Renew any hoses that

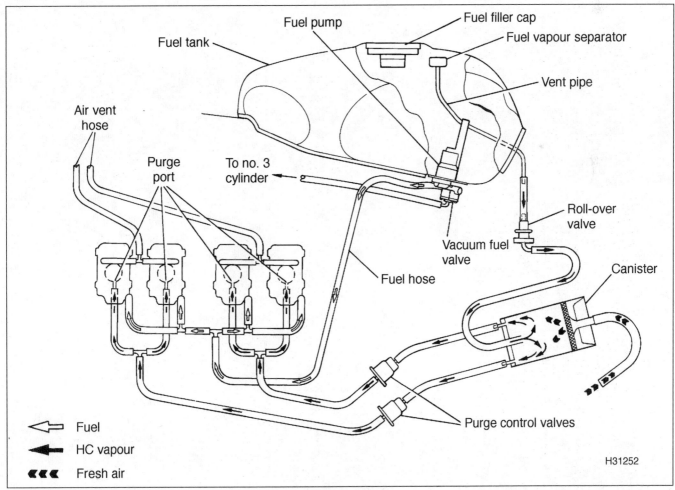

25.1 EVAP system

are cracked, split or generally deteriorated. Also check the other components for evidence of physical damage. The reed valves can be checked for any build-up of carbon – if any is found, install new reed valves. The control valve should allow air to pass through it only when a vacuum is applied to the vacuum union. As a specific vacuum range is required (270 to 450 mmHg), it is best to have the valve tested by a dealer. On later models, the reed valves and control valve are incorporated into one unit.

### Removal and installation

**11** Remove the fuel tank for access to the PAIR air cleaner. The control valve and reed valves are located between the radiator and the oil filter on the front of the engine.

**12** Before disconnecting any of the components from their mountings, label the hoses to ensure correct reconnection. It is not possible to dismantle or repair any of the PAIR components. If the metal pipes from the reed valve hoses to the cylinder head are removed, always use new gaskets at the cylinder joint on installation.

# Chapter 5
## Ignition system

## Contents

## Degrees of difficulty

| Easy, suitable for novice with little experience |  | Fairly easy, suitable for beginner with some experience |  | Fairly difficult, suitable for competent DIY mechanic |  | Difficult, suitable for experienced DIY mechanic | | Very difficult, suitable for expert DIY or professional | |

## Specifications

### General information
Firing order . . . . . . . . . . . . . . . . . . . . . . . . . . . . . . . . . . . . . . . . . . . 1–2–4–3
Cylinder identification . . . . . . . . . . . . . . . . . . . . . . . . . . . . . . . . . . . 1–2–3–4, from left to right
Spark plugs . . . . . . . . . . . . . . . . . . . . . . . . . . . . . . . . . . . . . . . . . . . see Chapter 1

### Ignition timing
At idle
  All GSX-R600 except US and California GSX-R600X . . . . . . . . . . . . 5° BTDC
  All GSX-R750 and US and California GSX-R600X . . . . . . . . . . . . . . 4° BTDC
Ignition rev limiter
  GSX-R600 . . . . . . . . . . . . . . . . . . . . . . . . . . . . . . . . . . . . . . . . . . . 13,400 rpm
  GSX-R750 . . . . . . . . . . . . . . . . . . . . . . . . . . . . . . . . . . . . . . . . . . . 13,200 rpm

### Pulse generator coil*
Resistance . . . . . . . . . . . . . . . . . . . . . . . . . . . . . . . . . . . . . . . . . . . 50 to 200 ohms
*Crankshaft position (CKP) sensor on GSX-R750 W and X models

### Ignition HT coils
GSX-R750T and V
  Primary winding resistance . . . . . . . . . . . . . . . . . . . . . . . . . . . . . . 2.3 to 3.3 ohms
  Secondary winding resistance (with plug lead and cap) . . . . . . . . . 30 to 40 K-ohms
GSX-R600 and GSX-R750W and X
  Primary winding resistance . . . . . . . . . . . . . . . . . . . . . . . . . . . . . . 0.07 to 0.11 ohms
  Secondary winding resistance . . . . . . . . . . . . . . . . . . . . . . . . . . . . 4.5 to 6.9 K-ohms

**5**

## 1 General information

All models are fitted with a fully transistorised electronic ignition system, which due to its lack of mechanical parts is totally maintenance free. The system comprises a rotor, pulse generator coil (crankshaft position sensor on GSX-R750W and X models), electronic control unit and ignition HT coils (refer to the wiring diagrams at the end of Chapter 9 for details).

The triggers on the rotor, which is fitted to the right-hand end of the crankshaft, magnetically operate the pulse generator coil as the crankshaft rotates. The pulse generator coil sends a signal to the ECU (electronic control unit) which then supplies the HT coils with the power necessary to produce a spark at the plugs.

On GSX-R750T and V models, the system uses two coils mounted on the inside of the right-hand frame spar. The top coil supplies Nos. 1 and 4 cylinder spark plugs and the bottom coil supplies Nos. 2 and 3 cylinder plugs.

On all GSX-R600 and GSX-R750W and X models, the coil for each spark plug is incorporated in the spark plug cap.

The ECU incorporates an electronic advance system controlled by signals generated by the pulse generator coil, and a limiter to prevent the engine exceeding its maximum rpm. On all models, the ECU is also

supplied with throttle position information from a sensor mounted on No. 4 carburettor or throttle body. On GSX-R750W and X (fuel injected) models, the crankshaft position sensor, gear position sensor and engine coolant temperature sensor also provide information which helps the ECU determine the optimum ignition timing for any situation.

The system incorporates a safety interlock circuit which will cut the ignition if the sidestand is put down whilst the engine is running and in gear, or if a gear is selected whilst the engine is running and the sidestand is down.

Because of their nature, the individual ignition system components can be checked but not repaired. If ignition system troubles occur, and the faulty component can be isolated, the only cure for the problem is to renew the part. Keep in mind that most electrical parts, once purchased, cannot be returned. To avoid unnecessary expense, make very sure the faulty component has been positively identified before buying a renewal part.

Note that there is no provision for checking or adjusting the ignition timing on these models.

## 2 Ignition system – check

**Warning: The energy levels in electronic systems can be very high. On no account should the ignition be switched on whilst the plugs or plug caps are being held. Shocks from the HT circuit can be most unpleasant. Secondly, it is vital that the engine is not turned over or run with any of the plug caps removed, and that the plugs are soundly earthed (grounded) when the system is checked for sparking. The ignition system components can be seriously damaged if the HT circuit becomes isolated.**

1 As no means of adjustment is available, any failure of the system can be traced to failure of a system component or a simple wiring fault. Of the two possibilities, the latter is by far the most likely. In the event of failure, check the system in a logical fashion, as described below.

2 Remove the air filter housing (see Chapter 4). On GSX-R750T and V models, pull the spark plug caps off the spark plugs. On GSX-R600 and GSX-R750W and X models, disconnect the ignition coil/plug cap wiring connectors, then pull the coil/ cap off each spark plug **(see illustrations)**. Connect each cap to a spare spark plug and lay each plug on the engine with the threads contacting the engine **(see illustration)**. If necessary, hold each spark plug with an insulated tool. Do not hold the plug against the valve cover or any other engine cover that is magnesium coated as the coating could be damaged.

**Warning: Do not remove any of the spark plugs from the engine to perform this check – atomised fuel being pumped out of the open spark plug hole could ignite, causing severe injury!**

3 Having observed the above precautions, check that the kill switch is in the RUN position and the transmission is in neutral, then turn the ignition switch ON and turn the engine over on the starter motor. If the system is in good condition a regular, fat blue spark should be evident at each plug electrode. If the spark appears thin or yellowish, or is non-existent, further investigation will be necessary. Before proceeding further, turn the ignition off and remove the key as a safety measure.

4 The ignition system must be able to produce a spark which is capable of jumping a particular size gap. Suzuki specify that a healthy system should produce a spark capable of jumping 8 mm. A simple testing tool can be made to test the minimum gap across which the spark will jump (see **Tool Tip**) or alternatively it is possible to buy an ignition spark gap tester tool and some of these tools are adjustable to alter the spark gap.

5 Connect one of the spark plug caps to the protruding electrode on the test tool, and clip the tool to a good earth (ground) on the

2.2a Disconnect the wiring connector . . .

2.2b . . . then pull the coil/plug cap off the spark plug

2.2c Ground (earth) the spark plug and operate the starter – bright blue sparks should be visible

TOOL TiP

A simple spark gap testing tool can be made from a block of wood, a large alligator clip and two nails, one of which is fashioned so that a spark plug cap or bare HT lead end can be connected to its end. Make sure the gap between the two nail ends is the same as specified

**2.5 Connect the tester as shown – when the engine is cranked sparks should jump the gap between the nails**

engine or frame (see illustration). Check that the kill switch is in the RUN position, turn the ignition switch ON and turn the engine over on the starter motor. If the system is in good condition a regular, fat blue spark should be seen to jump the gap between the nail ends. Repeat the test for the other coil. If the test results are good the entire ignition system can be considered good. If the spark appears thin or yellowish, or is non-existent, further investigation will be necessary.

6 Ignition faults can be divided into two categories, namely those where the ignition system has failed completely, and those which are due to a partial failure. The likely faults are listed below, starting with the most probable source of failure. Work through the list systematically, referring to the subsequent sections for full details of the necessary checks and tests. Note: Before checking the following items ensure that the battery is fully charged and that all fuses are in good condition.

a) Loose, corroded or damaged wiring connections, broken or shorted wiring between any of the component parts of the ignition system (see Chapter 9).
b) Faulty HT lead or spark plug cap (GSX-R750T and V only), faulty spark plug, dirty, worn or corroded plug electrodes, or incorrect gap between electrodes.
c) Faulty ignition (main) switch or engine kill switch (see Chapter 9).
d) Faulty clutch, neutral or sidestand switch (see Chapter 9).

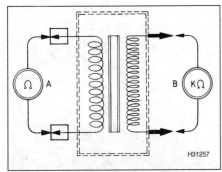

**3.5 Ignition HT coil test connections**

*A Primary winding test*
*B Secondary winding test*

e) Faulty pulse generator coil or damaged rotor.
f) Faulty ignition HT coil(s) - GSX-R750T and V only.
g) Faulty electronic control unit.

7 If the above checks don't reveal the cause of the problem, have the ignition system tested by a Suzuki dealer.

### 3 Ignition HT coils – check, removal and installation

*Check*

1 In order to determine conclusively that the ignition coils are defective, they should be tested by a Suzuki dealer.
2 However, the coils can be checked visually (for cracks and other damage) and the primary and secondary coil resistances can be measured with a multimeter. If the coils are undamaged, and if the resistance readings are as specified at the beginning of the Chapter, they are probably capable of proper operation.
3 Remove the rider's seat (see Chapter 8) and disconnect the battery negative (-ve) lead. To gain access to the coils, remove the air filter housing (see Chapter 4). On GSX-R750T and V models, the coils are mounted on the inside of the right-hand frame spar. The top coil supplies Nos. 1 and 4 cylinder spark plugs and the bottom coil supplies Nos. 2 and 3 cylinder plugs. On all GSX-R600 and GSX-R750W and X models, the coil for each spark plug is incorporated in the spark plug cap.

#### GSX-R750T and V models

4 Disconnect the primary circuit electrical connectors from the coil being tested and the pull the spark plug caps off the spark plugs. Mark the locations of all wires and leads before disconnecting them.
5 Set the meter to the ohms x 1 scale and measure the resistance between the primary circuit terminals (see illustration). This will give a resistance reading of the primary windings and should be consistent with the value given in the Specifications at the beginning of the Chapter.
6 To check the condition of the secondary windings, set the meter to the K-ohm scale. Connect one meter probe to one spark plug cap

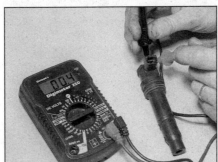

**3.9 To test the primary circuit resistance, connect the multimeter as shown**

and the other probe to the other spark plug cap (see illustration 3.5). If the reading obtained is not within the range shown in the Specifications, it is possible that the coil is defective, though it could be a spark plug cap or HT lead. The caps are available separately, but the leads are integral with the coil. Suzuki provide no test specifications for the caps, but it is worth substituting a known good one from another cylinder before consigning the coil to the bin.
7 Should any of the above checks not produce the expected result, have your findings confirmed by a Suzuki dealer. If the coil is confirmed to be faulty, it must be renewed; the coil is a sealed unit and cannot therefore be repaired.

#### GSX-R600 and GSX-R750W and X models

8 Disconnect the ignition coil/plug cap wiring connectors (see illustration 2.2a). Pull the coil/cap off each spark plug (see illustration 2.2b).
9 Set the meter to the ohms x 1 scale and measure the resistance between the primary circuit terminals on the coil/cap (see illustration). This will give a resistance reading of the primary windings and should be consistent with the value given in the Specifications at the beginning of the Chapter.
10 To check the condition of the secondary windings, set the meter to the K-ohm scale. Connect one meter probe to the negative primary circuit terminal and the other probe to the spark plug cap (see illustration). If the reading obtained is not within the range shown in the Specifications, it is possible that the coil is defective.
11 Should any of the above checks not produce the expected result, have your findings confirmed by a Suzuki dealer. If the coil is confirmed to be faulty, it must be renewed; the coil is a sealed unit and cannot therefore be repaired.

*Removal*

12 Remove the rider's seat (see Chapter 8) and disconnect the battery negative (-ve) lead, then remove the air filter housing (see Chapter 4).
13 On GSX-R750T and V models, disconnect the primary circuit electrical connectors from the coils and pull the spark plug caps off the spark plugs. Mark the locations of all wires and leads before disconnecting them.

**3.10 To test the secondary circuit resistance, connect the multimeter as shown**

**5**

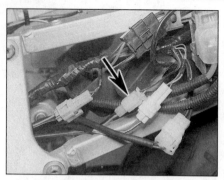

**4.2 Disconnect the pulse generator coil wiring connector (arrowed)**

Unscrew the two bolts securing each coil, noting the position of the spacers, and remove the coils. Note the routing of the HT leads.
14 On all GSX-R600 and GSX-R750W and X models, disconnect the ignition coil/plug cap wiring connectors **(see illustration 2.2a)**. Pull the coil/cap off each spark plug **(see illustration 2.2b)**.

## Installation

15 Installation is the reverse of removal. Make sure the wiring connectors and HT leads are securely connected.

## 4 Pulse generator coil assembly – check, removal and installation

**Note:** *The pulse generator coil is termed the crankshaft position (CKP) sensor on the GSX-R750W and X models.*

## Check

1 Remove the seat cowling (see Chapter 8) and disconnect the battery negative (-ve) lead.
2 Trace the pulse generator coil wiring back from the top of the right-hand side crankcase cover and disconnect it at the 2-pin connector with the black and green wires **(see illustration)**. Using a multimeter set to the ohms x 100 scale, measure the resistance between the terminals on the pulse generator coil side of the connector.
3 Compare the reading obtained with that given in the Specifications at the beginning of this Chapter. The pulse generator coil must be renewed if the reading obtained differs greatly

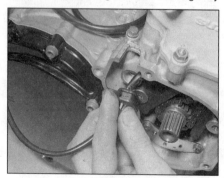

**4.11 . . . and fit the grommet into its cutout**

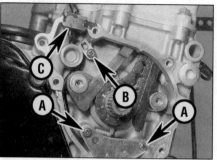

**4.8 Remove the mounting plate screws (A) and the clamp screw (B), and free the grommet (C) from its cutout**

from that given, particularly if the meter indicates a short circuit (no measurable resistance) or an open circuit (infinite, or very high resistance).
4 If the pulse generator coil is thought to be faulty, first check that this is not due to a damaged or broken wire from the coil to the connector; pinched or broken wires can usually be repaired. Note that the coil is not available individually but comes as an assembly with the mounting plate and wiring.

## Removal

5 Remove the seat cowling (see Chapter 8) and disconnect the battery negative (-ve) llead.
6 Trace the pulse generator coil switch wiring back from the top of the right-hand side crankcase cover and disconnect it at the 2-pin connector with the black and green wires **(see illustration 4.2)**. Free the wiring from any clips or ties and feed it through to its exit hole.
7 Remove the starter clutch (see Chapter 2).
8 Remove the screws securing the pulse generator coil assembly mounting plate to the crankcase cover and the screw securing the wiring clamp **(see illustration)**. Remove the rubber wiring grommet from its recess, then remove the coil assembly, noting how it fits.
9 Examine the rotor for signs of damage and install a new one if necessary (see Chapter 2, Section 9).

## Installation

10 Install the pulse generator coil assembly onto the crankcase and tighten its screws securely **(see illustration)**.
11 Apply a smear of sealant to the rubber

**5.3a Electronic control unit – GSX-R600 and GSX-R750T and V**

**4.10 Install the pulse generator coil . . .**

wiring seal and fit the grommet in its recess in the crankcase **(see illustration)**. Locate the wiring under its clamp and tighten the clamp screw **(see illustration 4.8)**.
12 Install the starter clutch (see Chapter 2).
13 Route the wiring up to the connector and reconnect it **(see illustration 4.2)**. Secure the wiring in its clips or ties.
14 Reconnect the battery negative (-ve) lead and install the seat cowling (see Chapter 8).

## 5 Electronic control unit (ECU) – check, removal and installation

## Check

1 If the tests shown in the preceding Sections have failed to isolate the cause of an ignition fault, it is likely that the electronic control unit itself is faulty. No test details are available with which the unit can be tested on home workshop equipment. Take the machine to a Suzuki dealer for testing.

## Removal

2 Remove the rider's seat (see Chapter 8) and disconnect the battery negative (-ve) lead.
3 Disconnect the wiring connectors from the electronic control unit **(see illustrations)**.
4 Free the control unit from its mounting and remove it.

## Installation

5 Installation is the reverse of removal. Make sure the wiring connectors are correctly and securely connected.

**5.3b Electronic control unit – GSX-R750W and X**

# Chapter 6
# Frame, suspension and final drive

## Contents

## Degrees of difficulty

| | | | |
|---|---|---|---|
| **Easy,** suitable for novice with little experience  | **Fairly easy,** suitable for beginner with some experience  | **Fairly difficult,** suitable for competent DIY mechanic | **Difficult,** suitable for experienced DIY mechanic | **Very difficult,** suitable for expert DIY or professional |

## Specifications

**Front forks**

| | |
|---|---|
| Fork oil type . . . . . . . . . . . . . . . . . . . . . . . . . . . . . . . . . . . . . . . . . . . | SAE 10W fork oil |
| Fork oil capacity | |
|   GSX-R600 . . . . . . . . . . . . . . . . . . . . . . . . . . . . . . . . . . . . . . . . . . | 533 cc |
|   GSX-R750T and V . . . . . . . . . . . . . . . . . . . . . . . . . . . . . . . . . . . . | 480 cc |
|   GSX-R750W and X . . . . . . . . . . . . . . . . . . . . . . . . . . . . . . . . . . . | 490 cc |
| Fork oil level* | |
|   GSX-R600 . . . . . . . . . . . . . . . . . . . . . . . . . . . . . . . . . . . . . . . . . . | 110 mm |
|   GSX-R750T and V . . . . . . . . . . . . . . . . . . . . . . . . . . . . . . . . . . . . | 105 mm |
|   GSX-R750W and X . . . . . . . . . . . . . . . . . . . . . . . . . . . . . . . . . . . | 99 mm |
| Fork spring free length (min) | |
|   GSX-R600V . . . . . . . . . . . . . . . . . . . . . . . . . . . . . . . . . . . . . . . . . | 251 mm |
|   GSX-R600W and X . . . . . . . . . . . . . . . . . . . . . . . . . . . . . . . . . . . | 261 mm |
|   GSX-R750 . . . . . . . . . . . . . . . . . . . . . . . . . . . . . . . . . . . . . . . . . . | 250 mm |
| Fork tube runout limit . . . . . . . . . . . . . . . . . . . . . . . . . . . . . . . . . . | 0.2 mm |
| Fork tube protrusion above top yoke (not inc. top bolt) | |
|   GSX-R600 . . . . . . . . . . . . . . . . . . . . . . . . . . . . . . . . . . . . . . . . . . | 3.2 mm |
|   GSX-R750 . . . . . . . . . . . . . . . . . . . . . . . . . . . . . . . . . . . . . . . . . . | 2.0 mm |

*Oil level is measured from the top of the tube with the fork spring removed and the leg fully compressed.*

**6**

## Rear suspension

Swingarm pivot bolt runout (max) ............................. 0.3 mm

## Final drive

Chain type
  GSX-R600 ................................................... RK525SMOZ2 (108 links, endless)
  GSX-R750T and V ........................................... RK50MFOZ1 (108 links, soft-link)
  GSX-R750W and X ........................................... RK525ROZ2 (108 links, soft-link)
Distance between outside of joining link and side plate (unstaked)
  (RK chain) – 750 models ..................................... 21.85 to 22.15 mm
Joining link staked ends diameter (RK chain) – 750 models ........ 5.45 to 5.85 mm

## Torque settings

Front footrest bracket bolts ................................... 39 Nm
Steering stem nut ............................................. 90 Nm
Fork clamp bolts (top and bottom yoke) ....................... 23 Nm
Handlebar set bolts .......................................... 10 Nm
Handlebar clamp bolts ....................................... 23 Nm
Front master cylinder clamp bolts ............................ 10 Nm
Fork top bolt ................................................ 35 Nm
Damper rod Allen bolt ........................................ 35 Nm
Damper rod locknut .......................................... 20 Nm
Steering head bearing adjuster nut (see text) ................. 45 Nm
Steering head bearing locknut ................................ 80 Nm
Steering stem nut ............................................ 90 Nm
Shock absorber upper mounting bracket nut
  GSX-R750T ................................................ 85 Nm
  All other models ........................................... 115 Nm
Rear shock absorber nut/bolt ................................. 50 Nm
Rear suspension linkage arm and linkage rod nuts ............. 78 Nm
Swingarm pivot boss nuts (750 models) ....................... 65 Nm
Swingarm pivot bolt .......................................... 15 Nm
Swingarm pivot nut ........................................... 100 Nm
Swingarm pivot bolt locknut .................................. 90 Nm
Front sprocket nut ........................................... 120 Nm
Speedometer rotor bolt ....................................... 13 Nm
Rear sprocket nuts ........................................... 60 Nm

## 1 General information

All models use a twin spar box-section aluminium frame which uses the engine as a stressed member.

Front suspension is by a pair of oil-damped telescopic forks. On GSX-R600 models, the forks have a cartridge damper and are adjustable for spring pre-load and rebound damping on all models, and also for compression damping on W and X models. On GSX-R750 models, the forks are upside-down with a cartridge damper and are adjustable for spring pre-load, rebound and compression damping on all models.

At the rear, an alloy swingarm acts on a single shock absorber via a three-way linkage. The shock absorber is adjustable for spring pre-load, rebound and compression damping on all models.

The drive to the rear wheel is by chain. GSX-R600 models use an endless chain, while 750 models use a soft-link type due to the construction of the swingarm.

## 2 Frame – inspection and repair

1 The frame should not require attention unless accident damage has occurred. In most cases, frame renewal is the only satisfactory remedy for such damage. A few frame specialists have the jigs and other equipment necessary for straightening the frame to the required standard of accuracy, but even then there is no simple way of assessing to what extent the frame may have been over stressed.
2 After the machine has accumulated a lot of miles, the frame should be examined closely for signs of cracking or splitting at the welded joints. Loose engine mount bolts can cause ovaling or fracturing of the mounting tabs. Minor damage can often be repaired by welding, depending on the extent and nature of the damage.
3 Remember that a frame which is out of alignment will cause handling problems. If misalignment is suspected as the result of an accident, it will be necessary to strip the machine completely so the frame can be thoroughly checked.

## 3 Footrests, brake pedal and gearchange lever – removal and installation

### Rider's footrests
#### Removal

1 Remove the split pin from the bottom of the footrest pivot pin, then withdraw the pivot pin and remove the footrest, noting the fitting of the return spring and spacer (see illustration).

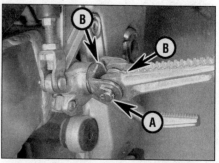

3.1 Remove the split pin (A) and withdraw the pin from the top. Note how the return spring ends (B) locate

**3.3 Remove the E-clip (A) and withdraw the pin from the top. Note how the detent plate, ball and spring (B) locate**

**3.5 Unscrew the bolts (arrowed) and displace the bracket**

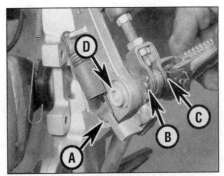

**3.6 Free the return spring end (A), remove the split pin and washer (B), and the clevis pin (C), then unscrew the bolt (D)**

### Installation

2 Installation is the reverse of removal.

## Passenger footrests

### Removal

3 Remove the E-clip from the bottom of the footrest pivot pin, then withdraw the pivot pin and remove the footrest, noting the fitting of the detent plate, ball and spring, and take care that they do not spring out when removing the footrest **(see illustration)**.

### Installation

4 Installation is the reverse of removal.

## Brake pedal

### Removal

5 The pedal pivots on the footrest holder. Unscrew the two bolts securing the footrest bracket to the frame, then lift the bracket to dislodge the brake light switch spring and turn it round to access the inside **(see illustration)**.

6 Unhook the brake pedal return spring **(see illustration)**.

7 Remove the split pin and washer from the clevis pin securing the brake pedal to the master cylinder pushrod **(see illustration 3.6)**. Remove the clevis pin and separate the pedal from the pushrod.

8 Remove the bolt on the inside of the footrest bracket and remove the footrest, its

holder and the brake pedal, then slide the pedal off the holder **(see illustration 3.6)**.

### Installation

9 Installation is the reverse of removal, noting the following:
a) Apply molybdenum disulphide grease to the brake pedal pivot.
b) Align the flat on the footrest holder with that in the bracket.
c) Apply a suitable non-permanent thread locking compound to the footrest holder bolt and tighten it securely
d) Use a new split pin on the clevis pin securing the brake pedal to the master cylinder pushrod.
e) Tighten the footrest bracket bolts to the torque setting specified at the beginning of the Chapter.
f) Check the operation of the rear brake light switch (see Chapter 1).

## Gearchange lever

### Removal

10 Slacken the gearchange lever linkage rod locknuts, then unscrew the rod and separate it from the lever and the arm (the rod is reverse-threaded on one end and so will simultaneously unscrew from both lever and arm when turned in the one direction) **(see illustration)**. Note the how far the rod is threaded into the lever and arm as this determines the height of the lever relative to the footrest.

11 The lever pivots on the footrest holder. Unscrew the two bolts securing the footrest bracket to the frame and turn it round to access the holder bolt **(see illustrations)**. Unscrew the bolt and remove the footrest, its holder and the lever, then slide the lever off the holder.

### Installation

12 Installation is the reverse of removal, noting the following:
a) Apply molybdenum disulphide grease to the gear lever pivot.
b) Align the flat on the footrest holder with that in the bracket.
c) Apply a suitable non-permanent thread locking compound to the footrest holder bolt and tighten it securely.
d) Tighten the footrest bracket bolts to the torque setting specified at the beginning of the Chapter.
e) Adjust the gear lever height as required by screwing the rod in or out of the lever and arm. Tighten the locknuts securely.

### 4 Sidestand – removal and installation

1 The sidestand is attached to a bracket on the frame. Springs between the bracket and the stand ensure that it is held in the retracted or extended position.

**3.10 Slacken the locknuts (arrowed) and unscrew the rod**

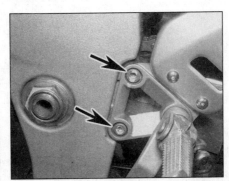

**3.11a Unscrew the bolts (arrowed) and displace the bracket . . .**

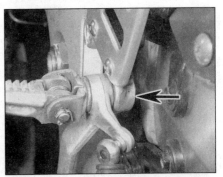

**3.11b . . . to access the bolt (arrowed) on the inside**

6

**4.3a Unscrew the nut (arrowed) and remove the pivot bolt . . .**

**4.3b . . . and free the spring ends**

**5.1 Disconnect the brake light switch wiring connectors (arrowed)**

**2** Support the bike using an auxiliary stand. If required, remove the sidestand switch (see Chapter 9).

**3** Unscrew the pivot bolt nut, then remove the pivot bolt from the inside of the bracket and remove the stand, releasing the springs as you do **(see illustrations)**.

**4** If required, unscrew the bolts securing the sidestand bracket to the frame and remove the bracket, noting that the top bolt is also the engine lower rear mounting bolt **(see illustration 4.4a)**. This must be tightened to the torque setting specified at the beginning of Chapter 2 on installation.

**5** On installation apply grease to the pivot bolt shank and tighten the nut securely. Check that the sidestand springs hold the stand securely up when not in use – an accident is almost certain to occur if the stand extends while the machine is in motion.

**6** Check the operation of the sidestand switch (see Chapter 1).

**5 Handlebars and levers –**
removal and installation

### Right handlebar removal

**1** Disconnect the brake light switch wires from the switch on the underside of the master cylinder assembly **(see illustration)**. Free the handlebar switch wiring from its guide under the top yoke **(see illustration 8.2)**. Release the throttle cables from the throttle pulley (see Chapter 4). Position the switch housing away from the handlebar.

**2** Unscrew the two front brake master cylinder assembly clamp bolts and the bolt securing the reservoir to the handlebar and position the assembly clear, making sure no strain is placed on the hydraulic hose **(see illustration)**. Keep the master cylinder reservoir upright to prevent possible fluid leakage.

**3** Slacken both the fork clamp bolts in the top yoke **(see illustration)**. Unscrew the set bolt securing the handlebar clamp to the top yoke **(see illustration)**. Unscrew and remove the steering stem nut and remove the washer **(see illustration)**.

**4** Raise the fuel tank and remove the air filter housing (see Chapter 4). Disconnect the ignition switch wiring connector to provide some slack and free the wiring from any clips or ties **(see illustration)**. Gently ease the top yoke upwards off the fork tubes and position it clear, using a rag to protect other components.

**5** Slacken the handlebar clamp bolt, then ease the handlebar up and off the fork **(see illustration 5.3a)**. If necessary, unscrew the handlebar end-weight retaining screw, then remove the weight from the end of the handlebar and slide off the throttle twistgrip.

### Left handlebar removal

**6** Disconnect the clutch switch wiring connector from the switch on the clutch lever

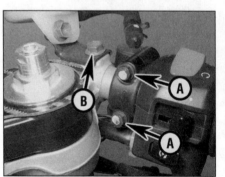

**5.2 Unscrew the clamp bolts (A) and the reservoir bolt (B)**

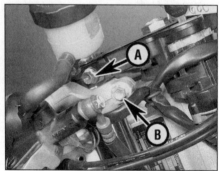

**5.3a Fork clamp bolt (A). Handlebar clamp bolt (B)**

**5.3b Handlebar set bolt (arrowed)**

**5.3c Steering stem nut (arrowed)**

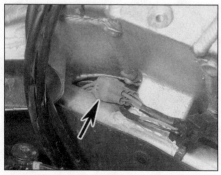

**5.4 Ignition switch wiring connector (arrowed)**

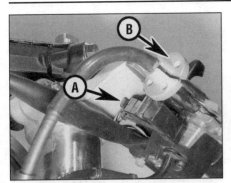

5.6 Clutch switch wiring connector (A), clutch cable adjuster (B)

5.7 Slacken the bracket bolt (arrowed)

5.11 Align the clamp mating surfaces with the punchmark (arrowed)

bracket **(see illustration)**. Free the handlebar switch wiring from its guide under the top yoke **(see illustration 8.2)**. Release the choke cable from the lever (see Chapter 4). Position the switch housing away from the handlebar.

7 Screw the clutch cable adjuster fully into the lever bracket **(see illustration 5.6)**. Align the slot in the adjuster with that in the bracket, then pull the outer cable end from the socket in the adjuster and release the inner cable from the lever. If there is not enough slack in the cable to free it from the adjuster, remove the clutch lever (see below). Slacken the clutch lever bracket bolt **(see illustration)**.

8 Slacken the fork clamp bolts in the top yoke **(see illustration 5.3a)**. Unscrew the set bolt securing the handlebar clamp to the top yoke **(see illustration 5.3b)**. Unscrew and remove the steering stem nut and remove the washer **(see illustration 5.3c)**.

9 Raise the fuel tank and remove the air filter housing (see Chapter 4). Disconnect the ignition switch wiring connector to provide some slack and free the wiring from any clips or ties **(see illustration 5.4)**. Gently ease the top yoke upwards off the fork tubes and position it clear, using a rag to protect other components.

10 Slacken the handlebar clamp bolt **(see illustration 5.3a)**, then ease the handlebar up and off the fork. If necessary, unscrew the handlebar end-weight retaining screw, then remove the weight from the end of the handlebar and remove the grip. It may be necessary to slit the grip open using a sharp

blade in order to remove it as they are usually stuck in place. This will mean using a new grip on assembly. The clutch lever bracket can now be slid off the handlebar.

### Handlebar installation

11 Installation is the reverse of removal, noting the following.

a) *Do not tighten the handlebar clamp bolt until the top yoke has been installed, and tighten the set bolt securing the handlebar to the yoke before the handlebar clamp bolt.*

b) *Refer to the Specifications at the beginning of the Chapter and tighten the steering stem nut, the fork clamp bolts, the handlebar set bolt and the handlebar clamp bolt to the specified torque settings, in that order.*

c) *Make sure the front brake lever assembly clamp is installed with the UP mark facing up, and align the clamp mating surface with the punchmark on the top of the handlebar (see illustration and 5.2). Tighten the brake master cylinder clamp bolts to the torque setting specified at the beginning of the Chapter.*

d) *Refer to Chapter 4 for installation of the throttle and choke cables. Make sure the pin in the upper half of each switch housing locates in the hole in the top of the handlebar.*

e) *If removed, apply a suitable non-permanent locking compound to the*

*handlebar end-weight retaining screws. If new grips are being fitted, secure them using a suitable adhesive.*

f) *Do not forget to reconnect the front brake light switch and clutch switch wiring connectors.*

### Clutch lever removal

12 Screw the clutch cable adjuster fully into the lever bracket to provide maximum freeplay in the cable **(see illustration)**. Unscrew the lever pivot bolt locknut, then unscrew the pivot bolt and remove the lever, detaching the cable nipple as you do.

### Front brake lever removal

13 Unscrew the lever pivot bolt locknut, then unscrew the pivot bolt and remove the lever **(see illustrations)**.

### Lever installation

14 Installation is the reverse of removal. Apply grease to the pivot bolt shafts and the contact areas between the lever and its bracket, and to the clutch cable nipple. Adjust the clutch cable freeplay (see Chapter 1).

### 6 Forks –
removal and installation

### Removal

1 Remove the fairing and the fairing side panels (see Chapter 4).

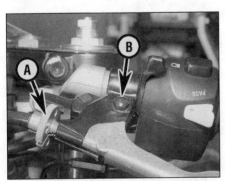

5.12 Clutch cable adjuster (A), lever pivot bolt (B)

5.13a Unscrew the locknut (arrowed) . . .

5.13b . . . then unscrew the pivot bolt (arrowed)

6

**6.4 Slacken the fork top bolt if required**

**6.5a Slacken the fork clamp bolts (arrowed) in the bottom yoke . . .**

**6.5b . . . and remove the fork**

**2** Remove the front wheel (see Chapter 7) and the mudguard (see Chapter 8). Work on each fork individually.

**3** Slacken the handlebar clamp bolt, the handlebar set bolt and the fork clamp bolt in the top yoke **(see illustrations 5.3a and b)**. Depending on the tools available, access to the right-hand fork clamp bolt may be restricted by the front brake reservoir bracket. If this is the case, unscrew the bracket bolt and displace the reservoir from the handlebar, making sure it stays upright and no strain is placed on the hose.

**4** If the forks are to be disassembled, or if the fork oil is being changed, it is advisable at this stage to slacken the fork top bolt **(see illustration)**.

**5** Slacken but do not remove the fork clamp bolts in the bottom yoke, and remove the fork by

twisting it and pulling it downwards **(see illustrations)**. Make sure the handlebar clamp does not get cocked in the fork as it is withdrawn as the lug for the set bolt could shear.

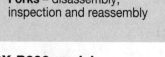 *If the fork legs are seized in the yokes, spray the area with penetrating oil and allow time for it to soak in before trying again.*

### Installation

**6** Remove all traces of corrosion from the fork tubes and the yokes. Install each fork individually. Slide the fork up through the bottom yoke and the handlebar and up into the top yoke, and set the fork in the yoke so that the amount of protrusion of the fork tube

above the top yoke is as specified at the beginning of the Chapter, and equal on both sides **(see illustrations)**.

**7** Tighten the fork clamp bolts in the bottom yoke to the torque setting specified at the beginning of the Chapter **(see illustration)**. If the fork has been dismantled or if the fork oil has been changed, the fork top bolt should now be tightened to the specified torque setting **(see illustration)**. Now tighten the fork clamp bolt in the top yoke, the handlebar set bolt and the handlebar clamp bolt to the specified torque setting **(see illustration)**.

**8** If displaced, position the front brake reservoir on the handlebar and tighten the bracket bolt securely.

**9** Install the front mudguard (see Chapter 8), and the front wheel (see Chapter 7).

**10** Install the fairing and fairing side panels (see Chapter 8).

**11** Check the operation of the front forks and brakes before taking the machine out on the road.

**7 Forks** – disassembly, inspection and reassembly

### GSX-R600 models
#### Disassembly

**1** Always dismantle the fork legs separately to avoid interchanging parts and thus causing an accelerated rate of wear. Store all

**6.6a Slide the fork up through the yokes and handlebar . . .**

**6.6b . . . and set it to the correct height**

**6.7a Tighten the bottom yoke clamp bolts . . .**

**6.7b . . . the fork top bolt (if necessary) . . .**

**6.7c . . . the top yoke clamp bolt and handlebar bolts to the specified torque settings**

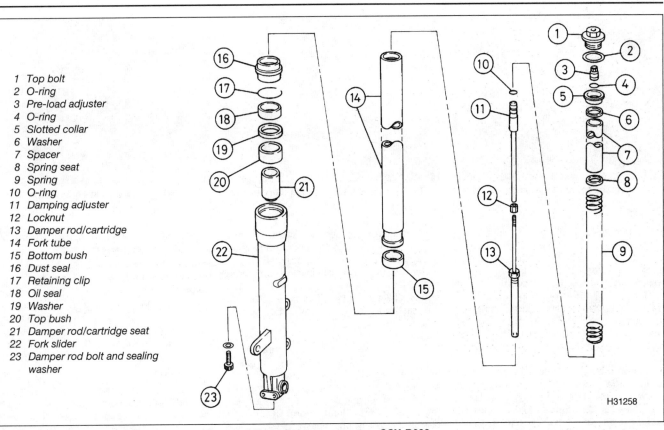

1 Top bolt
2 O-ring
3 Pre-load adjuster
4 O-ring
5 Slotted collar
6 Washer
7 Spacer
8 Spring seat
9 Spring
10 O-ring
11 Damping adjuster
12 Locknut
13 Damper rod/cartridge
14 Fork tube
15 Bottom bush
16 Dust seal
17 Retaining clip
18 Oil seal
19 Washer
20 Top bush
21 Damper rod/cartridge seat
22 Fork slider
23 Damper rod bolt and sealing
washer

H31258

**7.1 Front fork components – GSX-R600**

components in separate, clearly marked containers **(see illustration)**.
**2** Before dismantling the fork, it is advised that the damper rod bolt be slackened at this stage. Compress the fork tube in the slider so that the spring exerts maximum pressure on the damper rod head, then have an assistant slacken the damper rod bolt in the base of the fork slider **(see illustration)**. If an assistant is not available, clamp the brake caliper lugs on the fork slider between the padded jaws of a vice.
**3** If the fork top bolt was not slackened with the fork in situ, carefully clamp the fork tube between the padded jaws of a vice, taking care not to overtighten or score its surface, and slacken the top bolt **(see illustration 7.4)**.
**4** Unscrew the fork top bolt from the top of the fork tube **(see illustration)**. The pre-load adjuster will remain threaded on the damper rod.
**5** Carefully clamp the brake caliper lugs on the fork slider between the padded jaws of a vice and slide the fork tube down into the slider a little way (wrap a rag around the top of the tube to minimise oil spillage). Now grasp the spacer while, with the aid of an assistant if necessary, keep the damper rod fully extended and press down on the spacer, thereby compressing the spring, to expose the locknut, and slip a spanner onto it **(see illustration)**. Counter-hold the pre-load adjuster, then slacken the locknut and thread it to the base of its threads **(see illustration)**. Now counter-hold the locknut and

**7.2 Slacken the damper rod bolt**

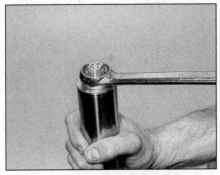

**7.4 Unscrew the fork top bolt**

**7.5a Push the spacer down to expose the locknut (arrowed)**

**7.5b Counter-hold the pre-load adjuster and slacken the locknut**

**6**

7.5c Draw the top bolt assembly out of the fork

7.8 Unscrew and remove the damper rod bolt

7.10 Prise out the dust seal using a flat-bladed screwdriver

thread the pre-load adjuster with the top bolt off the damper rod. Lift the top bolt assembly out of the fork (see illustration). If you want to disassemble the damping adjuster/pre-load adjuster/top bolt assembly, thread the top bolt off the top of the pre-load adjuster, then counter-hold the pre-load adjuster and screw the damping adjuster into and out of the bottom of the pre-load adjuster. If this is done, discard the O-rings as new ones should be used.

6 Remove the slotted collar by slipping it out to the side (see illustration 7.28), then remove the washer, the spacer and the spring seat (see illustrations 7.27d, c and b). Withdraw the spring from the tube, noting which way up it fits (see illustration 7.27a).

7.11 Prise out the retaining clip using a flat-bladed screwdriver

7 Invert the fork leg over a suitable container and pump the fork and damper rod vigorously to expel as much fork oil as possible.

8 Remove the previously slackened damper rod bolt and its sealing washer from the bottom of the slider (see illustration). Discard the washer as a new one must be used on reassembly.

9 Invert the fork and withdraw the damper rod from inside the fork tube (see illustration 7.25a). The damper rod seat may come away with the rod, otherwise remove it later.

10 Carefully prise out the dust seal from the top of the slider to gain access to the oil seal retaining clip (see illustration). Discard the dust seal as a new one must be used.

11 Carefully remove the retaining clip, taking care not to scratch the surface of the tube (see illustration).

12 To separate the tube from the slider it is necessary to displace the top bush and oil seal. The bottom bush should not pass through the top bush, and this can be used to good effect. Push the tube gently inwards until it stops against the damper rod seat. Take care not to do this forcibly or the seat may be damaged. Then pull the tube sharply outwards until the bottom bush strikes the top bush (see illustration). Repeat this operation until the top bush and seal are tapped out of the slider.

13 With the tube removed, slide off the oil seal, washer and top bush, noting which way

up they fit (see illustration). Discard the oil seal as a new one must be used.

*Caution: Do not remove the bottom bush from the tube unless it is to be renewed.*

14 If the damper rod seat did not come out with the rod, tip it out of the slider, noting which way up it fits. On W and X models, discard the O-ring as a new one should be used.

### Inspection

15 Clean all parts in solvent and blow them dry with compressed air, if available. Check the fork tube for score marks, scratches, flaking of the chrome finish and excessive or abnormal wear. Look for dents in the tube and renew the tube in both forks if any are found. Check the fork seal seat for nicks, gouges and scratches. If damage is evident, leaks will occur. Also check the oil seal washer for damage or distortion and renew it if necessary.

16 Check the fork tube for runout using V-blocks and a dial gauge, or have it done by a Suzuki dealer or suspension specialist (see illustration). If the amount of runout exceeds the service limit specified, the tube should be renewed.

⚠️ *Warning: If the tube is bent or exceeds the runout limit, it should not be straightened; renew it with a new one.*

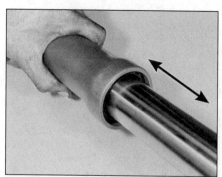

7.12 To separate the fork tube and slider, pull them apart firmly several times – the slide-hammer action will pull them apart

7.13 The oil seal (1), washer (2), top bush (3) and bottom bush (4) will come out with the fork tube

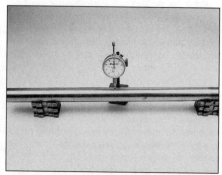

7.16 Check the fork tube for runout using V-blocks and a dial gauge

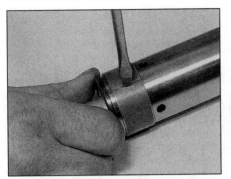

**7.18 Prise the bottom bush apart at its split using a flat-bladed screwdriver**

**7.20 Slide the fork tube into the slider**

**7.21a Install the top bush . . .**

**17** Check the spring for cracks and other damage. Measure the spring free length and compare the measurement to the specifications at the beginning of the Chapter. If it is defective or sagged below the service limit, renew the springs in both forks with new ones. Never renew only one spring.

**18** Examine the working surfaces of the two bushes; if worn or scuffed they must be renewed. Suzuki recommend new ones are fitted as a matter of course. To remove the bottom bush from the fork tube, prise it apart at the slit using a flat-bladed screwdriver and slide it off **(see illustration)**. Make sure the new one seats properly.

**19** Check the damper rod cartridge assembly for damage and wear, and renew it if necessary. Holding the outside of the cartridge, gently pump the rod in and out of the damper. If the rod does not move smoothly in the damper it must be renewed.

### Reassembly

**20** Oil the fork tube and bottom bush with the specified fork oil and insert the assembly into the slider **(see illustration)**.

**21** Push the fork tube fully into the slider, then oil the top bush and slide it down over the tube **(see illustration)**. Press the bush squarely into its recess in the slider as far as possible, then install the oil seal washer with its flat side facing up **(see illustration)**. Either use the service tool (Pt. No. 09940-52861) or a suitable piece of tubing to tap the bush fully

**7.21b . . . followed by the washer**

**7.22 Make sure the oil seal is the correct way up**

into place; the tubing must be slightly larger in diameter than the fork tube and slightly smaller in diameter than the bush recess in the slider. Take care not to scratch the fork tube during this operation; it is best to make sure that the fork tube is pushed fully into the slider so that any accidental scratching is confined to the area above the oil seal.

**22** When the bush is seated fully and squarely in its recess in the slider, (remove the washer to check, wipe the recess clean, then reinstall the washer), install the new oil seal. Smear the seal's lips with fork oil and slide it over the tube so that its markings face upwards and drive the seal into place as described in Step 21 until the retaining clip groove is visible above the seal **(see illustration)**.

**23** Once the seal is correctly seated, fit the

> **HAYNES HiNT** *Place the old oil seal on top of the new one to protect it when driving the seal into place.*

retaining clip, making sure it is correctly located in its groove **(see illustration)**.

**24** Lubricate the lips of the new dust seal then slide it down the fork tube and press it into position **(see illustration)**.

**25** On W and X models, fit a new O-ring onto the bottom of the damper rod seat. On all models, fit the damper rod seat onto the bottom of the rod. Keeping the assembly vertical to prevent the damper rod seat dropping out, insert the damper rod cartridge into the fork tube and slide it fully down **(see illustration)**. Fit

**7.23 Install the retaining clip . . .**

**7.24 . . . followed by the dust seal**

**7.25a Slide the damper rod cartridge into the fork tube**

**6**

**7.25b Apply a thread locking compound to the damper rod bolt and use a new sealing washer**

**7.25c Use wire as shown to keep the damper rod extended**

**7.26a Pour the oil into the top of the tube**

a new copper sealing washer to the damper rod bolt and apply a few drops of a suitable non-permanent thread locking compound, then install the bolt into the bottom of the slider **(see illustration)**. Tighten the bolt to the specified torque setting. If the damper rod cartridge rotates inside the tube, wait until the fork is fully reassembled before tightening the bolt. As the damper rod will have to be kept extended out of the slider later on, it is worth at this stage securing a piece of wire around the base of the locknut on the top of the rod to use as a holder **(see illustration)**.
26  Slowly pour in the specified quantity of the specified grade of fork oil and pump the fork and damper rod at least ten times each to distribute it evenly and expel all the air **(see illustration)**. It

may be necessary to pump the fork and rod even more, or to hold the fork upright for several minutes, before all the air bleeds out. The oil level should also be measured – fully compress the fork tube and damper rod into the slider and measure the fork oil level from the top of the tube **(see illustration)**. Add or subtract fork oil until it is at the level specified at the beginning of the Chapter.
27  Clamp the brake caliper lugs on the slider between the padded jaws of a vice, taking care not to overtighten and damage them. Pull the fork tube and damper rod out of the slider as far as possible then install the spring with its tapered end downwards **(see illustration)**. Install the spring seat, the spacer and the washer **(see illustrations)**.

28  Keeping the damper rod fully extended, slide the slotted collar into position between the washer and the nut on the damper rod – it may be necessary to compress the spring slightly by pushing down on the spacer to provide the clearance **(see illustration)**. You can now remove the piece of wire, if used.
29  If the damping adjuster/pre-load adjuster/top bolt assembly was disassembled, fit a new O-ring onto the damping adjuster rod and thread it into the pre-load adjuster so that it protrudes approximately 1.5 mm from the top. Fit a new O-ring onto the pre-load adjuster and thread the fork top bolt onto it.
30  Fit a new O-ring onto the fork top bolt,

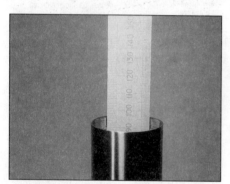

**7.26b Measure the oil level with the fork held vertical**

**7.27a Install the spring . . .**

**7.27b . . . followed by the spring seat . . .**

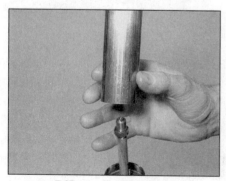

**7.27c . . . the spacer . . .**

**7.27d . . . and the washer**

**7.28 Slip the slotted collar under the locknut**

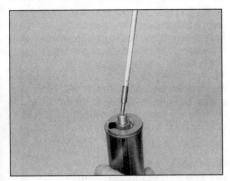

**7.30 Slide the damping adjuster into the damper rod**

then insert the damping adjuster/pre-load adjuster/top bolt assembly into the top of the damper rod and slide it fully down **(see illustration)**. Thread the pre-load adjuster onto the damper rod, holding the rod to prevent it from turning, until the wider section of the damping adjuster just seats on the top of the damper rod. Counter-hold the pre-load adjuster and tighten the locknut securely against it, to the specified torque if the correct tools are available **(see illustration 7.5b)**.

31 Withdraw the tube fully from the slider and carefully screw the top bolt into the fork tube making sure it is not cross-threaded **(see illustration 7.3)**. **Note:** *The top bolt can be tightened to the specified torque setting at this stage if the tube is held between the padded jaws of a vice, but do not risk distorting the tube by doing so. A better method is to tighten the top bolt when the fork leg has been installed and is securely held in the yokes.*

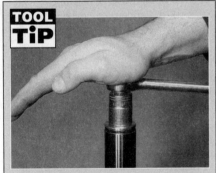

**Use a ratchet-type tool when installing the fork top bolt. This makes it unnecessary to remove the tool from the bolt whilst threading it in making it easier to maintain a downward pressure on the spring.**

If the damper rod Allen bolt requires tightening (see Step 25), clamp the brake caliper lugs on the fork slider between the padded jaws of a vice and have an assistant compress the tube into the slider so that maximum spring pressure is placed on the damper rod head – tighten the damper Allen bolt to the specified torque setting.

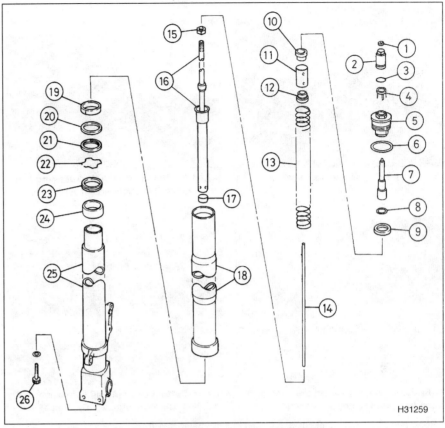

H31259

**7.33 Front fork components – GSX-R750**

| | | |
|---|---|---|
| 1 Snap-ring | 10 Spacer seat | 19 Bottom bush |
| 2 Pre-load adjuster | 11 Spacer | 20 Washer |
| 3 O-ring | 12 Spring seat | 21 Oil seal |
| 4 Adjuster tripod | 13 Spring | 22 Retaining clip |
| 5 Top bolt | 14 Damping adjuster rod | 23 Dust seal |
| 6 O-ring | 15 Locknut | 24 Top bush |
| 7 Damping adjuster | 16 Damper rod/cartridge | 25 Fork slider |
| 8 Washer | 17 Damper rod/cartridge seat | 26 Damper rod bolt and |
| 9 Top bolt rubber seat | 18 Fork tube | sealing washer |

32 Install the forks (see Section 6). Adjust the fork settings as required (see Section 12).

## GSX-R750 models

### Disassembly

33 Always dismantle the fork legs separately to avoid interchanging parts and thus causing an accelerated rate of wear. Store all components in separate, clearly marked containers **(see illustration)**.

34 Before dismantling the fork, it is advised that the damper rod bolt be slackened at this stage. Compress the fork tube in the slider so that the spring exerts maximum pressure on the damper rod head, then have an assistant slacken the damper rod bolt in the base of the fork slider **(see illustration 7.2)**. If an assistant is not available, clamp the brake caliper lugs on the fork slider between the padded jaws of a vice.

35 If the fork top bolt was not slackened with the fork in situ, carefully clamp the fork tube in

a vice equipped with soft jaws, taking care not to overtighten or score its surface, and slacken the top bolt **(see illustration 7.4)**.

36 Unscrew the fork top bolt from the top of the fork tube. The bolt will remain threaded on the damper rod.

37 Carefully clamp the brake caliper lugs on the fork slider between the padded jaws of a vice and slide the fork tube fully down onto the slider (wrap a rag around the top of the tube to minimise oil spillage) while, with the aid of an assistant if necessary, keeping the damper rod fully extended. Push down on the spacer and insert a suitably sized washer with a slot cut into it between the washer on the top of the spacer and the base of the locknut on the damper rod **(see illustration 7.28)**. This will keep the spacer and spring compressed while removing the top bolt assembly.

38 Using two spanners, one on the locknut and one on the flats on the base of the damping adjuster housing, counter-hold the

**6**

7.43 Prise off the dust seal . . .

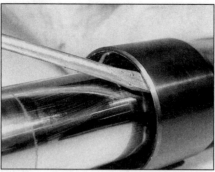

7.44 . . . then lever out the retaining clip using a flat-bladed screwdriver

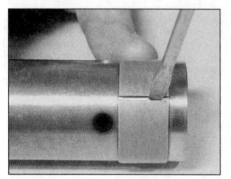

7.46a Carefully lever apart the ends of the top bush and remove it from the slider

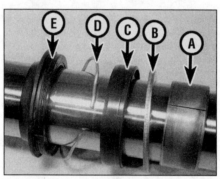

7.46b Bottom bush (A), oil seal washer (B), oil seal (C), retaining clip (D), dust seal (E)

housing and slacken the locknut, and thread it to the base of its threads. Now counter-hold the locknut and thread the damping adjuster/pre-load adjuster/top bolt assembly off the damper rod. Withdraw the damping adjuster rod from inside the damper rod. If you want to disassemble the damping adjuster/pre-load adjuster/top bolt assembly, remove the snap-ring from the top of the damping adjuster housing, then unscrew and remove the pre-load adjuster and withdraw the adjuster tripod. You may need either a magnet, or a piece of wire or welding rod, flattened at the end and hooked over slightly, to remove it. Again, if required, thread the top bolt off the top of the damping adjuster housing. Note the rubber seat on the base of the top bolt.

39 Remove the fabricated slotted washer used to hold the spacer down, then remove the washer, the spacer seat if loose (it fits into the top of the spacer and will probable stay with it), the spacer and the spring seat (which fits into the bottom of the spacer and will probably stay with it). Withdraw the spring from the tube, noting which way up it fits.

40 Invert the fork leg over a suitable container and gently pump the fork and damper rod to expel as much fork oil as possible.

41 Remove the previously slackened damper rod bolt and its sealing washer from the bottom of the slider (see illustration 7.8). Discard the sealing washer as a new one must be used on reassembly.

42 Invert the fork and withdraw the damper rod cartridge from inside the fork tube. The damper rod seat may come away with the cartridge, otherwise remove it later.

43 Carefully prise out the dust seal from the bottom of the tube to gain access to the oil seal retaining clip (see illustration). Discard the dust seal as a new one must be used.

44 Carefully remove the retaining clip, taking care not to scratch the surface of the tube (see illustration).

45 To separate the slider from the tube it is necessary to displace the bottom bush and oil seal. The top bush should not pass through the bottom bush, and this can be used to good effect. Push the slider gently inwards until it stops. Take care not to do this forcibly.

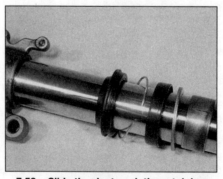

7.53a Slide the dust seal, the retaining clip, the oil seal, the oil seal washer and the bottom bush onto the slider as shown

Then pull the slider sharply outwards until the top bush strikes the bottom bush (see illustration 7.12). Repeat this operation until the bottom bush and seal are tapped out of the tube.

46 With the tube and slider separated, remove the top bush from the slider by carefully levering its ends apart using a screwdriver (see illustration). Slide the bottom bush, the oil seal washer, the oil seal, the retaining clip and the dust seal off the slider, noting which way up they fit (see illustration). Discard the oil seal and the dust seal as new ones must be used.

47 If the damper rod seat did not come out with the rod, tip it out of the slider, noting which way up it fits.

## Inspection

48 Clean all parts in solvent and blow them dry with compressed air, if available. Check the fork tube for score marks, scratches, flaking of the chrome finish and excessive or abnormal wear. Look for dents in the tube and renew the tube in both forks if any are found. Check the fork seal seat for nicks, gouges and scratches. If damage is evident, leaks will occur. Also check the oil seal washer for damage or distortion and renew it if necessary.

49 Check the fork slider for runout using V-blocks and a dial gauge, or have it done by a Suzuki dealer or suspension specialist (see illustration 7.16). If the amount of runout exceeds the service limit specified, the slider should be renewed.

 *Warning: If the slider is bent or exceeds the runout limit, it should not be straightened; renew it with a new one.*

50 Check the spring for cracks and other damage. Measure the spring free length and compare the measurement to the specifications at the beginning of the Chapter. If it is defective or sagged below the service limit, renew the springs in both forks with new ones. Never renew only one spring.

51 Examine the working surfaces of the two bushes; if worn or scuffed they must be renewed. Suzuki recommend new ones are fitted as a matter of course.

52 Check the damper rod cartridge assembly for damage and wear, and renew it if necessary. Holding the outside of the cartridge, pump the rod in and out of the damper. If the rod does not move smoothly in the damper it must be renewed.

## Reassembly

53 Wrap some insulating tape over the ridges on the end of the fork slider to protect the lips of the new oil seal as it is installed. Apply a smear of the specified clean fork oil to the lips of the oil seal and the inner surface of each bush, then slide the new dust seal, the retaining clip, the oil seal, the oil seal washer and the bottom bush onto the fork slider, making sure that the marked side of the oil seal faces the dust seal (see illustration).

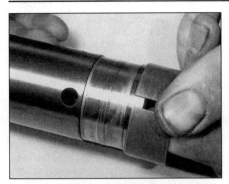

7.53b Make sure the top bush seats properly in its recess

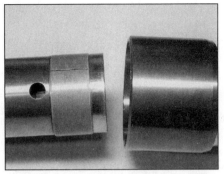

7.54 Fit the slider into the bottom of the fork tube

7.55 Make sure the bottom bush enters the fork tube squarely

Remove the insulating tape and fit the top bush into its recess in the slider (see illustration).

54 Apply a smear of the specified clean fork oil to the outer surface of each bush, then carefully insert the slider fully into the fork tube (see illustration).

55 Support the fork upside down, then press the bottom bush squarely into its recess in the fork tube as far as possible (see illustration). Slide the oil seal washer on top of the bush, and keep the oil seal, the retaining clip and the dust seal out of the way by sliding them up the slider. If necessary, tape them to the slider to prevent them from falling down and interfering as the bush is drifted into place.

56 Using either the special service tool (Pt. No. 09940-52861) or a suitable drift, carefully drive the bottom bush fully into its recess using the oil seal washer to prevent damaging the edges of the bush. Make sure the bush enters the recess squarely, and take care not to scratch or gouge the slider (it is best to make sure that the fork slider is pushed fully into the tube so that any accidental scratching is confined to the area that does not come into contact with the oil seal).

57 When the bush is seated fully and squarely in its recess in the tube, (remove the washer to check, wipe the recess clean, then reinstall the washer), drive the oil seal into place as described in Step 56 until the retaining clip groove is visible above the seal (see illustration).

58 Once the oil seal is correctly seated, fit the retaining clip, making sure it is correctly located in its groove, then press the dust seal into position (see illustrations).

59 Lay the fork flat and slide the slider fully into the tube. Fit the damper rod/cartridge seat onto the bottom of the damper rod/ cartridge, then insert the damper rod/cartridge into the top of the fork tube and into the slider until it seats on the bottom of the slider (see illustration). Fit a new sealing washer onto the damper rod bolt and apply a few drops of a suitable non-permanent thread locking compound, then install the bolt into the bottom of the slider and tighten it to the torque setting specified at the beginning of the Chapter (see illustration 7.25b). If the damper rod rotates inside the tube, wait until the fork is fully reassembled before tightening the bolt. As the damper rod will have to be kept extended out of the tube later on, it is worth at this stage securing a piece of wire around the base of the locknut on the top of the rod to use as a holder (see illustration 7.25c).

60 Stand the fork upright. Slowly pour in the specified quantity of the specified grade of fork oil and pump the fork and damper rod at least ten times each to distribute it evenly and expel all the air (see illustration 7.26a). It may be necessary to pump the fork and rod even more, or to hold the fork upright for several minutes, before all the air bleeds out. The oil level should also be measured – fully

compress the fork tube and damper rod onto the slider and measure the fork oil level from the top of the tube (see illustration 7.26b). Add or subtract fork oil until it is at the level specified at the beginning of the Chapter.

61 If removed, fit the spring seat into the bottom of the spacer and the spacer seat into the top. Withdraw the damper rod as far as possible out of the fork tube, and keep it extended using the aid of an assistant. Install the spring, with its tapered end upwards, into the fork tube, then fit the damping adjuster rod into the centre of the damper rod. Install the spacer, making sure the lip on the bottom of the spring seat fits into the top of the spring. Fit the washer onto the top of the spacer. Push down on the spacer and insert a suitably sized washer with a slot cut into it (as

7.57 Drive the oil seal into the bottom of the tube . . .

7.58a . . . and fit its retaining clip, making sure it is properly seated . . .

7.58b . . . then press the dust seal into place

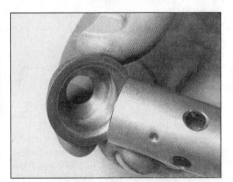

7.59 Fit the seat onto the end of the end of the damper rod/cartridge

6

**8.2 Free the wiring from the guide (arrowed)**

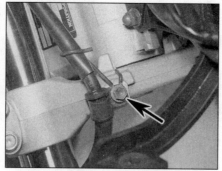

**8.3a Unscrew the bolt (arrowed) and detach the brake hose**

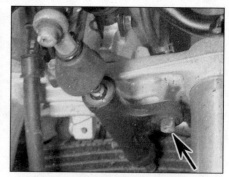

**8.3b Unscrew the bolt (arrowed) and detach the steering damper**

used on removal) between the washer on the top of the spacer and the base of the locknut on the damper rod. This will keep the spacer and spring compressed while installing the top bolt assembly. You can now remove the piece of wire.

**62** If the damping adjuster/pre-load adjuster/top bolt assembly was disassembled, set the damping adjuster so that it protrudes approximately 1.5 mm from the top of the adjuster housing. Fit a new O-ring onto the top bolt and thread it down onto the damping adjuster housing. Fit the pre-load adjuster tripod into the top bolt, making sure its legs locate into the three holes in the bottom. Fit a new O-ring onto the pre-load adjuster and thread it into the top bolt. Fit the snap-ring into its groove in the top of the damping adjuster housing.

**63** If removed, fit the rubber seat onto the base of the top bolt. Thread the damping adjuster/pre-load adjuster/top bolt assembly onto the damper rod, holding the rod to prevent it from turning, until the damper rod is felt to just seat on the inside of the housing. Counter-hold the flats on the base of the housing and tighten the locknut securely against it, to the specified torque if the correct tools are available.

**64** Apply a smear of the specified clean oil to the top bolt O-ring. Fully extend the fork tube and screw the bolt securely into the tube (see *Tool Tip on page 6•11*).

**65** Install the forks as described in Section 6. Adjust the fork settings as required (see Section 12).

## 8 Steering stem – removal and installation

### Removal

**1** Remove the front forks (see Section 6).
**2** Free the handlebar switch wiring from its guide under the top yoke **(see illustration)**. Remove the set bolt securing each handlebar to the top yoke and support the handlebars so they are out of the way **(see illustration 5.3b)**. Try to keep the master cylinder and reservoir

upright and make sure no strain is placed on the brake hose.

**3** Unscrew the bolt securing the front brake hose clamp to the bottom yoke **(see illustration)**. Where fitted, remove the bolt securing the steering damper to the bottom yoke and swing it aside **(see illustration)**.

**4** Raise the fuel tank (unless already removed) and remove the air filter housing (see Chapter 4). Disconnect the ignition switch wiring connector to provide some slack and free the wiring from its guide **(see illustration 5.4)**.

**5** Unscrew and remove the steering stem nut and remove the washer **(see illustration 5.3c)**. Gently ease the top yoke upwards and position it clear, using a rag to protect other components, or remove it completely.

**6** Unscrew the locknut using either a C-spanner, a peg spanner or a suitable drift located in one of the notches **(see illustration)**. Remove the lockwasher, noting how it fits.

**7** Supporting the bottom yoke, unscrew the adjuster nut using either a C-spanner, a peg-spanner or a suitable drift located in one of the notches, then remove the adjuster nut from the steering stem.

**8** Gently lower the bottom yoke and steering stem out of the steering head.

**9** Remove the bearing cover and the upper bearing from the top of the steering head. Remove all traces of old grease from the bearings and races and check them for wear or damage as described in Section 9. **Note:** *Do not attempt to remove the outer races*

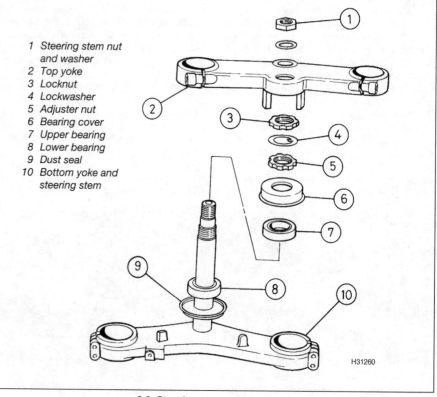

1 Steering stem nut and washer
2 Top yoke
3 Locknut
4 Lockwasher
5 Adjuster nut
6 Bearing cover
7 Upper bearing
8 Lower bearing
9 Dust seal
10 Bottom yoke and steering stem

H31260

**8.6 Steering stem components**

*from the frame or the lower bearing from the steering stem unless new ones are being installed.*

## Installation

**10** Smear a liberal quantity of grease on the bearing outer races in the frame. Work the grease well into both the upper and lower bearings.

**11** Carefully lift the steering stem/bottom yoke up through the steering head. Install the upper bearing in the top of the steering head, then install the bearing cover.

**12** Thread the adjuster nut onto the steering stem. If the correct tools are available, tighten the nut to the torque setting specified at the beginning of the Chapter, then turn the steering stem from lock to lock five or six times to settle the bearings, then slacken the adjuster nut by 1/4 to 1/2 a turn, until steering is able to move freely but without any freeplay. If the tools are not available, tighten the nut a little at a time until all freeplay is removed but also so that the steering is able to move freely, then tighten 1/2 a turn further. Now turn the steering stem from lock to lock five or six times to settle the bearings, then slacken the adjuster nut by 1/4 to 1/2 a turn, until steering is able to move freely but without any freeplay.

*Caution: Take great care not to apply excessive pressure because this will cause premature failure of the bearings. The object is to set the adjuster nut so that the bearings are under a very light loading, just enough to remove any freeplay.*

**13** Fit the washer onto the steering stem, aligning the tab on its inside with the groove in the stem. Fit the locknut and tighten it to the specified torque setting.

**14** Fit the top yoke onto the steering stem. Raise the fuel tank onto its support and reconnect the ignition switch wiring connector, making sure it is correctly routed, and secure it in its guide (**see illustration 5.4**). Install the air filter housing (see Chapter 4).

**15** Install the steering stem nut and its washer and tighten it finger-tight at this stage. Temporarily install one of the forks to align the top and bottom yokes, and secure it by

tightening the bottom yoke clamp bolts only. Tighten the steering stem nut to the specified torque setting.

**16** Attach the front brake hose clamp to the bottom yoke (**see illustration 8.3a**). Where fitted, also attach the steering damper to the bottom yoke (**see illustration 8.3b**).

**17** Locate each handlebar onto the underside of the top yoke and secure them with the set bolts, but leave them slack. Feed the handlebar switch wiring into its guide under the top yoke (**see illustration 8.2**).

**18** Where fitted, reconnect the steering damper. Install the front forks (see Section 6).

**19** Carry out a check of the steering head bearing freeplay as described in Chapter 1, and if necessary re-adjust.

## 9  Steering head bearings – inspection and renewal

### Inspection

**1** Remove the steering stem (see Section 8).

**2** Remove all traces of old grease from the bearings and races and check them for wear or damage.

**3** The outer races should be polished and free from indentations. Inspect the bearing balls for signs of wear, damage or discoloration, and examine their retainer cage for signs of cracks or splits. Spin the bearings by hand. They should spin freely and smoothly. If there are any signs of wear on any of the above components both upper and

lower bearing assemblies must be renewed as a set. Only remove the outer races from the frame if they need to be renewed – do not re-use them once they have been removed.

### Renewal

**4** The outer races are an interference fit in the frame steering head and can be tapped from position with a suitable drift (**see illustration**). Tap firmly and evenly around each race to ensure that it is driven out squarely. It may prove advantageous to curve the end of the drift slightly to improve access.

**5** Alternatively, the outer races can be removed using a slide-hammer type bearing extractor – these can often be hired from tool shops.

**6** The new outer races can be pressed into the steering head using a drawbolt arrangement (**see illustration**), or by using a large diameter tubular drift which bears only on the outer edge of the race. Ensure that the drawbolt washer or drift (as applicable) bears only on the outer edge of the race and does not contact the working surface. Alternatively, have the races installed by a Suzuki dealer equipped with the bearing race installing tools.

> **HAYNES HiNT** *Installation of new bearing outer races is made much easier if the races are left overnight in the freezer. This causes them to contract slightly making them a looser fit.*

**7** To remove the lower bearing from the steering stem, use two screwdrivers or cold chisels placed on opposite sides of the race to work it free. If the bearing is firmly in place it will be necessary to use a bearing puller, or in extreme circumstances to split the bearing's inner section (**see illustration**). Take the steering stem to a Suzuki dealer if required. Check the condition of the dust seal and fit a new one if necessary.

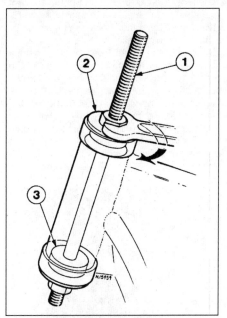

**9.6 Drawbolt arrangement for fitting steering head bearing outer races**

*1  Long bolt or threaded bar*
*2  Thick washer*
*3  Guide for lower outer race*

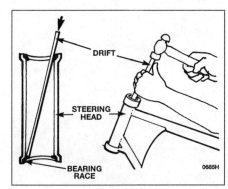

**9.4 Drive the bearing outer races out with a brass drift as shown**

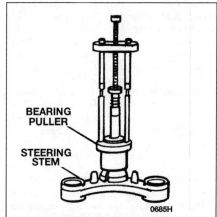

**9.7 It is best to remove the lower bearing using a puller**

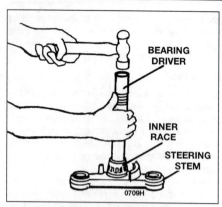

9.8 Drive the new bearing on using a suitable bearing driver or a length of pipe that bears only against the inner edge and not against the rollers or cage

8 Fit the new lower bearing onto the steering stem. A length of tubing with an internal diameter slightly larger than the steering stem will be needed to tap it into position (see illustration). Ensure that the drift bears only on the inner edge of the bearing and does not contact the balls or cage.

9 Install the steering stem (see Section 8).

## 10 Rear shock absorber – removal, inspection and installation

### Removal

1 Place the machine on an auxiliary stand. Position a support under the rear wheel so that it does not drop when the shock absorber is removed, but also making sure that the weight of the machine is off the rear suspension so that the shock is not compressed.

2 Remove the seat cowling and the lower fairing (see Chapter 8).

3 Unscrew the two bolts securing the front of the rear mudguard to the frame (see illustration).

4 Unscrew the bolt securing the bottom of the shock absorber to the suspension linkage arm (see illustration).

5 Access to the shock absorber upper mounting bolt and nut is best achieved using a socket extension via the hole in each side of the frame. Counter-hold the bolt and unscrew the nut (see illustration). Support the shock absorber and withdraw the bolt, then manoeuvre the shock absorber out through the top of the frame, pulling the front of the rear mudguard off its lugs on the frame and down to provide clearance (see illustration).

### Inspection

6 Inspect the shock absorber for obvious physical damage and the coil spring for looseness, cracks or signs of fatigue.

7 Inspect the damper rod for signs of bending, pitting and oil leakage (see illustration).

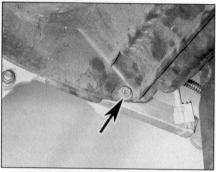

10.3 Unscrew the bolt (arrowed) on each side of the mudguard

10.5a . . . followed by the upper mounting bolt nut . . .

8 Inspect the pivot hardware at the top and bottom of the shock for wear or damage.

9 If the shock absorber is in any way damaged or worn a new one must be installed. Individual components are not available from Suzuki although it is worth checking whether the shock can be rebuilt by a suspension specialist.

10 Check the tightness of the shock absorber upper mounting bracket secured in the frame. If the bracket is loose, tighten the nut to the torque setting specified at the beginning of the Chapter. On 600 models if the bracket is disturbed for any reason, note that the white mark on the bracket should face the frame. On 750 models, don't remove the bracket from the frame unless you need to renew it; on GSX-R750T models there is a

10.7 Check the damper rod for oil leakage and corrosion

10.4 Unscrew the lower mounting bolt . . .

10.5b . . . then withdraw the upper bolt, pull the mudguard back and remove the shock

spacer between the adjuster bracket and frame.

### Installation

11 Installation is the reverse of removal, noting the following.

a) Apply general purpose grease to the pivot points and to the bearings in the linkage arm.

b) Install the upper mounting bolt first, but do not tighten the nut until the lower mounting bolt is installed.

c) Tighten the upper nut and lower bolt to the torque setting specified at the beginning of the Chapter (see illustration).

d) Adjust the suspension as required (see Section 12).

10.11 Tighten the upper nut and lower bolt to the specified torque

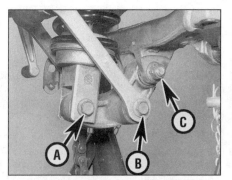

**11.3 Linkage arm to shock absorber bolt (A), linkage arm to linkage rods bolt (B), linkage arm to frame bolt (C)**

**11.6 Linkage rods to swingarm nut (arrowed)**

**11.7a Withdraw the spacers from the bearings**

## 11  Rear suspension linkage – removal, inspection and installation

### Removal

**1** Place the machine on an auxiliary stand. Position a support under the rear wheel so that it does not drop when the shock absorber is removed, but also making sure that the weight of the machine is off the rear suspension so that the shock is not compressed.

**2** Remove the lower fairing (see Chapter 8).

**3** Unscrew the bolt securing the linkage arm to the bottom of the shock absorber **(see illustration)**.

**4** Unscrew the nut and withdraw the bolt securing the linkage arm to the linkage rods **(see illustration 11.3)**.

**5** Unscrew the nut and withdraw the bolt securing the linkage arm to the frame, then remove the arm, noting the washers fitted between the arm and the frame **(see illustration 11.3)**.

**6** Unscrew the nut and withdraw the bolt securing the linkage rods to the swingarm and remove the rods **(see illustration)**.

### Inspection

**7** Withdraw the spacers from the linkage arm, noting their different sizes **(see illustration)**. Thoroughly clean all components, removing all traces of dirt, corrosion and grease **(see illustration)**.

**8** Inspect all components closely, looking for obvious signs of wear such as heavy scoring, or for damage such as cracks or distortion. Slip each spacer back into its bearing and check that there is not an excessive amount of freeplay between the two components. Renew any components as required.

**9** Check the condition of the needle roller bearings in the linkage arm and in the bottom of the swingarm. Refer to *Tools and Workshop Tips* (Section 5) in the Reference section for

more information on bearings. If the linkage rod bearings in the swingarm need to be renewed, remove the swingarm (see Section 13).

**10** Worn bearings can be drifted out of their bores, but note that removal will destroy them; new bearings should be obtained before work commences. The new bearings should be pressed or drawn into their bores rather than driven into position. In the absence of a press, a suitable drawbolt tool can be made up as described in

*Tools and Workshop Tips* in the Reference section.

**11** Lubricate the needle roller bearings and the pivot bolts with general purpose grease and install the spacers.

### Installation

**12** Installation is the reverse of removal, noting the following.

a) Apply general purpose grease to the bearings, spacers, pivot points and pivot bolts.

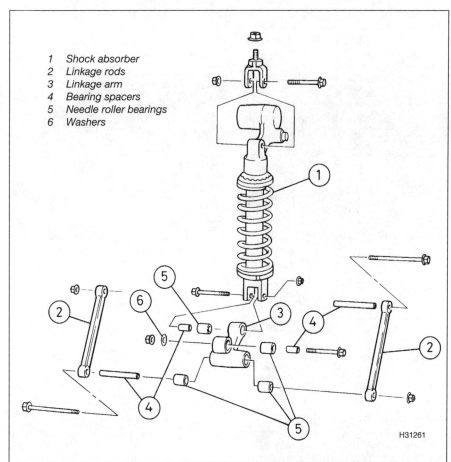

1  Shock absorber
2  Linkage rods
3  Linkage arm
4  Bearing spacers
5  Needle roller bearings
6  Washers

H31261

**11.7b  Suspension linkage components**

**6**

**11.12a Fit the washers between each side of the linkage arm and the frame**

**11.12b Tighten the nuts and bolt to the specified torque settings**

b) Do not forget to fit the washers between the linkage arm and the frame **(see illustration)**.
c) Do not fully tighten any of the bolts until they have all been installed.
d) Tighten the nuts and bolt to the torque setting specified at the beginning of the Chapter **(see illustration)**.
e) Check the operation of the rear suspension before taking the machine on the road.

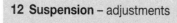
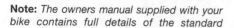

## 12 Suspension – adjustments

**Note:** *The owners manual supplied with your bike contains full details of the standard* suspension settings and recommended settings to suit the load carried and riding style.

### Front forks

**1** On GSX-R600V models, the forks are adjustable for spring pre-load and rebound damping. On all other 600 models and all 750 models the forks are adjustable for spring pre-load, rebound damping and compression damping.
**2** Spring pre-load is adjusted using a suitable spanner on the adjuster flats **(see illustrations)**. Turn it clockwise to increase pre-load and anti-clockwise to decrease it. The amount of pre-load is indicated by lines on the adjuster. Always make sure both adjusters are set equally.
**3** Rebound damping is adjusted using a screwdriver in the slot in the damping adjuster

rod protruding from the pre-load adjuster **(see illustration 12.2a or b)**. Turn it clockwise to increase damping and anti-clockwise to decrease it.
**4** Compression damping is adjusted using a screwdriver in the slot in the damping adjuster in the base of each fork **(see illustration)**. Turn it clockwise to increase damping and anti-clockwise to decrease it.

### *Rear shock absorber*

**5** On all models the rear shock absorber is adjustable for spring pre-load, rebound damping and compression damping.
**6** Spring pre-load is adjusted by turning the adjuster nut on the threads on the shock absorber body. Slacken the locknut, then turn the adjuster nut clockwise to increase pre-load and anti-clockwise to decrease it **(see illustration)**. Tighten the locknut securely after adjustment. Do not set the spring length to anything less than 190 mm, the hardest setting.
**7** Rebound damping is adjusted using a screwdriver in the slot in the adjuster at the bottom of the shock absorber **(see illustration)**. To increase the damping, turn the adjuster clockwise. To decrease the damping, turn the adjuster anti-clockwise.
**8** Compression damping is adjusted using a screwdriver in the slot in the adjuster at the top of the shock absorber **(see illustration)**. To increase the damping, turn the adjuster clockwise. To decrease the damping, turn the adjuster anti-clockwise.

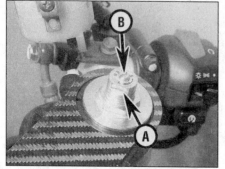

**12.2a Spring pre-load adjuster (A), rebound damping adjuster (B) – GSX-R600**

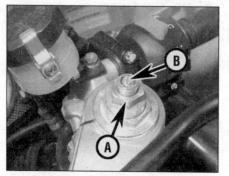

**12.2b Spring pre-load adjuster (A), rebound damping adjuster (B) – GSX-R750**

**12.4 Compression damping adjuster (arrowed)**

**12.6 Slacken the locknut (A) and turn the adjuster (B) as required to adjust pre-load**

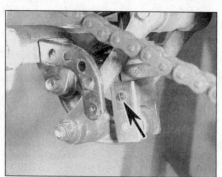

**12.7 Rebound damping adjuster (arrowed)**

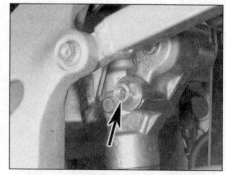

**12.8 Compression damping adjuster (arrowed)**

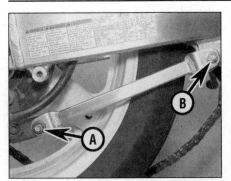

13.3a Detach the torque arm at either the caliper (A) or the swingarm (B)

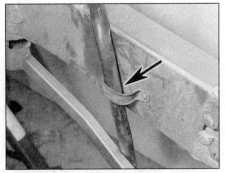

13.3b Feed the brake hose through the closed guide (arrowed) . . .

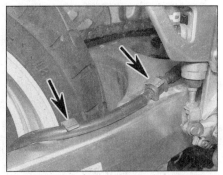

13.3c . . . and out of the open guides (arrowed)

## 13 Swingarm –
removal and installation

### Removal

**Note 1:** *Before removing the swingarm, it is advisable to perform the rear suspension checks described in Chapter 1 to assess the extent of any wear.*

**Note 2:** *The swingarm can be removed with the shock absorber and linkage assembly attached if required. Otherwise, the shock absorber must be removed, and the linkage assembly must either be removed completely, or it can remain attached either to the swingarm and removed with it after detaching it from the frame, or it can remain attached to the frame after detaching it from the swingarm. If the rear suspension is being removed as an assembly, but is later to be disassembled, it is advisable to slacken all the bolts before removing the assembly.*

**Note 3:** *The rear brake hose is fitted through a closed guide on the inside of the swingarm. The only way to separate the hose from the swingarm is to disconnect it from either the brake caliper or the master cylinder and feed it through. This will mean bleeding the brake system after installation. To prevent opening the system, it can be removed complete along with the swingarm – this is*

*better, unless a new swingarm is being installed, or extensive work is being carried out on the old one.*

**Note 4:** *On 600 models, the chain can remain on the front sprocket. On 750 models, due to the construction of the swingarm, the chain must either be split (see Section 15) or must be slipped off the front sprocket and removed along with the swingarm. If a new swingarm is being installed, or extensive work is being carried out on it, split the chain and remove it (see Section 15).*

### Removal

**1** Remove the seat cowling and the lower fairing (see Chapter 8).
**2** Remove the rear wheel (see Chapter 7).
**3** If the brake system is being removed along with the swingarm, secure the caliper bracket to the swingarm to prevent it dropping off, then refer to Chapter 7 and displace the master cylinder and reservoir and position them so they will come away with the swingarm. Otherwise, refer to Chapter 7 and separate the hydraulic hose from the caliper (following all precautions), then unscrew the nut and remove the bolt securing the brake torque arm to either the bracket or the swingarm and remove the caliper along with the bracket **(see illustration)**. Feed the hose through the closed guide, free it from the

other guides and secure it clear **(see illustrations)**.
**4** On GSX-R750 models, either remove the front sprocket cover and slip the chain off the sprocket (if the chain is being left intact and removed with the swingarm) (see Section 16), or split the chain and free it from the swingarm (see Section 15).
**5** Either remove the shock absorber (see Section 10), or if it is to be removed with the swingarm and suspension linkage, remove the shock absorber upper mounting bolt (see **Note 2** above) **(see illustration 10.5a)**.
**6** Either remove the suspension linkage completely (see Section 11), or separate it from either the swingarm (if it is to remain in place) or the frame (if it is being removed with the swingarm) as required (see **Note 2** above) **(see illustration 11.6 or 11.3)**.
**7** Before removing the swingarm it is advisable to re-check for play in the bearings (see Chapter 1). Any problems which may have been overlooked with the other suspension components attached to the frame are highlighted with them loose.
**8** Unscrew the locknut on the right-hand end of the swingarm pivot bolt **(see illustration)**. This requires the use of a Suzuki service tool (Pt. No. 09940-14970) or a suitable peg spanner, which can be fabricated using an old socket or an old nut (see **Tool Tip**).

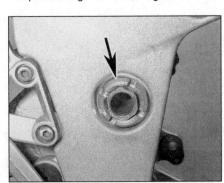

13.8 Unscrew and remove the locknut (arrowed)

A peg 'socket' can be made by cutting an old 32 mm socket as shown – measure the width and depth of the slots in the locknut to determine the size of the castellations on the socket (left). If an old socket is not available, a nut can be used and suitable pegs can be brazed or welded onto it (right).

 6

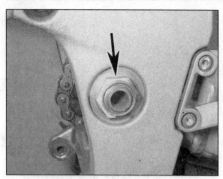

**13.9 Unscrew and remove the nut (arrowed)**

**13.10 Support the swingarm and withdraw the pivot bolt**

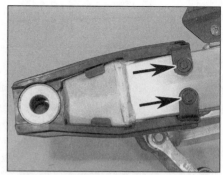

**13.11a The chain slider is secured by two bolts (arrowed) . . .**

**13.11b . . . and the chainguard by two screws (arrowed)**

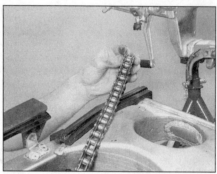

**13.17a Loop the chain around the front of the swingarm . . .**

**13.17b . . . then slide the pivot bolt through . . .**

9 Counter-hold the pivot bolt using a 27 mm socket or spanner and unscrew the nut on the left-hand end of the bolt using a 36 mm socket or spanner **(see illustration)**. Remove the washer.
10 Support the swingarm, then withdraw the pivot bolt and remove the swingarm **(see illustration)**. On 750 models, check that the pivot bosses in the frame are not worn or damaged and that they are tight in the frame. If they are loose, tighten the nuts on the inside of the frame to the torque setting specified at the beginning of the Chapter. Do not remove the bosses unless new ones are being fitted. If they are worn or damaged, new ones must be fitted.
11 Remove the chain slider, and if necessary the chainguard from the swingarm, noting how they fit **(see illustrations)**. If the chain

slider is badly worn or damaged, a new one should be fitted.
12 If attached, and if required, separate the suspension linkage from the swingarm (see Section 11).
13 Clean inspect and lubricate all components as described in Section 14.

### Installation

14 On 750 models, check that the pivot bosses in the frame are not worn or damaged and that they are tight in the frame. If they are loose, tighten the nuts on the inside of the frame to the torque setting specified at the beginning of the Chapter. Do not remove the bosses unless new ones are being fitted. If they are worn or damaged, new ones must be fitted.
15 If not already done, remove the dust

seals, washers and bearing spacers, then clean them and lubricate the bearings, spacers and the pivot bolt with grease **(see illustrations 14.2b and c)**. Install the bearing spacers, then fit the washers and dust seals.
16 Install the chain slider, and if removed the chainguard **(see illustrations 13.11a and b)**.
17 Offer up the swingarm, making sure the chain is correctly looped around it (unless removed on 750 models), and have an assistant hold it in place **(see illustration)**. Slide the pivot bolt through the swingarm from the right-hand side and tighten it to the torque setting specified at the beginning of the Chapter using a 27 mm socket **(see illustrations)**.
18 Thread the swingarm pivot nut with its washer finger-tight onto the left-hand end of the bolt **(see illustration)**. Counter-hold the

**13.17c . . . and tighten it to the specified torque**

**13.18a Fit the washer and nut . . .**

**13.18b . . . and tighten it while counter-holding the bolt**

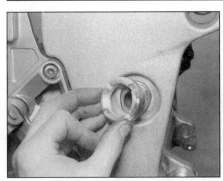

13.19a Fit the locknut . . .

13.19b . . . and tighten it to the specified torque setting

14.1 Clean off all accumulated chain lube and road dirt using a suitable degreaser

pivot bolt using a 27 mm socket or spanner and tighten the nut to the specified torque setting using a 36 mm socket **(see illustration)**.

**19** Thread the locknut finger-tight onto the right-hand end of the pivot bolt **(see illustration)**. Make a reference mark between the head of the pivot bolt and the frame as a check against the bolt turning when the locknut is tightened. Using the same tool as on removal, tighten the locknut to the specified torque setting **(see illustration)**. Check that the reference marks still align – if not remove the locknut and nut and slacken the pivot bolt, then repeat the tightening procedure.

**20** Install the rear shock absorber and linkage assembly as required by your removal procedure (see Sections 10 and 11).

**21** On 750 models, either fit the drive chain around the front sprocket, then install the sprocket cover (see Section 16), or fit the split chain and stake it using a new soft link as described in Section 15.

**22** Install the rear brake components as required by your removal procedure (see Chapter 7).

**23** Install the rear wheel (see Chapter 7), and the lower fairing and the seat cowling (see Chapter 8).

**24** Check and adjust the drive chain slack (see Chapter 1). Check the operation of the rear suspension and brake before taking the machine on the road.

## 14 Swingarm – inspection and bearing renewal

### Inspection

**1** Thoroughly clean the swingarm, removing all traces of dirt, corrosion and grease **(see illustration)**.

**2** Remove the dust seals, washers and bearing spacers **(see illustrations)**.

**3** Inspect all components closely, looking for obvious signs of wear such as heavy scoring, and cracks or distortion due to accident damage. Check the bearings for roughness,

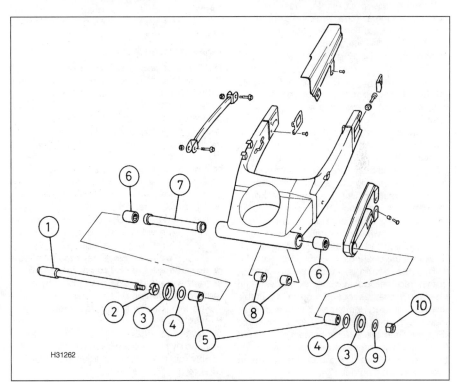

14.2a Swingarm components

| | | |
|---|---|---|
| 1 Pivot bolt | 5 Bearing spacer | 8 Linkage rod bearings |
| 2 Locknut | 6 Swingarm bearings | 9 Washer |
| 3 Dust seal | 7 Bearing spacer | 10 Pivot bolt nut |
| 4 Washer | | |

14.2b Remove the dust seal and washer . . .

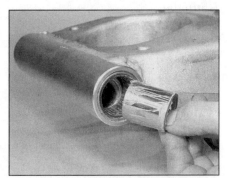

14.2c . . . and withdraw the spacer

6

looseness and any other damage, referring to *Tools and Workshop Tips* (Section 5) in the Reference section **(see illustration)**. Any damaged or worn component must be renewed.

**4** Check the swingarm pivot bolt for straightness by rolling it on a flat surface such as a piece of plate glass (first wipe off all old grease and remove any corrosion using fine emery cloth). If the equipment is available, place the axle in V-blocks and measure the runout using a dial gauge. If the axle is bent or the runout exceeds the limit specified, fit a new one.

### Bearing renewal

**5** Remove the dust seals, washers and bearing spacers **(see illustrations 14.2b and c)**. Refer to *Tools and Workshop Tips* (Section 5) in the Reference section for more information on bearing checks and renewal methods.

**6** Needle bearings can be drawn or driven out of their bores, but note that removal will destroy them; new bearings should be obtained before work commences. It may be possible to pass a long drift with a hooked end through the swingarm and locate it between the central spacer and the inner edge of the bearing. Tap the drift around the bearing's inner edge to ensure that it leaves its bore squarely. Once removed, withdraw the centre spacer and use the same method to extract the other bearing. If available, a slide-hammer with knife-edged bearing puller can be used, and is better than using a drift, to extract the bearings.

**7** The new bearings should be pressed or drawn into their bores rather than driven into position. In the absence of a press, a suitable drawbolt arrangement can be made up as described in *Tools and Workshop Tips* (Section 5) in the Reference section. Do not forget to install the centre spacer between the two bearings, and fit the bearings with their marked side facing out.

---

**15 Drive chain** – removal, cleaning and installation

---

### Removal

#### GSX-R600 models

**Note:** *The original equipment drive chain fitted to all 600 models is an endless chain. Removal requires the removal of the swingarm as detailed below.*

>  **Warning: NEVER install a drive chain which uses a clip-type master (split) link.**

**1** Remove the swingarm (see Section 13).
**2** Remove the front sprocket cover (see Section 16).
**3** Slip the chain off the front sprocket and remove it from the bike. If there is not enough clearance between the sprocket and the

**14.3 Check the bearings as described**

frame to remove the chain, remove the sprocket (see Section 16), then remove the chain.

#### GSX-R750 models

**Note:** *The original equipment drive chain fitted to these models has a staked -type master (soft) link which can be disassembled using either Suzuki service tool, Pt. No. 09922-22711, or one of several commercially-available drive chain cutting/staking tools. Such chains can be recognised by the soft link side plate's identification marks (and usually its different colour), as well as by the staked ends of the link's two pins which look as if they have been deeply centre-punched, instead of peened over as with all the other pins.*

>  **Warning: Use ONLY the correct service tools to disassemble the staked-type of soft link – if you do not have access to such tools or do not have the skill to operate them correctly, have the chain removed by a motorcycle dealer.**

**4** Remove the front sprocket cover (see Section 16).
**5** Locate the soft link in a suitable position to work on by rotating the back wheel.
**6** Slacken the drive chain as described in Chapter 1.
**7** Split the chain at the soft link using the chain cutter, following carefully the manufacturer's operating instructions (see also Section 8 in *Tools and Workshop Tips* in the Reference Section). Remove the chain from the bike, noting its routing through the swingarm.

### Cleaning

**8** Soak the chain in paraffin (kerosene) for approximately five or six minutes.
*Caution: Don't use gasoline (petrol), solvent or other cleaning fluids. Don't use high-pressure water. Remove the chain, wipe it off, then blow dry it with compressed air immediately. The entire process shouldn't take longer than ten minutes – if it does, the O-rings in the chain rollers could be damaged.*

### Installation

#### GSX-R600 models

**9** Installation is the reverse of removal. On completion adjust and lubricate the chain following the procedures described in Chapter 1.

#### GSX-R750 models

> **Warning: NEVER install a drive chain which uses a clip-type master (split) link. Use ONLY the correct service tools to secure the staked-type of soft link – if you do not have access to such tools or do not have the skill to operate them correctly, have the chain installed by a motorcycle dealer.**

**10** Slip the drive chain through the swingarm sections and around the front sprocket, leaving the two ends in a convenient position to work on.
**11** Refer to Section 8 in *Tools and Workshop Tips* in the Reference Section. Install the new soft link from the inside. Fit an O-ring onto each pin, then slide the link through and fit the other two O-rings. Install the new side plate with its identification marks facing out and press it into position. If fitting the original equipment type RK chain, measure the distance between the outer edges of the soft link and side plate and check they are within the measurements specified at the beginning of the Chapter **(see illustration)**.
**12** Stake the new link using the drive chain cutting/staking tool, following carefully the instructions of both the chain manufacturer and the tool manufacturer. DO NOT re-use old soft link components. After staking, check the soft link and staking for any signs of cracking. If there is any evidence of cracking,

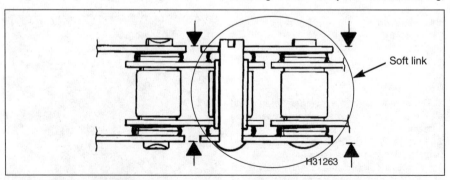

**15.11 Press sideplate on to specified distance (arrowed) on RK chain – 750 models**
*Soft link left-hand pin shown in cross-section*

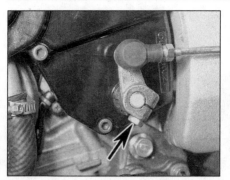

16.1  Unscrew the bolt (arrowed) and slide the arm off the shaft

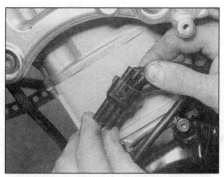

16.2  Disconnect the speedometer sensor wiring connector

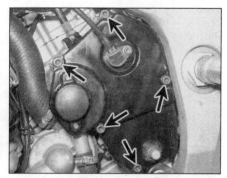

16.3  Sprocket cover bolts (arrowed)

the soft link, O-rings and side plate must be renewed. If fitting the original equipment type RK chain, measure the diameter of the staked ends in two directions and check that it is evenly staked and within the measurements specified at the beginning of the Chapter.

**13** Install the sprocket cover (see Section 16).
**14** On completion, adjust and lubricate the chain following the procedures described in Chapter 1.

## 16 Sprockets –
check and renewal

### Check

**1** Unscrew the gearchange linkage arm pinch bolt and remove the arm from the shaft, noting any alignment marks **(see illustration)**. If no marks are visible, make your own before removing the arm so that it can be correctly aligned with the shaft on installation.
**2** Trace the wiring from the speedometer sensor on the front sprocket cover and disconnect it at the connector **(see illustration)**.
**3** Unscrew the bolts securing the sprocket cover to the crankcase and move the cover aside **(see illustration)**. There is no need to detach the clutch cable from the cover. On W and X models, note the rubber bushing for the gearchange shaft and remove it from the cover if required.

**4** Check the wear pattern on both sprockets (see Chapter 1). If the sprocket teeth are worn excessively, renew the chain and both sprockets as a set. Whenever the sprockets are inspected, the drive chain should be inspected also (see Chapter 1). If you are fitting a new chain, fit new sprockets as well.
**5** Adjust and lubricate the chain following the procedures described in Chapter 1.

### Renewal

#### Front sprocket

**6** Unscrew the gearchange linkage arm pinch bolt and remove the arm from the shaft, noting any alignment marks **(see illustration 16.1)**. If no marks are visible, make your own before removing the arm so that it can be correctly aligned with the shaft on installation.
**7** Trace the wiring from the speedometer sensor on the front sprocket cover and disconnect it at the connector **(see illustration 16.2)**.
**8** Unscrew the bolts securing the sprocket cover to the crankcase and move the cover aside **(see illustration 16.3)**. There is no need to detach the clutch cable from the cover. On W and X models, note the rubber bushing for the gearchange shaft and remove it from the cover if required.
**9** Counter-hold the sprocket nut and unscrew the bolt securing the speedometer rotor **(see illustration)**. Remove the rotor, and on GSX-R750T models the washer.

**10** Have an assistant apply the rear brake hard. This will lock the sprocket and enable you to slacken and remove the nut. Unscrew the sprocket nut and remove it with the washer **(see illustration)**.
**11** Slide the sprocket and chain off the shaft, then slip the sprocket out of the chain **(see illustration)**. If the chain is too tight to allow the sprocket to be slid off the shaft, slacken the chain adjusters to provide some freeplay (see Chapter 1), or, if the rear sprocket is being renewed as well, remove the rear wheel (see Chapter 7).
**12** Engage the new sprocket with the chain and slide it on the shaft **(see illustration)**.
**13** Install the sprocket nut with its washer and tighten it to the torque setting specified at

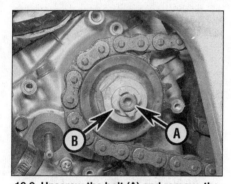

16.9  Unscrew the bolt (A) and remove the rotor (B)

16.10  Unscrew the nut (arrowed) . . .

16.11  . . . then slide the sprocket off the shaft and out of the chain

16.12  Fit the sprocket into the chain and onto the shaft . . .

6

16.13a . . . then fit the washer and nut . . .

16.13b . . . and tighten the nut to the specified torque

16.14 Fit the rotor and tighten its bolt to the specified torque

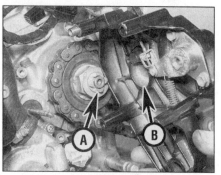

16.16a Locate the rotor (A) into the sensor (B)

16.16b Where fitted, and if removed, slide the rubber bush onto the shaft

16.21 The sprocket is secured by six nuts (arrowed)

the beginning of the Chapter, applying the rear brake as before to prevent the sprocket turning (see illustrations).

**14** Now install the speedometer rotor, on GSX-R750T models with its washer, and tighten the bolt to the specified torque setting while counter-holding the sprocket nut (see illustration).

**15** If detached, fit the clutch cable into the release mechanism in the sprocket cover (see Chapter 2).

**16** Make sure the dowels are either in the crankcase or the sprocket cover. Install the cover, making sure the speedometer rotor fits properly into the sensor and the dowels locate correctly, and tighten its bolts **(see illustration)**. On W and X models, if removed, fit the rubber bushing for the gearchange shaft into the cover **(see illustration)**.

**17** Slide the gearchange linkage arm onto the shaft, aligning the marks, and tighten the pinch bolt (see illustration 16.1).

**18** Reconnect the speedometer sensor wiring connector (see illustration 16.2).

**19** Adjust and lubricate the chain following the procedures described in Chapter 1.

### Rear sprocket

**20** Remove the rear wheel (see Chapter 7). *Caution: Do not lay the wheel down on the disc as it could become warped. Lay the wheel on wooden blocks so that the disc is off the ground.*

**21** Unscrew the nuts securing the sprocket to the wheel coupling, then remove the sprocket, noting which way round it fits **(see illustration)**.

**22** Before installing the new rear sprocket, check the wheel coupling and damper assembly components (see Section 17).

**23** Install the sprocket onto the coupling with the stamped mark facing out, then tighten the sprocket nuts to the torque setting specified at the beginning of the Chapter.

**24** Install the rear wheel (see Chapter 7).

**25** Adjust and lubricate the chain following the procedures described in Chapter 1.

### 17 Rear wheel coupling/rubber dampers – check and renewal

**1** Remove the rear wheel (see Chapter 7). *Caution: Do not lay the wheel down on the disc as it could become warped. Lay the wheel on wooden blocks so that the disc is off the ground.*

17.2 Lift the coupling out of the wheel . . .

**2** Lift the sprocket coupling out of the wheel leaving the rubber dampers in position in the wheel **(see illustration)**. Note the spacer inside the coupling. Check the coupling for cracks or any obvious signs of damage. Also check the sprocket studs for wear or damage, and that they are secure.

**3** Lift the rubber damper segments from the wheel and check them for cracks, hardening and general deterioration **(see illustration)**. Renew the rubber dampers as a set if necessary.

**4** Checking and renewal procedures for the sprocket coupling bearing are described in Chapter 7.

**5** Check that the coupling spacer is correctly located in the bearing in the coupling. Fit the coupling into the wheel, making sure the spacer also locates into the bearing in the wheel.

**6** Install the rear wheel (see Chapter 7).

17.3 . . . and check the damper segments

# Chapter 7
# Brakes, wheels and tyres

## Contents

## Degrees of difficulty

| | | | | |
|---|---|---|---|---|
| **Easy,** suitable for novice with little experience  | **Fairly easy,** suitable for beginner with some experience  | **Fairly difficult,** suitable for competent DIY mechanic 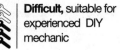 | **Difficult,** suitable for experienced DIY mechanic  | **Very difficult,** suitable for expert DIY or professional |

## Specifications

**Brakes**

Brake fluid type . . . . . . . . . . . . . . . . . . . . . . . . . . . . . . . . . . . DOT 4
Disc minimum thickness
  Front
    GSX-R600V and GSX-R750T and V models
      Standard . . . . . . . . . . . . . . . . . . . . . . . . . . . . . . . . . . 4.3 to 4.7 mm
      Service limit . . . . . . . . . . . . . . . . . . . . . . . . . . . . . . . . 4.0 mm
    GSX-R600W and X and GSX-R750W and X models
      Standard . . . . . . . . . . . . . . . . . . . . . . . . . . . . . . . . . . 4.8 to 5.2 mm
      Service limit . . . . . . . . . . . . . . . . . . . . . . . . . . . . . . . . 4.5 mm
  Rear
    Standard . . . . . . . . . . . . . . . . . . . . . . . . . . . . . . . . . . . . 4.8 to 5.2 mm
    Service limit . . . . . . . . . . . . . . . . . . . . . . . . . . . . . . . . . . 4.5 mm

**7**

## Brakes (continued)
Disc maximum runout (front and rear, all models) ................. 0.3 mm
Caliper bore ID
  Front
    GSX-R600
      Lower ................................................. 27.000 to 27.076 mm
      Upper ................................................. 30.230 to 30.306 mm
    GSX-R750
      Lower ................................................. 24.000 to 24.076 mm
      Middle and upper ............................. 27.000 to 27.076 mm
  Rear ...................................................... 38.180 to 38.256 mm
Caliper piston OD
  GSX-R600
    Lower ................................................. 26.920 to 26.970 mm
    Upper ................................................. 30.150 to 30.200 mm
  GSX-R750
    Lower ................................................. 23.925 to 23.975 mm
    Middle and upper ............................. 26.920 to 26.970 mm
  Rear ...................................................... 38.098 to 38.148 mm
Master cylinder bore ID
  Front
    GSX-R600 ........................................... 14.000 to 14.043 mm
    GSX-R750 ........................................... 15.870 to 15.913 mm
  Rear ...................................................... 12.700 to 12.743 mm
Master cylinder piston OD
  Front
    GSX-R600 ........................................... 13.957 to 13.984 mm
    GSX-R750 ........................................... 15.827 to 15.854 mm
  Rear ...................................................... 12.657 to 12.684 mm

## Wheels
Maximum wheel runout (front and rear)
  Axial (side-to-side) ................................... 2.0 mm
  Radial (out-of-round) ................................ 2.0 mm
Maximum axle runout (front and rear) ...................... 0.25 mm

## Tyres
Tyre pressures .......................................... see *Daily (pre-ride) checks*
Tyre sizes*
  GSX-R600
    Front ................................................. 120/70-ZR17 (58W)
    Rear .................................................. 180/55-ZR17 (73W)
  GSX-R750
    Front ................................................. 120/70-ZR17 (58W)
    Rear .................................................. 190/50-ZR17 (73W)
*Refer to the owners handbook or the tyre information label on the swingarm for approved tyre brands.*

## Torque settings
Front brake caliper joining bolts .............................. 23 Nm
Front brake caliper mounting bolts ............................ 39 Nm
Brake hose banjo bolts ...................................... 23 Nm
Front brake disc bolts ....................................... 23 Nm
Front brake master cylinder clamp bolts ....................... 10 Nm
Rear brake caliper joining bolts .............................. 33 Nm
Rear brake caliper mounting bolts ............................ 26 Nm
Rear brake torque arm nut ................................... 35 Nm
Rear brake disc bolts ....................................... 35 Nm
Rear brake master cylinder mounting bolts ..................... 10 Nm
Brake system bleed valves ................................... 8 Nm
Front axle clamp bolts and axle holder clamp bolts .............. 23 Nm
Front axle ................................................. 100 Nm
Rear axle nut .............................................. 100 Nm

**2.1 Unscrew the bolts (arrowed) and remove the pad spring**

**2.2a Remove the R-pin (arrowed) . . .**

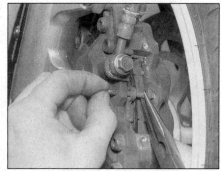

**2.2b . . . then withdraw the pad pin . . .**

## 1 General information

All models covered in this manual are fitted with cast alloy wheels designed for tubeless tyres only.

Both front and rear brakes are hydraulically operated disc brakes. On GSX-R600 models, the front has twin calipers with twin opposed pistons, the rear has a single caliper with single opposed pistons. On GSX-R750, the front has twin calipers with triple opposed pistons, the rear has a single caliper with single opposed pistons.

*Caution: Disc brake components rarely require disassembly. Do not disassemble components unless absolutely necessary. If a hydraulic brake line is loosened, the entire system must be disassembled, drained, cleaned and then properly filled and bled upon reassembly. Do not use solvents on internal brake components. Solvents will cause the seals to swell and distort. Use only clean brake fluid of the correct type for cleaning. Use care when working with brake fluid as it can injure your eyes and it will damage painted surfaces and plastic parts.*

## 2 Front brake pads – renewal

⚠️ *Warning: The dust created by the brake system may contain asbestos, which is harmful to your health. Never blow it out with compressed air and don't inhale any of it. An approved filtering mask should be worn when working on the brakes.*

**1** Unscrew the two bolts securing the pad spring and remove the spring **(see illustration)**.

**2** Remove the R-pin from the end of the pad retaining pin, then withdraw the pad pin **(see illustrations)**. Remove the pads from the caliper, noting how they fit **(see illustration)**.

**3** Inspect the surface of each pad for contamination and check that the friction material has not worn beyond its service limit (see Chapter 1, Section 11). If either pad is worn down to, or beyond, the service limit wear indicator (ie the wear indicator is no longer visible), fouled with oil or grease, or heavily scored or damaged by dirt and debris, both sets of pads must be renewed as a set.

Note that it is not possible to degrease the friction material; if the pads are contaminated in any way new ones must be fitted.

**4** If the pads are in good condition clean them carefully, using a fine wire brush which is completely free of oil and grease to remove all traces of road dirt and corrosion. Using a pointed instrument, clean out the grooves in the friction material and dig out any embedded particles of foreign matter. Any areas of glazing may be removed using emery cloth. Spray with a dedicated brake cleaner to remove any dust.

**5** Check the condition of the brake disc (see Section 4).

**6** Remove all traces of corrosion from the pad pin. Inspect the pin for signs of damage and renew it if necessary.

**7** Push the pistons as far back into the caliper as possible using hand pressure or a piece of wood as leverage **(see illustration)**. Due to the increased friction material thickness of new pads, it may be necessary to remove the master cylinder reservoir cover and diaphragm and siphon out some fluid.

**8** Smear the backs of the pads and the shank of the pad pin with copper-based grease, making sure that none gets on the front or sides of the pads.

**9** Insert the pads into the caliper so that the

**2.2c . . . and lift the pads out**

**2.7 Use a block of wood to press the pistons back**

**7**

2.9a Insert the pads . . .

2.9b . . . then slide in the pad pin . . .

2.9c . . . and fit the R-pin

2.10 Fit the pad spring

friction material of each pad faces the disc **(see illustration)**. Install the pad retaining pin, making sure it passes through the hole in each pad, and secure it with the R-pin, using a new one if necessary **(see illustrations)**.
**10** Fit the pad spring and secure it with the bolts **(see illustration)**.
**11** Top up the master cylinder reservoir if necessary (see *Daily (pre-ride) checks*), and renew the reservoir cover and diaphragm.
**12** Operate the brake lever several times to bring the pads into contact with the disc. Check the operation of the brake before riding the motorcycle.

## 3 Front brake calipers – removal, overhaul and installation

*Warning: If a caliper indicates the need for an overhaul (usually due to leaking fluid or sticky operation), all old brake fluid should be flushed from the system. Also, the dust created by the brake system may contain asbestos, which is harmful to your health. Never blow it out with compressed air and don't inhale any of it. An approved filtering mask should be worn when working on the brakes. Do not, under any circumstances, use petroleum-based solvents to clean brake parts. Use the specified clean brake fluid, dedicated brake cleaner or denatured alcohol only, as described.*

### Removal

**1** If the calipers are being overhauled, remove the brake pads (see Section 2). If the calipers are just being displaced or removed, the pads can be left in place **(see illustration)**.
**2** If the calipers are just being displaced and not completely removed or overhauled, do not disconnect the brake hose. If the calipers are being overhauled, remove the brake hose banjo bolt and detach the hose, noting its alignment with the caliper **(see illustration)**. When working on the right-hand caliper, note the double hose arrangement **(see

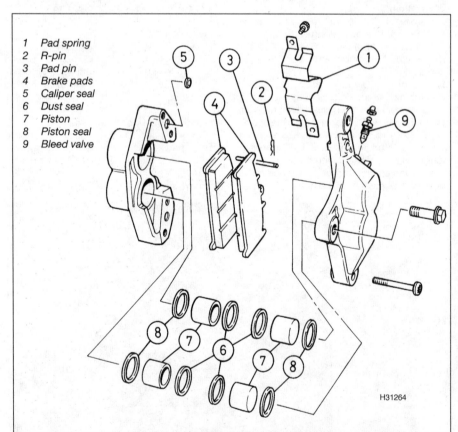

1 Pad spring
2 R-pin
3 Pad pin
4 Brake pads
5 Caliper seal
6 Dust seal
7 Piston
8 Piston seal
9 Bleed valve

H31264

3.1 Front brake caliper components. GSX-R600 shown – GSX-R750 models have an extra piston

3.2a Left-hand caliper banjo bolt (arrowed)

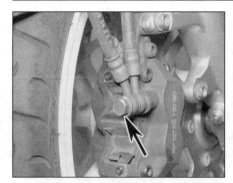

3.2b Right-hand caliper banjo bolt (arrowed) – note the double hose arrangement

3.3 Caliper body joining bolts (arrowed)

3.4a Unscrew the mounting bolts (arrowed) . . .

illustration). Plug the hose end(s) or wrap a plastic bag tightly around to minimise fluid loss and prevent dirt entering the system. Discard the sealing washers as new ones must be used on installation. **Note:** *If you are planning to overhaul the caliper and don't have a source of compressed air to blow out the pistons, just loosen the banjo bolt at this stage and retighten it lightly. The bike's hydraulic system can then be used to force the pistons out of the caliper once the pads have been removed. Disconnect the hose once the pistons have been sufficiently displaced.*

3 If the caliper body is to be split into its halves for overhaul, slacken the caliper body joining bolts at this stage and retighten them lightly **(see illustration)**.

4 Unscrew the caliper mounting bolts and slide the caliper off the disc **(see illustrations)**.

## Overhaul

5 Clean the exterior of the caliper with denatured alcohol or brake system cleaner.

6 Displace the pistons as far as possible from the caliper body, either by pumping them out by operating the front brake lever, or by forcing them out using compressed air – do not allow the piston heads to touch. If the compressed air method is used, place a wad of rag between the pistons and the caliper to act as a cushion, then use compressed air

directed into the fluid inlet to force the pistons out of the body. Use only low pressure to ease the pistons out and make sure all pistons are displaced at the same time. If the air pressure is too high and the pistons are forced out, the caliper and/or pistons may be damaged.

⚠️ **Warning: Never place your fingers in front of the pistons in an attempt to catch or protect them when applying compressed air, as serious injury could result.**

7 Unscrew the caliper body joining bolts and separate the body halves. Remove the pistons from each half. Mark each piston head and caliper body with a felt marker to ensure that the pistons can be matched to their original bores on reassembly. Note that two sizes of piston are used (see Specifications). Extract the caliper seal from whichever body half it is in and discard it as a new one must be used.

8 Using a wooden or plastic tool, remove the dust seals from the caliper bores **(see illustration)**. Discard them as new ones must be used on installation. If a metal tool is being used, take great care not to damage the caliper bores.

9 Remove and discard the piston seals in the same way.

10 Clean the pistons and bores with clean brake fluid of the specified type. If compressed air is available, use it to dry the

parts thoroughly (make sure it's filtered and unlubricated).

*Caution: Do not, under any circumstances, use a petroleum-based solvent to clean brake parts.*

11 Inspect the caliper bores and pistons for signs of corrosion, nicks and burrs and loss of plating. If surface defects are present, the caliper assembly must be renewed. If the necessary measuring equipment is available, compare the dimensions of the pistons and bores to those given in the Specifications Section of this Chapter, renewing any component that is worn beyond the service limit. If the caliper is in bad shape the master cylinder should also be checked.

12 Lubricate the new piston seals with clean brake fluid and install them in their grooves in the caliper bores, making sure the thicker side of the seal is facing the disc **(see illustration)**. Note that two sizes of bore and piston are used (see Specifications), and care must therefore be taken to ensure that the correct size seals are fitted to the correct bores. The same applies when fitting the new dust seals and pistons.

13 Lubricate the new dust seals with clean brake fluid and install them in their grooves in the caliper bores.

14 Lubricate the pistons with clean brake fluid and install them closed-end first into the

3.4b . . . and slide the caliper off the disc

3.8 Use a plastic or wooden tool (a pencil works well) to remove the seals

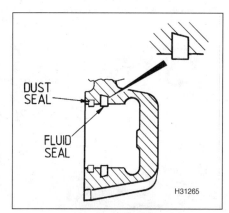

3.12 Ensure that the piston fluid seal is fitted correctly

DUST SEAL

FLUID SEAL

H31265

**7**

**3.16 Slide the caliper onto the disc . . .**

**3.17 . . . and tighten the mounting bolts to the specified torque setting**

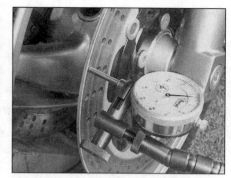

**4.2 Set up a dial gauge to contact the brake disc, then rotate the wheel to check for runout**

caliper bores. Using your thumbs, push the pistons all the way in, making sure they enter the bore squarely.

**15** Lubricate the new caliper seals with clean brake fluid and install them into one half of the caliper body. Join the two halves of the caliper body together, making sure that the caliper seals stay correctly seated in their recesses. Install the joining bolts and tighten them to the torque setting specified at the beginning of the Chapter. If it is not possible to tighten the bolts fully at this stage, tighten them as much as possible, then tighten them fully once the caliper has been installed on the machine.

### Installation

**16** Push the pistons a little way back into the caliper using hand pressure or a piece of wood as leverage. Slide the caliper onto the brake disc, making sure the pads sit squarely either side of the disc if they weren't removed **(see illustration)**.

**17** Install the caliper mounting bolts, and tighten them to the torque setting specified at the beginning of the Chapter **(see illustration)**.

**18** If the calipers were overhauled and if not already done, tighten the caliper body joining bolts to the specified torque setting **(see illustration 3.3)**.

**19** If removed, connect the brake hose(s) to the caliper, using new sealing washers on each side of the fitting(s). Align the hose(s) as

noted on removal **(see illustration 3.2a and b)**. Tighten the banjo bolt to the torque setting specified at the beginning of the Chapter. Top up the master cylinder reservoir with DOT 4 brake fluid (see *Daily (pre-ride) checks*) and bleed the hydraulic system as described in Section 11.

**20** If removed, install the brake pads (see Section 2).

**21** Check for leaks and thoroughly test the operation of the brake before riding the motorcycle.

---

### 4  Front brake disc – inspection, removal and installation

### Inspection

**1** Visually inspect the surface of the disc for score marks and other damage. Light scratches are normal after use and won't affect brake operation, but deep grooves and heavy score marks will reduce braking efficiency and accelerate pad wear. If a disc is badly grooved it must be machined or a new one fitted.

**2** To check disc runout, position the bike on an auxiliary stand and support it so that the front wheel is raised off the ground. Mount a dial gauge to a fork leg, with the plunger on the gauge touching the surface of the disc about 10 mm (1/2 in) from the outer edge **(see**

**illustration)**. Rotate the wheel and watch the gauge needle, comparing the reading with the limit listed in the Specifications at the beginning of the Chapter. If the runout is greater than the service limit, check the wheel bearings for play (see Chapter 1). If the bearings are worn, install new ones (see Section 16) and repeat this check. If the disc runout is still excessive, a new one will have to be fitted, although machining by an engineer may be possible.

**3** The disc must not be machined or allowed to wear down to a thickness less than the service limit as listed in this Chapter's Specifications and as marked on the disc itself **(see illustration)**. The thickness of the disc can be checked with a micrometer **(see illustration)**. If the thickness of the disc is less than the service limit, a new one must be fitted.

### Removal

**4** Remove the wheel (see Section 14).
*Caution: Do not lay the wheel down and allow it to rest on the disc – the disc could become warped. Set the wheel on wood blocks so the disc doesn't support the weight of the wheel.*

**5** Mark the relationship of the disc to the wheel, so it can be installed in the same position. Unscrew the disc retaining bolts, loosening them evenly and a little at a time in a criss-cross pattern to avoid distorting the disc, then remove the disc from the wheel **(see illustration)**.

**4.3a  The minimum disc thickness is marked on the disc**

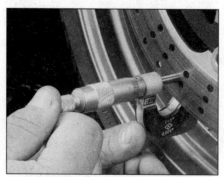

**4.3b  Using a micrometer to measure disc thickness**

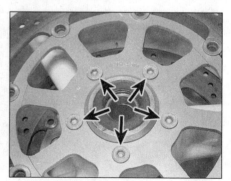

**4.5  The disc is secured by five bolts (arrowed)**

## Installation

**6** Install the disc on the wheel with its marked side facing out, aligning the previously applied matchmarks (if you're reinstalling the original disc).

**7** Clean the threads of the disc mounting bolts, then apply a suitable non-permanent thread locking compound. Install the bolts and tighten them evenly and a little at a time in a criss-cross pattern to the torque setting specified at the beginning of the Chapter. Clean off all grease from the brake disc using acetone or brake system cleaner. If a new brake disc has been installed, remove any protective coating from its working surfaces.

**8** Install the front wheel (see Section 14).

**9** Operate the brake lever several times to bring the pads into contact with the disc. Check the operation of the brakes carefully before riding the bike.

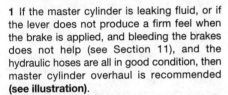

## 5 Front brake master cylinder – removal, overhaul and installation

**1** If the master cylinder is leaking fluid, or if the lever does not produce a firm feel when the brake is applied, and bleeding the brakes does not help (see Section 11), and the hydraulic hoses are all in good condition, then master cylinder overhaul is recommended **(see illustration)**.

**2** Before disassembling the master cylinder, read through the entire procedure and make sure that you have the correct rebuild kit. Also, you will need some new DOT 4 brake fluid, some clean rags and internal circlip pliers. **Note:** *To prevent damage to the paint from spilled brake fluid, always cover the fuel tank when working on the master cylinder.*
***Caution: Disassembly, overhaul and reassembly of the brake master cylinder must be done in a spotlessly clean work area to avoid contamination and possible failure of the brake hydraulic system components.***

### Removal

**3** Remove the reservoir cap clamp screw, then slacken the cap but do not fully unscrew it **(see illustration)**.

**4** Disconnect the electrical connectors from the brake light switch **(see illustration)**.

**5** Remove the front brake lever (see Chapter 6).

**6** Unscrew the brake hose banjo bolt and separate the hose from the master cylinder, noting its alignment **(see illustration)**. Discard the sealing washers as new ones must be used. Wrap the end of the hose in a clean rag and suspend it in an upright position or bend it down carefully and place the open end in a clean container. The objective is to prevent excessive loss of brake fluid, fluid spills and system contamination.

**7** Unscrew the bolt securing the reservoir

bracket to the handlebar **(see illustration 5.3)**. Unscrew the master cylinder clamp bolts, then lift the master cylinder and reservoir away from the handlebar **(see illustration)**.

**8** Unscrew the reservoir cap and remove the diaphragm plate and the diaphragm. Drain the

brake fluid from the master cylinder and reservoir into a suitable container. Release the clamp securing the reservoir hose to the union on the master cylinder and detach the hose **(see illustration 5.3)**. Wipe any remaining fluid out of the reservoir with a clean rag.

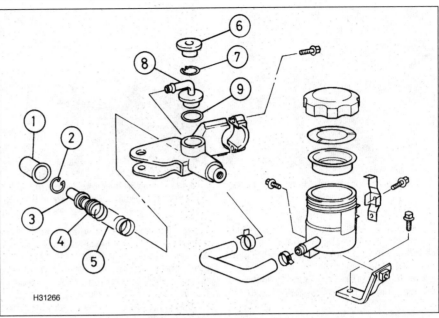

**5.1 Front brake master cylinder components**

| | | | | | |
|---|---|---|---|---|---|
| 1 | Rubber dust boot | 4 | Cup | 7 | Circlip |
| 2 | Circlip | 5 | Spring | 8 | Union |
| 3 | Piston assembly | 6 | Rubber cap | 9 | O-ring |

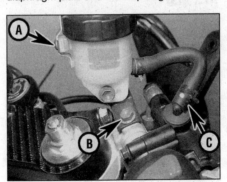

**5.3 Reservoir cap clamp screw (A), reservoir bracket bolt (B), hose union (C)**

**5.4 Brake light switch wiring connectors (A) and mounting screw (B)**

**5.6 Brake hose banjo bolt (arrowed)**

**5.7 Master cylinder clamp bolts (arrowed)**

**7**

5.10 Remove the rubber boot from the end of the master cylinder piston . . .

5.11a . . . then depress the piston and remove the circlip using a pair of internal circlip pliers

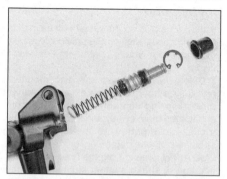

5.11b Lay out the internal parts as shown, even if new parts are being used, to avoid confusion on reassembly

**9** If required, remove the screw securing the brake light switch to the bottom of the master cylinder and remove the switch **(see illustration 5.4)**.
*Caution: Do not tip the master cylinder upside down or brake fluid will run out.*

## Overhaul

**10** Carefully remove the dust boot from the end of the piston **(see illustration)**.
**11** Using circlip pliers, remove the circlip and slide out the piston assembly and the spring, noting how they fit **(see illustration)**. Lay the parts out in the proper order to prevent confusion during reassembly **(see illustration)**.
**12** Remove the fluid reservoir hose union rubber cap, then remove the circlip and detach the union from the master cylinder. Discard the O-ring as a new one must be used. Inspect the reservoir hose for cracks or splits and renew it if necessary.
**13** Clean all parts with the correct type of clean brake fluid. If compressed air is available, use it to dry the parts thoroughly (make sure it's filtered and unlubricated).
*Caution: Do not, under any circumstances, use a petroleum-based solvent to clean brake parts.*
**14** Check the master cylinder bore for corrosion, scratches, nicks and score marks. If the necessary measuring equipment is available, compare the dimensions of the piston and bore to those given in the Specifications Section of this Chapter. If damage or wear is evident, the master cylinder must be renewed. If the master cylinder is in poor condition, then the calipers should be checked as well. Check that the fluid inlet and outlet ports in the master cylinder are clear.
**15** The dust boot, circlip, piston, seal, primary cup and spring are included in the rebuild kit. Use all of the new parts, regardless of the apparent condition of the old ones. If the seal and cup are not already on the piston, fit them according to the layout of the old piston assembly.
**16** Install the spring in the master cylinder so that its tapered end faces out towards the piston.
**17** Lubricate the piston, seal and cup with

clean brake fluid. Install the assembly into the master cylinder, making sure it is the correct way round **(see illustration 5.11b)**. Make sure the lips on the cup do not turn inside out when they are slipped into the bore. Depress the piston and install the new circlip, making sure that it locates in the master cylinder groove **(see illustration 5.11a)**.
**18** Install the rubber dust boot, making sure the lip is seated correctly in the piston groove **(see illustration 5.10)**.
**19** Fit a new O-ring onto the reservoir hose union, then press the union into the master cylinder and secure it with the circlip. Fit the rubber cap over the circlip.
**20** Inspect the reservoir cap rubber diaphragm and fit a new one it if it is damaged or deteriorated.

## Installation

**21** If removed, fit the brake light switch onto the bottom of the master cylinder **(see illustration 5.4)**.
**22** Attach the master cylinder to the handlebar and fit the clamp with its UP mark facing up **(see illustration 5.7)**. Align the clamp top mating surface with the punchmark in the handlebar, then tighten the upper bolt to the torque setting specified at the beginning of the Chapter, followed by the lower bolt **(see illustration)**.
**23** Connect the brake hose to the master cylinder, using new sealing washers on each side of the union, and aligning the hose as noted on removal **(see illustration 5.6)**.

5.22 Align the mating surfaces of the clamp with the punchmark (arrowed)

Tighten the banjo bolt to the torque setting specified at the beginning of this Chapter.
**24** Install the brake lever (see Chapter 6).
**25** Mount the reservoir onto the handlebar and tighten its bracket bolt securely **(see illustration 5.3)**. Connect the reservoir hose to the union and secure it with the clamp.
**26** Connect the brake light switch wiring **(see illustration 5.4)**.
**27** Fill the fluid reservoir with new DOT 4 brake fluid as described in *Daily (pre-ride) checks*. Refer to Section 11 of this Chapter and bleed the air from the system.
**28** Fit the rubber diaphragm, making sure it is correctly seated, the diaphragm plate and the cap onto the master cylinder reservoir. Tighten the cap and secure it with the clamp **(see illustration 5.3)**.
**29** Check the operation of the front brake before riding the motorcycle.

## 6 Rear brake pads – renewal

⚠️ *Warning: The dust created by the brake system may contain asbestos, which is harmful to your health. Never blow it out with compressed air and don't inhale any of it. An approved filtering mask should be worn when working on the brakes.*
**1** Prise off the brake pad cover using a flat-bladed screwdriver **(see illustration)**.

6.1 Prise off the cover . . .

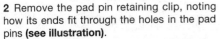

6.2 . . . then remove the pad pin retaining clip

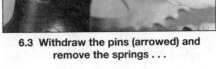

6.3 Withdraw the pins (arrowed) and remove the springs . . .

6.4 . . . then remove the pads and shims

**2** Remove the pad pin retaining clip, noting how its ends fit through the holes in the pad pins **(see illustration)**.

**3** Withdraw the pad pins from the caliper using a suitable pair of pliers and remove the pad springs, noting how they fit **(see illustration)**.

**4** Withdraw the pads from the caliper body and remove the anti-chatter shim from the back of each pad, noting how it fits **(see illustration)**.

**5** Inspect the surface of each pad for contamination and check that the friction material has not worn beyond its service limit (see Chapter 1, Section 11). If either pad is worn down to, or beyond, the service limit wear indicator (ie the wear indicator is no longer visible), fouled with oil or grease, or heavily scored or damaged by dirt and debris, both pads must be renewed as a set. Note that it is not possible to degrease the friction material; if the pads are contaminated in any way new ones must be fitted.

**6** If the pads are in good condition clean them carefully, using a fine wire brush which is completely free of oil and grease to remove all traces of road dirt and corrosion. Using a pointed instrument, clean out the grooves in the friction material and dig out any embedded particles of foreign matter. Any areas of glazing may be removed using emery cloth. Spray with a dedicated brake cleaner to remove any dust.

**7** Check the condition of the brake disc (see Section 8).

**8** Remove all traces of corrosion from the pad

pins. Inspect them for signs of damage, and renew them if necessary.

**9** Push the pistons as far back into the caliper as possible using hand pressure or a piece of wood as leverage **(see illustration 2.7)**. Due to the increased friction material thickness of new pads, it may be necessary to remove the master cylinder reservoir cover and diaphragm and siphon out some fluid. Remove the seat cowling to access the reservoir (see Chapter 8).

**10** Smear the backs of the pads and the shank of each pad pin with copper-based grease, making sure that none gets on the front or sides of the pads.

**11** Fit the anti-chatter shim onto the back of each pad with its open end facing forward **(see illustration)**. Insert the pads up into the caliper so that the friction material of each

6.11a Make sure the anti-chatter shims are the right way round

pad is facing the disc, then slide one pad pin, with its holed end on the outside, through the caliper and the holes in the pads **(see illustration)**. Slide the other pin into the outer pad only, then fit the pad springs, locating one end under the installed pad pin and onto the edge of the friction material, and fitting the central hooked section onto the bottom edge of the pad backing **(see illustration)**. Press up on the free end of the outer pad spring and slide the other pad pin over the spring end **(see illustration)**. Now press up on the inner spring end and slide the pin the rest of the way through. Secure the pins with the retaining clip, making sure that its ends fit through the holes in the pad pins – if necessary rotate the pad pins to align their holes correctly **(see illustration)**. Do not forget to install the pad cover.

6.11b Install one pin through both pads . . .

6.11c . . . and the other pin through one pad only, then install the springs . . .

6.11d . . . and push up on the spring end to locate it under the second pin as you slide it through

6.11e Do not forget the cover

7

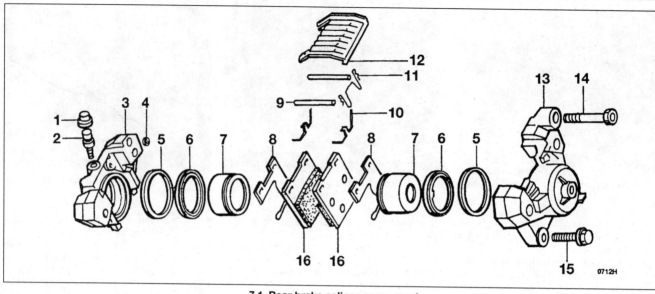

**7.1 Rear brake caliper components**

1 Bleed valve cap
2 Bleed valve
3 Caliper body half
4 Caliper seal

5 Piston seal
6 Dust seal
7 Piston
8 Anti-chatter shim

9 Pad pin
10 Pad spring
11 Pad pin clip
12 Brake pad cover

13 Caliper body half
14 Caliper joining bolt
15 Caliper mounting bolt
16 Brake pads

**12** Top up the master cylinder reservoir if necessary (see *Daily (pre-ride) checks*).
**13** Operate the brake pedal several times to bring the pads into contact with the disc. Check the operation of the brake before riding the motorcycle.

---

### 7 Rear brake caliper – removal, overhaul and installation

 **Warning: If a caliper indicates the need for an overhaul (usually due to leaking fluid or sticky operation), all old brake fluid should be flushed from the system. Also, the dust created by the brake system may contain asbestos, which is harmful to your health. Never blow it out with compressed air and don't inhale any of it. An approved filtering mask should be worn when working on the brakes. Do not, under any circumstances, use petroleum-based solvents to clean brake parts. Use the specified clean brake fluid, dedicated brake cleaner or denatured alcohol only, as described.**

#### Removal

**1** If the caliper is being overhauled, remove the brake pads (see Section 6). If the caliper is just being displaced or removed, the pads can be left in place **(see illustration)**.
**2** If the calipers are just being displaced and not completely removed or overhauled, do not disconnect the brake hose. If the calipers are being overhauled, note the alignment of the brake hose on the caliper then unscrew the

brake hose banjo bolt and separate the hose from the caliper **(see illustration)**. Plug the hose end or wrap a plastic bag tightly around it to minimise fluid loss and prevent dirt entering the system. Discard the sealing washers as new ones must be used on installation. **Note:** *If you are planning to overhaul the caliper and don't have a source of compressed air to blow out the pistons, just loosen the banjo bolt at this stage and retighten it lightly. The bike's hydraulic system can then be used to force the pistons out of the body once the pads have been removed. Disconnect the hose once the pistons have been sufficiently displaced.*
**3** If the caliper body is to be split into its halves for overhaul, slacken the caliper body joining bolts at this stage and retighten them lightly **(see illustration 7.2)**.
**4** Slacken the caliper mounting bolts, but do not yet remove them **(see illustration 7.2)**.

Unscrew the nut securing the brake torque arm to the caliper, but do not yet remove the bolt. **(see illustration 7.2)**.
**5** Unscrew the caliper mounting bolts, then support the caliper and withdraw the bolt from the torque arm. Drop the arm off the caliper and slide the caliper down off the disc **(see illustration)**.

#### Overhaul

**6** Clean the exterior of the caliper with denatured alcohol or brake system cleaner.
**7** Displace the pistons as far as possible from the caliper body, either by pumping them out by operating the rear brake pedal, or by forcing them out using compressed air – do not allow the piston heads to touch. If the compressed air method is used, place a wad of rag between the pistons to act as a cushion, then use compressed air directed into the fluid inlet to force the pistons out of

**7.2 Brake hose banjo bolt (A), caliper body joining bolts (B), caliper mounting bolts (C), torque arm nut (D)**

**7.5 Slide the caliper down off the disc**

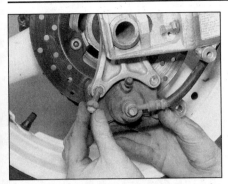

**7.18 Slide the caliper onto the disc and install the bolts**

**7.19a Locate the torque arm onto the caliper . . .**

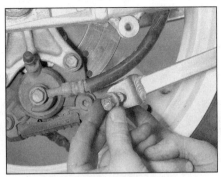

**7.19b . . . then fit the nut . . .**

the body. Use only low pressure to ease the pistons out. If the air pressure is too high and the pistons are forced out, the caliper and/or pistons may be damaged.

 *Warning: Never place your fingers in front of the piston in an attempt to catch or protect it when applying compressed air, as serious injury could result.*

**8** Unscrew the caliper body joining bolts and separate the body halves. Remove the piston from each half. Mark each piston head and caliper body with a felt marker to ensure that the pistons can be matched to their original bores on reassembly. Extract the caliper seal from whichever body half it is in and discard it as a new one must be used.

**9** Using a wooden or plastic tool, remove the dust seal from each caliper bore and discard them **(see illustration 3.8)**. New seals must be used on installation. If a metal tool is being used, take great care not to damage the caliper bore.

**10** Remove and discard the piston seals in the same way.

**11** Clean the pistons and bores with the correct type of clean brake fluid. If compressed air is available, use it to dry the parts thoroughly (make sure it's filtered and unlubricated).

*Caution: Do not, under any circumstances, use a petroleum-based solvent to clean brake parts.*

**12** Inspect the caliper bores and pistons for signs of corrosion, nicks and burrs and loss of plating. If surface defects are present, the caliper assembly must be renewed. If the necessary measuring equipment is available, compare the dimensions of the pistons and bores to those given in the Specifications Section of this Chapter, renewing any component that is worn beyond the service limit. If the caliper is in bad shape the master cylinder should also be checked.

**13** Lubricate the new piston seals with clean brake fluid and install them in their grooves in the caliper bores, making sure the thicker side of the seal is facing the disc **(see illustration 3.12)**.

**14** Lubricate the new dust seals with clean brake fluid and install each one in its groove in the caliper bore.

**15** Lubricate the pistons with clean brake fluid and install each one closed-end first into

**7.19c . . . and tighten it to the specified torque**

its caliper bore. Using your thumbs, push the pistons all the way in, making sure they enter the bores squarely.

**16** Lubricate the new caliper seal and install it into one half of the caliper body. Join the two halves of the caliper body together, making sure that the seal stays correctly seated in its recess. Install the caliper body joining bolts and tighten them to the torque setting specified at the beginning of the Chapter. If it is not possible to tighten the bolts fully at this stage, tighten them as much as possible, then tighten them fully once the caliper has been installed on the machine.

## Installation

**17** Push the pistons a little way back into the caliper using hand pressure or a piece of wood as leverage.

**18** Slide the caliper onto the brake disc, making

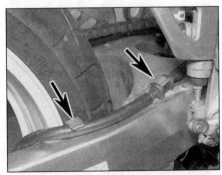

**7.21a Locate the hose in its open guides (arrowed) . . .**

**7.19d Now tighten the caliper mounting bolts to the specified torque**

sure the pads sit squarely either side of the disc if they weren't removed **(see illustration 7.5)**. Install the caliper mounting bolts, and tighten them finger-tight **(see illustration)**.

**19** Fit the brake torque arm onto the caliper and secure it with its bolt **(see illustration)**. Tighten the nut to the torque setting specified at the beginning of the Chapter **(see illustrations)**. Now tighten the caliper mounting bolts to the specified torque setting **(see illustration)**.

**20** If the calipers were overhauled and if not already done, tighten the caliper body joining bolts to the specified torque setting **(see illustration 7.2)**.

**21** If removed, connect the brake hose to the caliper, making sure it is routed through its guides on the swingarm, using new sealing washers on each side of the fitting **(see illustrations)**. Align the hose as noted on

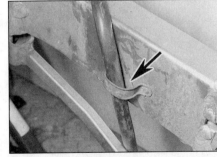

**7.21b . . . and make sure it passes through the closed guide on the inside of the swingarm (arrowed)**

**7**

**8.3 The disc is secured by five bolts (arrowed)**

removal **(see illustration 7.2)**. Tighten the banjo bolt to the torque setting specified at the beginning of the Chapter. Top up the master cylinder reservoir with DOT 4 brake fluid (see *Daily (pre-ride) checks*) and bleed the hydraulic system as described in Section 11.

**22** If removed, install the brake pads (see Section 6).

**23** Check for leaks and thoroughly test the operation of the brake before riding the motorcycle.

## 8 Rear brake disc – inspection, removal and installation

### Inspection

**1** Refer to Section 4 of this Chapter, noting that the dial gauge should be attached to the swingarm.

### Removal

**2** Remove the rear wheel (see Section 15).
**3** Mark the relationship of the disc to the wheel so it can be installed in the same position. Unscrew the disc retaining bolts, loosening them evenly and a little at a time in a criss-cross pattern to avoid distorting the disc, and remove the disc **(see illustration)**.

### Installation

**4** Install the disc on the wheel with its marked side facing out, aligning the previously applied matchmarks (if you're reinstalling the original disc).
**5** Clean the threads of the disc mounting bolts, then apply a suitable non-permanent thread locking compound. Install the bolts and tighten them evenly and a little at a time in a criss-cross pattern to the torque setting specified at the beginning of the Chapter. Clean off all grease from the brake disc using acetone or brake system cleaner. If a new brake disc has been installed, remove any protective coating from its working surfaces.
**6** Install the rear wheel (see Section 15).
**7** Operate the brake pedal several times to

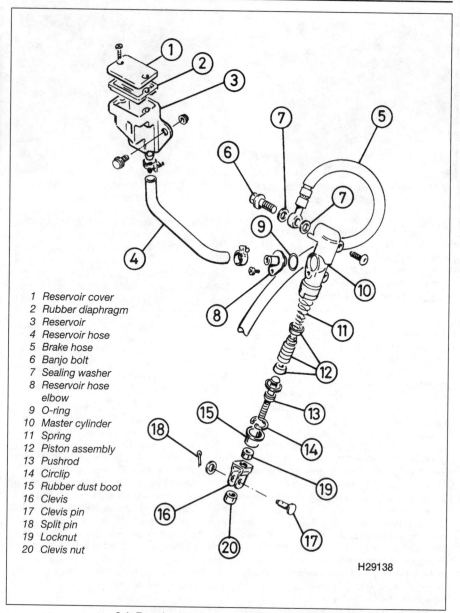

1 Reservoir cover
2 Rubber diaphragm
3 Reservoir
4 Reservoir hose
5 Brake hose
6 Banjo bolt
7 Sealing washer
8 Reservoir hose elbow
9 O-ring
10 Master cylinder
11 Spring
12 Piston assembly
13 Pushrod
14 Circlip
15 Rubber dust boot
16 Clevis
17 Clevis pin
18 Split pin
19 Locknut
20 Clevis nut

H29138

**9.1 Rear brake master cylinder components**

bring the pads into contact with the disc. Check the operation of the brake carefully before riding the motorcycle.

## 9 Rear brake master cylinder – removal, overhaul and installation

**1** If the master cylinder is leaking fluid, or if the lever does not produce a firm feel when the brake is applied, and bleeding the brakes does not help (see Section 11), and the hydraulic hoses are all in good condition, then master cylinder overhaul is recommended **(see illustration)**.
**2** Before disassembling the master cylinder, read through the entire procedure and make

sure that you have the correct rebuild kit. Also, you will need some new DOT 4 brake fluid, some clean rags and internal circlip pliers. **Note:** *To prevent damage to the paint from spilled brake fluid, always cover the surrounding components when working on the master cylinder.*
**Caution: Disassembly, overhaul and reassembly of the brake master cylinder must be done in a spotlessly clean work area to avoid contamination and possible failure of the brake hydraulic system components.**

### Removal

**3** Remove the seat cowling (see Chapter 8).
**4** Remove the master cylinder fluid reservoir cover screws, but leave the cover in place

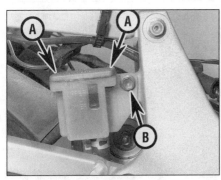

9.4a Reservoir cover screws (A), reservoir mounting bolt (B)

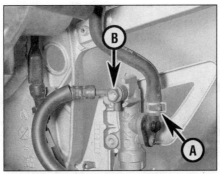

9.4b Reservoir hose clamp (A), brake hose banjo bolt (B)

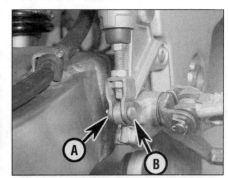

9.6 Remove the split pin and washer (A) and withdraw the clevis pin (B)

(see illustration). Unscrew the bolt securing the reservoir to the frame, then remove the reservoir cover and diaphragm and pour the fluid into a container. Release the clamp securing the reservoir hose to the union on the master cylinder and detach the hose – have a rag handy to catch any drips (see illustration).

5 Unscrew the brake hose banjo bolt and separate the brake hose from the master cylinder, noting its alignment (see illustration 9.4b). Discard the two sealing washers as they must be renewed. Wrap the end of the hose in a clean rag and suspend the hose in an upright position or bend it down carefully and place the open end in a clean container. The objective is to prevent excessive loss of brake fluid, fluid spills and system contamination.

6 Remove the split pin and washer from the clevis pin securing the master cylinder pushrod to the brake pedal (see illustration). Withdraw the clevis pin and separate the pushrod from the pedal. Discard the split pin as a new one must be used.

7 Unscrew the two bolts securing the heel plate and master cylinder to the bracket (see illustration).

### Overhaul

8 If required, mark the position of the clevis locknut on the pushrod, then slacken the locknut and thread the clevis and its base nut off the pushrod (see illustration).

9 Dislodge the rubber dust boot from the base of the master cylinder to reveal the pushrod retaining circlip (see illustration).

10 Depress the pushrod and, using circlip pliers, remove the circlip (see illustration). Slide out the piston assembly and spring. If they are difficult to remove, apply low pressure compressed air to the fluid outlet. Lay the parts out in the proper order to prevent confusion during reassembly.

11 Clean all of the parts with DOT 4 brake fluid.

Caution: Do not, under any circumstances, use a petroleum-based solvent to clean brake parts. If compressed air is available, use it to dry the parts thoroughly (make sure it's filtered and unlubricated).

12 Check the master cylinder bore for corrosion, scratches, nicks and score marks. If the necessary measuring equipment is available, compare the dimensions of the piston and bore to those given in the Specifications Section of this Chapter. If damage is evident, the master cylinder must be renewed. If the master cylinder is in poor condition, then the caliper should be checked as well.

13 Unscrew the fluid reservoir hose union screw and detach the union from the master cylinder. Discard the O-ring as a new one must be used. Inspect the reservoir hose for cracks or splits and renew it if necessary.

14 The dust boot, circlip, piston, seal, primary cup and spring are included in the

rebuild kit. Use all of the new parts, regardless of the apparent condition of the old ones. If the seal and cup are not already on the piston, fit them according to the layout of the old piston assembly.

15 Install the spring in the master cylinder so that its tapered end faces out towards the piston.

16 Lubricate the piston, seal and cup with clean brake fluid. Install the assembly into the master cylinder, making sure it is the correct way round (see illustration 9.1). Make sure the lips on the cup do not turn inside out when they are slipped into the bore.

17 Install and depress the pushrod, then fit a new circlip, making sure it is properly seated in the groove (see illustration 9.10).

18 Fit the rubber dust boot, making sure the

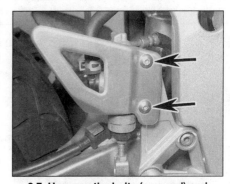

9.7 Unscrew the bolts (arrowed) and remove the heel plate and master cylinder

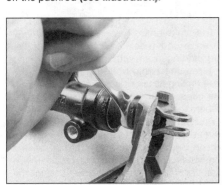

9.8 Hold the clevis and slacken the locknut

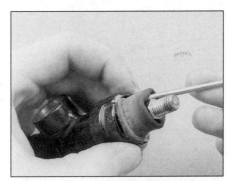

9.9 Remove the dust boot from the pushrod . . .

9.10 . . . then depress the piston and remove the circlip

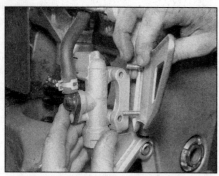

9.21 Locate the master cylinder and install the heel plate and bolts

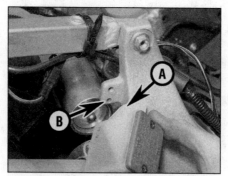

9.24 Locate the pin (A) in the hole (B)

10.2 Flex the brake hoses and check for cracks, bulges and leaking fluid

lip is seated properly in its groove (see illustration 9.9).

19 Fit a new O-ring onto the fluid reservoir hose union, then install the union onto the master cylinder and secure it with its screw.

## Installation

20 If removed, install the clevis locknut, the clevis and its base nut onto the master cylinder pushrod end. Position the clevis as noted on removal, but do not yet tighten the locknut.

21 Locate the master cylinder on the inside of the footrest bracket, then install the heel plate and tighten the mounting bolts to the torque setting specified at the beginning of the Chapter (see illustration).

22 Align the brake pedal with the master cylinder pushrod clevis, then slide in the clevis pin, fit the washer and secure it using a new

split pin (see illustration 9.6). If the clevis position on the pushrod was disturbed during overhaul, reset the brake pedal to its specified height (see Chapter 1, Section 12). Tighten the clevis locknut securely.

23 Connect the brake hose banjo bolt to the master cylinder, using a new sealing washer on each side of the banjo union (see illustration 9.4b). Ensure that the hose is positioned so that it butts against the lugs and tighten the banjo bolt to the specified torque setting.

24 Secure the fluid reservoir to the frame with its retaining bolt, making sure the pin on the reservoir locates in the lower hole (see illustration). Ensure that the hose is correctly routed behind the frame tube, then connect it to the union on the master cylinder and secure it with the clamp (see illustration 9.4b). Check that the hose is secure

and clamped at the reservoir end as well. If the clamps have weakened, use new ones.

25 Fill the fluid reservoir with new DOT 4 brake fluid (see Daily (pre-ride) checks) and bleed the system following the procedure in Section 11.

26 Fit the rubber diaphragm, making sure it is correctly seated, and the cover onto the master cylinder reservoir. Tighten the cover screws.

27 Install the seat cowling (see Chapter 8). Check the operation of the brake carefully before riding the motorcycle.

## 10 Brake hoses and unions – inspection and renewal

## Inspection

1 Brake hose condition should be checked regularly and the hoses renewed at the specified interval (see Chapter 1).

2 Twist and flex the rubber hoses while looking for cracks, bulges and seeping fluid (see illustration). Check extra carefully around the areas where the hoses connect with the banjo fittings, as these are common areas for hose failure.

3 Inspect the metal banjo union fittings connected to the brake hoses. If the fittings are rusted, scratched or cracked, fit new hoses.

## Renewal

4 The brake hoses have banjo union fittings on each end (see illustration). Cover the surrounding area with plenty of rags and unscrew the banjo bolt at each end of the hose, noting its alignment. Free the hose from any clips or guides and remove the hose. Discard the sealing washers.

5 Position the new hose, making sure it isn't twisted or otherwise strained, and abut the tab on the hose union with the lug on the component casting, where present. Otherwise align the hose as noted on removal. Install the banjo bolts, using new sealing washers on both sides of the unions, and tighten them to the torque setting specified at the beginning

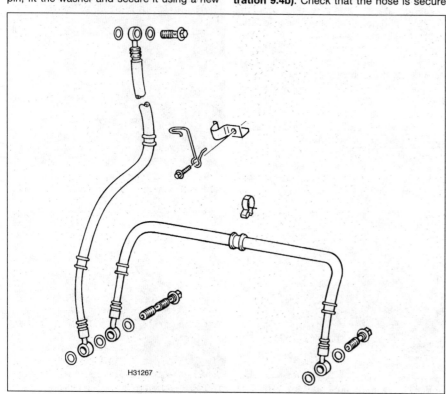

H31267

10.4 Front brake hose arrangement

**10.5 Use a new sealing washer on each side of the union**

**11.6a Remove the dust cap from the caliper bleed valve**

**11.6b To bleed the brakes you need a spanner to fit on the bleed valve, a short section of clear tubing, and a clear container part-filled with brake fluid so that the end of the tubing is submerged**

of this Chapter (see illustration). Make sure they are correctly aligned and routed clear of all moving components.

6 Flush the old brake fluid from the system, refill with new DOT 4 brake fluid (see *Daily (pre-ride) checks*) and bleed the air from the system (see Section 11). Check the operation of the brakes carefully before riding the motorcycle.

## 11 Brake system – bleeding

1 Bleeding the brakes is simply the process of removing all the air bubbles from the brake fluid reservoirs, the hoses and the brake calipers. Bleeding is necessary whenever a brake system hydraulic connection is loosened, when a component or hose is renewed, or when the master cylinder or caliper is overhauled. Leaks in the system may also allow air to enter, but leaking brake fluid will reveal their presence and warn you of the need for repair.

2 To bleed the brakes, you will need some new DOT 4 brake fluid, a length of clear vinyl or plastic tubing, a small container partially filled with clean brake fluid, some rags and a spanner to fit the brake caliper bleed valves.

3 Cover the fuel tank and other painted components to prevent damage in the event that brake fluid is spilled.

4 If bleeding the rear brake, remove the seat cowling (see Chapter 8) for access to the fluid reservoir.

5 Remove the reservoir cap or cover, diaphragm plate (front reservoir) and diaphragm and slowly pump the brake lever or pedal a few times, until no air bubbles can be seen floating up from the holes in the bottom of the reservoir. Doing this bleeds the air from the master cylinder end of the line. Loosely refit the reservoir cap or cover.

6 Pull the dust cap off the bleed valve (see illustration). Attach one end of the clear vinyl or plastic tubing to the bleed valve and submerge the other end in the brake fluid in the container (see illustration).

7 Remove the reservoir cap or cover and check the fluid level. Do not allow the fluid level to drop below the lower mark during the bleeding process.

8 Carefully pump the brake lever or pedal three or four times and hold it in (front) or down (rear) while opening the caliper bleed valve. When the valve is opened, brake fluid will flow out of the caliper into the clear tubing and the lever will move toward the handlebar or the pedal will move down.

9 Retighten the bleed valve, then release the brake lever or pedal gradually. Repeat the process until no air bubbles are visible in the brake fluid leaving the caliper, or if the fluid is being changed until new fluid is coming out, and the lever or pedal is firm when applied. On completion, disconnect the bleeding equipment, then tighten the bleed valve to the torque setting specified at the beginning of the chapter and install the dust cap.

> **HAYNES HINT** *Old brake fluid is invariably much darker in colour than new fluid, making it easy to see when all old fluid has been expelled from the system.*

10 Install the diaphragm, diaphragm plate (front reservoir) and cap or cover, not forgetting the cap clamp on the front reservoir. Wipe up any spilled brake fluid and check the entire system for leaks.

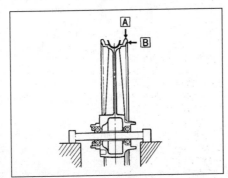

**12.2 Check the wheel for radial (out-of-round) runout (A) and axial (side-to-side) runout (B)**

> **HAYNES HINT** *If it's not possible to produce a firm feel to the lever or pedal the fluid my be aerated. Let the brake fluid in the system stabilise for a few hours and then repeat the procedure when the tiny bubbles in the system have settled out.*

## 12 Wheels – inspection and repair

1 In order to carry out a proper inspection of the wheels, it is necessary to support the bike upright so that the wheel being inspected is raised off the ground. Position the motorcycle on an auxiliary stand. Clean the wheels thoroughly to remove mud and dirt that may interfere with the inspection procedure or mask defects. Make a general check of the wheels (see Chapter 1) and tyres (see *Daily (pre-ride) checks*).

2 Attach a dial gauge to the fork or the swingarm and position its stem against the side of the rim (see illustration). Spin the wheel slowly and check the axial (side-to-side) runout of the rim. In order to accurately check radial (out of round) runout with the dial gauge, the wheel would have to be removed from the machine, and the tyre from the wheel. With the axle clamped in a vice and the dial gauge positioned on the top of the rim, the wheel can be rotated to check the runout.

3 An easier, though slightly less accurate, method is to attach a stiff wire pointer to the fork or the swingarm and position the end a fraction of an inch from the wheel (where the wheel and tyre join). If the wheel is true, the distance from the pointer to the rim will be constant as the wheel is rotated. **Note:** *If wheel runout is excessive, check the wheel or hub bearings very carefully before renewing the wheel.*

**7**

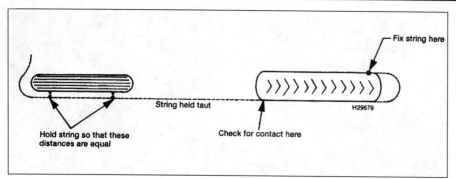

**13.5 Wheel alignment check using string**

**4** The wheels should also be visually inspected for cracks, flat spots on the rim and other damage. Look very closely for dents in the area where the tyre bead contacts the rim. Dents in this area may prevent complete sealing of the tyre against the rim, which leads to deflation of the tyre over a period of time. If damage is evident, or if runout in either direction is excessive, the wheel will have to be renewed. Never attempt to repair a damaged cast alloy wheel.

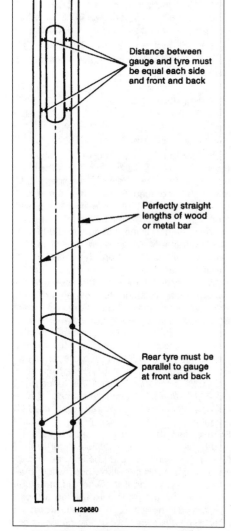

**13.7 Wheel alignment check using a straight-edge**

## 13 Wheels – alignment check

**1** Misalignment of the wheels, which may be due to a cocked rear wheel or a bent frame or fork yokes, can cause strange and possibly serious handling problems. If the frame or yokes are at fault, repair by a frame specialist or renewal with new parts are the only alternatives.
**2** To check the alignment you will need an assistant, a length of string or a perfectly straight piece of wood and a ruler. A plumb bob or other suitable weight will also be required.
**3** In order to make a proper check of the wheels it is necessary to support the bike in an upright position, using an auxiliary stand. Measure the width of both tyres at their widest points. Subtract the smaller measurement from the larger measurement, then divide the difference by two. The result is the amount of offset that should exist between the front and rear tyres on both sides.
**4** If a string is used, have your assistant hold one end of it about halfway between the floor and the rear axle, touching the rear sidewall of the tyre.
**5** Run the other end of the string forward and pull it tight so that it is roughly parallel to the floor **(see illustration)**. Slowly bring the string into contact with the front sidewall of the rear tyre, then turn the front wheel until it is parallel with the string. Measure the distance from the front tyre sidewall to the string.
**6** Repeat the procedure on the other side of the motorcycle. The distance from the front tyre sidewall to the string should be equal on both sides.
**7** As was previously pointed out, a perfectly straight length of wood or metal bar may be substituted for the string **(see illustration)**. The procedure is the same.

**8** If the distance between the string and tyre is greater on one side, or if the rear wheel appears to be cocked, refer to Chapter 1, Section 1 and check that the chain adjuster markings coincide on each side of the swingarm.
**9** If the front-to-back alignment is correct, the wheels still may be out of alignment vertically.
**10** Using the plumb bob, or other suitable weight, and a length of string, check the rear wheel to make sure it is vertical. To do this, hold the string against the tyre upper sidewall and allow the weight to settle just off the floor. When the string touches both the upper and lower tyre sidewalls and is perfectly straight, the wheel is vertical. If it is not, place thin spacers under one leg of the stand.
**11** Once the rear wheel is vertical, check the front wheel in the same manner. If both wheels are not perfectly vertical, the frame and/or major suspension components are bent.

## 14 Front wheel – removal and installation

### Removal

**1** Remove the fairing side panels (see Chapter 8). Position the motorcycle on an auxiliary stand and support it under the crankcase so that the front wheel is off the ground. Always make sure the motorcycle is properly supported.
**2** Remove the brake caliper mounting bolts and slide the calipers off the disc **(see illustration 3.4a and b)**. Support the calipers with pieces of wire, string or bungee cords so that no strain is placed on the hydraulic hoses. There is no need to disconnect the hoses from the calipers. **Note:** *Do not operate the front brake lever with the calipers removed.*
**3** Slacken the axle clamp bolts on the bottom of the right-hand fork, then unscrew the axle **(see illustration)**. Support the wheel (a good way to do this is to slide your foot part way under it), then withdraw the axle from the right-hand side, drawing the wheel to the right as you do so that it comes off the axle holder

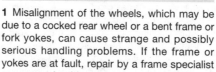

**14.3a Slacken the axle clamp bolts (A), then unscrew the axle (B)**

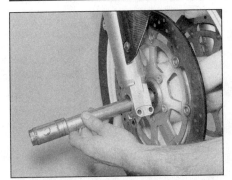

14.3b Withdraw the axle and remove the wheel

14.4 Remove the axle holder if required

14.9 Tighten the axle to the specified torque

in the bottom of the left-hand fork, and carefully lower the wheel **(see illustration)**.
**4** If required (ie if the forks are being disassembled), slacken the axle holder clamp bolts on the bottom of the left-hand fork and withdraw the holder **(see illustration)**.
*Caution: Don't lay the wheel down and allow it to rest on the disc – the disc could become warped. Set the wheel on wood blocks so the disc doesn't support the weight of the wheel.*
**5** Check the axle for straightness by rolling it on a flat surface such as a piece of plate glass (first wipe off all old grease and remove any corrosion using fine emery cloth). If the equipment is available, place the axle in V-blocks and measure the runout using a dial gauge. If the axle is bent or the runout exceeds the limit specified, fit a new one.
**6** Check the condition of the wheel bearings (see Section 16).

### Installation

**7** Manoeuvre the wheel into position, making sure the directional arrow is pointing in the normal direction of rotation. Apply a thin coat of grease to the axle and to the lips of the bearing seals.
**8** If removed, locate the axle holder into the bottom of the left-hand fork and push it in so that its flanged rim is pressed against the fork, then tighten the holder clamp bolts to the

torque setting specified at the beginning of the Chapter, making sure the holder remains pressed against the fork **(see illustration 14.4)**.
**9** Lift the wheel between the forks and slide the axle through from the right-hand side, and thread it into the holder **(see illustration 14.3b)**. Now slide the wheel to the left so that the inner end of the holder locates into the bearing seal, then tighten the axle to the torque setting specified at the beginning of the Chapter **(see illustration)**.
**10** Push the pistons a little way back into the caliper using hand pressure or a piece of wood on the pads as leverage. Slide the brake calipers onto the discs, making sure the pads sit squarely on each side of the discs **(see illustration 3.16)**. Tighten the caliper mounting bolts to the torque setting specified at the beginning of the Chapter **(see illustrations 3.17)**.
**11** Apply the front brake a few times to bring the pads back into contact with the discs. Move the motorcycle off its stand, apply the front brake and pump the front forks a few times to settle all components in position.
**12** Tighten the axle clamp bolts on the right-hand fork to the specified torque setting.
**13** Install the fairing side panels (see Chapter 8).
**14** Check for correct operation of the front brake before riding the motorcycle.

### 15 Rear wheel – removal and installation

### Removal

**1** Position the motorcycle on an auxiliary stand so that the wheel is just off the ground. If required, remove the lower fairing and/or fairing side panels so that the stand can be fitted (see Chapter 8).
**2** On US models, remove the split pin from the axle nut.
**3** Unscrew the axle nut, and on UK models remove the washer **(see illustration)**. Remove the chain adjuster block, noting how it fits **(see illustration)**.
**4** Support the wheel (a good way to do this is to slide your foot part way under it) then withdraw the axle along with the adjuster block from the right-hand side **(see illustration)**. Gently lower the wheel to the ground, making sure no strain is placed on the brake hose as the caliper lowers with it, then disengage the chain from the sprocket and draw the wheel back so the disc is clear of the caliper and remove the wheel. Note how the axle passes through the caliper mounting bracket.
**5** Remove the spacers from both sides of the

15.3a Unscrew the axle nut and washer (UK models) . . .

15.3b . . . and remove the chain adjuster block

15.4 Withdraw the axle from the right and lower the wheel

**15.5 Remove the spacers from the wheel**

**15.9 Fit the spacer into each side of the wheel**

**15.10 Locate the caliper onto the disc . . .**

wheel, noting which fits on which side **(see illustration)**.

*Caution: Do not lay the wheel down and allow it to rest on the disc or the sprocket – they could become warped. Set the wheel on wood blocks so the disc or the sprocket doesn't support the weight of the wheel. Do not operate the brake pedal with the wheel removed.*

6 Check the axle for straightness by rolling it on a flat surface such as a piece of plate glass (if the axle is corroded, first remove the corrosion with fine emery cloth). If the equipment is available, place the axle in V-blocks and measure the runout using a dial gauge. If the axle is bent or the runout exceeds the limit specified at the beginning of the Chapter, fit a new one.

7 Check the condition of the wheel bearings (see Section 16).

### Installation

8 Push the pistons a little way back into the brake caliper using hand pressure or a piece of wood on the pads as leverage.

9 Apply a thin coat of grease to the lips of each bearing seal, to the inside and the inner faces of the spacers where they contact the seals, and to the axle. Install the spacers into the wheel **(see illustration and 15.5)**. Slide the right-hand side adjuster block onto the axle, making sure it is the right way round.

10 Manoeuvre the wheel so that it is in between the ends of the swingarm and move

it forward so that the brake disc slides into the caliper, making sure the pads sit squarely on each side of the disc **(see illustration)**.

11 Engage the drive chain with the sprocket, then lift the wheel into position, making sure the caliper stays on the disc and the caliper bracket is correctly aligned with the wheel and the swingarm, and the spacers remain correctly in place in the wheel **(see illustration)**.

12 Install the axle from the right, making sure it passes through the caliper mounting bracket **(see illustration)**. Push it all the way through, locating the chain adjuster block in the swingarm and the flats on the axle head in the adjuster block. Check that everything is correctly aligned, then fit the left-hand side adjuster block, the washer (UK models) and the axle nut, but do not tighten it yet **(see illustrations 15.3b and a)**. If it is difficult to insert the axle due to the tension of the drive chain, back off the chain adjusters (see Chapter 1).

13 Adjust the chain slack as described in Chapter 1.

14 Tighten the axle nut to the torque setting specified at the beginning of the Chapter. On US models, fit a new split pin into the nut.

15 Operate the brake pedal several times to bring the pads into contact with the disc. Check the operation of the rear brake carefully before riding the bike.

## 16 Wheel bearings – removal, inspection and installation

### Front wheel bearings

**Note:** *Always renew the wheel bearings in pairs. Never renew the bearings individually. Avoid using a high pressure cleaner on the wheel bearing area.*

1 Remove the wheel (see Section 14).

2 Set the wheel on blocks so as not to allow the weight of the wheel to rest on the brake disc.

3 Lever out the bearing seal on each side of the wheel using a flat-bladed screwdriver, taking care not to damage the rim of the hub **(see illustration)**. Discard the seals as new ones should be used.

**HAYNES HiNT** *A small block of wood placed between the screwdriver and the rim will negate the possibility of damage and will improve leverage.*

4 Using a metal rod (preferably a brass drift punch) inserted through the centre of one bearing, tap evenly around the inner race of the other bearing to drive it from the hub **(see**

**15.11 . . . and fit the chain around the sprocket . . .**

**15.12 . . . then lift the wheel and slide in the axle**

**16.3 Lever out the bearing seals . . .**

**16.4a . . . then drive out the bearings . . .**

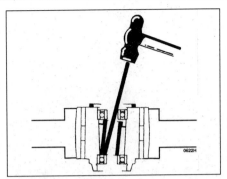

**16.4b . . . locating the drift as shown**

**16.9 Drive the new bearings into place . . .**

illustrations). The bearing spacer will also come out.

**5** Lay the wheel on its other side so that the remaining bearing faces down. Drive the bearing out of the wheel using the same technique as above.

**6** If the bearings are of the unsealed type or are only sealed on one side, clean them with a high flash-point solvent (one which won't leave any residue) and blow them dry with compressed air (don't let the bearings spin as you dry them). Apply a few drops of oil to the bearing. **Note:** *If the bearing is sealed on both sides don't attempt to clean it.*

**HAYNES HINT** *Refer to Tools and Workshop Tips (Section 5) for more information about bearings.*

**7** Hold the outer race of the bearing and rotate the inner race – if the bearing doesn't turn smoothly, has rough spots or is noisy, renew it.

**8** If the bearing is good and can be re-used, wash it in solvent once again and dry it, then pack the bearing with grease.

**9** Thoroughly clean the hub area of the wheel. First install the left-hand side bearing into its recess in the hub, with the marked or sealed side facing outwards. Using the old bearing (if new ones are being fitted), a bearing driver or a socket large enough to contact the outer race of the bearing, drive it

in until it's completely seated **(see illustration)**.

**10** Turn the wheel over and install the bearing spacer. Drive the right-hand side bearing into place as described above.

**11** Apply a smear of grease to the lips of the seals, then press them into the wheel, using a seal or bearing driver, a suitable socket or a flat piece of wood to drive it into place if necessary **(see illustration)**.

**12** Clean off all grease from the brake discs using acetone or brake system cleaner, then install the wheel (see Section 14).

### Rear wheel bearings

**13** Remove the rear wheel (see Section 15). Lift the sprocket coupling out of the wheel, noting how it fits **(see illustration)**. If not already done, remove the spacer from the right-hand side of the wheel **(see illustration 15.5)**.

**14** Set the wheel on blocks so as not to allow the weight of the wheel to rest on the brake disc.

**15** Lever out the bearing seal on the right-hand side of the wheel using a flat-bladed screwdriver, taking care not to damage the rim of the hub (see *Haynes Hint* after step 3) **(see illustration 16.3)**. Discard the seal as a new one should be used.

**16** Using a suitable socket located onto the rim of the bearing spacer, which fits inside the bearing, drive out the bearing on the other side **(see illustration)**. The bearing spacer will also come out.

**17** Lay the wheel on its other side so that the remaining bearing faces down. Drive the bearing out of the wheel using the same technique as above.

**18** Refer to Steps 6 to 8 above and check the bearings.

**19** Thoroughly clean the hub area of the wheel. First install the right-hand bearing into its recess in the hub, with the marked or sealed side facing outwards. Using the old bearing (if new ones are being fitted), a bearing driver or a socket large enough to contact the outer race of the bearing, drive it in squarely until it's completely seated **(see illustration 16.9)**.

**20** Turn the wheel over and install the bearing spacer. Drive the left-hand side bearing into place as described above **(see illustration)**.

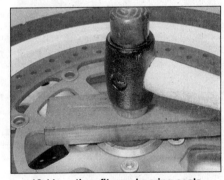

**16.11 . . . then fit new bearing seals**

**16.13 Lift the sprocket coupling out of the wheel**

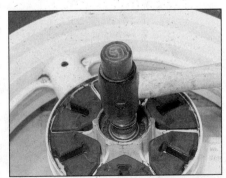

**16.16 Locate the socket inside the bearing and onto the rim of the spacer and drive out the opposite bearing**

**16.20 Drive in the new bearings using a suitable socket**

16.27 Drive the bearing out from the inside . . .

16.29 . . . and drive the new bearing in from the outside

16.30 Fit the spacer into the bearing

**21** Apply a smear of grease to the lips of the new grease seal, then press it into the right-hand side of the wheel, using a seal or bearing driver, a suitable socket or a flat piece of wood to drive it into place if necessary **(see illustration 16.11).**
**22** Clean off all grease from the brake disc using acetone or brake system cleaner. Fit the sprocket coupling into the wheel, making sure the coupling spacer locates into the bearing **(see illustration 16.13).**
**23** Install the wheel (see Section 15).

### Sprocket coupling bearing

**24** Remove the rear wheel (see Section 15). Lift the sprocket coupling out of the wheel, noting how it fits **(see illustration 16.13).**
**25** If not already done, remove the spacer from the outside of the sprocket coupling **(see illustration 15.9).** Also remove the spacer from the inside of the coupling, noting which way round it fits **(see illustration 16.30).**
**26** Lever out the bearing seal on the outside of the coupling using a flat-bladed screwdriver, taking care not to damage the rim

of the hub (see **Haynes Hint** after step 3). Discard the seal as a new one should be used.
**27** Support the coupling on blocks of wood and drive the bearing out from the inside using a bearing driver or socket **(see illustration).**
**28** Refer to Steps 6 to 8 above and check the bearings.
**29** Thoroughly clean the bearing recess then install the bearing into the outside of the coupling, with the marked or sealed side facing out. Using the old bearing (if new ones are being fitted), a bearing driver or a socket large enough to contact the outer race of the bearing, drive it in until it is completely seated.
**30** Fit the spacer into the inside of the coupling, making sure it locates into the bearing **(see illustration).**
**31** Apply a smear of grease to the lips of the new seal, then press it into the coupling, using a seal or bearing driver, a suitable socket or a flat piece of wood to drive it into place if necessary.
**32** Check the sprocket coupling/rubber damper (see Chapter 6).

**33** Clean off all grease from the brake disc using acetone or brake system cleaner. Fit the sprocket coupling into the wheel, making sure the coupling spacer locates into the bearing **(see illustration 16.13).**
**34** Install the wheel (see Section 15).

### 17 Tyres –
general information and fitting

#### General information

**1** The wheels fitted to all models are designed to take tubeless tyres only. Tyre sizes are given in the Specifications at the beginning of this chapter.
**2** Refer to the *Daily (pre-ride) checks* listed at the beginning of this manual for tyre maintenance.

#### Fitting new tyres

**3** When selecting new tyres, refer to the tyre information label on the swingarm and the tyre options listed in the owners handbook. Ensure that front and rear tyre types are compatible, the correct size and correct speed rating; if necessary seek advice from a Suzuki dealer or tyre fitting specialist **(see illustration).**
**4** It is recommended that tyres are fitted by a motorcycle tyre specialist rather than attempted in the home workshop. This is particularly relevant in the case of tubeless tyres because the force required to break the seal between the wheel rim and tyre bead is substantial, and is usually beyond the capabilities of an individual working with normal tyre levers. Additionally, the specialist will be able to balance the wheels after tyre fitting.
**5** Note that punctured tubeless tyres can in some cases be repaired. Repairs must be carried out by a motorcycle tyre fitting specialist. Suzuki advise that a repaired tyre should not be used at speeds above 50 mph (80 kmh) for the first 24 hours, and not above 80 mph (130 kmh) thereafter.

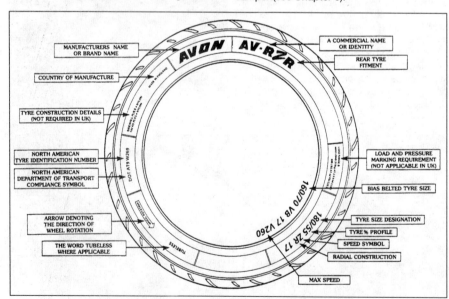

17.3 Common tyre sidewall markings

# Chapter 8
# Bodywork

## Contents

## Degrees of difficulty

| | | | | |
|---|---|---|---|---|
| **Easy,** suitable for novice with little experience  | **Fairly easy,** suitable for beginner with some experience  | **Fairly difficult,** suitable for competent DIY mechanic  | **Difficult,** suitable for experienced DIY mechanic  | **Very difficult,** suitable for expert DIY or professional |

## 1  General information

This Chapter covers the procedures necessary to remove and install the body parts. Since many service and repair operations on these motorcycles require the removal of the body parts, the procedures are grouped here and referred to from other Chapters.

In the case of damage to the body parts, it is usually necessary to remove the broken component and replace it with a new (or used) one. The material that the body panels are composed of doesn't lend itself to conventional repair techniques. Note that there are however some companies that specialise in 'plastic welding' and there are a number of bodywork repair kits now available for motorcycles.

When attempting to remove any body panel, first study it closely, noting any fasteners and associated fittings, to be sure of returning everything to its correct place on installation. In some cases the aid of an assistant will be required when removing panels, to help avoid the risk of damage to paintwork. Once the evident fasteners have been removed, try to withdraw the panel as described but DO NOT FORCE IT – if it will not release, check that all fasteners have been removed and try again. Where a panel engages another by means of tabs, be careful not to break the tab or its mating slot or to damage the paintwork. Remember that a few moments of patience at this stage will save you a lot of money in replacing broken fairing panels!

When installing a body panel, first study it closely, noting any fasteners and associated fittings removed with it, to be sure of returning everything to its correct place.

Check that all fasteners are in good condition, including all trim nuts or clips and damping/rubber mounts; any of these must be renewed if faulty before the panel is reassembled. Check also that all mounting brackets are straight and repair or renew them if necessary before attempting to install the panel.

Tighten the fasteners securely, but be careful not to overtighten any of them or the panel may break (not always immediately) due to the uneven stress.

 *Note that a small amount of lubricant (liquid soap or similar) applied to the mounting rubber grommets of the seat cowling will assist the lugs to engage without the need for undue pressure.*

**8**

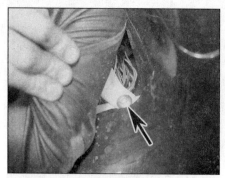

2.1a Lift up each corner and remove the bolt (arrowed) . . .

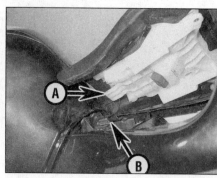

2.1b . . . then remove the seat, noting how the tab (A) locates in the bracket (B)

2.2a Turn the key in the lock and lift the front of the seat . . .

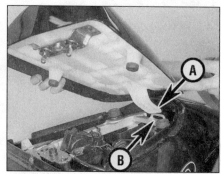

2.2b . . . then draw it forward to release the tab (A) from the bracket (B)

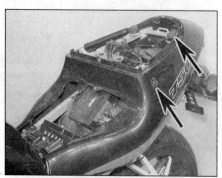

3.2a Remove the two bolts (arrowed) on each side . . .

3.2b . . . noting the collars and rubbers on the rear bolts

3.2c Remove the screws and clips joining the middle . . .

3.2d . . . and the screws at the back (arrowed) . . .

3.2e . . . then pull the sides away to free the lugs (arrowed) from their grommets and remove the cowling

## 2 Seats – removal and installation

### Removal

**1** To remove the rider's seat, lift up the rear corner on each side and unscrew the bolt **(see illustration)**. Remove the seat, noting how the tab at the front locates **(see illustration)**.

**2** To remove the passenger's seat, insert the ignition key into the seat lock located under the left-hand side of the seat cowling, and turn it clockwise to unlock the seat **(see illustration)**. Lift up the front of the seat and draw it forward, noting how the tab locates in the bracket **(see illustration)**.

### Installation

**3** Installation is the reverse of removal. Make sure the tab at the front of the rider's seat and the tab at the rear of the passenger's seat locate correctly into the brackets **(see illustrations 2.1b and 2.2b)**. Push down on the passenger's seat to engage the latch.

## 3 Seat cowling – removal and installation

### Removal

**1** Remove the seats (see Section 2).

**2** Remove the two bolts securing each side of the seat cowling, noting how the seat rubbers and collars fit **(see illustrations)**. Remove the screws securing the two clips joining the halves in the middle, and the two screws securing the underside at the back **(see illustrations)**. Carefully pull each side of the front of the cowling out away from the frame to free the two lugs on each side from their rubber grommets **(see illustration)**. Carefully draw the cowling rearwards and off the bike, taking care not to pull the front sides too far apart as this will stress the fasteners at the back.

### Installation

**3** Installation is the reverse of removal.

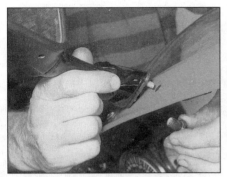

4.1 Unscrew the nuts and remove the mirror

5.1a Remove the screws securing each inner panel (arrowed)

5.1b Disconnect the wiring connectors

## 4 Rear view mirrors – removal and installation

### Removal

1 Unscrew the two nuts securing each mirror and remove the mirror along with its rubber insulator pad **(see illustration)**.

### Installation

2 Installation is the reverse of removal.

## 5 Fairing panels – removal and installation

### Fairing

**Removal**

1 Remove the screws securing the inner panels to the inside front of each fairing side panel and remove the inner panels **(see illustration)**. Disconnect the various wiring connectors, including the turn signal connectors **(see illustration)**.
2 Reach behind the instrument cluster, then pull back the rubber cover and disconnect the wiring connector **(see illustration)**.
3 Remove the two screws located below the instrument cluster **(see illustration)**.
4 Remove the screws securing each side of the fairing to the fairing side panels **(see illustration)**.
5 Remove the rear view mirrors (see Section 4).

6 Carefully draw the fairing forward and off the bike, bringing the left-hand air duct (with the fusebox attached – W and X models) with the fairing **(see illustration)**. The right-hand duct will stay on the bike – note how the fairing locates into it.

### Installation

7 Installation is the reverse of removal. Make sure the lugs on the headlight locate correctly into the rubber grommets in the mountings under the instrument cluster **(see**

5.2 Disconnect the instrument cluster wiring connector

5.3 Remove the screws (arrowed)

5.4 Remove the screws (arrowed) on each side

5.6 Carefully draw the fairing forward

**8**

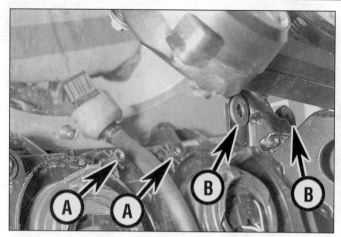

5.7 Locate the lugs (A) into the grommets (B)

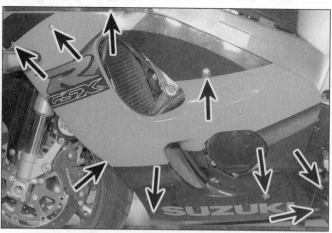

5.8a Remove the screws (arrowed) . . .

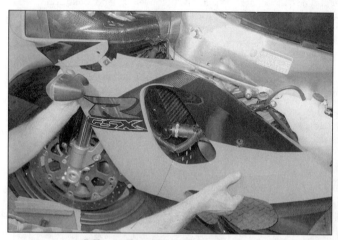

5.8b . . . then displace the panel . . .

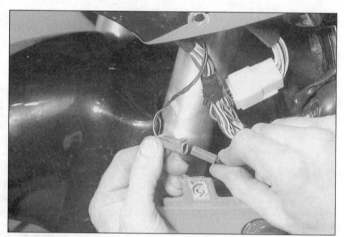

5.8c . . . and disconnect the turn signal wiring connector

illustration). Make sure the wiring connectors are correctly and securely connected.

## Fairing side panels

### Removal

8  To remove the left-hand panel only, remove the nine screws securing the panel, then carefully draw it down and away until the turn

5.8d  Note how the panels locate together on the underside

signal wiring connector becomes accessible **(see illustrations)**. Disconnect the connector and remove the panel, noting how it engages with the fairing along its top edge and the other side panel along its bottom edge **(see illustrations)**.

9  To remove the right-hand panel only, remove the nine screws securing the panel,

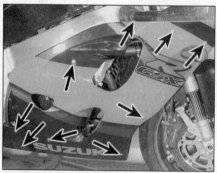

5.9  Remove the screws (arrowed)

then carefully draw it down and away until the turn signal wiring connector becomes accessible **(see illustration and 5.8b)**. Disconnect the connector and remove the panel, noting how it engages with the fairing along its top edge and the other side panel along its bottom edge **(see illustrations 5.8c and d)**.

10  If both panels are being removed, first remove the right-hand panel as described above. Now remove the left-hand panel, but do not remove the two lower front screws which secure the side panel to the centre panel, and bring the centre panel away with the side panel.

### Installation

11  Installation is the reverse of removal. Make sure the tabs along the top edge locate correctly with the fairing **(see illustration 5.8b)**, and the tabs on the bottom edge of the right-hand panel locate into the slots in the bottom edge of the left-hand panel **(see illustration 5.8d)**.

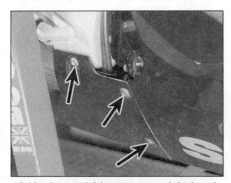

5.12a Lower fairing screws – right-hand side

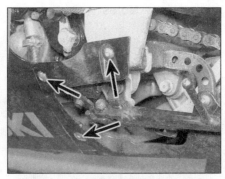

5.12b Lower fairing screws (arrowed) – left-hand side

6.1 Release the brake hoses as described . . .

## Lower fairing

### Removal

**12** Remove the screws securing each side, then carefully lower the fairing and manoeuvre it from under the bike **(see illustrations)**.

### Installation

**13** Installation is the reverse of removal.

6.2a . . . then unscrew the bolts (arrowed) on each side . . .

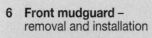

### 6 Front mudguard – removal and installation

### Removal

**1** Release the brake hoses from the mudguard **(see illustration)**. The hoses can either be prised out of the guides on the side, or the bolts securing the guides can be removed and the guides can come away with the hoses. There is a nut on each bolt on the inside of the mudguard – it is likely that after a while these could become corroded and prove difficult to remove, in which case it is best not to disturb them in case the mudguard is damaged. If you do remove them, apply some copper grease to the bolt threads on installation to prevent future problems. Release the central hose clip by pressing together the clip ends on the underside of the mudguard and drawing the clip out of the top.
**2** Unscrew the two bolts securing the mudguard to each fork, noting the arrangement of the washers, and remove the mudguard, noting how it fits **(see illustrations)**.

### Installation

**3** Installation is the reverse of removal.

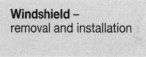

### 7 Windshield – removal and installation

### Removal

**1** Remove the screws securing the windshield to the fairing, noting the washers and nut inserts **(see illustration)**. Remove the windshield, noting how it fits.

### Installation

**2** Installation is the reverse of removal. Do not overtighten the screws.

6.2b . . . and remove the mudguard

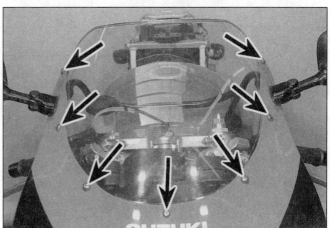

7.1 Windshield screws (arrowed)

**8**

**Notes**

# Chapter 9
# Electrical system

## Contents

## Degrees of difficulty

| **Easy,** suitable for novice with little experience |  | **Fairly easy,** suitable for beginner with some experience |  | **Fairly difficult,** suitable for competent DIY mechanic |  | **Difficult,** suitable for experienced DIY mechanic |  | **Very difficult,** suitable for expert DIY or professional | |
|---|---|---|---|---|---|---|---|---|---|

## Specifications

### Battery

| | |
|---|---|
| Capacity . . . . . . . . . . . . . . . . . . . . . . . . . . . . . . . . . . . . . . . . . . . . . . . | 12V, 8Ah |
| Electrolyte specific gravity . . . . . . . . . . . . . . . . . . . . . . . . . . . . . . . . . | 1.320 at 20°C |
| Current leakage . . . . . . . . . . . . . . . . . . . . . . . . . . . . . . . . . . . . . . . . . | 1 mA (max) |

### Charging system

| | |
|---|---|
| Alternator stator coil resistance | |
|   GSX-R600 and GSX-R750T and V models . . . . . . . . . . . . . . . . . . . . . | approx. 0.3 ohms |
|   GSX-R750W and X models . . . . . . . . . . . . . . . . . . . . . . . . . . . . . . . . . | 0.24 to 0.36 ohms |
| Alternator output (max) | |
|   GSX-R600 and GSX-R750T and V models . . . . . . . . . . . . . . . . . . . . . | approx. 378W @ 5000 rpm |
|   GSX-R750W and X models . . . . . . . . . . . . . . . . . . . . . . . . . . . . . . . . . | approx. 406W @ 5000 rpm |
| Unregulated voltage output (no-load) | |
|   GSX-R600 and GSX-R750T and V models . . . . . . . . . . . . . . . . . . . . . | min. 55V (ac) @ 5000 rpm |
|   GSX-R750W and X models . . . . . . . . . . . . . . . . . . . . . . . . . . . . . . . . . | min. 70V (ac) @ 5000 rpm |
| Regulated voltage output . . . . . . . . . . . . . . . . . . . . . . . . . . . . . . . . . . | 13.5 to 15.0V @ 5000 rpm |

**9**

## Starter motor

Brush length (min) . . . . . . . . . . . . . . . . . . . . . . . . . . . . . . . . . . . . . . . . . . . Not available
Starter relay resistance . . . . . . . . . . . . . . . . . . . . . . . . . . . . . . . . . . . 3.0 to 5.0 ohms

## Fuses

Main . . . . . . . . . . . . . . . . . . . . . . . . . . . . . . . . . . . . . . . . . . . . . . . . . . . . . . 30A
Headlight (high beam) . . . . . . . . . . . . . . . . . . . . . . . . . . . . . . . . . . . . . . . . . 15A
Headlight (low beam) . . . . . . . . . . . . . . . . . . . . . . . . . . . . . . . . . . . . . . . . . . 15A
Turn signal . . . . . . . . . . . . . . . . . . . . . . . . . . . . . . . . . . . . . . . . . . . . . . . . . . 15A
Ignition . . . . . . . . . . . . . . . . . . . . . . . . . . . . . . . . . . . . . . . . . . . . . . . . . . . . . 10A
Tail light (except GSX-R750W and X) . . . . . . . . . . . . . . . . . . . . . . . . . . . 10A
Fuel system (GSX-R750W and X) . . . . . . . . . . . . . . . . . . . . . . . . . . . . . . 10A

## Bulbs

Headlight
 GSX-R600 and GSX-R750T and V . . . . . . . . . . . . . . . . . . . . . . . . . . 55/50W H4 halogen x 2
 GSX-R750W and X . . . . . . . . . . . . . . . . . . . . . . . . . . . . . . . . . . . . . . 60/55W H4 halogen x 2
Sidelight (UK only) . . . . . . . . . . . . . . . . . . . . . . . . . . . . . . . . . . . . . . . . . . 5.0W
Brake/tail light . . . . . . . . . . . . . . . . . . . . . . . . . . . . . . . . . . . . . . . . . . . . . . 21/5W x 2
Turn signal lights . . . . . . . . . . . . . . . . . . . . . . . . . . . . . . . . . . . . . . . . . . . . 21W
Meter lights . . . . . . . . . . . . . . . . . . . . . . . . . . . . . . . . . . . . . . . . . . . . . . . . 1.7W
Turn signal indicator light . . . . . . . . . . . . . . . . . . . . . . . . . . . . . . . . . . . . . 1.7W
Neutral indicator light . . . . . . . . . . . . . . . . . . . . . . . . . . . . . . . . . . . . . . . . 1.7W
High beam indicator light . . . . . . . . . . . . . . . . . . . . . . . . . . . . . . . . . . . . . 1.7W
Fuel warning light . . . . . . . . . . . . . . . . . . . . . . . . . . . . . . . . . . . . . . . . . . . 1.7W

## Torque settings

Oil pressure switch . . . . . . . . . . . . . . . . . . . . . . . . . . . . . . . . . . . . . . . . . . 14 Nm
Alternator rotor bolt . . . . . . . . . . . . . . . . . . . . . . . . . . . . . . . . . . . . . . . . . 120 Nm

---

## 1 General information

All models have a 12-volt electrical system charged by a three-phase alternator with a separate regulator/rectifier.

The regulator maintains the charging system output within the specified range to prevent overcharging, and the rectifier converts the ac (alternating current) output of the alternator to dc (direct current) to power the lights and other components and to charge the battery. The alternator rotor is mounted on the left-hand end of the crankshaft.

The starter motor is mounted behind the cylinders. The starting system includes the motor, the battery, the relay and the various wires and switches. If the engine kill switch in the RUN position and the ignition (main) switch is ON, the starter relay allows the starter motor to operate only if the transmission is in neutral (neutral switch on) and the clutch lever is pulled in or, if the transmission is in gear, if the sidestand is up and the clutch lever is pulled in.

**Note:** *Keep in mind that electrical parts, once purchased, cannot be returned. To avoid unnecessary expense, make very sure the faulty component has been positively identified before buying a renewal part.*

## 2 Electrical system – fault finding

 *Warning: To prevent the risk of short circuits, the ignition (main) switch must always be OFF and the battery negative (-ve)* terminal should be disconnected before any of the bike's other electrical components are disturbed. Don't forget to reconnect the terminal securely once work is finished or if battery power is needed for circuit testing.

1 A typical electrical circuit consists of an electrical component, the switches, relays, etc. related to that component and the wiring and connectors that hook the component to both the battery and the frame. To aid in locating a problem in any electrical circuit, refer to the wiring diagrams at the end of this Chapter.

2 Before tackling any troublesome electrical circuit, first study the wiring diagram (see end of Chapter) thoroughly to get a complete picture of what makes up that individual circuit. Trouble spots, for instance, can often be narrowed down by noting if other components related to that circuit are operating properly or not. If several components or circuits fail at one time, chances are the fault lies in the fuse or earth (ground) connection, as several circuits often are routed through the same fuse and earth (ground) connections.

3 Electrical problems often stem from simple causes, such as loose or corroded connections or a blown fuse. Prior to any electrical fault finding, always visually check the condition of the fuse, wires and connections in the problem circuit. Intermittent failures can be especially frustrating, since you can't always duplicate the failure when it's convenient to test. In such situations, a good practice is to clean all connections in the affected circuit, whether or not they appear to be good. All of the connections and wires should also be wiggled to check for looseness which can cause intermittent failure.

4 If testing instruments are going to be utilised, use the wiring diagram to plan where you will make the necessary connections in order to accurately pinpoint the trouble spot.

5 The basic tools needed for electrical fault finding include a battery and bulb test circuit, a continuity tester, a test light, and a jumper wire. A multimeter capable of reading volts, ohms and amps is also very useful as an alternative to the above, and is necessary for performing more extensive tests and checks.

 *Refer to Fault Finding Equipment in the Reference section for details of how to use electrical test equipment.*

## 3 Battery – removal, installation, inspection and maintenance

**Caution: Be extremely careful when handling or working around the battery. The electrolyte is very caustic and an explosive gas (hydrogen) is given off when the battery is charging.**

### Removal and installation

1 Remove the rider's seat (see Chapter 8).
2 Unscrew the negative (-ve) terminal bolt first and disconnect the lead from the battery **(see illustration)**. Lift up the red insulating cover to access the positive (+ve) terminal, then unscrew the bolt and disconnect the lead. Lift the battery from the bike **(see illustration)**.
3 On installation, clean the battery terminals and lead ends with a wire brush or knife and emery paper. Reconnect the leads, connecting the positive (+ve) terminal first.

 **HAYNES HINT** *Battery corrosion can be kept to a minimum by applying a layer of petroleum jelly to the terminals after the cables have been connected.*

4 Install the seat (see Chapter 8).

### Inspection and maintenance

5 The battery fitted to the models covered in this manual is of the maintenance free (sealed) type, therefore requiring no regular maintenance. However, the following checks should still be regularly performed.
6 Check the battery terminals and leads for tightness and corrosion. If corrosion is evident, unscrew the terminal screws and disconnect the leads from the battery, disconnecting the negative (-ve) terminal first, and clean the terminals and lead ends with a wire brush or knife and emery paper. Reconnect the leads, connecting the negative (-ve) terminal last, and apply a thin coat of petroleum jelly to the connections to slow further corrosion.
7 The battery case should be kept clean to prevent current leakage, which can discharge the battery over a period of time (especially when it sits unused). Wash the outside of the case with a solution of baking soda and water. Rinse the battery thoroughly, then dry it.
8 Look for cracks in the case and renew the battery if any are found. If acid has been spilled on the frame or battery box, neutralise it with a baking soda and water solution, dry it thoroughly, then touch up any damaged paint.
9 If the motorcycle sits unused for long periods of time, disconnect the cables from the battery terminals, negative (-ve) terminal first. Refer to Section 4 and charge the battery once every month to six weeks.
10 The condition of the battery can be assessed by measuring the voltage present at the battery terminals. Connect the voltmeter

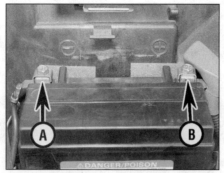

**3.2a  Disconnect the negative lead (A) first, then the positive lead (B) . . .**

positive (+ve) probe to the battery positive (+ve) terminal and the negative (-ve) probe to the battery negative (-ve) terminal. When fully charged there should be more than 12.5 volts present. If the voltage falls below 12.0 volts the battery must be removed, disconnecting the negative (-ve) terminal first, and recharged as described below in Section 4.

## 4 Battery – charging

**Caution: Be extremely careful when handling or working around the battery. The electrolyte is very caustic and an explosive gas (hydrogen) is given off when the battery is charging.**

1 Remove the battery (see Section 3). Connect the charger to the battery, making sure that the positive (+ve) lead on the charger is connected to the positive (+ve) terminal on the battery, and the negative (-ve) lead is connected to the negative (-ve) terminal.
2 Suzuki recommend that the battery is charged at a maximum rate of 0.9 amps for 5 hours. Exceeding this figure can cause the battery to overheat, buckling the plates and rendering it useless. Few owners will have access to an expensive current controlled charger, so if a normal domestic charger is used check that after a possible initial peak, the charge rate falls to a safe level **(see**

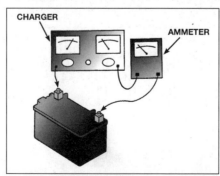

**4.2  If the charger doesn't have ammeter built in, connect one in series as shown. DO NOT connect the ammeter between the battery terminals or it will be ruined**

**3.2b  . . . and lift the battery out**

**illustration)**. If the battery becomes hot during charging **stop**. Further charging will cause damage. **Note:** *In emergencies the battery can be charged at a higher rate of around 4.0 amps for a period of 1 hour. However, this is not recommended and the low amp charge is by far the safer method of charging the battery.*
3 After charging, allow the battery to stand undisturbed for about 30 minutes, then check its voltage as described in Section 3. If the battery is still below 12.5 V, charge it some more. If the voltage is still low, the battery is failing and a new one should be installed.
4 If the recharged battery discharges rapidly if left disconnected it is likely that an internal short caused by physical damage or sulphation has occurred. A new battery will be required. A sound item will tend to lose its charge at about 1% per day.
5 Install the battery (see Section 3).
6 If the motorcycle sits unused for long periods of time, charge the battery once every month to six weeks and leave it disconnected.

## 5 Fuses – check and renewal

1 The electrical system is protected by fuses of different ratings. All except the main fuse are housed in the fusebox, which on T and V models is located below the instrument cluster, and on W and X models is on the inside of the left-hand air duct in the fairing **(see illustration)**. The main fuse is integral

**5.1  Fusebox (arrowed) – W and X models shown**

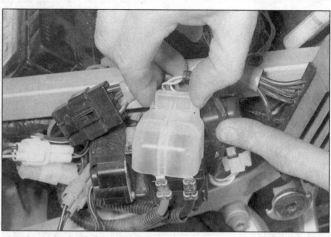

**5.2a Release the fusebox lid to access the fuses**

**5.2b Remove the starter relay cover . . .**

with the starter relay, which is located behind the left-hand side of the seat cowling **(see illustration 5.2c)**.

**2** To access the fusebox fuses, on T and V models remove the screw securing the retainer, then on all models unclip the fusebox lid **(see illustration)**. To access the main fuse, remove the seat cowling (see Chapter 8) and the starter relay cover **(see illustrations)**.

**3** The fuses can be removed and checked visually. If you can't pull the fuse out with your fingertips, use a pair of needle-nose pliers. A blown fuse is easily identified by a break in the element **(see illustration)**. Each fuse is clearly marked with its rating and must only be renewed by a fuse of the correct rating. A spare fuse of each rating is housed in the fusebox, and a spare main fuse is housed in the bottom of the starter relay **(see illustration 5.2c)**. If a spare fuse is used, always renew it so that a spare of each rating is carried on the bike at all times.

 *Warning: Never put in a fuse of a higher rating or bridge the terminals with any other substitute, however temporary it may be. Serious damage may be done to the circuit, or a fire may start.*

**4** If a fuse blows, be sure to check the wiring circuit very carefully for evidence of a short-circuit. Look for bare wires and chafed,

melted or burned insulation. If the fuse is renewed before the cause is located, the new fuse will blow immediately.

**5** Occasionally a fuse will blow or cause an open-circuit for no obvious reason. Corrosion of the fuse ends and fusebox terminals may occur and cause poor fuse contact. If this happens, remove the corrosion with a wire brush or emery paper, then spray the fuse end and terminals with electrical contact cleaner.

## 6   Lighting system – check

**1** The battery provides power for operation of the headlight, tail light, brake light and instrument cluster lights. If none of the lights operate, always check battery voltage before proceeding. Low battery voltage indicates either a faulty battery or a defective charging system. Refer to Section 3 for battery checks and Section 32 for charging system tests. Also, check the condition of the fuses (see Section 5).

### Headlight

**2** If the headlight fails to work, check the bulb first (see Section 7), then the fuse and the wiring connector, then check for battery voltage at the black/yellow (HI beam) and/or

black/green (LO beam) wire terminal on the supply side of the headlight wiring connector. If voltage is present, check the earth (ground) circuit for an open or poor connection.

**3** If no voltage is indicated, check the wiring between the headlight, the lighting switch (UK only) and the ignition switch, then check the switches themselves.

### Tail light

**4** If the tail light fails to work, check the bulb and the bulb terminals first, then the fuse and the wiring connector, then check for battery voltage at the brown wire terminal on the supply side of the tail light wiring connector. If voltage is present, check the earth (ground) circuit for an open or poor connection.

**5** If no voltage is indicated, check the wiring between the tail light, the lighting switch (UK only) and the ignition switch, then check the switches themselves.

### Brake light

**6** If the brake light fails to work, check the bulb and the bulb terminals first (see Section 9), then the fuse and the wiring connector, then check for battery voltage at the white/black wire terminal on the supply side of the tail light wiring connector, with the brake lever pulled in or the pedal depressed. If voltage is present, check the earth (ground) circuit for an open or poor connection.

**7** If no voltage is indicated, check the brake light switches (see Section 14), then the wiring between the tail light and the switches.

### Instrument and warning lights

**8** See Section 17 for instrument and warning light bulb renewal.

### Turn signal lights

**9** If one light fails to work, check the bulb and the bulb terminals first, then the wiring connector. If none of the turn signals work, first check the fuse.

**10** If the fuse is good, see Section 13 for the turn signal circuit check.

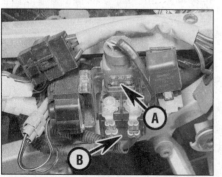

**5.2c . . . to access the main fuse (A). The spare is in the base of the relay (B)**

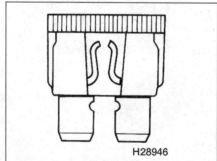

H28946

**5.3 A blown fuse can be identified by a break in its element**

**7.1a Disconnect the wiring connector . . .**

**7.1b . . . and remove the rubber cover**

**7.2a Release the retaining clip . . .**

**7.2b . . . and withdraw the bulb**

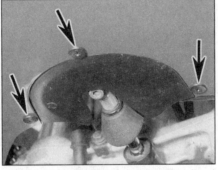

**7.6a Unscrew and remove the trim clips (arrowed) . . .**

**7.6b . . . and remove the panel**

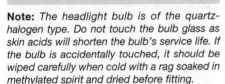

## 7 Headlight bulb and sidelight bulb – renewal

**Note:** *The headlight bulb is of the quartz-halogen type. Do not touch the bulb glass as skin acids will shorten the bulb's service life. If the bulb is accidentally touched, it should be wiped carefully when cold with a rag soaked in methylated spirit and dried before fitting.*

 **Warning: Allow the bulb time to cool before removing it if the headlight has just been on.**

### Headlight

**1** Disconnect the relevant wiring connector from the back of the headlight assembly and remove the rubber dust cover, noting how it fits **(see illustrations)**.

**2** Release the bulb retaining clip, noting how it fits, then remove the bulb **(see illustrations)**.

**3** Fit the new bulb, bearing in mind the information in the **Note** above. Make sure the tabs on the bulb fit correctly in the slots in the bulb housing, and secure it in position with the retaining clip.

**4** Install the dust cover, making sure it is

 **HAYNES HiNT** *Always use a paper towel or dry cloth when handling new bulbs to prevent injury if the bulb should break and to increase bulb life.*

correctly seated and with the 'TOP' mark at the top, and connect the wiring connector.

**5** Check the operation of the headlight.

### Sidelight

**6** Unscrew and remove the trim clips securing the access panel in the base of the fairing and remove the panel **(see illustrations)**.

**7** Pull the bulbholder out of its socket in the base of the headlight, then carefully pull the bulb out of the holder **(see illustrations)**.

**8** Install the new bulb in the bulbholder, then install the bulbholder by pressing it in. Make sure the rubber cover is correctly seated.

**9** Fit the access panel, then install the trim clips and press in their pins **(see illustration)**.

**10** Check the operation of the sidelight.

**7.7a Pull the bulbholder out of the headlight . . .**

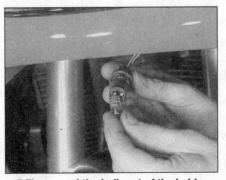

**7.7b . . . and the bulb out of the holder**

**7.9 Press the pins back into the clips**

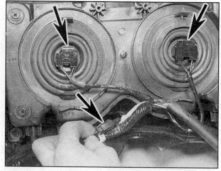

**8.2 Release the wiring from the clip (arrowed) . . .**

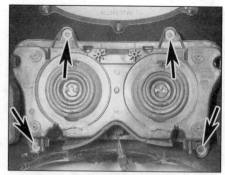

**8.3 . . . then disconnect the wiring connectors (arrowed)**

**8.4 Remove the screws (arrowed) and remove the headlight**

## 8 Headlight assembly – removal and installation

### Removal

**1** Remove the fairing (see Chapter 8).
**2** Move the air duct aside. Release the wiring loom from its clip on the lower left-hand side of the headlight **(see illustration)**.
**3** Disconnect the headlight and sidelight wiring connectors **(see illustration)**.
**4** Remove the screws securing the headlight to the fairing, noting the wiring clip secured by the lower left-hand screw **(see illustration)**. Remove the headlight, noting how it fits.

### Installation

**5** Installation is the reverse of removal. Make sure all the wiring is correctly connected and secured. Check the operation of the headlight and sidelight. Check the headlight aim (see Chapter 1).

## 9 Tail/brake light bulbs – renewal

**1** Remove the passenger seat (see Chapter 8).
**2** Turn the relevant bulbholder anti-clockwise

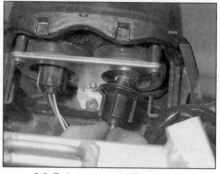

**9.2 Release the bulbholder . . .**

and withdraw it from the tail light **(see illustration)**.
**3** Push the bulb into the holder and twist it anti-clockwise to remove it **(see illustration)**.
**4** Check the socket terminals for corrosion and clean them if necessary. Line up the pins of the new bulb with the slots in the socket, then push the bulb in and turn it clockwise until it locks into place. **Note:** *The pins on the bulb are offset so it can only be installed one way. It is a good idea to use a paper towel or dry cloth when handling the new bulb to prevent injury if the bulb should break and to increase bulb life.*
**5** Fit the bulbholder into the tail light and turn it clockwise to secure it.
**6** Install the seat (see Chapter 8).

**9.3 . . . and remove the bulb**

## 10 Tail light assembly – removal and installation

### Removal

**1** Remove the seat cowling (see Chapter 8).
**2** Either turn the bulbholders anti-clockwise and withdraw them from the tail light **(see illustration 9.2)**, or trace the wiring from the tail light and disconnect it at the connector **(see illustration)**.
**3** Remove the screws securing the tail light assembly and carefully remove it **(see illustration)**.

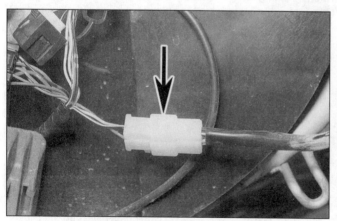

**10.2 Tail light wiring connector (arrowed)**

**10.3 The tail light is secured by three screws (arrowed)**

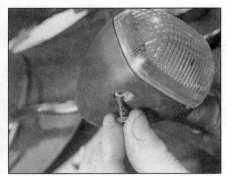

11.1a Remove the screw . . .

11.1b . . . and withdraw the lens

11.2 Release the bulbholder . . .

## Installation

4 Installation is the reverse of removal. Check the operation of the tail light and the brake light.

## 11 Turn signal bulbs – renewal

1 Remove the screw securing the turn signal lens and remove the lens, noting how it fits (see illustrations).
2 Turn the bulbholder anti-clockwise and withdraw it from the lens (see illustration).
3 Push the bulb into the holder and twist it anti-clockwise to remove it (see illustration). Check the socket terminals for corrosion and clean them if necessary. Line up the pins of the new bulb with the slots in the socket, then push the bulb in and turn it clockwise until it locks into place.
4 Fit the bulbholder back into the lens and turn it clockwise, making sure it is securely held.
5 Fit the lens into the holder, locating the tab on the side of the lens behind the plate in the housing, then install the screw (see illustration).

 **HAYNES HINT** *If the socket contacts are dirty or corroded, scrape them clean and spray with electrical contact cleaner before a new bulb is installed.*

## 12 Turn signal assemblies – removal and installation

### Front

#### Removal

1 Remove the screws securing the inner trim panel on the inside of the fairing side panel and remove the trim (see illustration).
2 Disconnect the turn signal wiring connector (see illustration 12.3).
3 Remove the screws securing the stalk to the inside of the fairing and remove the mounting plate, then twist the stalk to free the tabs and withdraw it from the fairing, noting

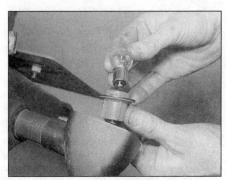

11.3 . . . and remove the bulb

how it fits (see illustration). Take care not to snag the wiring as you pull it through.

### Installation

4 Installation is the reverse of removal. Check the operation of the turn signals.

### Rear

#### Removal

5 Remove the passenger seat (see Chapter 8). Trace the wiring back from the turn signal and disconnect it at the connector, located behind the seat cowling on the left-hand side (see illustration). If the connectors are difficult to access, remove the seat cowling (see Chapter 8).
6 Unscrew the nut securing the turn signal assembly to the inside of the mudguard,

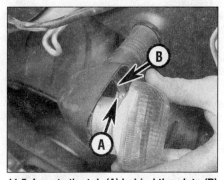

11.5 Locate the tab (A) behind the plate (B)

12.1 Remove the screws (arrowed) to free the trim panel

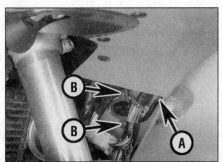

12.3 Disconnect the turn signal wiring connector (A), then remove the screws (B) and the mounting plate

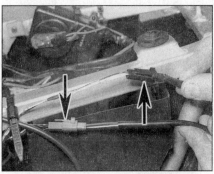

12.5 Disconnect the relevant wiring connector (arrowed) . . .

**9**

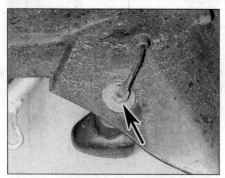

12.6 . . . then unscrew the nut (arrowed) and withdraw the turn signal

13.3a On W and X models the turn signal relay (arrowed) is next to the fusebox . . .

13.3b . . . and can be pulled off its connector

noting the washer, and draw the turn signal out of the mudguard (see illustration). Remove the spacer from the mounting hole to allow the wiring connector through. Take care not to snag the connector as you draw it through.

### Installation

7 Installation is the reverse of removal. Make sure the wiring is correctly routed and securely connected. Check the operation of the turn signals.

## 13 Turn signal circuit – check

1 Most turn signal problems are the result of a burned out bulb or corroded socket. This is especially true when the turn signals function properly in one direction, but fail to flash in the other direction. Check the bulbs and the sockets (see Section 11) and the wiring connectors. Also, check the fuse (see Section 5) and the switch (see Section 20).
2 The battery provides power for operation of the turn signal lights, so if they do not operate, also check the battery voltage. Low battery voltage indicates either a faulty battery or a defective charging system. Refer to Section 3 for battery checks and Section 32 for charging system tests.
3 If the all the above are good, check the relay, which on T and V models is located below the instrument cluster, and on W and X models is on the inside of the left-hand air duct in the fairing, next to the fusebox and integral with the sidestand relay and diode (see illustration). On T and V models, disconnect the relay wiring connector and release the relay from its mounting. On W and X models, pull the relay off its connector (see illustration). Check for battery voltage at the dark green wire terminal on the connector with the ignition ON. Connect the positive (+ve) probe of the meter to the terminal and the negative (-ve) to the frame or engine. Turn the ignition OFF when the check is complete and plug the relay back in.
4 If no power was present at the relay, check the wiring from the relay to the ignition (main) switch for continuity.

5 If power was present at the relay, trace the wiring from the relay to the connector block, but do not disconnect it. Check for battery voltage at the light blue terminal on the relay side of the connector with the ignition switch ON. Connect the positive (+ve) probe of the meter to the terminal and the negative (-ve) probe to the frame or engine. Turn the ignition OFF when the check is complete. If no power was present, and the wiring between the connector and the relay is good, the relay is probably faulty. As Suzuki provide no test data for the relay, the only way to test it is to substitute it with a known good one. If power was present at the connector, use the appropriate wiring diagram at the end of this Chapter and check the wiring between the relay, turn signal switch and turn signal lights for continuity.

## 14 Brake light switches – check and renewal

### Circuit check

1 Before checking any electrical circuit, check the bulb (see Section 9) and fuse (see Section 5).
2 The front brake light switch is mounted on the underside of the brake master cylinder (see illustration 14.6). The rear brake light switch is mounted on the inside of the frame on the right-hand side, above the brake pedal (see illustration 14.9). Disconnect the wiring connector(s) from the switch.

14.6 Front brake light switch wiring connectors (A) and mounting screw (B)

3 Using a multimeter or test light connected to a good earth (ground), check for voltage at the black/red (dark green on certain models) – front, or orange/green – rear, wire terminal on the connector with the ignition switch ON – there should be battery voltage. If there's no voltage present, check the wiring between the switch and the ignition switch (see the wiring diagrams at the end of this Chapter).
4 If voltage is available, reconnect the connector(s) and touch the probe of the meter or test light to the other terminal of the switch, then pull the brake lever in or depress the brake pedal. If no reading is obtained or the test light doesn't light up, renew the switch.
5 If a reading is obtained or the test light does light up, check the wiring between the switch and the brake light bulb (see the wiring diagrams at the end of this Chapter).

### Switch renewal

#### Front brake lever switch

6 The switch is mounted on the underside of the brake master cylinder. Disconnect the wiring connectors from the switch (see illustration).
7 Remove the single screw securing the switch to the bottom of the master cylinder and remove the switch.
8 Installation is the reverse of removal. The switch isn't adjustable.

#### Rear brake pedal switch

9 The switch is mounted on the inside of the frame on the right-hand side, above the brake pedal (see illustration). Pull up the rubber

14.9 Rear brake light switch (arrowed)

cover and disconnect the wiring connector from the switch.

**10** Detach the lower end of the switch spring from the brake pedal, then hold the adjusting nut and unscrew and remove the switch.

**11** Installation is the reverse of removal. Make sure the brake light is activated just before the rear brake pedal takes effect. If adjustment is necessary, either hold the switch and turn the adjusting nut on the switch body, or disconnect the wiring connector and turn the switch itself while holding the nut, until the brake light is activated when required.

## 15 Instrument cluster –
removed and installation

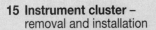

### Removal

**1** Remove the fairing (see Chapter 8).
**2** Unscrew the bolts securing the instrument cluster to the bracket and lift the cluster away **(see illustrations)**.

### Installation

**3** Installation is the reverse of removal. Check the condition of the rubber wiring grommets and fit new ones if they are damaged or deteriorated.

## 16 Instruments –
check and renewal

### Speedometer and speed sensor

#### Check

**1** Special equipment is needed to check the operation of the speedometer and sensor. If the speedometer doesn't work, take the motorcycle to a Suzuki dealer for assessment.

#### Renewal

**2** Remove the instrument cluster (see Section 15).

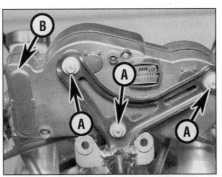

**15.2a Instrument cluster mounting bolts (A). Warning light cover (B)**

**15.2b Lift the instruments off the bracket, noting how the mounting lugs locate in the grommets**

**3** Remove the screws securing the rear cover and remove the cover **(see illustrations)**.
**4** Remove the screw securing the instruments in the front cover and lift them out of the cover **(see illustrations)**. The speedometer is not available individually from the other instruments, so the whole assembly must be renewed.
**5** Fit the new instruments into the front cover, then fit the back cover and install the cluster.
**6** To renew the sensor, disconnect its wiring connector, which is on the inside of the left-hand fairing side panel (remove the panel for improved access – see Chapter 8), then unscrew the bolt securing the sensor to the front sprocket cover and remove it **(see illustrations)**.

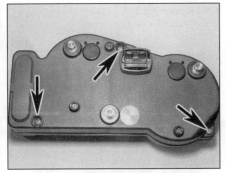

**16.3a Remove the screws (arrowed) . . .**

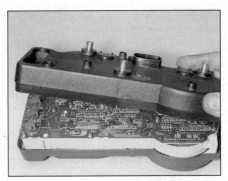

**16.3b . . . and lift off the cover**

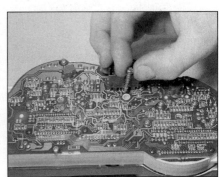

**16.4a Remove the single screw . . .**

**16.4b . . . and lift out the instruments**

**16.6a Disconnect the speed sensor wiring connector . . .**

**16.6b . . . then unscrew the bolt (arrowed) and remove the sensor**

## Tachometer

### Check

**7** No test procedure or data is provided. If the tachometer is not working, take the motorcycle to a Suzuki dealer for assessment.

### Renewal

**8** Remove the instrument cluster (see Section 15).
**9** Remove the screws securing the rear cover and remove the cover **(see illustrations 16.3a and b)**.
**10** Remove the screw securing the instruments in the front cover and lift them out of the cover **(see illustrations 16.4a and b)**. The tachometer is not available individually from the other instruments, so the whole assembly must be renewed.
**11** Fit the new instruments into the front cover, then fit the back cover and install the cluster.

## Coolant temperature display

### Check

**12** Special equipment is needed to check the operation of this circuit. If it's not working, and the temperature sensor is not faulty (see Chapter 3), take the motorcycle to a Suzuki dealer for assessment.

### Renewal

**13** See Steps 8 to 11 above.

## Oil pressure display

### Check

**14** Turn the ignition switch ON – the oil warning display should flicker until the engine is started, then it should go out.
**15** The oil pressure switch is screwed into the right-hand side of the crankcase – remove the right-hand fairing side panel for access (see Chapter 8). Remove the screw and detach the wiring connector from the switch **(see illustration 18.5)**. With the ignition switched ON, earth (ground) the wire on the crankcase and check that the display and warning light come on. If they don't, check for voltage at the wire terminal. If there is no voltage present, check the wire between the switch, the instrument cluster and fusebox for continuity (see the *wiring diagrams* at the end of this Chapter). If the wiring is good, then the display is faulty. If the display and light come on, check the oil pressure switch (see Section 18).
**16** If the display and warning light come on whilst the engine is running, yet the oil pressure is satisfactory, remove the screw and detach the wire from the oil pressure switch **(see illustration 18.5)**. With the wire detached and the ignition switched ON the display and light should be out. If they are illuminated, the wire between the switch and instrument cluster must be earthed (grounded) at some point. If the wiring is good, the switch must be assumed faulty and a new one must be fitted (see Section 18).

### Renewal

**17** See Steps 8 to 11 above.

## Fuel level warning display

### Check

**18** First check the bulb (see Section 17). If the bulb is good, raise the fuel tank (see Chapter 4) and disconnect the fuel pump wiring connector.
**19** Turn the ignition switch ON – the fuel warning light should come on for three seconds, after which it will go out if there are more than 4 litres of fuel in the tank, or will flicker if there are between 2.5 and 4 litres, or will remain on if there are less than 2.5 litres.
**20** Connect a jumper wire between the black/white and red/black terminals on the wiring loom side of the connector. With the ignition switched ON, the light should flicker. Now connect the jumper wire between the black/white and black/light green terminals on the wiring loom side of the connector. With the ignition switched ON, the light should be on. If not, check the wiring between the connector and the instruments. If the wiring is good, then the display is faulty.

### Renewal

**21** Remove the instrument cluster (see Section 15).
**22** Remove the screws securing the rear cover and remove the cover **(see illustrations 16.3a and b)**.
**23** Remove the screw securing the instruments in the front cover and lift them out of the cover **(see illustrations 16.4a and b)**. As individual parts are not available the whole assembly must be renewed.
**24** Fit the new instruments into the front cover, then fit the back cover and install the cluster.

## 17 Instrument and warning light bulbs – renewal

## Meter light bulbs

**1** Remove the instrument cluster (see Section 15).
**2** Remove the screws securing the rear cover and remove the cover **(see illustrations 16.3a and b)**.
**3** Twist the relevant bulbholder anticlockwise to release it, then carefully pull out the bulb **(see illustrations)**.
**4** Fit the new bulb, then install the holder.
**5** Fit the back cover and install the cluster.

## Warning light bulbs

**6** Remove the fairing (see Chapter 8).
**7** Remove the rubber cover from the back of the instrument cluster **(see illustration 15.2a)**.
**8** Twist the relevant bulbholder anticlockwise to release it, then carefully pull out the bulb.
**9** Fit the new bulb, then install the holder, the rubber cover and the fairing.

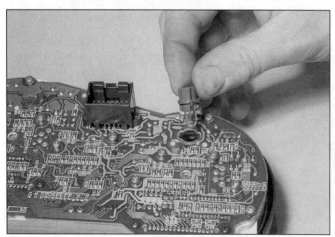

17.3a Release the bulbholder . . .

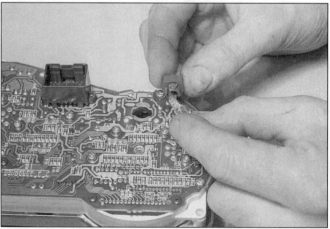

17.3b . . . and remove the bulb

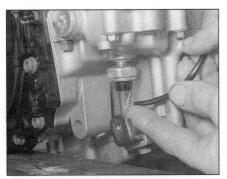

**18.5 Remove the screw and detach the wire from the switch**

## 18 Oil pressure switch – check, removal and installation

### Check

1 The oil pressure warning display should flicker and the warning light come on when the ignition (main) switch is turned ON, and they extinguish after the engine is started. If they come on as described whilst the engine is running, stop the engine immediately and carry out an oil pressure check as described in Chapter 1.

2 If the oil pressure warning light does not come on when the ignition is turned on, check the display (see Section 16).

3 If the display and wiring are good, the switch must be assumed faulty and a new one must be installed.

### Removal

4 Drain the engine oil (see Chapter 1).

5 The oil pressure switch is screwed into the right-hand side of the crankcase – remove the right-hand fairing side panel for access (see Chapter 8). Remove the screw and detach the wiring connector from the switch **(see illustration)**.

6 Unscrew the oil pressure switch and withdraw it from the crankcase.

### Installation

7 Apply a suitable sealant (Suzuki-Bond 1207B or equivalent) to the threads near the switch body, then install it in the crankcase and tighten it to the torque setting specified at the beginning of the Chapter.

8 Attach the wiring connector and tighten the screw **(see illustration 18.5)**.

9 Fill the engine with the correct type and quantity of oil as described in Chapter 1. Start the engine and check for leaks around the switch.

10 Install the fairing side panel (see Chapter 8).

## 19 Ignition (main) switch – check, removal and installation

> ⚠ **Warning: To prevent the risk of short circuits, disconnect the battery negative (-ve) lead before making any ignition (main) switch checks.**

### Check

1 Raise the fuel tank and remove the air filter housing (see Chapter 4). Disconnect the ignition switch wiring connector **(see illustration)**.

2 Using an ohmmeter or a continuity tester, check the continuity of the connector terminal pairs (see the *wiring diagrams* at the end of this Chapter). Continuity should exist between the terminals connected by a solid line on the diagram when the switch is in the indicated position.

3 If the switch fails any of the tests, renew it.

### Removal

4 Remove the fairing (see Chapter 8).

5 Raise the fuel tank and remove the air filter housing (see Chapter 4). Disconnect the ignition switch wiring connector, then free the wiring from its guide and feed it through to the switch **(see illustration 19.1)**.

6 Torx bolts are used to mount the ignition switch to the underside of the top yoke. Remove the two bolts, turning the handlebars as required to provide best access for your tools **(see illustration)**.

### Installation

7 Installation is the reverse of removal. Make sure the wiring is correctly routed and securely connected.

## 20 Handlebar switches – check

1 Generally speaking, the switches are reliable and trouble-free. Most troubles, when they do occur, are caused by dirty or corroded contacts, but wear and breakage of internal parts is a possibility that should not be overlooked. If breakage does occur, the entire switch and related wiring harness will have to be renewed, since individual parts are not available.

2 The switches can be checked for continuity using an ohmmeter or a continuity test light. Always disconnect the battery negative (-ve) lead, which will prevent the possibility of a short circuit, before making the checks.

3 Remove the screws securing the inner trim panel on the inside of the fairing side panel and remove the trim **(see illustration 12.1)**. Trace the wiring harness of the switch in question back to its connector and disconnect it **(see illustration)**. The black connector is for the right-hand switches and the yellow connector is for the left-hand switches.

4 Check for continuity between the terminals of the connector on the switch side, with the switch in the various positions (ie switch off – no continuity, switch on – continuity) – see the *wiring diagrams* at the end of this Chapter.

5 If the continuity check indicates a problem exists, refer to Section 21, remove the switch and spray the switch contacts with electrical contact cleaner. If they are accessible, the contacts can be scraped clean with a knife or polished with crocus cloth. If switch components are damaged or broken, it will be obvious when the switch is disassembled.

## 21 Handlebar switches – removal and installation

### Right-hand switch

#### Removal

1 If the switch is to be removed from the bike, rather than just displaced from the handlebar, remove the screws securing the inner trim

**19.1 Disconnect the ignition switch wiring connector (arrowed)**

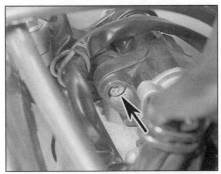

**19.6 Turn the handlebars for best access to each bolt (arrowed)**

**20.3 Handlebar switch wiring connectors (arrowed)**

**9**

panel on the inside of the fairing side panel and remove the trim **(see illustration 12.1)**. Trace the wiring harness of the switch in question back to its connector and disconnect it **(see illustration 20.3)**. The black connector is for the right-hand switches. Work back along the harness, freeing it from its guide, noting its correct routing.

**2** Disconnect the front brake light switch wiring connectors **(see illustration 14.6)**.

**3** Remove the throttle cables from the switch (see Chapter 4 – this procedure incorporates switch removal).

### Installation

**4** Installation is the reverse of removal. Refer to Chapter 4 for installation of the throttle cables. Make sure the locating pin in the upper half of the switch fits into hole in the top of the handlebar.

### *Left-hand switch*

#### Removal

**5** If the switch is to be removed from the bike, rather than just displaced from the handlebar, remove the screws securing the inner trim panel on the inside of the fairing side panel and remove the trim **(see illustration 12.1)**. Trace the wiring harness of the switch in question back to its connector and disconnect it **(see illustration 20.3)**. The yellow connector is for the left-hand switches. Work back along the harness, freeing it from its guide, noting its correct routing.

**6** Disconnect the clutch switch wiring connector **(see illustration 25.2)**.

**7** Remove the choke cable from the switch

(see Chapter 4 – this procedure incorporates switch removal).

### Installation

**8** Installation is the reverse of removal. Refer to Chapter 4 for installation of the choke cable. Make sure the locating pin in the upper half of the switch fits into hole in the top of the handlebar.

---

### 22 Neutral switch (gear position sensor) – check, removal and installation

### *Check*

**1** Before checking the electrical circuit, check the bulb (see Section 17) and fuse (see Section 5).

**2** Remove the seat cowling (see Chapter 8). Trace the neutral switch wiring from the left-hand side of the engine to the white connector with the blue and pink wires (T and V models) or blue, pink and black/white wires (W and X models), and disconnect it **(see illustration)**.

**3** Make sure the transmission is in neutral. With the connector disconnected and the ignition switched ON, the neutral light should be out. If not, the wire between the connector and instrument cluster must be earthed (grounded) at some point.

**4** Check for continuity between the blue wire terminal on the switch side of the wiring connector and the crankcase. With the transmission in neutral, there should be

continuity. With the transmission in gear, there should be no continuity. If the tests prove otherwise, then either the switch is faulty or the spring and plunger mechanism in the selector drum is faulty. Remove the switch (see below) and check the condition of the spring and plunger; make sure that the plunger moves freely in its hole. If there is any sign of wear or damage, renew the spring and plunger and check the operation of the switch before buying a new switch.

**5** If the continuity tests prove the switch is good, check for voltage at the blue wire terminal using a test light. If there's no voltage present, check the wire and components between the switch, diode, the instrument cluster and fusebox (see the *wiring diagrams* at the end of this Chapter).

### *Removal*

**6** Unscrew the gearchange linkage arm pinch bolt and remove the arm from the shaft, noting any alignment marks **(see illustration)**. If no marks are visible, make your own before removing the arm so that it can be correctly aligned with the shaft on installation.

**7** Trace the wiring from the speedometer sensor on the front sprocket cover and disconnect it at the connector – you may have to remove the left-hand fairing side panel to access it (see Chapter 8) **(see illustration 16.6a)**.

**8** Unscrew the bolts securing the sprocket cover to the crankcase and move the cover aside **(see illustration)**. There is no need to detach the clutch cable from the cover. On W and X models, note the rubber bushing for the gearchange shaft and remove it from the cover if required.

**9** Remove the seat cowling (see Chapter 8). Trace the neutral switch (gear position sensor) wiring from the left-hand side of the engine to the white connector with the blue and pink wires (T and V models) or blue, pink and black/white wires (W and X models), and disconnect it **(see illustration 22.2)**. Feed it through to the switch, releasing it from any clips or ties and noting its routing.

**10** Remove the two screws securing the switch to the crankcase and carefully remove it, together with the contact plunger(s) and spring(s) if required **(see illustrations)**.

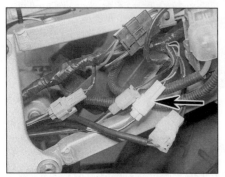

**22.2 Neutral switch wiring connector (arrowed)**

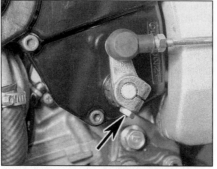

**22.6 Unscrew the bolt (arrowed) and slide the arm off the shaft**

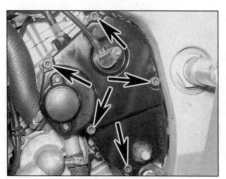

**22.8 Sprocket cover bolts (arrowed)**

**22.10a Remove the screws (arrowed) and pull out the switch**

**22.10b Remove the plungers and springs if required**

22.11a Install the springs and plungers . . .

22.11b . . . then fit a new O-ring onto the switch . . .

22.11c . . . and fit it onto the engine

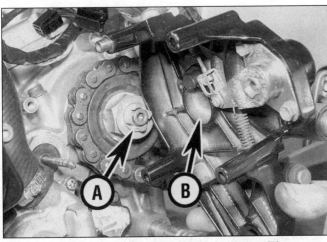
22.15a Locate the rotor (A) into the sensor (B)

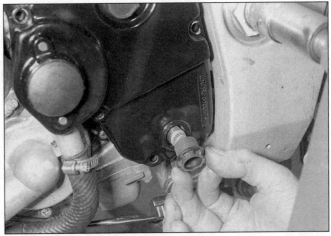
22.15b Where fitted and if removed, slide the rubber bush onto the shaft

Discard the O-ring as a new one must be used.

## Installation

11 If removed, install the spring(s) and plunger(s) into the hole(s) in the end of the selector drum, then install the switch using a new O-ring and tighten its screws securely **(see illustrations)**.

12 Route the wiring up to its connector and reconnect it **(see illustration 22.2)**. Secure the wiring with any clips or ties.

13 Check the operation of the neutral light.

14 If detached, fit the clutch cable into the release mechanism in the sprocket cover (see Chapter 2).

15 Make sure the dowels are either in the crankcase or the sprocket cover. Install the cover, making sure the speedometer rotor fits properly into the sensor and the dowels locate correctly, and tighten its bolts **(see illustration)**. On W and X models, if removed, fit the rubber bushing for the gearchange shaft into the cover **(see illustration)**.

16 Slide the gearchange linkage arm onto the shaft, aligning the marks, and tighten the pinch bolt **(see illustration 22.6)**.

17 Reconnect the speedometer sensor wiring connector **(see illustration 16.6a)**.

## 23 Sidestand switch – check and renewal

### Check

1 The sidestand switch is mounted on the sidestand bracket. The switch is part of the safety circuit which prevents or stops the engine running if the transmission is in gear whilst the sidestand is down, and prevents the engine from starting if the transmission is in gear unless the sidestand is up and the clutch lever is pulled in.

2 Remove the seat cowling (see Chapter 8). Trace the wiring back from the switch to the connector with the green and black/white wires and disconnect it **(see illustration)**.

3 Check the operation of the switch using an ohmmeter or continuity test light. Connect the meter between the terminals on the switch side of the connector. With the sidestand up there should be continuity (zero resistance) between the terminals, and with the stand down there should be no continuity (infinite resistance).

4 If the switch does not perform as expected, it is defective and must be renewed. Check

first that the fault is not caused by a sticking switch plunger due to the ingress of road dirt; spray the switch with a water dispersant aerosol.

5 If the switch is good, check the sidestand relay and diode as described in the relevant sections of this Chapter. Also check the wiring between the various components (see the *wiring diagrams* at the end of this chapter).

### Renewal

6 The sidestand switch is mounted on the sidestand bracket. Remove the seat cowling

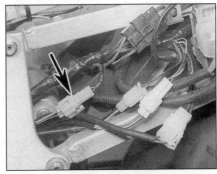
23.2 Disconnect the sidestand switch wiring connector (arrowed)

**9**

23.8a Unscrew the nuts (where fitted) (arrowed) . . .

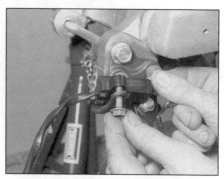

23.8b . . . then withdraw the bolts and remove the switch (nut/bolt arrangement differs according to model)

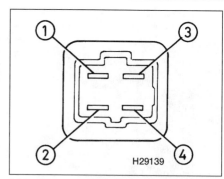

24.2 Sidestand relay terminal identification – T and V models

(see Chapter 8). Trace the wiring back from the switch to its connector and disconnect it **(see illustration 23.2)**.

7 Work back along the switch wiring, freeing it from any relevant retaining clips and ties, noting its correct routing.

8 Unscrew the nuts and/or remove the bolts (according to model) securing the switch to the frame **(see illustrations)**.

9 Fit the new switch onto the bracket, then apply a suitable non-permanent thread locking compound to the bolt threads and tighten the nuts securely.

10 Make sure the wiring is correctly routed up to the connector and retained by all the necessary clips and ties. Reconnect the wiring connector.

11 Install the seat cowling (see Chapter 8).

## 24 Sidestand relay – check and renewal

### Check

1 If the sidestand switch and wiring are good, the sidestand relay may be at fault. The relay is

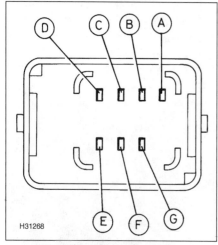

24.3 Sidestand relay/turn signal relay/diode terminal identification – W and X models

located behind the seat cowling on the left-hand side on T and V models (just ahead of the starter relay), and on the inside of the left-hand air duct in the fairing, next to the fusebox and integral with the turn signal relay and diode on W and X models **(see illustration 13.3a)**.

2 On T and V models, remove the seat cowling (see Chapter 8) and disconnect the relay wiring connector. Using an ohmmeter or continuity tester, connect the positive (+ve) lead to the No. 1 terminal on the relay and the negative (-ve) lead to the No. 2 terminal **(see illustration)**. There should be no continuity between the terminals. Using an auxiliary 12V battery and a set of leads, connect the battery positive (+ve) lead to the No. 3 terminal on the relay, and the battery negative (-ve) lead to the No. 4 terminal. With the battery connected, there should be continuity (zero resistance) between Nos. 1 and 2 terminals. If either of the above conditions do not exist, install a new relay.

3 On W and X models, unplug the sidestand relay/turn signal relay/diode from its connector **(see illustration 13.3b)**. Using an ohmmeter or continuity tester, connect the positive (+ve) lead to the D terminal on the relay and the negative (-ve) lead to the E terminal **(see illustration)**. There should be no continuity between the terminals. Using an auxiliary 12V battery and a set of leads, connect the battery positive (+ve) lead to the D terminal on the relay, and the battery negative (-ve) lead to the C terminal on the relay. With the battery connected, there

should be continuity (zero resistance) between D and E terminals. If either of the above conditions do not exist, install a new sidestand relay/turn signal relay/diode.

4 If the relay is good, check the other components in the starter circuit as described in the relevant sections of this Chapter. If all components are good, check the wiring between the various components (see the *wiring diagrams* at the end of this book).

### Renewal

5 The relay is located behind the seat cowling on the left-hand side on T and V models (just ahead of the starter relay), and on the inside of the left-hand air duct in the fairing, next to the fusebox and integral with the turn signal relay and diode on W and X models **(see illustration 13.3a)**.

6 On T and V models, remove the seat cowling (see Chapter 8) and disconnect the relay wiring connector, then remove the relay. Install the new relay and check the operation of the sidestand switch.

7 On W and X models, unplug the sidestand relay/turn signal relay/diode from its connector **(see illustration 13.3b)**. Install the new sidestand relay/turn signal relay/diode and check the operation of the sidestand switch.

## 25 Clutch switch – check and renewal

### Check

1 The clutch switch is situated on the underside of the clutch lever bracket. The switch is part of the safety circuit which prevents or stops the engine running if the transmission is in gear whilst the sidestand is down, and prevents the engine from starting if the transmission is in gear unless the sidestand is up and the clutch lever is pulled in.

2 To check the switch, disconnect the wiring connector **(see illustration)**. Connect the probes of an ohmmeter or a continuity test light to the two switch terminals. With the

25.2 Clutch switch wiring connector (arrowed)

clutch lever pulled in, continuity should be indicated. With the clutch lever out, no continuity (infinite resistance) should be indicated.

3 If the switch is good, check the other components in the starter circuit as described in the relevant sections of this Chapter. If all components are good, check the wiring between the various components (see the *wiring diagrams* at the end of this book).

### Renewal

4 Disconnect the wiring connector from the clutch switch (see illustration 25.2). Remove the screw and remove the switch.

5 Installation is the reverse of removal. The switch isn't adjustable.

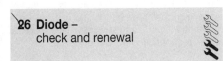

## 26 Diode – check and renewal

### Check

1 The diode is part of the safety circuit which prevents or stops the engine running if the transmission is in gear whilst the sidestand is down, and prevents the engine from starting if the transmission is in gear unless the sidestand is up and the clutch lever is pulled in. The diode is located under the fuel tank on T and V models, and on the inside of the left-hand air duct in the fairing, next to the fusebox and integral with the turn signal relay and sidestand relay on W and X models (see illustration 13.3a).

2 On T and V models, raise the fuel tank (see Chapter 4) and unplug the diode from its connector – it will probably have insulating tape wrapped round it securing it in the connector, so remove that and wind fresh tape around it on completion. Using an ohmmeter or continuity tester, connect the positive (+ve) probe to one of the outer terminals of the diode and the negative (-ve) probe to the middle terminal of the diode. The diode should show continuity. Now reverse the probes. The diode should show no continuity. Repeat the tests between the other outer terminal and the middle terminal. The same results should be achieved. If it does not behave as stated, install a new diode.

3 On W and X models, unplug the diode/turn signal relay/sidestand relay from its connector (see illustration 13.3b). Using an ohmmeter or continuity tester, connect the positive (+ve) probe to C terminal of the diode and the negative (-ve) probe to A terminal (see illustration 24.3). The diode should show continuity. Now reverse the probes. The diode should show no continuity. Repeat the tests between B terminal and A terminal. The same results should be achieved. If it doesn't behave as stated, install a new diode/turn signal relay/sidestand relay.

27.1a On 600 and 750T and V models, the horn is behind the bottom yoke

4 If the diode is good, check the other components in the starter circuit as described in the relevant sections of this Chapter. If all components are good, check the wiring between the various components (see the *wiring diagrams* at the end of this book).

### Renewal

5 On T and V models, raise the fuel tank (see Chapter 4) and unplug the diode from its connector – it will probably have insulating tape wrapped round it securing it in the connector, so remove that and wind fresh tape around it on completion. Plug in the new diode and check the circuit.

6 On W and X models, unplug the diode/turn signal relay/sidestand relay from its connector (see illustration 13.3b). Plug in the new diode/turn signal relay/sidestand relay and check the circuit.

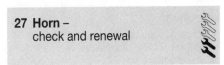

## 27 Horn – check and renewal

### Check

1 On GSX-R600 models and GSX-R750T and V models, the horn is mounted on the front of the frame below the steering head (see illustration). On GSX-R750W and X models, the horn is mounted on the top left-hand corner of the radiator (see illustration). The horn should be accessible without removing a fairing side panel (right-hand panel on GSX-R600 models and GSX-R750T and V models, left-hand panel on GSX-R750W and X models), but access is improved if you do so (see Chapter 8).

2 Disconnect the wiring connectors from the horn. Using two jumper wires, apply battery voltage directly to the terminals on the horn. If the horn sounds, check the switch (see Section 20) and the wiring between the switch and the horn (see the *wiring diagrams* at the end of this Chapter).

3 If the horn doesn't sound, install a new one.

### Renewal

4 On GSX-R600 models and GSX-R750T and

27.1b On 750W and X models, the horn is on the left-hand end of the radiator

V models, the horn is mounted on the front of the frame below the steering head (see illustration 27.1a). On GSX-R750W and X models, the horn is mounted on the top left-hand corner of the radiator (see illustration 27.1b). The horn should be accessible without removing a fairing side panel (right-hand panel on GSX-R600 models and GSX-R750T and V models, left-hand panel on GSX-R750W and X models), but access is improved if you do so (see Chapter 8).

5 Disconnect the wiring connectors from the horn, then remove the screw or bolt securing the horn and remove it from the bike.

6 Install the horn and securely tighten the screw or bolt. Connect the wiring connectors.

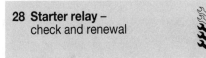

## 28 Starter relay – check and renewal

### Check

1 If the starter circuit is faulty, first check the fuse (see Section 5).

2 Remove the seat cowling (see Chapter 8). The starter relay is located on the rear sub-frame on the left-hand side. Disconnect the battery negative (-ve) lead. Remove the plastic cover on the top of the relay (see illustration). Unscrew the bolt securing the starter motor lead to its terminal and disconnect the lead

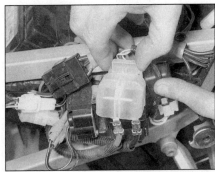

28.2a Remove the relay cover

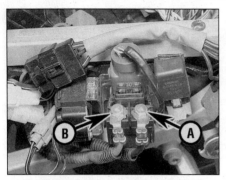

28.2b Starter motor lead terminal (A), battery lead terminal (B)

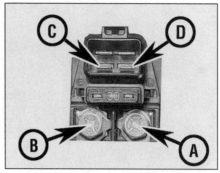

28.4 Starter relay terminal identification (see text)

28.9 Disconnect the relay wiring connector

(see illustration); position the lead away from the relay terminal. Reconnect the battery negative (-ve) lead. With the ignition switch ON, the engine kill switch in the RUN position, the transmission in neutral and the clutch pulled in, press the starter switch. The relay should be heard to click.

3 If the relay doesn't click, switch off the ignition, then remove the relay as described below and test it as follows.

4 Set a multimeter to the ohms x 1 scale and connect it across the relay's starter motor and battery lead terminals (A and B). Using a fully-charged 12 volt battery and two insulated jumper wires, connect the positive (+ve) battery lead to terminal C of the relay, and its negative (-ve) lead to terminal D (see illustration). At this point the relay should be heard to click and the multimeter should read 0 ohms (continuity). If this is the case the relay

is proved good. If the relay does not click when battery voltage is applied and indicates no continuity (infinite resistance) across its terminals, it is faulty and must be renewed.

5 To check the internal resistance of the relay, use a multimeter set to the ohms x 1 scale and connect its probes to terminals C and D of the relay (see illustration 28.4). The resistance reading obtained should be as specified at the beginning of the Chapter.

6 If the relay is good, check for battery voltage between the yellow/green and the black/white (GSX-R600 and GSX-R750T and V) or yellow/green and yellow/black (GSX-R750W and X) wire terminals on the connector when the starter button is pressed. If voltage is present, check the other components in the starter circuit as described in the relevant sections of this Chapter. If no voltage was present or if all components are good, check the wiring between the various components (see the *wiring diagrams* at the end of this chapter).

### Renewal

7 Remove the cowling (see Chapter 8). The starter relay is located on the rear sub-frame on the left-hand side.

8 Disconnect the battery terminals, remembering to disconnect the negative (-ve) terminal first.

9 Remove the plastic cover on the top of the relay (see illustration 28.2a). Unscrew the two bolts securing the starter motor and battery leads to the relay and detach the leads (see illustration 28.2b). Disconnect the relay wiring connector – you will probably need to displace

the relay to access the connector clip at the back (see illustration). Remove the relay.

10 Installation is the reverse of removal, ensuring the terminal bolts are securely tightened. Connect the negative (-ve) lead last when reconnecting the battery.

### 29 Starter motor – removal and installation

#### Removal

1 Remove the fuel tank (see Chapter 4). Disconnect the battery negative (-ve) lead.

2 Pull back the rubber cover on the starter motor terminal and remove the screw (600 models) or nut (750 models) securing the lead to the motor (see illustration).

3 Unscrew the two bolts securing the starter motor to the crankcase (see illustration).

4 Slide the starter motor out of the crankcase and remove it from the machine (see illustration 29.7).

5 Remove the O-ring on the end of the starter motor and discard it as a new one must be used (see illustration 29.6).

#### Installation

6 Install a new O-ring on the end of the starter motor and ensure it is seated in its groove (see illustration). Apply a smear of engine oil or grease to the O-ring to aid installation.

7 Manoeuvre the motor into position and slide it into the crankcase (see illustration).

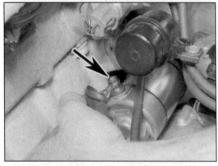

29.2 Remove the nut (arrowed) or screw and detach the lead

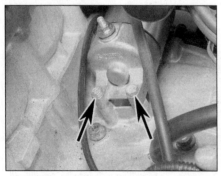

29.3 Unscrew the bolts (arrowed) and remove the starter motor

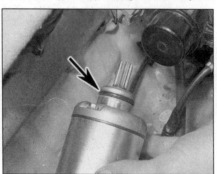

29.6 Fit a new O-ring (arrowed) . . .

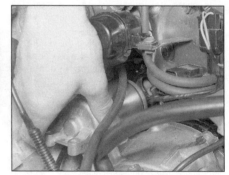

29.7 . . . then install the starter motor

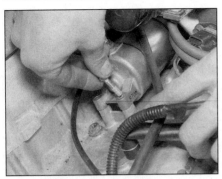

**29.8 Install the bolts . . .**

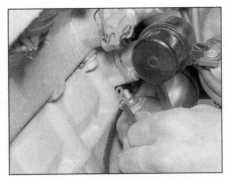

**29.9 . . . and connect the lead**

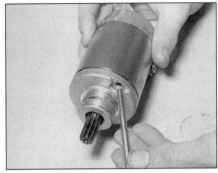

**30.3 Unscrew and remove the two long bolts**

Ensure that the starter motor teeth mesh correctly with those of the starter idle/reduction gear.

**8** Install the retaining bolts and tighten them securely, but not too tight **(see illustration)**.

**9** Connect the starter lead to the motor and secure it with the screw (600 models) or nut (750 models) **(see illustration)**. Make sure the rubber cover is correctly seated over the terminal.

**10** Install the fuel tank (see Chapter 4). Connect the battery negative (-ve) lead.

## 30 Starter motor – disassembly, inspection and reassembly

### GSX-R600 models

#### Disassembly

**1** Remove the starter motor (see Section 29).
**2** Note the alignment marks between the main housing and the front and rear covers, or make your own if they aren't clear.
**3** Unscrew the two long bolts and withdraw them from the starter motor **(see illustration)**. Discard their O-rings as new ones must be used.
**4** Remove the rear cover from the motor along with its O-ring and the brushplate assembly **(see illustration 30.15)**. The brushes are under spring pressure and will probably pop out when the armature is

removed – take care not to lose the springs.
**5** Wrap some insulating tape around the teeth on the end of the starter motor shaft – this will protect the oil seal from damage as the front cover is removed. Remove the front cover from the motor along with its O-ring **(see illustration 30.17d)**. Remove the shim from the front end of the armature shaft and the special washer from inside the front cover, noting how it fits **(see illustrations 30.17b and c)**.
**6** Withdraw the armature from the main housing, noting that it is held by the attraction of the magnets.

#### Inspection

**7** The parts of the starter motor that are most likely to require attention are the brushes. Suzuki give no specifications for the minimum

length of the brushes, however if they are obviously worn down and are close to the wire, cracked, chipped, or otherwise damaged, new ones should be installed. Draw all the brushes out of their holders and remove the springs **(see illustration)**. Remove the two screws securing the top brushes and remove them, noting how they fit **(see illustration)**. Lift out the brush holder plate, noting how it fits, then lift out the lower brushplate **(see illustrations)**. The top brushes can be renewed individually, the lower brushes come with the lower brushplate. Locate the lower brushplate into the rear cover, then fit the brush holder plate, making sure the lower brushes are correctly located. Install the top brushes, then secure them and the brush holder plate with the two screws **(see illustration)**.

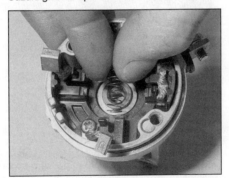

**30.7a Remove the springs from behind the brushes . . .**

**30.7b . . . then remove the screws (arrowed) and the top brushes**

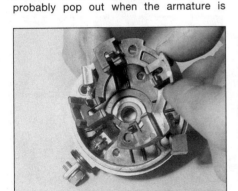

**30.7c Remove the brush holder plate . . .**

**30.7d . . . and the lower brush plate**

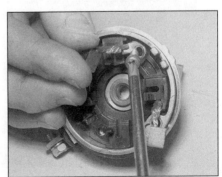

**30.7e Install the top brushes and screws**

**9**

30.9a Continuity should exist between the commutator bars

30.9b There should be no continuity between the commutator bars and the armature shaft

30.13 Check the seal and bearing in the front cover

8 Inspect the commutator bars on the armature for scoring, scratches and discoloration. The commutator can be cleaned and polished with crocus cloth, but do not use sandpaper or emery paper. After cleaning, wipe away any residue with a cloth soaked in electrical system cleaner or denatured alcohol. Also check that the insulation between each bar is not close to the level of the bars. If it is, scrape some away.

9 Using an ohmmeter or a continuity test light, check for continuity between the commutator bars (see illustration). Continuity should exist between each bar and all of the others. Also, check for continuity between the commutator bars and the armature shaft (see illustration). There should be no continuity (infinite resistance) between the commutator and the shaft. If the checks indicate otherwise, the armature is defective.

10 Check for continuity between each brush and the terminal bolt. There should be continuity (zero resistance). Check for continuity between the terminal bolt and the housing (when assembled). There should be no continuity (infinite resistance).

11 Check the front end of the armature shaft for worn, cracked, chipped and broken teeth. If the shaft is damaged or worn, install a new armature.

12 Check the end covers for signs of cracks or wear. Check the magnets in the main housing and the housing itself for cracks.

13 Check the front cover oil seal and bearing for signs of wear and damage and renew the front cover if necessary – the seal and bearing are not available separately (see illustration).

## Reassembly

14 Fit the O-ring onto the rear cover. Slide the springs and brushes back into their holders (see illustration). To make it easy to install the armature, it is necessary to draw the brushes as far back as possible in the holders and secure them there to provide clearance. A good way to do this is to cut up a cable tie into four sections, then use one for each brush, locating them between the brush wire and the wire guide on the holder (see illustrations). This should hold them in place.

15 Apply a smear of molybdenum disulphide grease to the armature shaft rear end. Insert the armature, then remove the cable tie pieces and locate the brushes on the commutator bars (see illustration). Check that each brush is securely pressed against the commutator by its spring and is free to move easily in its holder.

16 Fit the main housing over the armature, aligning the matchmarks on the housing and rear cover (see illustration). Note that the housing will be forcefully drawn onto the armature by the magnets.

17 Apply a smear of grease to the lips of the

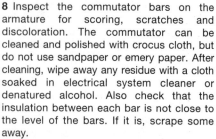

30.14a Install the spring . . .

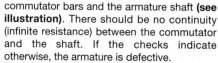

30.14b . . . then hold it back and insert the brush . . .

30.14c . . . and locate a piece of cable-tie between each brush wire and the wire guide to keep the brushes retracted

30.15 Fit the armature into the rear cover, making sure the brushes locate correctly . . .

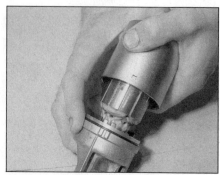

30.16 . . . then fit the main housing, being ready for the draw of the magnets

30.17a Fit a new O-ring onto the front cover

30.17b Slide the shim onto the shaft . . .

30.17c . . . and fit the special washer into the cover . . .

front cover oil seal and armature shaft and fit a new O-ring onto the cover (see illustration). Fit the shim onto the shaft and the special washer onto the front cover, making sure that its tabs locate correctly in the cover cutouts (see illustrations). Install the cover, aligning the matchmarks (see illustration). Remove the protective tape from the shaft end.

18 Make sure that the O-ring is in place on each of the long bolts, then install them and tighten them securely (see illustration 30.3).

19 Install the starter motor (see Section 29).

### GSX-R750 models

#### Disassembly

20 Remove the starter motor (see Section 29).

21 Note the alignment marks between the main housing and the front and rear covers, or make your own if they aren't clear (see illustration).

22 Unscrew the two long bolts and withdraw them from the starter motor (see illustration). Discard their O-rings as new ones must be used.

23 Wrap some insulating tape around the teeth on the end of the starter motor shaft – this will protect the oil seal from damage as the front cover is removed. Remove the front cover from the motor (see illustration). Remove the cover O-ring from the main housing and discard it as a new one must be used (see illustration 30.39b). Remove the shims from the front end of the armature shaft or the inside of the front cover, noting their correct fitted locations (see illustration 30.39a). Also

remove the special washer from the front cover (see illustration 30.39c).

24 Remove the rear cover and brushplate assembly from the motor (see illustration). Remove the cover O-ring from the main housing and discard it as a new one must be used (see illustration 30.38). Remove the shims from the rear end of the armature shaft or from inside the rear cover after the brushplate assembly has been removed (see illustration 30.37a).

25 Withdraw the armature from the main housing, noting that it is held by the attraction of the magnets.

26 Noting the correct fitted location of each component, unscrew the terminal nut and remove it along with its washer and the insulating washers (see illustration).

30.17d . . . then install the cover

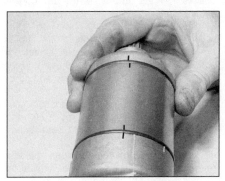

30.21 Note the alignment marks . . .

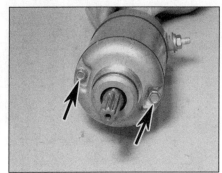

30.22 . . . then unscrew the bolts (arrowed) . . .

30.23 . . . and remove the front cover . . .

30.24 . . . and the rear cover

30.26 Unscrew the nut (arrowed) and remove the various washers

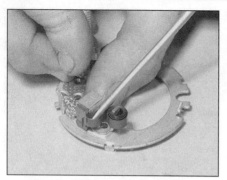

30.27a Lift the brush springs . . .

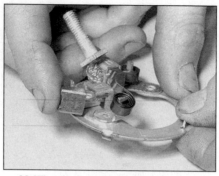

30.27b . . . and withdraw the brushes

30.36a Fit the insulator and O-ring . . .

Withdraw the terminal bolt and brushplate assembly from the rear cover (see illustration 30.36b).

27 Lift the brush springs and slide the brushes out from their holders (see illustrations).

## Inspection

28 The parts of the starter motor that are most likely to require attention are the brushes. Suzuki give no specifications for the minimum length of the brushes, however if they are obviously worn down and are close to the wire, cracked, chipped, or otherwise damaged, a new brushplate should be installed.

29 Inspect the commutator bars on the armature for scoring, scratches and

30.36b . . . then install the brushplate . . .

discoloration. The commutator can be cleaned and polished with crocus cloth, but do not use sandpaper or emery paper. After cleaning, wipe away any residue with a cloth soaked in electrical system cleaner or denatured alcohol. Also check that the insulation between each bar is not close to the level of the bars. If it is, scrape some away.

30 Using an ohmmeter or a continuity test light, check for continuity between the commutator bars (see illustration 30.9a). Continuity should exist between each bar and all of the others. Also, check for continuity between the commutator bars and the armature shaft (see illustration 30.9b). There should be no continuity (infinite resistance) between the commutator and the shaft. If the checks indicate otherwise, the armature is defective.

31 Check for continuity between each brush and the terminal bolt. There should be continuity (zero resistance). Check for continuity between the terminal bolt and the housing (when assembled). There should be no continuity (infinite resistance).

32 Check the front end of the armature shaft for worn, cracked, chipped and broken teeth. If the shaft is damaged or worn, install a new armature.

33 Check the end covers for signs of cracks or wear. Check the front cover oil seal for signs of wear and damage and renew the front cover if necessary – the seal and bearing

are not available separately. Check the magnets in the main housing and the housing itself for cracks.

34 Check the insulating washers and rubbers for signs of damage and renew them if necessary.

## Reassembly

35 Slide the brushes back into position in their holders and place the brush spring ends onto the brushes (see illustrations 30.27b and a). Check that the brushes slide freely in the holders.

36 Ensure that the inner rubber insulator is in place on the terminal bolt, then fit the O-ring if removed (see illustration). Insert the bolt through the rear cover and fit the brushplate assembly in the rear cover, making sure its slot is correctly located around the bolt bore in the cover (see illustration). Fit the insulating washers over the terminal, then fit the standard washer and the nut (see illustration).

37 Slide the shims onto the rear end of the armature shaft, then lubricate the shaft with a molybdenum disulphide grease (see illustration). Insert the armature into the rear cover, locating the brushes on the commutator bars as you do, taking care not to damage them (see illustration). Check that each brush is securely pressed against the commutator by its spring and is free to move easily in its holder.

38 Fit a new O-ring onto the main housing (see

30.36c . . . and fit the insulating washers, plain washer and nut

30.37a Slide the shims onto the shaft . . .

30.37b . . . then fit it into the rear cover, making sure the brushes locate correctly

30.38 Fit a new O-ring onto the main housing

30.39a Slide on the shims . . .

30.39b . . . and fit a new O-ring

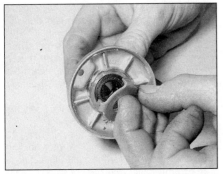

30.39c Fit the special washer into the front cover . . .

30.39d . . . then install the cover . . .

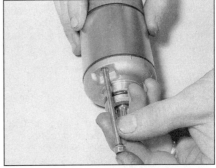

30.40 . . . and the long bolts

illustration), then fit the housing over the armature and onto the rear cover, aligning the marks made on removal (see illustration 30.24). Note that the housing will be forcefully drawn onto the armature by the magnets.

39 Slide the shims onto the front of the armature shaft, and fit a new O-ring onto the front of the main housing (see illustrations). Apply a smear of grease to the lips of the front cover oil seal. Fit the special washer onto the cover, making sure its tabs locate correctly (see illustration). Install the cover, aligning the marks made on removal (see illustration). Remove the protective tape from the shaft end.

40 Slide a new O-ring onto each of the long bolts. Check the marks made on removal are correctly aligned (see illustration 30.21), then install the long bolts and tighten them securely (see illustration).

41 Install the starter motor (see Section 29).

## 31 Charging system testing – general information and precautions

1 If the performance of the charging system is suspect, the system as a whole should be checked first, followed by testing of the individual components. **Note:** *Before beginning the checks, make sure the battery is fully charged and that all system connections are clean and tight.*

2 Checking the output of the charging system

and the performance of the various components within the charging system requires the use of a multimeter (with voltage, current and resistance checking facilities).

3 When making the checks, follow the procedures carefully to prevent incorrect connections or short circuits, as irreparable damage to electrical system components may result if short circuits occur.

4 If a multimeter is not available, the job of checking the charging system should be left to a Suzuki dealer.

## 32 Charging system – leakage and output test

1 If the charging system of the machine is thought to be faulty, remove the rider's seat (see Chapter 8) and perform the following checks.

### Leakage test

*Caution: Always connect an ammeter in series, never in parallel with the battery, otherwise it will be damaged. Do not turn the ignition ON or operate the starter motor when the ammeter is connected – a sudden surge in current will blow the meter's fuse.*

2 Turn the ignition switch OFF and disconnect the lead from the battery negative (-ve) terminal.

3 Set the multimeter to the Amps function

and connect its negative (-ve) probe to the battery negative (-ve) terminal, and positive (+ve) probe to the disconnected negative (-ve) lead (see illustration). Always set the meter to a high amps range initially and then bring it down to the mA (milli Amps) range; if there is a high current flow in the circuit it may blow the meter's fuse.

4 No current flow should be indicated. If current leakage is indicated (generally greater than 0.1 mA), there is a short circuit in the wiring. Disconnect the meter and reconnect the negative (-ve) lead to the battery, tightening it securely,

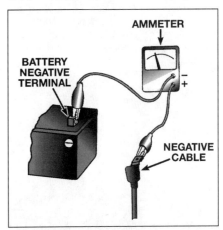

32.3 Checking the charging system leakage rate. Connect the meter as shown

**9**

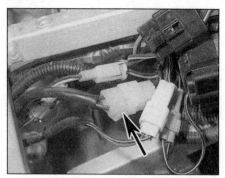

**33.2 Disconnect the alternator wiring connector (arrowed)**

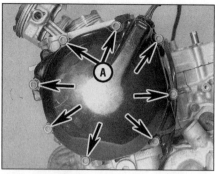

**33.6 Unscrew the bolts (arrowed), noting the ones with the sealing washers (A), and remove the cover**

**5** If leakage is indicated, use the wiring diagrams at the end of this book to systematically disconnect individual electrical components and repeat the test until the source is identified.

### Output test

**6** Start the engine and warm it up to normal operating temperature.

**7** To check the regulated voltage output, allow the engine to idle and connect a multimeter set to the 0-20 volts DC scale (voltmeter) across the terminals of the battery (positive (+ve) meter lead to battery positive (+ve) terminal, negative (-ve) meter lead to battery negative (-ve) terminal **(see illustration 3.2a))**. Slowly increase the engine speed to 5000 rpm and note the reading obtained. At this speed the voltage should be 13.5 to 15.0 volts. If the voltage is outside these limits, check the alternator and the regulator (see Sections 33 and 34).

**8** To check the unregulated output, remove the seat cowling (see Chapter 8). Trace the wiring back from the top of the alternator cover on the left-hand side of the engine and disconnect it at the white connector containing the three black wires **(see illustration 33.2)**. Using a multimeter set to 0-250 volts AC range, connect the meter probes to one pair of terminals on the alternator side of the connector. Start the engine and increase its speed to 5000 rpm. Check the voltage output and compare it to the minimum specified at the beginning of the

Chapter. Stop the engine, connect the meter to another pair of terminals, and repeat the test. Do this again to the other pair of terminals so that you have taken three readings in all. If any of the readings are below the minimum specified, check the stator coil resistance (see Section 33). If the readings are good, check the regulator/rectifier (see Section 34).

> **HAYNES HINT** *Clues to a faulty regulator are constantly blowing bulbs, with brightness varying considerably with engine speed, and battery overheating.*

### 33 Alternator – check, removal and installation

### Check

**1** Remove the seat cowling (see Chapter 8).
**2** Trace the wiring back from the top of the alternator cover on the left-hand side of the engine and disconnect it at the white connector containing the three black wires **(see illustration)**.
**3** Using a multimeter set to the ohms x 1 (ohmmeter) scale measure the resistance between each of the black wires on the alternator side of the connector, taking a total of three readings, then check for continuity between each terminal and ground (earth). If the

stator coil windings are in good condition the three readings should be within the range shown in the Specifications at the start of this Chapter and there should be no continuity (infinite resistance) between any of the terminals and ground (earth). If not, the alternator stator coil assembly is at fault and should be renewed.
**Note:** *Before condemning the stator coils, check the fault is not due to damaged wiring between the connector and coils.*

### Removal

**4** Remove the left-hand fairing side panel and the seat cowling (see Chapter 8). Trace the alternator wiring from the top of the alternator cover and disconnect it at the white connector containing the three black wires **(see illustration 33.2)**. Free the wiring from any clips or ties and feed it through to the alternator cover.
**5** Drain the engine oil (see Chapter 1).
**6** Unscrew the alternator cover bolts and remove the cover, being prepared to catch any residue oil **(see illustration)**. Discard the gasket as a new one must be used. Remove the dowels from either the cover or the crankcase if they are loose. Note the positions of the two bolts with sealing washers.
**7** To remove the rotor bolt it is necessary to stop the rotor from turning. If a rotor holding strap or tool is not available, and the engine is in the frame, place the transmission in gear and have an assistant apply the rear brake, then unscrew the bolt **(see illustration)**. There are also two flats machined into the boss in the rotor which can be used if a suitable holding tool is available **(see illustration)**; a large spanner can be applied to these flats, but note that there is some danger that it might slip due to the awkward angle involved.
**8** To remove the rotor from the crankshaft taper it is necessary to use a rotor puller. Thread the rotor puller into the centre of the rotor and turn it until the rotor is displaced from the shaft **(see illustration)**.
**9** To remove the stator from the cover, unscrew the bolts securing the stator, and the bolt securing the wiring clamp, then remove the assembly, noting how the rubber wiring grommet fits **(see illustration)**.

### Installation

**10** Install the stator onto the cover, aligning the rubber wiring grommet with the groove.

**33.7a Unscrew the rotor bolt using a holding tool**

**33.7b The flats (arrowed) can be used to hold the rotor if a suitable tool is available**

**33.8 Displace the rotor using a puller**

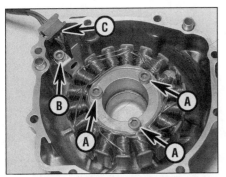

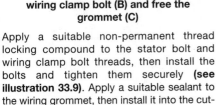

33.9 Unscrew the stator bolts (A) and the wiring clamp bolt (B) and free the grommet (C)

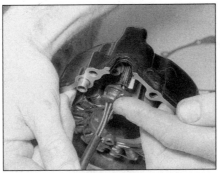

33.10 Apply sealant to the grommet

33.11 Slide the rotor onto the shaft . . .

Apply a suitable non-permanent thread locking compound to the stator bolt and wiring clamp bolt threads, then install the bolts and tighten them securely **(see illustration 33.9)**. Apply a suitable sealant to the wiring grommet, then install it into the cut-out in the cover **(see illustration)**.

**11** Clean the tapered end of the crankshaft and the corresponding mating surface on the inside of the rotor with a suitable solvent. Make sure that no metal objects have attached themselves to the magnet on the inside of the rotor, then slide the rotor onto the shaft **(see illustration)**.

**12** Apply a suitable non-permanent thread locking compound to the rotor bolt threads, then install the bolt with its

washer and tighten it to the torque setting specified at the beginning of the Chapter, using the method employed on removal to prevent the rotor from turning **(see illustrations)**.

**13** Apply a suitable sealant to the areas around the crankcase joints **(see illustration)**. If removed, insert the dowels in the cover or crankcase. Install the alternator cover using a new gasket, making sure it locates correctly onto the dowels, then install the cover bolts, using new sealing washers on the two top bolts in front of the wiring grommet **(see illustrations)**. Tighten the bolts evenly in a criss-cross sequence.

**14** Feed the alternator wiring back to its connector, making sure it is correctly routed

and secured by any clips or ties, and reconnect it **(see illustration 33.2)**.

**15** Refill the engine with oil (see Chapter 1).

**16** Install the fairing side panel and the seat cowling (see Chapter 8).

## 34 Regulator/rectifier –
check and renewal

### Check

**1** Remove the seat cowling (see Chapter 8). The regulator/rectifier is mounted on the left-hand side of the rear sub-frame. Disconnect the wiring connector **(see illustration)**.

**2** Using a multimeter or ohmmeter set to the

33.12a . . . then apply a thread-lock to the bolt . . .

33.12b . . . and tighten it to the specified torque

33.13a Apply a sealant to the crankcase joints (arrowed) . . .

33.13b . . . then locate the gasket over the dowels (arrowed) . . .

33.13c . . . and install the cover

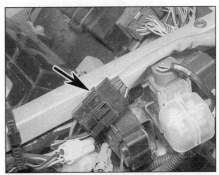

34.1 Disconnect the regulator/rectifier wiring connector

**9**

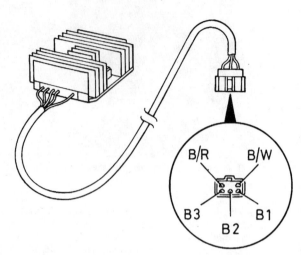

Unit: kΩ

| | | + Probe of tester to: | | | | |
|---|---|---|---|---|---|---|
| | | B/R | B₁ | B₂ | B₃ | B/W |
| − Probe of tester to: | B/R | | ∞ | ∞ | ∞ | ∞ |
| | B₁ | 1 to 10 | | ∞ | ∞ | ∞ |
| | B₂ | 1 to 10 | ∞ | | ∞ | ∞ |
| | B₃ | 1 to 10 | ∞ | ∞ | | ∞ |
| | B/W | 1 to 20 | 1 to 10 | 1 to 10 | 1 to 10 | |

∞ = infinity (very high infinite resistance)

H31269

**34.2 Regulator/rectifier test data and terminal identification**

B  Black        B/R  Black/red        B/W  Black/white

K-ohms scale, check the resistance between the various terminals on the regulator/rectifier as shown in the table **(see illustration)**. If the readings do not compare closely with those shown in the accompanying table the regulator/rectifier unit can be considered faulty. **Note:** *The use of certain multimeters could lead to false readings being obtained, as could a low battery in the meter and contact between the meter probes and your fingers. If the above check shows the regulator/rectifier unit to be faulty, take the unit to a Suzuki dealer for confirmation of its condition before renewing it. Suzuki have a special tester which will perform more detailed tests.*

**3** If the regulator appears to be good, check the wiring between the battery,

regulator/rectifier and alternator, and the wiring connectors (see the *wiring diagrams* at the end of this book).

### Renewal

**4** Remove the seat cowling (see Chapter 8).
**5** The regulator/rectifier is mounted on the left-hand side of the rear sub-frame. Disconnect the wiring connector **(see illustration 34.1)**.
**6** Remove the two screws securing the regulator/rectifier and remove it, noting the spacers behind it **(see illustration)**.
**7** Install the new unit and tighten its screws securely, not forgetting the spacers. Connect the wiring connector.
**8** Install the seat cowling (see Chapter 8).

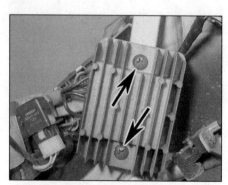

**34.6 The regulator/rectifier is secured by the two screws (arrowed)**

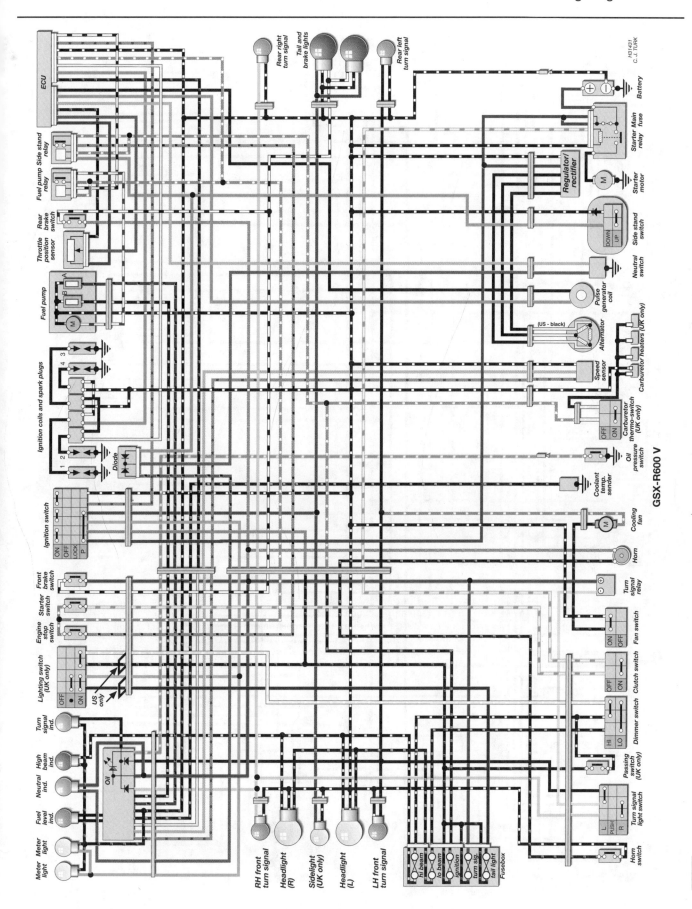

GSX-R600 V

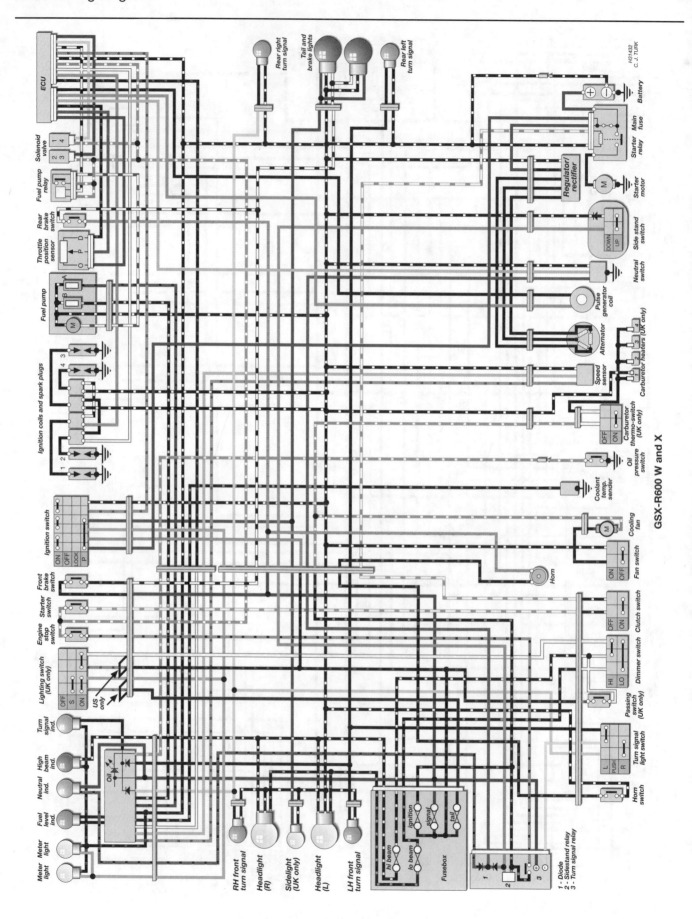

GSX-R600 W and X

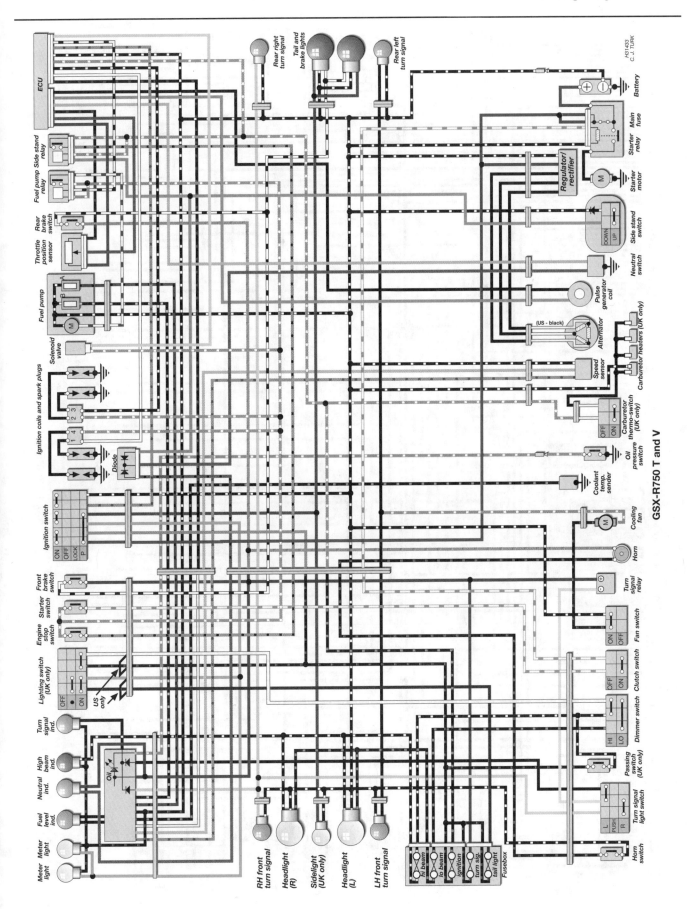

GSX-R750 T and V

9

GSX-R750 W and X

# Dimensions and weights

## GSX-R600 models

Wheelbase
  GSX-R600V . . . . . . . . . . . . . . . . . . . . . . . . . . . .1390 mm
  GSX-R600W and X . . . . . . . . . . . . . . . . . . . . . .1385 mm
Overall length . . . . . . . . . . . . . . . . . . . . . . . . . . . .2065 mm
Overall width . . . . . . . . . . . . . . . . . . . . . . . . . . . . .720 mm
Overall height
  GSX-R600V . . . . . . . . . . . . . . . . . . . . . . . . . . . .1135 mm
  GSX-R600W and X . . . . . . . . . . . . . . . . . . . . . .1165 mm
Seat height . . . . . . . . . . . . . . . . . . . . . . . . . . . . . .830 mm
Minimum ground clearance . . . . . . . . . . . . . . . . . . .130 mm
Weight (dry)
  UK and US models . . . . . . . . . . . . . . . . . . . . . . . . .174 kg
  California models . . . . . . . . . . . . . . . . . . . . . . . . . .175 kg

## GSX-R750 models

Wheelbase . . . . . . . . . . . . . . . . . . . . . . . . . . . . . .1400 mm
  GSX-R750T and V . . . . . . . . . . . . . . . . . . . . . . .1395 mm
  GSX-R750W and X . . . . . . . . . . . . . . . . . . . . . .2065 mm
Overall length
  GSX-R750T and V . . . . . . . . . . . . . . . . . . . . . . .2055 mm
  GSX-R750W and X . . . . . . . . . . . . . . . . . . . . . .2065 mm
Overall width . . . . . . . . . . . . . . . . . . . . . . . . . . . . .720 mm
Overall height
  GSX-R750T and V . . . . . . . . . . . . . . . . . . . . . . .1135 mm
  GSX-R750W and X . . . . . . . . . . . . . . . . . . . . . .1165 mm
Seat height . . . . . . . . . . . . . . . . . . . . . . . . . . . . . .830 mm
Minimum ground clearance . . . . . . . . . . . . . . . . . . .130 mm
Weight (dry)
  UK and US models . . . . . . . . . . . . . . . . . . . . . . . .179 kg
  California models . . . . . . . . . . . . . . . . . . . . . . . . . .180 kg

## Buying tools

A toolkit is a fundamental requirement for servicing and repairing a motorcycle. Although there will be an initial expense in building up enough tools for servicing, this will soon be offset by the savings made by doing the job yourself. As experience and confidence grow, additional tools can be added to enable the repair and overhaul of the motorcycle. Many of the specialist tools are expensive and not often used so it may be preferable to hire them, or for a group of friends or motorcycle club to join in the purchase.

As a rule, it is better to buy more expensive, good quality tools. Cheaper tools are likely to wear out faster and need to be renewed more often, nullifying the original saving.

> ⚠️ **Warning:** *To avoid the risk of a poor quality tool breaking in use, causing injury or damage to the component being worked on, always aim to purchase tools which meet the relevant national safety standards.*

The following lists of tools do not represent the manufacturer's service tools, but serve as a guide to help the owner decide which tools are needed for this level of work. In addition, items such as an electric drill, hacksaw, files, soldering iron and a workbench equipped with a vice, may be needed. Although not classed as tools, a selection of bolts, screws, nuts, washers and pieces of tubing always come in useful.

For more information about tools, refer to the Haynes *Motorcycle Workshop Practice Manual* (Bk. No. 3470).

## Manufacturer's service tools

Inevitably certain tasks require the use of a service tool. Where possible an alternative tool or method of approach is recommended, but sometimes there is no option if personal injury or damage to the component is to be avoided. Where required, service tools are referred to in the relevant procedure.

Service tools can usually only be purchased from a motorcycle dealer and are identified by a part number. Some of the commonly-used tools, such as rotor pullers, are available in aftermarket form from mail-order motorcycle tool and accessory suppliers.

# Maintenance and minor repair tools

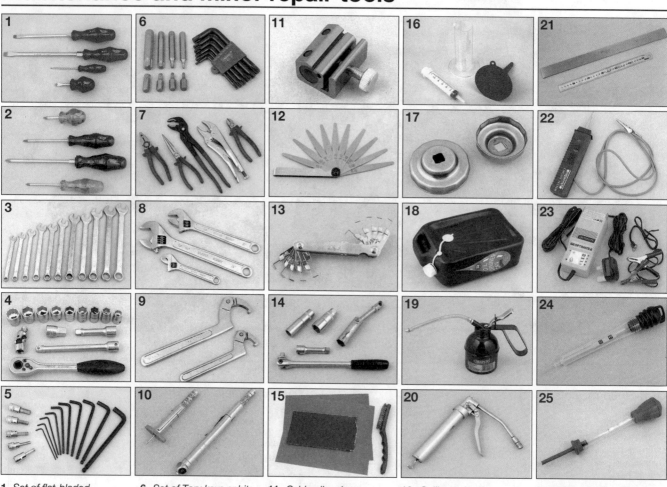

1  Set of flat-bladed screwdrivers
2  Set of Phillips head screwdrivers
3  Combination open-end and ring spanners
4  Socket set (3/8 inch or 1/2 inch drive)
5  Set of Allen keys or bits
6  Set of Torx keys or bits
7  Pliers, cutters and self-locking grips (Mole grips)
8  Adjustable spanners
9  C-spanners
10 Tread depth gauge and tyre pressure gauge
11 Cable oiler clamp
12 Feeler gauges
13 Spark plug gap measuring tool
14 Spark plug spanner or deep plug sockets
15 Wire brush and emery paper
16 Calibrated syringe, measuring vessel and funnel
17 Oil filter adapters
18 Oil drainer can or tray
19 Pump type oil can
20 Grease gun
21 Straight-edge and steel rule
22 Continuity tester
23 Battery charger
24 Hydrometer (for battery specific gravity check)
25 Anti-freeze tester (for liquid-cooled engines)

## Repair and overhaul tools

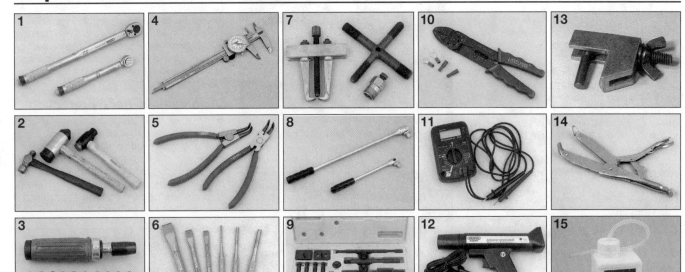

1  Torque wrench
   (small and mid-ranges)
2  Conventional, plastic or
   soft-faced hammers
3  Impact driver set

4  Vernier gauge
5  Circlip pliers (internal and
   external, or combination)
6  Set of cold chisels
   and punches

7  Selection of pullers
8  Breaker bars
9  Chain breaking/
   riveting tool set

10  Wire stripper and
    crimper tool
11  Multimeter (measures
    amps, volts and ohms)
12  Stroboscope (for
    dynamic timing checks)

13  Hose clamp
    (wingnut type shown)
14  Clutch holding tool
15  One-man brake/clutch
    bleeder kit

## Specialist tools

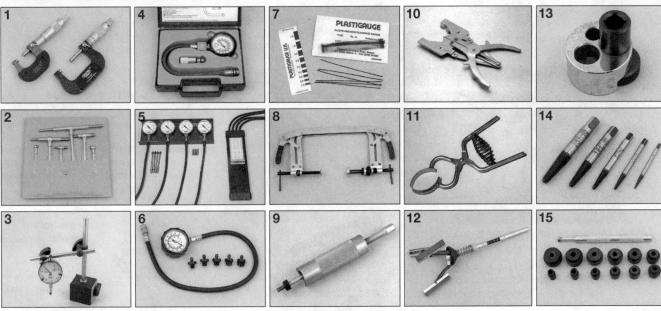

1  Micrometers
   (external type)
2  Telescoping gauges
3  Dial gauge

4  Cylinder
   compression gauge
5  Vacuum gauges (left) or
   manometer (right)
6  Oil pressure gauge

7  Plastigauge kit
8  Valve spring compressor
   (4-stroke engines)
9  Piston pin drawbolt tool

10  Piston ring removal and
    installation tool
11  Piston ring clamp
12  Cylinder bore hone
    (stone type shown)

13  Stud extractor
14  Screw extractor set
15  Bearing driver set

## 1 Workshop equipment and facilities

### The workbench

● Work is made much easier by raising the bike up on a ramp - components are much more accessible if raised to waist level. The hydraulic or pneumatic types seen in the dealer's workshop are a sound investment if you undertake a lot of repairs or overhauls **(see illustration 1.1)**.

**1.1 Hydraulic motorcycle ramp**

● If raised off ground level, the bike must be supported on the ramp to avoid it falling. Most ramps incorporate a front wheel locating clamp which can be adjusted to suit different diameter wheels. When tightening the clamp, take care not to mark the wheel rim or damage the tyre - use wood blocks on each side to prevent this.

● Secure the bike to the ramp using tie-downs **(see illustration 1.2)**. If the bike has only a sidestand, and hence leans at a dangerous angle when raised, support the bike on an auxiliary stand.

**1.2 Tie-downs are used around the passenger footrests to secure the bike**

● Auxiliary (paddock) stands are widely available from mail order companies or motorcycle dealers and attach either to the wheel axle or swingarm pivot **(see illustration 1.3)**. If the motorcycle has a centrestand, you can support it under the crankcase to prevent it toppling whilst either wheel is removed **(see illustration 1.4)**.

**1.3 This auxiliary stand attaches to the swingarm pivot**

**1.4 Always use a block of wood between the engine and jack head when supporting the engine in this way**

### Fumes and fire

● Refer to the Safety first! page at the beginning of the manual for full details. Make sure your workshop is equipped with a fire extinguisher suitable for fuel-related fires (Class B fire - flammable liquids) - it is not sufficient to have a water-filled extinguisher.

● Always ensure adequate ventilation is available. Unless an exhaust gas extraction system is available for use, ensure that the engine is run outside of the workshop.

● If working on the fuel system, make sure the workshop is ventilated to avoid a build-up of fumes. This applies equally to fume build-up when charging a battery. Do not smoke or allow anyone else to smoke in the workshop.

### Fluids

● If you need to drain fuel from the tank, store it in an approved container marked as suitable for the storage of petrol (gasoline) **(see illustration 1.5)**. Do not store fuel in glass jars or bottles.

**1.5 Use an approved can only for storing petrol (gasoline)**

● Use proprietary engine degreasers or solvents which have a high flash-point, such as paraffin (kerosene), for cleaning off oil, grease and dirt - never use petrol (gasoline) for cleaning. Wear rubber gloves when handling solvent and engine degreaser. The fumes from certain solvents can be dangerous - always work in a well-ventilated area.

### Dust, eye and hand protection

● Protect your lungs from inhalation of dust particles by wearing a filtering mask over the nose and mouth. Many frictional materials still contain asbestos which is dangerous to your health. Protect your eyes from spouts of liquid and sprung components by wearing a pair of protective goggles **(see illustration 1.6)**.

**1.6 A fire extinguisher, goggles, mask and protective gloves should be at hand in the workshop**

● Protect your hands from contact with solvents, fuel and oils by wearing rubber gloves. Alternatively apply a barrier cream to your hands before starting work. If handling hot components or fluids, wear suitable gloves to protect your hands from scalding and burns.

### What to do with old fluids

● Old cleaning solvent, fuel, coolant and oils should not be poured down domestic drains or onto the ground. Package the fluid up in old oil containers, label it accordingly, and take it to a garage or disposal facility. Contact your local authority for location of such sites or ring the oil care hotline.

**OIL CARE**
FOLLOW THE CODE
OIL BANK LINE
**0800 66 33 66**

*Note: It is antisocial and illegal to dump oil down the drain. To find the location of your local oil recycling bank, call this number free.*

*In the USA, note that any oil supplier must accept used oil for recycling.*

## 2 Fasteners -
### screws, bolts and nuts

### *Fastener types and applications*

#### Bolts and screws

● Fastener head types are either of hexagonal, Torx or splined design, with internal and external versions of each type **(see illustrations 2.1 and 2.2)**; splined head fasteners are not in common use on motorcycles. The conventional slotted or Phillips head design is used for certain screws. Bolt or screw length is always measured from the underside of the head to the end of the item **(see illustration 2.11)**.

**2.1 Internal hexagon/Allen (A), Torx (B) and splined (C) fasteners, with corresponding bits**

**2.2 External Torx (A), splined (B) and hexagon (C) fasteners, with corresponding sockets**

● Certain fasteners on the motorcycle have a tensile marking on their heads, the higher the marking the stronger the fastener. High tensile fasteners generally carry a 10 or higher marking. Never replace a high tensile fastener with one of a lower tensile strength.

#### Washers (see illustration 2.3)

● Plain washers are used between a fastener head and a component to prevent damage to the component or to spread the load when torque is applied. Plain washers can also be used as spacers or shims in certain assemblies. Copper or aluminium plain washers are often used as sealing washers on drain plugs.

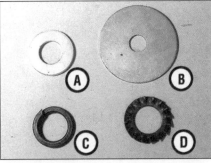

**2.3 Plain washer (A), penny washer (B), spring washer (C) and serrated washer (D)**

● The split-ring spring washer works by applying axial tension between the fastener head and component. If flattened, it is fatigued and must be renewed. If a plain (flat) washer is used on the fastener, position the spring washer between the fastener and the plain washer.

● Serrated star type washers dig into the fastener and component faces, preventing loosening. They are often used on electrical earth (ground) connections to the frame.

● Cone type washers (sometimes called Belleville) are conical and when tightened apply axial tension between the fastener head and component. They must be installed with the dished side against the component and often carry an OUTSIDE marking on their outer face. If flattened, they are fatigued and must be renewed.

● Tab washers are used to lock plain nuts or bolts on a shaft. A portion of the tab washer is bent up hard against one flat of the nut or bolt to prevent it loosening. Due to the tab washer being deformed in use, a new tab washer should be used every time it is disturbed.

● Wave washers are used to take up endfloat on a shaft. They provide light springing and prevent excessive side-to-side play of a component. Can be found on rocker arm shafts.

#### Nuts and split pins

● Conventional plain nuts are usually six-sided **(see illustration 2.4)**. They are sized by thread diameter and pitch. High tensile nuts carry a number on one end to denote their tensile strength.

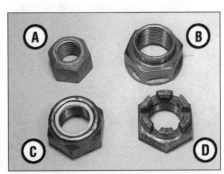

**2.4 Plain nut (A), shouldered locknut (B), nylon insert nut (C) and castellated nut (D)**

● Self-locking nuts either have a nylon insert, or two spring metal tabs, or a shoulder which is staked into a groove in the shaft - their advantage over conventional plain nuts is a resistance to loosening due to vibration. The nylon insert type can be used a number of times, but must be renewed when the friction of the nylon insert is reduced, ie when the nut spins freely on the shaft. The spring tab type can be reused unless the tabs are damaged. The shouldered type must be renewed every time it is disturbed.

● Split pins (cotter pins) are used to lock a castellated nut to a shaft or to prevent slackening of a plain nut. Common applications are wheel axles and brake torque arms. Because the split pin arms are deformed to lock around the nut a new split pin must always be used on installation - always fit the correct size split pin which will fit snugly in the shaft hole. Make sure the split pin arms are correctly located around the nut **(see illustrations 2.5 and 2.6)**.

**2.5 Bend split pin (cotter pin) arms as shown (arrows) to secure a castellated nut**

**2.6 Bend split pin (cotter pin) arms as shown to secure a plain nut**

*Caution: If the castellated nut slots do not align with the shaft hole after tightening to the torque setting, tighten the nut until the next slot aligns with the hole - never slacken the nut to align its slot.*

● R-pins (shaped like the letter R), or slip pins as they are sometimes called, are sprung and can be reused if they are otherwise in good condition. Always install R-pins with their closed end facing forwards **(see illustration 2.7)**.

**2.7  Correct fitting of R-pin.
Arrow indicates forward direction**

## Circlips (see illustration 2.8)

● Circlips (sometimes called snap-rings) are used to retain components on a shaft or in a housing and have corresponding external or internal ears to permit removal. Parallel-sided (machined) circlips can be installed either way round in their groove, whereas stamped circlips (which have a chamfered edge on one face) must be installed with the chamfer facing away from the direction of thrust load **(see illustration 2.9)**.

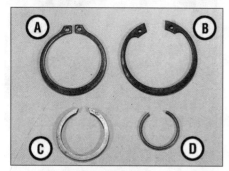

**2.8  External stamped circlip (A), internal stamped circlip (B), machined circlip (C) and wire circlip (D)**

● Always use circlip pliers to remove and install circlips; expand or compress them just enough to remove them. After installation, rotate the circlip in its groove to ensure it is securely seated. If installing a circlip on a splined shaft, always align its opening with a shaft channel to ensure the circlip ends are well supported and unlikely to catch **(see illustration 2.10)**.

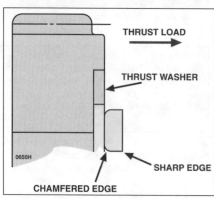

THRUST LOAD

THRUST WASHER

SHARP EDGE

CHAMFERED EDGE

0650H

**2.9  Correct fitting of a stamped circlip**

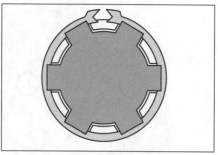

**2.10  Align circlip opening
with shaft channel**

● Circlips can wear due to the thrust of components and become loose in their grooves, with the subsequent danger of becoming dislodged in operation. For this reason, renewal is advised every time a circlip is disturbed.
● Wire circlips are commonly used as piston pin retaining clips. If a removal tang is provided, long-nosed pliers can be used to dislodge them, otherwise careful use of a small flat-bladed screwdriver is necessary. Wire circlips should be renewed every time they are disturbed.

## *Thread diameter and pitch*

● Diameter of a male thread (screw, bolt or stud) is the outside diameter of the threaded portion **(see illustration 2.11)**. Most motorcycle manufacturers use the ISO (International Standards Organisation) metric system expressed in millimetres, eg M6 refers to a 6 mm diameter thread. Sizing is the same for nuts, except that the thread diameter is measured across the valleys of the nut.
● Pitch is the distance between the peaks of the thread **(see illustration 2.11)**. It is expressed in millimetres, thus a common bolt size may be expressed as 6.0 x 1.0 mm (6 mm thread diameter and 1 mm pitch). Generally pitch increases in proportion to thread diameter, although there are always exceptions.
● Thread diameter and pitch are related for conventional fastener applications and the accompanying table can be used as a guide. Additionally, the AF (Across Flats), spanner or socket size dimension of the bolt or nut **(see illustration 2.11)** is linked to thread and pitch specification. Thread pitch can be measured with a thread gauge **(see illustration 2.12)**.

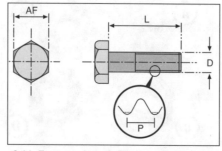

AF

L

D

P

**2.11  Fastener length (L), thread diameter (D), thread pitch (P) and head size (AF)**

**2.12  Using a thread gauge
to measure pitch**

| AF size | Thread diameter x pitch (mm) |
|---|---|
| 8 mm | M5 x 0.8 |
| 8 mm | M6 x 1.0 |
| 10 mm | M6 x 1.0 |
| 12 mm | M8 x 1.25 |
| 14 mm | M10 x 1.25 |
| 17 mm | M12 x 1.25 |

● The threads of most fasteners are of the right-hand type, ie they are turned clockwise to tighten and anti-clockwise to loosen. The reverse situation applies to left-hand thread fasteners, which are turned anti-clockwise to tighten and clockwise to loosen. Left-hand threads are used where rotation of a component might loosen a conventional right-hand thread fastener.

## *Seized fasteners*

● Corrosion of external fasteners due to water or reaction between two dissimilar metals can occur over a period of time. It will build up sooner in wet conditions or in countries where salt is used on the roads during the winter. If a fastener is severely corroded it is likely that normal methods of removal will fail and result in its head being ruined. When you attempt removal, the fastener thread should be heard to crack free and unscrew easily - if it doesn't, stop there before damaging something.
● A smart tap on the head of the fastener will often succeed in breaking free corrosion which has occurred in the threads **(see illustration 2.13)**.
● An aerosol penetrating fluid (such as WD-40) applied the night beforehand may work its way down into the thread and ease removal. Depending on the location, you may be able to make up a Plasticine well around the fastener head and fill it with penetrating fluid.

**2.13  A sharp tap on the head of a fastener
will often break free a corroded thread**

● If you are working on an engine internal component, corrosion will most likely not be a problem due to the well lubricated environment. However, components can be very tight and an impact driver is a useful tool in freeing them (see illustration 2.14).

**2.14 Using an impact driver
to free a fastener**

● Where corrosion has occurred between dissimilar metals (eg steel and aluminium alloy), the application of heat to the fastener head will create a disproportionate expansion rate between the two metals and break the seizure caused by the corrosion. Whether heat can be applied depends on the location of the fastener - any surrounding components likely to be damaged must first be removed (see illustration 2.15). Heat can be applied using a paint stripper heat gun or clothes iron, or by immersing the component in boiling water - wear protective gloves to prevent scalding or burns to the hands.

**2.15 Using heat to free a seized fastener**

● As a last resort, it is possible to use a hammer and cold chisel to work the fastener head unscrewed (see illustration 2.16). This will damage the fastener, but more importantly extreme care must be taken not to damage the surrounding component.

> *Caution: Remember that the component being secured is generally of more value than the bolt, nut or screw - when the fastener is freed, do not unscrew it with force, instead work the fastener back and forth when resistance is felt to prevent thread damage.*

**2.16 Using a hammer and chisel
to free a seized fastener**

## Broken fasteners and damaged heads

● If the shank of a broken bolt or screw is accessible you can grip it with self-locking grips. The knurled wheel type stud extractor tool or self-gripping stud puller tool is particularly useful for removing the long studs which screw into the cylinder mouth surface of the crankcase or bolts and screws from which the head has broken off (see illustration 2.17). Studs can also be removed by locking two nuts together on the threaded end of the stud and using a spanner on the lower nut (see illustration 2.18).

**2.17 Using a stud extractor tool to remove
a broken crankcase stud**

**2.18 Two nuts can be locked together to
unscrew a stud from a component**

● A bolt or screw which has broken off below or level with the casing must be extracted using a screw extractor set. Centre punch the fastener to centralise the drill bit, then drill a hole in the fastener (see illustration 2.19). Select a drill bit which is approximately half to three-quarters the

**2.19 When using a screw extractor,
first drill a hole in the fastener . . .**

diameter of the fastener and drill to a depth which will accommodate the extractor. Use the largest size extractor possible, but avoid leaving too small a wall thickness otherwise the extractor will merely force the fastener walls outwards wedging it in the casing thread.

● If a spiral type extractor is used, thread it anti-clockwise into the fastener. As it is screwed in, it will grip the fastener and unscrew it from the casing (see illustration 2.20).

**2.20 . . . then thread the extractor
anti-clockwise into the fastener**

● If a taper type extractor is used, tap it into the fastener so that it is firmly wedged in place. Unscrew the extractor (anti-clockwise) to draw the fastener out.

> *Warning: Stud extractors are very hard and may break off in the fastener if care is not taken - ask an engineer about spark erosion if this happens.*

● Alternatively, the broken bolt/screw can be drilled out and the hole retapped for an oversize bolt/screw or a diamond-section thread insert. It is essential that the drilling is carried out squarely and to the correct depth, otherwise the casing may be ruined - if in doubt, entrust the work to an engineer.

● Bolts and nuts with rounded corners cause the correct size spanner or socket to slip when force is applied. Of the types of spanner/socket available always use a six-point type rather than an eight or twelve-point type - better grip

**2.21 Comparison of surface drive ring spanner (left) with 12-point type (right)**

is obtained. Surface drive spanners grip the middle of the hex flats, rather than the corners, and are thus good in cases of damaged heads **(see illustration 2.21)**.

● Slotted-head or Phillips-head screws are often damaged by the use of the wrong size screwdriver. Allen-head and Torx-head screws are much less likely to sustain damage. If enough of the screw head is exposed you can use a hacksaw to cut a slot in its head and then use a conventional flat-bladed screwdriver to remove it. Alternatively use a hammer and cold chisel to tap the head of the fastener around to slacken it. Always replace damaged fasteners with new ones, preferably Torx or Allen-head type.

**HAYNES HiNT**

*A dab of valve grinding compound between the screw head and screw-driver tip will often give a good grip.*

### Thread repair

● Threads (particularly those in aluminium alloy components) can be damaged by overtightening, being assembled with dirt in the threads, or from a component working loose and vibrating. Eventually the thread will fail completely, and it will be impossible to tighten the fastener.

● If a thread is damaged or clogged with old locking compound it can be renovated with a thread repair tool (thread chaser) **(see illustrations 2.22 and 2.23)**; special thread

**2.22 A thread repair tool being used to correct an internal thread**

**2.23 A thread repair tool being used to correct an external thread**

chasers are available for spark plug hole threads. The tool will not cut a new thread, but clean and true the original thread. Make sure that you use the correct diameter and pitch tool. Similarly, external threads can be cleaned up with a die or a thread restorer file **(see illustration 2.24)**.

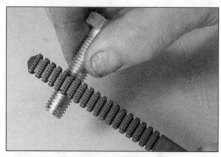

**2.24 Using a thread restorer file**

● It is possible to drill out the old thread and retap the component to the next thread size. This will work where there is enough surrounding material and a new bolt or screw can be obtained. Sometimes, however, this is not possible - such as where the bolt/screw passes through another component which must also be suitably modified, also in cases where a spark plug or oil drain plug cannot be obtained in a larger diameter threads size.

● The diamond-section thread insert (often known by its popular trade name of Heli-Coil) is a simple and effective method of renewing the thread and retaining the original size. A kit can be purchased which contains the tap, insert and installing tool **(see illustration 2.25)**. Drill out the damaged thread with the size drill specified **(see illustration 2.26)**. Carefully retap the thread **(see illustration 2.27)**. Install the

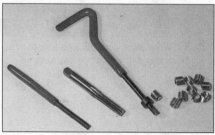

**2.25 Obtain a thread insert kit to suit the thread diameter and pitch required**

**2.26 To install a thread insert, first drill out the original thread . . .**

**2.27 . . . tap a new thread . . .**

**2.28 . . . fit insert on the installing tool . . .**

**2.29 . . . and thread into the component . . .**

**2.30 . . . break off the tang when complete**

insert on the installing tool and thread it slowly into place using a light downward pressure **(see illustrations 2.28 and 2.29)**. When positioned between a 1/4 and 1/2 turn below the surface withdraw the installing tool and use the break-off tool to press down on the tang, breaking it off **(see illustration 2.30)**.

● There are epoxy thread repair kits on the market which can rebuild stripped internal threads, although this repair should not be used on high load-bearing components.

## Thread locking and sealing compounds

● Locking compounds are used in locations where the fastener is prone to loosening due to vibration or on important safety-related items which might cause loss of control of the motorcycle if they fail. It is also used where important fasteners cannot be secured by other means such as lockwashers or split pins.

● Before applying locking compound, make sure that the threads (internal and external) are clean and dry with all old compound removed. Select a compound to suit the component being secured - a non-permanent general locking and sealing type is suitable for most applications, but a high strength type is needed for permanent fixing of studs in castings. Apply a drop or two of the compound to the first few threads of the fastener, then thread it into place and tighten to the specified torque. Do not apply excessive thread locking compound otherwise the thread may be damaged on subsequent removal.

● Certain fasteners are impregnated with a dry film type coating of locking compound on their threads. Always renew this type of fastener if disturbed.

● Anti-seize compounds, such as copper-based greases, can be applied to protect threads from seizure due to extreme heat and corrosion. A common instance is spark plug threads and exhaust system fasteners.

### 3    Measuring tools and gauges

## Feeler gauges

● Feeler gauges (or blades) are used for measuring small gaps and clearances (see illustration 3.1). They can also be used to measure endfloat (sideplay) of a component on a shaft where access is not possible with a dial gauge.

● Feeler gauge sets should be treated with care and not bent or damaged. They are etched with their size on one face. Keep them clean and very lightly oiled to prevent corrosion build-up.

**3.1 Feeler gauges are used for measuring small gaps and clearances - thickness is marked on one face of gauge**

● When measuring a clearance, select a gauge which is a light sliding fit between the two components. You may need to use two gauges together to measure the clearance accurately.

## Micrometers

● A micrometer is a precision tool capable of measuring to 0.01 or 0.001 of a millimetre. It should always be stored in its case and not in the general toolbox. It must be kept clean and never dropped, otherwise its frame or measuring anvils could be distorted resulting in inaccurate readings.

● External micrometers are used for measuring outside diameters of components and have many more applications than internal micrometers. Micrometers are available in different size ranges, eg 0 to 25 mm, 25 to 50 mm, and upwards in 25 mm steps; some large micrometers have interchangeable anvils to allow a range of measurements to be taken. Generally the largest precision measurement you are likely to take on a motorcycle is the piston diameter.

● Internal micrometers (or bore micrometers) are used for measuring inside diameters, such as valve guides and cylinder bores. Telescoping gauges and small hole gauges are used in conjunction with an external micrometer, whereas the more expensive internal micrometers have their own measuring device.

### External micrometer

**Note:** *The conventional analogue type instrument is described. Although much easier to read, digital micrometers are considerably more expensive.*

● Always check the calibration of the micrometer before use. With the anvils closed (0 to 25 mm type) or set over a test gauge (for

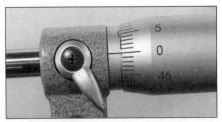

**3.2 Check micrometer calibration before use**

the larger types) the scale should read zero (see illustration 3.2); make sure that the anvils (and test piece) are clean first. Any discrepancy can be adjusted by referring to the instructions supplied with the tool. Remember that the micrometer is a precision measuring tool - don't force the anvils closed, use the ratchet (4) on the end of the micrometer to close it. In this way, a measured force is always applied.

● To use, first make sure that the item being measured is clean. Place the anvil of the micrometer (1) against the item and use the thimble (2) to bring the spindle (3) lightly into contact with the other side of the item (see illustration 3.3). Don't tighten the thimble down because this will damage the micrometer - instead use the ratchet (4) on the end of the micrometer. The ratchet mechanism applies a measured force preventing damage to the instrument.

● The micrometer is read by referring to the linear scale on the sleeve and the annular scale on the thimble. Read off the sleeve first to obtain the base measurement, then add the fine measurement from the thimble to obtain the overall reading. The linear scale on the sleeve represents the measuring range of the micrometer (eg 0 to 25 mm). The annular scale

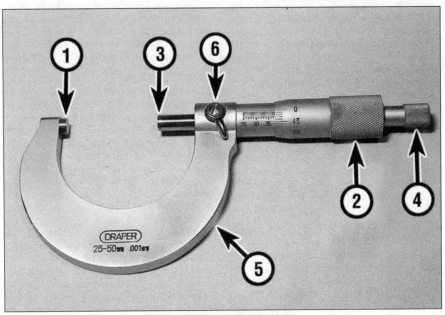

**3.3 Micrometer component parts**

| | | | |
|---|---|---|---|
| 1 | Anvil | 3 | Spindle | 5 | Frame |
| 2 | Thimble | 4 | Ratchet | 6 | Locking lever |

on the thimble will be in graduations of 0.01 mm (or as marked on the frame) - one full revolution of the thimble will move 0.5 mm on the linear scale. Take the reading where the datum line on the sleeve intersects the thimble's scale. Always position the eye directly above the scale otherwise an inaccurate reading will result.

In the example shown the item measures 2.95 mm **(see illustration 3.4)**:

| | |
|---|---|
| Linear scale | 2.00 mm |
| Linear scale | 0.50 mm |
| Annular scale | 0.45 mm |
| Total figure | **2.95 mm** |

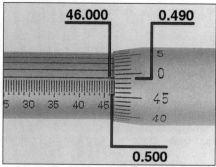

**3.5 Micrometer reading of 46.99 mm on linear and annular scales . . .**

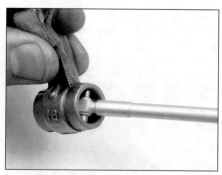

**3.7 Expand the telescoping gauge in the bore, lock its position . . .**

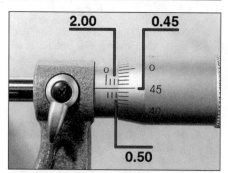

**3.4 Micrometer reading of 2.95 mm**

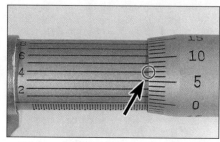

**3.6 . . . and 0.004 mm on vernier scale**

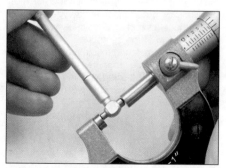

**3.8 . . . then measure the gauge with a micrometer**

Most micrometers have a locking lever (6) on the frame to hold the setting in place, allowing the item to be removed from the micrometer.
● Some micrometers have a vernier scale on their sleeve, providing an even finer measurement to be taken, in 0.001 increments of a millimetre. Take the sleeve and thimble measurement as described above, then check which graduation on the vernier scale aligns with that of the annular scale on the thimble **Note:** *The eye must be perpendicular to the scale when taking the vernier reading - if necessary rotate the body of the micrometer to ensure this.* Multiply the vernier scale figure by 0.001 and add it to the base and fine measurement figures.

In the example shown the item measures 46.994 mm **(see illustrations 3.5 and 3.6)**:

| | |
|---|---|
| Linear scale (base) | 46.000 mm |
| Linear scale (base) | 00.500 mm |
| Annular scale (fine) | 00.490 mm |
| Vernier scale | 00.004 mm |
| Total figure | **46.994 mm** |

### Internal micrometer

● Internal micrometers are available for measuring bore diameters, but are expensive and unlikely to be available for home use. It is suggested that a set of telescoping gauges and small hole gauges, both of which must be used with an external micrometer, will suffice for taking internal measurements on a motorcycle.
● Telescoping gauges can be used to

measure internal diameters of components. Select a gauge with the correct size range, make sure its ends are clean and insert it into the bore. Expand the gauge, then lock its position and withdraw it from the bore **(see illustration 3.7)**. Measure across the gauge ends with a micrometer **(see illustration 3.8)**.
● Very small diameter bores (such as valve guides) are measured with a small hole gauge. Once adjusted to a slip-fit inside the component, its position is locked and the gauge withdrawn for measurement with a micrometer **(see illustrations 3.9 and 3.10)**.

### Vernier caliper

**Note:** *The conventional linear and dial gauge type instruments are described. Digital types are easier to read, but are far more expensive.*
● The vernier caliper does not provide the precision of a micrometer, but is versatile in being able to measure internal and external diameters. Some types also incorporate a depth gauge. It is ideal for measuring clutch plate friction material and spring free lengths.
● To use the conventional linear scale vernier, slacken off the vernier clamp screws (1) and set its jaws over (2), or inside (3), the item to be measured **(see illustration 3.11)**. Slide the jaw into contact, using the thumb-wheel (4) for fine movement of the sliding scale (5) then tighten the clamp screws (1). Read off the main scale (6) where the zero on the sliding scale (5) intersects it, taking the whole number to the left of the zero; this provides the base measurement. View along the sliding scale and select the division which

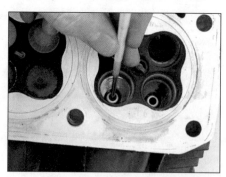

**3.9 Expand the small hole gauge in the bore, lock its position . . .**

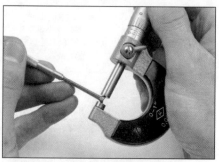

**3.10 . . . then measure the gauge with a micrometer**

lines up exactly with any of the divisions on the main scale, noting that the divisions usually represents 0.02 of a millimetre. Add this fine measurement to the base measurement to obtain the total reading.

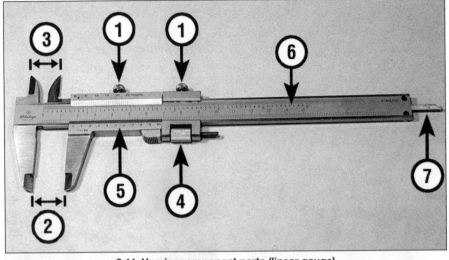

**3.11 Vernier component parts (linear gauge)**

| | | | |
|---|---|---|---|
| 1 Clamp screws | 3 Internal jaws | 5 Sliding scale | 7 Depth gauge |
| 2 External jaws | 4 Thumbwheel | 6 Main scale | |

In the example shown the item measures 55.92 mm **(see illustration 3.12)**:

| | |
|---|---|
| Base measurement | 55.00 mm |
| Fine measurement | 00.92 mm |
| Total figure | **55.92 mm** |

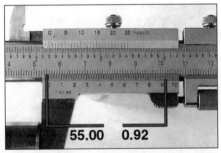

**3.12 Vernier gauge reading of 55.92 mm**

● Some vernier calipers are equipped with a dial gauge for fine measurement. Before use, check that the jaws are clean, then close them fully and check that the dial gauge reads zero. If necessary adjust the gauge ring accordingly. Slacken the vernier clamp screw (1) and set its jaws over (2), or inside (3), the item to be measured **(see illustration 3.13)**. Slide the jaws into contact, using the thumbwheel (4) for fine movement. Read off the main scale (5) where the edge of the sliding scale (6) intersects it, taking the whole number to the left of the zero; this provides the base measurement. Read off the needle position on the dial gauge (7) scale to provide the fine measurement; each division represents 0.05 of a millimetre. Add this fine measurement to the base measurement to obtain the total reading.

In the example shown the item measures 55.95 mm **(see illustration 3.14)**:

| | |
|---|---|
| Base measurement | 55.00 mm |
| Fine measurement | 00.95 mm |
| Total figure | **55.95 mm** |

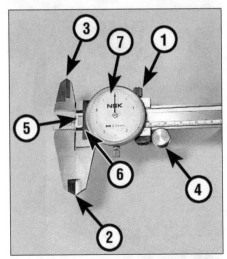

**3.13 Vernier component parts (dial gauge)**

| | |
|---|---|
| 1 Clamp screw | 5 Main scale |
| 2 External jaws | 6 Sliding scale |
| 3 Internal jaws | 7 Dial gauge |
| 4 Thumbwheel | |

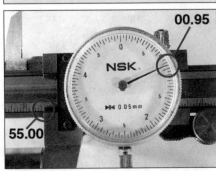

**3.14 Vernier gauge reading of 55.95 mm**

## Plastigauge

● Plastigauge is a plastic material which can be compressed between two surfaces to measure the oil clearance between them. The width of the compressed Plastigauge is measured against a calibrated scale to determine the clearance.
● Common uses of Plastigauge are for measuring the clearance between crankshaft journal and main bearing inserts, between crankshaft journal and big-end bearing inserts, and between camshaft and bearing surfaces. The following example describes big-end oil clearance measurement.
● Handle the Plastigauge material carefully to prevent distortion. Using a sharp knife, cut a length which corresponds with the width of the bearing being measured and place it carefully across the journal so that it is parallel with the shaft **(see illustration 3.15)**. Carefully install both bearing shells and the connecting rod. Without rotating the rod on the journal tighten its bolts or nuts (as applicable) to the specified torque. The connecting rod and bearings are then disassembled and the crushed Plastigauge examined.

**3.15 Plastigauge placed across shaft journal**

● Using the scale provided in the Plastigauge kit, measure the width of the material to determine the oil clearance **(see illustration 3.16)**. Always remove all traces of Plastigauge after use using your fingernails.

*Caution: Arriving at the correct clearance demands that the assembly is torqued correctly, according to the settings and sequence (where applicable) provided by the motorcycle manufacturer.*

**3.16 Measuring the width of the crushed Plastigauge**

## Dial gauge or DTI (Dial Test Indicator)

● A dial gauge can be used to accurately measure small amounts of movement. Typical uses are measuring shaft runout or shaft endfloat (sideplay) and setting piston position for ignition timing on two-strokes. A dial gauge set usually comes with a range of different probes and adapters and mounting equipment.

● The gauge needle must point to zero when at rest. Rotate the ring around its periphery to zero the gauge.

● Check that the gauge is capable of reading the extent of movement in the work. Most gauges have a small dial set in the face which records whole millimetres of movement as well as the fine scale around the face periphery which is calibrated in 0.01 mm divisions. Read off the small dial first to obtain the base measurement, then add the measurement from the fine scale to obtain the total reading.

In the example shown the gauge reads 1.48 mm **(see illustration 3.17)**:

| Base measurement | 1.00 mm |
|---|---|
| Fine measurement | 0.48 mm |
| Total figure | **1.48 mm** |

3.17 Dial gauge reading of 1.48 mm

● If measuring shaft runout, the shaft must be supported in vee-blocks and the gauge mounted on a stand perpendicular to the shaft. Rest the tip of the gauge against the centre of the shaft and rotate the shaft slowly whilst watching the gauge reading **(see illustration 3.18)**. Take several measurements along the length of the shaft and record the

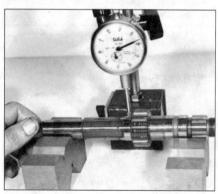

3.18 Using a dial gauge to measure shaft runout

maximum gauge reading as the amount of runout in the shaft. **Note:** *The reading obtained will be total runout at that point - some manufacturers specify that the runout figure is halved to compare with their specified runout limit.*

● Endfloat (sideplay) measurement requires that the gauge is mounted securely to the surrounding component with its probe touching the end of the shaft. Using hand pressure, push and pull on the shaft noting the maximum endfloat recorded on the gauge **(see illustration 3.19)**.

3.19 Using a dial gauge to measure shaft endfloat

● A dial gauge with suitable adapters can be used to determine piston position BTDC on two-stroke engines for the purposes of ignition timing. The gauge, adapter and suitable length probe are installed in the place of the spark plug and the gauge zeroed at TDC. If the piston position is specified as 1.14 mm BTDC, rotate the engine back to 2.00 mm BTDC, then slowly forwards to 1.14 mm BTDC.

## Cylinder compression gauges

● A compression gauge is used for measuring cylinder compression. Either the rubber-cone type or the threaded adapter type can be used. The latter is preferred to ensure a perfect seal against the cylinder head. A 0 to 300 psi (0 to 20 Bar) type gauge (for petrol/gasoline engines) will be suitable for motorcycles.

● The spark plug is removed and the gauge either held hard against the cylinder head (cone type) or the gauge adapter screwed into the cylinder head (threaded type) **(see illustration 3.20)**. Cylinder compression is measured with the engine turning over, but not running - carry out the compression test as described in

3.20 Using a rubber-cone type cylinder compression gauge

*Fault Finding Equipment*. The gauge will hold the reading until manually released.

## Oil pressure gauge

● An oil pressure gauge is used for measuring engine oil pressure. Most gauges come with a set of adapters to fit the thread of the take-off point **(see illustration 3.21)**. If the take-off point specified by the motorcycle manufacturer is an external oil pipe union, make sure that the specified replacement union is used to prevent oil starvation.

3.21 Oil pressure gauge and take-off point adapter (arrow)

● Oil pressure is measured with the engine running (at a specific rpm) and often the manufacturer will specify pressure limits for a cold and hot engine.

## Straight-edge and surface plate

● If checking the gasket face of a component for warpage, place a steel rule or precision straight-edge across the gasket face and measure any gap between the straight-edge and component with feeler gauges **(see illustration 3.22)**. Check diagonally across the component and between mounting holes **(see illustration 3.23)**.

3.22 Use a straight-edge and feeler gauges to check for warpage

3.23 Check for warpage in these directions

● Checking individual components for warpage, such as clutch plain (metal) plates, requires a perfectly flat plate or piece or plate glass and feeler gauges.

## 4  Torque and leverage

### What is torque?

● Torque describes the twisting force about a shaft. The amount of torque applied is determined by the distance from the centre of the shaft to the end of the lever and the amount of force being applied to the end of the lever; distance multiplied by force equals torque.

● The manufacturer applies a measured torque to a bolt or nut to ensure that it will not slacken in use and to hold two components securely together without movement in the joint. The actual torque setting depends on the thread size, bolt or nut material and the composition of the components being held.

● Too little torque may cause the fastener to loosen due to vibration, whereas too much torque will distort the joint faces of the component or cause the fastener to shear off. Always stick to the specified torque setting.

### Using a torque wrench

● Check the calibration of the torque wrench and make sure it has a suitable range for the job. Torque wrenches are available in Nm (Newton-metres), kgf m (kilograms-force metre), lbf ft (pounds-feet), lbf in (inch-pounds). Do not confuse lbf ft with lbf in.

● Adjust the tool to the desired torque on the scale (see illustration 4.1). If your torque wrench is not calibrated in the units specified, carefully convert the figure (see Conversion Factors). A manufacturer sometimes gives a torque setting as a range (8 to 10 Nm) rather than a single figure - in this case set the tool midway between the two settings. The same torque may be expressed as 9 Nm ± 1 Nm. Some torque wrenches have a method of locking the setting so that it isn't inadvertently altered during use.

**4.1  Set the torque wrench index mark to the setting required, in this case 12 Nm**

● Install the bolts/nuts in their correct location and secure them lightly. Their threads must be clean and free of any old locking compound. Unless specified the threads and flange should be dry - oiled threads are necessary in certain circumstances and the manufacturer will take this into account in the specified torque figure. Similarly, the manufacturer may also specify the application of thread-locking compound.

● Tighten the fasteners in the specified sequence until the torque wrench clicks, indicating that the torque setting has been reached. Apply the torque again to double-check the setting. Where different thread diameter fasteners secure the component, as a rule tighten the larger diameter ones first.

● When the torque wrench has been finished with, release the lock (where applicable) and fully back off its setting to zero - do not leave the torque wrench tensioned. Also, do not use a torque wrench for slackening a fastener.

### Angle-tightening

● Manufacturers often specify a figure in degrees for final tightening of a fastener. This usually follows tightening to a specific torque setting.

● A degree disc can be set and attached to the socket (see illustration 4.2) or a protractor can be used to mark the angle of movement on the bolt/nut head and the surrounding casting (see illustration 4.3).

**4.2  Angle tightening can be accomplished with a torque-angle gauge . . .**

**4.3  . . . or by marking the angle on the surrounding component**

### Loosening sequences

● Where more than one bolt/nut secures a component, loosen each fastener evenly a little at a time. In this way, not all the stress of the joint is held by one fastener and the components are not likely to distort.

● If a tightening sequence is provided, work in the REVERSE of this, but if not, work from the outside in, in a criss-cross sequence (see illustration 4.4).

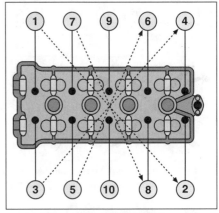

**4.4  When slackening, work from the outside inwards**

### Tightening sequences

● If a component is held by more than one fastener it is important that the retaining bolts/nuts are tightened evenly to prevent uneven stress build-up and distortion of sealing faces. This is especially important on high-compression joints such as the cylinder head.

● A sequence is usually provided by the manufacturer, either in a diagram or actually marked in the casting. If not, always start in the centre and work outwards in a criss-cross pattern (see illustration 4.5). Start off by securing all bolts/nuts finger-tight, then set the torque wrench and tighten each fastener by a small amount in sequence until the final torque is reached. By following this practice,

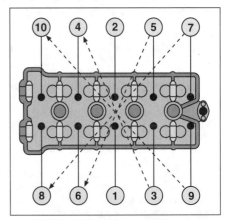

**4.5  When tightening, work from the inside outwards**

the joint will be held evenly and will not be distorted. Important joints, such as the cylinder head and big-end fasteners often have two- or three-stage torque settings.

### Applying leverage

● Use tools at the correct angle. Position a socket wrench or spanner on the bolt/nut so that you pull it towards you when loosening. If this can't be done, push the spanner without curling your fingers around it **(see illustration 4.6)** - the spanner may slip or the fastener loosen suddenly, resulting in your fingers being crushed against a component.

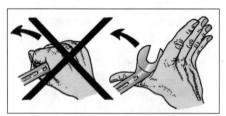

**4.6 If you can't pull on the spanner to loosen a fastener, push with your hand open**

● Additional leverage is gained by extending the length of the lever. The best way to do this is to use a breaker bar instead of the regular length tool, or to slip a length of tubing over the end of the spanner or socket wrench.
● If additional leverage will not work, the fastener head is either damaged or firmly corroded in place (see *Fasteners*).

## 5 Bearings

### Bearing removal and installation

#### Drivers and sockets

● Before removing a bearing, always inspect the casing to see which way it must be driven out - some casings will have retaining plates or a cast step. Also check for any identifying markings on the bearing and if installed to a certain depth, measure this at this stage. Some roller bearings are sealed on one side - take note of the original fitted position.
● Bearings can be driven out of a casing using a bearing driver tool (with the correct size head) or a socket of the correct diameter. Select the driver head or socket so that it contacts the outer race of the bearing, not the balls/rollers or inner race. Always support the casing around the bearing housing with wood blocks, otherwise there is a risk of fracture. The bearing is driven out with a few blows on the driver or socket from a heavy mallet. Unless access is severely restricted (as with wheel bearings), a pin-punch is not recommended unless it is moved around the bearing to keep it square in its housing.

● The same equipment can be used to install bearings. Make sure the bearing housing is supported on wood blocks and line up the bearing in its housing. Fit the bearing as noted on removal - generally they are installed with their marked side facing outwards. Tap the bearing squarely into its housing using a driver or socket which bears only on the bearing's outer race - contact with the bearing balls/rollers or inner race will destroy it **(see illustrations 5.1 and 5.2)**.
● Check that the bearing inner race and balls/rollers rotate freely.

**5.1 Using a bearing driver against the bearing's outer race**

**5.2 Using a large socket against the bearing's outer race**

#### Pullers and slide-hammers

● Where a bearing is pressed on a shaft a puller will be required to extract it **(see illustration 5.3)**. Make sure that the puller clamp or legs fit securely behind the bearing and are unlikely to slip out. If pulling a bearing

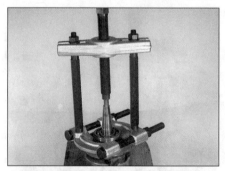

**5.3 This bearing puller clamps behind the bearing and pressure is applied to the shaft end to draw the bearing off**

off a gear shaft for example, you may have to locate the puller behind a gear pinion if there is no access to the race and draw the gear pinion off the shaft as well **(see illustration 5.4)**.

> *Caution: Ensure that the puller's centre bolt locates securely against the end of the shaft and will not slip when pressure is applied. Also ensure that puller does not damage the shaft end.*

**5.4 Where no access is available to the rear of the bearing, it is sometimes possible to draw off the adjacent component**

● Operate the puller so that its centre bolt exerts pressure on the shaft end and draws the bearing off the shaft.
● When installing the bearing on the shaft, tap only on the bearing's inner race - contact with the balls/rollers or outer race with destroy the bearing. Use a socket or length of tubing as a drift which fits over the shaft end **(see illustration 5.5)**.

**5.5 When installing a bearing on a shaft use a piece of tubing which bears only on the bearing's inner race**

● Where a bearing locates in a blind hole in a casing, it cannot be driven or pulled out as described above. A slide-hammer with knife-edged bearing puller attachment will be required. The puller attachment passes through the bearing and when tightened expands to fit firmly behind the bearing **(see illustration 5.6)**. By operating the slide-hammer part of the tool the bearing is jarred out of its housing **(see illustration 5.7)**.
● It is possible, if the bearing is of reasonable weight, for it to drop out of its housing if the casing is heated as described opposite. If this

**5.6 Expand the bearing puller so that it locks behind the bearing . . .**

**5.7 . . . attach the slide hammer to the bearing puller**

method is attempted, first prepare a work surface which will enable the casing to be tapped face down to help dislodge the bearing - a wood surface is ideal since it will not damage the casing's gasket surface. Wearing protective gloves, tap the heated casing several times against the work surface to dislodge the bearing under its own weight **(see illustration 5.8)**.

**5.8 Tapping a casing face down on wood blocks can often dislodge a bearing**

● Bearings can be installed in blind holes using the driver or socket method described above.

## Drawbolts

● Where a bearing or bush is set in the eye of a component, such as a suspension linkage arm or connecting rod small-end, removal by drift may damage the component. Furthermore, a rubber bushing in a shock absorber eye cannot successfully be driven out of position. If access is available to a engineering press, the task is straightforward. If not, a drawbolt can be fabricated to extract the bearing or bush.

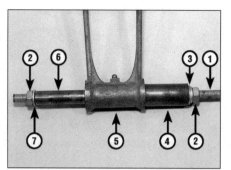

**5.9 Drawbolt component parts assembled on a suspension arm**

1  Bolt or length of threaded bar
2  Nuts
3  Washer (external diameter greater than tubing internal diameter)
4  Tubing (internal diameter sufficient to accommodate bearing)
5  Suspension arm with bearing
6  Tubing (external diameter slightly smaller than bearing)
7  Washer (external diameter slightly smaller than bearing)

**5.10 Drawing the bearing out of the suspension arm**

● To extract the bearing/bush you will need a long bolt with nut (or piece of threaded bar with two nuts), a piece of tubing which has an internal diameter larger than the bearing/bush, another piece of tubing which has an external diameter slightly smaller than the bearing/bush, and a selection of washers **(see illustrations 5.9 and 5.10)**. Note that the pieces of tubing must be of the same length, or longer, than the bearing/bush.

● The same kit (without the pieces of tubing) can be used to draw the new bearing/bush back into place **(see illustration 5.11)**.

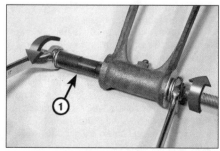

**5.11 Installing a new bearing (1) in the suspension arm**

## Temperature change

● If the bearing's outer race is a tight fit in the casing, the aluminium casing can be heated to release its grip on the bearing. Aluminium will expand at a greater rate than the steel bearing outer race. There are several ways to do this, but avoid any localised extreme heat (such as a blow torch) - aluminium alloy has a low melting point.

● Approved methods of heating a casing are using a domestic oven (heated to 100°C) or immersing the casing in boiling water **(see illustration 5.12)**. Low temperature range localised heat sources such as a paint stripper heat gun or clothes iron can also be used **(see illustration 5.13)**. Alternatively, soak a rag in boiling water, wring it out and wrap it around the bearing housing.

> ⚠ **Warning: All of these methods require care in use to prevent scalding and burns to the hands. Wear protective gloves when handling hot components.**

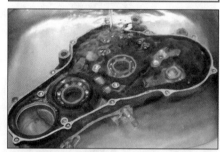

**5.12 A casing can be immersed in a sink of boiling water to aid bearing removal**

**5.13 Using a localised heat source to aid bearing removal**

● If heating the whole casing note that plastic components, such as the neutral switch, may suffer - remove them beforehand.

● After heating, remove the bearing as described above. You may find that the expansion is sufficient for the bearing to fall out of the casing under its own weight or with a light tap on the driver or socket.

● If necessary, the casing can be heated to aid bearing installation, and this is sometimes the recommended procedure if the motorcycle manufacturer has designed the housing and bearing fit with this intention.

● Installation of bearings can be eased by placing them in a freezer the night before installation. The steel bearing will contract slightly, allowing easy insertion in its housing. This is often useful when installing steering head outer races in the frame.

## Bearing types and markings

● Plain shell bearings, ball bearings, needle roller bearings and tapered roller bearings will all be found on motorcycles (see illustrations 5.14 and 5.15). The ball and roller types are usually caged between an inner and outer race, but uncaged variations may be found.

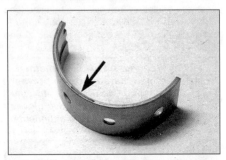

5.14 Shell bearings are either plain or grooved. They are usually identified by colour code (arrow)

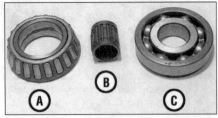

5.15 Tapered roller bearing (A), needle roller bearing (B) and ball journal bearing (C)

● Shell bearings (often called inserts) are usually found at the crankshaft main and connecting rod big-end where they are good at coping with high loads. They are made of a phosphor-bronze material and are impregnated with self-lubricating properties.
● Ball bearings and needle roller bearings consist of a steel inner and outer race with the balls or rollers between the races. They require constant lubrication by oil or grease and are good at coping with axial loads. Taper roller bearings consist of rollers set in a tapered cage set on the inner race; the outer race is separate. They are good at coping with axial loads and prevent movement along the shaft - a typical application is in the steering head.
● Bearing manufacturers produce bearings to ISO size standards and stamp one face of the bearing to indicate its internal and external diameter, load capacity and type (see illustration 5.16).
● Metal bushes are usually of phosphor-bronze material. Rubber bushes are used in suspension mounting eyes. Fibre bushes have also been used in suspension pivots.

5.16 Typical bearing marking

## Bearing fault finding

● If a bearing outer race has spun in its housing, the housing material will be damaged. You can use a bearing locking compound to bond the outer race in place if damage is not too severe.
● Shell bearings will fail due to damage of their working surface, as a result of lack of lubrication, corrosion or abrasive particles in the oil (see illustration 5.17). Small particles of dirt in the oil may embed in the bearing material whereas larger particles will score the bearing and shaft journal. If a number of short journeys are made, insufficient heat will be generated to drive off condensation which has built up on the bearings.

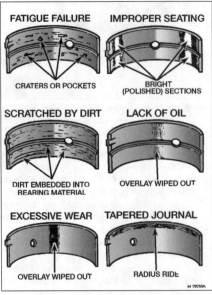

5.17 Typical bearing failures

● Ball and roller bearings will fail due to lack of lubrication or damage to the balls or rollers. Tapered-roller bearings can be damaged by overloading them. Unless the bearing is sealed on both sides, wash it in paraffin (kerosene) to remove all old grease then allow it to dry. Make a visual inspection looking to dented balls or rollers, damaged cages and worn or pitted races (see illustration 5.18).
● A ball bearing can be checked for wear by listening to it when spun. Apply a film of light oil to the bearing and hold it close to the ear - hold the outer race with one hand and spin the inner

5.18 Example of ball journal bearing with damaged balls and cages

5.19 Hold outer race and listen to inner race when spun

race with the other hand (see illustration 5.19). The bearing should be almost silent when spun; if it grates or rattles it is worn.

## 6 Oil seals

## Oil seal removal and installation

● Oil seals should be renewed every time a component is dismantled. This is because the seal lips will become set to the sealing surface and will not necessarily reseal.
● Oil seals can be prised out of position using a large flat-bladed screwdriver (see illustration 6.1). In the case of crankcase seals, check first that the seal is not lipped on the inside, preventing its removal with the crankcases joined.

6.1 Prise out oil seals with a large flat-bladed screwdriver

● New seals are usually installed with their marked face (containing the seal reference code) outwards and the spring side towards the fluid being retained. In certain cases, such as a two-stroke engine crankshaft seal, a double lipped seal may be used due to there being fluid or gas on each side of the joint.

● Use a bearing driver or socket which bears only on the outer hard edge of the seal to install it in the casing - tapping on the inner edge will damage the sealing lip.

## Oil seal types and markings

● Oil seals are usually of the single-lipped type. Double-lipped seals are found where a liquid or gas is on both sides of the joint.
● Oil seals can harden and lose their sealing ability if the motorcycle has been in storage for a long period - renewal is the only solution.
● Oil seal manufacturers also conform to the ISO markings for seal size - these are moulded into the outer face of the seal (see illustration 6.2).

**6.2 These oil seal markings indicate inside diameter, outside diameter and seal thickness**

## 7  Gaskets and sealants

## Types of gasket and sealant

● Gaskets are used to seal the mating surfaces between components and keep lubricants, fluids, vacuum or pressure contained within the assembly. Aluminium gaskets are sometimes found at the cylinder joints, but most gaskets are paper-based. If the mating surfaces of the components being joined are undamaged the gasket can be installed dry, although a dab of sealant or grease will be useful to hold it in place during assembly.
● RTV (Room Temperature Vulcanising) silicone rubber sealants cure when exposed to moisture in the atmosphere. These sealants are good at filling pits or irregular gasket faces, but will tend to be forced out of the joint under very high torque. They can be used to replace a paper gasket, but first make sure that the width of the paper gasket is not essential to the shimming of internal components. RTV sealants should not be used on components containing petrol (gasoline).
● Non-hardening, semi-hardening and hard setting liquid gasket compounds can be used with a gasket or between a metal-to-metal joint. Select the sealant to suit the application: universal non-hardening sealant can be used on virtually all joints; semi-hardening on joint faces which are rough or damaged; hard setting sealant on joints which require a permanent bond and are subjected to high temperature and pressure. **Note:** *Check first if the paper gasket has a bead of sealant*

*impregnated in its surface before applying additional sealant.*
● When choosing a sealant, make sure it is suitable for the application, particularly if being applied in a high-temperature area or in the vicinity of fuel. Certain manufacturers produce sealants in either clear, silver or black colours to match the finish of the engine. This has a particular application on motorcycles where much of the engine is exposed.
● Do not over-apply sealant. That which is squeezed out on the outside of the joint can be wiped off, whereas an excess of sealant on the inside can break off and clog oilways.

## Breaking a sealed joint

● Age, heat, pressure and the use of hard setting sealant can cause two components to stick together so tightly that they are difficult to separate using finger pressure alone. Do not resort to using levers unless there is a pry point provided for this purpose (see illustration 7.1) or else the gasket surfaces will be damaged.
● Use a soft-faced hammer (see illustration 7.2) or a wood block and conventional hammer to strike the component near the mating surface. Avoid hammering against cast extremities since they may break off. If this method fails, try using a wood wedge between the two components.

**Caution: If the joint will not separate, double-check that you have removed all the fasteners.**

**7.1 If a pry point is provided, apply gently pressure with a flat-bladed screwdriver**

**7.2 Tap around the joint with a soft-faced mallet if necessary - don't strike cooling fins**

## Removal of old gasket and sealant

● Paper gaskets will most likely come away complete, leaving only a few traces stuck on

*Most components have one or two hollow locating dowels between the two gasket faces. If a dowel cannot be removed, do not resort to gripping it with pliers - it will almost certainly be distorted. Install a close-fitting socket or Phillips screwdriver into the dowel and then grip the outer edge of the dowel to free it.*

the sealing faces of the components. It is imperative that all traces are removed to ensure correct sealing of the new gasket.
● Very carefully scrape all traces of gasket away making sure that the sealing surfaces are not gouged or scored by the scraper (see illustrations 7.3, 7.4 and 7.5). Stubborn deposits can be removed by spraying with an aerosol gasket remover. Final preparation of

**7.3 Paper gaskets can be scraped off with a gasket scraper tool . . .**

**7.4 . . . a knife blade . . .**

**7.5 . . . or a household scraper**

**7.6 Fine abrasive paper is wrapped around a flat file to clean up the gasket face**

**7.7 A kitchen scourer can be used on stubborn deposits**

the gasket surface can be made with very fine abrasive paper or a plastic kitchen scourer **(see illustrations 7.6 and 7.7)**.

● Old sealant can be scraped or peeled off components, depending on the type originally used. Note that gasket removal compounds are available to avoid scraping the components clean; make sure the gasket remover suits the type of sealant used.

## 8 Chains

### *Breaking and joining final drive chains*

● Drive chains for all but small bikes are continuous and do not have a clip-type connecting link. The chain must be broken using a chain breaker tool and the new chain securely riveted together using a new soft rivet-type link. Never use a clip-type connecting link instead of a rivet-type link, except in an emergency. Various chain breaking and riveting tools are available, either as separate tools or combined as illustrated in the accompanying photographs - read the instructions supplied with the tool carefully.

> ⚠ **Warning: The need to rivet the new link pins correctly cannot be overstressed - loss of control of the motorcycle is very likely to result if the chain breaks in use.**

● Rotate the chain and look for the soft link. The soft link pins look like they have been

**8.1 Tighten the chain breaker to push the pin out of the link . . .**

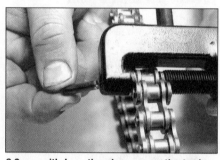

**8.2 . . . withdraw the pin, remove the tool . . .**

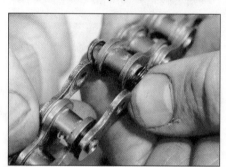

**8.3 . . . and separate the chain link**

deeply centre-punched instead of peened over like all the other pins **(see illustration 8.9)** and its sideplate may be a different colour. Position the soft link midway between the sprockets and assemble the chain breaker tool over one of the soft link pins **(see illustration 8.1)**. Operate the tool to push the pin out through the chain **(see illustration 8.2)**. On an O-ring chain, remove the O-rings **(see illustration 8.3)**. Carry out the same procedure on the other soft link pin.

> *Caution: Certain soft link pins (particularly on the larger chains) may require their ends to be filed or ground off before they can be pressed out using the tool.*

● Check that you have the correct size and strength (standard or heavy duty) new soft link - do not reuse the old link. Look for the size marking on the chain sideplates **(see illustration 8.10)**.

● Position the chain ends so that they are engaged over the rear sprocket. On an O-ring

**8.4 Insert the new soft link, with O-rings, through the chain ends . . .**

**8.5 . . . install the O-rings over the pin ends . . .**

**8.6 . . . followed by the sideplate**

chain, install a new O-ring over each pin of the link and insert the link through the two chain ends **(see illustration 8.4)**. Install a new O-ring over the end of each pin, followed by the sideplate (with the chain manufacturer's marking facing outwards) **(see illustrations 8.5 and 8.6)**. On an unsealed chain, insert the link through the two chain ends, then install the sideplate with the chain manufacturer's marking facing outwards.

● Note that it may not be possible to install the sideplate using finger pressure alone. If using a joining tool, assemble it so that the plates of the tool clamp the link and press the sideplate over the pins **(see illustration 8.7)**. Otherwise, use two small sockets placed over

**8.7 Push the sideplate into position using a clamp**

**8.8 Assemble the chain riveting tool over one pin at a time and tighten it fully**

**8.9 Pin end correctly riveted (A), pin end unriveted (B)**

the rivet ends and two pieces of the wood between a G-clamp. Operate the clamp to press the sideplate over the pins.

● Assemble the joining tool over one pin (following the maker's instructions) and tighten the tool down to spread the pin end securely **(see illustrations 8.8 and 8.9)**. Do the same on the other pin.

 *Warning: Check that the pin ends are secure and that there is no danger of the sideplate coming loose. If the pin ends are cracked the soft link must be renewed.*

### Final drive chain sizing

● Chains are sized using a three digit number, followed by a suffix to denote the chain type **(see illustration 8.10)**. Chain type is either standard or heavy duty (thicker sideplates), and also unsealed or O-ring/X-ring type.

● The first digit of the number relates to the pitch of the chain, ie the distance from the centre of one pin to the centre of the next pin **(see illustration 8.11)**. Pitch is expressed in eighths of an inch, as follows:

**8.10 Typical chain size and type marking**

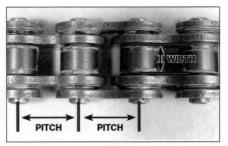

**8.11 Chain dimensions**

| Sizes commencing with a 4 (eg 428) have a pitch of 1/2 inch (12.7 mm) |
| Sizes commencing with a 5 (eg 520) have a pitch of 5/8 inch (15.9 mm) |
| Sizes commencing with a 6 (eg 630) have a pitch of 3/4 inch (19.1 mm) |

● The second and third digits of the chain size relate to the width of the rollers, again in imperial units, eg the 525 shown has 5/16 inch (7.94 mm) rollers **(see illustration 8.11)**.

## 9 Hoses

### Clamping to prevent flow

● Small-bore flexible hoses can be clamped to prevent fluid flow whilst a component is worked on. Whichever method is used, ensure that the hose material is not permanently distorted or damaged by the clamp.

a) A brake hose clamp available from auto accessory shops **(see illustration 9.1)**.
b) A wingnut type hose clamp **(see illustration 9.2)**.

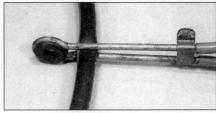

**9.1 Hoses can be clamped with an automotive brake hose clamp . . .**

**9.2 . . . a wingnut type hose clamp . . .**

c) Two sockets placed each side of the hose and held with straight-jawed self-locking grips **(see illustration 9.3)**.
d) Thick card each side of the hose held between straight-jawed self-locking grips **(see illustration 9.4)**.

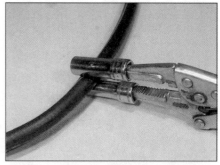

**9.3 . . . two sockets and a pair of self-locking grips . . .**

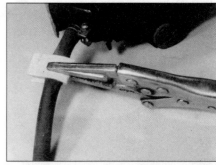

**9.4 . . . or thick card and self-locking grips**

### Freeing and fitting hoses

● Always make sure the hose clamp is moved well clear of the hose end. Grip the hose with your hand and rotate it whilst pulling it off the union. If the hose has hardened due to age and will not move, slit it with a sharp knife and peel its ends off the union **(see illustration 9.5)**.

● Resist the temptation to use grease or soap on the unions to aid installation; although it helps the hose slip over the union it will equally aid the escape of fluid from the joint. It is preferable to soften the hose ends in hot water and wet the inside surface of the hose with water or a fluid which will evaporate.

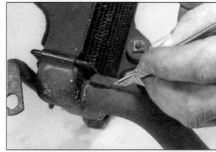

**9.5 Cutting a coolant hose free with a sharp knife**

# Conversion Factors

## Length (distance)

| | | | | |
|---|---|---|---|---|
| Inches (in) | x 25.4 | = Millimetres (mm) | x 0.0394 | = Inches (in) |
| Feet (ft) | x 0.305 | = Metres (m) | x 3.281 | = Feet (ft) |
| Miles | x 1.609 | = Kilometres (km) | x 0.621 | = Miles |

## Volume (capacity)

| | | | | |
|---|---|---|---|---|
| Cubic inches (cu in; in³) | x 16.387 | = Cubic centimetres (cc; cm³) | x 0.061 | = Cubic inches (cu in; in³) |
| Imperial pints (Imp pt) | x 0.568 | = Litres (l) | x 1.76 | = Imperial pints (Imp pt) |
| Imperial quarts (Imp qt) | x 1.137 | = Litres (l) | x 0.88 | = Imperial quarts (Imp qt) |
| Imperial quarts (Imp qt) | x 1.201 | = US quarts (US qt) | x 0.833 | = Imperial quarts (Imp qt) |
| US quarts (US qt) | x 0.946 | = Litres (l) | x 1.057 | = US quarts (US qt) |
| Imperial gallons (Imp gal) | x 4.546 | = Litres (l) | x 0.22 | = Imperial gallons (Imp gal) |
| Imperial gallons (Imp gal) | x 1.201 | = US gallons (US gal) | x 0.833 | = Imperial gallons (Imp gal) |
| US gallons (US gal) | x 3.785 | = Litres (l) | x 0.264 | = US gallons (US gal) |

## Mass (weight)

| | | | | |
|---|---|---|---|---|
| Ounces (oz) | x 28.35 | = Grams (g) | x 0.035 | = Ounces (oz) |
| Pounds (lb) | x 0.454 | = Kilograms (kg) | x 2.205 | = Pounds (lb) |

## Force

| | | | | |
|---|---|---|---|---|
| Ounces-force (ozf; oz) | x 0.278 | = Newtons (N) | x 3.6 | = Ounces-force (ozf; oz) |
| Pounds-force (lbf; lb) | x 4.448 | = Newtons (N) | x 0.225 | = Pounds-force (lbf; lb) |
| Newtons (N) | x 0.1 | = Kilograms-force (kgf; kg) | x 9.81 | = Newtons (N) |

## Pressure

| | | | | |
|---|---|---|---|---|
| Pounds-force per square inch (psi; lbf/in²; lb/in²) | x 0.070 | = Kilograms-force per square centimetre (kgf/cm²; kg/cm²) | x 14.223 | = Pounds-force per square inch (psi; lbf/in²; lb/in²) |
| Pounds-force per square inch (psi; lbf/in²; lb/in²) | x 0.068 | = Atmospheres (atm) | x 14.696 | = Pounds-force per square inch (psi; lbf/in²; lb/in²) |
| Pounds-force per square inch (psi; lbf/in²; lb/in²) | x 0.069 | = Bars | x 14.5 | = Pounds-force per square inch (psi; lbf/in²; lb/in²) |
| Pounds-force per square inch (psi; lbf/in²; lb/in²) | x 6.895 | = Kilopascals (kPa) | x 0.145 | = Pounds-force per square inch (psi; lbf/in²; lb/in²) |
| Kilopascals (kPa) | x 0.01 | = Kilograms-force per square centimetre (kgf/cm²; kg/cm²) | x 98.1 | = Kilopascals (kPa) |
| Millibar (mbar) | x 100 | = Pascals (Pa) | x 0.01 | = Millibar (mbar) |
| Millibar (mbar) | x 0.0145 | = Pounds-force per square inch (psi; lbf/in²; lb/in²) | x 68.947 | = Millibar (mbar) |
| Millibar (mbar) | x 0.75 | = Millimetres of mercury (mmHg) | x 1.333 | = Millibar (mbar) |
| Millibar (mbar) | x 0.401 | = Inches of water (inH₂O) | x 2.491 | = Millibar (mbar) |
| Millimetres of mercury (mmHg) | x 0.535 | = Inches of water (inH₂O) | x 1.868 | = Millimetres of mercury (mmHg) |
| Inches of water (inH₂O) | x 0.036 | = Pounds-force per square inch (psi; lbf/in²; lb/in²) | x 27.68 | = Inches of water (inH₂O) |

## Torque (moment of force)

| | | | | |
|---|---|---|---|---|
| Pounds-force inches (lbf in; lb in) | x 1.152 | = Kilograms-force centimetre (kgf cm; kg cm) | x 0.868 | = Pounds-force inches (lbf in; lb in) |
| Pounds-force inches (lbf in; lb in) | x 0.113 | = Newton metres (Nm) | x 8.85 | = Pounds-force inches (lbf in; lb in) |
| Pounds-force inches (lbf in; lb in) | x 0.083 | = Pounds-force feet (lbf ft; lb ft) | x 12 | = Pounds-force inches (lbf in; lb in) |
| Pounds-force feet (lbf ft; lb ft) | x 0.138 | = Kilograms-force metres (kgf m; kg m) | x 7.233 | = Pounds-force feet (lbf ft; lb ft) |
| Pounds-force feet (lbf ft; lb ft) | x 1.356 | = Newton metres (Nm) | x 0.738 | = Pounds-force feet (lbf ft; lb ft) |
| Newton metres (Nm) | x 0.102 | = Kilograms-force metres (kgf m; kg m) | x 9.804 | = Newton metres (Nm) |

## Power

| | | | | |
|---|---|---|---|---|
| Horsepower (hp) | x 745.7 | = Watts (W) | x 0.0013 | = Horsepower (hp) |

## Velocity (speed)

| | | | | |
|---|---|---|---|---|
| Miles per hour (miles/hr; mph) | x 1.609 | = Kilometres per hour (km/hr; kph) | x 0.621 | = Miles per hour (miles/hr; mph) |

## Fuel consumption*

| | | | | |
|---|---|---|---|---|
| Miles per gallon (mpg) | x 0.354 | = Kilometres per litre (km/l) | x 2.825 | = Miles per gallon (mpg) |

## Temperature

Degrees Fahrenheit = (°C x 1.8) + 32          Degrees Celsius (Degrees Centigrade; °C) = (°F - 32) x 0.56

*It is common practice to convert from miles per gallon (mpg) to litres/100 kilometres (l/100km), where mpg x l/100 km = 282*

A number of chemicals and lubricants are available for use in motorcycle maintenance and repair. They include a wide variety of products ranging from cleaning solvents and degreasers to lubricants and protective sprays for rubber, plastic and vinyl.

● **Contact point/spark plug cleaner** is a solvent used to clean oily film and dirt from points, grime from electrical connectors and oil deposits from spark plugs. It is oil free and leaves no residue. It can also be used to remove gum and varnish from carburettor jets and other orifices.

● **Carburettor cleaner** is similar to contact point/spark plug cleaner but it usually has a stronger solvent and may leave a slight oily reside. It is not recommended for cleaning electrical components or connections.

● **Brake system cleaner** is used to remove grease or brake fluid from brake system components (where clean surfaces are absolutely necessary and petroleum-based solvents cannot be used); it also leaves no residue.

● **Silicone-based lubricants** are used to protect rubber parts such as hoses and grommets, and are used as lubricants for hinges and locks.

● **Multi-purpose grease** is an all purpose lubricant used wherever grease is more practical than a liquid lubricant such as oil. Some multi-purpose grease is coloured white and specially formulated to be more resistant to water than ordinary grease.

● **Gear oil** (sometimes called gear lube) is a specially designed oil used in transmissions and final drive units, as well as other areas where high friction, high temperature lubrication is required. It is available in a number of viscosities (weights) for various applications.

● **Motor oil**, of course, is the lubricant specially formulated for use in the engine. It normally contains a wide variety of additives to prevent corrosion and reduce foaming and wear. Motor oil comes in various weights (viscosity ratings) of from 5 to 80. The recommended weight of the oil depends on the seasonal temperature and the demands on the engine. Light oil is used in cold climates and under light load conditions; heavy oil is used in hot climates and where high loads are encountered. Multi-viscosity oils are designed to have characteristics of both light and heavy oils and are available in a number of weights from 5W-20 to 20W-50.

● **Petrol additives** perform several functions, depending on their chemical makeup. They usually contain solvents that help dissolve gum and varnish that build up on carburettor and inlet parts. They also serve to break down carbon deposits that form on the inside surfaces of the combustion chambers. Some additives contain upper cylinder lubricants for valves and piston rings.

● **Brake and clutch fluid** is a specially formulated hydraulic fluid that can withstand the heat and pressure encountered in brake/clutch systems. Care must be taken that this fluid does not come in contact with painted surfaces or plastics. An opened container should always be resealed to prevent contamination by water or dirt.

● **Chain lubricants** are formulated especially for use on motorcycle final drive chains. A good chain lube should adhere well and have good penetrating qualities to be effective as a lubricant inside the chain and on the side plates, pins and rollers. Most chain lubes are either the foaming type or quick drying type and are usually marketed as sprays. Take care to use a lubricant marked as being suitable for O-ring chains.

● **Degreasers** are heavy duty solvents used to remove grease and grime that may accumulate on engine and frame components. They can be sprayed or brushed on and, depending on the type, are rinsed with either water or solvent.

● **Solvents** are used alone or in combination with degreasers to clean parts and assemblies during repair and overhaul. The home mechanic should use only solvents that are non-flammable and that do not produce irritating fumes.

● **Gasket sealing compounds** may be used in conjunction with gaskets, to improve their sealing capabilities, or alone, to seal metal-to-metal joints. Many gasket sealers can withstand extreme heat, some are impervious to petrol and lubricants, while others are capable of filling and sealing large cavities. Depending on the intended use, gasket sealers either dry hard or stay relatively soft and pliable. They are usually applied by hand, with a brush, or are sprayed on the gasket sealing surfaces.

● **Thread locking compound** is an adhesive locking compound that prevents threaded fasteners from loosening because of vibration. It is available in a variety of types for different applications.

● **Moisture dispersants** are usually sprays that can be used to dry out electrical components such as the fuse block and wiring connectors. Some types can also be used as treatment for rubber and as a lubricant for hinges, cables and locks.

● **Waxes and polishes** are used to help protect painted and plated surfaces from the weather. Different types of paint may require the use of different types of wax polish. Some polishes utilise a chemical or abrasive cleaner to help remove the top layer of oxidised (dull) paint on older vehicles. In recent years, many non-wax polishes (that contain a wide variety of chemicals such as polymers and silicones) have been introduced. These non-wax polishes are usually easier to apply and last longer than conventional waxes and polishes.

## About the MOT Test

In the UK, all vehicles more than three years old are subject to an annual test to ensure that they meet minimum safety requirements. A current test certificate must be issued before a machine can be used on public roads, and is required before a road fund licence can be issued. Riding without a current test certificate will also invalidate your insurance.

For most owners, the MOT test is an annual cause for anxiety, and this is largely due to owners not being sure what needs to be checked prior to submitting the motorcycle for testing. The simple answer is that a fully roadworthy motorcycle will have no difficulty in passing the test.

This is a guide to getting your motorcycle through the MOT test. Obviously it will not be possible to examine the motorcycle to the same standard as the professional MOT tester, particularly in view of the equipment required for some of the checks. However, working through the following procedures will enable you to identify any problem areas before submitting the motorcycle for the test.

It has only been possible to summarise the test requirements here, based on the regulations in force at the time of printing. Test standards are becoming increasingly stringent, although there are some exemptions for older vehicles. More information about the MOT test can be obtained from the TSO publications, *How Safe is your Motorcycle* and *The MOT Inspection Manual for Motorcycle Testing*.

Many of the checks require that one of the wheels is raised off the ground. If the motorcycle doesn't have a centre stand, note that an auxiliary stand will be required. Additionally, the help of an assistant may prove useful.

Certain exceptions apply to machines under 50 cc, machines without a lighting system, and Classic bikes - if in doubt about any of the requirements listed below seek confirmation from an MOT tester prior to submitting the motorcycle for the test.

Check that the frame number is clearly visible.

> **HAYNES HiNT**
>
> *If a component is in borderline condition, the tester has discretion in deciding whether to pass or fail it. If the motorcycle presented is clean and evidently well cared for, the tester may be more inclined to pass a borderline component than if the motorcycle is scruffy and apparently neglected.*

# Electrical System

### Lights, turn signals, horn and reflector

✔ With the ignition on, check the operation of the following electrical components. **Note:** *The electrical components on certain small-capacity machines are powered by the generator, requiring that the engine is run for this check.*

a) Headlight and tail light. Check that both illuminate in the low and high beam switch positions.

b) Position lights. Check that the front position (or sidelight) and tail light illuminate in this switch position.

c) Turn signals. Check that all flash at the correct rate, and that the warning light(s) function correctly. Check that the turn signal switch works correctly.

c) Hazard warning system (where fitted). Check that all four turn signals flash in this switch position.

d) Brake stop light. Check that the light comes on when the front and rear brakes are independently applied. Models first used on or after 1st April 1986 must have a brake light switch on each brake.

e) Horn. Check that the sound is continuous and of reasonable volume.

✔ Check that there is a red reflector on the rear of the machine, either mounted separately or as part of the tail light lens.

✔ Check the condition of the headlight, tail light and turn signal lenses.

### Headlight beam height

✔ The MOT tester will perform a headlight beam height check using specialised beam setting equipment **(see illustration 1)**. This equipment will not be available to the home mechanic, but if you suspect that the headlight is incorrectly set or may have been maladjusted in the past, you can perform a rough test as follows.

✔ Position the bike in a straight line facing a brick wall. The bike must be off its stand, upright and with a rider seated. Measure the height from the ground to the centre of the headlight and mark a horizontal line on the wall at this height. Position the motorcycle 3.8 metres from the wall and draw a vertical

**Headlight beam height checking equipment**

line up the wall central to the centreline of the motorcycle. Switch to dipped beam and check that the beam pattern falls slightly lower than the horizontal line and to the left of the vertical line **(see illustration 2)**.

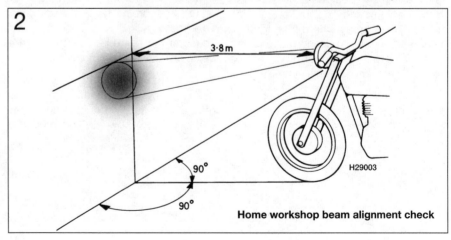

3·8 m

90°

90°

H29003

**Home workshop beam alignment check**

# Exhaust System and Final Drive

## Exhaust

✔ Check that the exhaust mountings are secure and that the system does not foul any of the rear suspension components.
✔ Start the motorcycle. When the revs are increased, check that the exhaust is neither holed nor leaking from any of its joints. On a linked system, check that the collector box is not leaking due to corrosion.

✔ Note that the exhaust decibel level ("loudness" of the exhaust) is assessed at the discretion of the tester. If the motorcycle was first used on or after 1st January 1985 the silencer must carry the BSAU 193 stamp, or a marking relating to its make and model, or be of OE (original equipment) manufacture. If the silencer is marked NOT FOR ROAD USE, RACING USE ONLY or similar, it will fail the MOT.

## Final drive

✔ On chain or belt drive machines, check that the chain/belt is in good condition and does not have excessive slack. Also check that the sprocket is securely mounted on the rear wheel hub. Check that the chain/belt guard is in place.
✔ On shaft drive bikes, check for oil leaking from the drive unit and fouling the rear tyre.

# Steering and Suspension

## Steering

✔ With the front wheel raised off the ground, rotate the steering from lock to lock. The handlebar or switches must not contact the fuel tank or be close enough to trap the rider's hand. Problems can be caused by damaged lock stops on the lower yoke and frame, or by the fitting of non-standard handlebars.
✔ When performing the lock to lock check, also ensure that the steering moves freely without drag or notchiness. Steering movement can be impaired by poorly routed cables, or by overtight head bearings or worn bearings. The tester will perform a check of the steering head bearing lower race by mounting the front wheel on a surface plate, then performing a lock to

lock check with the weight of the machine on the lower bearing **(see illustration 3)**.
✔ Grasp the fork sliders (lower legs) and attempt to push and pull on the forks **(see**

**Front wheel mounted on a surface plate for steering head bearing lower race check**

**illustration 4)**. Any play in the steering head bearings will be felt. Note that in extreme cases, wear of the front fork bushes can be misinterpreted for head bearing play.
✔ Check that the handlebars are securely mounted.
✔ Check that the handlebar grip rubbers are secure. They should by bonded to the bar left end and to the throttle cable pulley on the right end.

## Front suspension

✔ With the motorcycle off the stand, hold the front brake on and pump the front forks up and down **(see illustration 5)**. Check that they are adequately damped.

**Checking the steering head bearings for freeplay**

**Hold the front brake on and pump the front forks up and down to check operation**

Inspect the area around the fork dust seal for oil leakage (arrow)

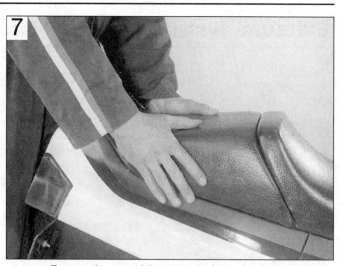

Bounce the rear of the motorcycle to check rear suspension operation

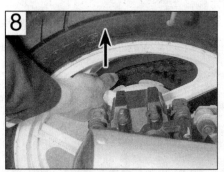

Checking for rear suspension linkage play

✔ Inspect the area above and around the front fork oil seals **(see illustration 6)**. There should be no sign of oil on the fork tube (stanchion) nor leaking down the slider (lower leg). On models so equipped, check that there is no oil leaking from the anti-dive units.

✔ On models with swingarm front suspension, check that there is no freeplay in the linkage when moved from side to side.

### Rear suspension

✔ With the motorcycle off the stand and an assistant supporting the motorcycle by its handlebars, bounce the rear suspension **(see illustration 7)**. Check that the suspension components do not foul on any of the cycle parts and check that the shock absorber(s) provide adequate damping.

✔ Visually inspect the shock absorber(s) and check that there is no sign of oil leakage from its damper. This is somewhat restricted on certain single shock models due to the location of the shock absorber.

✔ With the rear wheel raised off the ground, grasp the wheel at the highest point and attempt to pull it up **(see illustration 8)**. Any play in the swingarm pivot or suspension linkage bearings will be felt as movement. **Note:** *Do not confuse play with actual suspension movement.* Failure to lubricate suspension linkage bearings can lead to bearing failure **(see illustration 9)**.

✔ With the rear wheel raised off the ground, grasp the swingarm ends and attempt to move the swingarm from side to side and forwards and backwards - any play indicates wear of the swingarm pivot bearings **(see illustration 10)**.

Worn suspension linkage pivots (arrows) are usually the cause of play in the rear suspension

Grasp the swingarm at the ends to check for play in its pivot bearings

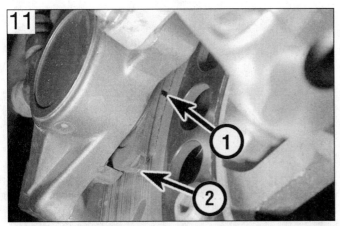

Brake pad wear can usually be viewed without removing the caliper. Most pads have wear indicator grooves (1) and some also have indicator tangs (2)

On drum brakes, check the angle of the operating lever with the brake fully applied. Most drum brakes have a wear indicator pointer and scale.

# Brakes, Wheels and Tyres

## Brakes

✔ With the wheel raised off the ground, apply the brake then free it off, and check that the wheel is about to revolve freely without brake drag.

✔ On disc brakes, examine the disc itself. Check that it is securely mounted and not cracked.

✔ On disc brakes, view the pad material through the caliper mouth and check that the pads are not worn down beyond the limit (see illustration 11).

✔ On drum brakes, check that when the brake is applied the angle between the operating lever and cable or rod is not too great (see illustration 12). Check also that the operating lever doesn't foul any other components.

✔ On disc brakes, examine the flexible hoses from top to bottom. Have an assistant hold the brake on so that the fluid in the hose is under pressure, and check that there is no sign of fluid leakage, bulges or cracking. If there are any metal brake pipes or unions, check that these are free from corrosion and damage. Where a brake-linked anti-dive system is fitted, check the hoses to the anti-dive in a similar manner.

✔ Check that the rear brake torque arm is secure and that its fasteners are secured by self-locking nuts or castellated nuts with split-pins or R-pins (see illustration 13).

✔ On models with ABS, check that the self-check warning light in the instrument panel works.

✔ The MOT tester will perform a test of the motorcycle's braking efficiency based on a calculation of rider and motorcycle weight. Although this cannot be carried out at home, you can at least ensure that the braking systems are properly maintained. For hydraulic disc brakes, check the fluid level, lever/pedal feel (bleed of air if its spongy) and pad material. For drum brakes, check adjustment, cable or rod operation and shoe lining thickness.

## Wheels and tyres

✔ Check the wheel condition. Cast wheels should be free from cracks and if of the built-up design, all fasteners should be secure. Spoked wheels should be checked for broken, corroded, loose or bent spokes.

✔ With the wheel raised off the ground, spin the wheel and visually check that the tyre and wheel run true. Check that the tyre does not foul the suspension or mudguards.

✔ With the wheel raised off the ground, grasp the wheel and attempt to move it about the axle (spindle) (see illustration 14). Any play felt here indicates wheel bearing failure.

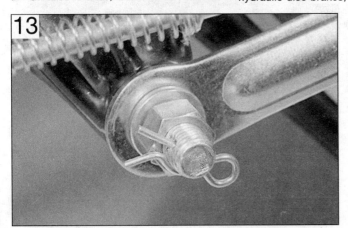

Brake torque arm must be properly secured at both ends

Check for wheel bearing play by trying to move the wheel about the axle (spindle)

Checking the tyre tread depth

Tyre direction of rotation arrow can be found on tyre sidewall

Castellated type wheel axle (spindle) nut must be secured by a split pin or R-pin

Two straightedges are used to check wheel alignment

✔ If the tyre sidewall carries a direction of rotation arrow, this must be pointing in the direction of normal wheel rotation (see illustration 16).

✔ Check that the wheel axle (spindle) nuts (where applicable) are properly secured. A self-locking nut or castellated nut with a split-pin or R-pin can be used (see illustration 17).

✔ Wheel alignment is checked with the motorcycle off the stand and a rider seated. With the front wheel pointing straight ahead, two perfectly straight lengths of metal or wood and placed against the sidewalls of both tyres (see illustration 18). The gap each side of the front tyre must be equidistant on both sides. Incorrect wheel alignment may be due to a cocked rear wheel (often as the result of poor chain adjustment) or in extreme cases, a bent frame.

✔ Check the tyre tread depth, tread condition and sidewall condition (see illustration 15).

✔ Check the tyre type. Front and rear tyre types must be compatible and be suitable for road use. Tyres marked NOT FOR ROAD USE, COMPETITION USE ONLY or similar, will fail the MOT.

# General checks and condition

✔ Check the security of all major fasteners, bodypanels, seat, fairings (where fitted) and mudguards.

✔ Check that the rider and pillion footrests, handlebar levers and brake pedal are securely mounted.

✔ Check for corrosion on the frame or any load-bearing components. If severe, this may affect the structure, particularly under stress.

# Sidecars

A motorcycle fitted with a sidecar requires additional checks relating to the stability of the machine and security of attachment and swivel joints, plus specific wheel alignment (toe-in) requirements. Additionally, tyre and lighting requirements differ from conventional motorcycle use. Owners are advised to check MOT test requirements with an official test centre.

# Preparing for storage

## Before you start

If repairs or an overhaul is needed, see that this is carried out now rather than left until you want to ride the bike again.

Give the bike a good wash and scrub all dirt from its underside. Make sure the bike dries completely before preparing for storage.

## Engine

● Remove the spark plug(s) and lubricate the cylinder bores with approximately a teaspoon of motor oil using a spout-type oil can **(see illustration 1)**. Reinstall the spark plug(s). Crank the engine over a couple of times to coat the piston rings and bores with oil. If the bike has a kickstart, use this to turn the engine over. If not, flick the kill switch to the OFF position and crank the engine over on the starter **(see illustration 2)**. If the nature on the ignition system prevents the starter operating with the kill switch in the OFF position,

remove the spark plugs and fit them back in their caps; ensure that the plugs are earthed (grounded) against the cylinder head when the starter is operated **(see illustration 3)**.

⚠️ **Warning: It is important that the plugs are earthed (grounded) away from the spark plug holes otherwise there is a risk of atomised fuel from the cylinders igniting.**

> **HAYNES HINT** On a single cylinder four-stroke engine, you can seal the combustion chamber completely by positioning the piston at TDC on the compression stroke.

● Drain the carburettor(s) otherwise there is a risk of jets becoming blocked by gum deposits from the fuel **(see illustration 4)**.

● If the bike is going into long-term storage, consider adding a fuel stabiliser to the fuel in the tank. If the tank is drained completely, corrosion of its internal surfaces may occur if left unprotected for a long period. The tank can be treated with a rust preventative especially for this purpose. Alternatively, remove the tank and pour half a litre of motor oil into it, install the filler cap and shake the tank to coat its internals with oil before draining off the excess. The same effect can also be achieved by spraying WD40 or a similar water-dispersant around the inside of the tank via its flexible nozzle.

● Make sure the cooling system contains the correct mix of antifreeze. Antifreeze also contains important corrosion inhibitors.

● The air intakes and exhaust can be sealed off by covering or plugging the openings. Ensure that you do not seal in any condensation; run the engine until it is hot,

Squirt a drop of motor oil into each cylinder

Flick the kill switch to OFF . . .

. . . and ensure that the metal bodies of the plugs (arrows) are earthed against the cylinder head

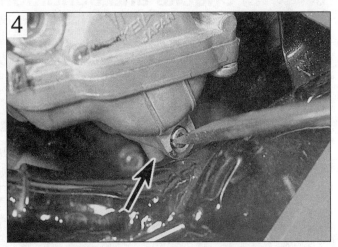

Connect a hose to the carburettor float chamber drain stub (arrow) and unscrew the drain screw

Exhausts can be sealed off with a plastic bag

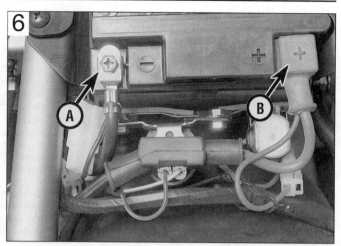

Disconnect the negative lead (A) first, followed by the positive lead (B)

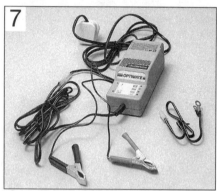

Use a suitable battery charger - this kit also assess battery condition

then switch off and allow to cool. Tape a piece of thick plastic over the silencer end(s) **(see illustration 5)**. Note that some advocate pouring a tablespoon of motor oil into the silencer(s) before sealing them off.

## Battery

● Remove it from the bike - in extreme cases of cold the battery may freeze and crack its case **(see illustration 6)**.

● Check the electrolyte level and top up if necessary (conventional refillable batteries). Clean the terminals.
● Store the battery off the motorcycle and away from any sources of fire. Position a wooden block under the battery if it is to sit on the ground.
● Give the battery a trickle charge for a few hours every month **(see illustration 7)**.

## Tyres

● Place the bike on its centrestand or an auxiliary stand which will support the motorcycle in an upright position. Position wood blocks under the tyres to keep them off the ground and to provide insulation from damp. If the bike is being put into long-term storage, ideally both tyres should be off the ground; not only will this protect the tyres, but will also ensure that no load is placed on the steering head or wheel bearings.
● Deflate each tyre by 5 to 10 psi, no more or the beads may unseat from the rim, making subsequent inflation difficult on tubeless tyres.

## Pivots and controls

● Lubricate all lever, pedal, stand and

footrest pivot points. If grease nipples are fitted to the rear suspension components, apply lubricant to the pivots.
● Lubricate all control cables.

## Cycle components

● Apply a wax protectant to all painted and plastic components. Wipe off any excess, but don't polish to a shine. Where fitted, clean the screen with soap and water.
● Coat metal parts with Vaseline (petroleum jelly). When applying this to the fork tubes, do not compress the forks otherwise the seals will rot from contact with the Vaseline.
● Apply a vinyl cleaner to the seat.

## Storage conditions

● Aim to store the bike in a shed or garage which does not leak and is free from damp.
● Drape an old blanket or bedspread over the bike to protect it from dust and direct contact with sunlight (which will fade paint). This also hides the bike from prying eyes. Beware of tight-fitting plastic covers which may allow condensation to form and settle on the bike.

# Getting back on the road

## Engine and transmission

● Change the oil and replace the oil filter. If this was done prior to storage, check that the oil hasn't emulsified - a thick whitish substance which occurs through condensation.
● Remove the spark plugs. Using a spout-type oil can, squirt a few drops of oil into the cylinder(s). This will provide initial lubrication as the piston rings and bores comes back into contact. Service the spark plugs, or fit new ones, and install them in the engine.

● Check that the clutch isn't stuck on. The plates can stick together if left standing for some time, preventing clutch operation. Engage a gear and try rocking the bike back and forth with the clutch lever held against the handlebar. If this doesn't work on cable-operated clutches, hold the clutch lever back against the handlebar with a strong elastic band or cable tie for a couple of hours **(see illustration 8)**.
● If the air intakes or silencer end(s) were blocked off, remove the bung or cover used.
● If the fuel tank was coated with a rust

Hold clutch lever back against the handlebar with elastic bands or a cable tie

preventative, oil or a stabiliser added to the fuel, drain and flush the tank and dispose of the fuel sensibly. If no action was taken with the fuel tank prior to storage, it is advised that the old fuel is disposed of since it will go off over a period of time. Refill the fuel tank with fresh fuel.

## Frame and running gear

● Oil all pivot points and cables.
● Check the tyre pressures. They will definitely need inflating if pressures were reduced for storage.
● Lubricate the final drive chain (where applicable).
● Remove any protective coating applied to the fork tubes (stanchions) since this may well destroy the fork seals. If the fork tubes weren't protected and have picked up rust spots, remove them with very fine abrasive paper and refinish with metal polish.
● Check that both brakes operate correctly. Apply each brake hard and check that it's not possible to move the motorcycle forwards, then check that the brake frees off again once released. Brake caliper pistons can stick due to corrosion around the piston head, or on the sliding caliper types, due to corrosion of the slider pins. If the brake doesn't free after repeated operation, take the caliper off for examination. Similarly drum brakes can stick due to a seized operating cam, cable or rod linkage.
● If the motorcycle has been in long-term storage, renew the brake fluid and clutch fluid (where applicable).
● Depending on where the bike has been stored, the wiring, cables and hoses may have been nibbled by rodents. Make a visual check and investigate disturbed wiring loom tape.

## Battery

● If the battery has been previously removal and given top up charges it can simply be reconnected. Remember to connect the positive cable first and the negative cable last.
● On conventional refillable batteries, if the battery has not received any attention, remove it from the motorcycle and check its electrolyte level. Top up if necessary then charge the battery. If the battery fails to hold a charge and a visual checks show heavy white sulphation of the plates, the battery is probably defective and must be renewed. This is particularly likely if the battery is old. Confirm battery condition with a specific gravity check.
● On sealed (MF) batteries, if the battery has not received any attention, remove it from the motorcycle and charge it according to the information on the battery case - if the battery fails to hold a charge it must be renewed.

## Starting procedure

● If a kickstart is fitted, turn the engine over a couple of times with the ignition OFF to distribute oil around the engine. If no kickstart is fitted, flick the engine kill switch OFF and the ignition ON and crank the engine over a couple of times to work oil around the upper cylinder components. If the nature of the ignition system is such that the starter won't work with the kill switch OFF, remove the spark plugs, fit them back into their caps and earth (ground) their bodies on the cylinder head. Reinstall the spark plugs afterwards.
● Switch the kill switch to RUN, operate the choke and start the engine. If the engine won't start don't continue cranking the engine - not only will this flatten the battery, but the starter motor will overheat. Switch the ignition off and try again later. If the engine refuses to start, go through the fault finding procedures in this manual. **Note:** *If the bike has been in storage for a long time, old fuel or a carburettor blockage may be the problem. Gum deposits in carburettors can block jets - if a carburettor cleaner doesn't prove successful the carburettors must be dismantled for cleaning.*

● Once the engine has started, check that the lights, turn signals and horn work properly.

● Treat the bike gently for the first ride and check all fluid levels on completion. Settle the bike back into the maintenance schedule.

This Section provides an easy reference-guide to the more common faults that are likely to afflict your machine. Obviously, the opportunities are almost limitless for faults to occur as a result of obscure failures, and to try and cover all eventualities would require a book. Indeed, a number have been written on the subject.

Successful troubleshooting is not a mysterious 'black art' but the application of a bit of knowledge combined with a systematic and logical approach to the problem. Approach any troubleshooting by first accurately identifying the symptom and then checking through the list of possible causes, starting with the simplest or most obvious and progressing in stages to the most complex.

Take nothing for granted, but above all apply liberal quantities of common sense.

The main symptom of a fault is given in the text as a major heading below which are listed the various systems or areas which may contain the fault. Details of each possible cause for a fault and the remedial action to be taken are given, in brief, in the paragraphs below each heading. Further information should be sought in the relevant Chapter.

## 1 Engine doesn't start or is difficult to start
- [ ] Starter motor doesn't rotate
- [ ] Starter motor rotates but engine does not turn over
- [ ] Starter works but engine won't turn over (seized)
- [ ] No fuel flow
- [ ] Engine flooded
- [ ] No spark or weak spark
- [ ] Compression low
- [ ] Stalls after starting
- [ ] Rough idle

## 2 Poor running at low speed
- [ ] Spark weak
- [ ] Fuel/air mixture incorrect
- [ ] Compression low
- [ ] Poor acceleration

## 3 Poor running or no power at high speed
- [ ] Firing incorrect
- [ ] Fuel/air mixture incorrect
- [ ] Compression low
- [ ] Knocking or pinking
- [ ] Miscellaneous causes

## 4 Overheating
- [ ] Engine overheats
- [ ] Firing incorrect
- [ ] Fuel/air mixture incorrect
- [ ] Compression too high
- [ ] Engine load excessive
- [ ] Lubrication inadequate
- [ ] Miscellaneous causes

## 5 Clutch problems
- [ ] Clutch slipping
- [ ] Clutch not disengaging completely

## 6 Gearchanging problems
- [ ] Doesn't go into gear, or lever doesn't return
- [ ] Jumps out of gear
- [ ] Overshifts

## 7 Abnormal engine noise
- [ ] Knocking or pinking
- [ ] Piston slap or rattling
- [ ] Valve noise
- [ ] Other noise

## 8 Abnormal driveline noise
- [ ] Clutch noise
- [ ] Transmission noise
- [ ] Final drive noise

## 9 Abnormal frame and suspension noise
- [ ] Front end noise
- [ ] Shock absorber noise
- [ ] Brake noise

## 10 Oil pressure warning light comes on
- [ ] Engine lubrication system
- [ ] Electrical system

## 11 Excessive exhaust smoke
- [ ] White smoke
- [ ] Black smoke
- [ ] Brown smoke

## 12 Poor handling or stability
- [ ] Handlebar hard to turn
- [ ] Handlebar shakes or vibrates excessively
- [ ] Handlebar pulls to one side
- [ ] Poor shock absorbing qualities

## 13 Braking problems
- [ ] Brakes are spongy, don't hold
- [ ] Brake lever or pedal pulsates
- [ ] Brakes drag

## 14 Electrical problems
- [ ] Battery dead or weak
- [ ] Battery overcharged

# 1 Engine doesn't start or is difficult to start

### Starter motor doesn't rotate

☐ Engine kill switch OFF.
☐ Fuse blown. Check main fuse and ignition circuit fuse (Chapter 9).
☐ Battery voltage low. Check and recharge battery (Chapter 9).
☐ Starter motor defective. Make sure the wiring to the starter is secure. Make sure the starter relay clicks when the start button is pushed. If the relay clicks, then the fault is in the wiring or motor.
☐ Starter relay faulty. Check it according to the procedure in Chapter 9.
☐ Starter switch not contacting. The contacts could be wet, corroded or dirty. Disassemble and clean the switch (Chapter 9).
☐ Wiring open or shorted. Check all wiring connections and harnesses to make sure that they are dry, tight and not corroded. Also check for broken or frayed wires that can cause a short to ground (earth) (see wiring diagram, Chapter 9).
☐ Ignition (main) switch defective. Check the switch according to the procedure in Chapter 9. Renew the switch if it is defective.
☐ Engine kill switch defective. Check for wet, dirty or corroded contacts. Clean or renew the switch as necessary (Chapter 9).
☐ Faulty neutral (gear position), sidestand or clutch switch. Check the wiring to each switch and the switch itself according to the procedures in Chapter 9.
☐ Faulty diode. Check as described in Chapter 9.

### Starter motor rotates but engine does not turn over

☐ Starter motor clutch defective. Inspect and repair or renew (Chapter 2).
☐ Damaged idler or starter gears. Inspect and renew the damaged parts (Chapter 2).

### Starter works but engine won't turn over (seized)

☐ Seized engine caused by one or more internally damaged components. Failure due to wear, abuse or lack of lubrication. Damage can include seized valves, followers, camshafts, pistons, crankshaft, connecting rod bearings, or transmission gears or bearings. Refer to Chapter 2 for engine disassembly.

### No fuel flow

☐ No fuel in tank.
☐ Fuel tank breather hose obstructed.
☐ Fuel valve not opening (carburettor models). Check the valve (Chapter 4).
☐ Fuel pump faulty, or strainer and/or filter is blocked (see Chapter 4).
☐ Fuel line clogged. Pull the fuel line loose and carefully blow through it.
☐ Float needle valve (carburettor models) or injector (injection models) clogged. For all of the valves to be clogged, either a very bad batch of fuel with an unusual additive has been used, or some other foreign material has entered the tank. Many times after a machine has been stored for many months without running, the fuel turns to a varnish-like liquid and forms deposits on the components.

### Engine flooded

☐ Float height too high (carburettor models). Check as described in Chapter 4.
☐ Float needle valve worn or stuck open (carburettor models). A piece of dirt, rust or other debris can cause the valve to seat improperly, causing excess fuel to be admitted to the float chamber. In this case, the float chamber should be cleaned and the needle valve and seat inspected. If the needle and seat are worn, then the leaking will persist and the parts should be renewed (Chapter 4).
☐ Starting technique incorrect. Under normal circumstances (ie, if all the carburettor functions or fuel injection system are sound) the machine should start with little or no throttle. When the engine is cold, the choke should be operated and the engine started without opening the throttle. When the engine is at operating temperature, only a very slight amount of throttle should be necessary.

### No spark or weak spark

☐ Ignition switch OFF.
☐ Engine kill switch turned to the OFF position.
☐ Battery voltage low. Check and recharge the battery as necessary (Chapter 9).
☐ Spark plugs dirty, defective or worn out. Locate reason for fouled plugs using spark plug condition chart on the inside rear cover and follow the plug maintenance procedures (Chapter 1).
☐ Spark plug caps or secondary (HT) wiring faulty (GSX-R750T and V models). Check condition. Renew either or both components if cracks or deterioration are evident (Chapter 5).
☐ Spark plug cap/coil defective (GSX-R600 and GSX-R750W and X models). Test and renew if necessary (Chapter 5).
☐ Spark plug caps not making good contact. Make sure that the plug caps fit snugly over the plug ends.
☐ Electronic control unit defective. Check the unit, referring to Chapter 5 for details.
☐ Pulse generator coil (crankshaft position sensor on fuel injected models) defective. Check the unit, referring to Chapter 5 for details.
☐ Ignition HT coils defective. Check the coils, referring to Chapter 5.
☐ Ignition or kill switch shorted. This is usually caused by water, corrosion, damage or excessive wear. The switches can be disassembled and cleaned with electrical contact cleaner. If cleaning does not help, renew the switches (Chapter 9).
☐ Wiring shorted or broken between:
   a)   Ignition (main) switch and engine kill switch (or blown fuse)
   b)   Electronic control unit and engine kill switch
   c)   Electronic control unit and ignition HT coils
   d)   Ignition HT coils and spark plugs (GSX-R750T and V models)
   e)   Electronic control unit and pulse generator
☐ Make sure that all wiring connections are clean, dry and tight. Look for chafed and broken wires (Chapters 5 and 9).

### Compression low

☐ Spark plugs loose. Remove the plugs and inspect their threads. Reinstall and tighten to the specified torque (Chapter 1).
☐ Cylinder head not sufficiently tightened down. If a cylinder head is suspected of being loose, then there's a chance that the gasket or head is damaged if the problem has persisted for any length of time. The head bolts should be tightened to the proper torque in the correct sequence (Chapter 2).
☐ Improper valve clearance. This means that the valve is not closing completely and compression pressure is leaking past the valve. Check and adjust the valve clearances (Chapter 1).
☐ Cylinder and/or piston worn. Excessive wear will cause compression pressure to leak past the rings. This is usually accompanied by worn rings as well. A top-end overhaul is necessary (Chapter 2).
☐ Piston rings worn, weak, broken, or sticking. Broken or sticking piston rings usually indicate a lubrication or carburation problem that causes excess carbon deposits or seizures to form on the pistons and rings. Top-end overhaul is necessary (Chapter 2).
☐ Piston ring-to-groove clearance excessive. This is caused by excessive wear of the piston ring lands. Piston renewal is necessary (Chapter 2).
☐ Cylinder head gasket damaged. If a head is allowed to become loose, or if excessive carbon build-up on the piston crown and combustion chamber causes extremely high compression, the head gasket may leak. Retorquing the head is not always sufficient to restore the seal, so gasket renewal is necessary (Chapter 2).
☐ Cylinder head warped. This is caused by overheating or improperly tightened head bolts. Machine shop resurfacing or head renewal is necessary (Chapter 2).
☐ Valve spring broken or weak. Caused by component failure or wear; the springs must be renewed (Chapter 2).

# 1 Engine doesn't start or is difficult to start (continued)

☐ Valve not seating properly. This is caused by a bent valve (from over-revving or improper valve adjustment), burned valve or seat (improper carburation) or an accumulation of carbon deposits on the seat (from carburation or lubrication problems). The valves must be cleaned and/or renewed and the seats serviced if possible (Chapter 2).

## Stalls after starting

☐ Improper choke action (carburettor models). Make sure the choke linkage shaft is getting a full stroke and staying in the out position (Chapter 4).
☐ Ignition malfunction. See Chapter 5.
☐ Carburettor or fuel injection system malfunction. See Chapter 4.
☐ Fuel contaminated. The fuel can be contaminated with either dirt or water, or can change chemically if the machine is allowed to sit for several months or more. Drain the tank and fuel system components (Chapter 4).
☐ Inlet air leak. Check for loose carburettor/throttle body-to-inlet

manifold connections, loose or missing vacuum gauge adapter screws, caps or hoses (Chapter 4).
☐ Engine idle speed incorrect. Turn idle adjusting screw until the engine idles at the specified rpm (Chapter 1).

## Rough idle

☐ Ignition malfunction. See Chapter 5.
☐ Idle speed incorrect. See Chapter 1.
☐ Carburettors or throttle bodies not synchronised. Adjust them with vacuum gauge or manometer set as described in Chapter 1.
☐ Carburettor or fuel injection system malfunction. See Chapter 4.
☐ Fuel contaminated. The fuel can be contaminated with either dirt or water, or can change chemically if the machine is allowed to sit for several months or more. Drain the tank and float chambers or fuel rail (Chapter 4).
☐ Inlet air leak. Check for loose carburettor/throttle body-to-inlet manifold connections, loose or missing vacuum gauge adapter screws, caps or hoses, or loose carburettor tops (Chapter 4).
☐ Air filter clogged. Renew the air filter element (Chapter 1).

# 2 Poor running at low speeds

## Spark weak

☐ Battery voltage low. Check and recharge battery (Chapter 9).
☐ Spark plugs fouled, defective or worn out. Refer to Chapter 1 for spark plug maintenance.
☐ Spark plug caps or secondary (HT) wiring faulty (GSX-R750T and V models). Check condition. Renew either or both components if cracks or deterioration are evident (Chapter 5).
☐ Spark plug cap/coil defective (GSX-R600 and GSX-R750W and X models). Test and renew if necessary (Chapter 5).
☐ Spark plug caps not making contact.
☐ Incorrect spark plugs. Wrong type, heat range or cap configuration. Check and install correct plugs listed in Chapter 1.
☐ Electronic control unit defective. See Chapter 5.
☐ Pulse generator coil (crankshaft position sensor on GSX-R750W and X models) defective. See Chapter 5.
☐ Ignition HT coils defective. See Chapter 5.

## Fuel/air mixture incorrect

☐ Pilot screws out of adjustment (Chapter 4). Pilot jet or air passage clogged. Remove and overhaul the carburettors/throttle bodies (Chapter 4).
☐ Fuel injector clogged or fuel injection system malfunction (see Chapter 4).
☐ Air bleed holes clogged. Remove carburettor and blow out all passages (Chapter 4).
☐ Air filter clogged, poorly sealed or missing (Chapter 1).
☐ Air filter housing poorly sealed. Look for cracks, holes or loose clamps and renew or repair defective parts.
☐ Fuel level too high or too low (carburettor models). Check the float height (Chapter 4).
☐ Fuel tank breather hose obstructed.
☐ Carburettor/throttle body inlet manifolds loose. Check for cracks, breaks, tears or loose clamps. Renew the rubber inlet manifold joints if split or perished.

## Compression low

☐ Spark plugs loose. Remove the plugs and inspect their threads. Reinstall and tighten to the specified torque (Chapter 1).
☐ Cylinder heads not sufficiently tightened down. If a cylinder head is suspected of being loose, then there's a chance that the gasket and head are damaged if the problem has persisted for any length of time. The head bolts should be tightened to the proper torque in the correct sequence (Chapter 2).

☐ Improper valve clearance. This means that the valve is not closing completely and compression pressure is leaking past the valve. Check and adjust the valve clearances (Chapter 1).
☐ Cylinder and/or piston worn. Excessive wear will cause compression pressure to leak past the rings. This is usually accompanied by worn rings as well. A top-end overhaul is necessary (Chapter 2).
☐ Piston rings worn, weak, broken, or sticking. Broken or sticking piston rings usually indicate a lubrication or carburation problem that causes excess carbon deposits or seizures to form on the pistons and rings. Top-end overhaul is necessary (Chapter 2).
☐ Piston ring-to-groove clearance excessive. This is caused by excessive wear of the piston ring lands. Piston renewal is necessary (Chapter 2).
☐ Cylinder head gasket damaged. If a head is allowed to become loose, or if excessive carbon build-up on the piston crown and combustion chamber causes extremely high compression, the head gasket may leak. Retorquing the head is not always sufficient to restore the seal, so gasket renewal is necessary (Chapter 2).
☐ Cylinder head warped. This is caused by overheating or improperly tightened head bolts. Machine shop resurfacing or head renewal is necessary (Chapter 2).
☐ Valve spring broken or weak. Caused by component failure or wear; the springs must be renewed (Chapter 2).
☐ Valve not seating properly. This is caused by a bent valve (from over-revving or improper valve adjustment), burned valve or seat (improper carburation) or an accumulation of carbon deposits on the seat (from carburation, lubrication problems). The valves must be cleaned and/or renewed and the seats serviced if possible (Chapter 2).

## Poor acceleration

☐ Carburettors/throttle bodies leaking or dirty. Overhaul them (Chapter 4).
☐ Timing not advancing. The pulse generator coil (crankshaft position sensor on GSX-R750W and X models) or the electronic control module may be defective. If so, they must be renewed.
☐ Carburettors/throttle bodies not synchronised. Adjust them with a vacuum gauge set or manometer (Chapter 1).
☐ Engine oil viscosity too high. Using a heavier oil than that recommended in Chapter 1 can damage the oil pump or lubrication system and cause drag on the engine.
☐ Brakes dragging. Usually caused by debris which has entered the brake piston seals, or from a warped disc or bent axle. Repair as necessary (Chapter 7).

# 3 Poor running or no power at high speed

## Firing incorrect

☐ Air filter restricted. Clean or renew filter (Chapter 1).
☐ Spark plugs fouled, defective or worn out. See Chapter 1 for spark plug maintenance.
☐ Spark plug caps or secondary (HT) wiring faulty (GSX-R750T and V models). Check condition. Renew either or both components if cracks or deterioration are evident (Chapter 5).
☐ Spark plug cap/coil defective (GSX-R600 and GSX-R750W and X models). Test and renew if necessary (Chapter 5).
☐ Spark plug caps not in good contact. See Chapter 5.
☐ Incorrect spark plugs. Wrong type, heat range or cap configuration. Check and install correct plugs listed in Chapter 1.
☐ Electronic control unit defective. See Chapter 5.
☐ Ignition HT coils defective. See Chapter 5.

## Fuel/air mixture incorrect

☐ Main jet or fuel injector clogged or wrong size. Dirt, water or other contaminants can clog them. Clean the fuel strainer and/or filter, and the carburettors or injectors (Chapter 4). The standard jetting is for sea level atmospheric pressure and oxygen content.
☐ Fuel injector clogged or fuel injection system malfunction (see Chapter 4).
☐ Carburettor throttle shaft-to-carburettor body clearance excessive.
☐ Carburettor air bleed holes clogged. Remove and overhaul carburettors (Chapter 4).
☐ Air filter clogged, poorly sealed, or missing (Chapter 1).
☐ Air filter housing poorly sealed. Look for cracks, holes or loose clamps, and renew or repair defective parts.
☐ Carburettor fuel level too high or too low. Check the float height (Chapter 4).
☐ Fuel tank breather hose obstructed.
☐ Carburettor/throttle body inlet manifolds loose. Check for cracks, breaks, tears or loose clamps. Renew the rubber inlet manifolds if they are split or perished (Chapter 4).

## Compression low

☐ Spark plugs loose. Remove the plugs and inspect their threads. Reinstall and tighten to the specified torque (Chapter 1).
☐ Cylinder heads not sufficiently tightened down. If a cylinder head is suspected of being loose, then there's a chance that the gasket and head are damaged if the problem has persisted for any length of time. The head bolts should be tightened to the proper torque in the correct sequence (Chapter 2).
☐ Improper valve clearance. This means that the valve is not closing completely and compression pressure is leaking past the valve. Check and adjust the valve clearances (Chapter 1).
☐ Cylinder and/or piston worn. Excessive wear will cause compression pressure to leak past the rings. This is usually accompanied by worn rings as well. A top-end overhaul is necessary (Chapter 2).
☐ Piston rings worn, weak, broken, or sticking. Broken or sticking piston rings usually indicate a lubrication or carburation problem

that causes excess carbon deposits or seizures to form on the pistons and rings. Top-end overhaul is necessary (Chapter 2).
☐ Piston ring-to-groove clearance excessive. This is caused by excessive wear of the piston ring lands. Piston renewal is necessary (Chapter 2).
☐ Cylinder head gasket damaged. If a head is allowed to become loose, or if excessive carbon build-up on the piston crown and combustion chamber causes extremely high compression, the head gasket may leak. Retorquing the head is not always sufficient to restore the seal, so gasket renewal is necessary (Chapter 2).
☐ Cylinder head warped. This is caused by overheating or improperly tightened head bolts. Machine shop resurfacing or head renewal is necessary (Chapter 2).
☐ Valve spring broken or weak. Caused by component failure or wear; the springs must be renewed (Chapter 2).
☐ Valve not seating properly. This is caused by a bent valve (from over-revving or improper valve adjustment), burned valve or seat (improper carburation) or an accumulation of carbon deposits on the seat (from carburation or lubrication problems). The valves must be cleaned and/or renewed and the seats serviced if possible (Chapter 2).

## Knocking or pinking

☐ Carbon build-up in combustion chamber. Use of a fuel additive that will dissolve the adhesive bonding the carbon particles to the crown and chamber is the easiest way to remove the build-up. Otherwise, the cylinder head will have to be removed and decarbonised (Chapter 2).
☐ Incorrect or poor quality fuel. Old or improper grades of fuel can cause detonation. This causes the piston to rattle, thus the knocking or pinking sound. Drain old fuel and always use the recommended fuel grade.
☐ Spark plug heat range incorrect. Uncontrolled detonation indicates the plug heat range is too hot. The plug in effect becomes a glow plug, raising cylinder temperatures. Install the proper heat range plug (Chapter 1).
☐ Improper air/fuel mixture. This will cause the cylinders to run hot, which leads to detonation. Clogged jets or an air leak can cause this imbalance. See Chapter 4.

## Miscellaneous causes

☐ Throttle valve doesn't open fully. Adjust the throttle grip freeplay (Chapter 1).
☐ Clutch slipping. May be caused by loose or worn clutch components. Refer to Chapter 2 for clutch overhaul procedures.
☐ Timing not advancing.
☐ Engine oil viscosity too high. Using a heavier oil than the one recommended in Chapter 1 can damage the oil pump or lubrication system and cause drag on the engine.
☐ Brakes dragging. Usually caused by debris which has entered the brake piston seals, or from a warped disc or bent axle. Repair as necessary.

# 4 Overheating

## Engine overheats

☐ Coolant level low. Check and add coolant (Chapter 1).
☐ Leak in cooling system. Check cooling system hoses and radiator for leaks and other damage. Repair or renew parts as necessary (Chapter 3).
☐ Thermostat sticking open or closed. Check and renew as described in Chapter 3.
☐ Faulty radiator cap. Remove the cap and have it pressure tested.
☐ Coolant passages clogged. Have the entire system drained and flushed, then refill with fresh coolant.
☐ Water pump defective. Remove the pump and check the components (Chapter 3).
☐ Clogged radiator fins. Clean them by blowing compressed air through the fins from the backside.
☐ Cooling fan or fan switch fault (Chapter 3).

## Firing incorrect

☐ Spark plugs fouled, defective or worn out. See Chapter 1 for spark plug maintenance.
☐ Incorrect spark plugs.
☐ Electronic control unit defective. See Chapter 5.
☐ Faulty ignition HT coils (Chapter 5).

## Fuel/air mixture incorrect

☐ Main jet or fuel injector clogged. Dirt, water or other contaminants can clog them. Clean the fuel strainer and/or filter, and the carburettors or injectors (Chapter 4). The standard jetting is for sea level atmospheric pressure and oxygen content.
☐ Fuel injection system malfunction (see Chapter 4).
☐ Throttle shaft-to-carburettor body clearance excessive. Refer to Chapter 4.
☐ Carburettor air bleed holes clogged. Remove and overhaul carburettors (Chapter 4).
☐ Air filter clogged, poorly sealed, or missing (Chapter 1).
☐ Air filter housing poorly sealed. Look for cracks, holes or loose clamps, and renew or repair defective parts.
☐ Carburettor fuel level too high or too low. Check the float height (Chapter 4).
☐ Fuel tank breather hose obstructed.

☐ Carburettor/throttle body inlet manifolds loose. Check for cracks, breaks, tears or loose clamps. Renew the rubber inlet manifolds if they are split or perished (Chapter 4).

## Compression too high

☐ Carbon build-up in combustion chamber. Use of a fuel additive that will dissolve the adhesive bonding the carbon particles to the piston crown and chamber is the easiest way to remove the build-up. Otherwise, the cylinder head will have to be removed and decarbonised (Chapter 2).
☐ Improperly machined head surface or installation of incorrect gasket during engine assembly.

## Engine load excessive

☐ Clutch slipping. Can be caused by damaged, loose or worn clutch components. Refer to Chapter 2 for overhaul procedures.
☐ Engine oil level too high. The addition of too much oil will cause pressurisation of the crankcase and inefficient engine operation. Check Specifications and drain to proper level (Chapter 1).
☐ Engine oil viscosity too high. Using a heavier oil than the one recommended in Chapter 1 can damage the oil pump or lubrication system as well as cause drag on the engine.
☐ Brakes dragging. Usually caused by debris which has entered the brake piston seals, or from a warped disc or bent axle. Repair as necessary.

## Lubrication inadequate

☐ Engine oil level too low. Friction caused by intermittent lack of lubrication or from oil that is overworked can cause overheating. The oil provides a definite cooling function in the engine. Check the oil level (Chapter 1).
☐ Poor quality engine oil or incorrect viscosity or type. Oil is rated not only according to viscosity but also according to type. Some oils are not rated high enough for use in this engine. Check the Specifications section and change to the correct oil (Chapter 1).

## Miscellaneous causes

☐ Modification to exhaust system. Most aftermarket exhaust systems cause the engine to run leaner, which make them run hotter. When installing an accessory exhaust system, always rejet the carburettors.

# 5 Clutch problems

## Clutch slipping

☐ Insufficient clutch cable freeplay. Check and adjust (Chapter 1).
☐ Friction plates worn or warped. Overhaul the clutch assembly (Chapter 2).
☐ Plain plates warped (Chapter 2).
☐ Clutch diaphragm springs broken or weak. Old or heat-damaged (from slipping clutch) springs should be renewed (Chapter 2).
☐ Clutch release mechanism defective. Renew any defective parts (Chapter 2).
☐ Clutch centre or housing unevenly worn. This causes improper engagement of the plates. Renew the damaged or worn parts (Chapter 2).

## Clutch not disengaging completely

☐ Excessive clutch cable freeplay. Check and adjust (Chapter 1).
☐ Clutch plates warped or damaged. This will cause clutch drag, which in turn will cause the machine to creep. Overhaul the clutch assembly (Chapter 2).

☐ Clutch diaphragm spring fatigued or broken. Check and renew the spring (Chapter 2).
☐ Engine oil deteriorated. Old, thin, worn out oil will not provide proper lubrication for the plates, causing the clutch to drag. Renew the oil and filter (Chapter 1).
☐ Engine oil viscosity too high. Using a heavier oil than recommended in Chapter 1 can cause the plates to stick together, putting a drag on the engine. Change to the correct weight oil (Chapter 1).
☐ Clutch housing guide seized on mainshaft. Lack of lubrication, severe wear or damage can cause the guide to seize on the shaft. Overhaul of the clutch, and perhaps transmission, may be necessary to repair the damage (Chapter 2).
☐ Clutch release mechanism defective. Overhaul the clutch cover components (Chapter 2).
☐ Loose clutch centre nut. Causes housing and centre misalignment putting a drag on the engine. Engagement adjustment continually varies. Overhaul the clutch assembly (Chapter 2).

# 6 Gearchanging problems

## Doesn't go into gear or lever doesn't return

☐ Clutch not disengaging. See above.
☐ Selector fork(s) bent or seized. Often caused by dropping the machine or from lack of lubrication. Overhaul the transmission (Chapter 2).
☐ Gear(s) stuck on shaft. Most often caused by a lack of lubrication or excessive wear in transmission bearings and bushings. Overhaul the transmission (Chapter 2).
☐ Selector drum binding. Caused by lubrication failure or excessive wear. Renew the drum and bearing (Chapter 2).
☐ Gearchange lever return spring weak or broken (Chapter 2).
☐ Gearchange lever broken. Splines stripped out of lever or shaft, caused by allowing the lever to get loose or from dropping the machine. Renew necessary parts (Chapter 2).

☐ Gearchange mechanism stopper arm broken or worn. Full engagement and rotary movement of selector drum results. Renew the arm (Chapter 2).

## Jumps out of gear

☐ Selector fork(s) worn. Overhaul the transmission (Chapter 2).
☐ Gear groove(s) worn. Overhaul the transmission (Chapter 2).
☐ Gear dogs or dog slots worn or damaged. The gears should be inspected and renewed. No attempt should be made to service the worn parts.

## Overshifts

☐ Stopper arm spring weak or broken (Chapter 2).
☐ Gearshift shaft return spring post broken or distorted (Chapter 2).

# 7 Abnormal engine noise

## Knocking or pinking

☐ Carbon build-up in combustion chamber. Use of a fuel additive that will dissolve the adhesive bonding the carbon particles to the piston crown and chamber is the easiest way to remove the build-up. Otherwise, the cylinder head will have to be removed and decarbonised (Chapter 2).
☐ Incorrect or poor quality fuel. Old or improper fuel can cause detonation. This causes the pistons to rattle, thus the knocking or pinking sound. Drain the old fuel and always use the recommended grade fuel (Chapter 4).
☐ Spark plug heat range incorrect. Uncontrolled detonation indicates that the plug heat range is too hot. The plug in effect becomes a glow plug, raising cylinder temperatures. Install the proper heat range plug (Chapter 1).
☐ Improper air/fuel mixture. This will cause the cylinders to run hot and lead to detonation. Clogged jets/injectors or an air leak can cause this imbalance. See Chapter 4.

## Piston slap or rattling

☐ Cylinder-to-piston clearance excessive. Caused by improper assembly. Inspect and overhaul top-end parts (Chapter 2).
☐ Connecting rod bent. Caused by over-revving, trying to start a badly flooded engine or from ingesting a foreign object into the combustion chamber. Renew the damaged parts (Chapter 2).
☐ Piston pin or piston pin bore worn or seized from wear or lack of lubrication. Renew damaged parts (Chapter 2).
☐ Piston ring(s) worn, broken or sticking. Overhaul the top-end (Chapter 2).
☐ Piston seizure damage. Usually from lack of lubrication or overheating. Renew the pistons and cylinder block, as necessary (Chapter 2).

☐ Connecting rod upper or lower end clearance excessive. Caused by excessive wear or lack of lubrication. Renew worn parts.

## Valve noise

☐ Incorrect valve clearances. Adjust the clearances by referring to Chapter 1.
☐ Valve spring broken or weak. Check and renew weak valve springs (Chapter 2).
☐ Camshaft or cylinder head worn or damaged. Lack of lubrication at high rpm is usually the cause of damage. Insufficient oil or failure to change the oil at the recommended intervals are the chief causes. Since there are no replaceable bearings in the head, the head itself will have to be renewed if there is excessive wear or damage (Chapter 2).

## Other noise

☐ Cylinder head gasket leaking.
☐ Exhaust pipe leaking at cylinder head connection. Caused by improper fit of pipe(s) or loose exhaust flange. All exhaust fasteners should be tightened evenly and carefully. Failure to do this will lead to a leak.
☐ Crankshaft runout excessive. Caused by a bent crankshaft (from over-revving) or damage from an upper cylinder component failure. Can also be attributed to dropping the machine on either of the crankshaft ends.
☐ Engine mounting bolts loose. Tighten all engine mount bolts (Chapter 2).
☐ Crankshaft bearings worn (Chapter 2).
☐ Cam chain rattle, due to worn chain or defective tensioner. Also worn chain tensioner/guide blades. Renew according to the procedure in Chapter 2.

# 8 Abnormal driveline noise

### Clutch noise
☐ Clutch housing/friction plate clearance excessive (Chapter 2).
☐ Wear between the clutch housing splines and input shaft splines (Chapter 2).
☐ Worn release bearing (Chapter 2).

### Transmission noise
☐ Bearings worn. Also includes the possibility that the shafts are worn. Overhaul the transmission (Chapter 2).
☐ Gears worn or chipped (Chapter 2).
☐ Metal chips jammed in gear teeth. Probably pieces from a broken clutch, gear or selector mechanism that were picked up by the gears. This will cause early bearing failure (Chapter 2).
☐ Engine oil level too low. Causes a howl from transmission. Also affects engine power and clutch operation (Chapter 1).

### Final drive noise
☐ Chain not adjusted properly or excessively worn (Chapter 1).
☐ Front or rear sprocket loose. Tighten fasteners (Chapter 6).
☐ Sprockets worn. Renew sprockets (Chapter 6).
☐ Rear sprocket warped. Renew sprockets (Chapter 6).
☐ Rubber dampers in rear wheel worn (Chapter 6).

# 9 Abnormal frame and suspension noise

### Front end noise
☐ Low fluid level or improper viscosity oil in forks. This can sound like spurting and is usually accompanied by irregular fork action (Chapter 6).
☐ Spring weak or broken. Makes a clicking or scraping sound. Fork oil, when drained, will have a lot of metal particles in it (Chapter 6).
☐ Steering head bearings loose or damaged. Clicks when braking. Check and adjust or renew as necessary (Chapters 1 and 6).
☐ Fork yokes loose. Make sure all clamp pinch bolts are tightened to the specified torque (Chapter 6).
☐ Forks bent. Good possibility if machine has been dropped. Renew forks (Chapter 6).
☐ Front axle bolt or axle clamp bolts loose. Tighten them to the specified torque (Chapter 7).
☐ Loose or worn wheel bearings. Check and renew as needed (Chapters 1 and 7).

### Shock absorber noise
☐ Fluid level incorrect. Indicates a leak caused by defective seal. Shock will be covered with oil. Renew shock or seek advice on repair from a suspension specialist (Chapter 6).
☐ Defective shock absorber with internal damage. This is in the body of the shock and can't be remedied. The shock must be renewed or rebuilt (Chapter 6).

☐ Bent or damaged shock body. Renew the shock (Chapter 6).
☐ Loose or worn suspension linkage components. Check and renew as necessary (Chapter 6).

### Brake noise
☐ Squeal caused by pad shim not installed or positioned correctly (where fitted) (Chapter 7).
☐ Squeal caused by dust on brake pads. Usually found in combination with glazed pads. Clean using brake cleaning solvent (Chapter 7).
☐ Contamination of brake pads. Oil, brake fluid or dirt causing brake to chatter or squeal. Clean or renew pads (Chapter 7).
☐ Pads glazed. Caused by excessive heat from prolonged use or from contamination. Do not use sandpaper, emery cloth, carborundum cloth or any other abrasive to roughen the pad surfaces as abrasives will stay in the pad material and damage the disc. A very fine flat file can be used, but pad renewal is suggested as a cure (Chapter 7).
☐ Disc warped. Can cause a chattering, clicking or intermittent squeal. Usually accompanied by a pulsating lever and uneven braking. Renew the disc (Chapter 7).
☐ Loose or worn wheel bearings. Check and renew as needed (Chapters 1 and 7).

# 10 Oil pressure warning light comes on

### Engine lubrication system
☐ Engine oil pump defective, blocked oil strainer gauze or failed pressure regulator. Carry out an oil pressure check (Chapter 1).
☐ Engine oil level low. Inspect for leak or other problem causing low oil level and add recommended oil (Daily (pre-ride) checks).
☐ Engine oil viscosity too low. Very old, thin oil or an improper weight of oil used in the engine. Change to correct oil (Chapter 1).
☐ Camshaft or crankshaft journals worn. Excessive wear causing drop in oil pressure. Abnormal wear could be caused by oil starvation at high rpm from low oil level or improper weight or type of oil (Chapter 1).

### Electrical system
☐ Oil pressure switch defective. Check the switch according to the procedure in Chapter 9. Renew it if it is defective.
☐ Oil pressure warning light circuit or display defective. Check for pinched, shorted, disconnected or damaged wiring (Chapter 9).

# 11 Excessive exhaust smoke

## White smoke

☐ Piston oil ring worn. The ring may be broken or damaged, causing oil from the crankcase to be pulled past the piston into the combustion chamber. Renew the rings (Chapter 2).

☐ Cylinders worn, cracked, or scored. Caused by overheating or oil starvation. Install a new cylinder block (Chapter 2).

☐ Valve oil seal damaged or worn. Renew oil seals (Chapter 2).

☐ Valve guide worn. Perform a complete valve job (Chapter 2).

☐ Engine oil level too high, which causes the oil to be forced past the rings. Drain oil to the proper level (Daily (pre-ride) checks).

☐ Head gasket broken between oil return and cylinder. Causes oil to be pulled into the combustion chamber. Renew the head gasket and check the head for warpage (Chapter 2).

☐ Abnormal crankcase pressurisation, which forces oil past the rings. Clogged breather is usually the cause.

## Black smoke

☐ Air filter clogged. Clean or renew the element (Chapter 1).

☐ Carburettor main jet too large or loose. Compare the jet size to the Specifications (Chapter 4).

☐ Choke cable or linkage shaft stuck (carburettor models), causing fuel to be pulled through choke circuit (Chapter 4).

☐ Fuel level too high (carburettor models). Check and adjust the float height(s) as necessary (Chapter 4).

☐ Float needle valve held off needle seat (Carburettor models). Clean the float chambers and fuel line and renew the needles and seats if necessary (Chapter 4).

☐ Fuel injection system malfunction (Chapter 4).

## Brown smoke

☐ Main jet too small or clogged (carburettor models). Lean condition caused by wrong size main jet or by a restricted orifice. Clean float chambers and jets and compare jet size to Specifications (Chapter 4).

☐ Fuel flow insufficient (carburettor models). Float needle valve stuck closed due to chemical reaction with old fuel. Float height incorrect. Restricted fuel line. Clean line and float chamber and adjust floats if necessary.

☐ Fuel pump faulty (Chapter 4).

☐ Carburettor/throttle body inlet manifold clamps loose (Chapter 4).

☐ Air filter poorly sealed or not installed (Chapter 1).

☐ Fuel injection system malfunction (Chapter 4).

# 12 Poor handling or stability

## Handlebar hard to turn

☐ Steering head bearing adjuster nut too tight. Check adjustment as described in Chapter 1.

☐ Bearings damaged. Roughness can be felt as the bars are turned from side-to-side. Renew bearings (Chapter 6).

☐ Races dented or worn. Denting results from wear in only one position (eg, straight ahead), from a collision or hitting a pothole or from dropping the machine. Renew bearings (Chapter 6

☐ Steering stem lubrication inadequate. Causes are grease getting hard from age or being washed out by high pressure car washes. Disassemble steering head and repack bearings (Chapter 6).

☐ Steering stem bent. Caused by a collision, hitting a pothole or by dropping the machine. Renew damaged part. Don't try to straighten the steering stem (Chapter 6).

☐ Front tyre air pressure too low (Chapter 1).

## Handlebar shakes or vibrates excessively

☐ Tyres worn or out of balance (Chapter 7).

☐ Swingarm bearings worn. Renew worn bearings (Chapter 6).

☐ Failed steering damper.

☐ Wheel rim(s) warped or damaged. Inspect wheels for runout (Chapter 7).

☐ Wheel bearings worn. Worn front or rear wheel bearings can cause poor tracking. Worn front bearings will cause wobble (Chapters 1 and 7).

☐ Handlebar clamp bolts loose (Chapter 6).

☐ Fork yoke bolts loose. Tighten them to the specified torque (Chapter 6).

☐ Engine mounting bolts loose. Will cause excessive vibration with increased engine rpm (Chapter 2).

## Handlebar pulls to one side

☐ Frame bent. Definitely suspect this if the machine has been dropped. May or may not be accompanied by cracking near the bends. Renew the frame (Chapter 6).

☐ Wheels out of alignment. Caused by improper location of axle spacers or from bent steering stem or frame (Chapter 6).

☐ Swingarm bent or twisted. Renew the arm (Chapter 6).

☐ Steering stem bent. Caused by impact damage or by dropping the motorcycle. Renew the steering stem (Chapter 6).

☐ Forks bent. Disassemble the forks and renew the damaged parts (Chapter 6).

☐ Fork oil level uneven. Check and add or drain as necessary (Chapter 6).

## Poor shock absorbing qualities

☐ Too hard:
  a)  Fork oil level excessive (Chapter 6).
  b)  Fork oil viscosity too high. Use a lighter oil (see the Specifications in Chapter 6).
  c)  Fork tube bent. Causes a harsh, sticking feeling (Chapter 6).
  d)  Shock shaft or body bent or damaged (Chapter 6).
  e)  Fork internal damage (Chapter 6).
  f)  Shock internal damage.
  g)  Tyre pressure too high (Chapter 1).
  h)  Suspension settings incorrect.

☐ Too soft:
  a)  Fork or shock oil insufficient and/or leaking (Chapter 6).
  b)  Fork oil level too low (Chapter 6).
  c)  Fork oil viscosity too light (Chapter 6).
  d)  Fork springs weak or broken (Chapter 6).
  e)  Shock internal damage or leakage (Chapter 6).
  f)  Suspension settings incorrect.

# 13 Braking problems

## Brakes are spongy, don't hold

☐ Air in brake line. Caused by inattention to master cylinder fluid level or by leakage. Locate problem and bleed brakes (Chapter 7).
☐ Pad or disc worn (Chapters 1 and 7).
☐ Brake fluid leak. See paragraph 1.
☐ Contaminated pads. Caused by contamination with oil, grease, brake fluid, etc. Clean or renew pads. Clean disc thoroughly with brake cleaner (Chapter 7).
☐ Brake fluid deteriorated. Fluid is old or contaminated. Drain system, replenish with new fluid and bleed the system (Chapter 7).
☐ Master cylinder internal parts worn or damaged causing fluid to bypass (Chapter 7).
☐ Master cylinder bore scratched by foreign material or broken spring. Repair or renew master cylinder (Chapter 7).
☐ Disc warped. Renew disc (Chapter 7).

## Brake lever or pedal pulsates

☐ Disc warped. Renew disc (Chapter 7).
☐ Axle bent. Renew axle (Chapter 7).
☐ Brake caliper bolts loose (Chapter 7).
☐ Wheel warped or otherwise damaged (Chapter 7).
☐ Wheel bearings damaged or worn (Chapters 1 and 7).

## Brakes drag

☐ Master cylinder piston seized. Caused by wear or damage to piston or cylinder bore (Chapter 7).
☐ Lever balky or stuck. Check pivot and lubricate (Chapter 7).
☐ Brake caliper piston seized in bore. Caused by corrosion or ingestion of dirt past deteriorated seal (Chapter 7).
☐ Brake pad damaged. Pad material separated from backing plate. Usually caused by faulty manufacturing process or from contact with chemicals. Renew pads (Chapter 7).
☐ Pads improperly installed (Chapter 7).

# 14 Electrical problems

## Battery dead or weak

☐ Battery faulty. Caused by sulphated plates which are shorted through sedimentation. Also, broken battery terminal making only occasional contact (Chapter 9).
☐ Battery cables making poor contact (Chapter 9).
☐ Load excessive. Caused by addition of high wattage lights or other electrical accessories.
☐ Ignition (main) switch defective. Switch either grounds (earths) internally or fails to shut off system. Renew the switch (Chapter 9).
☐ Regulator/rectifier defective (Chapter 9).
☐ Alternator stator coil open or shorted (Chapter 9).
☐ Charging system fault. Check for current leakage (Chapter 9).
☐ Wiring faulty. Wiring grounded (earthed) or connections loose in ignition, charging or lighting circuits (Chapter 9).

## Battery overcharged

☐ Regulator/rectifier defective. Overcharging is noticed when battery gets excessively warm (Chapter 9).
☐ Battery defective. Renew battery with a new one (Chapter 9).
☐ Battery amperage too low, wrong type or size. Install manufacturer's specified amp-hour battery to handle charging load (Chapter 9).

## Checking engine compression

● Low compression will result in exhaust smoke, heavy oil consumption, poor starting and poor performance. A compression test will provide useful information about an engine's condition and if performed regularly, can give warning of trouble before any other symptoms become apparent.

● A compression gauge will be required, along with an adapter to suit the spark plug hole thread size. Note that the screw-in type gauge/adapter set up is preferable to the rubber cone type.

● Before carrying out the test, first check the valve clearances as described in Chapter 1.

1 Run the engine until it reaches normal operating temperature, then stop it and remove the spark plug(s), taking care not to scald your hands on the hot components.

2 Install the gauge adapter and compression gauge in No. 1 cylinder spark plug hole **(see illustration 1)**.

**Screw the compression gauge adapter into the spark plug hole, then screw the gauge into the adapter**

3 On kickstart-equipped motorcycles, make sure the ignition switch is OFF, then open the throttle fully and kick the engine over a couple of times until the gauge reading stabilises.

4 On motorcycles with electric start only, the procedure will differ depending on the nature of the ignition system. Flick the engine kill switch (engine stop switch) to OFF and turn the ignition switch ON; open the throttle fully and crank the engine over on the starter motor for a couple of revolutions until the gauge reading stabilises. If the starter will not operate with the kill switch OFF, turn the ignition switch OFF and refer to the next paragraph.

5 Install the spark plugs back into their suppressor caps and arrange the plug electrodes so that their metal bodies are earthed (grounded) against the cylinder head; this is essential to prevent damage to the ignition system as the engine is spun over **(see illustration 2)**. Position the plugs well

**All spark plugs must be earthed (grounded) against the cylinder head**

away from the plug holes otherwise there is a risk of atomised fuel escaping from the combustion chambers and igniting. As a safety precaution, cover the top of the valve cover with rag. Now turn the ignition switch ON and kill switch ON, open the throttle fully and crank the engine over on the starter motor for a couple of revolutions until the gauge reading stabilises.

6 After one or two revolutions the pressure should build up to a maximum figure and then stabilise. Take a note of this reading and on multi-cylinder engines repeat the test on the remaining cylinders.

7 The correct pressures are given in Chapter 2 Specifications. If the results fall within the specified range and on multi-cylinder engines all are relatively equal, the engine is in good condition. If there is a marked difference between the readings, or if the readings are lower than specified, inspection of the top-end components will be required.

8 Low compression pressure may be due to worn cylinder bores, pistons or rings, failure of the cylinder head gasket, worn valve seals, or poor valve seating.

9 To distinguish between cylinder/piston wear and valve leakage, pour a small quantity of oil into the bore to temporarily seal the piston rings, then repeat the compression tests **(see illustration 3)**. If the readings show

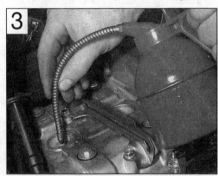

**Bores can be temporarily sealed with a squirt of motor oil**

a noticeable increase in pressure this confirms that the cylinder bore, piston, or rings are worn. If, however, no change is indicated, the cylinder head gasket or valves should be examined.

10 High compression pressure indicates excessive carbon build-up in the combustion chamber and on the piston crown. If this is the case the cylinder head should be removed and the deposits removed. Note that excessive carbon build-up is less likely with the used on modern fuels.

## Checking battery open-circuit voltage

 *Warning: The gases produced by the battery are explosive - never smoke or create any sparks in the vicinity of the battery. Never allow the electrolyte to contact your skin or clothing - if it does, wash it off and seek immediate medical attention.*

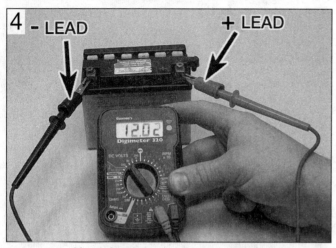

Measuring open-circuit battery voltage

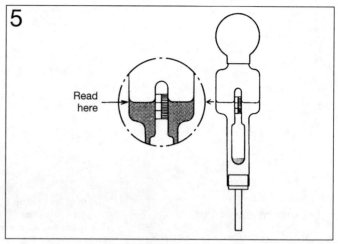

Float-type hydrometer for measuring battery specific gravity

● Before any electrical fault is investigated the battery should be checked.

● You'll need a dc voltmeter or multimeter to check battery voltage. Check that the leads are inserted in the correct terminals on the meter, red lead to positive (+ve), black lead to negative (-ve). Incorrect connections can damage the meter.

● A sound fully-charged 12 volt battery should produce between 12.3 and 12.6 volts across its terminals (12.8 volts for a maintenance-free battery). On machines with a 6 volt battery, voltage should be between 6.1 and 6.3 volts.

1 Set a multimeter to the 0 to 20 volts dc range and connect its probes across the battery terminals. Connect the meter's positive (+ve) probe, usually red, to the battery positive (+ve) terminal, followed by the meter's negative (-ve) probe, usually black, to the battery negative terminal (-ve) (see illustration 4).

2 If battery voltage is low (below 10 volts on a 12 volt battery or below 4 volts on a six volt battery), charge the battery and test the voltage again. If the battery repeatedly goes flat, investigate the motorcycle's charging system.

## Checking battery specific gravity (SG)

 Warning: The gases produced by the battery are explosive - never smoke or create any sparks in the vicinity of the battery. Never allow the electrolyte to contact your skin or clothing - if it does, wash it off and seek immediate medical attention.

● The specific gravity check gives an indication of a battery's state of charge.

● A hydrometer is used for measuring specific gravity. Make sure you purchase one

which has a small enough hose to insert in the aperture of a motorcycle battery.

● Specific gravity is simply a measure of the electrolyte's density compared with that of water. Water has an SG of 1.000 and fully-charged battery electrolyte is about 26% heavier, at 1.260.

● Specific gravity checks are not possible on maintenance-free batteries. Testing the open-circuit voltage is the only means of determining their state of charge.

1 To measure SG, remove the battery from the motorcycle and remove the first cell cap. Draw

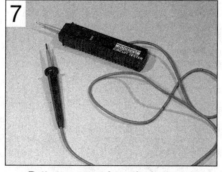

Digital multimeter can be used for all electrical tests

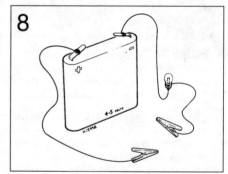

Battery-powered continuity tester

some electrolyte into the hydrometer and note the reading (see illustration 5). Return the electrolyte to the cell and install the cap.

2 The reading should be in the region of 1.260 to 1.280. If SG is below 1.200 the battery needs charging. Note that SG will vary with temperature; it should be measured at 20°C (68°F). Add 0.007 to the reading for every 10°C above 20°C, and subtract 0.007 from the reading for every 10°C below 20°C. Add 0.004 to the reading for every 10°F above 68°F, and subtract 0.004 from the reading for every 10°F below 68°F.

3 When the check is complete, rinse the hydrometer thoroughly with clean water.

## Checking for continuity

● The term continuity describes the uninterrupted flow of electricity through an electrical circuit. A continuity check will determine whether an open-circuit situation exists.

● Continuity can be checked with an ohmmeter, multimeter, continuity tester or battery and bulb test circuit (see illustrations 6, 7 and 8).

Battery and bulb test circuit

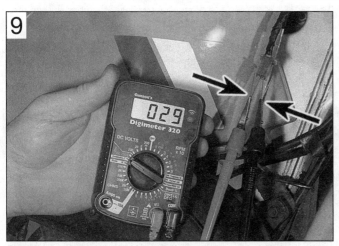

Continuity check of front brake light switch using a meter - note split pins used to access connector terminals

Continuity check of rear brake light switch using a continuity tester

● All of these instruments are self-powered by a battery, therefore the checks are made with the ignition OFF.

● As a safety precaution, always disconnect the battery negative (-ve) lead before making checks, particularly if ignition switch checks are being made.

● If using a meter, select the appropriate ohms scale and check that the meter reads infinity (∞). Touch the meter probes together and check that meter reads zero; where necessary adjust the meter so that it reads zero.

● After using a meter, always switch it OFF to conserve its battery.

## Switch checks

1 If a switch is at fault, trace its wiring up to the wiring connectors. Separate the wire connectors and inspect them for security and condition. A build-up of dirt or corrosion here will most likely be the cause of the problem - clean up and apply a water dispersant such as WD40.

2 If using a test meter, set the meter to the ohms x 10 scale and connect its probes across the wires from the switch **(see illustration 9)**. Simple ON/OFF type switches, such as brake light switches, only have two wires whereas combination switches, like the ignition switch, have many internal links. Study the wiring diagram to ensure that you are connecting across the correct pair of wires. Continuity (low or no measurable resistance - 0 ohms) should be indicated with the switch ON and no continuity (high resistance) with it OFF.

3 Note that the polarity of the test probes doesn't matter for continuity checks, although care should be taken to follow specific test procedures if a diode or solid-state component is being checked.

4 A continuity tester or battery and bulb circuit can be used in the same way. Connect its probes as described above **(see illustration 10)**. The light should come on to indicate continuity in the ON switch position, but should extinguish in the OFF position.

## Wiring checks

● Many electrical faults are caused by damaged wiring, often due to incorrect routing or chaffing on frame components.

● Loose, wet or corroded wire connectors can also be the cause of electrical problems, especially in exposed locations.

1 A continuity check can be made on a single length of wire by disconnecting it at each end and connecting a meter or continuity tester across both ends of the wire **(see illustration 11)**.

2 Continuity (low or no resistance - 0 ohms) should be indicated if the wire is good. If no continuity (high resistance) is shown, suspect a broken wire.

### Checking for voltage

● A voltage check can determine whether current is reaching a component.

● Voltage can be checked with a dc voltmeter, multimeter set on the dc volts scale, test light or buzzer **(see illustrations 12 and 13)**. A meter has the advantage of being able to measure actual voltage.

● When using a meter, check that its leads are inserted in the correct terminals on the meter, red to positive (+ve), black to negative (-ve). Incorrect connections can damage the meter.

● A voltmeter (or multimeter set to the dc volts scale) should always be connected in parallel (across the load). Connecting it in series will destroy the meter.

● Voltage checks are made with the ignition ON.

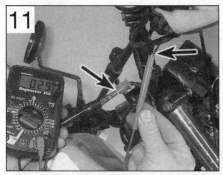

Continuity check of front brake light switch sub-harness

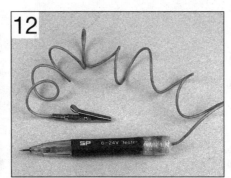

A simple test light can be used for voltage checks

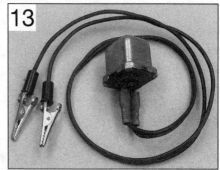

A buzzer is useful for voltage checks

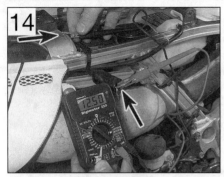

**Checking for voltage at the rear brake light power supply wire using a meter . . .**

**1** First identify the relevant wiring circuit by referring to the wiring diagram at the end of this manual. If other electrical components share the same power supply (ie are fed from the same fuse), take note whether they are working correctly - this is useful information in deciding where to start checking the circuit.

**2** If using a meter, check first that the meter leads are plugged into the correct terminals on the meter (see above). Set the meter to the dc volts function, at a range suitable for the battery voltage. Connect the meter red probe (+ve) to the power supply wire and the black probe to a good metal earth (ground) on the motorcycle's frame or directly to the battery negative (-ve) terminal **(see illustration 14)**. Battery voltage should be shown on the meter

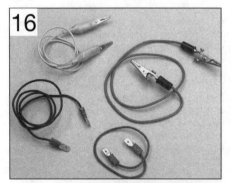

**A selection of jumper wires for making earth (ground) checks**

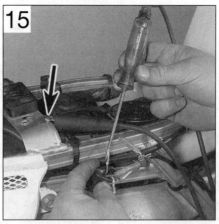

**. . . or a test light - note the earth connection to the frame (arrow)**

with the ignition switched ON.

**3** If using a test light or buzzer, connect its positive (+ve) probe to the power supply terminal and its negative (-ve) probe to a good earth (ground) on the motorcycle's frame or directly to the battery negative (-ve) terminal **(see illustration 15)**. With the ignition ON, the test light should illuminate or the buzzer sound.

**4** If no voltage is indicated, work back towards the fuse continuing to check for voltage. When you reach a point where there is voltage, you know the problem lies between that point and your last check point.

## Checking the earth (ground)

● Earth connections are made either directly to the engine or frame (such as sensors, neutral switch etc. which only have a positive feed) or by a separate wire into the earth circuit of the wiring harness. Alternatively a short earth wire is sometimes run directly from the component to the motorcycle's frame.
● Corrosion is often the cause of a poor earth connection.
● If total failure is experienced, check the security of the main earth lead from the

negative (-ve) terminal of the battery and also the main earth (ground) point on the wiring harness. If corroded, dismantle the connection and clean all surfaces back to bare metal.

**1** To check the earth on a component, use an insulated jumper wire to temporarily bypass its earth connection **(see illustration 16)**. Connect one end of the jumper wire between the earth terminal or metal body of the component and the other end to the motorcycle's frame.

**2** If the circuit works with the jumper wire installed, the original earth circuit is faulty. Check the wiring for open-circuits or poor connections. Clean up direct earth connections, removing all traces of corrosion and remake the joint. Apply petroleum jelly to the joint to prevent future corrosion.

## Tracing a short-circuit

● A short-circuit occurs where current shorts to earth (ground) bypassing the circuit components. This usually results in a blown fuse.

● A short-circuit is most likely to occur where the insulation has worn through due to wiring chafing on a component, allowing a direct path to earth (ground) on the frame.

**1** Remove any bodypanels necessary to access the circuit wiring.

**2** Check that all electrical switches in the circuit are OFF, then remove the circuit fuse and connect a test light, buzzer or voltmeter (set to the dc scale) across the fuse terminals. No voltage should be shown.

**3** Move the wiring from side to side whilst observing the test light or meter. When the test light comes on, buzzer sounds or meter shows voltage, you have found the cause of the short. It will usually shown up as damaged or burned insulation.

**4** Note that the same test can be performed on each component in the circuit, even the switch.

## A

**ABS (Anti-lock braking system)** A system, usually electronically controlled, that senses incipient wheel lockup during braking and relieves hydraulic pressure at wheel which is about to skid.

**Aftermarket** Components suitable for the motorcycle, but not produced by the motorcycle manufacturer.

**Allen key** A hexagonal wrench which fits into a recessed hexagonal hole.

**Alternating current (ac)** Current produced by an alternator. Requires converting to direct current by a rectifier for charging purposes.

**Alternator** Converts mechanical energy from the engine into electrical energy to charge the battery and power the electrical system.

**Ampere (amp)** A unit of measurement for the flow of electrical current. Current = Volts ÷ Ohms.

**Ampere-hour (Ah)** Measure of battery capacity.

**Angle-tightening** A torque expressed in degrees. Often follows a conventional tightening torque for cylinder head or main bearing fasteners **(see illustration)**.

**Angle-tightening cylinder head bolts**

**Antifreeze** A substance (usually ethylene glycol) mixed with water, and added to the cooling system, to prevent freezing of the coolant in winter. Antifreeze also contains chemicals to inhibit corrosion and the formation of rust and other deposits that would tend to clog the radiator and coolant passages and reduce cooling efficiency.

**Anti-dive** System attached to the fork lower leg (slider) to prevent fork dive when braking hard.

**Anti-seize compound** A coating that reduces the risk of seizing on fasteners that are subjected to high temperatures, such as exhaust clamp bolts and nuts.

**API** American Petroleum Institute. A quality standard for 4-stroke motor oils.

**Asbestos** A natural fibrous mineral with great heat resistance, commonly used in the composition of brake friction materials. Asbestos is a health hazard and the dust created by brake systems should never be inhaled or ingested.

**ATF** Automatic Transmission Fluid. Often used in front forks.

**ATU** Automatic Timing Unit. Mechanical device for advancing the ignition timing on early engines.

**ATV** All Terrain Vehicle. Often called a Quad.

**Axial play** Side-to-side movement.

**Axle** A shaft on which a wheel revolves. Also known as a spindle.

## B

**Backlash** The amount of movement between meshed components when one component is held still. Usually applies to gear teeth.

**Ball bearing** A bearing consisting of a hardened inner and outer race with hardened steel balls between the two races.

**Bearings** Used between two working surfaces to prevent wear of the components and a build-up of heat. Four types of bearing are commonly used on motorcycles: plain shell bearings, ball bearings, tapered roller bearings and needle roller bearings.

**Bevel gears** Used to turn the drive through 90°. Typical applications are shaft final drive and camshaft drive **(see illustration)**.

**Bevel gears are used to turn the drive through 90°**

**BHP** Brake Horsepower. The British measurement for engine power output. Power output is now usually expressed in kilowatts (kW).

**Bias-belted tyre** Similar construction to radial tyre, but with outer belt running at an angle to the wheel rim.

**Big-end bearing** The bearing in the end of the connecting rod that's attached to the crankshaft.

**Bleeding** The process of removing air from an hydraulic system via a bleed nipple or bleed screw.

**Bottom-end** A description of an engine's crankcase components and all components contained there-in.

**BTDC** Before Top Dead Centre in terms of piston position. Ignition timing is often expressed in terms of degrees or millimetres BTDC.

**Bush** A cylindrical metal or rubber component used between two moving parts.

**Burr** Rough edge left on a component after machining or as a result of excessive wear.

## C

**Cam chain** The chain which takes drive from the crankshaft to the camshaft(s).

**Canister** The main component in an evaporative emission control system (California market only); contains activated charcoal granules to trap vapours from the fuel system rather than allowing them to vent to the atmosphere.

**Castellated** Resembling the parapets along the top of a castle wall. For example, a castellated wheel axle or spindle nut.

**Catalytic converter** A device in the exhaust system of some machines which converts certain pollutants in the exhaust gases into less harmful substances.

**Charging system** Description of the components which charge the battery, ie the alternator, rectifer and regulator.

**Circlip** A ring-shaped clip used to prevent endwise movement of cylindrical parts and shafts. An internal circlip is installed in a groove in a housing; an external circlip fits into a groove on the outside of a cylindrical piece such as a shaft. Also known as a snap-ring.

**Clearance** The amount of space between two parts. For example, between a piston and a cylinder, between a bearing and a journal, etc.

**Coil spring** A spiral of elastic steel found in various sizes throughout a vehicle, for example as a springing medium in the suspension and in the valve train.

**Compression** Reduction in volume, and increase in pressure and temperature, of a gas, caused by squeezing it into a smaller space.

**Compression damping** Controls the speed the suspension compresses when hitting a bump.

**Compression ratio** The relationship between cylinder volume when the piston is at top dead centre and cylinder volume when the piston is at bottom dead centre.

**Continuity** The uninterrupted path in the flow of electricity. Little or no measurable resistance.

**Continuity tester** Self-powered bleeper or test light which indicates continuity.

**Cp** Candlepower. Bulb rating commonly found on US motorcycles.

**Crossply tyre** Tyre plies arranged in a criss-cross pattern. Usually four or six plies used, hence 4PR or 6PR in tyre size codes.

**Cush drive** Rubber damper segments fitted between the rear wheel and final drive sprocket to absorb transmission shocks **(see illustration)**.

**Cush drive rubbers dampen out transmission shocks**

## D

**Degree disc** Calibrated disc for measuring piston position. Expressed in degrees.

**Dial gauge** Clock-type gauge with adapters for measuring runout and piston position. Expressed in mm or inches.

**Diaphragm** The rubber membrane in a master cylinder or carburettor which seals the upper chamber.

**Diaphragm spring** A single sprung plate often used in clutches.

**Direct current (dc)** Current produced by a dc generator.

**Decarbonisation** The process of removing carbon deposits - typically from the combustion chamber, valves and exhaust port/system.

**Detonation** Destructive and damaging explosion of fuel/air mixture in combustion chamber instead of controlled burning.

**Diode** An electrical valve which only allows current to flow in one direction. Commonly used in rectifiers and starter interlock systems.

**Disc valve (or rotary valve)** A induction system used on some two-stroke engines.

**Double-overhead camshaft (DOHC)** An engine that uses two overhead camshafts, one for the intake valves and one for the exhaust valves.

**Drivebelt** A toothed belt used to transmit drive to the rear wheel on some motorcycles. A drivebelt has also been used to drive the camshafts. Drivebelts are usually made of Kevlar.

**Driveshaft** Any shaft used to transmit motion. Commonly used when referring to the final driveshaft on shaft drive motorcycles.

# E

**Earth return** The return path of an electrical circuit, utilising the motorcycle's frame.

**ECU (Electronic Control Unit)** A computer which controls (for instance) an ignition system, or an anti-lock braking system.

**EGO** Exhaust Gas Oxygen sensor. Sometimes called a Lambda sensor.

**Electrolyte** The fluid in a lead-acid battery.

**EMS (Engine Management System)** A computer controlled system which manages the fuel injection and the ignition systems in an integrated fashion.

**Endfloat** The amount of lengthways movement between two parts. As applied to a crankshaft, the distance that the crankshaft can move side-to-side in the crankcase.

**Endless chain** A chain having no joining link. Common use for cam chains and final drive chains.

**EP (Extreme Pressure)** Oil type used in locations where high loads are applied, such as between gear teeth.

**Evaporative emission control system** Describes a charcoal filled canister which stores fuel vapours from the tank rather than allowing them to vent to the atmosphere. Usually only fitted to California models and referred to as an EVAP system.

**Expansion chamber** Section of two-stroke engine exhaust system so designed to improve engine efficiency and boost power.

# F

**Feeler blade or gauge** A thin strip or blade of hardened steel, ground to an exact thickness, used to check or measure clearances between parts.

**Final drive** Description of the drive from the transmission to the rear wheel. Usually by chain or shaft, but sometimes by belt.

**Firing order** The order in which the engine cylinders fire, or deliver their power strokes, beginning with the number one cylinder.

**Flooding** Term used to describe a high fuel level in the carburettor float chambers, leading to fuel overflow. Also refers to excess fuel in the combustion chamber due to incorrect starting technique.

**Free length** The no-load state of a component when measured. Clutch, valve and fork spring lengths are measured at rest, without any preload.

**Freeplay** The amount of travel before any action takes place. The looseness in a linkage, or an assembly of parts, between the initial application of force and actual movement. For example, the distance the rear brake pedal moves before the rear brake is actuated.

**Fuel injection** The fuel/air mixture is metered electronically and directed into the engine intake ports (indirect injection) or into the cylinders (direct injection). Sensors supply information on engine speed and conditions.

**Fuel/air mixture** The charge of fuel and air going into the engine. See **Stoichiometric ratio**.

**Fuse** An electrical device which protects a circuit against accidental overload. The typical fuse contains a soft piece of metal which is calibrated to melt at a predetermined current flow (expressed as amps) and break the circuit.

# G

**Gap** The distance the spark must travel in jumping from the centre electrode to the side electrode in a spark plug. Also refers to the distance between the ignition rotor and the pickup coil in an electronic ignition system.

**Gasket** Any thin, soft material - usually cork, cardboard, asbestos or soft metal - installed between two metal surfaces to ensure a good seal. For instance, the cylinder head gasket seals the joint between the block and the cylinder head.

**Gauge** An instrument panel display used to monitor engine conditions. A gauge with a movable pointer on a dial or a fixed scale is an analogue gauge. A gauge with a numerical readout is called a digital gauge.

**Gear ratios** The drive ratio of a pair of gears in a gearbox, calculated on their number of teeth.

**Glaze-busting** see **Honing**

**Grinding** Process for renovating the valve face and valve seat contact area in the cylinder head.

**Gudgeon pin** The shaft which connects the connecting rod small-end with the piston. Often called a piston pin or wrist pin.

# H

**Helical gears** Gear teeth are slightly curved and produce less gear noise that straight-cut gears. Often used for primary drives.

**Installing a Helicoil thread insert in a cylinder head**

**Helicoil** A thread insert repair system. Commonly used as a repair for stripped spark plug threads **(see illustration)**.

**Honing** A process used to break down the glaze on a cylinder bore (also called glaze-busting). Can also be carried out to roughen a rebored cylinder to aid ring bedding-in.

**HT (High Tension)** Description of the electrical circuit from the secondary winding of the ignition coil to the spark plug.

**Hydraulic** A liquid filled system used to transmit pressure from one component to another. Common uses on motorcycles are brakes and clutches.

**Hydrometer** An instrument for measuring the specific gravity of a lead-acid battery.

**Hygroscopic** Water absorbing. In motorcycle applications, braking efficiency will be reduced if DOT 3 or 4 hydraulic fluid absorbs water from the air - care must be taken to keep new brake fluid in tightly sealed containers.

# I

**lbf ft** Pounds-force feet. An imperial unit of torque. Sometimes written as ft-lbs.

**lbf in** Pound-force inch. An imperial unit of torque, applied to components where a very low torque is required. Sometimes written as in-lbs.

**IC** Abbreviation for Integrated Circuit.

**Ignition advance** Means of increasing the timing of the spark at higher engine speeds. Done by mechanical means (ATU) on early engines or electronically by the ignition control unit on later engines.

**Ignition timing** The moment at which the spark plug fires, expressed in the number of crankshaft degrees before the piston reaches the top of its stroke, or in the number of millimetres before the piston reaches the top of its stroke.

**Infinity (∞)** Description of an open-circuit electrical state, where no continuity exists.

**Inverted forks (upside down forks)** The sliders or lower legs are held in the yokes and the fork tubes or stanchions are connected to the wheel axle (spindle). Less unsprung weight and stiffer construction than conventional forks.

# J

**JASO** Quality standard for 2-stroke oils.

**Joule** The unit of electrical energy.

**Journal** The bearing surface of a shaft.

# K

**Kickstart** Mechanical means of turning the engine over for starting purposes. Only usually fitted to mopeds, small capacity motorcycles and off-road motorcycles.

**Kill switch** Handebar-mounted switch for emergency ignition cut-out. Cuts the ignition circuit on all models, and additionally prevent starter motor operation on others.

**km** Symbol for kilometre.

**kmh** Abbreviation for kilometres per hour.

# L

**Lambda (λ) sensor** A sensor fitted in the exhaust system to measure the exhaust gas oxygen content (excess air factor).

**Lapping** see **Grinding**.
**LCD** Abbreviation for Liquid Crystal Display.
**LED** Abbreviation for Light Emitting Diode.
**Liner** A steel cylinder liner inserted in a aluminium alloy cylinder block.
**Locknut** A nut used to lock an adjustment nut, or other threaded component, in place.
**Lockstops** The lugs on the lower triple clamp (yoke) which abut those on the frame, preventing handlebar-to-fuel tank contact.
**Lockwasher** A form of washer designed to prevent an attaching nut from working loose.
**LT Low Tension** Description of the electrical circuit from the power supply to the primary winding of the ignition coil.

# M

**Main bearings** The bearings between the crankshaft and crankcase.
**Maintenance-free (MF) battery** A sealed battery which cannot be topped up.
**Manometer** Mercury-filled calibrated tubes used to measure intake tract vacuum. Used to synchronise carburettors on multi-cylinder engines.
**Micrometer** A precision measuring instrument that measures component outside diameters **(see illustration)**.

**Tappet shims are measured with a micrometer**

**MON (Motor Octane Number)** A measure of a fuel's resistance to knock.
**Monograde oil** An oil with a single viscosity, eg SAE80W.
**Monoshock** A single suspension unit linking the swingarm or suspension linkage to the frame.
**mph** Abbreviation for miles per hour.
**Multigrade oil** Having a wide viscosity range (eg 10W40). The W stands for Winter, thus the viscosity ranges from SAE10 when cold to SAE40 when hot.
**Multimeter** An electrical test instrument with the capability to measure voltage, current and resistance. Some meters also incorporate a continuity tester and buzzer.

# N

**Needle roller bearing** Inner race of caged needle rollers and hardened outer race. Examples of uncaged needle rollers can be found on some engines. Commonly used in rear suspension applications and in two-stroke engines.
**Nm** Newton metres.
**NOx** Oxides of Nitrogen. A common toxic pollutant emitted by petrol engines at higher temperatures.

# O

**Octane** The measure of a fuel's resistance to knock.
**OE (Original Equipment)** Relates to components fitted to a motorcycle as standard or replacement parts supplied by the motorcycle manufacturer.
**Ohm** The unit of electrical resistance. Ohms = Volts ÷ Current.
**Ohmmeter** An instrument for measuring electrical resistance.
**Oil cooler** System for diverting engine oil outside of the engine to a radiator for cooling purposes.
**Oil injection** A system of two-stroke engine lubrication where oil is pump-fed to the engine in accordance with throttle position.
**Open-circuit** An electrical condition where there is a break in the flow of electricity - no continuity (high resistance).
**O-ring** A type of sealing ring made of a special rubber-like material; in use, the O-ring is compressed into a groove to provide the sealing action.
**Oversize (OS)** Term used for piston and ring size options fitted to a rebored cylinder.
**Overhead cam (sohc) engine** An engine with single camshaft located on top of the cylinder head.
**Overhead valve (ohv) engine** An engine with the valves located in the cylinder head, but with the camshaft located in the engine block or crankcase.
**Oxygen sensor** A device installed in the exhaust system which senses the oxygen content in the exhaust and converts this information into an electric current. Also called a Lambda sensor.

# P

**Plastigauge** A thin strip of plastic thread, available in different sizes, used for measuring clearances. For example, a strip of Plastigauge is laid across a bearing journal. The parts are assembled and dismantled; the width of the crushed strip indicates the clearance between journal and bearing.
**Polarity** Either negative or positive earth (ground), determined by which battery lead is connected to the frame (earth return). Modern motorcycles are usually negative earth.
**Pre-ignition** A situation where the fuel/air mixture ignites before the spark plug fires. Often due to a hot spot in the combustion chamber caused by carbon build-up. Engine has a tendency to 'run-on'.
**Pre-load (suspension)** The amount a spring is compressed when in the unloaded state. Preload can be applied by gas, spacer or mechanical adjuster.
**Premix** The method of engine lubrication on older two-stroke engines. Engine oil is mixed with the petrol in the fuel tank in a specific ratio. The fuel/oil mix is sometimes referred to as "petroil".
**Primary drive** Description of the drive from the crankshaft to the clutch. Usually by gear or chain.
**PS** Pfedestärke - a German interpretation of BHP.
**PSI** Pounds-force per square inch. Imperial measurement of tyre pressure and cylinder pressure measurement.
**PTFE** Polytetrafluroethylene. A low friction substance.

**Pulse secondary air injection system** A process of promoting the burning of excess fuel present in the exhaust gases by routing fresh air into the exhaust ports.

# Q

**Quartz halogen bulb** Tungsten filament surrounded by a halogen gas. Typically used for the headlight **(see illustration)**.

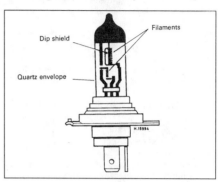

**Quartz halogen headlight bulb construction**

# R

**Rack-and-pinion** A pinion gear on the end of a shaft that mates with a rack (think of a geared wheel opened up and laid flat). Sometimes used in clutch operating systems.
**Radial play** Up and down movement about a shaft.
**Radial ply tyres** Tyre plies run across the tyre (from bead to bead) and around the circumference of the tyre. Less resistant to tread distortion than other tyre types.
**Radiator** A liquid-to-air heat transfer device designed to reduce the temperature of the coolant in a liquid cooled engine.
**Rake** A feature of steering geometry - the angle of the steering head in relation to the vertical **(see illustration)**.

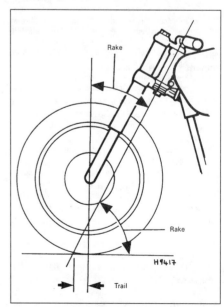

**Steering geometry**

**Rebore** Providing a new working surface to the cylinder bore by boring out the old surface. Necessitates the use of oversize piston and rings.

**Rebound damping** A means of controlling the oscillation of a suspension unit spring after it has been compressed. Resists the spring's natural tendency to bounce back after being compressed.

**Rectifier** Device for converting the ac output of an alternator into dc for battery charging.

**Reed valve** An induction system commonly used on two-stroke engines.

**Regulator** Device for maintaining the charging voltage from the generator or alternator within a specified range.

**Relay** A electrical device used to switch heavy current on and off by using a low current auxiliary circuit.

**Resistance** Measured in ohms. An electrical component's ability to pass electrical current.

**RON (Research Octane Number)** A measure of a fuel's resistance to knock.

**rpm** revolutions per minute.

**Runout** The amount of wobble (in-and-out movement) of a wheel or shaft as it's rotated. The amount a shaft rotates `out-of-true'. The out-of-round condition of a rotating part.

# S

**SAE (Society of Automotive Engineers)** A standard for the viscosity of a fluid.

**Sealant** A liquid or paste used to prevent leakage at a joint. Sometimes used in conjunction with a gasket.

**Service limit** Term for the point where a component is no longer useable and must be renewed.

**Shaft drive** A method of transmitting drive from the transmission to the rear wheel.

**Shell bearings** Plain bearings consisting of two shell halves. Most often used as big-end and main bearings in a four-stroke engine. Often called bearing inserts.

**Shim** Thin spacer, commonly used to adjust the clearance or relative positions between two parts. For example, shims inserted into or under tappets or followers to control valve clearances. Clearance is adjusted by changing the thickness of the shim.

**Short-circuit** An electrical condition where current shorts to earth (ground) bypassing the circuit components.

**Skimming** Process to correct warpage or repair a damaged surface, eg on brake discs or drums.

**Slide-hammer** A special puller that screws into or hooks onto a component such as a shaft or bearing; a heavy sliding handle on the shaft bottoms against the end of the shaft to knock the component free.

**Small-end bearing** The bearing in the upper end of the connecting rod at its joint with the gudgeon pin.

**Spalling** Damage to camshaft lobes or bearing journals shown as pitting of the working surface.

**Specific gravity (SG)** The state of charge of the electrolyte in a lead-acid battery. A measure of the electrolyte's density compared with water.

**Straight-cut gears** Common type gear used on gearbox shafts and for oil pump and water pump drives.

**Stanchion** The inner sliding part of the front forks, held by the yokes. Often called a fork tube.

**Stoichiometric ratio** The optimum chemical air/fuel ratio for a petrol engine, said to be 14.7 parts of air to 1 part of fuel.

**Sulphuric acid** The liquid (electrolyte) used in a lead-acid battery. Poisonous and extremely corrosive.

**Surface grinding (lapping)** Process to correct a warped gasket face, commonly used on cylinder heads.

# T

**Tapered-roller bearing** Tapered inner race of caged needle rollers and separate tapered outer race. Examples of taper roller bearings can be found on steering heads.

**Tappet** A cylindrical component which transmits motion from the cam to the valve stem, either directly or via a pushrod and rocker arm. Also called a cam follower.

**TCS** Traction Control System. An electronically-controlled system which senses wheel spin and reduces engine speed accordingly.

**TDC** Top Dead Centre denotes that the piston is at its highest point in the cylinder.

**Thread-locking compound** Solution applied to fastener threads to prevent slackening. Select type to suit application.

**Thrust washer** A washer positioned between two moving components on a shaft. For example, between gear pinions on gearshaft.

**Timing chain** See **Cam Chain.**

**Timing light** Stroboscopic lamp for carrying out ignition timing checks with the engine running.

**Top-end** A description of an engine's cylinder block, head and valve gear components.

**Torque** Turning or twisting force about a shaft.

**Torque setting** A prescribed tightness specified by the motorcycle manufacturer to ensure that the bolt or nut is secured correctly. Undertightening can result in the bolt or nut coming loose or a surface not being sealed. Overtightening can result in stripped threads, distortion or damage to the component being retained.

**Torx key** A six-point wrench.

**Tracer** A stripe of a second colour applied to a wire insulator to distinguish that wire from another one with the same colour insulator. For example, Br/W is often used to denote a brown insulator with a white tracer.

**Trail** A feature of steering geometry. Distance from the steering head axis to the tyre's central contact point.

**Triple clamps** The cast components which extend from the steering head and support the fork stanchions or tubes. Often called fork yokes.

**Turbocharger** A centrifugal device, driven by exhaust gases, that pressurises the intake air. Normally used to increase the power output from a given engine displacement.

**TWI** Abbreviation for Tyre Wear Indicator. Indicates the location of the tread depth indicator bars on tyres.

# U

**Universal joint or U-joint (UJ)** A double-pivoted connection for transmitting power from a driving to a driven shaft through an angle. Typically found in shaft drive assemblies.

**Unsprung weight** Anything not supported by the bike's suspension (ie the wheel, tyres, brakes, final drive and bottom (moving) part of the suspension).

# V

**Vacuum gauges** Clock-type gauges for measuring intake tract vacuum. Used for carburettor synchronisation on multi-cylinder engines.

**Valve** A device through which the flow of liquid, gas or vacuum may be stopped, started or regulated by a moveable part that opens, shuts or partially obstructs one or more ports or passageways. The intake and exhaust valves in the cylinder head are of the poppet type.

**Valve clearance** The clearance between the valve tip (the end of the valve stem) and the rocker arm or tappet/follower. The valve clearance is measured when the valve is closed. The correct clearance is important - if too small the valve won't close fully and will burn out, whereas if too large noisy operation will result.

**Valve lift** The amount a valve is lifted off its seat by the camshaft lobe.

**Valve timing** The exact setting for the opening and closing of the valves in relation to piston position.

**Vernier caliper** A precision measuring instrument that measures inside and outside dimensions. Not quite as accurate as a micrometer, but more convenient.

**VIN** Vehicle Identification Number. Term for the bike's engine and frame numbers.

**Viscosity** The thickness of a liquid or its resistance to flow.

**Volt** A unit for expressing electrical "pressure" in a circuit. Volts = current x ohms.

# W

**Water pump** A mechanically-driven device for moving coolant around the engine.

**Watt** A unit for expressing electrical power. Watts = volts x current.

**Wear limit** see **Service limit**

**Wet liner** A liquid-cooled engine design where the pistons run in liners which are directly surrounded by coolant **(see illustration).**

**Wet liner arrangement**

**Wheelbase** Distance from the centre of the front wheel to the centre of the rear wheel.

**Wiring harness or loom** Describes the electrical wires running the length of the motorcycle and enclosed in tape or plastic sheathing. Wiring coming off the main harness is usually referred to as a sub harness.

**Woodruff key** A key of semi-circular or square section used to locate a gear to a shaft. Often used to locate the alternator rotor on the crankshaft.

**Wrist pin** Another name for gudgeon or piston pin.

**Note:** *References throughout this index are in the form – "Chapter number" • "page number"*

# Haynes Motorcycle Manuals – The Complete List

| Title | Book No |
|---|---|
| **BMW** | |
| **BMW 2-valve Twins (70 - 96)** | 0249 |
| **BMW K100 & 75 2-valve Models (83 - 96)** | 1373 |
| **BMW R850 & R1100 4-valve Twins (93 - 97)** | 3466 |
| **BSA** | |
| BSA Bantam (48 - 71) | 0117 |
| BSA Unit Singles (58 - 72) | 0127 |
| BSA Pre-unit Singles (54 - 61) | 0326 |
| BSA A7 & A10 Twins (47 - 62) | 0121 |
| BSA A50 & A65 Twins (62 - 73) | 0155 |
| **DUCATI** | |
| **Ducati 600, 750 & 900 2-valve V-Twins (91 - 96)** | 3290 |
| **Ducati 748, 916 & 996 4-valve V-Twins (94 - 01)** | 3756 |
| **HARLEY-DAVIDSON** | |
| Harley-Davidson Sportsters (70 - 00) | 0702 |
| Harley-Davidson Big Twins (70 - 99) | 0703 |
| **HONDA** | |
| Honda NB, ND, NP & NS50 Melody (81 - 85) ◊ | 0622 |
| Honda NE/NB50 Vision & SA50 Vision Met-in (85 - 95) ◊ | 1278 |
| Honda MB, MBX, MT & MTX50 (80 - 93) | 0731 |
| Honda C50, C70 & C90 (67 - 99) | 0324 |
| Honda XR80R & XR100R (85 - 96) | 2218 |
| Honda XL/XR 80, 100, 125, 185 & 200 2-valve Models (78 - 87) | 0566 |
| Honda H100 & H100S Singles (80 - 92) ◊ | 0734 |
| Honda CB/CD125T & CM125C Twins (77 - 88) ◊ | 0571 |
| Honda CG125 (76 - 00) ◊ | 0433 |
| Honda NS125 (86 - 93) ◊ | 3056 |
| Honda MBX/MTX125 & MTX200 (83 - 93) ◊ | 1132 |
| Honda CD/CM185 200T & CM250C 2-valve Twins (77 - 85) | 0572 |
| Honda XL/XR 250 & 500 (78 - 84) | 0567 |
| Honda XR250L, XR250R & XR400R (86 - 01) | 2219 |
| Honda CB250 & CB400N Super Dreams (78 - 84) ◊ | 0540 |
| Honda CR Motocross Bikes (86 - 01) | 2222 |
| Honda Elsinore 250 (73 - 75) | 0217 |
| **Honda CBR400RR Fours (88 - 99)** | 3552 |
| **Honda VFR400 (NC30) & RVF400 (NC35) V-Fours (89 - 98)** | 3496 |
| **Honda CB500 (93 - 01)** | 3753 |
| Honda CB400 & CB550 Fours (73 - 77) | 0262 |
| Honda CX/GL500 & 650 V-Twins (78 - 86) | 0442 |
| Honda CBX550 Four (82 - 86) ◊ | 0940 |
| Honda XL600R & XR600R (83 - 00) | 2183 |
| **Honda CBR600F1 & 1000F Fours (87 - 96)** | 1730 |
| **Honda CBR600F2 & F3 Fours (91 - 98)** | 2070 |
| **Honda CBR600F4 (99 - 02)** | 3911 |
| **Honda CB600F Hornet** | 3915 |
| Honda CB650 sohc Fours (78 - 84) | 0665 |
| **Honda NTV600/650/Deauville V-Twins (88 - 01)** | 3243 |
| Honda Shadow VT600 & 750 (USA) (88 - 99) | 2312 |
| Honda CB750 sohc Four (69 - 79) | 0131 |
| Honda V45/65 Sabre & Magna (82 - 88) | 0820 |
| **Honda VFR750 & 700 V-Fours (86 - 97)** | 2101 |
| **Honda VFR800 V-Fours (97 - 99)** | 3703 |
| Honda CB750 & CB900 dohc Fours (78 - 84) | 0535 |
| **Honda VTR1000 (FireStorm, Super Hawk) & XL1000V (Varadero) (97 - 00)** | 3744 |
| **Honda CBR900RR FireBlade (92 - 99)** | 2161 |
| **Honda CBR1100 XX Super Blackbird (96 - 01)** | 3901 |
| **Honda ST1100 Pan European V-Fours (90 - 01)** | 3384 |
| Honda Shadow VT1100 (USA) (85 - 98) | 2313 |

| Title | Book No |
|---|---|
| Honda GL1000 Gold Wing (75 - 79) | 0309 |
| Honda GL1100 Gold Wing (79 - 81) | 0669 |
| Honda Gold Wing 1200 (USA) (84 - 87) | 2199 |
| Honda Gold Wing 1500 (USA) (88 - 00) | 2225 |
| **KAWASAKI** | |
| Kawasaki AE/AR 50 & 80 (81 - 95) | 1007 |
| Kawasaki KC, KE & KH100 (75 - 99) | 1371 |
| Kawasaki KMX125 & 200 (86 - 96) ◊ | 3046 |
| Kawasaki 250, 350 & 400 Triples (72 - 79) | 0134 |
| Kawasaki 400 & 440 Twins (74 - 81) | 0281 |
| Kawasaki 400, 500 & 550 Fours (79 - 91) | 0910 |
| Kawasaki EN450 & 500 Twins (Ltd/Vulcan) (85 - 93) | 2053 |
| **Kawasaki EX & ER500 (GPZ500S & ER-5) Twins (87 - 99)** | 2052 |
| **Kawasaki ZX600 (Ninja ZX-6, ZZ-R600) Fours (90 - 00)** | 2146 |
| **Kawasaki ZX-6R Ninja Fours (95 - 98)** | 3541 |
| **Kawasaki ZX600 (GPZ600R, GPX600R, Ninja 600R & RX & ZX750 (GPX750R, Ninja 750R) Fours (85 - 97)** | 1780 |
| **Kawasaki 650 Four (76 - 78)** | 0373 |
| Kawasaki 750 Air-cooled Fours (80 - 91) | 0574 |
| **Kawasaki ZR550 & 750 Zephyr Fours (90 - 97)** | 3382 |
| **Kawasaki ZX750 (Ninja ZX-7 & ZXR750) Fours (89 - 96)** | 2054 |
| **Kawasaki Ninja ZX-7R & ZX-9R (ZX750P, ZX900B/C/D/E) (94 - 00)** | 3721 |
| Kawasaki 900 & 1000 Fours (73 - 77) | 0222 |
| **Kawasaki ZX900, 1000 & 1100 Liquid-cooled Fours (83 - 97)** | 1681 |
| **Moto Guzzi** | |
| Moto Guzzi 750, 850 & 1000 V-Twins (74 - 78) | 0339 |
| **MZ ETZ** | |
| MZ ETZ Models (81 - 95) ◊ | 1680 |
| **NORTON** | |
| Norton 500, 600, 650 & 750 Twins (57 - 70) | 0187 |
| Norton Commando (68 - 77) | 0125 |
| **PIAGGIO** | |
| Piaggio (Vespa) Scooters (91 - 98) | 3492 |
| **SUZUKI** | |
| Suzuki GT, ZR & TS50 (77 - 90) ◊ | 0799 |
| Suzuki TS50X (84 - 00) ◊ | 1599 |
| Suzuki 100, 125, 185 & 250 Air-cooled Trail bikes (79 - 89) | 0797 |
| Suzuki GP100 & 125 Singles (78 - 93) ◊ | 0576 |
| Suzuki GS, GN, GZ & DR125 Singles (82 - 99) ◊ | 0888 |
| Suzuki GT250X7, GT200X5 & SB200 Twins (78 - 83) ◊ | 0469 |
| Suzuki GS/GSX250, 400 & 450 Twins (79 - 85) | 0736 |
| **Suzuki GS500E Twin (89 - 97)** | 3238 |
| Suzuki GS550 (77 - 82) & GS750 Fours (76 - 79) | 0363 |
| Suzuki GS/GSX550 4-valve Fours (83 - 88) | 1133 |
| **Suzuki GSX-R600 & 750 (96 - 99)** | 3553 |
| **Suzuki GSF600 & 1200 Bandit Fours (95 - 01)** | 3367 |
| Suzuki GS850 Fours (78 - 88) | 0536 |
| Suzuki GS1000 Four (77 - 79) | 0484 |
| **Suzuki GSX-R750, GSX-R1100 (85 - 92), GSX600F, GSX750F, GSX1100F (Katana) Fours (88 - 96)** | 2055 |
| Suzuki GS/GSX1000, 1100 & 1150 4-valve Fours (79 - 88) | 0737 |
| **TRIUMPH** | |
| Triumph 350 & 500 Unit Twins (58 - 73) | 0137 |
| Triumph Pre-Unit Twins (47 - 62) | 0251 |
| Triumph 650 & 750 2-valve Unit Twins (63 - 83) | 0122 |
| Triumph Trident & BSA Rocket 3 (69 - 75) | 0136 |
| **Triumph Fuel Injected Triples (97 - 00)** | 3755 |
| **Triumph Triples & Fours (carburettor engines) (91 - 99)** | 2162 |
| **VESPA** | |
| Vespa P/PX125, 150 & 200 Scooters (78 - 95) | 0707 |
| Vespa Scooters (59 - 78) | 0126 |

| Title | Book No |
|---|---|
| **YAMAHA** | |
| Yamaha DT50 & 80 Trail Bikes (78 - 95) ◊ | 0800 |
| Yamaha T50 & 80 Townmate (83 - 95) ◊ | 1247 |
| Yamaha YB100 Singles (73 - 91) ◊ | 0474 |
| Yamaha RS/RXS100 & 125 Singles (74 - 95) | 0331 |
| Yamaha RD & DT125LC (82 - 87) ◊ | 0887 |
| Yamaha TZR125 (87 - 93) & DT125R (88 - 95) ◊ | 1655 |
| Yamaha TY50, 80, 125 & 175 (74 - 84) ◊ | 0464 |
| Yamaha XT & SR125 (82 - 96) | 1021 |
| Yamaha Trail Bikes (81 - 00) | 2350 |
| Yamaha 250 & 350 Twins (70 - 79) | 0040 |
| Yamaha XS250, 360 & 400 sohc Twins (75 - 84) | 0378 |
| Yamaha RD250 & 350LC Twins (80 - 82) | 0803 |
| Yamaha RD350 YPVS Twins (83 - 95) | 1158 |
| Yamaha RD400 Twin (75 - 79) | 0333 |
| Yamaha XT, TT & SR500 Singles (75 - 83) | 0342 |
| Yamaha XZ550 Vision V-Twins (82 - 85) | 0821 |
| Yamaha FJ, FZ, XJ & YX600 Radian (84 - 92) | 2100 |
| **Yamaha XJ600S (Diversion, Seca II) & XJ600N Fours (92 - 99)** | 2145 |
| **Yamaha YZF600R Thundercat & FZS600 Fazer (96 - 00)** | 3702 |
| **Yamaha YZF-R6 (98 - 01)** | 3900 |
| Yamaha 650 Twins (70 - 83) | 0341 |
| Yamaha XJ650 & 750 Fours (80 - 84) | 0738 |
| Yamaha XS750 & 850 Triples (76 - 85) | 0340 |
| **Yamaha TDM850, TRX850 & XTZ750 (89 - 99)** | 3540 |
| **Yamaha YZF750R & YZF1000R Thunderace (93 - 00)** | 3720 |
| **Yamaha FZR600, 750 & 1000 Fours (87 - 96)** | 2056 |
| **Yamaha XV V-Twins (81 - 96)** | 0802 |
| **Yamaha XJ900F Fours (83 - 94)** | 3239 |
| **Yamaha XJ900S Diversion (94 - 01)** | 3739 |
| **Yamaha YZF-R1 (98 - 01)** | 3754 |
| **Yamaha FJ1100 & 1200 Fours (84 - 96)** | 2057 |
| **ATVs** | |
| Honda ATC70, 90, 110, 185 & 200 (71 - 85) | 0565 |
| Honda TRX300 Shaft Drive ATVs (88 - 95) | 2125 |
| Honda TRX300EX & TRX400EX ATVs (93 - 99) | 2318 |
| Kawasaki Bayou 220/300 & Prairie 300 ATVs (86 - 01) | 2351 |
| Polaris ATVs (85 to 97) | 2302 |
| Yamaha YT, YFM, YTM & YTZ ATVs (80 - 85) | 1154 |
| Yamaha YFS200 Blaster ATV (88 - 98) | 2317 |
| Yamaha YFB250 Timberwolf ATV (92 - 96) | 2217 |
| Yamaha YFM350 (ER and Big Bear) ATVs (87 - 99) | 2126 |
| Yamaha Warrior and Banshee ATVs (87 - 99) | 2314 |
| ATV Basics | 10450 |
| **MOTORCYCLE TECHBOOKS** | |
| Motorcycle Basics TechBook (2nd Edition) | 3515 |
| Motorcycle Electrical TechBook (3rd Edition) | 3471 |
| Motorcycle Fuel Systems TechBook | 3514 |
| Motorcycle Workshop Practice TechBook (2nd Edition) | 3470 |

◊ = not available in the USA  **Bold type** = *Superbike*

The manuals on this page are available through good motorcycle dealers and accessory shops. In case of difficulty, contact: **Haynes Publishing** (UK) +44 1963 442030   (USA) +1 805 4986703 (FR) +33 1 47 78 50 50   (SV) +46 18 124016 (Australia/New Zealand) +61 3 9763 8100

MCL12.10/01

# Preserving Our Motoring Heritage

< The Model J Duesenberg Derham Tourster. Only eight of these magnificent cars were ever built – this is the only example to be found outside the United States of America

Almost every car you've ever loved, loathed or desired is gathered under one roof at the Haynes Motor Museum. Over 300 immaculately presented cars and motorbikes represent every aspect of our motoring heritage, from elegant reminders of bygone days, such as the superb Model J Duesenberg to curiosities like the bug-eyed BMW Isetta. There are also many old friends and flames. Perhaps you remember the 1959 Ford Popular that you did your courting in? The magnificent 'Red Collection' is a spectacle of classic sports cars including AC, Alfa Romeo, Austin Healey, Ferrari, Lamborghini, Maserati, MG, Riley, Porsche and Triumph.

## A Perfect Day Out

Each and every vehicle at the Haynes Motor Museum has played its part in the history and culture of Motoring. Today, they make a wonderful spectacle and a great day out for all the family. Bring the kids, bring Mum and Dad, but above all bring your camera to capture those golden memories for ever. You will also find an impressive array of motoring memorabilia, a comfortable 70 seat video cinema and one of the most extensive transport book shops in Britain. The Pit Stop Cafe serves everything from a cup of tea to wholesome, home-made meals or, if you prefer, you can enjoy the large picnic area nestled in the beautiful rural surroundings of Somerset.

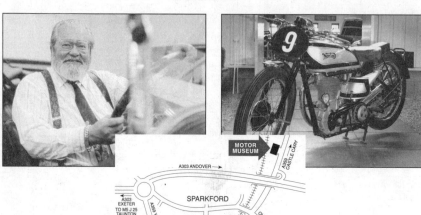

> John Haynes O.B.E., Founder and Chairman of the museum at the wheel of a Haynes Light 12.

< The 1936 490cc sohc-engined International Norton – well known for its racing success

The Museum is situated on the A359 Yeovil to Frome road at Sparkford, just off the A303 in Somerset. It is about 40 miles south of Bristol, and 25 minutes drive from the M5 intersection at Taunton.
Open 9.30am - 5.30pm (10.00am - 4.00pm Winter) 7 days a week, *except Christmas Day, Boxing Day and New Years Day*
Special rates available for schools, coach parties and outings  Charitable Trust No. 292048